THE WEB COLLECTION

PREMIUM

REVEALED

ADOBE FLASH CS4
DREAMWEAVER C
& PHOTOSHOP C

SHERRY BISHOP, JIM SHUMAN & ELIZABETH EISNER REDING

DELMAR
CENGAGE Learning™

Australia • Brazil • Japan • Korea • Mexico • Singapore • Spain • United Kingdom • United States

DELMAR
CENGAGE Learning™

The Web Collection Revealed Premium Edition:
Adobe Dreamweaver CS4,
Flash CS4, and Photoshop CS4

Sherry Bishop, Jim Shuman, and Elizabeth Eisner Reding

Vice President, Career and Professional Editorial: Dave Garza

Director of Learning Solutions: Sandy Clark

Senior Acquisitions Editor: Jim Gish

Managing Editor: Larry Main

Product Managers: Jane Hosie-Bounar, Nicole Calisi

Editorial Assistant: Sarah Timm

Vice President Marketing, Career and Professional: Jennifer McAvey

Executive Marketing Manager: Deborah S. Yarnell

Marketing Manager: Erin Brennan

Marketing Coordinator: Jonathan Sheehan

Production Director: Wendy Troeger

Senior Content Project Manager: Kathryn B. Kucharek

Developmental Editors: Barbara Clemens, Pam Conrad, Karen Stevens, Barbara Waxer

Technical Editors: John Shanley, Sasha Vodnik, Susan Whalen

Art Directors: Bruce Bond, Joy Kocsis

Cover Design: Lisa Kuhn, Curio Press, LLC

Cover Art: Lisa Kuhn, Curio Press, LLC

Text Designer: Ann Small

Proofreader: Harold Johnson

Indexer: Alexandra Nickerson

Technology Project Manager: Christopher Catalina

Production Technology Analyst: Tom Stover

Some of the images used in this book are royalty-free and the property of Getty Images, Inc. and morguefile.com. The Getty images include artwork from the following royalty-free CD-ROM collections: Education Elements, Just Flowers, Portraits of Diversity, Sports and Recreation, Texture and Light, Tools of the Trade, Travel Souvenirs, Travel & Vacation Icons, and Working Bodies. Morguefile images include artwork from the following categories: Objects, Scenes, Animals, and People. All websites pictured in this book are printed with the permission of the website copyright holders.

Adobe® Photoshop®, Adobe® InDesign®, Adobe® Illustrator®, Adobe® Flash®, Adobe® Dreamweaver®, Adobe® Fireworks®, Adobe® Flash® Player, Adobe® PostScript®, Adobe® Shockwave®, and Adobe® Creative Suite® are trademarks or registered trademarks of Adobe Systems, Inc. in the United States and/or other countries. Third party products, services, company names, logos, design, titles, words, or phrases within these materials may be trademarks of their respective owners. The Trademark BlackBerry® is owned by Research In Motion Limited and is registered in the United States and may be pending or registered in other countries. Delmar Cengage Learning is not endorsed, sponsored, affiliated with or otherwise authorized by Research In Motion Limited. Coca-Cola® is a registered trademark of The Coca-Cola Company. RealPlayer® and RealNetworks® are registered trademarks of RealNetworks, Inc.

Library of Congress Control Number: 2008943842

Hardcover edition:
ISBN-13: 978-1-4354-8264-7
ISBN-10: 1-4354-8264-6

Soft cover edition:
ISBN-13: 978-1-4354-4196-5
ISBN-10: 1-4354-4196-6

Delmar
5 Maxwell Drive
Clifton Park, NY 12065-2919
USA

Cengage Learning is a leading provider of customized learning solutions with office locations around the globe, including Singapore, the United Kingdom, Australia, Mexico, Brazil, and Japan. Locate your local office at:
international.cengage.com/region

Cengage Learning products are represented in Canada by Nelson Education, Ltd.

To learn more about Delmar, visit
www.cengage.com/delmar

Purchase any of our products at your local college store or at our preferred online store **www.ichapters.com**

Notice to the Reader

Printed in the United States of America
2 3 4 5 6 7 13 12 11 10 09

Revealed Series Vision

The Revealed Series is your guide to today's hottest multimedia applications. These comprehensive books teach the skills behind the application, showing you how to apply smart design principles to multimedia products such as dynamic graphics, animation, websites, software authoring tools, and digital video.

A team of design professionals including multimedia instructors, students, authors, and editors worked together to create this series. We recognized the unique learning environment of the multimedia classroom and created a series that:

- Gives you comprehensive step-by-step instructions
- Offers in-depth explanation of the "Why" behind a skill
- Includes creative projects for additional practice
- Explains concepts clearly using full-color visuals

It was our goal to create a book that speaks directly to the multimedia and design community—one of the most rapidly growing computer fields today. We think we've done just that, with a sophisticated and instructive book design.

—The Revealed Series

Authors' Visions

This book will introduce you to three fascinating programs that will hopefully inspire you to create rich and exciting websites. Through the work of many talented and creative individuals, this text was created for you. The Product Manager, Jane Hosie-Bounar, guided and directed the team from start to finish. She is a talented and tireless individual—the ultimate professional and visionary. Working with Barbara Clemens, the Development Editor, is always a joy. It is a bit bittersweet when a project with her is completed. She is such an encourager, both by her words and her example. Although we live thousands of miles apart, I always feel a void when our working time together is over.

The copyright content was generously provided by my dear friend Barbara Waxer. Additional information on locating media on the Internet and determining its legal use is available in her Revealed Series book *Internet Surf and Turf Revealed: The Essential Guide to Copyright, Fair Use, and Finding Media.*

John Shanley and Susan Whalen, the Dreamweaver Technical Editors, carefully tested each step to make sure that the end product was error-free. They gave exceptional feedback as they reviewed each chapter. This part of the publishing process is what truly sets Delmar Cengage Learning apart from other publishers. They have a challenging job and are so appreciated by all of us.

Tintu Thomas and Kathy Kucharek, our Content Product Managers, kept the schedule on track. We thank them for keeping up with the many details and deadlines. The work is beautiful.

Janice Jutras patiently contacted the websites we used as examples to obtain permission for their inclusion.

Harold Johnson quietly worked behind the scenes to ensure that my grammatical and punctuation errors were corrected. Paula Melton authored the test banks.

Special thanks go to Jim Gish, Senior Acquisitions Editor, and Sandy Clark, the Director of Learning Solutions. They have embraced the Revealed books with enthusiasm and grace.

SERIES & AUTHORS' VISION

The Beach Club in Gulf Shores, Alabama (www.beachclubal.com), generously allowed us to use several photographs of their beautiful property for The Striped Umbrella website. Florence Pruitt, the club director, was extremely helpful and gracious.

Typically, your family is the last to be thanked. My husband, Don, continues to support and encourage me every day, as he has for the last thirty-eight years. Our travels with our children and grandchildren provide happy memories for me and content for the websites. You will see the faces of my precious grandchildren Jacob, Emma, Thomas, and Caroline peeking out from some of the pages.
—Sherry Bishop

I would like to thank Jane Hosie-Bounar for her leadership in guiding us through this project. A very special thanks to Pam Conrad (for her word wizardry and wit) and to my co-authors Barbara, Sherry, and Liz. I also want to give a heartfelt thanks to my wife, Barbara, for her patience and support.
—Jim Shuman

Another 18 months, another version of the Adobe Creative Suite. While it might seem unusual to some, this is what we in the computer textbook publishing biz have come to call normal. It seems as though we thrive on this hurry-up-and-wait syndrome otherwise known as a new product release. To the reader, a book magically appears on the shelf with each software revision, but to those of us "making it happen" it means not only working under ridiculous deadlines (which we're used to), but it also means working with slightly different teams with slightly different ways of doing things. Karen Stevens, Susan Whalen, Jane Hosie-Bounar, and I have all worked together before on a variety of projects that have spanned more years than we care to admit. Added to the mix are Jim Gish, Nicole Calisi, Sarah Timm, Kathy Kucharek, and Tintu Thomas. The majority of us have never met face-to-face, yet once again we managed to work together in a professional manner, while defying the time-space continuum with its many time zones, cultural holidays, and countless vacation plans.

I would also like to thank my husband, Michael, who is used to my disappearing acts when I'm facing deadlines, and to Phoebe, Bix, and Jet, who know when it's time to take a break for some good old-fashioned head-scratching.
—Elizabeth Eisner Reding

Introduction to The Web Collection, Premium Edition

Welcome to *The Web Collection Premium Edition: Adobe Dreamweaver CS4, Flash CS4, and Photoshop CS4—Revealed.* This book offers creative projects, concise instructions, and coverage of basic Dreamweaver, Flash, Photoshop, and Creative Suite integration skills, helping you to create polished, professional-looking websites and art work. Use this book both in the classroom and as your own reference guide.

This text is organized into 17 chapters. In these chapters, you will learn many skills, including how to move amongst the Creative Suite applications, which, in this release, provide familiar functionality from one application to the next.

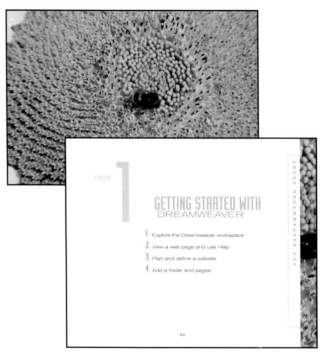

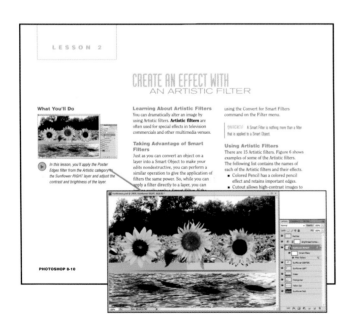

What You'll Do

A What You'll Do figure begins every lesson. This figure gives you an at-a-glance look at what you'll do in the chapter, either by showing you a file from the current project or a tool you'll be using.

Comprehensive Conceptual Lessons

Before jumping into instructions, in-depth conceptual information tells you "why" skills are applied. This book provides the "how" and "why" through the use of professional examples. Also included in the text are tips and sidebars to help you work more efficiently and creatively, or to teach you a bit about the history or design philosophy behind the skill you are using.

Step-by-Step Instructions

This book combines in-depth conceptual information with concise steps to help you learn CS4. Each set of steps guides you through a lesson where you will create, modify, or enhance a CS4 file. Step references to large colorful images and quick step summaries round out the lessons. The Data Files for the steps are provided on the CD at the back of this book.

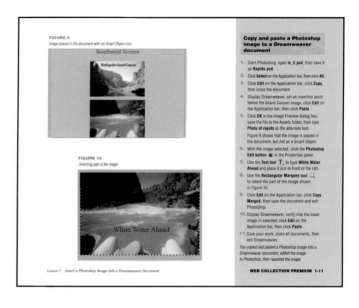

Projects

This book contains a variety of end-of-chapter materials for additional practice and reinforcement. The Skills Review contains hands-on practice exercises that mirror the progressive nature of the lesson material. The chapter concludes with four projects; two Project Builders, one Design Project, and one Portfolio Project. The Project Builders and the Design Project require you to apply the skills you've learned in the chapter. Portfolio Projects encourage students to address and solve challenges based on the content explored in the chapter in order to create portfolio-quality work.

Dreamweaver

Chapter 1 Getting Started With Dreamweaver
Lesson 1 Explore the Dreamweaver workspace 1-4
2 View a Web page and use Help 1-12
3 Plan and define a website 1-18
4 Add a folder and pages 1-26

Chapter 2 Developing a web page
Lesson 1 Create head content and set page properties 2-4
2 Create, import, and format text 2-10
3 Add links to Web pages 2-18
4 Use the History panel and edit code 2-24
5 Modify and test Web pages 2-30

Chapter 3 Working with Text and Images
Lesson 1 Create unordered and ordered lists 3-4
2 Create, apply, and edit Cascading Style Sheets 3-10
3 Add rules and attach Cascading Style Sheets 3-18
4 Insert and align Graphics 3-22
5 Enhance an image and use alternate text 3-28
6 Insert a background image and perform site maintenance 3-34

Chapter 4 Working With Links
Lesson 1 Create external and internal links 4-4
2 Create internal links to named anchors 4-10
3 Create, modify, and copy a navigation bar 4-16
4 Create an image map 4-24
5 Manage Website links 4-28

Chapter 5 Using HTML Tables to Lay Out a Page
Lesson 1 Create a Page Using CSS Layouts 5-4
2 Add content to CSS Layout Blocks 5-8
3 Edit Content in CSS Layout Blocks 5-12
4 Create a Table 5-18
5 Resize, split, and merge cells 5-22
6 Insert and align Images in Table cells 5-28
7 Insert text and format cell content 5-32

Chapter 6 Managing a Web Server and Files
Lesson 1 Perform Website maintenance 6-4
2 Publish a Website and transfer files 6-14
3 Check files out and in 6-22
4 Cloak files 6-26
5 Import and export a site definition 6-30
6 Evaluate Web content for legal use 6-34

Flash

Chapter 1 Getting Started with Adobe Flash CS4
Lesson 1 Understand the Adobe Flash CS4 workspace 1-4
2 Open a document and play a movie 1-12
3 Create and save a movie 1-18
4 Work with the Timeline 1-30
5 Distribute an Adobe Flash movie 1-36
6 Plan an application or a Website 1-40

Chapter 2 Drawing Objects in ADOBE Flash
Lesson 1 Use the Flash drawing tools 2-4
2 Select Objects and Apply Colors 2-14
3 Work with drawn objects 2-20
4 Work with text and text objects 2-28
5 Work with layers and objects 2-34

Chapter 3 Working with Symbols and interactivity
Lesson 1 Create symbols and instances 3-4
2 Work with Libraries 3-10
3 Create buttons 3-16
4 Assign actions to frames and buttons 3-22

Chapter 4 Creating Animations
Lesson 1 Create motion tween animations 4-4
2 Create classic tween animations 4-20
3 Create frame-by-frame animations 4-24
4 Create Shape Tween animations 4-30
5 Create movie clips 4-36
6 Animate text 4-42

BRIEF CONTENTS

vii

Chapter 5 Creating Special Effects

Lesson 1 Create a mask effect 5-4
2 Add sound 5-8
3 Add video 5-12
4 Create an animated naviagation bar 5-18
5 Create Character animations using inverse kinematics 5-26
6 Create 3D effects 5-34

Photoshop

Chapter 1 Getting Started with Adobe Photoshop CS4

Lesson 1 Start Adobe Photoshop CS4 1-4
2 Learn how to open and save an image 1-8
3 Use organizational and management features 1-14
4 Examine the Photoshop window 1-16
5 Use the Layers and History panels 1-24
6 Learn about Photoshop by using Help 1-28
7 View and print an image 1-32
8 Close a file and exit Photoshop 1-38

Chapter 2 Working with Layers

Lesson 1 Examine and convert layers 2-4
2 Add and delete layers 2-8
3 Add a selection from one image to another 2-12
4 Organize layers with layer groups and colors 2-16

Chapter 3 Making Selections

Lesson 1 Make a selection using shapes 3-4
2 Modify a marquee 3-12
3 Select using color and modify a selection 3-16
4 Add a vignette effect to a selection 3-23

Chapter 4 Incorporating Color Techniques

Lesson 1 Work with color to transform an image 4-4
2 Use the Color Picker and the Swatches palette 4-10
3 Place a border around an image 4-16
4 Blend colors using the Gradient Tool 4-18
5 Add color to a grayscale image 4-22
6 Use filters, opacity, and blending modes 4-26
7 Match colors 4-32

Chapter 5 Placing Type in an Image

Lesson 1 Learn about type and how it is created 5-4
2 Change spacing and adjust baseline shift 5-8
3 Use the Drop Shadow style 5-12
4 Apply anti-aliasing to type 5-16
5 Modify type with the Bevel and Emboss style 5-20
6 Apply special effects to type using filters 5-24
7 Create text on a path 5-28

Integration

Chapter 1 Integrating Adobe CS4 Web Premium

Lesson 1 Insert a Photoshop image into a Dreamweaver document 1-4
2 Create a Photoshop document and import it into Flash 1-12
3 Insert and edit a Flash movie in Dreamweaver 1-18

Data Files 1

Glossary 13

Index 29

Art Credits 48

Dreamweaver CS4

CHAPTER 1   GETTING STARTED WITH DREAMWEAVER

INTRODUCTION
Getting Started With Dreamweaver 1-2
Introduction 1-2
Using Dreamweaver Tools 1-2

LESSON 1
Explore the Dreamweaver Workspace 1-4
Examining the Dreamweaver Workspace 1-4
Working with Dreamweaver Views 1-7
Tasks   Start Dreamweaver (Windows) 1-8
      Start Dreamweaver (Macintosh) 1-9
      Change views and view panels 1-10

LESSON 2
View a Web Page and Use Help 1-12
Opening a Web Page 1-12
Viewing Basic Web Page Elements 1-12
Getting Help 1-13
Tasks   Open a web page and view basic
      page elements 1-14
      Use Dreamweaver Help 1-16

LESSON 3
Plan and Define a website 1-18
Understanding the Total Process 1-18
Planning a website 1-18
Setting Up the Basic Structure 1-19
Creating the Web Pages and Collecting
the Page Content 1-20
Testing the Pages 1-21
Modifying the Pages 1-21
Publishing the Site 1-21
Tasks   Select the location for your website 1-22
      Create a root folder 1-23
      Define a website 1-24
      Set up web server access 1-25

LESSON 4
Add a Folder and Pages 1-26
Adding a Folder to a Website 1-26
Creating the Home Page 1-27
Adding Pages to a Website 1-27
Tasks   Add a folder to a website (Windows) 1-28
      Add a folder to a website
      (Macintosh) 1-28
      Set the default images folder 1-29
      Set the default images folder 1-25
      Create the home page 1-30
      Save an image file in the assets
      folder 1-31
      Add pages to a website (Windows) 1-32
      Add pages to a website (Macintosh) 1-33

CHAPTER 2   **DEVELOPING A WEB PAGE**

INTRODUCTION
Developing a Web Page 2-2
Introduction 2-2
Understanding Page Layout 2-2

LESSON 1
Create Head Content and Set Page Properties 2-4
Creating the Head Content 2-4
Setting Web Page Properties 2-5
Tasks   Edit a page title 2-6
     Enter keywords 2-7
     Enter a description 2-8
     Set the page background color 2-9

LESSON 2
Create, Import, and Format Text 2-10
Creating and Importing Text 2-10
Formatting Text Using the Property Inspector 2-11
Using HTML Tags Compared to using CSS 2-11
Changing Fonts 2-11
Changing Font Sizes 2-11
Formatting Paragraphs 2-11
Tasks   Enter text 2-12
     Format text 2-13
     Save an image file in the assets folder 2-14
     Import text 2-15
     Set text properties 2-16
     Checking Spelling 2-17

LESSON 3
Add Links to Web Pages 2-18
Adding Links to Web Pages 2-18
Using Navigation Bars 2-19
Tasks   Create a navigation bar 2-20
     Insert a horizontal rule 2-20
     Add links to web pages 2-21
     Create an email link 2-22
     View the email link in the Assets panel 2-23

LESSON 4
Use the History Panel and Edit Code 2-24
Using the History Panel 2-24
Viewing HTML Code in the Code Inspector 2-25
Tasks   Use the History panel 2-26
     Use the Code Inspector 2-27
     Use the Reference panel 2-28
     Insert a date object 2-29

LESSON 5
Modify and Test Web Pages 2-30
Testing and Modifying web Pages 2-30
Testing a Web Page Using Different Browsers and Screen Sizes 2-31
Testing a Web Page as Rendered in a Mobile Device 2-31
Tasks   Modify a web page 2-32
     Test web pages by viewing them in a browser 2-33

INTRODUCTION

Working with Text and Images 3-2
Introduction 3-2
Formatting Text as Lists 3-2
Using Cascading Style Sheets 3-2
Using Images to Enhance Web Pages 3-2

LESSON 1

Create Unordered and Ordered Lists 3-4
Creating Unordered Lists 3-4
Formatting Unordered Lists 3-4
Creating Ordered Lists 3-4
Formatting Ordered Lists 3-5
Creating Definition Lists 3-5
Tasks   Create an unordered list 3-6
        Format an unordered list 3-7
        Create an ordered list 3-8
        Format an ordered list 3-9

LESSON 2

**Create, Apply, and Edit Cascading Style
Sheets** 3-10
Understanding Cascading Style Sheets 3-10
Using the CSS Styles Panel 3-10
Comparing the Advantages of Using Style
Sheets 3-11
Understanding CSS Style Sheet Code 3-11
Tasks   Create a Cascading Style Sheet
        and a rule 3-12
        Apply a rule in a Cascading
        Style Sheet 3-14
        Edit a rule in a Cascading
        Style Sheet 3-15
View code with the Code Navigator 3-16
Use the Code Navigator to edit a rule 3-17

LESSON 3

**Add Rules and Attach Cascading Style
Sheets** 3-18
Understanding External and Embedded Style
Sheets 3-18
Tasks   Add rules to a Cascading Style Sheet 3-20
        Attach a style sheet 3-21

LESSON 4

Insert and Align Graphics 3-22
Understanding Graphic File Formats 3-22
Understanding the Assets Panel 3-22
Inserting Files with Adobe Bridge 3-23
Aligning Images 3-23
Tasks   Insert a graphic 3-24
        Use Adobe Bridge 3-25
        Align an image 3-26

LESSON 5

**Enhance an Image and Use Alternate
Text** 3-28
Enhancing an Image 3-28
Using Alternate Text 3-29
Tasks   Add a border 3-30
        Add horizontal and vertical space 3-30
        Edit image settings 3-31
        Edit alternate text 3-32
        Set the alternate text
        accessibility option 3-33

LESSON 6

**Insert a Background Image and Perform
Site Maintenance** 3-34
Inserting a Background Image 3-34
Managing Images 3-34
Removing Colors from a website 3-35
Tasks   Insert a background image 3-36
        Remove a background image from a
        page 3-37
        Delete files from a website 3-38
        Check for Non-web-safe colors 3-39

CHAPTER 4 — WORKING WITH LINKS

INTRODUCTION

Working with Links 4-2
Introduction 4-2
Understanding Internal and External Links 4-2

LESSON 1

Create External and Internal Links 4-4
Creating External Links 4-4
Creating Internal Links 4-5
Tasks   Create an external link 4-6
        Create an internal link 4-8
        View links in the Assets panel 4-9

LESSON 2

Create Internal Links to Named Anchors 4-10
Inserting Named Anchors 4-10
Creating Internal Links to Named Anchors 4-11
Tasks   Insert a named anchor 4-12
        Create an internal link to a named anchor 4-14

LESSON 3

Create, Modify, and Copy a Navigation Bar 4-16
Creating a Navigation Bar Using Images 4-16
Copying and Modifying a Navigation Bar 4-17
Tasks   Create a navigation bar using images 4-18
        Add elements to a navigation bar 4-20
        Copy and paste a navigation bar 4-22
        Modify a navigation bar 4-22

LESSON 4

Create an Image Map 4-24
Tasks   Create an image map 4-26

LESSON 5

Manage Website Links 4-28
Managing Website Links 4-28
Tasks   Manage website links 4-29
        Update a page 4-30

INTRODUCTION
Positioning Objects with CSS AND TABLES 5-2
Introduction 5-2
Using Div Tags Versus Tables for Page Layout 5-2

LESSON 1
Create a Page Using CSS Layouts 5-4
Understanding Div Tags 5-4
Using CSS Page Layouts 5-4
Viewing CSS Layout Blocks 5-5
Tasks　Create a page with a CSS layout 5-6

LESSON 2
Add content to CSS Layout Blocks 5-8
Understanding Div Tag Content 5-8
Understanding CSS Code 5-9
Tasks　Add text to a CSS container 5-10
　　　Add images to a CSS container 5-11

LESSON 3
Edit Content in CSS Layout Blocks 5-12
Edit Content in CSS Layout Blocks 5-12
Tasks　Format content in CSS layout blocks 5-13
　　　Edit styles in CSS layout blocks 5-15
　　　Edit CSS layout block properties 5-15
　　　Edit page properties 5-17

LESSON 4
Create a Table 5-18
Understanding Table Modes 5-18
Creating a Table 5-18
Using Expanded Tables Mode 5-19
Setting Table Accessibility Preferences 5-19
Tasks　Create a table 5-20
　　　Set table properties 5-21

LESSON 5
Resize, split, and merge cells 5-22
Resizing Table Elements 5-22
Tasks　Resize columns 5-24
　　　Resize rows 5-25
　　　Split cells 5-26
　　　Merge cells 5-27

LESSON 6
Insert and Align Images in Table Cells 5-28
Inserting Images in Table Cells 5-28
Aligning Images in Table Cells 5-29
Tasks　Insert images in table cells 5-30
　　　Align graphics in table cells 5-31

LESSON 7
Insert Text and Format Cell Content 5-32
Inserting Text in a Table 5-32
Formatting Cell Content 5-32
Formatting Cells 5-33
Tasks　Insert text 5-34
　　　Format cell content 5-35
　　　Format cells 5-36
　　　Modify cell content 5-37
　　　Check layout 5-37

CHAPTER 6 **MANAGING A WEB SERVER AND FILES**

INTRODUCTION
Managing a Web Server and Files 6-2
Introduction 6-2
Preparing to Publish a Site 6-2

LESSON 1
Perform Website Maintenance 6-4
Maintaining a Website 6-4
Using the Assets Panel 6-4
Checking Links Sitewide 6-4
Using Site Reports 6-4
Validating Markup 6-5
Testing Pages 6-5
Tasks   Check for broken links 6-6
        Check for orphaned files 6-6
        Verify that all colors are web-safe 6-7
        Check for untitled documents 6-8
        Check for missing alternate text 6-9
        Enable Design Notes 6-10
        Associate a Design Note with a file 6-11
        Edit a Design Note 6-12

LESSON 2
Publish a Website and Transfer Files 6-14
Defining a Remote Site 6-14
Viewing a Remote Site 6-14
Transferring Files to and from a Remote Site 6-15
Synchronizing Files 6-16
Tasks   Set up web server access on an FTP site 6-17
        Set up web server access on a local or network folder 6-18
        View a website on a remote server 6-19
        Upload files to a remote server 6-20
        Synchronize files 6-21

LESSON 3
Check Files Out and In 6-22
Managing a Website with a Team 6-22
Checking Out and Checking In Files 6-22
Enabling the Check In/Check Out Feature 6-23
Tasks   Enable the Check In/Check Out feature 6-24
        Check out a file 6-24
        Check in a file 6-25

LESSON 4
Cloak Files 6-26
Understanding Cloaking Files 6-26
Cloaking a Folder 6-26
Cloaking Selected File Types 6-27
Tasks   Cloak and uncloak a folder 6-28
        Cloak selected file types 6-29

LESSON 5
Import and Export a Site Definition 6-30
Exporting a Site Definition 6-30
Importing a Site Definition 6-30
Tasks   Export a site definition 6-31
        Import a site definition 6-32
        View the imported site 6-33

LESSON 6
Evaluate Web Content for Legal Use 6-34
Can I Use Downloaded Media? 6-34
Understanding Intellectual Property 6-34
Understanding Copyright Law 6-34
What Exactly Does the Copyright Owner Own? 6-35
Understanding Fair Use 6-35
How Do I Use Work Properly? 6-35
Understanding Licensing Agreements 6-35
Obtaining Permission or a License 6-36
Posting a Copyright Notice 6-36
References 6-37

Flash CS4

CHAPTER 1   GETTING STARTED WITH ADOBE FLASH CS4

INTRODUCTION
Getting Started with Adobe Flash CS4 1-2
Introduction 1-2

LESSON 1
Understand the Adobe Flash CS4 Workspace 1-4
Organizing the Flash Workspace 1-4
Stage 1-4
Timeline (Frames and Layers) 1-5
Panels 1-5
Tools Panel 1-6
Tasks   Start Adobe Flash and work
        with panels 1-9
        Change the Stage view and display of the
        Timeline 1-11

LESSON 2
Open a Document and Play a Movie 1-12
Opening a Movie in Flash 1-12
Previewing a Movie 1-12
Control Menu Commands
(and Keyboard Shortcuts) 1-12
Controller 1-13
Testing a Movie 1-13
Documents, Movies, and Applications 1-14
Using the Flash Player 1-14
Tasks   Open and play a movie using the
        Control menu and the Controller 1-14
        Test a movie 1-15
        Change the Document Properties 1-17

LESSON 3
Create and Save a Movie 1-18
Creating a Flash Movie 1-18
Creating an Animation 1-19
The Motion Tween Animation Process 1-20
Motion Presets 1-21
Adding Effects to an Object 1-21
Tasks   Create objects using drawing tools 1-22
        Create a motion tween animation 1-23
        Reshaping the Motion Path 1-24
        Changing the transparency of
        an object 1-25
        Resize an object 1-26
        Add a filter to an object 1-27
        Add a motion preset 1-28

LESSON 4
Work with the Timeline 1-30
Understanding the Timeline 1-30
Using Layers 1-30
Using Frames 1-30
Using the Playhead 1-31
Understanding Scenes 1-31
Working with the Timeline 1-32
Tasks   Add a layer 1-33
        Create a second animation 1-33
        Work with layers and view Timeline
        features 1-34
        Modify the frame rate 1-35

LESSON 5
Distribute an Adobe Flash Movie 1-36
Distributing Movies 1-36
Tasks   Publish a movie for distribution
        on the web 1-38
        Create a projector file 1-39

LESSON 6
Plan an Application or a Website 1-40
Planning an Application or a Website 1-40
Using Screen Design Guidelines 1-42
Using Interactive Design Guidelines 1-43
The Flash Workflow Process 1-44
Task   Use Flash Help 1-45

CHAPTER 2   DRAWING OBJECTS IN ADOBE FLASH

INTRODUCTION
Drawing Objects in Adobe Flash 2-2
Introduction 2-2

LESSON 1
Use the Flash Drawing Tools 2-4
Using Flash Drawing and Editing Tools 2-4
Working with Grouped Tools 2-6
Working with Tool Options 2-6
Tools for Creating Vector Graphics 2-6
Positioning Objects on the Stage 2-6
Tasks   Show gridlines and check settings 2-8
        Use the Rectangle, Oval, and
        Line tools 2-9
        Use the Pen, Pencil, and Brush tools 2-10
        Modify an object using tool options 2-11
        Use the Spray tool with a symbol 2-12

LESSON 2
Select Objects and Apply Colors 2-14
Selecting Objects 2-14
Using the Selection Tool 2-14
Using the Lasso Tool 2-14
Drawing Model Modes 2-14
Working with Colors 2-15
Working with Gradients 2-15
Tasks   Select a drawing using the
        Selection tool 2-16
        Change fill and stroke colors 2-17
        Create a gradient and make changes
        to the gradient 2-18
        Work with the Object Drawing
        Model mode 2-19

LESSON 3
Work with Drawn Objects 2-20
Copying and Moving Objects 2-20
Transforming Objects 2-20
Resizing an Object 2-20
Rotating and Skewing an Object 2-21
Distorting an Object 2-21
Reshaping a Segment of an Object 2-21
Flipping an Object 2-21
Tasks   Copy and move an object 2-22
        Resize and reshape an object 2-23
        Rotate, skew, and flip an object 2-24
        Use the Zoom, Subselection,
        and Selection tools 2-25
        Use the Primitive Rectangle and
        Oval tools 2-26

LESSON 4
Work with Text and Text Objects 2-28
Learning About Text 2-28
Entering Text and Changing
the Text Block 2-28
Changing Text Attributes 2-28
Working with Paragraphs 2-29
Transforming Text 2-29
Tasks   Enter text and change text attributes 2-30
        Add a Filter effect to text 2-31
        Skew text and align objects 2-32
        Reshape and apply a gradient to text 2-33

LESSON 5
Work with Layers and Objects 2-34
Learning About Layers 2-34
Working with Layers 2-35
Using a Guide Layer 2-36
Distributing Text to Layers 2-37
Using Folder Layers 2-37
Tasks   Create and reorder layers 2-38
        Rename and delete layers and expand the
        Timeline 2-39
        Hide, lock, and display layer outlines 2-40
        Create a guide for a Guide layer 2-41
        Add objects to a Guide layer 2-42
        Adding text on top of an object 2-43

CHAPTER 3   WORKING WITH SYMBOLS AND INTERACTIVITY

INTRODUCTION
Working with Symbols and Interactivity 3-2
Introduction 3-2

LESSON 1
Create Symbols and Instances 3-4
Creating a Graphic Symbol 3-4
Working with Instances 3-4
Tasks   Create a symbol 3-6
        Create and edit an instance 3-7
        Edit a symbol in the edit window 3-8
        Break apart an instance 3-9

LESSON 2
Work with Libraries 3-10
Understanding the Library 3-10
Tasks   Create folders in the Library panel 3-12
        Organize items within Library panel
        folders 3-13
        Display the properties of symbols, rename
        symbols, and delete a symbol 3-14
        Use multiple Library panels 3-15

LESSON 3
Create Buttons 3-16
Understanding Buttons 3-16
Tasks   Create a button 3-18
        Edit a button and specify a Hit area 3-19
        Test a button 3-20

LESSON 4
Assign Actions to Frames and Buttons 3-22
Understanding Actions 3-22
Analyzing ActionScript 3-22
ActionScript 2.0 and 3.0 3-22
Tasks   Assign a stop action to frames 3-26
        Assign a play action to a button 3-27
        Assign a goto frame action
        to a button 3-28
        Assign a second event to a button 3-29

LESSON 5
Importing Graphics 3-30
Understanding Graphic Types 3-30
Importing and Editing Graphics 3-31
Task   Importing graphics 3-32

CONTENTS

xvii

CHAPTER 4   CREATING ANIMATIONS

INTRODUCTION
Creating Animations 4-2
Introduction 4-2
How Does Animation Work? 4-2
Flash Animation 4-2

LESSON 1
Create Motion Tween Animations 4-4
Understanding Motion Tween
Animations 4-4
Tween Spans 4-5
Motion Path 4-5
Property Keyframes 4-6
Tasks   Create a motion tween animation 4-7
         Edit a motion path 4-8
         Change the ease value of an
         animation 4-10
         Resize and reshape an object 4-11
         Create a color effect 4-12
         Orient an object to a path 4-13
         Copy a motion path 4-14
         Rotate an object 4-16
         Remove a motion tween 4-17
         Work with multiple motion tweens 4-18

LESSON 2
Create Classic Tween Animations 4-20
Understanding Classic Tweens 4-20
Understanding Motion Guides 4-20
Transformation Point and Registration
Point 4-21
Tasks   Create a classic tween
         animation 4-22
         Add a motion guide and orient the
         object to the guide 4-22

LESSON 3
Create Frame-By-Frame Animations 4-24
Understanding Frame-by-Frame
Animations 4-24
Creating a Frame-by-Frame Animation 4-25
Using the Onion Skin Feature 4-25
Tasks   Create an in-place frame-by-frame
         animation 4-26
         Copy frames and add a moving
         background 4-27
         Create a frame-by-frame animation of a
         moving object 4-28

LESSON 4
Create Shape Tween Animations 4-30
Shape Tweening 4-30
Using Shape Tweening to Create a
Morphing Effect 4-30
Properties Panel Options 4-31
Shape Hints 4-31
Tasks   Create a shape tween animation 4-32
         Create a morphing effect 4-33
         Adjust the rate of change in a shape tween
         animation 4-34
         Use shape hints 4-35

LESSON 5
Create Movie Clips 4-36
Understanding Movie Clip Symbols 4-36
Tasks   Break apart a graphic symbol and select
         parts of the object to separate from the
         graphic 4-38
         Create and edit a movie clip 4-39
         Animate a movie clip 4-40

LESSON 6
Animate Text 4-42
Animating Text 4-42
Tasks   Select, copy, and paste frames 4-44
         Create animated text 4-45
         Create rotating text 4-46
         Resize and fade in text 4-47
         Make a text block into a button 4-48
         Add an action to the button 4-49

CHAPTER 5　CREATING SPECIAL EFFECTS

INTRODUCTION
Creating Special Effects 5-2
Introduction 5-2

LESSON 1
Create a Mask Effect 5-4
Understanding Mask Layers 5-4
Tasks　Create a mask layer 5-6
　　　Create a masked layer 5-7

LESSON 2
Add Sound 5-8
Incorporating Animation and Sound 5-8
Tasks　Add sound to a movie 5-10
　　　Add sound to a button 5-11

LESSON 3
Add Video 5-12
Incorporating Video 5-12
Using the Adobe Media Encoder 5-13
Using the Import Video Wizard 5-13
Tasks　Import a video 5-14
　　　Attach actions to video control
　　　buttons 5-16
　　　Synchronize sound to a video clip 5-17

LESSON 4
Create an Animated Navigation Bar 5-18
Understanding Animated
Navigation Bars 5-18
Using Frame Labels 5-19
Tasks　Position the drop-down buttons 5-20
　　　Add a mask layer 5-21
　　　Assign an action to a
　　　drop-down button 5-22
　　　Add a frame label and
　　　assign a rollover action 5-23
　　　Add an invisible button 5-24

LESSON 5
**Create Character Animations Using Inverse
Kinematics** 5-26
Understanding Inverse Kinematics 5-26
Creating the Bone Structure 5-26
Animating the IK Object 5-27
Creating a Movie Clip with an IK Object 5-28
Runtime Feature 5-28
Tasks　Create the bone structure 5-29
　　　Animate the character 5-30
　　　Create a movie clip of the IK 5-31
　　　Apply an ease value 5-32
　　　Set the play to runtime 5-33

LESSON 6
Create 3D Effects 5-34
The 3D Tools 5-34
Using a Motion Tween with a 3D Effect 5-35
Task　Create a 3D animation 5-36

CONTENTS

Photoshop CS4

CONTENTS

CHAPTER 1   GETTING STARTED WITH ADOBE PHOTOSHOP CS4

INTRODUCTION
Getting Started with Adobe
Photoshop CS4 1-2
Using Photoshop 1-2
Understanding Platform User Interfaces 1-2
Understanding Sources 1-2

LESSON 1
Start Adobe Photoshop CS4 1-4
Defining Image-Editing Software 1-4
Understanding Images 1-4
Using Photoshop Features 1-4
Starting Photoshop and Creating a File 1-5
Tasks   Start Photoshop (Windows) 1-6
      Start Photoshop (Macintosh) 1-7

LESSON 2
Learn How to Open and Save an Image 1-8
Opening and Saving Files 1-8
Customizing How You Open Files 1-8
Browsing Through Files 1-9
Understanding the Power of Bridge 1-10
Creating a PDF Presentation 1-10
Using Save As Versus Save 1-10
Tasks   Open a file using the Application bar 1-11
      Open a file using Folders panel in
      Adobe Bridge 1-11
      Use the Save As command 1-12
      Change from Tabbed to Floating
      Documents
      Rate and filter with Bridge 1-13

LESSON 3
Use Organizational and Management
Features 1-14
Learning about Version Cue 1-14
Understanding Version Cue
Workspaces 1-14
Using Version Cue's Administrative
Functions 1-15
Making Use of Bridge 1-15

LESSON 4
Examine the Photoshop Window 1-16
Learning About the Workspace 1-16
Finding Tools Everywhere 1-16
Using Tool Shortcut Keys 1-18
Customizing Your Environment 1-18
Tasks   Select a tool 1-19
      Select a tool from the Tool Preset
      picker 1-20
      Add a tool to the Tool Preset
      picker 1-21
      Change the default display 1-21
      Show and hide panels 1-22
      Create a customized workspace 1-23

LESSON 5
Use the Layers and History panels 1-24
Learning About Layers 1-24
Understanding the Layers Panel 1-25
Displaying and Hiding Layers 1-25
Using the History Panel 1-25
Tasks   Hide and display a layer 1-26
      Move a layer on the Layers panel
      and delete a state on the
      History panel 1-27

LESSON 6
Learn About Photoshop
by Using Help 1-28
Understanding the Power of Help 1-28
Using Help Topics 1-28
Tasks   Find information in Contents 1-29
      Get help and support 1-30
      Find information using Search 1-31

LESSON 7
View and Print an Image 1-32
Getting a Closer Look 1-32
Printing Your Image 1-32
Understanding Color Handling in
Printing 1-33
Viewing an Image in Multiple Views 1-33
Tasks   Use the Zoom Tool 1-34
      Modify print settings 1-35
      Create a PDF with Bridge 1-36
      Create a Web Gallery with Bridge 1-37

LESSON 8
Close a File and Exit Photoshop 1-38
Concluding Your Work Session 1-38
Closing Versus Exiting 1-38
Tasks   Close a file and exit Photoshop 1-39

INTRODUCTION
Working with Layers 2-2
Layers Are Everything 2-2
Understanding the Importance of Layers 2-2
Using Layers to Modify an Image 2-2

LESSON 1
Examine and Convert Layers 2-4
Learning About the Layers Panel 2-4
Recognizing Layer Types 2-4
Organizing Layers 2-5
Converting Layers 2-6
Tasks   Convert an image layer into
         a Background layer 2-7

LESSON 2
Add and Delete Layers 2-8
Adding Layers to an Image 2-8
Naming a Layer 2-9
Deleting Layers from an Image 2-9
Tasks   Add a layer using the Layer menu 2-10
         Delete a layer 2-11
         Add a layer using the Layers panel 2-11

LESSON 3
**Add a Selection from One Image
to Another** 2-12
Understanding Selections 2-12
Understanding the Extract and Color
Range Commands 2-12
Making a Selection and Moving a Selection 2-13
Defringing Layer Contents 2-13
Tasks   Make a color range selection 2-14
         Move a selection to another image 2-15
         Defringe the selection 2-15

LESSON 4
**Organize Layers with Layer groups
and Colors** 2-16
Understanding Layer Groups 2-16
Organizing Layers into Groups 2-16
Adding Color to a Layer 2-17
Flattening an Image 2-17
Understanding Layer Comps 2-18
Using Layer Comps 2-18
Tasks   Create a layer group 2-19
         Move layers to the layer group 2-19
         Rename a layer and adjust opacity 2-20
         Create layer comps 2-20
         Flatten an image 2-21

CONTENTS

CHAPTER 3 ■ **MAKING SELECTIONS**

INTRODUCTION
Making Selections 3-2
Combining Images 3-2
Understanding Selection Tools 3-2
Understanding Which Selection Tool to Use 3-2
Combining Imagery 3-2

LESSON 1
Make a Selection Using Shapes 3-4
Selecting by Shape 3-4
Creating a Selection 3-4
Using Fastening Points 3-4
Selecting, Deselecting, and Reselecting 3-5
Placing a Selection 3-6
Using Guides 3-6
Tasks   Create a selection with the
             Rectangular Marquee Tool 3-7
             Position a selection with the Move Tool 3-8
             Deselect a selection 3-9
             Create a selection with the
             Magnetic Lasso Tool 3-10
             Move a complex selection to an
             existing image 3-11

LESSON 2
Modify a Marquee 3-12
Changing the Size of a Marquee 3-12
Modifying a Marquee 3-12
Moving a Marquee 3-13
Using the Quick Selection Tool 3-13
Tasks   Move and enlarge a marquee 3-14
             Use the Quick Selection tool 3-15

LESSON 3
**Select Using Color and
Modify a Selection** 3-16
Selecting with Color 3-16
Using the Magic Wand Tool 3-16
Using the Color Range Command 3-17
Transforming a Selection 3-17
Understanding the Healing Brush Tool 3-17
Using the Healing Brush Tool 3-17
Tasks   Select using color range 3-18
             Select using the Magic Wand tool 3-19
             Flip a selection 3-20
             Fix imperfections with the
             Healing Brush tool 3-21

LESSON 4
**Add a Vignette Effect to a
Selection** 3-23
Understanding Vignettes 3-22
Creating a Vignette 3-22
Task   Create a vignette 3-23

INTRODUCTION
Incorporating Color Techniques 4-2
Using Color 4-2
Understanding Color Modes and Color
Models 4-2
Displaying and Printing Images 4-2

LESSON 1
**Work with Color to Transform
an Image** 4-4
Learning About Color Models 4-4
Lab Model 4-5
HSB Model 4-5
RGB Mode 4-5
CMYK Mode 4-6
Understanding the Bitmap and
Grayscale Modes 4-6
Changing Foreground and
Background Colors 4-6
Tasks   Set the default foreground
        and background colors 4-7
        Change the background color using
        the Color panel 4-8
        Change the background color using
        the Eyedropper tool 4-9

LESSON 2
**Use the Color Picker and
the Swatches panel** 4-10
Making Selections from the
Color Picker 4-10
Using the Swatches Panel 4-11
Tasks   Select a color using the
        Color Picker dialog box 4-12
        Select a color using the
        Swatches panel 4-12
        Add a new color to the
        Swatches panel 4-13
        Use kuler from a web browser 4-14
        Use kuler from Photoshop 4-15

LESSON 3
Place a Border Around an Image 4-16
Emphasizing an Image 4-16
Locking Transparent Pixels 4-16
Task   Create a border 4-17

LESSON 4
Blend Colors Using the Gradient Tool 4-18
Understanding Gradients 4-18
Using the Gradient Tool 4-19
Customizing Gradients 4-19
Tasks   Create a gradient from a
        sample color 4-20
        Apply a gradient fill 4-21

LESSON 5
Add Color to a Grayscale Image 4-22
Colorizing Options 4-22
Converting Grayscale and Color Modes 4-22
Tweaking adjustments 4-23
Colorizing a Grayscale Image 4-23
Tasks   Change the color mode 4-24
        Colorize a grayscale image 4-25

LESSON 6
**Use Filters, Opacity and
Blending Modes** 4-26
Manipulating an Image 4-26
Understanding Filters 4-26
Choosing Blending Modes 4-27
Understanding Blending
Mode Components 4-27
Softening Filter Effects 4-27
Balancing Colors 4-27
Tasks   Adjust brightness and contrast 4-29
        Work with a filter, a blending
        mode, and an opacity setting 4-30
        Adjust color balance 4-31

LESSON 7
Match Colors 4-32
Finding the Right Color 4-32
Using Selections to Match Colors 4-32
Task   Match a color 4-33

CONTENTS

CHAPTER 5   **PLACING TYPE IN AN IMAGE**

INTRODUCTION
Placing Type in an Image 5-2
Learning About Type 5-2
Understanding the Purpose of Type 5-2
Getting the Most Out of Type 5-2

LESSON 1
**Learn About Type and
How It is Created** 5-4
Introducing Type Types 5-4
Getting to Know Font Families 5-4
Measuring Type Size 5-5
Acquiring Fonts 5-5
Tasks   Create and modify type 5-6
     Change type color using an
     existing image color 5-7

LESSON 2
**Change Spacing and
Adjust Baseline Shift** 5-8
Adjusting Spacing 5-8
Understanding Character and
Line Spacing 5-8
Using the Character Panel 5-9
Adjusting the Baseline Shift 5-9
Tasks   Kern characters 5-10
     Shift the baseline 5-11

LESSON 3
Use the Drop Shadow Style 5-12
Adding Effects to Type 5-12
Using the Drop Shadow 5-12
Applying a Style 5-12
Controlling a Drop Shadow 5-13
Tasks   Add a drop shadow 5-14
     Modify drop shadow settings 5-15

LESSON 4
Apply Anti-Aliasing to Type 17-16
Eliminating the "Jaggies" 5-16
Knowing When to Apply Anti-Aliasing 5-16
Understanding Anti-Aliasing 5-17
Tasks   Apply anti-aliasing 5-18
     Undo anti-aliasing 5-19

LESSON 5
**Modify Type with the Bevel and
Emboss Style** 5-20
Using the Bevel and Emboss Style 5-20
Understanding Bevel and
Emboss Settings 5-20
Tasks   Add the Bevel and Emboss style
     with the Layer menu 5-22
     Modify Bevel and Emboss
     settings 5-23

LESSON 6
**Apply Special Effects to Type
Using Filters** 5-24
Understanding Filters 5-24
Creating Special Effects 5-24
Producing Distortions 5-24
Using Textures and Relief 5-25
Blurring Imagery 5-25
Tasks   Rasterize a type layer 5-26
     Modify filter settings 5-27

LESSON 7
Create Text on a Path 5-28
Understanding Text on a Path 5-28
Creating Text on a Path 5-28
Task   Create a path and add type 5-29

Integration

INTRODUCTION
Integrating Adobe CS4 Web Premium 1-2
Introduction 1-2

LESSON 1
**Insert a Photoshop Image into a
Dreamweaver Document** 1-4
Inserting a Photoshop Image into
Dreamweaver 1-4
Setting Photoshop as the Primary External
Image Editor 1-5
Setting up the Folder Structure for
the Files 1-6
Using Design Notes 1-6
Tasks   Designate the primary external image
         editor 1-7
         Edit a Photoshop document 1-8
         Insert a Photoshop image into a
         Dreamweaver document 1-9
         Edit a Photoshop image from a
         Dreamweaver document 1-10
         Copy and paste a Photoshop image to a
         Dreamweaver document 1-11

LESSON 2
**Create a Photoshop Document and Import
it into Flash** 1-12
Importing a Photoshop Document into
Flash 1-12
Tasks   Create a Photoshop image with several
         layers 1-14
         Import a Photoshop document into
         Flash 1-15
         Edit a Photoshop image that has been
         imported into Flash 1-16
         Create an animation using a Photoshop-
         created text 1-17

LESSON 3
**Insert and Edit a Flash Movie in
Dreamweaver** 1-18
Inserting a Flash Movie into a Dreamweaver
Document 1-18
Using the Properties Panel with the
Movie 1-18
Tasks   Insert a Flash movie into Dreamweaver 1-20
         Play a Flash movie and change settings
         from Dreamweaver 1-21
         Edit a Flash movie from
         Dreamweaver 1-22

Data Files 1

Glossary 13

Index 29

Art Credits 48

What Instructor Resources Are Available with This Book?

The Instructor Resources CD-ROM is Delmar's way of putting the resources and information needed to teach and learn effectively into your hands. All the resources are available for both Macintosh and Windows operating systems.

Instructor's Manual

Available as an electronic file, the Instructor's Manual includes chapter overviews and detailed lecture topics for each chapter, with teaching tips. The Instructor's Manual is available on the Instructor Resources CD-ROM.

PowerPoint Presentations

Each chapter has a corresponding PowerPoint presentation that you can use in lectures, distribute to your students, or customize to suit your course.

Data Files for Students

To complete most of the chapters in this book, your students will need Data Files. The Data Files are available on the CD at the back of this text book. Instruct students to use the Data Files List at the end of this book. This list gives instructions on organizing files.

Solutions to Exercises

Solution Files are Data Files completed with comprehensive sample answers. Use these files to evaluate your students' work. Or distribute them electronically so students can verify their work. Sample solutions to all lessons and end-of-chapter material are provided.

Test Bank and Test Engine

ExamView is a powerful testing software package that allows instructors to create and administer printed and computer (LAN-based) exams. ExamView includes hundreds of questions that correspond to the topics covered in this text, enabling students to generate detailed study guides that include page references for further review. The computer-based and LAN-based/online testing component allows students to take exams using the EV, Player and also saves the instructor time by grading each exam automatically.

Intended Audience

This text is designed for the beginner or intermediate user who wants to learn how to use Dreamweaver CS4, Flash CS4, and Photoshop CS4. The book is designed to provide basic and in-depth material that not only educates, but also encourages you to explore the nuances of these exciting programs.

Approach

The text allows you to work at your own pace through step-by-step tutorials. A concept is presented and the process is explained, followed by the actual steps. To learn the most from the use of the text, you should adopt the following habits:

- Proceed slowly: Accuracy and comprehension are more important than speed.
- Understand what is happening with each step before you continue to the next step.
- After finishing a skill, ask yourself if you could do it on your own, without referring to the steps. If the answer is no, review the steps.

Icons, Buttons, and Pointers

Symbols for icons, buttons, and pointers are shown in the step each time they are used. Icons may look different in the files panel depending on the file association settings on your computer.

Skills Reference

As a bonus, a Power User Shortcuts table is included at the end of Dreamweaver and Photoshop chapters. This table contains the quickest method of completing tasks covered in the chapter. It is meant for the more experienced user, or for the user who wants to become more experienced. Tools are shown, not named.

Fonts

The Data Files contain a variety of commonly used fonts, but there is no guarantee that these fonts will be available on your computer. In a few cases, fonts other than those common to a PC or a Macintosh are used. If any of the fonts in use is not available on your computer, you can make a substitution, realizing that the results may vary from those in the book.

Windows and Macintosh

Adobe Creative Suite works virtually the same on Windows and Macintosh operating systems. In those cases where there is a significant difference, the abbreviations (Win) and (Mac) are used.

Data Files

To complete the lessons in this book, you need the Data Files on the CD in the back of this book. Your instructor will tell you where to store the files as you work, such as the hard drive, a network server, or a USB storage device. The instructions in the lessons will refer to "where you store your Data Files" when referring to the Data Files for the book.

When you copy the Data Files to your computer, you may see lock icons that indicate that the files are read-only when you view them in the Dreamweaver Files panel. To unlock the files, right-click on the locked file name in the Files panel, then click Turn off Read Only.

Images vs. Graphics

Many times these terms seem to be used interchangeably. For the purposes of the Dreamweaver chapters, the term images is used when referring to pictures on a web page. The term graphics is used as a more encompassing term that refers to non-text items on a web page such as photographs, logos, navigation bars, Flash animations, graphs, background images, and drawings. You may define these terms in a slightly different way, depending on your professional background or business environment.

Preference Settings

The learning process will be much easier if you can see the file extensions for the files you will use in the lessons. To do this in Windows, open Windows Explorer, click Organize, Folder and Search Options, click the View tab, then uncheck the box Hide Extensions for Known File Types. To do this for a

Mac, go to the Finder, click the Finder menu, and then click Preferences. Click the Advanced tab, then select the Show all file extensions check box.

To view the Flash content that you will be creating, you must set a preference in your browser to allow active content to run. Otherwise, you will not be able to view objects such as Flash buttons. To set this preference in Internet Explorer, click Tools, Internet Options, Advanced, then check the box Allow active content to run in files on My Computer. Your browser settings may be slightly different, but look for similar wording. When using Windows Internet Explorer 7, you can also click the information bar when prompted to allow blocked content.

Creating a Portfolio
The Portfolio Project, and Project Builders allow students to use their creativity to come up with original Dreamweaver, Flash, and Photoshop designs. You might suggest that students create a portfolio in which they can store their original work.

Dreamweaver CS4
System Requirements
For a Windows operating system:

- 2GHz or faster processor
- Microsoft Windows® XP with Service Pack 2 (Service Pack 3 recommended) or Windows Visa Home Premium, Business, Ultimate, or Enterprise with Service Pack 1 (certified for 32-bit Windows XP and Windows Vista)
- 1GB of RAM or more recommended
- 9.3 GB of available hard-disk space for installation; additional free space required during installation (cannot install on flash-based storage devices)
- 1,024×768 display (1,280×800 recommended) with 16-bit video card
- Some GPU-accelerated features require graphics support for Shader Model 3.0 and OpenGL 2.0
- Some features in Adobe®Bridge rely on a DirectX9-capable graphics card with at least 64MB of VRAM
- DVD-ROM drive
- Quicktime 7.4.5 software required for multimedia features
- Broadband Internet connection required for online services

For a Macintosh operating system:

- PowerPC® G5 or multicore Intel® processor
- Mac OS X v10.4.11–10.5.4

- Java™ Runtime Environment 1.5 required for Adobe Version Cue® Server
- 1GB of RAM or more recommended 10.3GB of available hard-disk space for installation; additional hard-disk space required during installation (cannot install on a volume that uses a case-sensitive file system or on flash-based storage devices)
- 1,024×768 display (1,280×800 recommended) with 16-bit video card
- Some GPU-accelerated features require graphics support for Shader Model 3.0 and OpenGL 2.0
- DVD-ROM drive
- QuickTime 7.4.5 software required for multimedia features
- Broadband Internet connection required for online services*

Windows and Macintosh
Adobe Dreamweaver CS4 works virtually the same on Windows and Macintosh operating systems. In those cases where there is a significant difference, the abbreviations (Win) and (Mac) are used.

Memory Challenges
If, instead of seeing an image on an open page, you see an image placeholder with a large X across it, your RAM is running low. Try closing any other applications that are running to free up memory.

Building a Website

You will create and develop a website called The Striped Umbrella in the lesson material in this book. Because each chapter builds off of the previous chapter, it is recommended that you work through the chapters in consecutive order.

Websites Used in Figures

Each time a website is used for illustration purposes in a lesson, where necessary, a statement acknowledging that we obtained permission to use the website is included, along with the URL of the website. Sites whose content is in the public domain, such as federal government websites, are acknowledged as a courtesy.

Data Files

To complete the lessons in this book, you need the Data Files on the CD in the back of this book. Your instructor will tell you where to store the files as you work, such as the hard drive, a network server, or a USB storage device. The instructions in the lessons will refer to "where you store your Data Files" when referring to the Data Files for the book.

When you copy the Data Files to your computer, you may see lock icons that indicate that the files are read-only when you view them in the Dreamweaver Files panel. To unlock the files, right-click on the locked file name in the Files panel, and then click Turn off Read Only.

Flash CS4
System Requirements
For a Windows operating system:

- 1GHz or faster processor
- Microsoft® Windows® XP with Service Pack 2 (Service Pack 3 recommended) or Windows Vista™ Home Premium, Business, Ultimate, or Enterprise with Service Pack 1 (certified for 32-bit editions)
- 1GB of RAM
- 3.5GB of available hard-disk space (additional free space required during installation)
- 1,024 × 768 monitor resolution with 16-bit video card
- DVD-ROM drive
- QuickTime 7.1.2 software required for multimedia features

For a Macintosh operating system:

- PowerPC® G5 or multicore Intel® processor
- Mac OS X v10.4.11–10.5.4
- 1G of RAM
- 4GB of available hard-disk space (additional free space required during installation)
- 1,024 × 768 display (1,280×800 recommended) with 16-bit video card
- DVD-ROM drive
- QuickTime 7.1.2 software required for multimedia features

Projects

Several projects are presented that allow students to apply the skills they have learned in a chapter. Two projects, Ultimate Tours and the Portfolio, build from chapter to chapter. You will need to contact your instructor if you plan to work on these without having completed the previous chapter's project.

READ THIS BEFORE YOU BEGIN

Photoshop CS4
System Requirements

For a Windows operating system:

- Intel® Pentium® 4, Intel Centrino®, Intel Xeon®, or Intel Core™ Duo (or compatible) processor
- Microsoft® Windows® XP with Service Pack 2 or Windows Vista™ Home Premium, Business, Ultimate, or Enterprise (certified for 32-bit editions)
- 512MB of RAM
- 64MB of video RAM
- 1GB of available hard-disk space (additional free space required during installation)
- 1,024×768 monitor resolution with 16-bit video card
- DVD-ROM drive
- QuickTime 7 software required for multimedia features
- Internet or phone connection required for product activation
- Broadband Internet connection required for Adobe Stock Photos* and other services

For a Macintosh operating system:

- PowerPC® G4 or G5 or multicore Intel processor
- Mac OS X v.10.4.8
- 512MB of RAM
- 64MB of video RAM
- 2GB of available hard-disk space (additional free space required during installation)
- 1,024x768 monitor resolution with 16-bit video card
- DVD-ROM drive
- QuickTime 7 software required for multimedia features
- Internet or phone connection required for product activation
- Broadband Internet connection required for Adobe Stock Photos* and other services

File Identification

Instead of printing a file, the owner of a Photoshop image can be identified by reading the File Info dialog box. Use the following instructions to add your name to an image:

1. Click File on the menu bar, then click File Info.
2. Click the Description, if necessary.
3. Click the Author text box.
4. Type your name, course number, or other identifying information.
5. Click OK.

There are no instructions with this text to use the File Info feature other than when it is introduced in Chapter 1. It is up to each user to use this feature so that his or her work can be identified.

Measurements

When measurements are shown, needed, or discussed, they are given in pixels. Use the following instructions to change the units of measurement to pixels:

1. Click Edit on the menu or Application bar, point to Preferences, then click Units & Rulers.

2. Click the Rulers list arrow, then click pixels.

3. Click OK.

You can display rulers by clicking View on the menu or Application bar, then clicking Rulers, or by pressing [Ctrl][R] (Win) or ⌘[R] (Mac). A check mark to the left of the Rulers command indicates that the Rulers are displayed. You can hide visible rulers by clicking View on the menu bar, then clicking Rulers, or by pressing [Ctrl][R] (Win) or ⌘[R] (Mac).

Menu Commands in Tables

In tables, menu commands are abbreviated using the following format: Edit ➤ Preferences ➤ Units & Rulers. This command translates as follows: Click Edit on the menu bar, point to Preferences, then click Units & Rulers.

Grading Tips

Many students have web-ready accounts where they can post their completed assignments. The instructor can access the student accounts using a browser and view the images online. Using this method, it is not necessary for the student to include his/her name on a type layer, because all of their assignments are in an individual password-protected account.

Creating a Portfolio

One method for students to submit and keep a copy of all of their work is to create a portfolio of their projects that is linked to a simple web page that can be saved on a CD-ROM. If it is necessary for students to print completed projects, work can be printed and mounted at a local copy shop; a student's name can be printed on the back of the image.

chapter 1

GETTING STARTED WITH
DREAMWEAVER

1. Explore the Dreamweaver workspace

2. View a web page and use Help

3. Plan and define a website

4. Add a folder and pages

ADOBE DREAMWEAVER CS4

chapter 1

GETTING STARTED WITH
DREAMWEAVER

Introduction

Adobe Dreamweaver CS4 is a web development tool that lets you create dynamic, interactive web pages containing text, images, hyperlinks, animation, sounds, video, and other elements. You can use Dreamweaver to create individual web pages or complex websites consisting of many web pages. A **website** is a group of related web pages that are linked together and share a common interface and design. You can use Dreamweaver to create design elements such as text, tables, and interactive buttons, or you can import elements from other software programs. You can save Dreamweaver files in many different file formats, including XHTML, HTML, JavaScript, CSS, or XML, to name a few. **XHTML** is the acronym for eXtensible HyperText Markup Language, the current standard language used to create web pages. You can still use **HTML** (HyperText Markup Language) in Dreamweaver; however, it is no longer considered the standard language. In Dreamweaver, you can easily convert exist-

ing HTML code to XHTML-compliant code. You use a web browser to view your web pages on the Internet. A **web browser** is a program, such as Microsoft Internet Explorer or Mozilla Firefox, that lets you display HTML-developed web pages.

Using Dreamweaver Tools

Creating an excellent website is a complex task. Fortunately, Dreamweaver has an impressive number of tools that can help. Using Dreamweaver's design tools, you can create dynamic and interactive web pages without writing a word of code. However, if you prefer to write code, Dreamweaver makes it easy to type and edit the code directly and see the visual results of the code instantly. Dreamweaver also contains organizational tools that help you work with a team of people to create a website. You can also use Dreamweaver's management tools to help you manage a website. For instance, you can use the **Files panel** to create folders to organize and store the various files for your website, and add pages to your website.

Tools You'll Use

Property inspector

Collapse to Icons button

Show Code and Design views button *Switch Design View to Live View button*

Show Code view button *Show Design view button*

EXPLORE THE
DREAMWEAVER WORKSPACE

What You'll Do

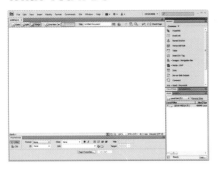

In this lesson, you will start Dreamweaver, examine the components that make up the Dreamweaver workspace, and change views.

Examining the Dreamweaver Workspace

The **Dreamweaver workspace** is designed to provide you with easy access to all the tools you need to create web pages. Refer to Figure 1 as you locate the components described below.

The **Document window** is the large white area in the Dreamweaver program window where you create and edit web pages. The **Application bar**, located above the Document window, includes menu names (Windows only), a Workspace switcher, and other application commands. To choose a menu command, click the menu name to open the menu, then click the menu command. The Insert panel is displayed at the top of the Dreamweaver workspace on the right side of the screen. The **Insert panel** includes eight categories of buttons displayed through a drop-down menu: Common, Layout, Forms, Data, Spry, InContext Editing, Text, and Favorites. Clicking a category in the Insert panel displays the buttons and menus associated with that category. For example, if you click the Layout category, you will find buttons for using div tags, used for creating blocks of content on pages; Table buttons, used for inserting and editing tables; and the Frames button, used for selecting one of 13 different frame layouts.

> **QUICK**TIP
>
> Two additional options are also available through the Insert panel drop-down menu. To display the icons in color, click Color Icons, or right-click the Insert panel, then click Color Icons. To hide the button labels, click Hide Labels.

The **Document toolbar** contains buttons and drop-down menus you can use to change the current work mode, preview web pages, debug web pages, choose visual aids, and view file-management options. There are two toolbars that are not displayed by default. They are the Style Rendering toolbar and the Standard toolbar. The **Standard toolbar** contains buttons you can use to execute frequently used commands also available on the File and Edit menus. The **Style Rendering toolbar** contains buttons that can be used to render different media types, but is available only if your document uses media-dependent style sheets. An example of a media-dependent style sheet would be one used to create and format pages for a cell phone. The Style Rendering toolbar also includes a button that allows you to enable or disable CSS styles while you are working. To display or hide the Document, Standard, and Style Rendering toolbars, right-click an empty area of an open toolbar, then click the toolbar name you wish

to display or hide or use the View, Toolbars menu. The **Related Files toolbar** is located below an open document's filename tab and displays the names of any related files. **Related files** are files that are linked to a document and are necessary for the document to display and function correctly. An external CSS style sheet is a good example of a related file. The **Coding toolbar** contains buttons that are used when working directly in the code and is not visible unless you are in Code view.

When visible, it appears on the left side of the Document window.

The **Property inspector**, located at the bottom of the Dreamweaver window, lets you view and change the properties of a selected object. The Property inspector is context sensitive, which means it changes according to what is selected in the Document window. The **status bar** is located below the Document window. The left side of the status bar displays the **tag selector**, which shows

FIGURE 1
Dreamweaver CS4 workspace

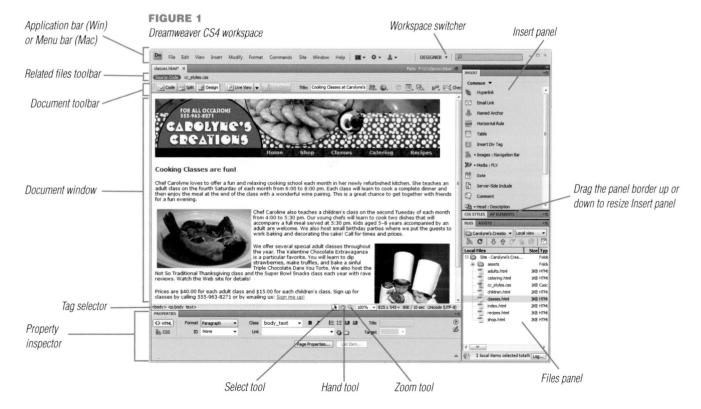

Application bar (Win) or Menu bar (Mac)

Related files toolbar

Document toolbar

Document window

Tag selector

Property inspector

Workspace switcher

Insert panel

Drag the panel border up or down to resize Insert panel

Files panel

Select tool   Hand tool   Zoom tool

the HTML tags used at the insertion point location. The right side displays the window size and estimated download time for the current page, as well as the Select tool, used for page editing; the Hand tool, used for panning; and the Zoom tool, used for magnifying.

A **panel** is a window that displays information on a particular topic or contains related commands. **Panel groups** are sets of related panels that are grouped together. A collection of panels or panel groups is called a **dock**. To view the contents of a panel in a panel group, click the panel tab. Panels are docked by default on the right side of the screen. They can be undocked or "floated" by dragging the panel tab. To collapse or expand a panel group, double-click the panel tab or click the blank area in the panel title bar, as shown in Figure 2. When you first start Dreamweaver, the Insert, CSS Styles, AP Elements, Files, and Assets panels appear by default. Panels can be opened using the Window menu commands or the corresponding shortcut keys.

FIGURE 2
Panels in panel group

Collapse to Icons button

Active panel tab

Click to collapse panel group

Your drive or folder may differ

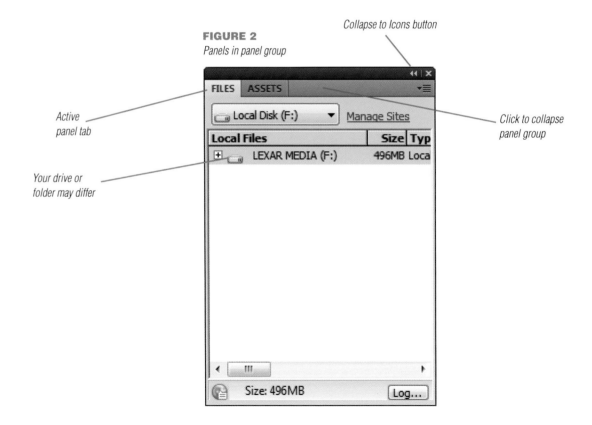

Working with Dreamweaver Views

A **view** is a particular way of displaying page content. Dreamweaver has three working views. **Design view** shows the page as it would appear in a browser and is primarily used for designing and creating a web page. **Code view** shows the underlying HTML code for the page; use this view to read or edit the underlying code.

Show Code and Design views is a combination of Code view and Design view. Show Code and Design views is the best view for **debugging** or correcting errors because you can immediately see how code modifications change the appearance of the page. The view buttons are located on the Document toolbar.

Start Dreamweaver
(Windows)

1. Click the **Start button** 🔵 on the taskbar.

2. Point to **All Programs**, click **Adobe Web Premium CS4** (if necessary), then click **Adobe Dreamweaver CS4**, as shown in Figure 3.

   TIP   The name of your Adobe suite may differ from the figure.

3. If the Default Editor dialog box opens, click **OK**.

You started Dreamweaver CS4 for Windows.

FIGURE 3
Starting Dreamweaver CS4 (Windows)

Click Adobe Dreamweaver CS4

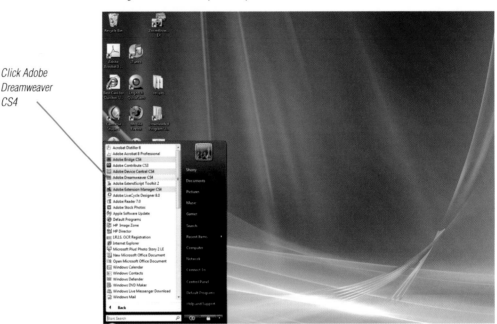

Choosing a workspace layout

The Dreamweaver interface is an integrated workspace, which means that all of the document windows and panels are arranged in a single application window. However, individual panels can be "floated" or undocked from their set position and moved to any position on the screen. (The Mac OS interface is slightly different, in that documents can either be tabbed together in a single window or displayed in separate windows.) To view a tabbed document, click the tab with the document's file name. The **Workspace switcher** is a drop-down menu located in the top right corner on the Application bar. The Workspace switcher allows you to change the workspace layout. The default layout is the Designer workspace layout, where the panels are docked on the right side of the screen and Design view is the default view. In the Coder workspace layout, the panels are docked on the left side of the screen and Code view is the default view. However, the panels may be docked on either side of the screen in both Coder and Designer layouts. Other views include App Developer, App Developer Plus, Classic, Coder Plus, Designer Compact, and Dual Screen. To change the workspace layout, click the Workspace switcher, then click the desired layout; or click Window in the Application bar, point to Workspace Layout, then click the desired layout. You can also rearrange the workspace using your own choices for panel placement and save the workspace with a unique name using the "New Workspace" and "Manage Workspaces" commands on the Workspace switcher. The Reset' current view' option will reset the workspace layout to return to the default positions on the screen.

FIGURE 4
Starting Dreamweaver CS4 (Macintosh)

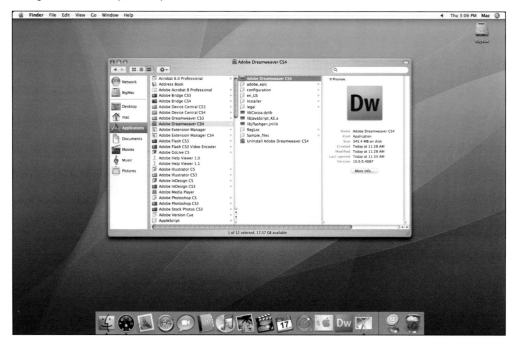

Start Dreamweaver (Macintosh)

1. Click **Finder** in the Dock, then click **Applications**.

2. Click the **Adobe Dreamweaver CS4 folder**, then double-click the **Dreamweaver CS4 application,** as shown in Figure 4.

   > TIP   Once Dreamweaver is running, you can add it to the Dock permanently by [control]-clicking the Dreamweaver icon, then clicking Keep In Dock.

   You started Dreamweaver CS4 for Macintosh.

Using two monitors for optimum workspace layout

One option you have for workspace layout is Dual Screen layout. **Dual Screen layout** is the layout you would choose when you are using two monitors while working with Dreamweaver. The Document window and Property inspector are displayed on the first monitor and the panels are displayed on the second monitor. It is quite seamless to work between the two monitors and provides optimum workspace by allowing you to have multiple panels open without compromising your Document window space.

Change views and view panels

1. Click **HTML** in the Create New category on the Dreamweaver Welcome Screen.

   The Dreamweaver Welcome Screen provides shortcuts for opening files and for creating new files or websites.

   TIP If you do not want the Dreamweaver Welcome Screen to appear each time you start Dreamweaver, click the Don't show again check box on the Welcome Screen or remove the check mark next to Show Welcome Screen in the General category in the Preferences dialog box.

2. Click the **Show Code view button** 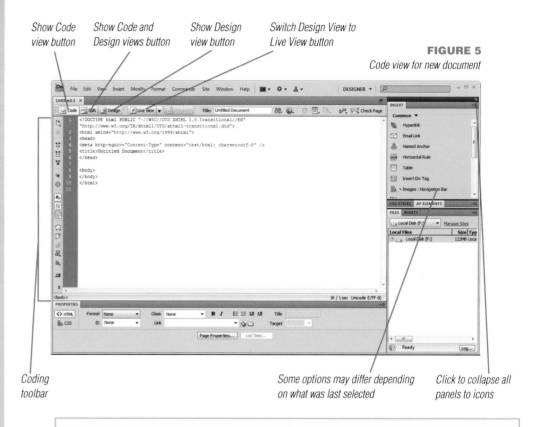 on the Document toolbar.

   The default code for a new document appears in the Document window, as shown in Figure 5.

   TIP The Coding toolbar is available only in Code view and the Code window in Split view.

3. Click the **Show Code and Design views button** Split on the Document toolbar.

4. Click the **Show Design view button** Design on the Document toolbar.

   TIP If your icons are not displayed in color and you would like to display them in color, click the Insert panel drop-down menu, then click Color Icons.

   (continued)

Show Code view button   Show Code and Design views button   Show Design view button   Switch Design View to Live View button

FIGURE 5
Code view for new document

Coding toolbar

Some options may differ depending on what was last selected

Click to collapse all panels to icons

Using the Switch Design View to Live View button

The Switch Design View to Live View button is a new feature in Dreamweaver CS4. When you click this button, the open document will appear as if it were being viewed in a browser, with interactive elements active and functioning. The Switch Design View to Live View button is similar to using the Preview in Browser button. Next to the Live View button is the Shows the Live View source in code view button. When the Switch Design View to Live View button is active, the Shows the Live View source in code view button can be toggled on or off. When you click the Live View button the first time, you may see a message that you need to install the Flash plug-in from HYPERLINK "http://www.adobe.com" www.adobe.com. Download the plug-in and your page can then be viewed using Live View.

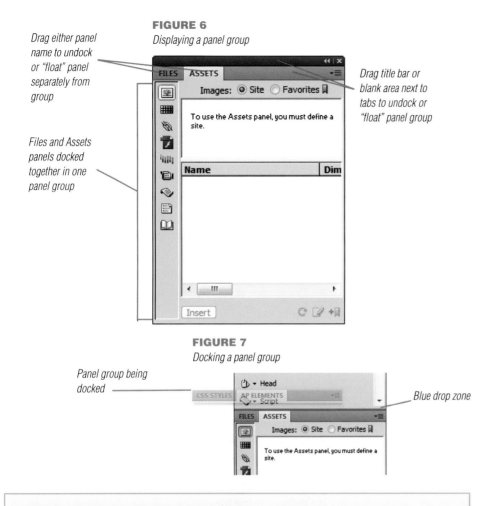

FIGURE 6
Displaying a panel group

Drag either panel name to undock or "float" panel separately from group

Drag title bar or blank area next to tabs to undock or "float" panel group

Files and Assets panels docked together in one panel group

FIGURE 7
Docking a panel group

Panel group being docked

Blue drop zone

Hiding and Displaying Toolbars

To hide or display the Style Rendering, Document, or Standard toolbars, click View on the Application bar (Win) or Menu bar (Mac), point to Toolbars, then click Style Rendering, Document, or Standard. The Coding toolbar is available only in Code view and the Code window in Split view, and appears vertically in the Document window. By default, the Document toolbar appears in the workspace.

5. Click the **Assets panel tab**, then compare your screen to Figure 6.

   TIP If the Assets panel is not visible on the screen, click Window on the Application bar (Win) or Menu bar (Mac), then click Assets.

6. Click each panel name tab to display the contents of each panel.

7. Double-click **Assets** to collapse the panel group.

8. View the contents of the CSS Styles and AP Elements panels.

9. Click and drag the **blank area** next to the AP Elements tab to the middle of the document window.

   The panel group is now in a floating window.

10. Click and drag the **panel title bar** back to its original position, then drop it to dock the panel group.

    Release the mouse only when you see the blue drop zone. **The blue drop zone** is a heavy blue line that appears when the panel is in the correct position to be docked. See Figure 7.

    TIP If you have rearranged the panels from their original positions and want to reset them back to their default positions, click the Workspace switcher drop-down menu, then click "Reset 'Designer'." You will also have to reset the Color Icons, as color icons are not part of the default Designer workspace.

11. Click File on the Application bar (Win) or Menu bar (Mac), then click **Close** to close the open document.

You viewed a new web page using three views, opened panel groups, viewed their contents, then closed panel groups.

VIEW A WEB PAGE
AND USE HELP

What You'll Do

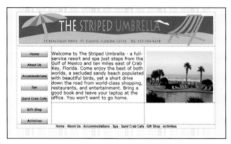

▶ In this lesson, you will open a web page, view several page elements, and access the Help system.

Opening a Web Page

After starting Dreamweaver, you can create a new website, create a new web page, or open an existing website or web page. The first web page that appears when viewers go to a website is called the **home page**. The home page sets the look and feel of the website and directs viewers to the rest of the pages in the website.

Viewing Basic Web Page Elements

There are many elements that make up web pages. Web pages can be very simple and designed primarily with text, or they can be media-rich with text, images sound, and movies, creating an enhanced interactive web experience. Figure 8 is an example of a web page with several different page elements that work together to create a simple and attractive page.

Most information on a web page is presented in the form of **text**. You can type text directly onto a web page in Dreamweaver or import text created in other programs. You can then use the Property inspector to format text so that it is attractive and easy to read. Text should be short and to the point to prevent viewers from losing interest and leaving your site.

Hyperlinks, also known as **links**, are image or text elements on a web page that users click to display another location on the page, another web page on the same website, or a web page on a different website.

Images add visual interest to a web page. The saying that "less is more" is certainly true with images, though. Too many images cause the page to load slowly and discourage viewers from waiting for the page to download. Many pages have **banners**, which are images displayed across the top of the screen that can incorporate a company's logo, contact information, and links to the other pages in the site.

Navigation bars are bars that contain multiple links that are usually organized in rows or columns. Sometimes navigation bars are used with an image map. An **image map** is an image that has been divided into sections, each of which contains a link.

The way that navigation bars and other internal links are used on your pages is referred to as the **navigation structure** of the site.

Rich media content is a comprehensive term that refers to attractive and engaging images, interactive elements, video, or animations. Some of this content can be created in Dreamweaver, but much of it is created with other programs such as Adobe Flash, Fireworks, Photoshop, or Illustrator.

Getting Help

Dreamweaver has an excellent Help feature that is both comprehensive and easy to use. When questions or problems arise, you can use the commands on the Help menu to find the answers you need. Clicking the Dreamweaver Help command opens the Dreamweaver Help page that contains a list of topics and subtopics by category.

The Search text box at the top of the window lets you enter a keyword to search for a specific topic. Context-specific help can be accessed by clicking the Help button on the Property inspector.

FIGURE 8
Common web page elements

National Endowment for the Arts website – www.arts.endow.gov

Open a web page and view basic page elements

1. Click **File** on the Application bar (Win) or Menu bar (Mac), then click **Open**.

2. Click the **Look in list arrow** (Win), or **navigation list arrow** (Mac), locate the drive and folder where you store your Data Files, then double-click the **chapter_1 folder** (Win), or click the **chapter_1 folder** (Mac).

3. Click **dw1_1.html**, then click **Open**.
   You may not see the .html file extension if the option for hiding file extensions for known file types is selected on your operating system.

   TIP If you want your screen to match the figures in this book, make sure the Document window is maximized.

4. Locate each of the web page elements shown in Figure 9.

   TIP Because you are opening a single page that is not in a website with access to the other pages, the links will not work.

   (continued)

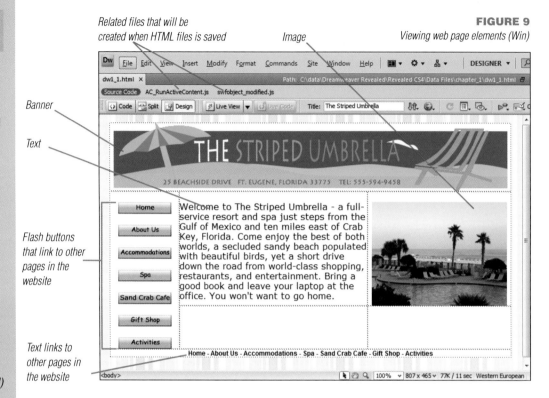

FIGURE 9

Viewing web page elements (Win)

Related files that will be created when HTML files is saved

Image

Banner

Text

Flash buttons that link to other pages in the website

Text links to other pages in the website

Understanding Related Page Files

When an HTML file is opened that is linked to other files necessary to display the page content, these files are called **related files.** If the dw1_1.html file you just opened was saved to your computer, two supporting files would be created to enable the page content to work. Although you can see file tabs for them, these files will not be created until the page is saved. These files are AC_RunActiveContent.js and swfobject_modified.js. See Figure 9. Related files are automatically opened when the page they support is opened. These two files will support the Flash buttons on the page and are required to make the buttons work in a browser. **Adobe Flash** is a program that is used to create animations and video content for the web. You will learn about Flash content in the media chapter.

FIGURE 9
Viewing web page elements (Mac)

Menu bar —

Related files
toolbar

Your Flash
buttons may
appear as
placeholders

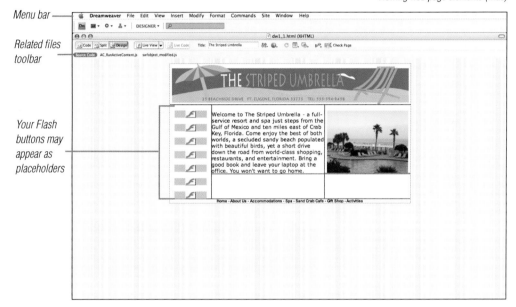

5. Click the **Show Code view button** to
view the code for the page.

6. Scroll down to view all the code, then click
the **Show Design view button** to
return to Design view.

> TIP To view the code for a particular page
> element, select the page element in Design
> view, then click the Show Code view button.

7. Click **File** on the Application bar (Win) or
Menu bar (Mac), then click **Close** to close the
open page without saving it.

> TIP You can also click the X in the filename
> tab to close the page.

*You opened a web page, located several page
elements, viewed the code for the page, then
closed the page without saving it.*

Use Dreamweaver Help

1. Click **Help** on the Application bar (Win) or Menu bar (Mac), then click **Dreamweaver Help.**

   The Dreamweaver Help and Support window opens.

   > TIP You can also open the Help feature by pressing [F1].

2. Click the **Dreamweaver help (web)** link in the top right corner of the Dreamweaver Help and Support window, as shown in Figure 10.

   > TIP If you don't see the link, enlarge or maximize the window.

3. Click the **plus sign** next to Workspace in the left column, click the **plus sign** next to Working in the Document window, then click **Switch between views in the Document window**.

   The topic opens on the right side of the Help window, as shown in Figure 11, and the plus signs change to minus signs, indicating that the topics are expanded.

4. Read the text in the content side of the Help window, then close the Adobe Dreamweaver CS4 window.

   (continued)

FIGURE 10

Dreamweaver Help and Support web page

Dreamweaver help (web) link

FIGURE 11

Displaying Help content

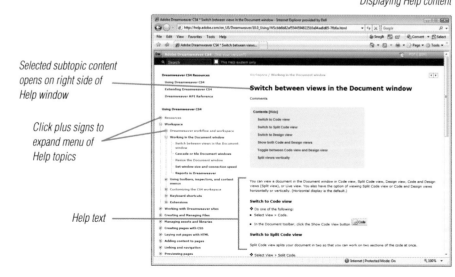

Selected subtopic content opens on right side of Help window

Click plus signs to expand menu of Help topics

Help text

Getting Started with Dreamweaver

FIGURE 12

Searching for a topic in Help

Type the search terms
in the search text box

Relevant topics
are listed

Click the list arrow
to change Adobe
applications

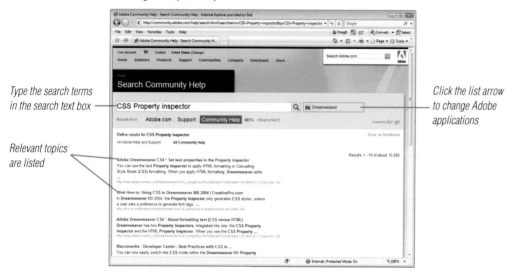

5. In the Dreamweaver Help and Support window, type **CSS Property inspector** in the search text box, notice that the Community Help button is selected, then press [Enter] (Win) or [Return] (Mac).

   A list of topics related to the search terms opens in the bottom of the window as shown in Figure 12.

6. Click one of the links to read information about one of the topics of your choice.

   You can either search the Adobe website, the Support Center, or the Community Help by clicking each link under the Search text box.

7. Close the Search Community Help window.

You used Dreamweaver Help to read information in the Adobe Dreamweaver CS4 documentation and in the Community Help files.

Using Adobe Community Help

When you access the Help feature in Dreamweaver, you have a choice of using offline help (which is similar to searching in a Dreamweaver manual) or using online help. The online help feature is called Adobe Community Help. **Adobe Community Help** is a collection of materials such as tutorials, published articles, or blogs, in addition to the regular help content. All content is monitored and approved by the Adobe Community Expert program.

PLAN AND DEFINE A WEBSITE

What You'll Do

In this lesson, you will review a website plan for The Striped Umbrella, a beach resort and spa. You will also create a root folder for The Striped Umbrella website, and then define the website.

Understanding the Total Process

Creating a website is a complex process. It can often involve a large team of people working in various roles to ensure that the website contains accurate information, looks good, and works smoothly.

Figure 13 illustrates the phases in a website development project.

Planning a Website

Planning is probably the most important part of any successful project. Planning is an *essential* part of creating a website, and

FIGURE 13
Phases of a website development project

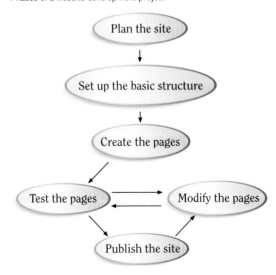

is a continuous process that overlaps the subsequent phases. To start planning your website, you need to create a checklist of questions and answers about the site. For example, what are your goals for the site? Who is the audience you want to target? Teenagers? Children? Sports enthusiasts? Senior citizens? How can you design the site to appeal to the target audience? The more questions you can answer about the site, the more prepared you will be when you begin the developmental phase. Because

of the public demand for "instant" information, your plan should include not just how to get the site up and running, but how to keep it current. Table 1 lists some of the basic questions you need to answer during the planning phase for almost any type of website. From your checklist, you should create a statement of purpose and scope, a timeline for all due dates, a budget, a task list with work assignments, and a list of resources needed. You should also include a list of deliverables, such as a preliminary

storyboard, page drafts, and art for approval. The due dates for each deliverable should be included in the timeline.

Setting Up the Basic Structure

Once you complete the planning phase, you need to set up the structure of the site by creating a storyboard. A **storyboard** is a small sketch that represents every page in a website. Like a flowchart, a storyboard shows the relationship of each page in the site to all the other pages. Storyboards are very

TABLE 1: Website Planning Checklist

question	examples
1. Who is the target audience?	Seniors, teens, children
2. How can I tailor the site to reach that audience?	Specify an appropriate reading level, decide the optimal amount of media content, use formal or casual language
3. What are the goals for the site?	Sell a product, provide information
4. How will I gather the information?	Recruit other employees, write it myself, use content from in-house documents
5. What are my sources for media content?	Internal production department, outside production company, my own photographs
6. What is my budget?	Very limited, well financed
7. What is the timeline?	Two weeks, one month, six months
8. Who is on my project team?	Just me, a complete staff of designers
9. How often should the site be updated?	Every 10 minutes, once a month
10. Who will update the site?	Me, other team members

helpful when planning a website, because they allow you to visualize how each page in the site is linked to others. You can sketch a storyboard by using a pencil and paper or by using a graphics program on a computer. The storyboard shown in Figure 14 shows all the pages that will be contained in The Striped Umbrella website that you will create in this book. Notice that the home page appears at the top of the storyboard, and that it has four pages linked to it. The home page is called the **parent page**, because it is at a higher level in the web hierarchy and has pages linked to it. The pages linked below it are called **child pages**. The Activities page, which is a child page to the home page, is also a parent page to the Cruises and Fishing pages. You can refer to this storyboard as you create the actual links in Dreamweaver. More detailed storyboards will also include all document names, images, text files, and link information.

QUICKTIP

You can create a storyboard on a computer using a software program such as Microsoft Word, PowerPoint, or Paint; Corel Paintshop Pro; or Adobe Illustrator. You might find it easier to make changes to a computer-generated storyboard than to one created on paper.

In addition to creating a storyboard for your site, you should also create a folder hierarchy for all of the files that will be used in the site. Start by creating a folder for the site with a descriptive name, such as the name of the company. This folder,

known as the **root folder** or **local root folder**, will store all the pages or HTML files for the site. Then create a subfolder called **assets** in which you store all of the files that are not pages, such as images and sound files.

QUICKTIP

You should avoid using spaces, special characters, or uppercase characters in your folder names to ensure that all your files can be read and linked successfully on all web servers, whether they are Windows- or UNIX-based.

After you create the root folder, you need to define your site. When you **define** a site, the root folder and any folders and files it contains appear in the **Files panel**, the

panel you use to manage your website's files and folders. Using the Files panel to manage your files ensures that the site links work correctly when the website is published. You also use the Files panel to add or delete pages.

Creating the Web Pages and Collecting the Page Content

This is the fun part! After you create your storyboard, you need to gather the files that will be used to create the pages, including text, images, buttons, video, and animation. Some of these files will

FIGURE 14
The Striped Umbrella website storyboard

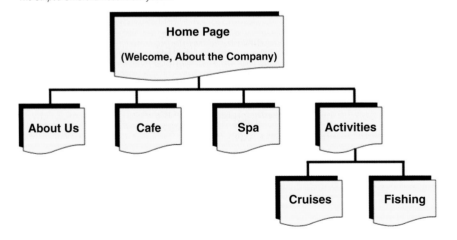

come from other software programs, and some you will create in Dreamweaver. For example, you can create text in a word-processing program and insert it into Dreamweaver, or you can create and format text in Dreamweaver.

Images, tables, colors, and horizontal rules all contribute to making a page attractive and interesting. In choosing your elements, however, you should always carefully consider the file size of each page. A page with too many graphical elements might take a long time to load, which could cause visitors to leave your site.

Testing the Pages

Once all your pages are completed, you need to test the site to make sure all the links work and that everything looks good. It is important to test your web pages using different browser software. The two most common browsers are Microsoft Internet Explorer and Mozilla Firefox. You should also test your site using different versions of each browser. Older versions of Internet Explorer do not support the latest web technology. You should also test your site using a variety of screen sizes. Some viewers may have small monitors, while others may have

large, high-resolution monitors. You should also consider connection download time. Although more people use cable modems or DSL (digital subscriber line), some still use slower dial-up modems. Testing is a continuous process, for which you should allocate plenty of time.

Modifying the Pages

After you create a website, you'll probably find that you need to keep making changes to it, especially when information on the site needs to be updated. Each time you make a change, such as adding a new button or image to a page, you should test the site again. Modifying and testing pages in a website is an ongoing process.

Publishing the Site

Publishing a website means that you transfer all the files for the site to a **web server**, a computer that is connected to the Internet with an IP (Internet Protocol) address, so that it is available for viewing on the Internet. A website must be published or users of the Internet cannot view it. There are several options for publishing a website. For instance, many

Internet Service Providers (ISPs) provide space on their servers for customers to publish websites, and some commercial websites provide limited free space for their viewers. Although publishing happens at the end of the process, it's a good idea to set up web server access in the planning phase. Use the Files panel to transfer your files using Dreamweaver's FTP capability. **FTP (File Transfer Protocol)** is the process of uploading and downloading files to and from a remote site.

Dreamweaver also gives you the ability to transfer files using the FTP process without creating a site first. You simply enter login information to an FTP site to establish a connection by clicking New in the Manage Sites dialog box, and then clicking the FTP option. You would then use the Files panel to transfer the files, just as if you were transferring files in a website.

Select the location for your website

1. Open or expand the Files panel if necessary to view the contents.

2. Click the **drive or folder** that is currently displayed in the pop-up menu in the Files panel. See Figure 15.

3. Click to select the **drive or folder** (or subfolder) in the list where you will store your folders and files for your websites.

   Dreamweaver will store all of the folders and files you create inside this drive or folder.

You selected the drive or folder where you will create your website.

Click to display the pop-up menu

FIGURE 15
Selecting a drive in the Files panel

Click to select the drive that you will use to store your files (your drive or folder may differ)

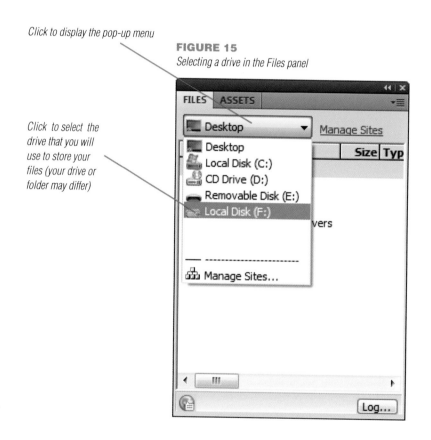

FIGURE 16

Creating a root folder using the Files panel

*Your drive
or folder
may differ*

*If you just see a drive or folder name here,
you do not currently have a website open*

*striped_umbrella
root folder*

FIGURE 17

Viewing an open website in the files panel

*If you see the word "Site" here, you do have
a website open and the toolbar appears.*

*striped_umbrella
root folder*

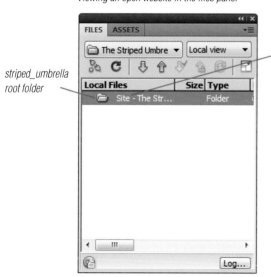

Create a root folder

1. Select the drive or folder in the Files panel,
    right-click (Windows) or **control-click**
    (Macintosh), then click **New Folder**.

2. Type **striped_umbrella** to rename the folder,
    then press **[Enter]**.

    The folder is renamed striped_umbrella, as
    shown in Figure 16.

    When you see a drive or folder in the pop-up
    menu, you do not have a website open.
    Notice the difference between Figure 16 and
    Figure 17. In Figure 16, you have only cre-
    ated the root folder, not the website. In
    Figure 17, The Striped Umbrella website has
    been created and is open. You have not cre-
    ated a website yet. You have just created the
    folder that will serve as the root folder after
    the site is created.

*You created a new folder to serve as the root
folder for The Striped Umbrella website.*

Define a website

1. Click **Site** on the Application bar (Win) or Menu bar (Mac), then click **New Site.**

2. Click the **Advanced tab** (if necessary), then type **The Striped Umbrella** in the Site name text box.

   The Basic tab can be used instead of the Advanced tab if you prefer to use a wizard.

   > TIP It is acceptable to use uppercase letters in the site name because it is not the name of a folder or a file.

3. Click the **Browse for File icon** 🗀 next to the Local root folder text box, click the **Select list arrow** (Win) or the **navigation list arrow** (Mac) in the **Choose local root folder for site The Striped Umbrella dialog box,** click the **drive and folder** where your website files will be stored, then click the **striped_umbrella folder.**

4. Click **Open** (Win) or **Choose** (Mac), then click **Select** (Win).

5. Verify that the Links relative to option button is set to Document.

6. Verify that the Enable cache check box is checked, as shown in Figure 18.

   This setting is very important to make sure your links work correctly.

You created a website and defined it with the name The Striped Umbrella. You then verified that the correct options were selected in the Site Definition dialog box.

FIGURE 18

Site Definition for The Striped Umbrella dialog box

Advanced tab

Website name

Browse for File icon

Local root folder text box – your drive may differ

Links relative to: option

Enable cache check box

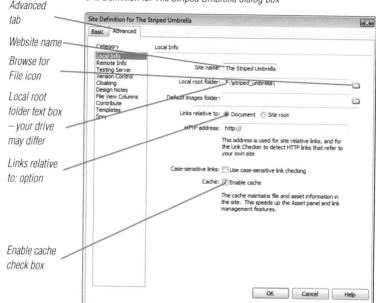

Understanding IP addresses and domain names

To be accessible over the Internet, a website must be published to a web server with a permanent IP address. An **IP address** is an assigned series of numbers, separated by periods, that designates an address on the Internet. To access a web page, you can enter either an IP address or a domain name in the address text box of your browser window. A **domain name** is a web address that is expressed in letters instead of numbers and usually reflects the name of the business represented by the website. For example, the domain name of the Adobe website is *www.adobe.com,* but the IP address is 192.150.20.61. Because domain names use descriptive text instead of numbers, they are much easier to remember. Compare an IP address to your Social Security number and a domain name to your name. Both your Social Security number and your name are used to refer to you as a person, but your name is much easier for your friends and family to use than your Social Security number. You can type the IP address or the domain name in the address text box of the browser window to access a website. The domain name is also referred to as a URL, or Uniform Resource Locator.

FIGURE 19

Setting the Remote Access for The Striped Umbrella website

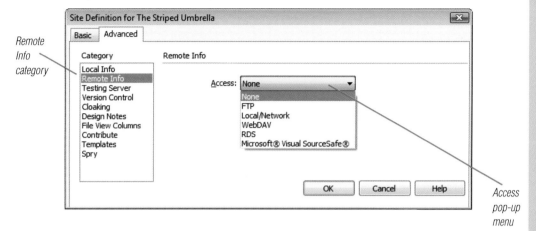

Remote
Info
category

Access
pop-up
menu

1. Click **Remote Info** in the Category list, click the **Access pop-up menu** then choose the method you will use to publish your website, as shown in Figure 19.

    TIP If you do not have the information to publish your website, choose None. You can specify this information later.

2. Enter any necessary information in the Site Definition dialog box based on the setting you chose in Step 1, then click **OK**.

    TIP Your network administrator or web hosting service will give you the necessary information to publish your website.

    You set up the remote access information to prepare you for publishing your website.

Understanding the process of publishing a website

Before publishing a website so that viewers of the web can access it, you should first create a local root folder, called the **local site**, to house all the files for your website, as you did on page 1-23. This folder usually resides on your hard drive. Next, you need to gain access to a remote server. A **remote server** is a web server that hosts websites and is not directly connected to the computer housing the local site. Many Internet Service Providers, or ISPs, provide space for publishing websites on their servers. Once you have access to a remote server, you can then use the Remote Info category in the Site Definition dialog box to enter information such as the FTP host, host directory, login, and password. After entering this information, you can then use the Put File(s) button in the Files panel to transfer the files to the designated remote server. Once the site is published to a remote server, it is called a **remote site**.

ADD A FOLDER AND PAGES

What You'll Do

 In this lesson, you will use the Files panel to create a new folder and new pages for the website.

Adding a Folder to a Website

After defining a website, you need to create folders to organize the files that will make up the site. Creating a folder called **assets** is a good beginning. There is nothing magic about the word "assets," though. You can name your folder anything that makes sense to you as long as you follow proper folder naming conventions such as avoiding the use of spaces. You can use the assets folder to store all non-HTML files, such as images or sound files. After you create the assets folder, it is a good idea to set it as the default location to store the website images. This saves a step when you import new images into the website.

DESIGNTIP **Creating an effective navigation structure**

When you create a website, it's important to consider how your viewers will navigate from page to page within the site. A navigation bar is a critical tool for moving around a website, so it's important that all text, buttons, and icons used in a navigation bar have a consistent look across all pages. If a complex navigation bar is used, such as one that incorporates JavaScript or Flash, it's a good idea to include plain text links in another location on the page for accessibility. Otherwise, viewers might become confused or lost within the site. A navigation structure can include more links than those included in a navigation bar, however. For instance, it can contain other sets of links that relate to the content of a specific page and which are placed at the bottom or sides of a page in a different format. No matter which navigation structure you use, make sure that every page includes a link back to the home page. Don't make viewers rely on the Back button on the browser toolbar to find their way back to the home page. It's possible that the viewer's current page might have opened as a result of a search and clicking the Back button will take the viewer out of the website.

QUICKTIP

Because complex websites might contain many types of files, you might want to create subfolders within the assets folder for each type of file. For instance, you could create subfolders named text, images, and sound.

Creating the Home Page

The **home page** of a website is the first page that viewers see when they visit your site. Most websites contain many other pages that all connect back to the home page. The home page filename usually has the name index.html (.htm), or default.html (.htm).

Adding Pages to a Website

Websites might be as simple as one page or might contain hundreds of pages. When you create a website, you can add all the pages and specify where they should be placed in the website folder structure in the root folder. Once you add and name all the pages in the website, you can then add the content, such as text and graphics, to each page. It is better to add as many blank pages as you think you will need in the beginning, rather than adding them one at a time with all the content in place. This will enable you to set up the navigation structure of the website at the beginning of the development process and view how each page is linked to others. When you are satisfied with the overall structure, you can then add the content to each page. This is strictly a personal preference, however. You can also choose to add and link pages as they are created, and that will work just fine, too.

You have a choice of several default document types you can generate when you create new HTML pages. The default document type is designated in the Preferences dialog box. XHTML 1.0 Transitional is the default document type when you install Dreamweaver and will be used throughout this book. It's important to understand the terminology—the pages are still called HTML pages and the file extension is still HTML, but the document type will be XHTML 1.0 Transitional.

QUICKTIP

You can also convert existing HTML documents into XHTML-compliant documents. To do this, open an existing HTML document, click File, point to Convert, then choose the XHTML document type.

Using the Files panel for file management

You should definitely use the Files panel to add, delete, move, or rename files and folders in a website. It is very important that you perform these file-maintenance tasks in the Files panel rather than in Windows Explorer (Win) or in the Finder (Mac). Working outside of Dreamweaver, such as in Windows Explorer, can cause linking errors. You cannot take advantage of Dreamweaver's simple yet powerful site-management features unless you use the Files panel for all file-management activities. You may choose to use Windows Explorer (Win) or the Finder (Mac) only to create the root folder or to move or copy the root folder of a website to another location. If you move or copy the root folder to a new location, you will have to define the site again in the Files panel, as you did in Lesson 3 of this chapter. Defining a site is not difficult and will become routine for you after you practice a bit. If you are using Dreamweaver on multiple computers, such as in labs or at home, you will have to define your sites the first time you change to a different computer.

Add a folder to a website (Windows)

1. Right-click **Site - The Striped Umbrella** in the Files panel, then click **New Folder**.

2. Type **assets** in the folder text box, then press **[Enter]**.

   TIP To rename a folder, click the folder name once, pause, click again, then type the new name.

3. Compare your screen to Figure 20.

You used the Files panel to create a new folder in the striped_umbrella folder and named it 'assets'.

Add a folder to a website (Macintosh)

1. Press and hold **[control]**, click the **striped_umbrella folder**, then click **New Folder**.

2. Type **assets** in the new folder name text box, then press **[return]**.

   TIP To rename a folder, click the folder name text box, type the new name, then press **[return]**.

3. Compare your screen to Figure 21.

You used the Files panel to create a new folder in the striped_umbrella folder and named it 'assets'.

FIGURE 20
The Striped Umbrella site in Files panel with assets folder created (Windows)

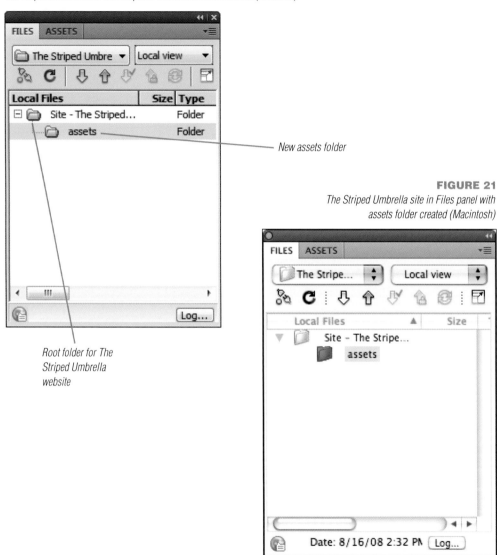

New assets folder

FIGURE 21
The Striped Umbrella site in Files panel with assets folder created (Macintosh)

Root folder for The Striped Umbrella website

Getting Started with Dreamweaver

FIGURE 22

Site Definition for The Striped Umbrella dialog box with assets folder set as the default images folder

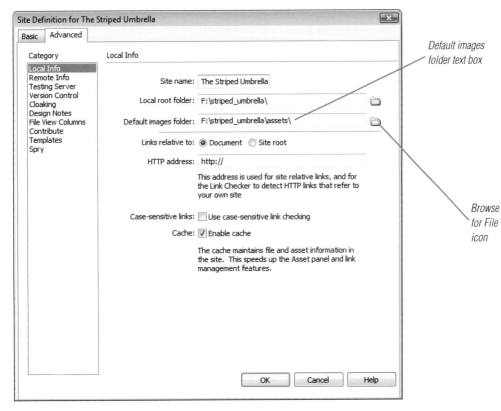

Default images folder text box

Browse for File icon

1. Click **The Striped Umbrella** in the Site list box in the Files panel, click **Manage Sites**, then click **Edit**.

2. Click the **Browse for File icon** 📁 next to the Default images folder text box.

3. If necessary, navigate to your striped_umbrella folder, double-click the **assets folder** (Win) or click the **assets folder** (Mac) in the Choose local images folder for site The Striped Umbrella: dialog box, then click **Select** (Win) or **Choose** (Mac).

   Compare your screen to Figure 22.

4. Click **OK**, then click **Done**.

You set the assets folder as the default images folder so that imported images will be automatically saved in it.

Create the home page

1. Open **dw1_2.html** from where you store your Data Files.

   The file has several elements in it, including a banner image.

2. Click **File** on the Application bar (Win) or Menu bar (Mac), click **Save As**, click the **Save in list arrow** (Win) or the **Where list arrow** (Mac), navigate to the striped_umbrella folder, select **dw1_2.html** in the File name text box (Win) or select **dw1_2** in the Save As text box (Mac), then type **index.html**.

   Windows users do not have to type the file extension. It will be added automatically.

3. Click **Save**, then click **No** when asked to update links.

   TIP As shown in Figure 23, the drive where the root folder is stored, the root folder name, and the filename of the page are displayed to the right of the document tab if the page is not open in a separate window. If open in a separate window, they are displayed on the document title bar. This information is called the **path**, or location of the open file in relation to other folders in the website.

   The banner image is no longer visible and the page contains a broken link to the image. This is because although you saved the .html file under a new name in the website's root folder, you have not yet copied the image file into the website's assets folder. The link to the banner image is still linked to the Data Files folder. You will fix this in the next set of steps.

   You opened a file, then saved it with the filename index.

FIGURE 23

index.html placed in the striped_umbrella root folder

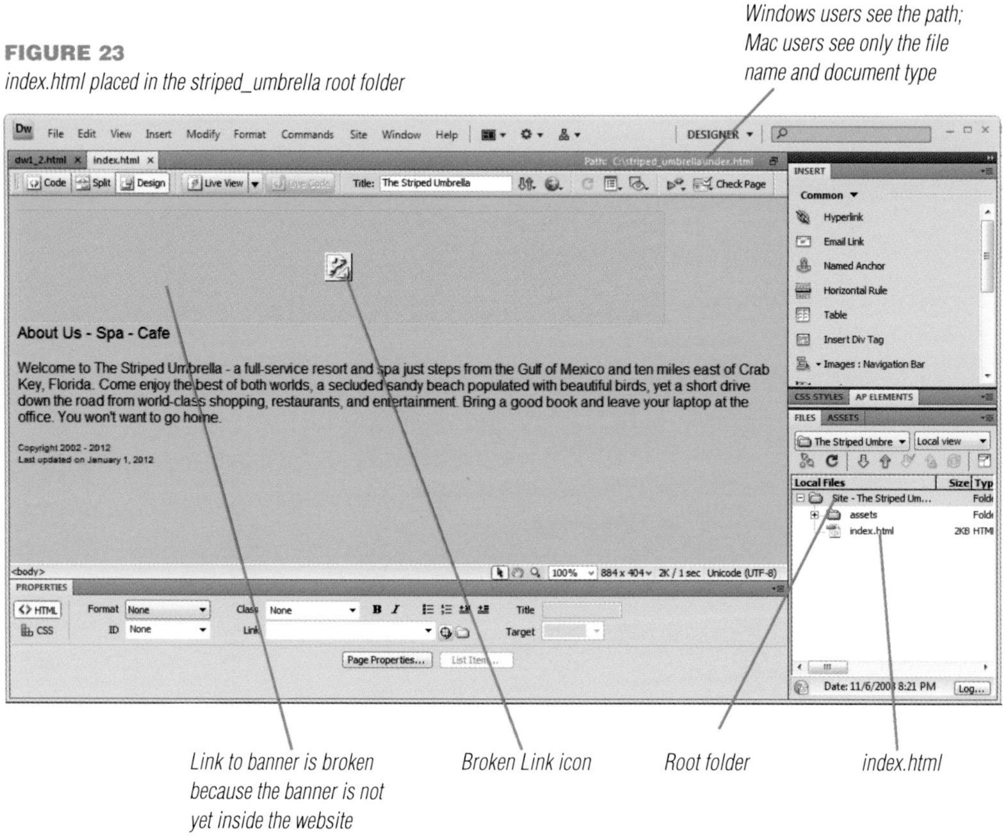

Windows users see the path; Mac users see only the file name and document type

Link to banner is broken because the banner is not yet inside the website

Broken Link icon

Root folder

index.html

The Striped
Umbrella banner

Selection
handles

FIGURE 24
Property inspector showing properties of The Striped Umbrella banner

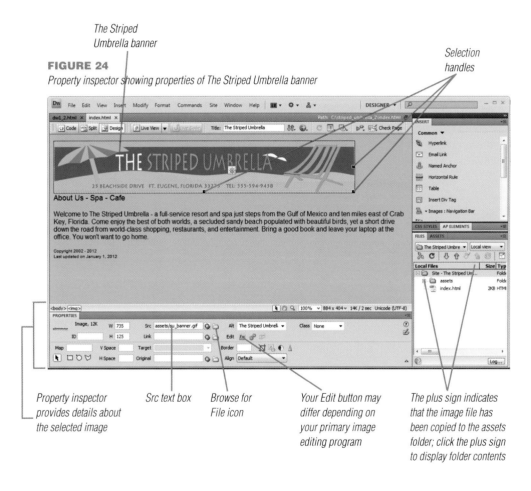

Property inspector
provides details about
the selected image

Src text box

Browse for
File icon

Your Edit button may
differ depending on
your primary image
editing program

The plus sign indicates
that the image file has
been copied to the assets
folder; click the plus sign
to display folder contents

1. Click **The Striped Umbrella banner broken link placeholder** to select it.

   Selection handles appear around the broken link. To correct the broken link, you must copy the image file from the Data Files folder into the assets folder of your website.

2. Click the **Browse for File icon** 🗀 next to the Src text box in the Property inspector, click the **Look in list arrow** (Win) or **navigation list arrow** (Mac), navigate to the assets folder in your Data Files folder for this chapter, click **su_banner.gif**, click **OK** (Win) or **Choose** (Mac), then click in a blank part of the page. (Click the banner placeholder image again if the banner still doesn't appear.)

   The file for The Striped Umbrella banner, su_banner.gif, is automatically copied to the assets folder of The Striped Umbrella website, the folder that you designated as the default images folder. The Src text box shows the path of the banner to the assets folder in the website, and the banner image is visible on the page.

   TIP If you do not see the su-banner.gif file listed in the Files panel, click the Refresh button 🔁 on the Files panel toolbar.

3. Select the banner to view the banner properties in the Property inspector, then compare your screen to Figure 24.

   TIP Until you copy a graphic from an outside folder to your website, the graphic is not part of the website and the image will appear as a broken link.

You saved The Striped Umbrella banner in the assets folder.

Add pages to a website (Windows)

1. Click the **plus sign** to the left of the assets folder (if necessary) to open the folder and view its contents, su_banner.gif.

   TIP If you do not see a file listed in the assets folder, click the Refresh button ⟳ on the Files panel toolbar.

2. Right-click the **striped_umbrella root folder**, click **New File**, type **about_us.html** to replace untitled.html, then press **[Enter]**.

   Each new file is a page in the website. These pages do not have page content or page titles yet.

   TIP If you create a new file in the Files panel, you must type the filename extension (.html) manually. However, if you create a new file using the File menu or the Welcome Screen the filename extension will be added automatically.

3. Repeat Step 2 to add five more blank pages to The Striped Umbrella website, naming the new files **spa.html**, **cafe.html**, **activities.html**, **cruises.html**, and **fishing.html**.

   TIP Make sure to add the new files to the root folder, not the assets folder. If you accidentally add them to the assets folder, just drag them to the root folder.

4. Click the **Refresh button** ⟳ on the Files panel to list the files alphabetically, then compare your screen to Figure 25.

5. Click **File** on the Application bar then click **Exit**.

   TIP If you are prompted to save changes, click No.

You added the following six pages to The Striped Umbrella website: about_us, activities, cafe, cruises, fishing, and spa.

FIGURE 25
New pages added to The Striped Umbrella website (Windows)

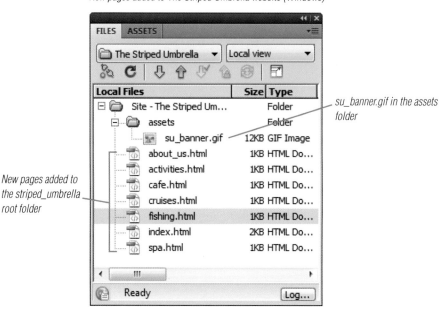

su_banner.gif in the assets folder

New pages added to the striped_umbrella root folder

DESIGNTIP Adding page titles

When you view a web page in a browser, its page title appears in the browser window title bar. The page title should reflect the page content and set the tone for the page. It is especially important to use words in your page title that are likely to match keywords viewers might enter when using a search engine. Search engines compare the text in page titles to the keywords typed into the search engine. When a title bar displays "Untitled Document," the designer has neglected to give the page a title. This is like giving up free "billboard space" and looks unprofessional.

FIGURE 26

New pages added to The Striped Umbrella website (Macintosh)

New pages added to the striped_umbrella root folder

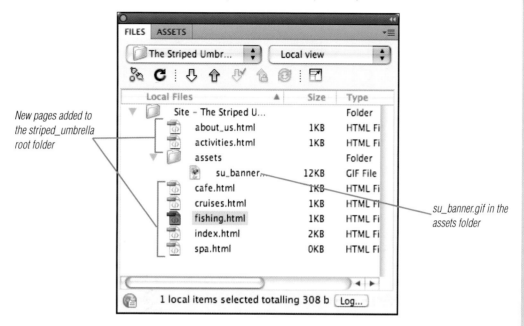

su_banner.gif in the assets folder

| to do this: | use this shortcut: |

POWER USER SHORTCUTS

to do this:	use this shortcut:
Open a file	[Ctrl][O] (Win) or ⌘ [O] (Mac)
Close a file	[Ctrl][W] (Win) or ⌘ [W] (Mac)
Create a new file	[Ctrl][N] (Win) or ⌘ [N] (Mac)
Save a file	[Ctrl][S] (Win) or ⌘ [S] (Mac)
Dreamweaver Help	F1
Show/Hide panels	F4
Switch between Code view and Design view	[Ctrl][`] (Win) or [Ctrl][`] (Mac)

Add pages to a website (Macintosh)

1. Click the **triangle** to the left of the assets folder to open the folder and view its contents.

   TIP If you do not see a file listed in the assets folder, click the Refresh button ↻ on the Files panel.

2. [control]-click the **striped_umbrella root folder**, click **New File**, type **about_us.html** to replace untitled.html, then press **[return]**.

   TIP If you create a new file in the Files panel, you must type the filename extension (.html) manually.

3. Repeat Step 3 to add five more blank pages to The Striped Umbrella website, naming the new files **spa.html**, **cafe.html**, **activities.html**, **cruises.html**, and **fishing.html**.

4. Click the **Refresh button** ↻ to list the files alphabetically, then compare your screen to Figure 26.

5. Click **Dreamweaver** on the Menu bar, and then click **Quit Dreamweaver**.

   TIP If you are prompted to save changes, click No.

You added six pages to The Striped Umbrella website: about_us, activities, cafe, cruises, fishing, spa.

Explore the Dreamweaver workspace.

1. Start Dreamweaver.
2. Create a new document.
3. Change the view to Code view.
4. Change the view to Code and Design views.
5. Change the view to Design view.
6. Collapse the panels to icons.
7. Expand the panels.
8. Undock the Files panel and float it to the middle of the document window. Dock the Files panel back to its original position.
9. View the Assets panel.
10. Close the page without saving it.

View a web page and use Help.

1. Open the file dw1_3.html from where you store your Data Files.
2. Locate the following page elements: a table, a banner, an image, and some formatted text.
3. Change the view to Code view.
4. Change the view to Design view.
5. Use the Dreamweaver Help command to search for information on docking panels.
6. Display and read one of the topics you find.
7. Close the Dreamweaver Help window.
8. Close the page without saving it.

Plan and define a website.

1. Use the Files panel to select the drive and folder where you store your website files.
2. Create a new root folder in this folder or drive called **blooms**.
3. Create a new site called **blooms & bulbs**.
4. Specify the blooms folder as the Local root folder.
5. Verify that the Links Relative to is set to Document and the Enable cache check box is selected.
6. Use the Remote Info category in the Site Definition for blooms & bulbs dialog box to set up web server access. (*Hint:* Specify None if you do not have the necessary information to set up web server access.)
7. Click OK, then click Done to close the Manage Sites dialog box.

Add a folder and pages and set the home page.

1. Create a new folder in the blooms root folder called **assets**.
2. Edit the site to set the assets folder as the default location for the website images.

3. Open the file dw1_4.html from where you store your Data Files, save this file in the blooms root folder as **index.html**, then click No to updating the links.
4. Select the broken image for the blooms & bulbs banner on the page.
5. Use the Property inspector to browse for blooms_banner.jpg, then select it to automatically save it in the assets folder of the blooms & bulbs website. (Remember to click off of the banner anywhere else on the page to show the banner as it replaces the broken image if necessary.)
6. Create seven new pages in the Files panel, and name them: **plants.html**, **classes.html**, **newsletter.html**, **annuals.html**, **perennials.html**, **water_plants.html**, and **tips.html**.
7. Refresh the view to list the new files alphabetically, then compare your screen to Figure 27.
8. Close all open pages.

FIGURE 27
Completed Skills Review

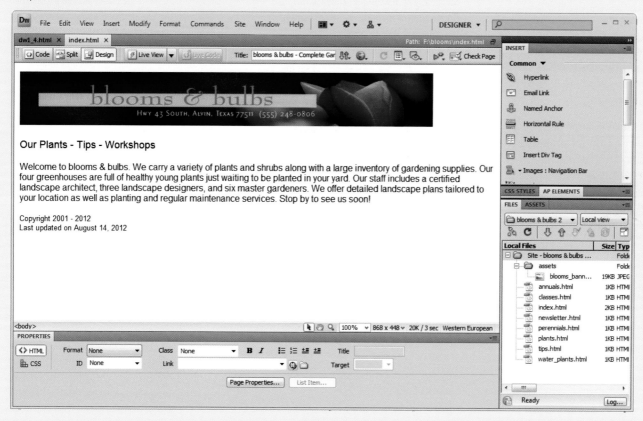

You have been hired to create a website for a travel outfitter called TripSmart. TripSmart specializes in travel products and services. In addition to selling travel products, such as luggage and accessories, they sponsor trips and offer travel advice. Their clients range from college students to families to vacationing professionals. The owner, Thomas Howard, has requested a dynamic website that conveys the excitement of traveling.

1. Using the information in the preceding paragraph, create a storyboard for this website, using either a pencil and paper or a software program such as Microsoft Word. Include the home page with links to four child pages named **catalog.html**, **newsletter.html**, **services.html**, and **destinations.html**. Include two child pages under the destinations page named **amazon.html** and **kenya.html**.

2. Create a new root folder named **tripsmart** in the drive and folder where you store your website files.

3. Start Dreamweaver, then create a site with the name **TripSmart**. Set the tripsmart folder as the local root folder for the site.

4. Create an assets folder and set it as the default location for images.

5. Open the file dw1_5.html from where you store your Data Files, then save it in the tripsmart root folder as **index.html**. (Remember not to update links.)

6. Correct the path for the banner by selecting the banner on the page, browsing to the original source in the Data Files folder, then selecting the file to copy it automatically to your TripSmart assets folder.

7. Create six additional pages for the site, and name them as follows: **catalog.html**, **newsletter.html**, **services.html**, **destinations.html**, **amazon.html**, and **kenya.html**. Use your storyboard and Figure 28 as a guide.

8. Refresh the Files panel.

9. Close all open pages.

FIGURE 28
Completed Project Builder 1

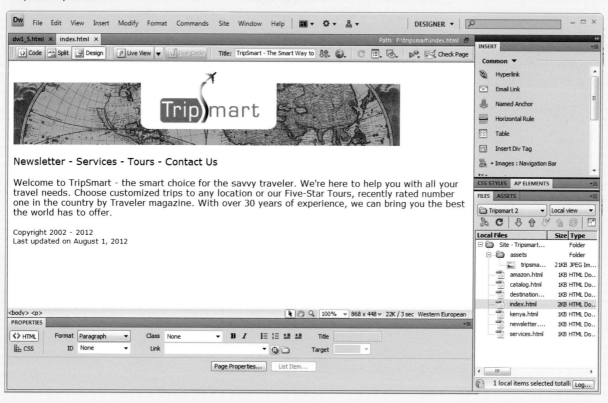

Your company has been selected to design a website for a catering business called Carolyne's Creations. In addition to catering, Carolyne's services include cooking classes and daily specials available as take-out meals. She also has a retail shop that stocks gourmet treats and kitchen items.

1. Create a storyboard for this website that includes a home page and child pages named **shop.html, classes.html, catering.html,** and **recipes.html.** Create two more child pages under the classes.html page called **children.html** and **adults.html**.

2. Create a new root folder for the site in the drive and folder where you save your website files, then name it **cc**.

3. Create a website with the name **Carolyne's Creations**, using the cc folder for the root folder.

4. Create an assets folder for the site and set the assets folder as the default location for images.

5. Open dw1_6.html from the where you store your Data Files then save it as **index.html** in the cc folder.

6. Reset the source for the banner to automatically save the cc_banner.jpg file in the assets folder.

7. Using Figure 29 and your storyboard as guides, create the additional pages shown for the website.

8. Refresh the Files panel to sort the files alphabetically.

9. Close all open pages.

FIGURE 29

Completed Project Builder 2

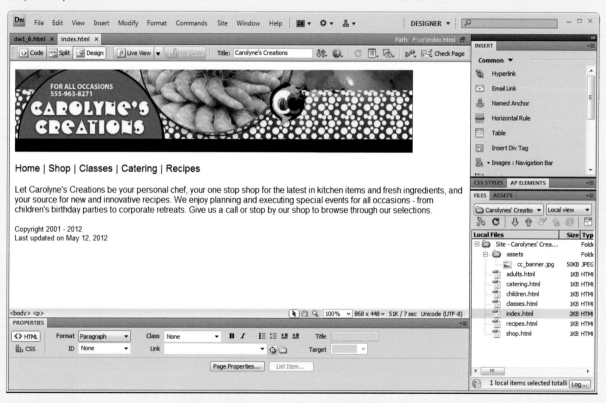

Figure 30 shows the Audi website, a past selection for the Adobe Site of the Day. To visit the current Audi website, connect to the Internet, then go to www.audi.com. The current page might differ from the figure because dynamic websites are updated frequently to reflect current information. Also, your page may default to the Audi of America site. The main navigation structure is accessed through the links along the right side of the page. The page title is Audi Worldwide > Home.

Go to the Adobe website at www.adobe.com, click the Showcase link under the Company menu, then click the current Site of the Day. Explore the site and answer the following questions:

1. Do you see page titles for each page you visit?
2. Do the page titles accurately reflect the page content?
3. View the pages using more than one screen resolution, if possible. For which resolution does the site appear to be designed?

4. Is the navigation structure clear?
5. How is the navigation structure organized?

6. Why do you think this site was chosen as a Site of the Day?

FIGURE 30
Design Project

Audi website used with permission from Audi AG – www.audi.com

PORTFOLIO PROJECT

The Portfolio Project will be an ongoing project throughout the book, in which you will plan and create an original website without any Data Files supplied. The focus of the site can be on any topic, organization, sports team, club, or company that you would like. You will build on this site from chapter to chapter, so you must do each Portfolio Project assignment in each chapter to complete your website. When you finish this book, you should have a completed site that would be an excellent addition to a professional portfolio.

1. Decide what type of site you would like to create. It can be a personal site about you, a business site that promotes a fictitious or real company, or an informational site that provides information about a topic, cause, or organization.
2. Write a list of questions and answers about the site you have decided to create.
3. Create a storyboard for your site to include at least four pages. The storyboard should include the home page with at least three child pages under it.
4. Create a root folder and an assets folder to house the assets, then define your site using the root folder as the website local root folder and the assets folder as the default images folder.
5. Create a blank page named **index.html** as a placeholder for the home page.
6. Begin collecting content, such as pictures or text to use in your website. You can use a digital camera to take photos, use a scanner to scan pictures, or create your own graphics using a program such as Adobe Fireworks or Adobe Illustrator. Gather the content in a central location that will be accessible to you as you develop your site.

chapter

2

DEVELOPING A
WEB PAGE

1. Create head content and set page properties

2. Create, import, and format text

3. Add links to web pages

4. Use the History panel and edit code

5. Modify and test web pages

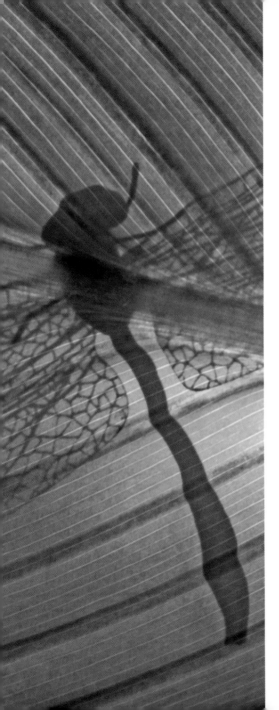

CHAPTER 2 DEVELOPING A WEB PAGE

Introduction

The process of developing a web page requires several steps. If the page is a home page, you need to spend some time crafting the head content. The head content contains information used by search engines to help viewers find your website. You also need to choose the colors for the page background and text. You then need to add the page content, format it attractively, and add links to other pages in the site or to other websites. Finally, to ensure that all links work correctly and are current, you need to test them regularly.

Understanding Page Layout

Before you add content to a page, consider the following guidelines for laying out pages:

Use White Space Effectively. A living room crammed with too much furniture makes it difficult to appreciate the individual pieces. The same is true of a web page. Too many text blocks, links, animations, and images can be distracting. Consider leaving some white space on each page. **White space**, which is not necessarily white, is the area on a page that contains no text or graphics.

Limit Media Elements. Too many media elements, such as images, video clips, or sounds, may result in a page that takes too much time to load. Viewers may leave your site before the entire page finishes loading. Use media elements only if you have a good reason.

Keep It Simple. Often the simplest websites are the most appealing and are also the easiest to create and maintain. A simple, well-designed site that works well is far superior to a complex one that contains errors.

Use an Intuitive Navigation Structure. Make sure the navigation structure is easy to use. Viewers should always know where they are in the site and be able to easily find their way back to the home page. If viewers get lost, they may leave the site rather than struggle to find their way around.

Apply a Consistent Theme. To help give pages in your website a consistent appearance, consider designing your pages using elements that relate to a common theme. Consistency in the use of color and fonts, the placement of the navigation links, and the overall page design gives a website a unified look and promotes greater ease-of-use and accessibility. Template-based pages and style sheets make this task much easier.

2-2

Tools You'll Use

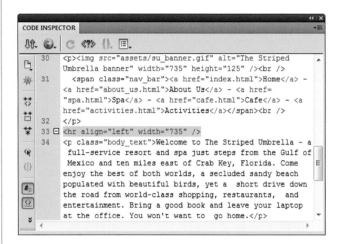

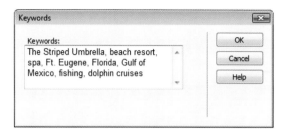

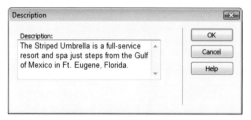

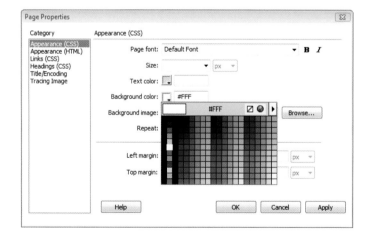

CREATE HEAD CONTENT AND
SET PAGE PROPERTIES

What You'll Do

In this lesson, you will learn how to enter titles, keywords, and descriptions in the head content section of a web page. You will also change the background color for a web page.

Creating the Head Content

A web page is composed of two distinct sections: the head content and the body. The **head content** includes the page title that appears in the title bar of the browser and some important page elements, called meta tags, that are not visible in the browser. **Meta tags** are HTML codes that include information about the page, such as the page title, keywords and descriptions. Meta tags are read by screen readers (for viewers who have visual impairments) and are also used to provide the server information such as the PICS rating for the page. PICS is the acronym for **Platform for Internet Content Selection**. This is a rating system for web pages that is similar to rating systems used for movies. **Keywords** are words that relate to the content of the website.

QUICKTIP

Page titles are not to be confused with filenames, the name used to store each file on the server.

DESIGNTIP   **Using web-safe colors**

Prior to 1994, colors appeared differently on different types of computers. In 1994, Netscape developed the first **web-safe color palette**, a set of colors that appears consistently in all browsers and on Macintosh, Windows, and UNIX platforms. The evolution of video cards has made this less relevant today, although understanding web-safe colors may still prove important given the limitations of other online devices, such as cell phones and PDAs. If you want your web pages to be viewed across a wide variety of computer platforms, choose web-safe colors for all your page elements. Dreamweaver has two web-safe color palettes, Color Cubes and Continuous Tone, each of which contains 216 web-safe colors. Color Cubes is the default color palette. To choose a different color palette, click Modify on the Application bar (Win) or Menu bar (Mac) click Page Properties, click the Appearance (CSS) or Appearance (HTML) category, click the Background, Text, or Links color box to open the color picker, click the color picker list arrow, and then click the color palette you want.

A **description** is a short paragraph that describes the content and features of the website. For instance, the words "beach" and "resort" would be appropriate keywords for The Striped Umbrella website. Search engines find web pages by matching the title, description, and keywords in the head content of web pages with keywords that viewers enter in search engine text boxes. Therefore, it is important to include concise, useful information in the head content. The **body** is the part of the page that appears in a browser window. It contains all the page content that is visible to viewers, such as text, images, and links.

Setting Web Page Properties

When you create a web page, one of the first design decisions that you should make is choosing the **background color**, or the color that fills the entire page. The background color should complement the colors used for text, links, and images that are placed on the page. Many times, images are used for backgrounds for either the entire page or a part of the page, such as a table background or Cascading Style Sheet (CSS) block.

QUICKTIP

A **CSS block** is a section of a web page defined and formatted using a Cascading Style Sheet.
A **Cascading Style Sheet** is a file used to assign sets of common formatting characteristics to page elements such as text, objects, tags, and tables. We will initially use the Page Properties dialog box to set page properties such as the background color. Later we will learn to do this using Cascading Style Sheets.

A strong contrast between the text color and the background color makes it easier for viewers to read the text on your web page.

You can choose a light background color with a dark text color, or a dark background color with a light text color. A white background with dark text, though not terribly exciting, provides good contrast and is the easiest to read for most viewers. Another design decision you need to make is whether to change the **default font** and **default link colors**, which are the colors used by the browser to display text, links, and visited links. The default color for **unvisited links**, or links that the viewer has not clicked yet, is blue. In Dreamweaver, unvisited links are simply called **links**. The default color for **visited links**, or links that have been previously clicked, is purple. You change the background color, text, and link colors using the color picker in the Page Properties dialog box. You can choose colors from one of the five Dreamweaver color palettes, as shown in Figure 1.

FIGURE 1
Color picker showing color palettes

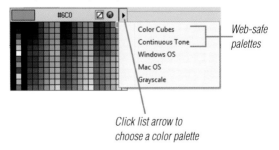

Web-safe palettes

Click list arrow to choose a color palette

Edit a page title

1. Start Dreamweaver, click the **Site list arrow** on the Files panel, then click **The Striped Umbrella** (if necessary).

2. Double-click **index.html** in the Files panel to open The Striped Umbrella home page, click **View** on the Application bar (Win) or Menu bar (Mac), then click **Head Content**.

   The Meta icon , Title icon , and CSS icon are now visible in the head content section.

3. Click the **Title icon** in the head content section.

   The page title The Striped Umbrella appears in the Title text box in the Property inspector, and the selected Title icon in the head content section changes to a blue color, as shown in Figure 2.

4. Click after the end of The Striped Umbrella text in the Title text box in the Property inspector, press **[Spacebar]**, type **beach resort and spa, Ft. Eugene, Florida**, then press **[Enter]** (Win) or **[return]** (Mac).

   Compare your screen with Figure 3. The new title is better, because it incorporates the words "beach resort" and "spa" and the location of the resort—words that potential customers might use as keywords when using a search engine.

   | TIP   You can also change the page title using the Title text box on the Document toolbar.

You opened The Striped Umbrella website, opened the home page in Design view, viewed the head content section, and changed the page title.

FIGURE 2
Viewing the head content

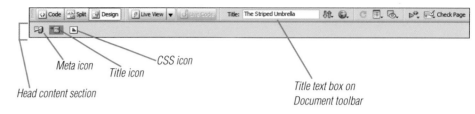

Meta icon   ~~CSS icon~~ CSS icon
Title icon
Head content section

Title text box on
Document toolbar

FIGURE 3
Property inspector displaying new page title

Scroll with arrow key to
see the rest of the title

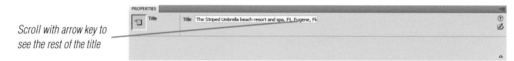

DESIGNTIP   **Using appropriate content for your target audience**

When you begin developing the content for your website, you need to decide what content to include and how to arrange each element on each page. You must design the content with the audience in mind. What is the age group of your audience? What reading level is appropriate? Should you use a formal or informal tone? Should the pages be simple, consisting mostly of text, or rich with images and media files? Your content should fit your target audience. Look at the font sizes used, the number and size of images and animations used, the reading level, and the amount of technical expertise needed to navigate your site, and then evaluate them to see if they fit your audience. If they do not, you will be defeating your purpose. Usually, the first page that your audience will see when they visit your site is the home page. The home page should be designed so that viewers will understand your site's purpose and feel comfortable finding their way around the pages in your site. To ensure that viewers do not get lost in your site, make sure you design all the pages with a consistent look and feel. You can use templates and Cascading Style Sheets to maintain a common look for each page. **Templates** are web pages that contain the basic layout for each page in the site, including the location of a company logo or a menu of buttons. **Cascading Style Sheets** are sets of formatting attributes that are used to format web pages to provide a consistent presentation for content across the site. Cascading Style Sheets make it easy to separate your site content from the site design. The content is stored on web pages, and the formatting styles are stored in a separate style sheet file.

FIGURE 4
Insert bar displaying the
Common category

Common category

Head list arrow

Your icon may differ depending on what was last selected

Keywords command

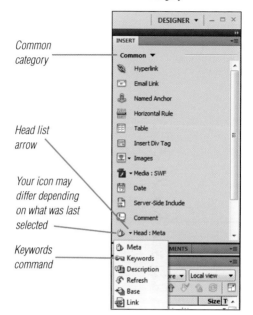

Enter keywords

1. Click the **Common category** on the Insert panel (if necessary).

2. Click the **Head list arrow**, as shown in Figure 4, then click **Keywords**.

   TIP   Some buttons on the Insert panel include a list arrow indicating that there is a menu of choices beneath the current button. The button that you select last will appear on the Insert panel until you select another.

3. Type **The Striped Umbrella, beach resort, spa, Ft. Eugene, Florida, Gulf of Mexico, fishing, dolphin cruises** in the Keywords text box, as shown in Figure 5, then click **OK**

   The Keywords icon appears in the head content section; click it and the keywords will appear in the Keywords text box in the Property inspector.

You added keywords relating to the beach to the head content of The Striped Umbrella home page.

FIGURE 5
Keywords dialog box

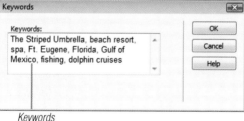

Keywords

DESIGNTIP   **Entering keywords and descriptions**

Search engines use keywords, descriptions, and titles to find pages after a user enters search terms. Therefore, it is very important to anticipate the search terms your potential customers would use and include these words in the keywords, description, and title. Many search engines display page titles and descriptions in their search results. Some search engines limit the number of keywords that they will index, so make sure you list the most important keywords first. Keep your keywords and descriptions short and concise to ensure that all search engines will include your site. To choose effective keywords, many designers incorporate the use of focus groups to have a more representative sample of words that potential customers or clients might use. A **focus group** is a marketing tool that asks a group of people for feedback about a product, such as its impact in a television ad or the effectiveness of a website design.

Enter a description

1. Click the **Head list arrow** on the Insert panel, then click **Description**.

2. In the Description text box, type **The Striped Umbrella is a full-service resort and spa just steps from the Gulf of Mexico in Ft. Eugene, Florida**.

   Your screen should resemble Figure 6.

3. Click **OK**, then click the **Description icon** 🔲 in the Head Content.

   The Description icon 🔲 appears in the Head Content section and the description appears in the Description text box in the Property inspector.

4. Click the **Show Code view button** 〈〉 Code on the Document toolbar.

   Notice that the title, keywords, and description appear in the HTML code in the document window, as shown in Figure 7.

   | TIP   You can also enter and edit the meta tags directly in the code in Code view.

5. Click the **Show Design view button** 🔲 Design to return to Design view.

6. Click **View** on the Application bar (Win) or Menu bar (Mac), then click **Head Content** to close the head content section.

You added a description of The Striped Umbrella resort to the head content of the home page. You then viewed the page in Code view and examined the HTML code for the head content.

FIGURE 6
Description dialog box

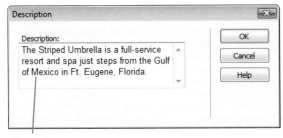

Description

FIGURE 7
Head Content displayed in Code view

Opening Head tag

Title tag

Your head content line numbers may differ

Keywords tag

Description tag

Closing Head tag

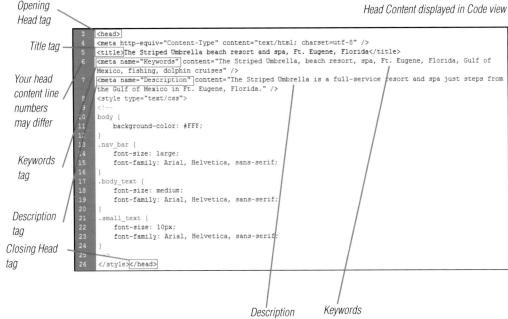

Description   Keywords

Developing a Web Page

FIGURE 8

Page Properties dialog box

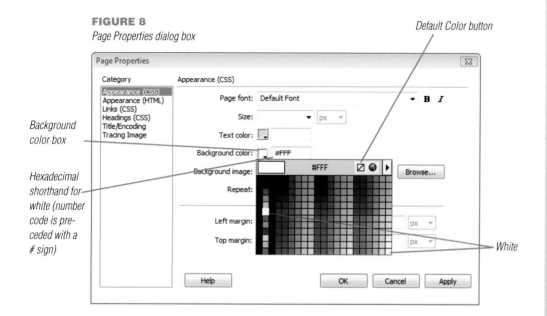

Default Color button

Background color box

Hexadecimal shorthand for white (number code is preceded with a # sign)

White

Understanding hexadecimal values

Each color is assigned a **hexadecimal RGB value**, a value that represents the amount of red, green, and blue present in the color. For example, white, which is made of equal parts of red, green, and blue, has a hexadecimal value of FFFFFF. This is also referred to as an RGB triplet in hexadecimal format (**hex triplet**). Each pair of characters in the hexadecimal value represents the red, green, and blue values. The hexadecimal number system is based on 16, rather than 10 in the decimal number system. Because the hexadecimal number system includes only numbers up to 9, values after 9 use the letters of the alphabet. "A" represents the number 10 in the hexadecimal number system. "F" represents the number 15. The hexadecimal values are entered in the code using a form of shorthand that shortens the six characters to three characters. For instance: FFFFFF become FFF; 0066CC becomes 06C. The number value for a color is preceded by a pound sign (#) in HTML code.

Set the page background color

1. Click **Modify** on the Application bar (Win) or Menu bar (Mac), then click **Page Properties** to open the Page Properties dialog box.

2. Click the **Background color box** [ ] to open the color picker, as shown in Figure 8.

3. Click the rightmost color in the bottom row (white).

4. Click **Apply**, then click **OK**.

   Clicking Apply lets you see the changes you made to the web page without closing the Page Properties dialog box.

   > TIP   If you don't like the color you chose, click the Default Color button ☑ in the color picker to switch to the default color.

   The background color of the web page is now white. The black text against the white background provides a nice contrast and makes the text easy to read.

5. Save your work.

You used the Page Properties dialog box to change the background color to white.

CREATE, IMPORT, AND
FORMAT TEXT

What You'll Do

In this lesson, you will apply HTML heading styles and HTML text styles to text on The Striped Umbrella home page. You will also import a file and set text properties for the text on the new page.

Creating and Importing Text

Most information in web pages is presented in the form of text. You can type text directly in Dreamweaver, import, or copy and paste it from another software program. (Macintosh users do not have the option to import text. They must open a text file, copy the text, then paste it into an HTML document.) When using a Windows computer to import text from a Microsoft Word file, you use the Import Word Document command. Not only will the formatting be preserved, but Dreamweaver will generate clean HTML code. Clean HTML code is code that does what it is supposed to do without using unnecessary instructions, which take up memory. When you format text, it is important to keep in mind that visitors to your site must have the same fonts installed on their computers as the fonts you use. Otherwise, the text may appear incorrectly. Some software programs can convert text into graphics so that the text retains the same appearance no matter which fonts are installed. However, text converted into graphics is no longer editable. If text does not have a font specified, the default font will apply. This means that the default font on

Using keyboard shortcuts

When working with text, the standard Windows keyboard shortcuts for Cut, Copy, and Paste are very useful. These are [Ctrl][X] (Win) or ⌘[X] (Mac) for Cut, [Ctrl][C] (Win) or ⌘[C] (Mac) for Copy, and [Ctrl][V] (Win) or ⌘[V] (Mac) for Paste. You can view all Dreamweaver keyboard shortcuts using the Keyboard Shortcuts dialog box, which lets you view existing shortcuts for menu commands, tools, or miscellaneous functions, such as copying HTML or inserting an image. You can also create your own shortcuts or assign shortcuts that you are familiar with from using them in other software programs. To view or modify keyboard shortcuts, click the Keyboard Shortcuts command on the Edit menu (Win) or Dreamweaver menu (Mac), then select the shortcut key set you want. The Keyboard Shortcuts feature is also available in Adobe Fireworks and Flash. Each chapter in this book includes a list of keyboard shortcuts relevant to that chapter.

the user's computer will be used to display the text. Keep in mind that some fonts may not appear the same on both a Windows and a Macintosh computer. The way fonts are rendered (drawn) on the screen differs because Windows and Macintosh computers use different technologies to render them. It is wise to stick to the standard fonts that work well with both systems. Test your pages using both operating systems.

Formatting Text Using the Property Inspector

Because text is more difficult and tiring to read on a computer screen than on a printed page, you should make the text in your website attractive and easy to read. You can format text in Dreamweaver by changing its font, size, and color, just as you would in other software programs. To apply formatting to text, you first select the text you want to enhance, and then use the Property inspector to apply formatting attributes, such as font type, size, color, alignment, and indents.

Using HTML Tags Compared to Using CSS

The standard practice today is to use Cascading Style Sheets (CSS) to handle the formatting and placement of web page elements. In fact, the default preference in Dreamweaver is to use CSS rather than HTML tags.

QUICKTIP

Tags are the parts of the code that specify formatting for all elements in the document.

However, this is a lot to learn when you are just beginning, so we are going to begin by using HTML tags for formatting until we study CSS in depth in the next chapter. At that point, we will use CSS instead of HTML tags. To change from CSS to HTML and vice versa, you select the CSS or HTML Property inspector. The Property inspector options will change according to which button is selected. Even if you have the HTML Property inspector selected, styles will be created automatically when you apply most formatting attributes.

Changing Fonts

You can format your text with different fonts by choosing a font combination from the Font list in the CSS Property inspector. A **font combination** is a set of three font choices that specify which fonts a browser should use to display the text on your web page. Font combinations are used so that if one font is not available, the browser will use the next one specified in the font combination. For example, if text is formatted with the font combination Arial, Helvetica, sans serif; the browser will first look on the viewer's system for Arial. If Arial is not available, then it will look for Helvetica. If Helvetica is not available, then it will look for a sans-serif font to apply to the text. Using fonts within the default settings is wise, because fonts set outside the default settings may not be available on all viewers' computers.

Changing Font Sizes

There are two ways to change the size of text using the Property inspector. When the CSS option is selected, you can select a numerical value for the size from 9 to 36 pixels or you can use a size expressed in words from xx-small to larger. On the HTML Property inspector, you do not have font sizes available.

Formatting Paragraphs

The HTML Property inspector displays options to format blocks of text as paragraphs or as different sizes of headings. To format a paragraph as a heading, click anywhere in the paragraph, and then select the heading size you want from the Format list in the Property inspector. The Format list contains six different heading formats. Heading 1 is the largest size, and Heading 6 is the smallest size. Browsers display text formatted as headings in bold, setting them off from paragraphs of text. You can also align paragraphs with the alignment buttons on the CSS Property inspector and indent paragraphs using the Text Indent and Text Outdent buttons on the HTML Property inspector.

QUICKTIP

Mixing too many different fonts and formatting attributes on a web page can result in pages that are visually confusing or difficult to read.

Enter text

1. Position the insertion point directly after "want to go home." at the end of the paragraph, press **[Enter]** (Win) or **[return]** (Mac), then type **The Striped Umbrella**.

   Pressing [Enter] (Win) or [return] (Mac) creates a new paragraph. The HTML code for a paragraph break is <p>. The tag is closed with </p>.

   > TIP If the new text does not assume the formatting attributes as the paragraph above it, click the Show Code and Design views button ![Split] position the cursor right after the period after "home", then go back to the page in Design view and insert a new paragraph.

2. Press and hold **[Shift]**, press **[Enter]** (Win) or **[return]** (Mac), then type **25 Beachside Drive**.

   Pressing and holding [Shift] while you press [Enter] (Win) or [return] (Mac) creates a line break. A **line break** places a new line of text on the next line down without creating a new paragraph. Line breaks are useful when you want to add a new line of text directly below the current line of text and keep the same formatting. The HTML code for a line break is <br />.

3. Add the following text below the 25 Beachside Drive text, using line breaks after each line:

   Ft. Eugene, Florida 33775
   555-594-9458

4. Compare your screen with Figure 9.

   You entered text for the address and telephone number on the home page.

FIGURE 9
Entering the address and telephone number on The Striped Umbrella home page

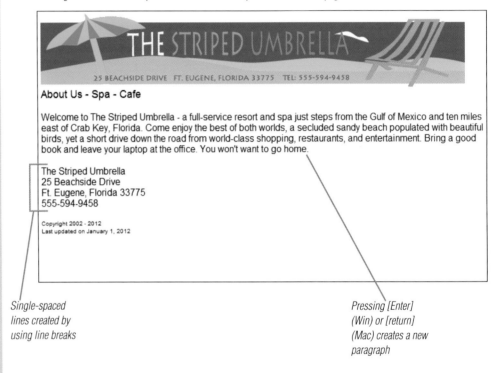

Single-spaced lines created by using line breaks

Pressing [Enter] (Win) or [return] (Mac) creates a new paragraph

Preventing data loss

When you are ready to stop working with a file in Dreamweaver, it is a good idea to save your changes, close the page or pages on which you are working, and exit Dreamweaver. Doing this will prevent the loss of data if power is interrupted. In some cases, loss of power can corrupt an open file and render it unusable.

FIGURE 10

Formatting the address on The Striped Umbrella home page

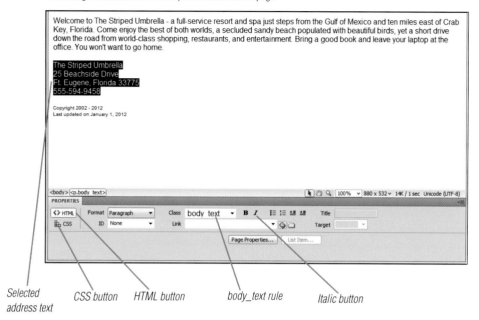

Selected address text

CSS button   HTML button   body_text rule   Italic button

FIGURE 11

Viewing the HTML code for the address and phone number

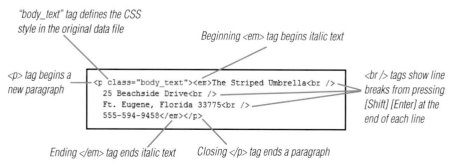

"body_text" tag defines the CSS style in the original data file

Beginning <em> tag begins italic text

<p> tag begins a new paragraph

 tags show line breaks from pressing [Shift] [Enter] at the end of each line

Ending </em> tag ends italic text   Closing </p> tag ends a paragraph

Format text

1. Select the entire address and telephone number, as shown in Figure 10, then click the **HTML button** `<> HTML` in the Property inspector (if it is not already selected) to change to the HTML Property inspector, as shown in Figure 10.

2. Click the **Italic button** _I_ in the Property inspector to italicize the text, then click after the text to deselect it.

    The HTML tag for italic text is <em>.

    > TIP   The HTML tag for bold text is <strong></strong>. The HTML tag for underlined text is <u></u>.

3. Click the **Show Code view button** `<> Code` to view the HTML code, as shown in Figure 11.

    It is always helpful to learn what the HTML code means. As you edit and format your pages, read the code to see how it is written for each element. The more familiar you are with the code, the more comfortable you will feel with Dreamweaver and web design. A strong knowledge of HTML is a necessary skill for professional web designers.

4. Click the **Show Design view button** `Design` to return to Design view.

5. Save your work, then close the page.

You changed the Property inspector options from CSS to HTML, then formatted the address and phone number for The Striped Umbrella by changing the font style to italic.

Save an image file in the assets folder

1. Open dw2_1.html from where you store your Data Files, save it as **spa.html** in the striped_umbrella folder, overwriting the existing file, then click **No** in the Update Links dialog box.

2. Select **The Striped Umbrella** banner.

   Updating links ties the image or hyperlink to the Data Files folder. Because you already copied su_banner.gif to the website, the banner image is visible. Notice that the Src text box shows the link is to the website assets folder, not to the Data Files folder.

3. Click the **Spa image broken link placeholder** to select it, click the **Browse for File icon** in the Property inspector next to the Src text box, navigate to the chapter_2 assets folder, click **the_spa.jpg**, then click **OK** (Win) or **Choose** (Mac).

   Because this image was not in the website, it appeared as a broken link. Using the Browse for File icon selects the source of the original image file. Dreamweaver automatically copies the file to the assets folder of the website and it is visible on the page. You may have to deselect the new image to see it replace the broken link.

4. Click the **Refresh button** on the Files panel toolbar if necessary, then click the **plus sign** (Win) or **expander arrow** (Mac) next to the assets folder in the Files panel, (if necessary).

   A copy of the_spa.jpg file appears in the assets folder, as shown in Figure 12.

   You opened a new file, saved it as the new spa page, and fixed a broken link by copying the image to the assets folder.

FIGURE 12
Image file added to The Striped Umbrella assets folder

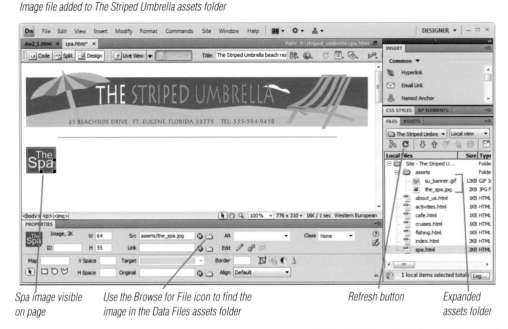

Spa image visible on page

Use the Browse for File icon to find the image in the Data Files assets folder

Refresh button

Expanded assets folder

Choosing filenames for HTML web pages

When you choose a name for a web page, you should use a descriptive name that reflects the contents of the page. For example, if the page is about your company's products, you could name it products.html. You should also follow some general rules for naming web pages, such as naming the home page **index.html**. Most file servers look for the file named index.html to use as the initial page for a website. Do not use spaces, special characters, or punctuation in web page filenames or in the names of any images that will be inserted in your site. Spaces in filenames can cause errors when a browser attempts to read a file, and may cause your images to load incorrectly; use underscores in place of spaces. Forbidden characters include * & ^ % $ # @ ! / and \. You should also never use a number for the first character of a filename. To ensure that everything will load properly on all platforms, including UNIX, assume that filenames are case-sensitive and use lowercase characters. HTML web pages can be saved with the .htm or .html file extension. Although either file extension is appropriate, Dreamweaver uses the default file extension of .html.

FIGURE 13
Clean Up Word HTML dialog box

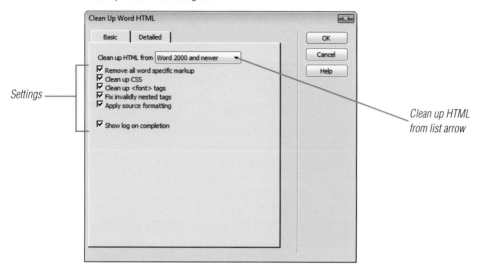

Settings

Clean up HTML
from list arrow

Importing and linking Microsoft Office documents (Windows)

Adobe makes it easy to transfer data between Microsoft Office documents and Dreamweaver web pages. When importing a Word or Excel document, click File on the Application bar, point to Import, then click either Word Document or Excel Document. Select the file want to import, then click the Formatting list arrow to choose between importing Text only; Text with structure (paragraphs, lists, and tables); Text, structure, basic formatting (bold, italic); Text, structure, full formatting (bold, italic, styles) before you click Open. The option you choose depends on the importance of the original structure and formatting. Always use the Clean Up Word HTML command after importing a Word file. You can also create a link to a Word or Excel document on your web page. To do so, drag the Word or Excel document from its current location to the location on the page where you would like the link to appear. (If the document is located outside the site, you can browse for it using the Site list arrow on the Files panel, Windows Explorer, or Mac Finder.) Next, select the Create a link option button in the Insert Document dialog box, then save the file in your root folder so it will be uploaded when you publish your site. If it is not uploaded, the link will be broken.

Import text

1. With the insertion point to the right of the spa graphic on the spa.html page, press **[Enter]** (Win) or **[return]** (Mac).

2. Click **File** on the Application bar, point to **Import**, click **Word Document**, double-click the **chapter_2 folder** from where you store your Data Files, then double-click **spa.doc** (Win); or double-click **spa.doc** from where you store your Data Files, select all, copy, close spa.doc, then paste the copied text on the spa page in Dreamweaver (Mac).

3. Click **Commands** on the Application bar (Win) or Menu bar (Mac), then click **Clean Up Word HTML**.

   TIP If a dialog box appears stating that Dreamweaver was unable to determine the version of Word used to generate this document, click OK, click the Clean up HTML from list arrow, then choose the Word 2000 and newer version of Word if it isn't already selected.

4. Make sure each check box in the Clean Up Word HTML dialog box is checked, as shown in Figure 13, click **OK**, then click **OK** again to close the results window.

You imported a Word document, then used the Clean Up Word HTML command.

Set text properties

1. Click the Common category on the Insert panel if necessary, then scroll up and place the insertion point anywhere within the words "Spa Services."

2. Click the **Format list arrow** in the HTML Property inspector, click **Heading 4,** click the **Show Code and Design views button** ⬚ Split on the Document toolbar, then compare your screen to Figure 14.

   The Heading 4 format is applied to the paragraph. Even a single word is considered a paragraph if there is a hard return or paragraph break after it. The HTML code for a Heading 4 tag is <h4>. The tag is then closed with </h4>. The level of the heading tag follows the h, so the code for a Heading 1 tag is <h1>.

3. Click **Format** on the Application bar (Win) or Menu bar (Mac), point to **Align,** then click **Center**.

   When the paragraph is centered, the HTML code 'align="center"' is added to the <h4> tag.

You applied a heading format to a heading, viewed the HTML code, then centered the heading.

FIGURE 14

Viewing the heading tag in Show Code and Design views

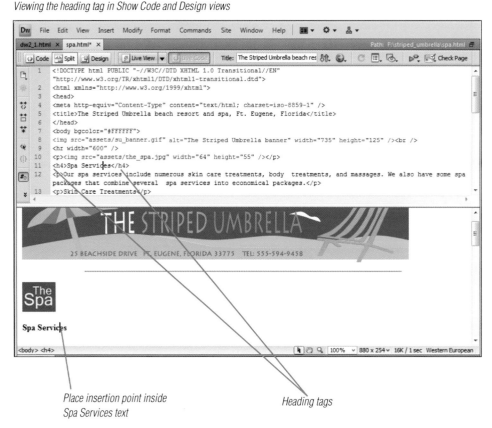

Place insertion point inside
Spa Services text

Heading tags

Developing a Web Page

FIGURE 15
Check Spelling dialog box

Our spa services include numerous skin care treatments, body treatments, and massages. We also have some spa packages that combine several spa se...

Skin Care Treatments

Revitalizing Facial
A light massage that moisturizes the sk...

Gentlemen's Facial
A cleansing facial that includes a neck...

Milk Mask
A mask applied to soften and moisturi...

Body Treatments

Salt Glow
Imported sea salts are masaged into the skin, exfoliating and cleansing the pores.

Mud Body Wrap
Relief for your aches and pains.

Check Spelling

Word not found in dictionary:
masaged

Add to Personal

Change to: massaged

Suggestions:
massaged
massage
messaged
massages
managed
massager
message
massacred

Ignore
Change
Ignore All
Change All

Close   Help

Misspelled word

Click "Change" to correct spelling

Checking for spelling errors

It is very important to check for spelling and grammatical errors before publishing a page. A page that is published with errors will cause the viewer to immediately judge the site as unprofessional and carelessly made, and the accuracy of the data presented will be in question. If a file you create in a word processor will be imported into Dreamweaver, run a spell check in the word processor first. Then spell check the imported text again in Dreamweaver so you can add words such as proper names to the Dreamweaver dictionary so the program will not flag them again. Click the Add to Personal button in the Check Spelling dialog box to add a new word to the dictionary. Even though you may have checked a page using the spell check feature, you still must proofread the content yourself to catch usage errors such as "to," "too," and "two." Accuracy in both content and delivery is critical.

Check spelling

1. Click the **Show Design view button** [Design] to return to Design view.

2. Place the insertion point in front of the text "Spa Services".

    It is a good idea to start a spelling check at the top of the document because Dreamweaver searches from the insertion point down. If your insertion point is in the middle of the document, you will receive a message asking if you want to check the rest of the document. Starting from the beginning just saves time.

3. Click **Commands** on the Application bar (Win) or Menu bar (Mac), then click **Check Spelling.**

    The word "masaged" is highlighted on the page as a misspelled word and suggestions are listed to correct it in the Check Spelling dialog box, as shown in Figure 15.

4. Click **massaged** in the Suggestions list if necessary, then click **Change.**

    The word is corrected on the page.

5. Click **OK** to close the Dreamweaver dialog box stating that the Spelling Check is completed.

6. Save and close the spa page, then close the dw2_1.html page.

You checked the page for spelling errors.

ADD LINKS TO
WEB PAGES

What You'll Do

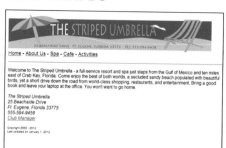

 In this lesson, you will open the home page and add links to the navigation bar that link to the About Us, Spa, Cafe, and Activities pages. You will then insert an email link at the bottom of the page.

Adding Links to Web Pages

Links provide the real power for web pages. Links make it possible for viewers to navigate all the pages in a website and to connect to other pages anywhere on the web. Viewers are more likely to return to websites that have a user-friendly navigation structure. Viewers also enjoy websites that have interesting links to other web pages or other websites.

To add links to a web page, first select the text or image that you want to serve as a link, and then specify a path to the page to which you want to link in the Link text box in the Property inspector.

When you create links on a web page, it is important to avoid **broken links**, or links that cannot find their intended destinations. You can accidentally cause a broken link by typing the incorrect address for the link in the Link text box. Broken links are often caused by companies merging, going out of business, or simply moving their website addresses.

In addition to adding links to your pages, you should provide a **point of contact**, or a place on a web page that provides viewers with a means of contacting the company. A common point of contact is a **mailto: link**, which is an email address that viewers with questions or problems can use to contact someone at the company's headquarters.

Using Navigation Bars

A **navigation bar** is an area on a web page that contains links to the main pages of a website. Navigation bars are usually located at the top or side of the main pages of a website and can be created with text, images, or a combination of the two. To make navigating a website as easy as possible, you should place navigation bars in the same position on each page. Navigation bars are the backbone of a website's navigation structure, which includes all navigation aids for moving around a website. You can, however, include additional links to the main pages of the website elsewhere on the page. The web page in Figure 16 shows an example of a navigation bar that contains both text and image links that use JavaScript. Notice that when the mouse is placed on an item in the navigation bar, the image expands to include more information.

Navigation bars can also be simple and contain only text-based links to the pages in the site. You can create a simple navigation bar by typing the names of your website's pages at the top of your web page, formatting the text, and then adding links to each page name. It is always a good idea to provide plain text links for accessibility, regardless of the type of navigation structure you choose to use.

FIGURE 16
The CIA website

Additional information appears

Navigation bar with text links using JavaScript

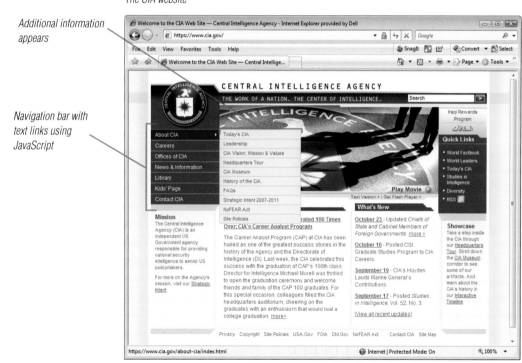

Create a navigation bar

1. Open **index.html**.

2. Position the insertion point to the left of "A" in About Us, then drag to select **About Us - Spa - Cafe**.

3. Type **Home - About Us - Spa - Cafe - Activities,** as shown in Figure 17.

   These five text labels will serve as a navigation bar. You will add the links later.

You created a new navigation bar using text, replacing the original navigation bar.

Insert a horizontal rule

1. Click after the end of the word "Activities" if necessary, then press **[Shift][Enter]** (Win) **or [Shift][return]** (Mac).

2. Click **Horizontal Rule** in the Common category on the Insert panel to insert a horizontal rule under the navigation bar.

   A horizontal rule is a line used to separate page elements or to organize information on a page.

3. Compare your screen to Figure 18, then save your work.

   TIP   An asterisk after the filename in the title bar indicates that you have altered the page since you last saved it. After you save your work, the asterisk does not appear.

You added a horizontal rule to separate the navigation bar from the page content.

FIGURE 17
Viewing the new navigation bar

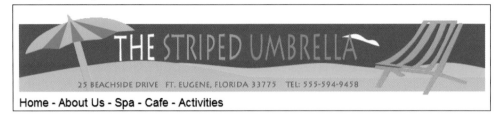

Home - About Us - Spa - Cafe - Activities

FIGURE 18
Inserting a horizontal rule

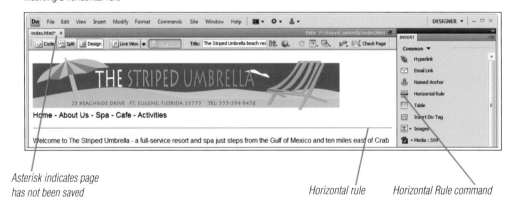

Asterisk indicates page
has not been saved

Horizontal rule   Horizontal Rule command

FIGURE 19

Selecting text for the Home link

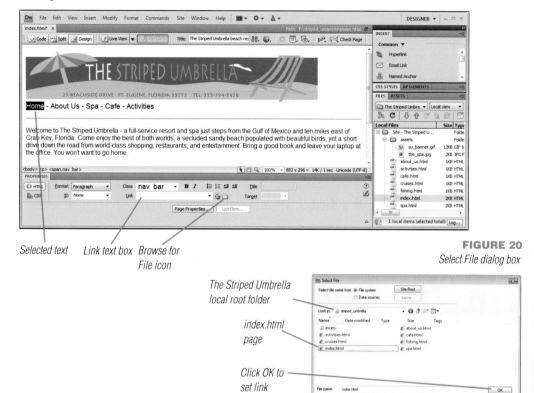

FIGURE 20

Select File dialog box

Selected text   Link text box Browse for
                                 File icon

The Striped Umbrella
local root folder

index.html
page

Click OK to
set link

Relative to:
list arrow

FIGURE 21

Links added to navigation bar

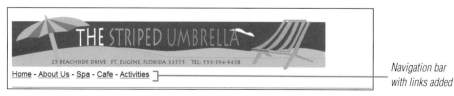

Navigation bar
with links added

Add links to web pages

1. Double-click **Home** to select it, as shown in Figure 19.

2. Click the **Browse for File icon** 📁 next to the Link text box in the HTML Property inspector, then navigate to the striped_umbrella root folder (if necessary).

3. Verify that the link is set Relative to Document in the Relative to: list.

4. Click **index.html** as shown in Figure 20, click **OK** (Win) or **Choose** (Mac), then click anywhere on the page to deselect Home.

   TIP Your file listing may differ depending on your view settings.

   Home now appears in blue with an underline, indicating it is a link. However, clicking Home will not open a new page because the link is to the home page. It might seem odd to create a link to the same page on which the link appears, but this will be helpful when you copy the navigation bar to other pages in the site. Always provide viewers a link to the home page.

5. Repeat Steps 1–4 to create links for About Us, Spa, Cafe, and Activities to their corresponding pages in the striped_umbrella root folder.

6. When you finish adding the links to the other four pages, deselect all, then compare your screen to Figure 21.

You created a link for each of the five navigation bar elements to their respective web pages in The Striped Umbrella website.

Create an email link

1. Place the insertion point after the last digit in the telephone number, then insert a line break.

2. Click **Email Link** in the Common category on the Insert panel to insert an email link.

3. Type **Club Manager** in the Text text box, type **manager@stripedumbrella.com** in the E-Mail text box, as shown in Figure 22, then click **OK** to close the Email Link dialog box.

   If the text does not not retain the formatting from the previous line use the Edit, Undo command to undo Steps 1–3. Switch to Code view and place the insertion point immediately to the right of the telephone number, then repeat the steps again in Design view.

4. Save your work.

   The text "mailto:manager@striped_ umbrella.com," appears in the Link text box in the HTML Property inspector. When a viewer clicks this link, a blank email message window opens in the viewer's default email software, where the viewer can type a message. See Figure 23.

   TIP   You must enter the correct email address in the E-Mail text box for the link to work. However, you can enter any descriptive name, such as customer service or Bob Smith in the Text text box. You can also enter the email address as the text if you want to show the actual email address on the web page.

You inserted an email link to serve as a point of contact for The Striped Umbrella.

FIGURE 22
Email Link dialog box

Text for email link on the page (this could also be a person's name or position or the actual email link)

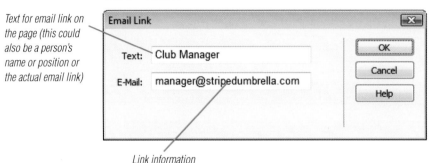

Link information

FIGURE 23
mailto: link on the Property inspector

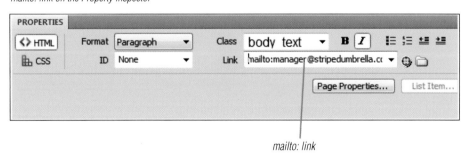

mailto: link

FIGURE 24

The Assets panel URL category

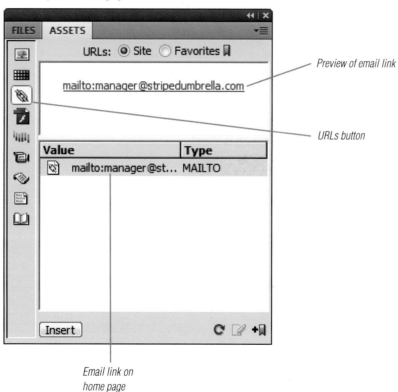

Preview of email link

URLs button

Email link on
home page

1. Click the **Assets panel tab** to view the
   Assets panel.

2. Click the **URLs button** to display the URLs
   in the website, as shown in Figure 24.

   URL stands for **Uniform Resource Locator**. The
   URLs listed in the Assets panel show all of the
   external links, or links pointing outside of the
   website. An email link is outside the website, so
   it is an external link. You will learn more about
   URLs and links in Chapter 4. The links you
   created to the site pages are internal links
   (inside the website), and are not listed in the
   Assets panel.

3. Click the **Files panel tab** to view the Files panel.

*You viewed the email link from the home page in
the Assets panel.*

USE THE HISTORY
PANEL AND EDIT CODE

What You'll Do

In this lesson, you will use the History panel to undo formatting changes you make to a horizontal rule. You will then use the Code Inspector to view the HTML code for the horizontal rule. You will also insert a date object and then view its code in the Code Inspector.

Using the History Panel

Throughout the process of creating a web page, it's likely that you will make mistakes along the way. Fortunately, you have a tool named the History panel to undo your mistakes. The **History panel** records each editing and formatting task performed and displays them in a list in the order in which they were completed. Each task listed in the History panel is called a **step**. You can drag the **slider** on the left side of the History panel to undo or redo steps, as shown in Figure 25. You can also click in the bar to the left of a step to undo all steps below it. You click the step to select it. By default, the History panel records 50 steps. You can change the number of steps the History panel records in the General category of the Preferences dialog box. However, keep in mind that setting this number too high might require additional memory and could affect Dreamweaver's performance.

Understanding other History panel features

Dragging the slider up and down in the History panel is a quick way to undo or redo steps. However, the History panel offers much more. It has the capability to "memorize" certain tasks and consolidate them into one command. This is a useful feature for steps that you perform repetitively on web pages. Some Dreamweaver features, such as drag and drop, cannot be recorded in the History panel and are noted by a red "x" placed next to them. The History panel does not show steps performed in the Files panel.

Viewing HTML Code in the Code Inspector

If you enjoy writing code, you occasionally might want to make changes to web pages by entering the code rather than using the panels and tools in Design view. You can view the code in Dreamweaver using Code view, Code and Design views, or the Code Inspector. The **Code Inspector**, shown in Figure 26, is a separate window that displays the current page in Code view. The advantage of using the Code Inspector is that you can see a full-screen view of your page in Design view while viewing the underlying code in a floating window that you can resize and position wherever you want.

You can add advanced features, such as JavaScript functions, to web pages by copying and pasting code from one page to another in the Code Inspector. A **JavaScript** function is a block of code that adds dynamic content such as rollovers or interactive forms to a web page. A **rollover** is a special effect that changes the appearance of an object when the mouse moves over it.

QUICK TIP

If you are new to HTML, you can use the Reference panel to find answers to your HTML questions. The Reference panel is accessed through the Code Inspector or the Results panel and contains many resources besides HTML help, such as JavaScript help.

FIGURE 25
The History panel

FIGURE 26
The Code Inspector

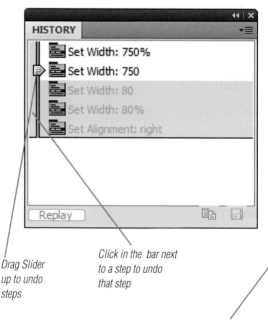

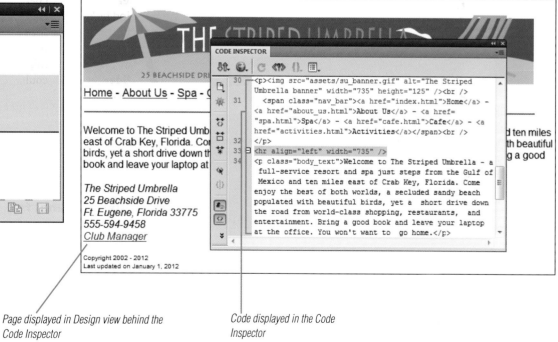

Drag Slider up to undo steps

Click in the bar next to a step to undo that step

Page displayed in Design view behind the Code Inspector

Code displayed in the Code Inspector

Use the History panel

1. Click **Window** on the Application bar (Win) or Menu bar (Mac), then click **History**.

   The History panel opens and displays steps you have recently performed.

2. Click the **History panel options menu button** , click **Clear History**, as shown in Figure 27, then click **Yes** to close the warning box.

3. Select the **horizontal rule** on the home page.

   The Property inspector shows the properties of the selected horizontal rule.

4. Click the W text box in the Property inspector, type **750**, click the **Align list arrow**, click **Left**, then compare your Property inspector to Figure 28.

   TIP Horizontal rule widths can be set in pixels or as a percent of the width of the window. If the width is expressed in pixels, the code will only show the number without the word "pixels". Pixels is understood as the default width setting.

5. Using the Property inspector, change the W text box value to **80**, change the measurement unit to **%**, click the **Align list arrow**, then click **Right**.

6. Drag the **slider** on the History panel up to Set Alignment: Left, as shown in Figure 29.

   The bottom three steps in the History panel appear gray, indicating that these steps have been undone.

7. Right-click (Win) or Control-click (Mac) the **History panel title bar,** then click **Close** to close the History panel.

You formatted the horizontal rule, made changes to it, then used the History panel to undo some of the changes.

FIGURE 27

Clearing the History panel

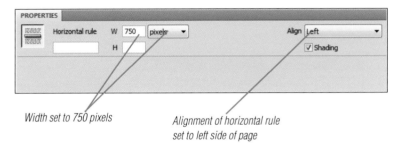

Options menu button

You will see a additional commands if your panel is displayed in a tab group

Clear History command

FIGURE 28

Property inspector settings for horizontal rule

Width set to 750 pixels

Alignment of horizontal rule set to left side of page

FIGURE 29

Undoing steps using the History panel

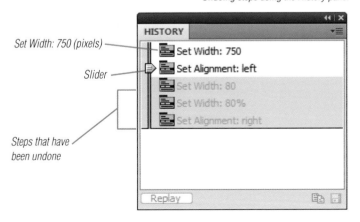

Set Width: 750 (pixels)

Slider

Steps that have been undone

FIGURE 30

Viewing the Options menu in the Code Inspector

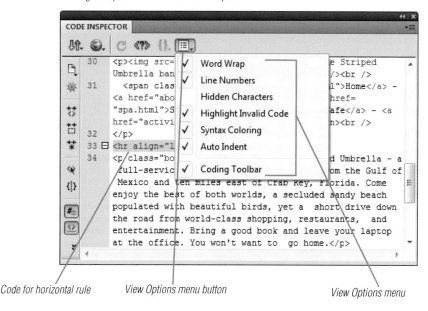

Code for horizontal rule   View Options menu button   View Options menu

POWER USER SHORTCUTS	
to do this:	**use this shortcut:**
Select All	[Ctrl][A] (Win) or ⌘ [A] (Mac)
Copy	[Ctrl][C] (Win) or ⌘ [C] (Mac)
Cut	[Ctrl][X] (Win) or ⌘ [X] (Mac)
Paste	[Ctrl][V] (Win) or ⌘ [V] (Mac)
Line Break	[Shift][Enter] (Win) or [Shift][return] (Mac)
Show or hide the Code Inspector	[F10] (Win) or [option][F10] (Mac)
Preview in browser	[F12] (Win) or [option][F12] (Mac)
Check spelling	[Shift][F7]

Use the Code Inspector

1. Click the **horizontal rule** to select it (if necessary), click **Window** on the Application bar (Win) or Menu bar (Mac), then click **Code Inspector**.

   Because the horizontal rule on the page is selected, the corresponding code is highlighted in the Code Inspector.

   TIP   You can also press [F10](Win) or [option][F10] (Mac) to display the Code Inspector.

2. Click the **View Options menu button** on the Code Inspector toolbar to display the View Options menu, then click **Word Wrap** (if necessary), to activate Word Wrap.

   The Word Wrap feature forces text to stay within the confines of the Code Inspector window, allowing you to read without scrolling sideways.

3. Click the **View Options menu button**, then verify that the Word Wrap, Line Numbers, Highlight Invalid Code, Syntax Coloring, Auto Indent, and the Coding Toolbar menu items are checked, as shown in Figure 30. If they are not checked, check them.

4. Select **750** in the horizontal rule width code, then type **735**.

You changed the width of the horizontal rule by changing the code in the Code Inspector.

Use the Reference panel

1. Click the **Reference button** <?> on the Code Inspector toolbar, as shown in Figure 31, to open the Results Tab Group with the Reference panel visible.

   TIP   Verify that the horizontal rule is still selected, or you will not see the horizontal rule description in the Reference panel.

2. Read the information about horizontal rules in the Reference panel, as shown in Figure 32, right-click in an empty area of the **Results Tab Group title bar,** then click **Close Tab Group** (Win) or click the **Panel Options menu button** then click **Close Tab Group** (Mac and Win) to close the Results Tab Group.

3. Close the Code Inspector.

You read information about horizontal rule settings in the Reference panel.

FIGURE 31
Reference button on the Code Inspector toolbar

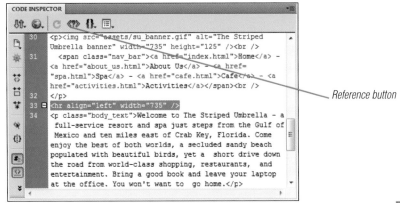

Reference button

FIGURE 32
Viewing the Reference panel

Results tab group

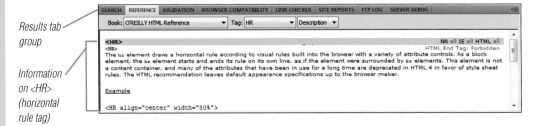

Information on <HR> (horizontal rule tag)

Inserting comments

A handy Dreamweaver feature is the ability to insert comments into HTML code. Comments can provide helpful information describing portions of the code, such as a JavaScript function. You can create comments in any Dreamweaver view, but you must turn on Invisible Elements to see them in Design view. Use the Edit (Win) or Dreamweaver (Mac), Preferences, Invisible Elements, Comments option to enable viewing of comments; then use the View, Visual Aids, Invisible Elements menu option to display them on the page. To create a comment, click the Common category on the Insert panel, click Comment, type a comment in the Comment dialog box, and then click OK. Comments are not visible in browser windows.

FIGURE 33
Insert Date dialog box

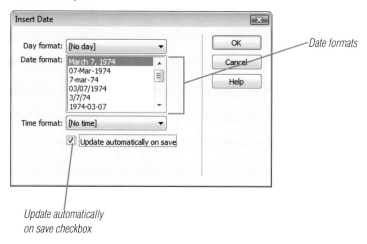

Date formats

Update automatically
on save checkbox

FIGURE 34
Viewing the date object code

```
35   <p class="body_text"><em>The Striped Umbrella<br />
36     25 Beachside Drive<br />
37     Ft. Eugene, Florida 33775<br />
38     555-594-9458<br />
39   <a href="mailto:manager@stripedumbrella.com">Club Manager</a></em></p>
40
41   <p class="small_text">Copyright 2002 - 2012 <br />
42   Last updated on
43     <!-- #BeginDate format:Am1 -->July 4, 2008<!-- #EndDate -->
44   </p>
45   </body>
46   </html>
47
```

Code for date object

Insert a date object

1. Scroll down the page (if necessary) to select **January 1, 2012**, then press **[Delete]** (Win) or **[delete]** (Mac).

2. Click **Date** in the Common category in the Insert panel, then click **March 7, 1974** if necessary in the Date format list box.

3. Click the **Update automatically on save checkbox**, as shown in Figure 33, click **OK**, then deselect the text.

4. Change to Code and Design views.

   The code has changed to reflect the date object, which is set to today's date, as shown in Figure 34. (Your date will be different.) The new code is highlighted with a light yellow background, indicating that it is a date object, automatically coded by Dreamweaver, rather than a date that has been manually typed on the page by the designer.

5. Return to Design view, then save the page.

You inserted a date object that will be updated automatically when you open and save the home page.

MODIFY AND TEST
WEB PAGES

What You'll Do

In this lesson, you will preview the home page in the browser to check for typographical errors, grammatical errors, broken links, and overall appearance. After previewing, you will make slight formatting adjustments to the page to improve its appearance.

Testing and Modifying web pages

Testing web pages is a continuous process. You never really finish a website, because there are always additions and corrections to make. As you add and modify pages, you must test each page as part of the development process. The best way to test a web page is to preview it in a browser window to make sure that all text and image elements appear the way you expect them to. You should also test your links to make sure they work properly. You also need to proofread your text to make sure it contains all the necessary information for the page with no typographical or grammatical errors. Designers typically view a page in a browser, return to Dreamweaver to make necessary changes, and then view the page in a browser again. This process may be repeated many times before the page is ready for publishing. In fact, it is sometimes difficult to stop making improvements to a page and move on to another project. You need to strike a balance among quality, creativity, and productivity.

DESIGN TIP **Using "Under Construction" or "Come back later" pages**

Many people are tempted to insert an unfinished page as a placeholder for a page that will be finished later. Rather than have real content, these pages usually contain text or an image that indicates the page is not finished, or "under construction." You should not publish a web page that has a link to an unfinished page. It is frustrating to click a link for a page you want to open only to find an "under construction" note or image displayed. You want to make the best possible impression on your viewing audience. If you cannot complete a page before publishing it, at least provide enough information on it to make it "worth the trip."

Developing a Web Page

Testing a Web Page Using Different Browsers and Screen Sizes

Because users access the Internet using a wide variety of computer systems, it is important to design your pages so that all browsers and screen sizes can display them well. You should test your pages using different browsers and a wide variety of screen sizes to ensure the best view of your page by the most people possible. Although the most common screen size that designers use today is 1024 × 768, some viewers restore down (reduce) individual program windows to a size comparable to 800 × 600 to be able to have more windows open simultaneously on their screen. In other words, people use their "screen real estate" according to their personal work style. To view your page using different screen sizes, click the Window Size pop-up menu in the status bar, then choose the setting you want to use. Table 1 lists the Dreamweaver default window screen sizes. Remember also to check your pages using Windows and Macintosh platforms. Some page elements such as fonts, colors, table borders, layers, and horizontal rules may not appear consistently in both.

Testing a Web Page as Rendered in a Mobile Device

Dreamweaver has another preview feature that allows you to see what a page would look like if it were viewed on a mobile hand-held device, such as a BlackBerry smartphone. To use this feature, click the Preview/Debug in Browser button on the Document toolbar, then click Preview in Device Central.

TABLE 1: Dreamweaver default window screen sizes

window size (inside dimensions of the browser window without borders)	monitor size
592W	
536 × 196	640 × 480, default
600 × 300	640 × 480, maximized
760 × 420	800 × 600, maximized
795 × 470	832 × 624, maximized
955 × 600	1024 × 768, maximized

Modify a web page

1. Click the **Restore Down button** on the index.html title bar to decrease the size of the home page window (Win) or skip to Step 2 (Mac).

   | TIP You cannot use the Window Size options if your Document window is maximized (Win).

2. Click the current window size on the status bar, as shown in Figure 35, then click **600 × 300 (640 × 480, Maximized)**, (if necessary).

   A viewer using this setting will be forced to use the horizontal scroll bar to view the entire page.

3. Click the current window size on the status bar, then click **760 × 420 (800 × 600, Maximized)**.

4. Replace the period after the last sentence, "You won't want to go home." with an exclamation point.

5. Click the **Maximize button** on the index.html title bar to maximize the home page window.

6. Save your work.

You viewed the home page using two different window sizes and you made simple formatting changes to the page.

FIGURE 35
Window screen sizes

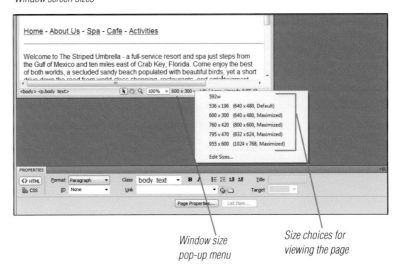

Window size pop-up menu

Size choices for viewing the page

Using smart design principles in web page layout

As you view your pages in the browser, take a critical look at the symmetry of the page. Is it balanced? Are there too many images compared to text, or vice versa? Does everything "heavy" seem to be on the top or bottom of the page, or do the page elements seem to balance with the weight evenly distributed between the top, bottom, and sides? Use design principles to create a site-wide consistency for your pages. Horizontal symmetry means that the elements are balanced across the page. Vertical symmetry means that they are balanced down the page. Diagonal symmetry balances page elements along the invisible diagonal line of the page. Radial symmetry runs from the center of the page outward, like the petals of a flower. These principles all deal with balance; however, too much balance is not good, either. Sometimes it adds interest to place page elements a little off center or to have an asymmetric layout. Color, white space, text, and images should all complement each other and provide a natural flow across and down the page. The rule of thirds—dividing a page into nine squares like a tic-tac-toe grid—states that interest is increased when your focus is on one of the intersections in the grid. The most important information should be at the top of the page where it is visible without scrolling, or "above the fold," as they say in the newspaper business.

FIGURE 36
Viewing The Striped Umbrella home page in the Firefox browser

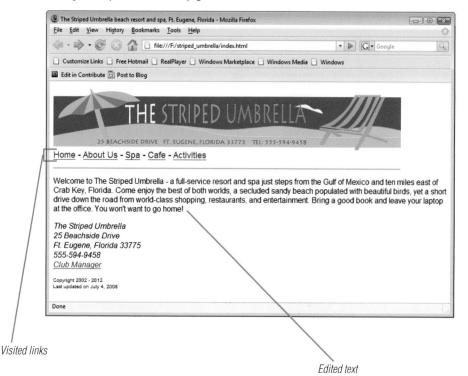

Visited links

Edited text

1. Click the **Preview/Debug in browser button** 🌐 on the Document toolbar, then choose your browser from the menu that opens.

   The Striped Umbrella home page opens in your default browser.

   TIP   If previewing the page in Internet Explorer 7, click the Information bar when prompted, click Allow Blocked Content, then click Yes to close the Security Warning dialog box.

2. Click each link on the navigation bar, then after each click, use the Back button on the browser toolbar to return to the home page.

   Pages with no content at this point will appear as blank pages. Compare your screen to Figure 36.

3. Close your browser window, then close all open pages in Dreamweaver.

You viewed The Striped Umbrella home page in your browser and tested each link on the navigation bar.

DESIGN TIP   **Choosing a window size**

Today, the majority of viewers are using a screen resolution of 1024 × 768 or higher. Because of this, more content can be displayed at one time on a computer monitor. Some people may use their whole screen to view pages on the Internet. Others may choose to allocate a smaller area of their screen to the browser window. In other words, people tend to use their "screen real estate" in different ways. The ideal web page will not be so small that it tries to spread out over a larger screen size or so large that the viewer has to use horizontal scroll bars to read the page content. Achieving the best balance is one of the design decisions that must be made during the planning process.

Create head content and set page properties.

1. Open the blooms & bulbs website.
2. Open the index page and view the head content.
3. Add the word "Your" to the page title to read **blooms & bulbs - Your Complete Garden Center**.
4. Insert the following keywords: **garden**, **plants**, **nursery**, **flowers**, **landscape**, **blooms & bulbs**.
5. Insert the following description: **blooms & bulbs is a premier supplier of garden plants for both professional and home gardeners.**
6. Switch to Code view to view the HTML code for the head content, then switch back to Design view.
7. Open the Page Properties dialog box to view the current page properties.
8. Change the background color to a color of your choice.
9. Change the background color to white, then save your work.

Create, import, and format text.

1. Create a new paragraph after the paragraph of text and type the following text, inserting a line break after each line.
   blooms & bulbs
   Highway 43 South
   Alvin, Texas 77511
   (555) 248-0806

2. Verify that the HTML button is selected in the Property inspector, and select it if it is not.
3. Italicize the address and phone number lines.
4. Change to Code view to view the formatting code for the italicized text.
5. Save your work, then close the home page.
6. Open dw2_2.html and save it as **tips.html** in the blooms & bulbs website, overwriting the existing file, but not updating links.
7. Click the broken image link below the blooms & bulbs banner, use the Property inspector to browse to the chapter_2 Data Files folder, select the file garden_tips.jpg in the assets folder, then click OK to save a copy of it in the blooms & bulbs website.
8. Place the insertion point under the Garden Tips graphic.
9. Import gardening_tips.doc from where you store your Data Files, using the Import Word Document command (Win) or copy and paste the text (Mac).
10. Use the Clean Up Word HTML command to correct or remove any unnecessary code.
11. Select the Seasonal Gardening Checklist heading, use the Application bar (Win) or Menu bar (Mac) to center the text, then delete the colon.
12. Use the Property inspector to format the selected text with a Heading 3 format.
13. Check the page for spelling errors by using the Check Spelling command.

14. Save your work and close the tips page and the data file.

Add links to web pages.

1. Open the index page, then select the current navigation bar and replace it with **Home, Featured Plants, Garden Tips,** and **Classes**. Between each item, use a hyphen with a space on either side to separate the items.
2. Add a horizontal rule under the navigation bar, then remove any extra space between the navigation bar and the horizontal rule, so it looks like Figure 37.
3. Use the Property inspector to link Home on the navigation bar to the index.html page in the blooms & bulbs website.
4. Link Featured Plants on the navigation bar to the plants.html page.
5. Link Garden Tips on the navigation bar to the tips.html page.
6. Link Classes on the navigation bar to the classes.html page.
7. Using the Insert panel, create an email link under the telephone number.
8. Type **Customer Service** in the Text text box and **mailbox@blooms.com** in the E-Mail text box.
9. Save your work.
10. View the email link in the Assets panel, then view the Files panel. You may need to click the Refresh button to see the new link.

Use the History panel and edit code.

1. Open the History panel, then clear its contents.
2. Select the horizontal rule under the navigation bar, then change the width to 700 pixels and the alignment to Left.
3. Change the width to 70% and the alignment to Center.
4. Use the History panel to restore the horizontal rule settings to 700 pixels wide, left aligned.
5. Close the History panel.
6. Open the Code inspector and verify that Word Wrap is selected.
7. Edit the code in the Code inspector to change the width of the horizontal rule to 735 pixels.
8. Open the Reference panel and scan the information about horizontal rules.

9. Close the Code inspector and close the Reference panel tab group.
10. Delete the current date in the Last updated on statement on the home page and replace it with a date that will update automatically when the file is saved.
11. Examine the code for the date at the bottom of the page to verify that the code that forces it to update on save is included in the code. (*Hint*: The code should be highlighted with a light yellow background.)
12. Save your work.

Modify and test web pages.

1. Using the Window Size pop-up menu, view the home page at 600×300 (640×480, Maximized) and 760×420 (800×600, Maximized), then maximize the Document window.

2. View the page in your browser. (*Hint:* If previewing the page in Internet Explorer 7, click the Information bar when prompted to allow blocked content.)
3. Verify that all links work correctly, then close the browser.
4. On the home page, change the text "Stop by and see us soon!" to **We ship overnight**!
5. Save your work, then view the pages in your browser, comparing your pages to Figure 37 and Figure 38.
6. Close your browser.
7. Adjust the spacing (if necessary), save your work, then preview the home page in the browser again.
8. Close the browser, then save and close all open pages.

FIGURE 37
Completed Skills Review, home page

FIGURE 38
Completed Skills Review, tips page

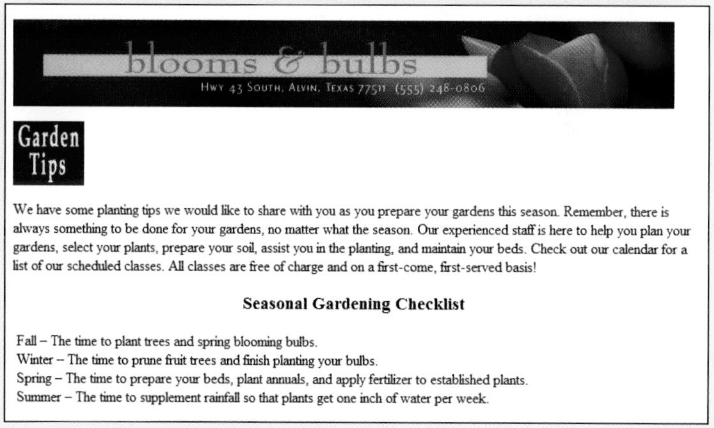

You have been hired to create a website for a TripSmart, a travel outfitter. You have created the basic framework for the website and are now ready to format and edit the home page to improve the content and appearance.

1. Open the TripSmart website, then open the home page.
2. Enter the following keywords: **TripSmart, travel**, **traveling**, **trips**, **vacations**, and **tours**.
3. Enter the following description: **TripSmart is a comprehensive travel store. We can help you plan trips, make travel arrangements, and supply you with travel gear**.
4. Change the page title to **TripSmart - Serving All Your Travel Needs**.

5. Select the existing navigation bar and replace it with the following text links: **Home**, **Catalog**, **Services**, **Destinations**, and **Newsletter**. Between each item, use a hyphen with a space on either side to separate the items.
6. Replace the date in the last updated statement with a date that will update automatically on save.
7. Type the following address two lines below the paragraph about the company, using line breaks after each line:
TripSmart
1106 Beechwood
Fayetteville, AR 72704
555-848-0807

8. Insert an email link in the line below the telephone number, using **Customer Service** for the Text text box and **mailbox@tripsmart.com** for the E-Mail text box in the Email Link dialog box.
9. Italicize TripSmart, the address, phone number, and email link.
10. Link the navigation bar entries to index.html, catalog.html, services.html, destinations.html, and newsletter.html.
11. View the HTML code for the page.
12. Insert a horizontal rule between the paragraph of text and the address.

13. Change the horizontal rule width to 720 pixels and align to the left side of the page.
14. Save your work.

15. View the page using two different window sizes, then test the links in your browser window.

16. Compare your page to Figure 39, close the browser, then close all open pages.

FIGURE 39
Completed Project Builder 1

Home - Catalog - Services - Destinations - Newsletter

Welcome to TripSmart - the smart choice for the savvy traveler. We're here to help you with all your travel needs. Choose customized trips to any location or our Five-Star Tours, recently rated number one in the country by Traveler magazine. With over 30 years of experience, we can bring you the best the world has to offer.

TripSmart
1106 Beechwood
Fayetteville, AR 72704
555.848.0807
Customer Service

Copyright 2002 - 2012
Last updated on July 6, 2008

Your company has been selected to design a website for a catering business named Carolyne's Creations. You are now ready to add content to the home page and apply formatting options to improve the page's appearance, using Figure 40 as a guide.

1. Open the Carolyne's Creations website, then open the home page.
2. Edit the page title to read **Carolyne's Creations - Premier Gourmet Food Shop.**
3. Add the description **Carolyne's Creations is a full service gourmet food shop. We offer cooking classes, take-out meals, and catering services. We also have a retail shop that stocks gourmet treats and kitchen accessories.**

4. Add the keywords **Carolyne's Creations, gourmet, catering, cooking classes, kitchen accessories, take-out.**
5. Place the insertion point in front of the sentence beginning "Give us a call" and type **Feel like a guest at your own party**.
6. Add the following address below the paragraph using line breaks after each line:
   Carolyne's Creations
   496 Maple Avenue
   Seven Falls, Virginia 52404
   555-963-8271
7. Enter another line break after the telephone number and type **Email**, add a space, then add an email link using Carolyne Kate for the text and carolyne@carolynescreations.com for the email address.

8. Create links from each navigation bar element to its corresponding web page.
9. Replace the date that follows the text "Last updated on" with a date object, then save your work.
10. Insert a horizontal rule below the navigation bar.
11. Set the width of the horizontal rule to 360 pixels.
12. Left-align the horizontal rule.

13. Save your work, view the completed page in your default browser, then test each link. (*Hint*: If previewing the page in Internet Explorer 7, click the Information bar when prompted to allow blocked content.)

14. Close your browser.

15. Close all open pages.

FIGURE 40
Completed Project Builder 2

Angela Lou is a freelance photographer. She is searching the Internet looking for a particular type of paper to use in printing her digital images. She knows that websites use keywords and descriptions in order to receive "hits" with search engines. She is curious about how they work. Follow the steps below and write your answers to the questions.

1. Connect to the Internet, then go to *www.snapfish.com* to see the Snapfish website's home page, as shown in Figure 41.

2. View the page source by clicking View on the Application bar, then clicking Source (Internet Explorer) or Page Source (Mozilla Firefox).

3. Can you locate a description and keywords? If so, what are they?

4. How many keywords do you find?

5. Is the description appropriate for the website? Why or why not?

6. Look at the numbers of keywords and words in the description. Is there an appropriate number? Or are there too many or not enough?

7. Use a search engine such as Google at www.google.com, then type the words **photo quality paper** in the Search text box.

8. Click the first link in the list of results and view the source code for that page. Do you see keywords and a description? Do any of them match the words you used in the search?

FIGURE 41
Design Project

Snapfish website used with permission from Snapfish - www.snapfish.com

In this assignment, you will continue to work on the website you defined in Chapter 1. In Chapter 1, you created a storyboard for your website with at least four pages. You also created a local root folder for your site and an assets folder to store the site asset files. You set the assets folder as the default storage location for your images. You began to collect information and resources for your site and started working on the home page.

1. Think about the head content for the home page. Add the title, keywords, and a description.
2. Create the main page content for the home page and format it attractively.
3. Add the address and other contact information to the home page, including an email address.
4. Consult your storyboard and design the navigation bar.
5. Link the navigation bar items to the appropriate pages.

6. Add a last updated on statement to the home page with a date that will automatically update when the page is saved.
7. Edit and format the page content until you are satisfied with the results.
8. Verify that all links, including the email link, work correctly.
9. When you are satisfied with the home page, review the checklist questions shown in Figure 42, then make any necessary changes.
10. Save your work.

FIGURE 42
Portfolio Project

Website Checklist
1. Does the home page have a page title?
2. Does the home page have a description and keywords?
3. Does the home page contain contact information, including an email address?
4. Does the home page have a navigation bar that includes a link to itself?
5. Does the home page have a "last updated on" statement that will automatically update when the page is saved?
6. Do all paths for links and images work correctly?
7. Does the home page look good using at least two different browsers and screen resolutions?

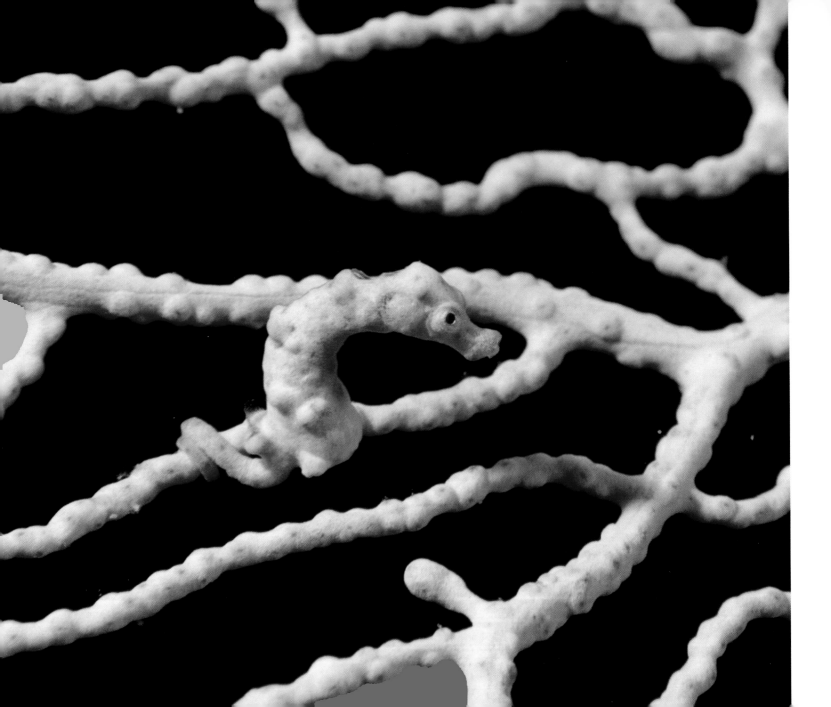

3

WORKING WITH TEXT
AND IMAGES

1. Create unordered and ordered lists

2. Create, apply, and edit Cascading Style Sheets

3. Add rules and attach Cascading Style Sheets

4. Insert and align graphics

5. Enhance an image and use alternate text

6. Insert a background image and perform site maintenance

chapter **3** WORKING WITH TEXT
AND IMAGES

Introduction

Most web pages contain a combination of text and images. Dreamweaver provides many tools for working with text and images that you can use to make your web pages attractive and easy to read. Dreamweaver also has tools that help you format text quickly and ensure a consistent appearance of text elements across all your web pages.

Formatting Text as Lists

If a web page contains a large amount of text, it can be difficult for viewers to digest it all. You can break up the monotony of large blocks of text by dividing them into smaller paragraphs or organizing them as lists. You can create three types of lists in Dreamweaver: unordered lists, ordered lists, and definition lists.

Using Cascading Style Sheets

You can save time and ensure that all your page elements have a consistent appearance by using **Cascading Style Sheets (CSS)**. CSS are sets of formatting instructions, usually stored in a separate file, that control the appearance of content on a web page

or throughout a website. You can use CSS to define consistent formatting attributes for page elements such as text and tables throughout your website. You can then apply the formatting attributes you define to any element in a single document or to all of the pages in a website.

Using Images to Enhance Web Pages

Images make web pages visually stimulating and more exciting than pages that contain only text. However, you should use images sparingly. If you think of text as the meat and potatoes of a website, the images would be the seasoning. You should add images to a page just as you would add seasoning to food. A little seasoning enhances the flavor and brings out the quality of the dish. Too much seasoning overwhelms the dish and masks the flavor of the main ingredients. Too little seasoning results in a bland dish. There are many ways to work with images so that they complement the content of pages in a website. There are specific file formats used to save images for websites to ensure maximum quality with minimum file size. You should store images in a separate folder in an organized fashion.

Tools You'll Use

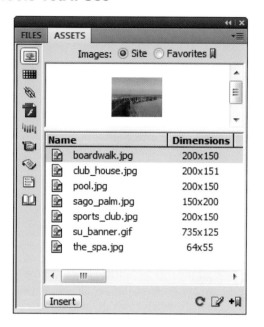

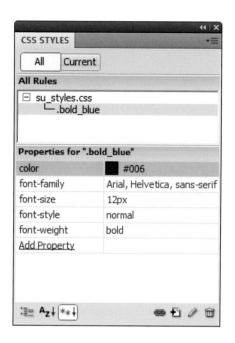

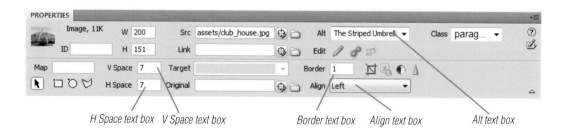

H Space text box   V Space text box   Border text box   Align text box   Alt text box

CREATE UNORDERED AND ORDERED LISTS

What You'll Do

Spa Packages

- Spa Sampler
  Mix and match any three of our services.
- Girl's Day Out
  One hour massage, a facial, a manicure, and a pedicure.

Call the Spa desk for prices and reservations. Our desk is open from 7:00 a.m. until 5:00 p.m.

Questions you may have

1. How do I schedule Spa services?
   Please make appointments by calling The Club desk at least 24 hours in advance. Please arrive 15 minutes before your appointment to allow enough time to shower or use the sauna.
2. Will I be charged if I cancel my appointment?
   Please cancel 24 hours before your service to avoid a cancellation charge. No-shows and cancellations without adequate notice will be charged for the full service.
3. Are there any health safeguards I should know about?
   Please advise us of medical conditions or allergies you have. Heat treatments like hydrotherapy and body wraps should be avoided if you are pregnant, have high blood pressure, or any type of heart condition or diabetes.
4. What about tipping?
   Gratuities are at your sole discretion, but are certainly appreciated.

In this lesson, you will create an unordered list of spa services on the spa page. You will also import text with questions and format them as an ordered list.

Creating Unordered Lists

Unordered lists are lists of items that do not need to be placed in a specific sequence. A grocery list that lists items in a random order is a good example of an unordered list. Items in unordered lists are usually preceded by a **bullet**, or a small dot or similar icon. Unordered lists that contain bullets are sometimes called **bulleted lists**. Although you can use paragraph indentations to create an unordered list, bullets can often make lists easier to read. To create an unordered list, first select the text you want to format as an unordered list, then use the Unordered List button in the HTML Property inspector to insert bullets at the beginning of each paragraph of the selected text.

Formatting Unordered Lists

In Dreamweaver, the default bullet style is a round dot. To change the bullet style to a square, click inside a bulleted item, expand the Property inspector to its full size, as shown in Figure 1, click the List Item button in the HTML Property inspector to open the List Properties dialog box, and then set the style for bulleted lists to Square. Be aware, however, that not all browsers display square bullets correctly, in which case the bullets will appear differently.

Creating Ordered Lists

Ordered lists, which are sometimes called **numbered lists**, are lists of items that are presented in a specific sequence and that are preceded by sequential numbers or letters. An ordered list is appropriate for a list in which each item must be executed according to its specified order. A list that provides numbered directions for driving from Point A to Point B or a list that provides instructions for assembling a bicycle are both examples of ordered lists.

Formatting Ordered Lists

You can format an ordered list to show different styles of numbers or letters by using the List Properties dialog box, as shown in Figure 2. You can apply numbers, Roman numerals, lowercase letters, or uppercase letters to an ordered list.

Creating Definition Lists

Definition lists are similar to unordered lists but do not have bullets. They are often used with terms and definitions, such as in a dictionary or glossary. To create a definition list, select the text to use for the list, click Format on the Application bar (Win) or Menu bar (Mac), point to List, and then click Definition List.

FIGURE 1

Expanded Property inspector

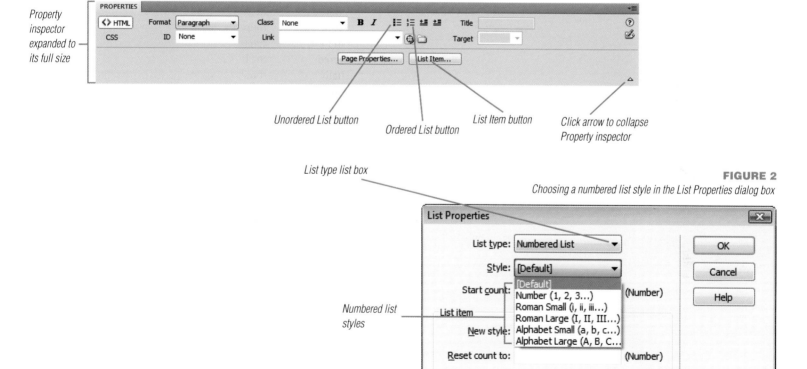

Property inspector expanded to its full size

Unordered List button

Ordered List button

List Item button

Click arrow to collapse Property inspector

List type list box

FIGURE 2

Choosing a numbered list style in the List Properties dialog box

Numbered list styles

Create an unordered list

1. Open the spa page in The Striped Umbrella website.

2. Select the three items under the Skin Care Treatments heading.

3. Click the **HTML button** in the Property inspector to switch to the HTML Property inspector if necessary, click the **Unordered List button** 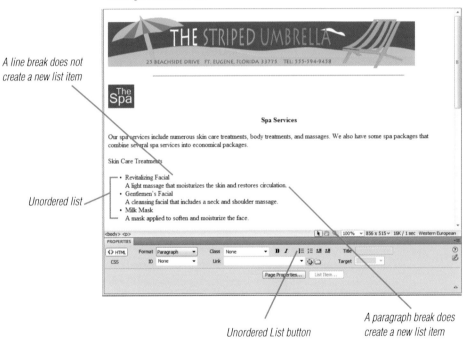 to format the selected text as an unordered list, click anywhere to deselect the text, then compare your screen to Figure 3.

   Each spa service item and its description is separated by a line break. That is why each description is indented under its corresponding item, rather than formatted as a new list item. You must enter a paragraph break to create a new list item.

4. Repeat Step 3 to create unordered lists of the items under the Body Treatments, Massages, and Spa Packages headings, being careful not to include the contact information in the last sentence on the page as part of your last list.

   TIP Pressing [Enter] (Win) or [return] (Mac) once at the end of an unordered list creates another bulleted item. To end an unordered list, press [Enter] (Win) or [return] (Mac) twice.

You opened the spa page in Design view and formatted four spa services lists as unordered lists.

FIGURE 3
Creating an unordered list

A line break does not create a new list item

Unordered list

Unordered List button

A paragraph break does create a new list item

FIGURE 4
List Properties dialog box

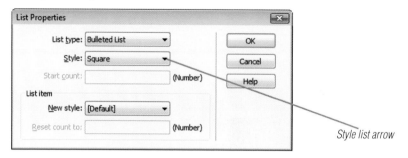

Style list arrow

FIGURE 5
HTML tags in Code view for unordered list

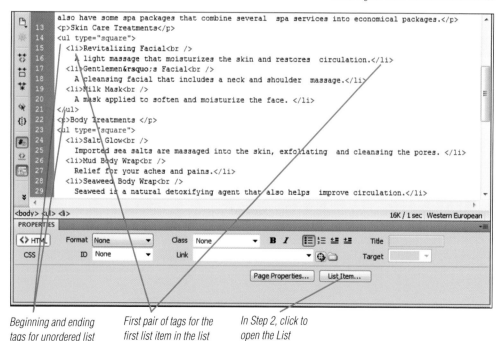

Beginning and ending tags for unordered list

First pair of tags for the first list item in the list

In Step 2, click to open the List Properties dialog box

Format an unordered list

1. Click any of the items in the first unordered list to place the insertion point in the list.

2. Expand the Property inspector (if necessary), click **List Item** in the HTML Property inspector to open the List Properties dialog box, click the **Style list arrow**, click **Square**, as shown in Figure 4, then click **OK**.

   The bullets in the unordered list now have a square shape.

3. Repeat Step 2 to format the next three unordered lists.

4. Position the insertion point to the left of the first item in the first unordered list, then click the **Show Code view button** 〔Code〕 on the Document toolbar to view the code for the unordered list, as shown in Figure 5.

   Notice that there is a pair of HTML tags surrounding each type of element on the page. The first tag in each pair begins the code for a particular element, and the last tag ends the code for the element. For instance, the tags <ul></ul> surround the unordered list. The tags <li> and </li> surround each item in the list.

5. Click the **Show Design view button** 〔Design〕 on the Document toolbar.

6. Save your work.

You used the List Properties dialog box to apply the Square bullet style to the unordered lists. You then viewed the HTML code for the unordered lists in Code view.

Create an ordered list

1. Place the insertion point at the end of the page, after the word "5:00 p.m."

2. Use the Import, Word Document command to import questions.doc from where you store your Data Files (Win) or open questions.doc from where you store your Data Files, select all, copy, then paste the copied text on the page (Mac).

   The inserted text appears on the same line as the existing text.

3. Use the Clean Up Word HTML command, place the insertion point to the left of the text "Questions you may have," then click **Horizontal Rule** in the Common category on the Insert panel.

   A horizontal rule appears and separates the unordered list from the text you just imported.

4. Select the text beginning with "How do I schedule" and ending with the last sentence on the page.

5. Click the **Ordered List button** in the HTML Property inspector to format the selected text as an ordered list.

6. Deselect the text, then compare your screen to Figure 6.

You imported text on the spa page. You also added a horizontal rule to help organize the page. Finally, you formatted selected text as an ordered list.

FIGURE 6
Creating an ordered list

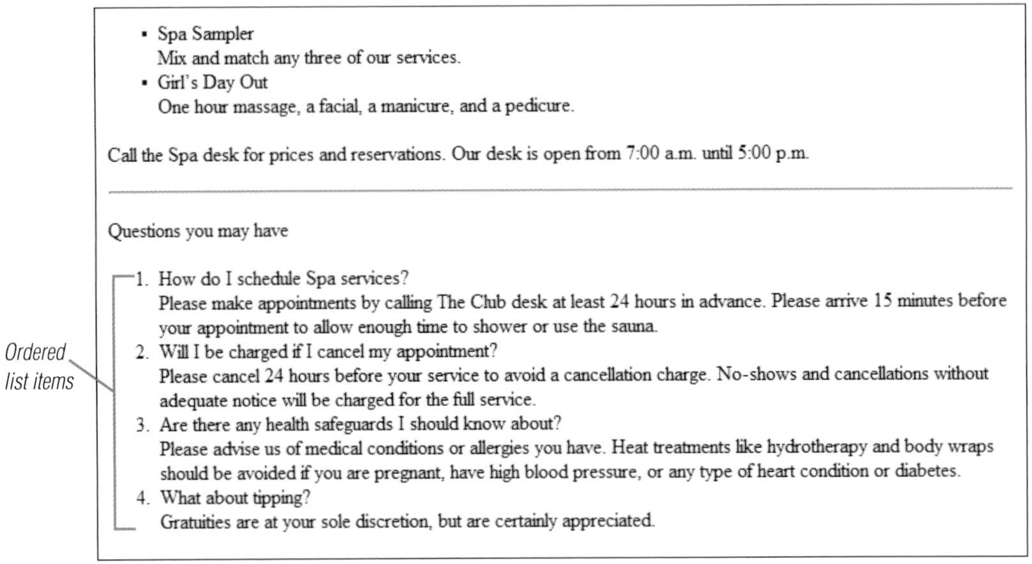

- Spa Sampler
  Mix and match any three of our services.
- Girl's Day Out
  One hour massage, a facial, a manicure, and a pedicure.

Call the Spa desk for prices and reservations. Our desk is open from 7:00 a.m. until 5:00 p.m.

Questions you may have

Ordered list items

1. How do I schedule Spa services?
   Please make appointments by calling The Club desk at least 24 hours in advance. Please arrive 15 minutes before your appointment to allow enough time to shower or use the sauna.
2. Will I be charged if I cancel my appointment?
   Please cancel 24 hours before your service to avoid a cancellation charge. No-shows and cancellations without adequate notice will be charged for the full service.
3. Are there any health safeguards I should know about?
   Please advise us of medical conditions or allergies you have. Heat treatments like hydrotherapy and body wraps should be avoided if you are pregnant, have high blood pressure, or any type of heart condition or diabetes.
4. What about tipping?
   Gratuities are at your sole discretion, but are certainly appreciated.

FIGURE 7
Spa page with ordered list

Formatted heading

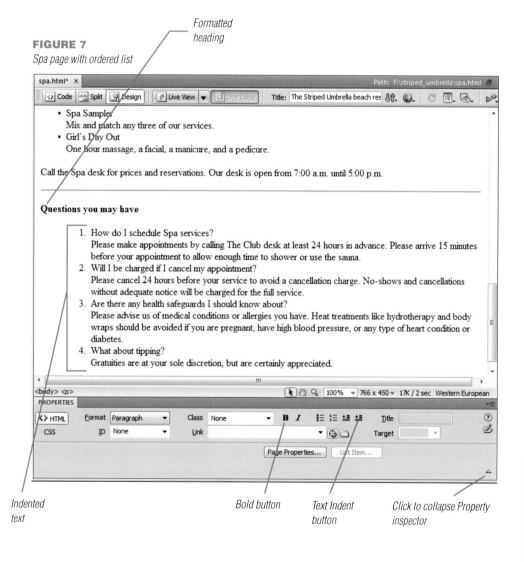

Indented text

Bold button

Text Indent button

Click to collapse Property inspector

Format an ordered list

1. Select the heading "Questions you may have," then click the **Bold button** **B** in the HTML Property inspector.

2. Select the four questions and answers text, click the **Text Indent button** in the HTML Property inspector, deselect the text, then compare your screen to Figure 7. The Text Indent and Text Outdent buttons are used to indent selected text or remove an indent from selected text.

   TIP If you want to see more of your web page in the Document window, you can collapse the Property inspector.

3. Save your work.

You formatted the "Questions you may have" heading. You also indented the four questions and answers text.

CREATE, APPLY, AND EDIT
CASCADING STYLE SHEETS

What You'll Do

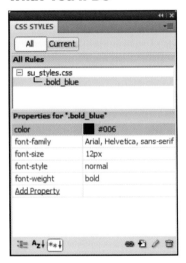

 In this lesson, you will create a Cascading Style Sheet file for The Striped Umbrella website. You will also create a rule named bold_blue and apply it to text on the spa page.

Understanding Cascading Style Sheets

CSS are made up of sets of formatting attributes called **rules,** which define the formatting attributes for individual styles, and are classified by where the code is stored. Sometime "style" and "rule" are used interchangeably, but this is not technically accurate. The code can be saved in a separate file (**external style sheet**), as part of the head content of an individual web page (**internal or embedded styles**) or as part of the body of the HTML code (**inline styles**). External CSS style sheets are saved as files with the .css extension and are stored in the directory structure of a website. Figure 8 shows a style sheet named su_styles.css. This style sheet contains a rule called bold_blue. External style sheets are the preferred method for creating and using styles.

CSS are also classified by their type. A **Class type** can be used to format any page element. An **ID type** and a **Tag type** are used to redefine an HTML tag. A **Compound** type is used to format a selection. In this chapter, we will use class type stored in external style sheet files.

Using the CSS Styles Panel

You use the buttons on the CSS Styles panel to create, edit, and apply rules. To add a rule, use the New CSS Rule dialog box to name the rule and specify whether to add it to a new or existing style sheet. You then use the CSS Rule definition dialog box to set the formatting attributes for the rule. Once you add a new rule to a style sheet, it appears in a list in the CSS Styles panel. To apply a rule, you select the text to which you want to apply the rule, and then choose a rule from the Targeted Rule list in the CSS Property inspector. You can apply CSS styles to elements on a single web page or to all of the pages in a website. When you make a change to a rule, all page elements formatted with that rule are automatically updated. Once you create a CSS style sheet, you can attach it to the remaining pages in your website.

The CSS Styles panel is used for managing your styles. The Properties pane displays properties for a selected rule at the bottom of the panel. You can easily change a property's value by clicking an option from a drop-down window.

Comparing the Advantages of Using Style Sheets

You can use CSS styles to save an enormous amount of time. Being able to define a rule and then apply it to page elements on all the pages of your website means that you can make hundreds of formatting changes in a few minutes. In addition, style sheets create a more uniform look from page to page and they generate cleaner code. Using style sheets separates the development of content from the way the content is presented. Pages formatted with CSS styles are much more compliant with current accessibility standards than those with manual formatting.

QUICKTIP

For more information about Cascading Style Sheets, visit www.w3.org or play the audio/video tutorials at www.adobe.com/go/vid0152.

Understanding CSS Style Sheet Code

You can see the code for a CSS rule by opening a style sheet file. A CSS style consists of two parts: the selector and the declaration. The **selector** is the name of the tag to which the style declarations have been assigned. The **declaration** consists of the property and the value. For example, Figure 9 shows the code for the su_styles.css style sheet. In this example, the first property listed for the .bold_blue rule is font-family. The value for this property is Arial, Helvetica, sans-serif. When you create a new CSS, you will see it as an open document in the Document window. Save this file as you make changes to it.

FIGURE 8

Cascading Style Sheet file created in striped_umbrella root folder

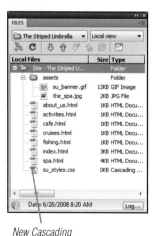

New Cascading Style Sheet file

Property   Value   **FIGURE 9**

su_styles.css file

```
1  .bold_blue {
2      font-family: Arial, Helvetica, sans-serif;
3      font-size: 14px;
4      font-style: normal;
5      font-weight: bold;
6      color: #306;
7  }
8  .heading {
9      font-family: Arial, Helvetica, sans-serif;
10     font-size: 16px;
11     font-style: normal;
12     font-weight: bold;
13     color: #036;
14     text-align: center;
15 }
16 .paragraph_text {
17     font-family: Arial, Helvetica, sans-serif;
18     font-size: 14px;
19     font-style: normal;
20 }
21
```

Create a Cascading Style Sheet and a rule

1. Click the **CSS button** [⬛ CSS] in the Property inspector to switch to the CSS Property inspector, as shown in Figure 10.

   From this point forward, we will use CSS rather than HTML tags to format most text.

2. Click **Window** on the Application bar (Win) or Menu bar (Mac), then click **CSS Styles** to open the CSS Styles panel.

3. Click the **Switch to All (Document) Mode button** [All], click the **New CSS Rule button** [🔁] in the CSS Styles panel to open the New CSS Rule dialog box, verify that Class (can apply to any HTML element) is selected under Selector Type, then type **bold_blue** in the Selector Name text box.

   TIP Class names are preceded by a period. If you don't enter a period when you type the name, Dreamweaver will add the period for you.

4. Click the **Rule Definition list arrow**, click **(New Style Sheet File)**, compare your screen with Figure 11, then click **OK**.

5. Type **su_styles** in the File name text box (Win) or the Save As text box (Mac), then click **Save** to open the CSS Rule Definition for .bold_blue in su_styles.css dialog box.

   The .bold_blue rule will be stored within the su_styles.css file.

   (continued)

FIGURE 10
Property inspector after choosing CSS rather than HTML tags option

CSS button

Options in the Property inspector change depending on whether the HTML or CSS button is selected

FIGURE 11
New CSS Rule Dialog box

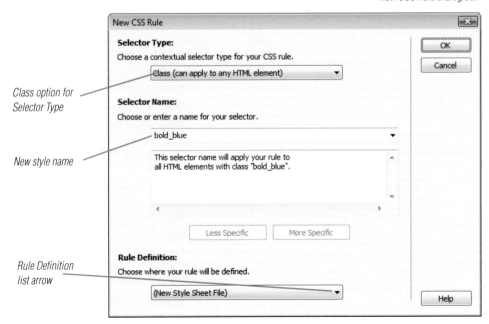

Class option for Selector Type

New style name

Rule Definition list arrow

FIGURE 12

CSS Rule Definition for .bold_blue in the su_styles.css dialog box

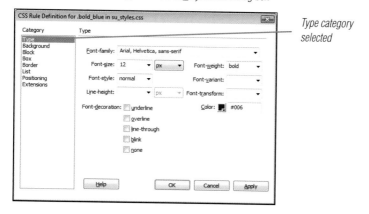

Type category
selected

FIGURE 13

CSS Styles panel with bold_blue rule added

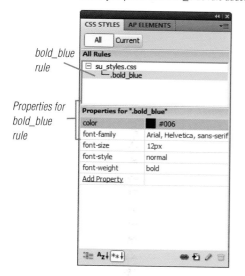

bold_blue
rule

Properties for
bold_blue
rule

6. Verify that Type is selected in the Category list, set the Font-family to **Arial, Helvetica, sans-serif,** set the Font-size to **12 px,** set the Font-weight to **bold,** set the Font-style to **normal,** set the Color to **#006,** compare your screen to Figure 12, then click **OK.**

   TIP You can modify the font combinations in the Font-family list by clicking Format on the Application bar (Win) or Menu bar (Mac), pointing to Font, then clicking Edit Font List.

7. Click the **plus sign** (Win) or the **expander arrow** (Mac) next to su_styles.css in the CSS Styles panel and expand the panel (if necessary) to list the bold_blue style, then select the **bold_blue style.**

   The CSS rule named .bold_blue and the properties appear in the CSS Styles panel, as shown in Figure 13.

   You created a Cascading Style Sheet file named su_styles.css and a rule called .bold_blue.

DESIGNTIP **Choosing fonts**

There are two classifications of fonts: sans-serif and serif. Sans-serif fonts are block-style characters that are often used for headings and subheadings. The headings in this book use a sans-serif font. Examples of sans-serif fonts include Arial, Verdana, and Helvetica. Serif fonts are more ornate and contain small extra strokes at the beginning and end of the characters. Some people consider serif fonts easier to read in printed material, because the extra strokes lead your eye from one character to the next. This paragraph you are reading uses a serif font. Examples of serif fonts include Times New Roman, Times, and Georgia. Many designers feel that a sans-serif font is preferable when the content of a website is primarily intended to be read on the screen, but that a serif font is preferable if the content will be printed. When you choose fonts, you need to keep in mind the amount of text each page will contain and whether most viewers will read the text on-screen or print it. A good rule of thumb is to limit each website to no more than three font variations.

Apply a rule in a Cascading Style Sheet

1. Click **View** on the Application bar (Win) or Menu bar (Mac), point to **Toolbars**, then click **Style Rendering**.

   TIP You can also right-click on an empty area on an open toolbar to see the displayed and hidden toolbars. The displayed toolbars have a check next to them. To display or hide a toolbar, click it.

2. Verify that the **Toggle Displaying of CSS Styles button** ![CSS] on the Style Rendering toolbar is active, as shown in Figure 14.

   TIP You can determine if the Toggle Displaying of CSS Styles button is active if it has an outline around the button. As long as this button is active, you do not have to display the toolbar on the screen.

   You use the Toggle Displaying of CSS Styles button to see how styles affect your page. If it is not active, you will not see the effects of your styles.

3. Select the text "Revitalizing Facial," as shown in Figure 15, click the **Targeted Rule text box** in the Property inspector, then click **bold_blue**, as shown in Figure 15.

4. Repeat Step 3 to apply the bold_blue style to each of the spa services bulleted items in the unordered lists, then compare your screen to Figure 16.

   TIP You can use the keyboard shortcut [Ctrl][Y] (Win) or [Command][Y] (Mac) to repeat the previous action.

   You applied the bold_blue style to each item in the Spa Services category lists.

FIGURE 14
Style Rendering toolbar

Toggle Displaying of CSS Styles button

FIGURE 15
Applying a CSS rule to selected text   *Toggle Displaying of CSS Styles button*

Rule applied

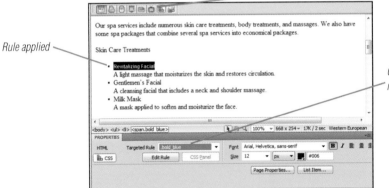

Click to apply bold_blue rule to selected text

FIGURE 16
Unordered list with bold_blue rule applied

bold_blue rule applied to each of the Spa Services items

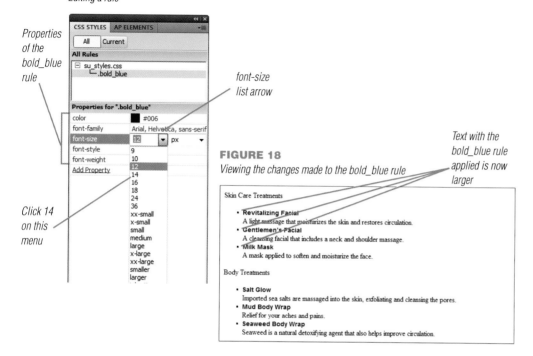

FIGURE 17
Editing a rule

Properties
of the
bold_blue
rule

font-size
list arrow

FIGURE 18
Viewing the changes made to the bold_blue rule

Text with the
bold_blue rule
applied is now
larger

Click 14
on this
menu

Skin Care Treatments

- **Revitalizing Facial**
  A light massage that moisturizes the skin and restores circulation.
- **Gentlemen's Facial**
  A cleansing facial that includes a neck and shoulder massage.
- **Milk Mask**
  A mask applied to soften and moisturize the face.

Body Treatments

- **Salt Glow**
  Imported sea salts are massaged into the skin, exfoliating and cleansing the pores.
- **Mud Body Wrap**
  Relief for your aches and pains.
- **Seaweed Body Wrap**
  Seaweed is a natural detoxifying agent that also helps improve circulation.

Edit a rule in a Cascading Style Sheet

1. Click **.bold_blue** in the CSS Styles panel.

   The rule's properties and values appear in the Properties pane, the bottom part of the CSS Styles panel.

   TIP   Click the plus sign (Win) or expander arrow (Mac) to the left of su_styles.css in the CSS Styles panel if you do not see .bold_blue. Click the plus sign (Win) or expander arrow (Mac) to the left of <style> if you do not see su_styles.css.

2. Click **12px** in the CSS Styles panel, click the **font-size list arrow**, click **14** as shown in Figure 17, then compare your screen to Figure 18.

   All of the text to which you applied the bold_blue style is larger, reflecting the changes you made to the bold_blue rule. You can also click the **Edit Rule button** in the CSS Styles panel to open the CSS Rule Definition for .bold_blue dialog box.

   TIP   If you position the insertion point in text that has a CSS rule applied to it, that rule is displayed in the Targeted Rule text box in the Property inspector.

3. Use the File, Save All command to save the spa page and the style sheet file.

4. Hide the Style Rendering toolbar.

You edited the bold_blue style to change the font size to 14 pixels. You then viewed the results of the edited rule in the unordered list.

Using the Style Rendering toolbar

The Style Rendering toolbar allows you to render your page as different media types, such as print, TV, or handheld. To display it when a page is open, click View on the Application bar (Win); or Menu bar (Mac), point to Toolbars, and then click Style Rendering. The buttons on the Style Rendering toolbar allow you to see how your page will look as you select different media types. The next to the last button on the toolbar is the Toggle Displaying of CSS Styles button, which you can use to view how a page looks with styles applied. It works independently of the other buttons. The last button is the Design-time Style Sheets button, which you can use to show or hide particular combinations of styles while you are working in the Document window.

View code with the Code Navigator

1. Point to the text "Revitalizing Facial" and hover until the Click indicator to bring up the Code Navigator icon ☀ is displayed, as shown in Figure 19.

2. Click the **Click indicator to bring up the Code Navigator icon** ☀.

    A window opens, as shown in Figure 20, with the name of the style sheet that is linked to this page (su_styles.css) and the name of the rule in the style sheet that has been applied to this text (bold_blue).

    > TIP You can also [Alt]-click (Win) or [Command][Option]-click (Mac) the text on the page to display the Code Navigator.

3. Position your cursor over the bold_blue rule name to see the properties of the rule displayed, as shown in Figure 21.

You displayed the Code Navigator to view the properties of the bold_blue rule.

FIGURE 19
Viewing the Click indicator to bring up the Code Navigator icon

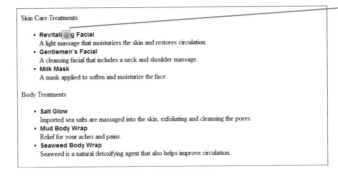

Click indicator to bring up the Code Navigator icon

FIGURE 20
Viewing the Code Navigator

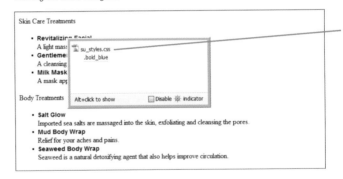

Window displays the name of the style sheet file and rule applied from the style sheet

FIGURE 21
Viewing rule properties and values

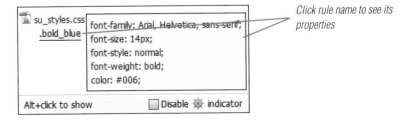

Click rule name to see its properties

Working with Text and Images

FIGURE 22

Using Code and Design views to view rule properties

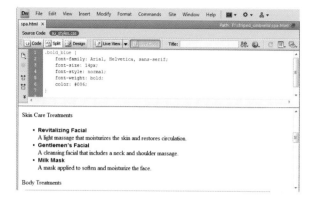

FIGURE 23

Using Code and Design views to edit a rule

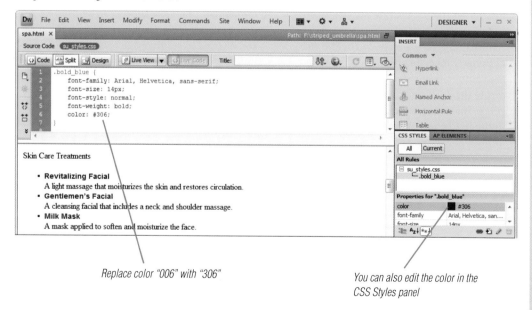

Replace color "006" with "306"

You can also edit the color in the
CSS Styles panel

1. Click **.bold_blue** in the Code Navigator.

   The document window is split into two sections. The top section displays the code for the CSS file and the bottom section displays the page in Design view, as shown in Figure 22.

2. Type directly in the code to replace the color "006" with the color "306" as shown in Figure 23.

3. Save all files.

   The font color has changed in Design view to reflect the new shade of blue in the rule.

   > TIP You can also edit the rule properties in the CSS Styles panel.

4. Click the Show Design view button ⬚ Design .

You changed the color property in the .bold_blue rule.

ADD RULES AND ATTACH
CASCADING STYLE SHEETS

What You'll Do

In this lesson, you will add a style to a Cascading Style Sheet. You will then attach the style sheet file to the index page and apply one of the styles to text on the page.

Understanding External and Embedded Style Sheets

When you are first learning about CSS, the terminology can be very confusing. In the last lesson, you learned that external style sheets are a separate file in a website saved with the .css file extension. You also learned that CSS can be part of an HTML file, rather than a separate file. These are called internal, or embedded, style sheets. External CSS files are created by the web designer. Embedded style sheets are created automatically if the designer does not create them, using default names for the rules. The code for these rules will reside in the head content for that page. These rules will be automatically named style1, style2, and so on. You can rename the rules as they are created to make them more recognizable for you to use, for example, paragraph_text, subheading, or address. Embedded style sheets apply only to a single page, although you can copy them into the code in other pages. Remember that style sheets can be used to format much more than text objects. They can be used to set the page background, link properties, tables, or determine the appearance of almost any object on the page. Figure 24 shows the code for some embedded rules. The code resides in the head content of the web page.

When you have several pages in a website, you will probably want to use the same CSS style sheet for each page to ensure that all your elements have a consistent appearance. To attach a style sheet to another document, click the Attach Style Sheet button on the CSS Styles panel to open the Attach External Style Sheet dialog box, make sure the Add as Link option is selected, browse to locate the file you want to attach, and then click OK. The rules contained in the attached style sheet will appear in the CSS Styles panel, and you can use them to apply rules to text on the page. External style sheets can be attached, or linked, to any page. This is an extremely powerful tool. If you decide to make a change in a rule, it will automatically be made to every object that it formats.

FIGURE 24

Code for embedded rules shown in Code view

Rules are embedded in the head content rather than in an external style sheet file

```
1   <!DOCTYPE html PUBLIC "-//W3C//DTD XHTML 1.0 Transitional//EN"
    "http://www.w3.org/TR/xhtml1/DTD/xhtml1-transitional.dtd">
2   <html xmlns="http://www.w3.org/1999/xhtml">
3   <head>
4   <meta http-equiv="Content-Type" content="text/html; charset=utf-8" />
5   <title>The Striped Umbrella beach resort and spa, Ft. Eugene, Florida</title>
6   <style type="text/css">
7   <!--
8   body {
9       background-color: #FFF;
10  }
11  .nav_bar {
12      font-size: large;
13      font-family: Arial, Helvetica, sans-serif;
14  }
15  .body_text {
16      font-size: medium;
17      font-family: Arial, Helvetica, sans-serif;
18  }
19  .small_text {
20      font-size: 10px;
21      font-family: Arial, Helvetica, sans-serif;
22  }
23  -->
24  </style>
```

Add rules to a Cascading Style Sheet

1. Click the **New CSS Rule button** 🗗 in the CSS Styles panel.

2. Type **heading** in the Selector Name text box, as shown in Figure 25, then click **OK**.

3. Set the Font-family to **Arial**, **Helvetica**, **sans-serif**, set the Font-size to **16**, set the Font-style to **normal**, set the Font-weight to **bold**, set the Color to **#036**, compare your screen to Figure 26, then click **OK**.

4. Click the **Edit Rule button** 🖉.

5. Click the **Block category** in the CSS Rule Definition for .heading in su_styles.css dialog box, click the **Text align list arrow**, click **center**, as shown in Figure 27, then click **OK**.

6. Select the heading text "Spa Services," click the **HTML button** `<> HTML` in the Property inspector, set the Format to **Paragraph**, then click the **CSS button** `🖹 CSS` in the Property inspector.

   TIP Before you apply a style to selected text, you need to remove all formatting attributes such as font and color from that text, or the style will not be applied correctly.

7. Click the **Targeted Rule list arrow** in the Property inspector, then click **heading** to apply it to the Spa Services heading.

8. Repeat Steps 1 through 3 to add another rule called **paragraph_text** with the **Arial**, **Helvetica**, **sans-serif** Font-family, size **14**, and **normal** style.

9. Repeat Steps 6 and 7 to apply the paragraph_text style to the all the text on the page except for the blue text that already has the bold_blue style applied to it and the heading text "Questions you may have."

(continued)

FIGURE 25
Adding a rule to a CSS Style sheet

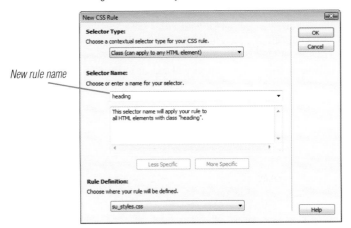

New rule name

FIGURE 26

Formatting options for heading rule

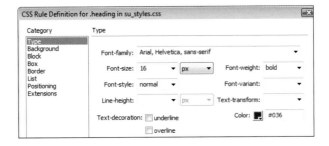

FIGURE 27

Setting text alignment for heading rule

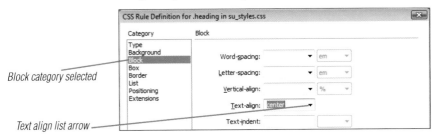

Block category selected

Text align list arrow

Working with Text and Images

FIGURE 28

Spa page with style sheet applied to rest of text on page

heading rule
applied

Spa Services

Our spa services include numerous skin care treatments, body treatments, and massages. We also have
some spa packages that combine several spa services into economical packages.

Skin Care Treatments

paragraph_text
rule applied

- **Revitalizing Facial**
  A light massage that moisturizes the skin and restores circulation.
- **Gentlemen's Facial**
  A cleansing facial that includes a neck and shoulder massage.
- **Milk Mask**
  A mask applied to soften and moisturize the face.

su_styles.css style sheet selected

FIGURE 29

Attaching a style sheet to a file

Link option
button

Attach External Style Sheet

File/URL: su_styles.css   Browse...   OK

Add as: ● Link   Preview

○ Import   Cancel

Media:

You may also enter a comma-separated list of media types.

Dreamweaver has sample style sheets to get you started.   Help

FIGURE 30

Viewing the code to link the CSS style sheet file

```
26  <meta name="Description" content="The Striped Umbrella is a full-service resort and spa
    just steps from the Gulf of Mexico in Ft. Eugene, Florida." />
27  <link href="su_styles.css" rel="stylesheet" type="text/css" />
28  </head>
29
30  <body>
31  <p><img src="assets/su_banner.gif" alt="The Striped Umbrella banner" width="735" height=
    "125" /><br />
32    <span class="nav_bar"><a href="index.html">Home</a> - <a href="about_us.html">About Us</a
    > - <a href="spa.html">Spa</a> - <a href="cafe.html">Cafe</a> - <a href="activities.html">
    Activities</a></span><br />
33  </p>
34  <hr align="left" width="735" />
35  <p class="paragraph_text">Welcome to The Striped Umbrella - a full-service resort and spa
    just steps from the Gulf of Mexico and ten miles east of Crab Key, Florida. Come enjoy the
    best of both worlds, a secluded sandy beach populated with beautiful birds, yet a  short
    drive down the road from world-class shopping, restaurants,  and entertainment. Bring a
    good book and leave your laptop at the office. You won't want to  go home!</p>
```

Code linking external style
sheet file to the index page

Code that applies the paragraph_text rule from the
external style sheet to the paragraph

10. Select the heading text **Questions you may
    have**, click the **HTML button** ⟨⟩ HTML , click
    the **Bold button** B to remove the bold set-
    ting, click the **CSS button** 🖿 CSS , click the
    Targeted Rule list arrow, then click **heading**
    to apply the heading rule.

11. Click **File** on the Application bar (Win) or
    Menu bar (Mac), then click **Save All**, to save
    both the spa page and the su_styles.css file.

    The styles are saved and applied to the text,
    as shown in Figure 28.

    > TIP You must save the open su_styles.css file
    > after editing it, or you will lose your changes.

*You added two new rules called heading and para-
graph_text to the su_styles.css file. You then
applied the two rules to selected text.*

Attach a style sheet

1. Close the spa page and open the index page.

2. Click the **Attach Style Sheet button** 🔗 on
   the CSS Styles panel.

3. Browse to select the file su_styles.css (if necessary), click **OK** (Win) or click **Choose** (Mac),
   verify that the **Link option button** is selected,
   as shown in Figure 29, then click **OK**.

4. Select the opening paragraph text and the
   contact information paragraph, click the **HTML
   button** ⟨⟩ HTML , set the Format to **Paragraph**,
   click the **CSS button** 🖿 CSS , click the **Targeted
   Rule text box**, then click **paragraph_text**.

5. Click the **Show Code view button** ⟨⟩ Code and
   view the code that links the su_styles.css file to
   the index page, as shown in Figure 30.

6. Click the **Show Design view button** 🔲 Design ,
   save your work, then close the index page.

*You attached the su_styles.css file to the index.html
page and applied the paragraph_text rule to selected
text on the page.*

INSERT AND ALIGN
GRAPHICS

What You'll Do

In this lesson, you will insert five images on the about_us page in The Striped Umbrella website. You will then stagger the alignment of the images on the page to make the page more visually appealing.

Understanding Graphic File Formats

When you add graphics to a web page, it's important to choose the appropriate file format. The three primary graphic file formats used in web pages are **GIF** (Graphics Interchange Format), **JPEG** (Joint Photographic Experts Group), and **PNG** (Portable Network Graphics). GIF files download very quickly, making them ideal to use on web pages. Though limited in the number of colors they can represent, GIF files have the ability to show transparent areas. JPEG files can display many colors. Because they often contain many shades of the same color, photographs are often saved in JPEG format. Files saved with the PNG format can display many colors and use various degrees of transparency, called **opacity**. While the GIF format is subject to licensing restrictions, the PNG format is free to use. However, not all older browsers support the PNG format.

> **QUICK**TIP
>
> The status bar displays the download time for the page. Each time you add a new graphic to the page, you can see how much additional time is added to the total download time.

Understanding the Assets Panel

When you add a graphic to a website, it is automatically added to the Assets panel. The **Assets panel**, located in the Files panel group, displays all the assets in a website. The Assets panel contains nine category buttons that you use to view your assets by category. These include Images, Colors, URLs, SWF, Shockwave, Movies, Scripts, Templates, and Library. To view a particular type of asset, click the appropriate category button. The Assets panel is split into two panes. When you click the Images button, as shown in Figure 31, the lower pane displays a list of all the images in your site and is divided into five columns. The top pane displays a thumbnail of the selected image in the list. You can view assets in each category in two ways. You can use the Site option button to view all the assets in a website, or you can use the Favorites option button to view those assets that you have designated as **favorites**, or assets that you expect to use repeatedly while you work on the site. You can use the Assets panel to add an asset to a web page by dragging the asset from the Assets panel to the page or by using the Insert button on the Assets panel.

QUICKTIP

You might need to resize the Assets panel to see all five columns when it is docked. To resize the Assets panel, undock the Files tab group and drag a side or corner of the panel border.

Inserting Files with Adobe Bridge

You can manage project files, including video and Camera Raw files, with a file-management tool called Adobe Bridge. Bridge is an easy way to view files outside the website before bringing them into the website. It is an integrated application, working with other Adobe programs such as Photoshop and Illustrator. You can also use Bridge to add meta tags and search text to your files. To open Bridge, click the Browse in Bridge command on the File menu or click the Browse In Bridge button on the Standard toolbar.

Aligning Images

When you insert an image on a web page, you need to position it in relation to other elements on the page. Positioning an image is referred to as **aligning** an image. By default, when you insert an image in a paragraph, its bottom edge aligns with the baseline of the first line of text or any other element in the same paragraph. When you select an image, the Align text box in the Property inspector displays the alignment setting for the image. You can change the alignment setting using the options in the Align menu in the Property inspector.

QUICKTIP

The Align menu options function differently from the Align buttons in the Property inspector. You use the Align buttons to center, left-align, or right-align an element without regard to how the element is aligned in relation to other elements. The Align menu options align an image in relation to other elements on the page.

FIGURE 31
The Assets panel

Drag title bar to undock tab group

Site option button

Images button

Favorites option button

Category buttons

Thumbnail of selected image

List of images in website

Drag any panel border or corner to resize

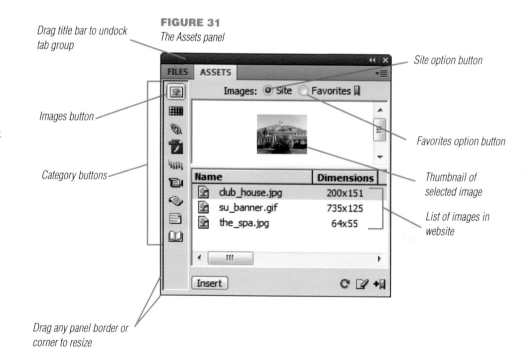

Insert a graphic

1. Open dw3_1.html from where you store your Data Files, then save it as **about_us.html** in the striped_umbrella root folder.

2. Click **Yes** (Win) or **Replace** (Mac) to overwrite the existing file, click **No** to Update Links, then close dw3_1.html.

3. Click the **Attach Style Sheet button** 🔲 in the CSS Styles panel, attach the su_styles.css style sheet, select the paragraphs of text on the page, click the **HTML button** <> HTML, verify that the Style is set to **Paragraph**, click the **CSS button** 🔲 CSS then apply the paragraph_text rule to all of the paragraph text on the page.

4. Place the insertion point before "When" in the first paragraph, click the **Images list arrow** in the Common category in the Insert panel if necessary, then click **Image** to open the Select Image Source dialog box.

5. Navigate to the assets folder where you store your Data Files, double-click **club_house.jpg**, type the alternate text **Club House** if prompted, click **OK**, open the Files panel if necessary, then verify that the file was copied to your assets folder in the striped_umbrella root folder.

   Compare your screen to Figure 32.

6. Click the **Assets panel tab** in the Files tab group, click the **Images button** 🖾 in the Assets panel (if necessary), then click the **Refresh Site List button** 🔁 in the Assets panel to update the list of images in The Striped Umbrella website.

   The Assets panel displays a list of all the images in The Striped Umbrella website, as shown in Figure 33.

   You inserted one image on the about_us page and copied it to the assets folder of the website.

FIGURE 32

The Striped Umbrella about_us page with inserted image

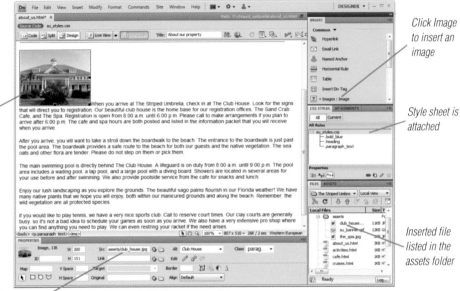

Click Image to insert an image

Style sheet is attached

Inserted file listed in the assets folder

club_house.jpg file inserted

Path should begin with the word "assets"

FIGURE 33

Image files for The Striped Umbrella website listed in Assets panel

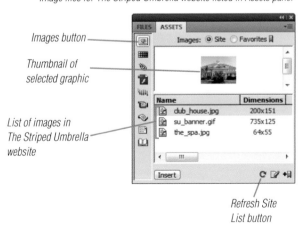

Images button

Thumbnail of selected graphic

List of images in The Striped Umbrella website

Refresh Site List button

FIGURE 34

Using Adobe Bridge

Your path may
differ

Folders
panel

Folders
tab

boardwalk.jpg
image is selected
in Content panel

Preview panel

Metadata and
Keywords
panels

Using Favorites in the Assets panel

The assets in the Assets panel can be listed two ways: Site and Favorites. The Site option
lists all of the assets in the website in the selected category in alphabetical order. As your
list of assets grows, you can designate some of the assets that are used more frequently
as Favorites for quicker access. To add an asset to the Favorites list, right-click (Win) or
[control]-click (Mac) the asset name in the Site list, and then click Add to Favorites.
When an asset is placed in the Favorites list, it is still included in the Site list. To delete an
asset from the Favorites list, click the Favorites option button in the Assets panel, select
the asset you want to delete, and then press [Delete] or the Remove from Favorites button on the Assets panel. If you delete an asset from the Favorites list, it still remains in
the Site list. You can further organize your Favorites list by creating folders for similar
assets and grouping them inside the folders.

Use Adobe Bridge

1. Click to place the insertion point before the
word "After" at the beginning of the second
paragraph.

2. Click **File** on the Application bar (Win) or
Menu bar (Mac) click **Browse in Bridge**, close
the dialog box asking if you want Bridge to
start at login (if necessary), click the **Folders
tab**, navigate to where you store your Data
Files, then click the thumbnail image **board-
walk.jpg** in the assets folder, as shown in
Figure 34. If a dialog box opens asking if you
want Bridge to launch at startup, click **Yes** or
No, depending on your personal preference.

   Bridge is divided into several panels; files and
folders are listed in the Folders Panel. The
files in the selected folder appear in the
Content Panel. A picture of the file appears in
the Preview Panel. The Metadata and
Keywords Panels list any tags that have been
added to the file.

3. Click **File** on the Application bar (Win) or
Menu bar (Mac), point to **Place**, then click
In Dreamweaver.

4. Type the alternate text **Boardwalk to the
beach,** if prompted, then click **OK**.

   The image appears on the page.

   TIP You can also click the Browse in Bridge
button on the Standard toolbar to
open Bridge.

(continued)

5. Repeat Steps 1–4 to place the **pool.jpg, sago_palm.jpg**, and **sports_club.jpg** files at the beginning of each of the succeeding paragraphs, adding appropriate alternate text if prompted for the pool, sago palm, and sports club images.

After refreshing, your Assets panel should resemble Figure 35.

You inserted four images using Adobe Bridge on the about_us page and copied each image to the assets folder of The Striped Umbrella website.

Align an image

1. Scroll to the top of the page, click the **club house image**, then expand the Property inspector (if necessary).

Because an image is selected, the Property inspector displays tools for setting the properties of an image.

2. Click the **Align list arrow** in the Property inspector, then click **Left**.

The club house photo is now left-aligned with the text and the paragraph text flows around its right edge, as shown in Figure 36.

(continued)

FIGURE 35
Assets panel with seven images

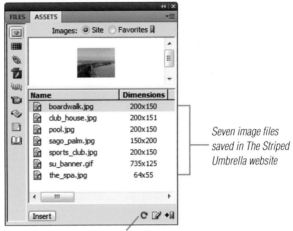

Seven image files saved in The Striped Umbrella website

Click Refresh Site List button to refresh file list

FIGURE 36
Left-aligned club house image

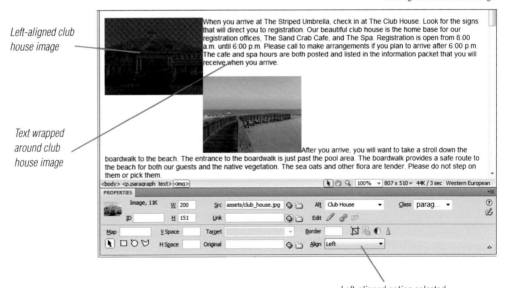

Left-aligned club house image

Text wrapped around club house image

Left-aligned option selected

FIGURE 37

Aligned images on the about_us page

3. Select the boardwalk image, click the **Align list arrow** in the Property inspector, then click **Right**.

4. Align the pool image, using the **Left Align** option.

5. Align the sago palm image, using the **Right Align** option.

6. Align the sports club image, using the **Left Align** option.

7. Save your work.

8. Preview the web page in your browser, compare your screen to Figure 37, then close your browser.

9. Close Adobe Bridge.

You used the Property inspector to set the alignment for the five images. You then previewed the page in your browser.

Graphics versus images

Two terms that sometimes seem to be used interchangeably are graphics and images. For the purposes of discussion in this text, we will use the term **graphics** to refer to the appearance of most non-text items on a web page such as photographs, logos, navigation bars, Flash animations, graphs, background images, and drawings. Files such as these are called graphic files. They are referred to by their file type, or graphic file format, such as JPEG (Joint Photographic Experts Group), GIF (Graphics Interchange Format), or PNG (Portable Network Graphics). We will refer to the actual pictures that you see on the pages as images. Don't worry about which term to use. Many people use one term or the other according to habit or region, or use them interchangeably.

Lesson 4   Insert and Align Graphics

ENHANCE AN IMAGE AND
USE ALTERNATE TEXT

What You'll Do

In this lesson, you will add borders to images, add horizontal and vertical space to set them apart from the text, and then add alternate text to each image on the page.

Enhancing an Image

After you place an image on a web page, you have several options for **enhancing** it, or improving its appearance. To make changes to the image itself, such as removing scratches from it, or erasing parts of it, you need to use an image editor such as Adobe Fireworks or Adobe Photoshop. To edit an image directly in Fireworks from Dreamweaver, first select the image, and then click Edit in the Property inspector. This will open the Fireworks program if it is installed on your computer.

Complete your editing, and then click Done to return to Dreamweaver.

QUICKTIP
You can copy a Photoshop PSD file directly into Dreamweaver. After inserting the image, Dreamweaver will prompt you to optimize the image for the web.

You can use Dreamweaver to enhance certain aspects of how images appear on a page. For example, you can add borders around an image or add horizontal and

---

DESIGNTIP **Resizing graphics using an external editor**

Each image on a web page takes a specific number of seconds to download, depending on the size of the file. Larger files (in kilobytes, not width and height) take longer to download than smaller files. It's important to determine the smallest acceptable size for an image on your web page. Then, if you need to resize an image to reduce the file size, use an external image editor to do so, *instead* of resizing it in Dreamweaver. Although you can adjust the width and height settings of an image in the Property inspector to change the size of the image as it appears on your screen, these settings do not affect the file size. Decreasing the size of an image using the H (height) and W (width) settings in the Property inspector does *not* reduce the time it will take the file to download. Ideally you should use images that have the smallest file size and the highest quality possible, so that each page downloads as quickly as possible.

vertical space. **Borders** are frames that surround an image. Horizontal and vertical space is blank space above, below, and on the sides of an image that separates the image from text or other elements on the page. Adding horizontal or vertical space is the same as adding white space, and helps images stand out on a page. In the web page shown in Figure 38, the horizontal and vertical space around the images helps make these images more prominent. Adding horizontal or vertical space does not affect the width or height of the image. Spacing around web page objects can also be created by using "spacer" images, or clear images that act as placeholders.

Using Alternate Text

One of the easiest ways to make your web page viewer-friendly and accessible to people of all abilities is to use alternate text. **Alternate text** is descriptive text that appears in place of an image while the image is downloading or when the mouse pointer is placed over it. You can program some browsers to display only alternate text and to download images manually. Alternate text can be "read" by a **screen reader**, a device used by persons with visual impairments to convert written text on a computer monitor to spoken words. Screen readers and alternate text make it possible for viewers who have visual impairments to have an image described to them in detail. One of the default preferences in Dreamweaver is to

prompt you to enter alternate text whenever you insert an image on a page.

The use of alternate text is the first checkpoint listed in the World Wide Web Consortium (W3C) list of Priority 1 accessibility checkpoints. The Priority 1 checkpoints dictate the most basic level of

accessibility standards to be used by web developers today. The complete list of these and the other priority-level checkpoints are listed on the W3C website, www.w3.org (use the search "text accessibility level checkpoints"). You should always strive to meet these criteria for all web pages.

FIGURE 38
National Park Service website

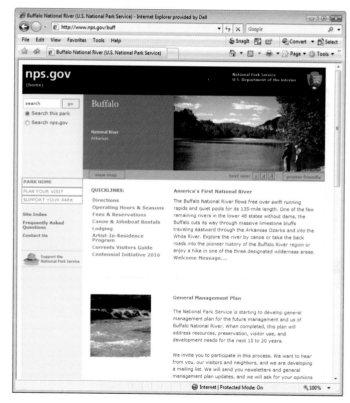

National Park Service website – www.nps.gov

Add a border

1. Select the club house image, then expand the Property inspector (if necessary).

2. Type **1** in the Border text box, press **[Tab]** to apply the border to the club house image, then select the image, as shown in Figure 39.

   The border setting is not visible until you preview the page in a browser.

3. Repeat Step 2 to add borders to the other four images.

You added a 1-pixel border to each image on the about_us page.

Add horizontal and vertical space

1. Select the club house image, type **7** in the V Space text box in the Property inspector, press **[Tab]**, type **7** in the H Space text box, press **[Tab]**, then compare your screen to Figure 40.

   The text is more evenly wrapped around the image and is easier to read, because it is not so close to the edge of the image.

2. Repeat Step 1 to set the V Space and H Space to 7 for the other four images.

   The spacing under each picture differs because of the difference in the lengths of the paragraphs.

You added horizontal spacing and vertical spacing around each image on the about_us page.

FIGURE 39

Using the Property inspector to add a border

Selected image with 1-pixel border

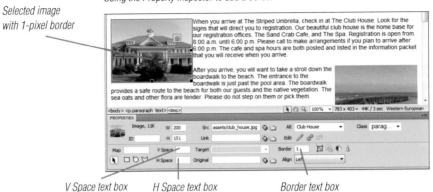

V Space text box   H Space text box   Border text box

FIGURE 40

Comparing images with and without horizontal and vertical space

Image with horizontal and vertical space

Image without horizontal and vertical space

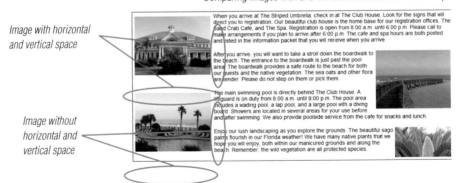

FIGURE 41

Viewing the Image Preview dialog box

Options tab

File tab

Format list arrow

Format options

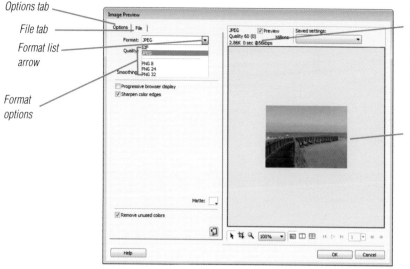

The file size and download time will increase or decrease as you edit the settings

Preview panel shows a thumbnail of the selected image

Integrating Photoshop CS4 with Dreamweaver

Dreamweaver has many functions integrated with Photoshop CS4. This new partnership includes the ability to copy and paste a Photoshop PSD file directly from Photoshop into Dreamweaver. After using the Paste command, Dreamweaver will prompt you to optimize the image by choosing a file format and settings for the web. After optimization, Dreamweaver will then paste the image on the page. If you want to edit the image later, simply double-click the image in Dreamweaver and it will open in Photoshop.

Photoshop users can set Photoshop as the default image editor in Dreamweaver. Click Edit on the Application bar, click Preferences, (Win) or click Dreamweaver, click Preferences (Mac) click File Types/Editors, click the Editors plus sign button, select a file format, then use the dialog box to browse to Photoshop (if you don't see it listed already), and then click Make Primary. Search the Adobe website for a tutorial on Photoshop and Dreamweaver integration.

Edit image settings

1. Select the **boardwalk image**.

2. Click the **Edit Image Settings button** 🖻 in the Property inspector, then click the **Format list arrow** on the Options tab, as shown in Figure 41.

   You can use this dialog box to save a copy of the image using a different file format. File property options will be displayed depending on which format you choose. It is important to note that no matter which settings you choose in this dialog box, the original file will not be altered. A duplicate copy of the file will be altered and saved when you finish editing the image.

3. Choose a PNG format, then notice the difference in file size displayed in the Preview panel.

4. Experiment with different file formats and settings, then click **Cancel** to close the dialog box without making any changes to the image.

   TIP In addition to being able to save an image using different file formats on the Options tab, you can also use the File tab to scale or resize an image.

You experimented with file format settings in the Image Preview dialog box, then closed the dialog box without making any changes.

Edit alternate text

1. Select the club house image, select any existing text in the Alt text box in the Property inspector (if necessary), type **The Striped Umbrella Club House** as shown in Figure 42, then press **[Enter]** (Win) or **[return]** (Mac).

2. Save your work, preview the page in your browser, then point to the **club house image** until the alternate text appears, as shown in Figure 43. (*Hint*: You may not see the alternate text in some browsers.)

3. Close your browser.

4. Select the boardwalk image, type **The board-walk to the beach** in the Alt text box, replacing any existing text, then press **[Enter]** (Win) or **[return]** (Mac).

5. Repeat Step 4 to add the alternate text **The pool area** to the pool image.

6. Repeat Step 4 to add the alternate text **Lush sago palm** to the sago palm image.

7. Repeat Step 4 to add the alternate text **The Sports Club** to the sports club image.

8. Save your work.

9. Preview the page in your browser, view the alternate text for each image, then close your browser.

You edited the alternate text for five images on the page, then you viewed the alternate text in your browser.

FIGURE 42
Alternate text setting in the Property inspector

Alt text box

FIGURE 43
Alternate text displayed in browser

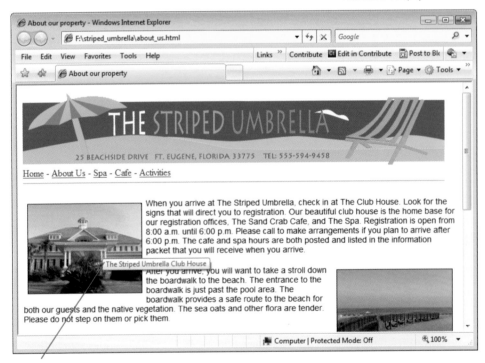

Alternate text appears when triggered by the mouse pointer

FIGURE 44

Preferences dialog box with Accessibility category selected

Accessibility category

Check boxes for Form objects, Frames, Media, and Images

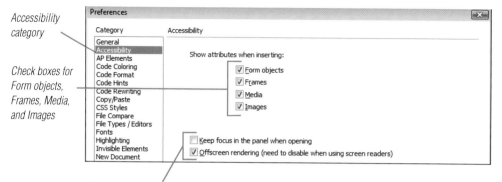

These options are not available in Mac OS X

Set the alternate text accessibility option

1. Click **Edit** on the Application bar (Win) or **Dreamweaver** (Mac) on the Menu bar, click **Preferences** to open the Preferences dialog box, then click the **Accessibility category**.

2. Verify that the four attributes check boxes are checked, as shown in Figure 44, check them if they are not checked, then click **OK**.

    TIP   Once you set the Accessibility preferences, they will be in effect for all websites that you develop, not just the one that's open when you set them.

You set the Accessibility preferences to prompt you to enter alternate text each time you insert a form object, frame, media, image, or object on a web page.

INSERT A BACKGROUND IMAGE
AND PERFORM SITE
MAINTENANCE

What You'll Do

 In this lesson, you will insert two types of background images. You will then use the Assets panel to delete them both from the website. You will also check for non-web-safe colors in the Assets panel.

Inserting a Background Image

You can insert a background image on a web page to provide depth and visual interest to the page, or to communicate a message or mood. **Background images** are image files used in place of background colors. Although you can use background images to create a dramatic effect, you should avoid inserting them on web pages where they would not provide the contrast necessary for reading page text. Even though they might seem too plain, standard white backgrounds are usually the best choice for web pages. If you choose to use a background image on a web page, it should be small in file size. You can insert either a small image file that is tiled, or repeated, across the page or a larger image that is not repeated across the page. A tiled image will download much faster than a large image. A **tiled image** is a small image that repeats across and down a web page, appearing as individual squares or rectangles. When you create a web page, you can use either a background color or a background image,

but not both, unless you have a need for the background color to be displayed while the background image finishes downloading. The background in the web page shown in Figure 45 uses an ocean-wave graphic, which ties to the restaurant name "Mermaids" and the ocean theme for the restaurant decor. This image background does not compete with the text on the page, however, because a solid black background is placed behind the text and in front of the image background. This can be done using tables or CSS blocks.

Managing Images

As you work on a website, you might find that you accumulate files in your assets folder that the website does not use. To avoid accumulating unnecessary files, it's a good idea to look at an image first, before you place it on the page and copy it to the assets folder. If you inadvertently copy an unwanted file to the assets folder, you should delete it or move it to another location. This is a good website management practice that will prevent the assets folder from filling up with unwanted image files.

Removing an image from a web page does not remove it from the assets folder in the local root folder of the website. To remove an asset from a website, you first locate the file you want to remove in the Assets panel. You then use the Locate in Site command to open the Files panel with the unwanted file selected. You can then use the Delete command to remove the file from the site.

QUICKTIP

You cannot use the Assets panel to delete a file. You must use the Files panel to delete files and perform all file-management tasks.

Removing Colors from a Website

You can use the Assets panel to locate non-web-safe colors in a website. **Non-web-safe** colors are colors that may not be displayed uniformly across computer platforms. After you replace a non-web-safe color with another color, you should use the Refresh Site List button on the Assets panel to verify that the color has been removed. Sometimes it's necessary to press [Ctrl] (Win) or ⌘ (Mac) while you click the Refresh Site List button. If refreshing the Assets panel does not work, try re-creating the site cache, and then refreshing the Assets panel.

QUICKTIP

To re-create the site cache, click Site on the Application bar (Win) or Menu bar (Mac), point to Advanced, then click Recreate Site Cache.

FIGURE 45
Mermaids website

Mermaids website used with permission from Mermaids Restaurant and Catering - www.mermaids.ws

Insert a background image

1. Click **Modify** on the Application bar (Win) or Menu bar (Mac), then click **Page Properties** to open the Page Properties dialog box.

2. Click the **Appearance (CSS) category**, if necessary.

3. Click **Browse** next to the Background image text box, navigate to the assets folder where you store your Data Files, then double-click **umbrella_back.gif**.

4. Click **OK** to close the Page Properties dialog box, then click the **Refresh Site List button** to refresh the file list in the Assets panel. The umbrella_back.gif file is automatically copied to The Striped Umbrella assets folder.

   A file with a single umbrella forms a background made up of individual squares, replacing the white background, as shown in Figure 46. It is much too busy and makes it difficult to read the page.

5. Repeat Steps 1–4 to replace the umbrella_back.gif background image with stripes_back.gif, located in the chapter_3 assets folder.

   As shown in Figure 47, the striped background is also tiled, but with vertical stripes, so you aren't aware of the small squares making up the pattern. It is still too busy, though.

You applied a tiled background to the about_us page. Then you replaced the tiled background with another tiled background that was not as busy.

FIGURE 46

The About Us page with a busy tiled background

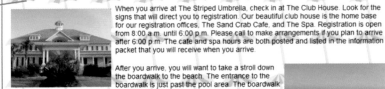

Each umbrella is a small square that forms a tiled background

FIGURE 47

The about_us page with a more subtle tiled background

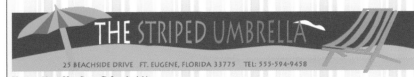

It is harder to tell where each square ends

FIGURE 48

Removing a background image

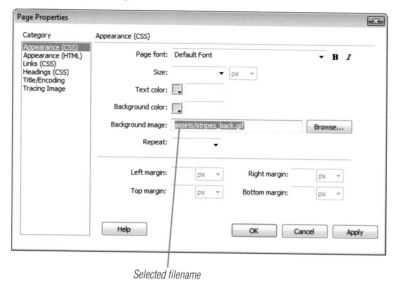

Selected filename

1. Click **Modify** on the Application bar (Win) or Menu bar (Mac), click **Page Properties**, then click **Appearance (CSS)**.

2. Select the text in the Background image text box, as shown in Figure 48, press **[Delete]**, then click **OK**.

   The background of the about_us page is white again.

3. Save your work.

You deleted the link to the background image file to change the about_us page background back to white.

Understanding HTML body tags

When you are setting page preferences, it is helpful to understand the HTML tags that are being generated. Sometimes it's much easier to make changes to the code, rather than use menus and dialog boxes. The <body> </body> tags define the beginning and end of the body section of a web page. The page content falls between these two tags. If you want to change the page properties, additional codes must be added to the <body> tag. Adding a color to the background will add a style to the page; for example, "body { Background-color:#000; }". If you insert an image for a background, the code will read "body { background-image: url assets/stripes.gif); }".

Delete files from a website

1. Click the **Assets panel tab**, then click the **Images button** 🖼 (if necessary).

2. Refresh the Assets panel, right-click (Win) or [control]-click (Mac) **stripes_back.gif** in the Assets panel, click **Locate in Site** to open the Files panel, select **stripes_back.gif** on the Files panel (if necessary), press **[Delete]**, then click **Yes** in the dialog box that appears.

   TIP Refresh the Assets panel if you still see the file listed.

3. Click the Assets panel tab, then repeat Step 2 to remove umbrella_back.gif from the website, open the Assets panel, then refresh the Assets panel.

   TIP If you delete a file on the Files panel that has an active link to it, you will receive a warning message. If you rename a file on the Files panel that has a link to it, the Files panel will update the links to correctly link to the renamed file. To rename a file, right-click (Win) or [control]-click (Mac) the file you want to rename, point to Edit, click Rename, then type the new name.

   Your Assets panel should resemble Figure 49.

You removed two image files from The Striped Umbrella website, then refreshed the Assets panel.

FIGURE 49
Images listed in Assets panel

Images file list after removing umbrella_back.gif and stripes_back.gif

Managing image files

It is a good idea to store original unedited copies of your website image files in a separate folder, outside the assets folder of your website. If you edit the original files, save them again using different names. Doing this ensures that you will be able to find a file in its original, unaltered state. You may have files on your computer that you are currently not using at all; however, you may need to use them in the future. Storing currently unused files also helps keep your assets folder free of clutter. Storing copies of original website image files in a separate location also ensures that you have back-up copies in the event that you accidentally delete a file from the website.

FIGURE 50

Colors listed in Assets panel

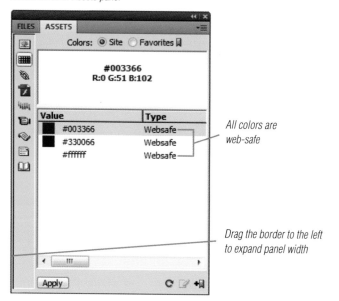

All colors are
web-safe

Drag the border to the left
to expand panel width

1. Click the **Colors button** ⊞ in the Assets
    panel to display the colors used in the website,
    then drag the left border of the Assets panel to
    display the second column, (if necessary), as
    shown in Figure 50.

    The two blue colors listed are not actually in
    the page code for the about_us page, but are
    in the attached style sheet.

    The Assets panel does not list any
    non-web-safe colors.

    > TIP If you see a non-web-safe color listed,
    > click Site on the Application bar (Win) or
    > Menu bar (Mac), point to Advanced, then
    > click Recreate Site Cache. The non-web-safe
    > color should then be removed from the
    > Assets panel. This should also remove any
    > colors you have experimented with, unless
    > you have saved a page with a color left on it.
    > If you see an extra color, use the Find and
    > Replace command to locate it, then remove
    > it from the page and refresh the Assets
    > panel again.

2. Save your work, preview the page in your
    browser, close your browser, then close all
    open files.

*You checked for non-web-safe colors in the Assets
panel list of colors.*

Using color in compliance with accessibility guidelines

The second guideline listed in the World Wide Web Consortium (W3C) list of Priority 1
Checkpoints is to not rely on the use of color alone. This means that if your website
content is dependent on your viewer correctly seeing a color, then you are not providing for those people who cannot distinguish between certain colors or do not have
monitors that display color.

Be especially careful when choosing color used with text to provide a good
contrast between the text and the background. It is better to reference colors as
numbers, rather than names. For example, use "#FFF" instead of "white." Using style
sheets for specifying color formats is the preferred method for coding. For more
information, see the complete list of priority level checkpoints listed on the W3C
website, www.w3.org.

Create unordered and ordered lists.

1. Open the blooms & bulbs website.
2. Open the tips page.
3. Select the four lines of text below the Seasonal Gardening Checklist heading and format them as an unordered list. (*Hint*: If each line does not become a separate list item, enter a paragraph break between each line, then remove any extra spaces.)
4. Select the lines of text below the Basic Gardening Tips heading and format them as an ordered list. (Refer to the Step 3 hint if each line does not become a separate list item.)
5. Indent the unordered list items one stop, then change the bullet format to square.
6. Save your work.

Create, apply, and edit Cascading Style Sheets.

1. Create a new CSS rule named **bold_blue**, making sure that the Class option button is selected in the Selector Type section and that the (New Style Sheet File) option button is selected in the Rule Definition section of the New CSS Rule dialog box.
2. Click OK, name the style sheet file **blooms_styles** in the Save Style Sheet File As dialog box, then click Save.
3. Choose the following settings for the bold_blue style: Font-family = Arial, Helvetica, sans-serif; Font-size = large; Font-style = normal; Font-weight = bold; and Font-color = #036.

4. Apply the bold_blue style to the names of the seasons in the Seasonal Gardening Checklist: Fall, Winter, Spring, and Summer.
5. Edit the bold_blue style by changing the font size to 16 pixels.

Add rules and attach Cascading Style Sheets.

1. Add an additional style called **headings** in the blooms_styles.css file and define this style choosing the following type settings: Font-family = Arial, Helvetica, sans-serif; Font-size = large; Font-style = normal; Font-weight = bold; and Font-color = #036.
2. Apply the headings style to the two sub-headings on the page: Seasonal Gardening Checklist and Basic Gardening Tips. (*Hint*: Make sure you remove any manual formatting before applying the style.)
3. Create a new rule named **paragraph_text** in the blooms_styles.css file with the Arial, Helvetica, sans-serif, size 14 font.
4. Apply the paragraph_text rule to the rest of the text on the page that has not been previously formatted with a rule, then save the page.
5. Open the index page and attach the blooms_styles.css file.
6. Select both the introductory paragraph and the contact information paragraph, remove the body_text rule from the text, and apply the paragraph_text rule. If necessary, add a paragraph break after the introductory paragraph.
7. Click File on the Application bar (Win) or Menu bar (Mac), click Save All, then view

both pages in the browser. (*Hint*: If previewing the page in Internet Explorer 7, click the Information bar when prompted to allow blocked content.)
8. Close the browser and all open pages.

Insert and align graphics.

1. Open dw3_2.html from where you store your Data Files, then save it as **plants.html** in the blooms & bulbs website, overwriting the existing plants.html. Do not update links.
2. Verify that the path of the blooms & bulbs banner is set correctly to the assets folder in the blooms root folder.
3. Set the Accessibility preferences to prompt you to add alternate text to images (if necessary).
4. Use Adobe Bridge to insert the petunias.jpg file from the assets folder where you store your Data Files to the left of the words "Pretty petunias" and add **Petunias** as alternate text.
5. Use Bridge to insert the verbena.jpg file from assets folder where you store your Data Files in front of the words "Verbena is one" and add **Verbena** as alternate text.
6. Insert the lantana.jpg file from the assets folder where you store your Data Files in front of the words "Dramatic masses" and add **Lantana** as alternate text.
7. Refresh the Files panel to verify that all three images were copied to the assets folder.
8. Left-align the petunias image.
9. Right-align the verbena image.
10. Left-align the lantana image.
11. Save your work.

Enhance an image and use alternate text.

1. Apply a 1-pixel border, vertical spacing of 10 pixels, and horizontal spacing of 20 pixels around the petunias image.

2. Apply a 1-pixel border, vertical spacing of 10 pixels, and horizontal spacing of 20 pixels around the verbana image.

3. Apply a 1-pixel border, vertical spacing of 10 pixels, and horizontal spacing of 20 pixels around the lantana image.

4. Attach the blooms_styles.css file to the page, then apply the headings style to the heading at the top of the page and the paragraph_text to the rest of the text on the page.

5. Save your work, preview it in the browser, then compare your screen to Figure 51.

6. Close the browser and open the tips page and add V Space of 10 and H Space of 10 to the garden_tips.jpg image.

7. Left-align the garden tips image, then compare your screen to Figure 52.

8. Save your work.

Insert a background image and perform site maintenance.

1. Switch to the plants page, then insert the **daisies.jpg** file as a background image from the assets folder where you store your Data Files.

2. Save your work.

3. Preview the web page in your browser, then close your browser.

4. Remove the daisies.jpg file from the background.

5. Open the Assets panel, then refresh the Files list.

6. Use the Files panel to delete the daisies.jpg file from the list of images.

7. Refresh the Assets panel, then verify that the daisies.jpg file has been removed from the website.

8. View the colors used in the site in the Assets panel, then verify that all are web-safe.

9. Save your work, then close all open pages.

FIGURE 51
Completed Skills Review

FIGURE 52
Completed Skills Review

Drop by to see our Featured Spring Plants

Pretty petunias blanket your beds with lush green leaves and bright blooms in assorted colors. Shown is the Moonlight White Petunia (Mini-Spreading). This variety is fast-growing and produces spectacular blooms. Cut them back in July for blooms that will last into the fall. Full sun to partial shade. Great for border plants or hanging baskets.

Verbena is one of our all-time favorites. The variety shown is Blue Silver. Verbena grows rapidly and is a good choice for butterfly gardens. The plants can spread up to two feet wide, so it makes excellent ground cover. Plant in full sun. Heat resistant. Beautiful also in rock gardens. We have several other varieties equally as beautiful.

Dramatic masses of Lantana display summer color for your beds or containers. The variety shown is Golden Dream. Blooms late spring through early fall. This variety produces outstanding color. Plant in full sun with well-drained soil. We carry tall, dwarf, and trailing varieties. You can also overwinter with cuttings.

Stop by to see us soon. We will be happy to help you with your selections.

 Garden Tips

We have some planting tips we would like to share with you as you prepare your gardens this season. Remember, there is always something to be done for your gardens, no matter what the season. Our experienced staff is here to help you plan your gardens, select your plants, prepare your soil, assist you in the planting, and maintain your beds. Check out our calendar for a list of our scheduled classes. All classes are free of charge and on a first-come, first-served basis!

Seasonal Gardening Checklist:

- **Fall** – The time to plant trees and spring blooming bulbs.
- **Winter** – The time to prune fruit trees and finish planting your bulbs.
- **Spring** – The time to prepare your beds, plant annuals, and apply fertilizer to established plants.
- **Summer** – The time to supplement rainfall so that plants get one inch of water per week.

Basic Gardening Tips

1. Select plants according to your climate.
2. In planning your garden, consider the composition, texture, structure, depth, and drainage of your soil.
3. Use compost to improve the structure of your soil.
4. Choose plant foods based on your garden objectives.
5. Generally, plants should receive one inch of water per week.
6. Use mulch to conserve moisture, keep plants cool, and cut down on weeding.

Working with Text and Images

Use Figures 53 and 54 as guides to continue your work on the TripSmart website that you began in Project Builder 1 in Chapter 1, and continued to work on in Chapter 2. You are now ready to format text on the newsletter page and begin work on the destinations page that showcases one of the featured tours to Kenya. You want to include some colorful pictures and attractively formatted text on the page.

1. Open the TripSmart website.
2. Open dw3_3.html from where you store your Data Files and save it in the tripsmart root folder as **newsletter.html**, overwriting the existing newsletter.html file and not updating the links.
3. Verify that the path for the banner is correctly set to the assets folder of the TripSmart website. Create an unordered list from the text beginning "Expandable clothesline" to the end of the page.
4. Create a new CSS rule called **paragraph_text** making sure that the Class option is selected in the Selector Type section and that the (New Style Sheet File) option is selected in the Rule Definition section of the New CSS Rule dialog box.
5. Save the style sheet file as **tripsmart_styles.css** in the TripSmart website root folder.

6. Choose a font, size, style, color, and weight of your choice for the paragraph_text style.
7. Apply the **paragraph_text** style to all of the text on the page except the "Ten Packing Essentials" heading.
8. Create another style called **heading** with a font, size, style, color, and weight of your choice and apply it to the "Ten Packing Essentials" heading.
9. Type **Travel Tidbits** in the Title text box on the Document toolbar, save and close the newsletter page and the tripsmart_styles file, then close the dw3_3.html page.

10. Open dw3_4.html from where you store your Data Files and save it in the tripsmart root folder as **destinations.html**, overwriting the existing destinations.html file. Do not update links.
11. Attach the tripsmart_styles.css style sheet to the page.
12. Insert **zebra_mothers.jpg** from the assets folder where you store your Data Files to the left of the sentence beginning "Our next," then add appropriate alternate text.

FIGURE 53
Sample Project Builder 1

13. Insert lion.jpg from the assets folder where you store your Data Files to the left of the sentence beginning "This lion", then add appropriate alternate text.

14. Align both images using the Align list arrow in the Property inspector with alignments of your choice, then add horizontal spacing, vertical spacing, or borders if desired.

15. Apply the heading style to the "Destination: Kenya" heading and the paragraph_text style to the rest of the text on the page. Add any necessary paragraph breaks to separate the paragraphs of text.

16. Apply any additional formatting to enhance the page appearance, then add the page title **Destination: Kenya**.

17. Save your work, then preview the destinations page in your browser. (*Hint:* If previewing the page in Internet Explorer 7, click the Information bar when prompted to allow blocked content.)

18. Close your browser, then close all open files.

FIGURE 54
Sample Project Builder 2

Destination: Kenya

Our next Photo Safari to Kenya has now been scheduled with a departure date of May 5 and a return date of May 23. Come join us and take some beautiful pictures like these two Grevy's zebras nursing their young at Samburu National Reserve. Our flight will leave New York for London, where you will have dayrooms reserved before flying all night to Nairobi, Kenya. To provide the finest in personal attention, this tour will be limited to no more than sixteen persons. Game drives will take place early each morning and late afternoon to provide maximum opportunity for game viewing, as the animals are most active at these times. We will visit five game reserves to allow for a variety of animal populations and scenery.

This lion is relaxing in the late afternoon sun. Notice the scar under his right ear. He might have received that when he was booted out of his pride as a young lion. We will be spending most nights in tented camps listening to the night sounds of hunters such as this magnificent animal. Enjoy visiting native villages and trading with the local businessmen. Birding enthusiasts will enjoy adding to their bird lists with Kenya's over 300 species of birds. View the beginning of the annual migration of millions of wildebeest, a spectacular sight. The wildebeest are traveling from the Serengeti Plain to the Mara in search of water and grass. Optional excursions include ballooning over the Masai Mara, fishing on Lake Victoria, camel rides at Amboseli Serena Lodge, and golfing at the Aberdare Country Club. Lake Victoria is the largest freshwater lake in the world.

Working with Text and Images

PROJECT BUILDER 2

In this exercise, you continue your work on the Carolyne's Creations website that you started in Project Builder 2 in Chapter 1, and continued to build in Chapter 2. You are now ready to add two new pages to the website. One page will display featured items in the kitchen store and one will be used to showcase a recipe. Figures 55 and 56 show possible solutions for this exercise. Your finished pages will look different if you choose different formatting options.

1. Open the Carolyne's Creations website.
2. Open dw3_5.html from where you store your Data Files, save it to the website root folder as **recipes.html**, overwriting the existing file and not updating the links.
3. Format the list of ingredients as an unordered list.
4. Create a CSS rule named **paragraph_text** and save it in a style sheet filenamed **cc_styles.css** in the website root folder. Use any formatting options that you like, and then apply the paragraph_text rule to all text except the navigation bar and the text "Cranberry Ice" and "Directions."

FIGURE 55
Completed Project Builder 2

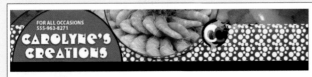

Home | Shop | Classes | Catering | Recipes

This is one of our most requested desserts. It is simple, elegant, and refreshing. You will need a small electric ice cream maker to produce the best results.

Cranberry Ice

- 3 pts. fresh cranberries
- 1 1/2 pts. sugar
- juice of 1 1/2 lemons
- 1 cup whipping cream
- dash salt

Directions:

Boil cranberries in 3 pints of water. When soft, strain. Add the sugar to the juice and bring to a brisk boil. Cool. Add the lemon juice and freeze to a soft mush. Stir in whipping cream and freeze in an ice cream maker. Serves 14.

This recipe was given to us by Cosie Simmons, who served it as one of her traditions at Thanksgiving and Christmas family gatherings.

FIGURE 56
Completed Project Builder 2

Home | Shop | Classes | Catering | Recipes

Our small storefront is filled with wonderful kitchen accessories and supplies. We also have a large assortment of gourmet items from soup mixes to exotic teas and coffee — perfect for gift baskets for any occasion. We deliver to homes and offices, as well as dorms and hospitals.

January Specials: Multifunctional Pot and Cutlery Set

We try to feature special items each month and love to promote local foods. This month's features: A large multifunctional pot for tempting soups and stews and a professional grade cutlery set.

The pot is made of polished stainless steel with a tempered glass lid so you can peak without lifting the lid to monitor progress. A pasta insert lifts out for draining. Each piece is dishwasher safe. The handles remain cool to the touch while the pot is heating on the stovetop.

The knife blades are solid stainless steel, precision forged as one single piece. The heavy bolsters provide balance and control. The cutting edge holds its sharpness well. The five knives come with a handsome butcher block knife stand. They are dishwasher safe, but hand washing is recommended.

5. Create another rule called **heading** using appropriate formatting options and apply it to the text "Cranberry Ice" and "Directions."

6. Create another rule called **nav_bar** using appropriate formatting options and apply it to the navigation bar.

7. Insert the file cranberry_ice.jpg from where you store your Data Files, then place it on the page, using alignment, horizontal space, and vertical space settings. (*Hint*: In Figure 55 the align setting is set to left, H space is set to 30, and V space is set to 10.)

8. Add appropriate alternate text to the banner, then save and close the page and the style sheet file.

9. Open dw3_6.html from where you store your Data Files and save it as **shop.html**, overwriting the existing file and not updating the links.

10. Attach the cc_styles.css style sheet and create a new rule named **sub_head** to use in formatting the text "January Specials - Multifunctional Pot and Cutlery Set." Use any formatting options that you like. Apply the nav_bar rule to the navigation bar. Apply the **paragraph_text** rule to the rest of the text on the page.

11. Insert the pot_knives.jpg image from the assets folder where you store your Data Files next to the paragraph beginning

"We try," choosing your own alignment and spacing settings and adding appropriate alternate text.

12. Save the shop page and the style sheet file, then preview both new pages in the browser, (*Hint:* If previewing the page in Internet Explorer 7, click the Information bar when prompted to allow blocked content.)

13. Close your browser, then close all open pages.

Working with Text and Images

Don Chappell is a new sixth-grade history teacher. He is reviewing educational websites for information he can use in his classroom.

1. Connect to the Internet, then navigate to the Library of Congress website at www.loc.gov. The Library of Congress website is shown in Figure 57.

2. Which fonts are used for the main content on the home—serif or sans-serif? Are the same fonts used consistently on the other pages in the site?

3. Do you see ordered or unordered lists on any pages in the site? If so, how are they used?

4. Use the Source command on the View menu to view the source code to see if a style sheet was used.

5. Do you see the use of Cascading Style Sheets noted in the source code?

FIGURE 57
Design Project

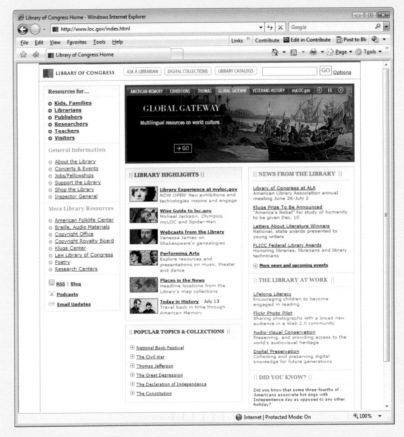

The Library of Congress website - www.loc.gov

In this assignment, you will continue to work on the website that you started in Chapter 1, and continued to build in Chapter 2. No Data Files are supplied. You are building this site from chapter to chapter, so you must do each Portfolio Project assignment in each chapter to complete your website.

You continue building your website by designing and completing a page that contains a list, headings, paragraph_text, images, and a background. During this process, you will develop a style sheet and add several rules to it. You will insert appropriate images on your page and enhance them for maximum effect. You will also check for non-web-safe colors and remove any that you find.

1. Consult your storyboard and decide which page to create and develop for this chapter.
2. Plan the page content for the page and make a sketch of the layout. Your sketch should include at least one ordered or unordered list, appropriate headings, paragraph text, several images, and a background color or image. Your sketch should also show where the paragraph text and headings should be placed on the page and what rules should be used for each type of text. You should plan on creating at least two rules.
3. Create the page using your sketch for guidance.
4. Create a Cascading Style Sheet for the site and add to it the rules you decided to use. Apply the rules to the appropriate content.
5. Access the images you gathered in Chapter 2, and place them on the page so that the page matches the sketch you created in Step 2. Add a background image if you want, and appropriate alternate text for each image.
6. Remove any non-web-safe colors.
7. Identify any files in the Assets panel that are currently not used in the site. Decide which of these assets should be removed, then delete these files.
8. Preview the new page in a browser, then check for page layout problems and broken links. Make any necessary corrections in Dreamweaver, then preview the page again in the browser. Repeat this process until you are satisfied with the way the page looks in the browser. (*Hint:* If previewing the page in Internet Explorer 7, click the Information bar when prompted to allow blocked content.)
9. Use the checklist in Figure 58 to check all the pages in your site.
10. Close the browser, then close the open pages.

FIGURE 58
Portfolio Project checklist

Website Checklist

1. Does each page have a page title?
2. Does the home page have a description and keywords?
3. Does the home page contain contact information?
4. Does every page in the site have consistent navigation links?
5. Does the home page have a last updated statement that will automatically update when the page is saved?
6. Do all paths for links and images work correctly?
7. Do all images have alternate text?
8. Are all colors web-safe?
9. Are there any unnecessary files you can delete from the assets folder?
10. Is there a style sheet with at least two rules?
11. Did you apply the rules to all text blocks?
12. Do all pages look good using at least two different browsers?

4 WORKING WITH
LINKS

1. Create external and internal links

2. Create internal links to named anchors

3. Create, modify, and copy a navigation bar

4. Create an image map

5. Manage website links

chapter **4** WORKING WITH
LINKS

Introduction

What makes websites so powerful are the
links that connect one page to another
within a website or to any page on the web.
Although you can add graphics, animations, movies, and other enhancements to
a website to make it visually attractive, the
links you include are often a site's most
essential components. Links that connect
the pages within a site are always very
important because they help viewers navigate between the pages of the site.
However, if one of your goals is to keep
viewers from leaving your website, you
might want to avoid including links to
other websites. For example, most e-commerce sites include only links to other
pages in the site to discourage shoppers
from leaving the site. In this chapter, you
will create links to other pages in The
Striped Umbrella website and to other sites
on the web. You will also insert a navigation bar that contains images instead of
text, and check the links in The Striped

Umbrella website to make sure they all
work correctly.

Understanding Internal and External Links

Web pages contain two types of links:
internal links and external links.
Internal links are links to web pages in
the same website, and **external links** are
links to web pages in other websites or to
email addresses. Both internal and external links have two important parts that
work together. The first part of a link is
the element that viewers see and click on
a web page, for example, text, an image,
or a button. The second part of a link is
the **path**, or the name and location of the
web page or file that will open when the
element is clicked. Setting and maintaining the correct paths for all your links is
essential to avoid having broken links in
your site, which can easily cause a visitor
to click away immediately.

Tools You'll Use

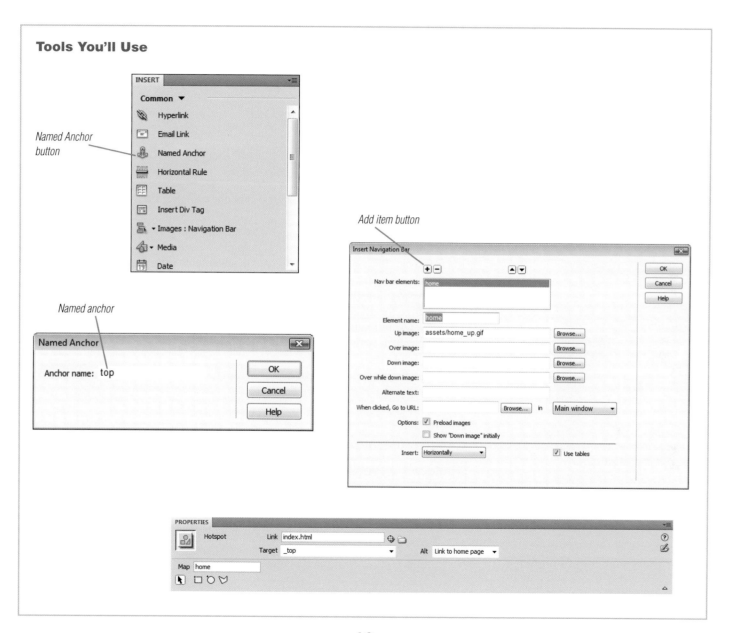

Named Anchor button

Named anchor

Add item button

CREATE EXTERNAL AND
INTERNAL LINKS

What You'll Do

 In this lesson, you will create external links on The Striped Umbrella activities page that link to websites related to area attractions. You will also create internal links to other pages within The Striped Umbrella website.

Creating External Links

A good website often includes a variety of external links to other related websites so that viewers can get more information on a particular topic. To create an external link, you first select the text or object that you want to serve as a link, then you type the absolute path to the destination web page in the Link text box in the Property inspector. An **absolute path** is a path used for external links that includes the complete address for the destination page, including the protocol (such as http://) and the complete **URL** (Uniform Resource Locator), or address, of the destination page. When necessary, the web page filename and folder hierarchy are also part of an absolute path. Figure 1 shows an example of an absolute path showing the protocol, URL, and filename. An example for the code for an external link would be <a href="http://www.adobe.com"> Adobe website</a>.

FIGURE 1
An example of an absolute path

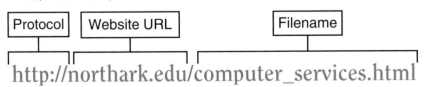

| Protocol | Website URL | | Filename |

http://northark.edu/computer_services.html

Creating Internal Links

Each page in a website usually focuses on an individual category or topic. You should make sure that the home page provides links to each major page in the site, and that all pages in the site contain numerous internal links so that viewers can move easily from page to page. To create an internal link, you first select the text element or image that you want to use to make a link, and then use the Browse for File icon next to the Link text box in the HTML Property inspector to specify the relative path to the destination page. A **relative path** is a type of path used to reference web pages and image files within the same website. Relative paths include the filename and folder location of a file. Figure 2 shows an example of a relative path. Table 1 describes absolute paths and relative paths. Relative paths can either be site-root relative or document-relative. You can also use the Point to File icon in the HTML Property inspector to point to the file you want to use for the link, or drag the file you want to use for the link from the Files panel into the Link text box in the Property inspector.

You should take great care in managing your internal links to make sure they work correctly and are timely and relevant to the page content. You should design the navigation structure of your website so that viewers are never more than three or four clicks away from the page they are seeking. An example for the code for a relative internal link would be <a href="activities.html"> Activities</a>.

FIGURE 2
An example of a relative path

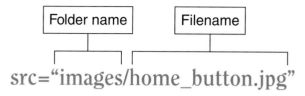

src="images/home_button.jpg"

TABLE 1: Description of absolute and relative paths

type of path	description	examples
Absolute path	Used for external links and specifies protocol, URL, and filename of destination page	http://www.yahoo.com/recreation
Relative path	Used for internal links and specifies location of file relative to the current page	spa.html or assets/heron.gif
Root-relative path	Used for internal links when publishing to a server that contains many websites or where the website is so large it requires more than one server	/striped_umbrella/activities.html
Document-relative path	Used in most cases for internal links and specifies the location of file relative to current page	cafe.html or assets/heron.gif

Create an external link

1. Open The Striped Umbrella website, open dw4_1.html from where you store your Chapter 4 Data Files, then save it as **activities** in the striped_umbrella root folder, overwriting the existing activities page, but not updating links.

2. Attach the su_styles.css file, then apply the **paragraph_text rule** to the paragraphs of text on the page (not to the navigation bar).

3. Select the first broken image link, click the **Browse for File icon** next to the Src text box, then select the **heron_waiting_small.jpg** in the Data Files assets folder to save the image in your assets folder.

4. Click on the page next to the broken image link to see the heron_waiting_small image, as shown in Figure 3.

(continued)

FIGURE 3
Saving an image file in the assets folder

Broken image is replaced when file is saved in the assets folder

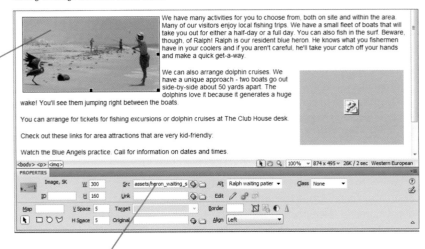

Image is saved in assets folder

Typing URLs

Typing URLs in the Link text box in the Property inspector can be very tedious. When you need to type a long and complex URL, it is easy to make mistakes and create a broken link. You can avoid such mistakes by copying and pasting the URL from the Address text box (Internet Explorer) or Location bar (Mozilla Firefox) to the Link text box in the Property inspector. Copying and pasting a URL ensures that the URL is entered correctly.

FIGURE 4

Assets panel with two new images added

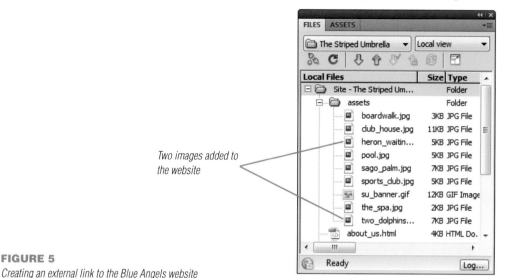

Two images added to
the website

FIGURE 5

Creating an external link to the Blue Angels website

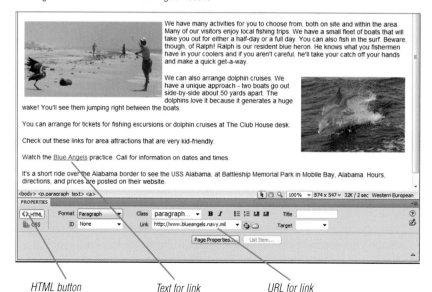

HTML button   Text for link   URL for link

5. Repeat Step 3 for the second image, **two_dolphins_small.jpg.** The two new files are copied into the assets folder, as shown in Figure 4.

6. Scroll down, then select the text "Blue Angels."

7. Click the **HTML button** `<> HTML` in the Property inspector to switch to the HTML Property inspector, click in the Link text box, type **http://www.blueangels.navy.mil**, press [**Enter**] (Win) or [**return**] (Mac), deselect the link, then compare your screen to Figure 5.

8. Repeat Steps 6 and 7 to create a link for the USS Alabama site in the next paragraph: **http://www.ussalabama.com.**

9. Save your work, preview the page in your browser, test all the links to make sure they work, then close your browser.

TIP   You must have an active Internet connection to test the links. If clicking a link does not open a page, make sure you typed the URL correctly in the Link text box.

You opened The Striped Umbrella website, replaced the existing activities page, attached the su_styles.css.file, applied the paragraph_text style to the text, then imported the new images into the site. You added two external links to other sites on the page, then tested each link in your browser.

Create an internal link

1. Select the text "fishing excursions" in the third paragraph.

2. Click the **Browse for File icon** 🗀 next to the Link text box in the HTML Property inspector, then double-click **fishing.html** in the Select File dialog box to set the relative path to the fishing page.

   Notice that fishing.html appears in the Link text box in the Property inspector, as shown in Figure 6.

   > TIP Pressing [F4] will hide or redisplay all panels, including the ones on the right side of the screen.

3. Select the text "dolphin cruises" in the same sentence.

4. Click the **Browse for File icon** 🗀 next to the Link text box in the HTML Property inspector, then double-click **cruises.html** in the Select File dialog box to specify the relative path to the cruises page.

   The words "dolphin cruises" are now a link to the cruises page.

5. Save your work, preview the page in your browser to verify that the internal links work correctly, then close your browser.

   The fishing and cruises pages do not have page content yet, but serve as placeholders until they do.

You created two internal links on the activities page, and then tested the links in your browser.

FIGURE 6
Creating an internal link on the activities page

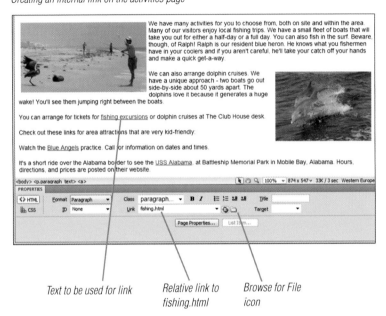

Text to be used for link   Relative link to fishing.html   Browse for File icon

Using case-sensitive links
When text is said to be "case sensitive," it means that the text will be treated differently when it is typed using uppercase letters rather than lowercase letters, or vice-versa. With some operating systems, such as Windows, it doesn't matter which case you use when you enter URLs. However, with other systems, such as UNIX, it does matter. To be sure that your links will work with all systems, use lowercase letters for all links. This is another good reason to select and copy a URL from the browser address bar, and then paste it in the link text box or code in Dreamweaver when creating an external link. You won't have to worry about missing a case change.

View links in the Assets panel

1. Click the **Assets panel tab** to view the Assets panel.

2. Click the **URLs button** in the Assets panel.

3. Click the **Refresh Site List button**.

   Three links are listed in the Assets panel: one external link for the email link and two external links to the Blue Angels and USS Alabama websites, as shown in Figure 7. Notice that the internal links are not displayed in the Assets panel.

4. Click the **Files panel tab** to view the Files panel.

5. Close the activities page and the dw4_1.html page.

You viewed the external links on the activities page in the Assets panel.

FIGURE 7
Assets panel with three external links

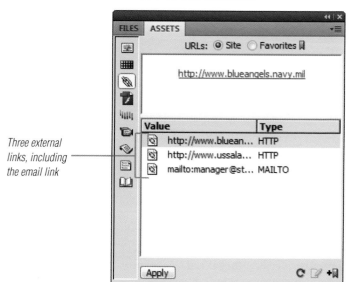

Three external links, including the email link

Lesson 1   Create External and Internal Links

CREATE INTERNAL LINKS
TO NAMED ANCHORS

What You'll Do

In this lesson, you will insert five named anchors on the spa page: one for the top of the page and four for each of the spa services lists. You will then create internal links to each named anchor.

Inserting Named Anchors

Some web pages have so much content that viewers must scroll repeatedly to get to the bottom of the page and then back up to the top of the page. To make it easier for viewers to navigate to specific areas of a page without scrolling, you can use a combination of internal links and named anchors. A **named anchor** is a specific location on a web page that has a descriptive name. Named anchors act as targets for internal links and make it easy for viewers to jump to a particular place on the same page quickly. A **target** is the location on a web page that a browser displays when an internal link is clicked. For example, you can insert a named anchor called "top" at the top of a web page, and then create a link to it from the bottom of the page.

You can also insert named anchors in strategic places on a web page, such as at the beginning of paragraph headings.

You insert a named anchor using the Named Anchor button in the Common category on the Insert panel, as shown in Figure 8. You then enter the name of the anchor in the Named Anchor dialog box. You should choose short names that describe the named anchor location on the page. Named anchors are represented by yellow anchor icons on a web page when viewed in Design view. Selected anchors are represented by blue icons. You can show or hide named anchor icons by clicking View on the Application bar (Win) or Menu bar (Mac), bar, pointing to Visual Aids, and then clicking Invisible Elements.

Creating Internal Links to Named Anchors

Once you create a named anchor, you can create an internal link to it using one of two methods. You can select the text or image on the page that you want to use to make a link, and then drag the Point to File icon from the Property inspector to the named anchor icon on the page. Or, you can select the text or image to which you want to use to make a link, then type # followed by the named anchor name (such as "#top") in the Link text box in the Property inspector.

QUICKTIP

To avoid possible errors, you should create a named anchor before you create a link to it.

FIGURE 8
Using the Point to File icon

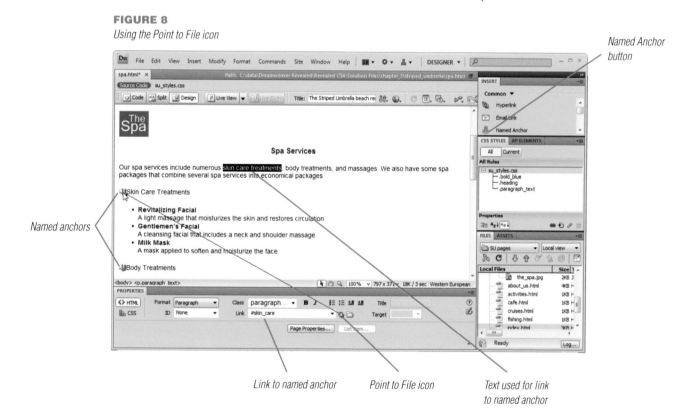

Named Anchor button

Named anchors

Link to named anchor   Point to File icon   Text used for link to named anchor

Insert a named anchor

1. Open the spa page, click the **banner image** to select it, then press [←] to place the insertion point to the left of the banner.

2. Click **View** on the Application bar (Win) or Menu bar (Mac), point to **Visual Aids**, then verify that Invisible Elements is checked.

   TIP If there is no check mark next to Invisible Elements, this feature is turned off. Click Invisible Elements to turn this feature on.

3. Click the **Common** category on the Insert panel (if necessary).

4. Click **Named Anchor** on the Insert panel to open the Named Anchor dialog box, type **top** in the Anchor name text box, compare your screen with Figure 9, then click **OK**.

   An anchor icon now appears before The Striped Umbrella banner.

   TIP Use lowercase letters, no spaces, and no special characters in named anchor names. You should also avoid using a number as the first character in a named anchor name.

   (continued)

(continued)

FIGURE 9
Named Anchor dialog box

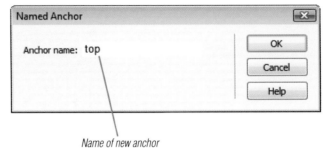

Name of new anchor

FIGURE 10
Named anchors on the activities page

Named anchor icons

Selected named anchor icon

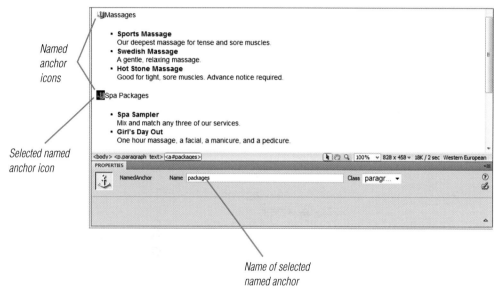

Name of selected named anchor

5. Click to the left of the Skin Care Treatments heading, then insert a named anchor named **skin_care**.

6. Insert named anchors to the left of the Body Treatments, Massages, and Spa Packages headings using the following names: **body_treatments**, **massages**, and **packages**.

Your screen should resemble Figure 10.

You created five named anchors on the activities page; one at top of the page, and four that will help viewers quickly access the Spa Services headings on the page.

Create an internal link to a named anchor

1. Select the words "skin care treatments" in the first paragraph, then drag the **Point to File icon** ⊕ from the Property inspector to the anchor named skin_care, as shown in Figure 11.

   The words "skin care treatments" are now linked to the skin_care named anchor. When viewers click the words "skin care treatments" the browser will display the Skin Care Treatments heading at the top of the browser window.

   | TIP The name of a named anchor is always preceded by a pound (#) sign in the Link text box in the Property inspector.

2. Create internal links for body treatments, massages, and spa packages in the first paragraph by first selecting each of these words or phrases, then dragging the **Point to File icon** ⊕ to the appropriate named anchor icon.

   The words "body treatments," "massages," and "spa packages" are now links that connect to the Body Treatments, Massages, and Spa Packages headings.

   | TIP Once you select the text on the page you want to link, you might need to scroll down to view the named anchor on the screen. Once you see the named anchor on your screen, you can drag the Point to File icon on top of it. You can also move the pointer to the edge of the page window (still in the white area of the page) to scroll the page.

   (continued)

FIGURE 11
Dragging the Point to File icon to a named anchor

Text to link to named anchor

Point to File icon dragged to named anchor

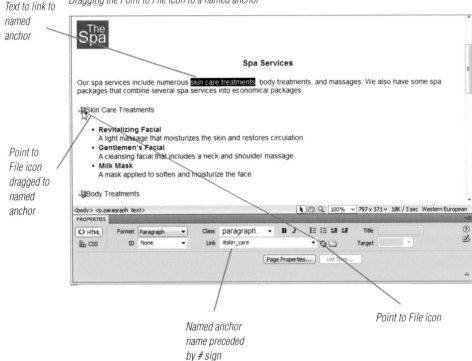

Named anchor name preceded by # sign

Point to File icon

FIGURE 12

Spa page in Mozilla Firefox with internal links to named anchors

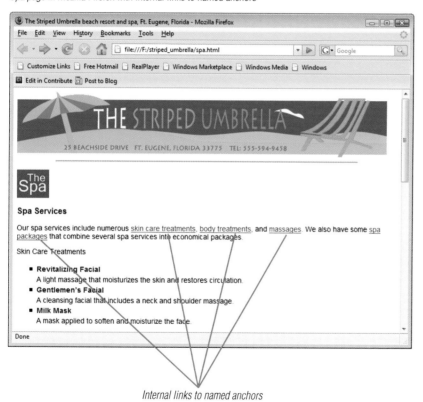

Internal links to named anchors

3. Scroll down to the bottom of the page, then place the insertion point at the end of the last sentence on the page.

4. Press [**Enter**] (Win) or [**return**] (Mac) twice to insert two paragraph breaks, then type **Top of page**.

5. Click the **CSS button** [🔳 CSS] to switch to the CSS Property inspector, then apply the paragraph_text rule to "Top of Page."

6. Click the **HTML button** [<> HTML] to switch to the HTML Property inspector, then use the Point to File icon to link the text to the top named anchor.

7. Save your work, preview the page in your browser, as shown in Figure 12, then test the links to each named anchor.

   Notice that when you click the spa packages link in the browser, the associated named anchor appears in the middle of the page instead of at the top. This happens because the spa page is not long enough to position this named anchor at the top of the page.

8. Close your browser.

You created internal links to the named anchors next to the Spa Services headings and to the top of the spa page. You then previewed the page in your browser and tested each link.

CREATE, MODIFY, AND COPY
A NAVIGATION BAR

What You'll Do

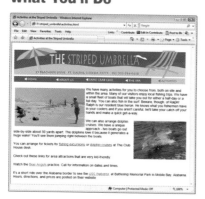

 In this lesson, you will create a navigation bar on the spa page that can be used to link to each major page in the website. The navigation bar will have five elements: home, about _us, cafe, spa, and activities. You will also copy the new navigation bar to other pages in the website. On each page you will modify the appropriate element state to reflect the current page.

Creating a Navigation Bar Using Images

To make your website more visually appealing, you can create a navigation bar with images rather than text. Any images you use in a navigation bar must be created in a graphics software program, such as Adobe Fireworks or Adobe Illustrator. For a browser to display a navigation bar correctly, all image links in the navigation bar must be exactly the same size. You insert a navigation bar by clicking Insert on the Application bar (Win) or Menu bar (Mac), pointing to Image Objects, then clicking Navigation Bar. The Insert Navigation Bar dialog box appears. You use this dialog box to specify the appearance of each link, called an **element**, in each of four possible states. A **state** is the condition of the element relative to the mouse pointer. The four states are as follows: **Up image** (the state when the mouse pointer is not on top of the element), **Over image** (the state when the mouse pointer is positioned on top of the element), **Down image** (the state when you click the element), and **Over while down image** (the state when the mouse

pointer is positioned over an element that has been clicked). You can create a rollover effect by using different colors or images to represent each element state. You can add many special effects to navigation bars or to links on a web page. For instance, the website shown in Figure 13 contains a navigation bar that uses rollovers and also contains images that link to featured items in the website.

When a navigation bar is inserted on a web page using the Insert Navigation Bar command, JavaScript code is added to the page to make the interaction work with the navigation bar elements. Dreamweaver also creates a Scripts folder and adds it to the root folder to store the newly created AC-RunActiveContent.js file. When a viewer views a web page with one of these navigation bars, the JavaScript that runs is stored on the user's, or client's, computer.

QUICKTIP

You can insert only one navigation bar using the Insert, Image Objects, Navigation Bar command or by clicking the Common category in the Insert panel and then selecting Navigation Bar from the Images menu.

Copying and Modifying a Navigation Bar

After you create a navigation bar, you can reuse it and save time by copying and pasting it to the other main pages in your site. Make sure you place the navigation bar in the same position on each page. This practice ensures that the navigation bar will look the same on each page, making it much easier for viewers to navigate to all the pages in your website. If you are even one line or one pixel off, the navigation bar will appear to "jump" as it changes position from page to page.

You use the Modify Navigation Bar dialog box to customize the appearance of the copied navigation bar on each page. For example, you can change the appearance of the spa navigation bar element on the spa page so that it appears in a different color. Highlighting the navigation element for the current page provides a visual reminder so that viewers can quickly tell which page they are viewing. This process ensures that the navigation bar will not only look consistent across all pages, but will be customized for each page.

FIGURE 13
NASA website

Navigation bar
with rollovers

Navigation links
with rollovers

Rollover images
serving as links

Create a navigation bar using images

1. Select the banner on the spa page, press the **right arrow key,** then press **[Shift][Enter]** (Win) or **[Shift][return]** (Mac) to enter a line break after the banner.

   The insertion point is now positioned between the banner and the horizontal rule.

2. Click the **Common** category on the Insert panel (if necessary), click the **Images list arrow**, then click **Navigation Bar**.

3. Type **home** in the Element name text box, in the Insert Navigation Bar dialog box, click the **Insert list arrow** as shown in Figure 14, click **Horizontally** (if necessary), to specify that the navigation bar be placed horizontally on the page.

   Be sure to choose Horizontally for the navigation bar orientation. The two options below the horizontal rule will not be available in the Modify Navigation Bar dialog box. If you miss these settings now, you will either have to make your corrections directly in the code or start over.

4. Click **Browse** next to the Up image text box, navigate to the assets folder where you store your Data Files, then double-click **home_up.gif**.

   The path to the file home_up.gif appears in the Up image text box, as shown in Figure 14.

5. Click **Browse** next to the Over image text box to specify a path to the file home_down.gif located in the chapter_4 Data Files assets folder.

6. Click **Browse** next to the Down image text box to specify a path to the file home_down.gif

   (continued)

FIGURE 14
Insert Navigation Bar dialog box

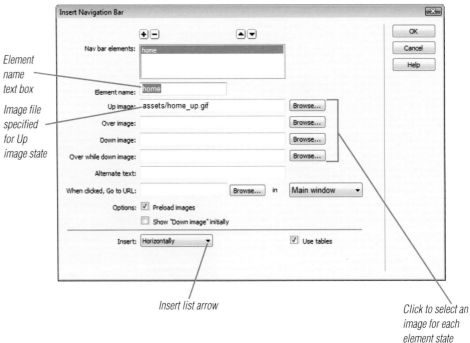

Element name text box

Image file specified for Up image state

Insert list arrow

Click to select an image for each element state

FIGURE 15
Insert Navigation Bar dialog box

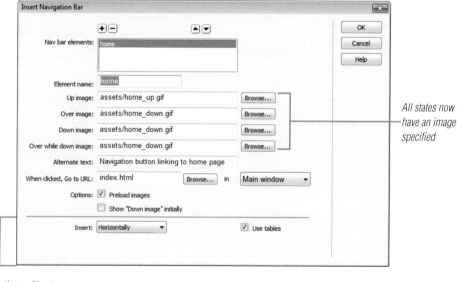

These options will not
be available in the
Modify Navigation
Bar dialog box

All states now
have an image
specified

located in the chapter_4 Data Files assets folder, overwriting the existing file.

Because this is a simple navigation bar, you use the home_down.gif image for the Over, Down, and Over while down image states.

TIP Instead of clicking Browse in Steps 6 and 7, you could copy the path of the home_down.gif file in the Over image text box and paste it to the Down image and Over while down image text boxes. You could also reference the home_down.gif file in The Striped Umbrella assets folder once it is copied there in Step 5.

7. Click **Browse** next to the Over while down image text box to specify a path to the file home_down.gif located in the chapter_4 Data Files assets folder, overwriting the existing file.

By specifying one graphic for the Up image state, and another graphic for the Over image, Down image, and Over while down image states, you will create a rollover effect.

8. Type **Navigation button linking to home page** in the Alternate text text box, click **Browse** next to the When clicked, Go to URL text box, double-click **index.html** in the striped_umbrella root folder, then compare your screen to Figure 15.

You used the Insert Navigation Bar dialog box to create a navigation bar for the spa page and added the home element to it. You used one image for the Up state and one for the other three states.

Add elements to a navigation bar

1. Click the **Add item button** ⊞ in the Insert Navigation Bar dialog box, then type **about_us** in the Element name text box.

   TIP You use the Add item button ⊞ to add a new navigation element to the navigation bar, and the Delete item button ⊟ to delete a selected navigation bar element from the navigation bar.

2. Click **Browse** next to the Up image text box, navigate to the chapter_4 assets folder, click **about_us_up.gif**, then click **OK** (Win) or **Choose** (Mac).

3. Click **Browse** next to the Over image text box to specify a path to the file **about_us_down.gif** located in the chapter_4 assets folder.

4. Click **Browse** next to the Down image text box to specify a path to the file **about_us_down.gif** located in the chapter_4 assets folder, over-writing the existing file.

5. Repeat Step 4 for the Over while down image.

6. Type **Navigation button linking to about_us page** in the Alternate text text box, click **Browse** next to the When clicked, Go to URL text box, double-click **about_us.html**, then compare your screen to Figure 16.

   (continued)

FIGURE 16
Add elements to a navigation bar

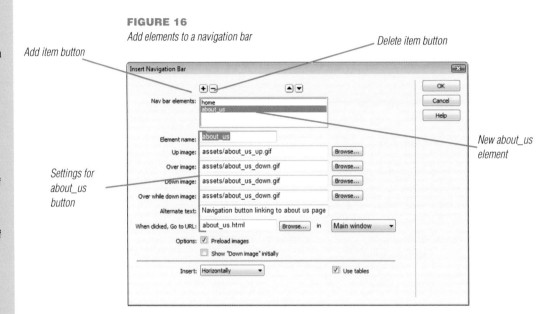

Add item button

Delete item button

New about_us element

Settings for about_us button

FIGURE 17

Navigation bar with all elements added

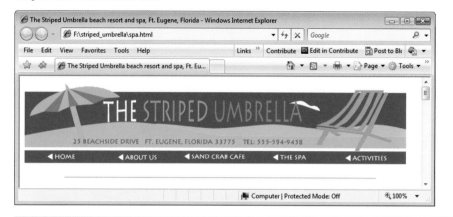

TABLE 2: Settings to use in the Insert Navigation Bar dialog box for each new element

dialog box item	cafe element	spa element	activities element
Up image file	cafe_up.gif	spa_up.gif	activities_up.gif
Over image file	cafe_down.gif	spa_down.gif	activities_down.gif
Down image file	cafe_down.gif	spa_down.gif	activities_down.gif
Over while down image file	cafe_down.gif	spa_down.gif	activities_down.gif
Alternate text	Navigation button linking to cafe page	Navigation button linking to spa page	Navigation button linking to activities page
When clicked, Go to URL	cafe.html	spa.html	activities.html

7. Using the information provided in Table 2, add three more navigation bar elements in the Insert Navigation Bar dialog box called **cafe**, **spa**, and **activities.**

   TIP All files listed in the table are located in the assets folder of the chapter_4 folder where you store your Data Files.

8. Click **OK** to close the Insert Navigation Bar dialog box.

9. Save your work, preview the page in your browser, compare your screen to Figure 17, check each link to verify that each element works correctly, then close your browser.

You completed The Striped Umbrella navigation bar by adding four more elements to it, each of which contain links to four pages in the site. All images added to the navigation bar are now stored in the assets folder of The Striped Umbrella website.

Copy and paste a navigation bar

1. Place the insertion point to the left of the navigation bar, press and hold **[Shift]**, then click to the right of the navigation bar. Since this navigation bar was created using the tables option in the Insert Navigation Bar dialog box, table tags are used to place the navigation bar. To make sure you have selected the entire table that formats the navigation bar, verify in the Tag selector that the <table> tag is selected, as shown in Figure 18.

2. Click **Edit** on the Application bar (Win) or Menu bar (Mac) then click **Copy**.

3. Double-click **activities.html** on the Files panel to open the activities page.

4. Select the original navigation bar on the page, click **Edit** on the Application bar (Win) or Menu bar (Mac) click **Paste**, then compare your screen to Figure 19.

You copied the navigation bar from the spa page and pasted it on the activities page.

Modify a navigation bar

1. Click **Modify** on the Application bar (Win) or Menu bar (Mac), then click **Navigation Bar** to open the Modify Navigation Bar dialog box.

2. Scroll down and click **activities** in the Nav bar elements list box, then click the **Show "Down image" initially check box**, as shown in Figure 20.

   An asterisk appears next to activities in the Nav bar elements list box, indicating that this element will be displayed in the Down image state initially. The sand-colored activities navigation

(continued)

FIGURE 18
Table tag selected in Tag selector

Table tag is selected

FIGURE 19
Navigation bar copied to the activities page

FIGURE 20
Changing settings for the activities element

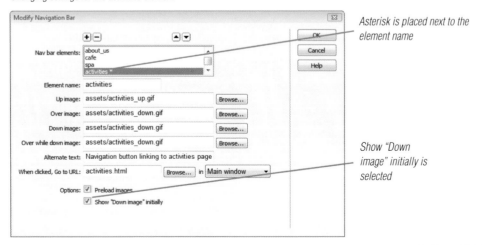

Asterisk is placed next to the element name

Show "Down image" initially is selected

FIGURE 21

About Us page with the modified navigation bar

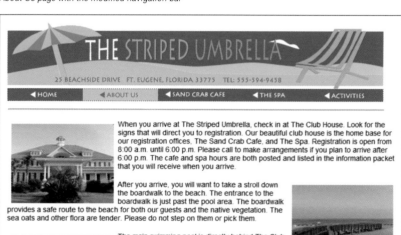

element normally used for the Down image state of the activities navigation bar element will remind viewers that they are on the activities page.

3. Click **OK** to save the new settings and close the Modify Navigation Bar dialog box, then save and close the activities page.

4. Repeat Steps 1 through 3 to modify the navigation bar on the spa page to show the Down image initially for the spa element, then save and close the spa page.

> TIP The Show "Down image" initially check box should be checked only for the element that links to the current page.

5. Open the home page, paste the navigation bar on top of the original navigation bar, then modify the navigation bar to show the Down image initially for the home element.

6. Save and close the home page.

7. Open the about_us page, paste the navigation bar on top of the original navigation bar, then use the Modify Navigation Bar dialog box to specify that the Down image be displayed initially for the about_us element, then compare your screen to Figure 21.

8. Save your work, preview the current page in your browser, test the navigation bar on the home, about_us, spa, and activities pages, then close your browser.

The cafe page is blank at this point, so use the Back button when you test the cafe link to return to the page you were viewing previously.

You modified the navigation bar on the activities page to show the activities element in the Down state initially. You then copied the navigation bar to two additional pages in The Striped Umbrella website, modifying the navigation bar elements each time to show the Down image state initially.

CREATE AN
IMAGE MAP

In this lesson, you will create an image map by placing a hotspot on The Striped Umbrella banner that will link to the home page.

Another way to create links for web pages is to combine them with images by creating an image map. An **image map** is an image that has one or more hotspots placed on top of it. A **hotspot** is a clickable area on an image that, when clicked, links to a different location on the page or to another web page. For example, a map of the United States could have a hotspot placed on each individual state so that viewers could click a state to link to information about that state. The National Park Service website is shown in Figure 22. As you place your mouse over a state, the state name, a photo, and introductory sentences from that state's page are displayed. When you click a state, you will be linked to information about national parks in that state. You

can create hotspots by first selecting the image on which you want to place a hotspot, and then using one of the hotspot tools in the Property inspector to define its shape.

There are several ways to create image maps to make them user-friendly and accessible. One way is to be sure to include alternate text for each hotspot. Another is to draw the hotspot boundaries a little larger than they need to be to cover the area you want to set as a link. This allows viewers a little leeway when they place their mouse over the hotspot by creating a larger target area for them.

The hotspot tools in Dreamweaver make creating image maps a snap. In addition to the Rectangle Hotspot Tool, there is a

Circle Hotspot Tool and a Polygon Hotspot Tool for creating different shapes. These tools can be used to create any shape hotspot that you need. For instance, on a map of the United States, you can draw an outline around each state with the Polygon Hotspot Tool.

You can then make each state "clickable." Hotspots can be easily changed and rearranged on the image. Use the Pointer Hotspot Tool to select the hotspot you would like to edit. You can drag one of the hotspot selector handles to change the size or shape of a hotspot. You can also

move the hotspot by dragging it to a new position on the image. It is a good idea to limit the number of complex hotspots in an image because the code can become too lengthy for the page to download in a reasonable length of time.

FIGURE 22
Viewing an image map on the National Park Service website

Clicking on an individual state will link to information about parks in that state

The pointer is over Hawaii, which causes a window with a photo and introductory text about Hawaii to display

National Park Service website - www.nps.gov

Create an image map

1. Open the activities page, if necessary, select the banner, then click the **Rectangle Hotspot Tool** ☐ in the Property inspector.

2. Drag the **pointer** to create a rectangle over the umbrella in the banner, as shown in Figure 23, then click **OK** to close the dialog box that reminds you to supply alternate text for the hotspot.

   TIP To adjust the shape of a hotspot, click the Pointer Hotspot Tool ▶ in the Property inspector, then drag a sizing handle on the hotspot.

3. Drag the **Point to File icon** ⊕ in the Property inspector to the index.html file on the Files panel to link the index page to the hotspot.

4. Replace the default text "Map" with **home** in the Map text box in the Property inspector to give the image map a unique name.

5. Click the **Target list arrow** in the Property inspector, then click **_top**.

   When the hotspot is clicked, the _top option causes the home page to open in the same window. See Table 3 for an explanation of the four target options.

   (continued)

FIGURE 23
Properties of the rectangular hotspot on the banner

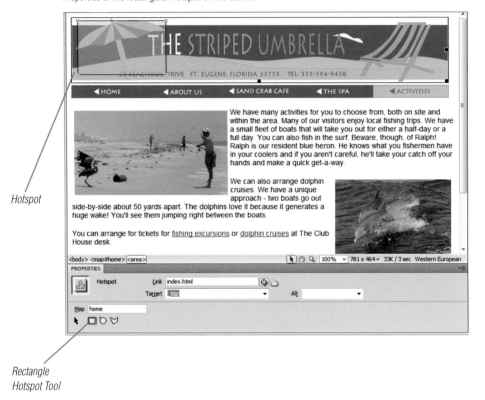

Hotspot

Rectangle
Hotspot Tool

TABLE 3: Options in the Target list

target	result
_blank	Displays the destination page in a separate browser window
_parent	Displays the destination page in the parent frameset (replaces the frameset)
_self	Displays the destination page in the same frame or window
_top	Displays the destination page in the whole browser window

FIGURE 24
Hotspot properties

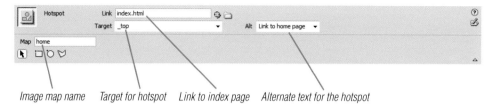

Image map name   Target for hotspot   Link to index page   Alternate text for the hotspot

FIGURE 25

Image map preview on the activities page in the browser

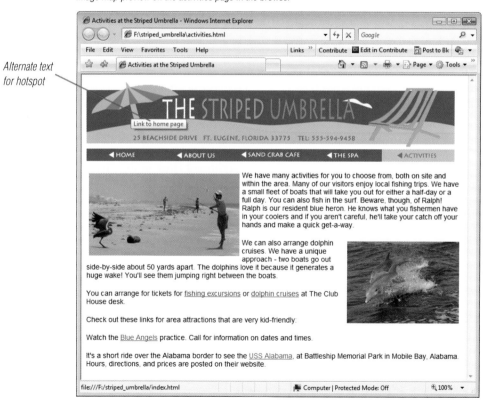

Alternate text for hotspot

6. Type **Link to home page** in the Alt text box in the Property inspector, as shown in Figure 24. then press **[Enter]** (Win) or **[return]** (Mac).

7. Save your work, preview the page in your browser, then place the pointer over the image map.

   As you place the pointer over the hotspot, you see the alternate text displayed and the pointer indicates the link (Win), as shown in Figure 25.

8. Click the link to test it, close the browser, then close all open pages.

You created an image map on the banner of the activities page using the Rectangle Hotspot Tool. You then linked the hotspot to the home page.

MANAGE WEBSITE
LINKS

What You'll Do

In this lesson, you will use some of Dreamweaver's reporting features to check The Striped Umbrella website for broken links and orphaned files.

Managing Website Links

Because the World Wide Web changes constantly, websites may be up one day and down the next. If a website changes server locations or goes down due to technical difficulties or a power failure, the links to it become broken. Broken links, like misspelled words on a web page, indicate that a website is not being maintained diligently.

Checking links to make sure they work is an ongoing and crucial task you need to perform on a regular basis. You must check external links manually by reviewing your website in a browser and clicking each link to make sure it works correctly. The Check Links Sitewide feature is a helpful tool for managing internal links. You can use it to check your entire website for the total number of links and the number of links that are okay, external, or broken, and then view the results in the Link Checker panel. The Link Checker panel also provides a list of all of the files used in a website, including those that are **orphaned files**, or files that are not linked to any pages in the website.

DESIGNTIP **Considering navigation design issues**

As you work on the navigation structure for a website, you should try to limit the number of links on each page to no more than is necessary. Too many links may confuse visitors to your website. You should also design links so that viewers can reach the information they want within a few clicks. If finding information takes more than three or four clicks, the viewer may become discouraged or lost in the site. It's a good idea to provide visual clues on each page to let viewers know where they are, much like a "You are here" marker on a store directory at the mall, or a bread crumbs trail. A **bread crumbs trail** is a list of links that provides a path from the initial page you opened in a website to the page that you are currently viewing.

FIGURE 26

Link Checker panel displaying external links

List of external links   Show list arrow

FIGURE 27

Link Checker panel displaying no orphaned files

No orphaned
files shown

Show list arrow

FIGURE 28

Assets panel displaying links

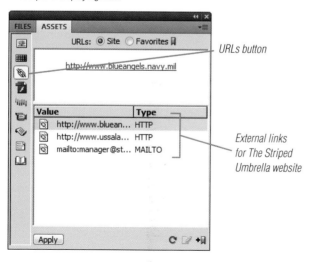

URLs button

External links
for The Striped
Umbrella website

Manage website links

1. Click **Site** on the Application bar (Win) or Menu bar (Mac), point to **Advanced**, then click **Recreate Site Cache**.

2. Click **Site** on the Application bar (Win) or Menu bar (Mac), then click **Check Links Sitewide**.

   The Results tab group opens with the Link Checker panel displayed. By default, the Link Checker panel initially displays any broken internal links found in the website. The Striped Umbrella website has no broken links.

3. Click the **Show list arrow** in the Link Checker panel, click **External Links**, then compare your screen to Figure 26.

4. Click the **Show list arrow**, then click **Orphaned Files** to view the orphaned files in the Link Checker panel, as shown in Figure 27.

   The Striped Umbrella website has no orphaned files.

5. Right-click in an empty area of the Results tab group title bar, then click **Close tab group**.

6. Display the Assets panel (if necessary), then click the **URLs button** 🖉 in the Assets panel if necessary to display the list of links in the website.

   The Assets panel displays the external links used in the website, as shown in Figure 28.

You used the Link Checker panel to check for broken links, external links, and orphaned files in The Striped Umbrella website. You also viewed the external links in the Assets panel.

Update a page

1. Open dw4_2.html from where you store your Data Files, then save it as **fishing.html** in the striped_umbrella root folder, overwriting the existing fishing page, but not updating the links.

2. Click the broken link image placeholder, click the **Browse for File icon** 📁 next to the Src text box in the Property inspector, then browse to the chapter_4 Data Files folder and select the file **heron_small.jpg** to copy the file to the striped_umbrella assets folder.

3. Deselect the image placeholder and the image will appear as shown in Figure 29.

   Notice that the text is automatically updated with the paragraph_text style. The code was already in place on the page linking the su_styles.css to the file.

4. Save and close the fishing page, then close the dw4_2.html page.

(continued)

FIGURE 29
Fishing page updated

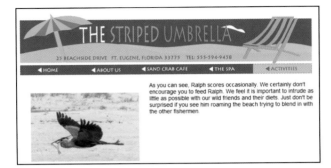

As you can see, Ralph scores occasionally. We certainly don't encourage you to feed Ralph. We feel it is important to intrude as little as possible with our wild friends and their diets. Just don't be surprised if you see him roaming the beach trying to blend in with the other fishermen.

POWER USER SHORTCUTS

to do this:	use this shortcut:
Close a file	[Ctrl][W] (Win) or ⌘[W] (Mac)
Close all files	[Ctrl][Shift][W] (Win) or ⌘[Shift][W] (Mac)
Print Code	[Ctrl][P] (Win) or ⌘[P] (Mac)
Check page links	[Shift][F8]
Undo	[Ctrl][Z], [Alt][BkSp] (Win) or ⌘[Z], [option][delete] (Mac)
Redo	[Ctrl][Y], [Ctrl][Shift][Z] (Win) or ⌘[Y], ⌘[Shift][Z] (Mac)
Refresh Design View	[F5]
Hide all Visual Aids	[Ctrl][Shift][I] (Win) or ⌘[Shift][I] (Mac)
Insert a Named Anchor	[Ctrl][Alt][A] (Win) or ⌘[option][A] (Mac)
Make a Link	[Ctrl][L] (Win) or ⌘[L] (Mac)
Remove a Link	[Ctrl][Shift][L] (Win) or ⌘[Shift][L] (Mac)
Check Links Sitewide	[Ctrl][F8] (Win) or ⌘[F8] (Mac)
Show Files tab group	[F8] (Win) or ⌘[Shift][F] (Mac)

FIGURE 30
Cruises page updated

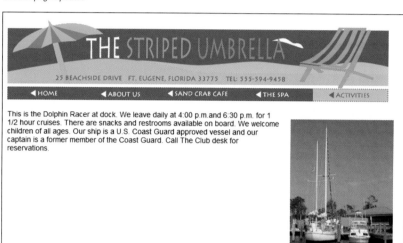

5. Open dw4_3.html from where you store your Data Files, then save it as **cruises.html** in the striped_umbrella root folder, overwriting the existing cruises page, but not updating the links.

6. Click the broken link graphic placeholder, click the **Browse for File icon** 📁 next to the Src text box in the Property inspector, then browse to the chapter_4 Data Files folder and select the file **boats.jpg** to copy the file to the striped_umbrella assets folder.

7. Deselect the image placeholder and the image will appear as shown in Figure 30.

   Notice that the text is automatically updated with the paragraph_text style. The code was already in place on the page linking the su_styles.css to the file.

8. Save and close the page.

9. Open each page that has a horizontal rule under the navigation bar, delete the horizontal rule, then save each page.

   Each page did not have a horizontal rule. By deleting each existing horizontal rule after the navigation bars were added, all pages now have a consistent look.

10. Preview each page in the browser, close the browser, then close all open pages.

You added content to two previously blank pages in the website, then deleted horizontal rules under navigation bars to provide a consistent look for each page in the site.

Create external and internal links.

1. Open the blooms & bulbs website.
2. Open dw4_4.html from where you store your Data Files, then save it as **newsletter.html** in the blooms & bulbs website, overwriting the existing file without updating the links. Close dw4_4.html.
3. Verify that the banner path is set correctly to the assets folder in the website and correct it, if it is not.
4. Scroll to the bottom of the page, then link the National Gardening Association text to http://www.garden.org.
5. Link the Organic Gardening text to http://www.organicgardening.com.
6. Link the Southern Living text to http://www.southernliving.com/southern.
7. Save the file, then preview the page in your browser, verifying that each link works correctly.
8. Close your browser, then return to the newsletter page in Dreamweaver.
9. Scroll to the paragraph about gardening issues, select the gardening tips text in the last sentence, then link the selected text to the tips.html file in the blooms root folder.
10. Apply the paragraph_text rule from the blooms_styles.css file to all of the text on the page except the subheadings and heading.

11. Apply the headings rule to the text "Gardening Matters," and the bold_blue rule to the sub-headings on the page.
12. Change the page title to **Gardening Matters**, then save your work.
13. Open the plants page and add the following sentence to the end of the last paragraph: **We have many annuals, perennials, and water plants that have just arrived**.
14. Link the "annuals" text to the annuals.html file, link the "perennials" text to the perennials.html file, and the "water plants" text to the water_plants.html file.
15. Save your work, test the links in your browser, then close your browser. (*Hint*: These pages do not have content yet, but are serving as placeholders.)

Create internal links to named anchors.

1. Show Invisible Elements (if necessary).
2. Click the Common category in the Insert panel.
3. Switch to the newsletter page, then insert a named anchor in front of the Grass heading named **grass**.
4. Insert a named anchor in front of the Plants heading named **plants**.
5. Insert a named anchor in front of the Trees heading named **trees**.

6. Use the Point to File icon in the Property inspector to create a link from the word "grass" in the Gardening Issues paragraph to the anchor named "grass."
7. Create a link from the word "trees" in the Gardening Issues paragraph to the anchor named "trees."
8. Create a link from the word "plants" in the Gardening Issues paragraph to the anchor named "plants."
9. Save your work, view the page in your browser, test all the links to make sure they work, then close your browser.

Create, modify, and copy a navigation bar.

1. Select the banner, press the right arrow key, click the Images list arrow on the Insert panel, then click Navigation Bar to insert a horizontal navigation bar at the top of the newsletter page below the banner. Verify that the option to use tables is selected.
2. Type **home** as the first element name, then use the **b_home_up.jpg** file for the Up image state. This file is in the assets folder where you store your Data Files.
3. Specify the file **b_home_down.jpg** for the three remaining states. This file (and all files for the remainder of this exercise) are in the assets folder where you store your Data Files.
4. Enter **Link to home page** as the alternate text, then set the index.html file as the link for the home element.
5. Create a new element named **plants** and use the **b_plants_up.jpg** file for the Up image state and the **b_plants_down.jpg** file for the remaining three states.
6. Enter **Link to plants page** as the alternate text, then set the **plants.html** file as the link for the plants element.

7. Create a new element named **tips** and use the **b_tips_up.jpg** file for the Up image state and the **b_tips_down.jpg** file for the remaining three states.
8. Enter **Link to tips page** as the alternate text, then set the **tips.html** file as the link for the tips element.
9. Create a new element named **classes** and use the **b_classes_up.jpg** file for the Up image state and the **b_classes_down.jpg** file for the remaining three states.
10. Enter **Link to classes page** as the alternate text, then set the **classes.html** file as the link for the classes element.
11. Create a new element named **newsletter**, then use the **b_newsletter_up.jpg** file for the Up image state and the **b_newsletter_down.jpg** file for the remaining three states.
12. Enter the alternate text **Link to newsletter page**, then set the **newsletter.html** file as the link for the newsletter element.
13. Save the page and test the links in your browser, then close the browser.
14. Select and copy the navigation bar, then open the home page.
15. Delete the current navigation bar on the home page, paste the new navigation bar

under the banner, then delete the horizontal rule under the navigation bar. Remove any space between the banner and navigation bar if necessary. (*Hint*: The easiest way to remove any extra space is to go to Code view and delete any space between the end of the banner code and the beginning table tag for the navigation bar.)
16. Modify the home element on the navigation bar to show the Down image state initially.
17. Save the page, test the links in your browser, then close the browser and the page.
18. Modify the navigation bar on the newsletter page so the Down image is shown initially for the newsletter element.
19. Paste the navigation bar on the plants page and the tips page, making the necessary modifications so that the Down image is shown initially for each element.

20. Save your work, preview all the pages in your browser, compare your newsletter page to Figure 31, test all the links, then close your browser.

Create an image map.

1. Use the Rectangle Hotspot Tool to draw an image map across the left side of the banner on the newsletter page that will link to the home page.

2. Name the image map **home** and set the target to **_top**.

3. Add the alternate text **Link to home page**, save the page, then preview it in the browser to test the link. (*Hint*: In the Internet Explorer browser, you may see a space between the banner and the navigation bar that is caused by the image map on the banner. Mozilla Firefox will display the page correctly without the space.)

4. Close the page.

Manage website links.

1. Use the Link Checker panel to view and fix broken links and orphaned files in the blooms & bulbs website.

2. Open dw4_5.html from where you store your Data Files, then save it as **annuals.html**, replacing the original file. Do not update links, but save the file **fuschia.jpg** in the assets folder of the website. Close dw4_5.html.

3. Repeat Step 2 using **dw4_6.html** to replace **perennials.html**, saving the **iris.jpg** file in

the assets folder and using **dw4_7.html** to replace **water_plants.html**, saving the **water_hyacinth.jpg** file in the assets folder.

4. Save your work, then close all open pages.

FIGURE 31
Completed Skills Review

Gardening Matters

Welcome, fellow gardeners. My name is Cosie Simmons, and I am the owner of blooms & bulbs. My passion has always been my gardens. Ever since I was a small child, I was drawn to my back yard where all varieties of beautiful plants flourished. A lush carpet of thick grass bordered with graceful beds is truly a haven for all living creatures. With proper planning and care, your gardens will draw a variety of birds and butterflies and become a great pleasure to you.

Gardening Issues

There are several areas to concentrate on when formulating your landscaping plans. One is your grass. Another is the number and variety of trees you plant. The third is the combination of plants you select. All of these decisions should be considered in relation to the climate in your area. Be sure and check out our gardening tips before you begin work.

Grass

Lawn experts classify grass into two categories: cool-climate and warm-climate. The northern half of the United States would be considered cool-climate. Examples of cool-climate grass are Kentucky bluegrass and ryegrass. Bermuda grass is a warm-climate grass. Before planting grass, whether by seeding, sodding, sprigging, or plugging, the ground must be properly prepared. The soil should be tested for any nutritional deficiencies and cultivated. Come by or call to make arrangements to have your soil tested.

Plants

There are so many types of plants available that it can become overwhelming. Do you want border plants, shrubs, ground covers, annuals, perennials, vegetables, fruits, vines, or bulbs? In reality, a combination of several of these works well. Water plants are quite popular now. We will be happy to help you sort out your preferences and select a harmonious combination of plants for you.

Trees

Before you plant trees, you should evaluate your purpose. Are you interested in shade, privacy, or color? Do you want to attract wildlife? Attract birds? Create a shady play area? Your purpose will determine what variety of tree you should plant. Of course, you also need to consider your climate and available space. We carry many varieties of trees and are happy to help you make your selections to fit your purpose.

Further Research

These are some of my favorite gardening links. Take the time to browse through some of the information they offer, then give me a call at *(555) 248-0806* or e-mail me at *cosie@blooms&bulbs.com*

National Gardening Association
Organic Gardening
Southern Living

Use Figure 32 as a guide to continue your work on the TripSmart website that you began in Project Builder 1 in Chapter 1 and developed in the previous chapters. You have been asked to create a new page for the website that lists helpful links for customers. You will also add content to the destinations, kenya, and amazon pages.

1. Open the TripSmart website.
2. Open dw4_8.html from where you store your Data Files, then save it as **services.html** in the TripSmart website root folder, replacing the existing file and not updating links. Close dw4_8.html.
3. Verify that the TripSmart banner is in the assets folder of the root folder.
4. Apply the paragraph_text rule to the paragraphs of text and the heading rule to the four main paragraph headings.
5. Create named anchors named **reservations, outfitters, tours**, and **links** in front of the respective headings on the page, then link each named anchor to "Reservations," "Travel Outfitters," "Escorted Tours," and "Helpful Links in Travel Planning" in the first paragraph.

6. Link the text "on-line catalog" in the Travel Outfitters paragraph to the catalog.html page.
7. Link the text "CNN Travel Channel" under the heading Travel Information Sites to http://www.cnn.com/TRAVEL.
8. Repeat Step 7 to create links for the rest of the websites listed:
   US Department of State:
   http://travel.state.gov
   Yahoo!:
   http://yahoo.com/Recreation/Travel
   MapQuest:
   http://www.mapquest.com
   Rand McNally:
   http://www.randmcnally.com
   AccuWeather:
   http://www.accuweather.com
   The Weather Channel:
   http://www.weather.com
9. Save the services page, then open the index page.
10. Reformat the navigation bar on the home page with a style of your choice. If you decide to use graphics for the navigation bar, you will have to create your own graphic files using a graphics program. There are no Data Files for you to use.

(*Hint*: If you create your own graphic files, be sure to create two graphic files for each element: one for the Up image state and one for the Down image state.) To design a navigation bar using text, you simply type the text for each navigation bar element, format the text appropriately using styles, and insert links to each text element as you did in Chapter 2. The navigation bar should contain the following elements: Home, Catalog, Services, Destinations, and Newsletter. In Figure 32, the navigation bar style was edited to incorporate letter spacing to spread the text slightly. Indents were then used to center the navigation bar under the banner. (Letter spacing and indents are in the Block category in the CSS Rule definition dialog box. You can also use the Text Indent button on the HTML Property inspector.)
11. Copy the navigation bar, then place it on each completed page of the website.

12. Save each page, then check for broken links and orphaned files. (*Hint*: The two orphaned files will be removed after completing the next steps.)

13. Open the destinations.html file in your root folder and save it as **kenya.html**, overwriting the existing file, then close the file.

14. Open dw4_9.html from where you store your Data Files, then save it as **amazon.html**, overwriting the existing file. Do not update links, but save the **water_lily.jpg** and **sloth.jpg** files in the assets folder of the website, then save and close the file. Close dw4_9.html.

15. Open dw4_10.html from where you store your Data Files, then save the file as **destinations.html**, overwriting the existing file. Do not update links, but save the **parrot.jpg** and **giraffe.jpg** files in the assets folder of the website. Close dw4_10.html.

16. Link the text "Amazon" in the second sentence of the first paragraph to the **amazon.html** file.

17. Link the text "Kenya" in the first sentence in the second paragraph to the **kenya.html** file.

18. Copy your customized navigation bar to the two new pages so they will match the other pages.

19. Check all text on all pages to make sure each text block uses a style for formatting. Correct those that don't.

20. Save all files.

21. Test all links in your browser, close your browser, then close all open pages.

FIGURE 32

Sample Project Builder 1

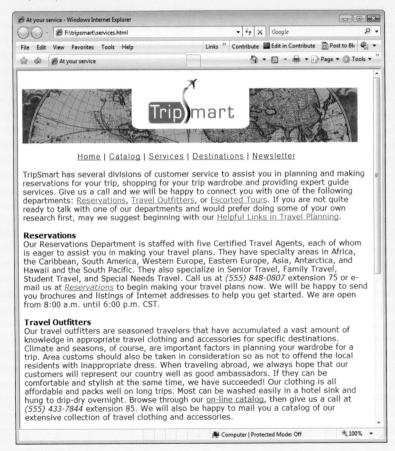

Working with Links

You are continuing your work on the Carolyne's Creations website, that you started in Project Builder 2 in Chapter 1 and developed in the previous chapters. Chef Carolyne has asked you to create a page describing her cooking classes offered every month. You will create the content for that page and individual pages describing the children's classes and the adult classes. Refer to Figures 33-36 for possible solutions.

1. Open the Carolyne's Creations website.
2. Open dw4_11.html from where you store your Data Files, save it as **classes.html** in the root folder of the Carolyne's Creations website, overwriting the existing file and not updating the links. Close dw4_11.html.
3. Check the path of the banner to make sure it is linking to the banner in the assets folder of the website. Notice that styles have already been applied to the text, because the CSS code was already in the Data File.
4. Select the text "adults' class" in the last paragraph, then link it to the adults.html page. (*Hint*: This page has not been developed yet.)
5. Select the text "children's class" in the last paragraph and link it to the children.html page. (*Hint*: This page has not been developed yet.)

6. Create an email link from the text "Sign me up!" that links to **carolyne@carolynescreations.com**
7. Insert the file **fish.jpg** from the assets folder where you store your Data Files at the beginning of the second paragraph, add

appropriate alternate text, then choose your own alignment and formatting settings.
8. Add the file **children_cooking.jpg** from the assets folder where you store your Data Files at the beginning of the third paragraph.

FIGURE 33
Completed Project Builder 2

Cooking Classes are fun!

Chef Carolyne loves to offer a fun and relaxing cooking school each month in her newly refurbished kitchen. She teaches an **adult class** on the fourth Saturday of each month from 6:00 to 8:00 pm. Each class will learn to cook a complete dinner and then enjoy the meal at the end of the class with a wonderful wine pairing. This is a great chance to get together with friends for a fun evening.

Chef Caroline also teaches a **children's class** on the second Tuesday of each month from 4:00 to 5:30 pm. Our young chefs will learn to cook two dishes that will accompany a full meal served at 5:30 pm. Kids aged 5–8 years accompanied by an adult are welcome. We also host small birthday parties where we put the guests to work baking and decorating the cake! Call for times and prices.

We offer several special adult classes throughout the year. The **Valentine Chocolate Extravaganza** is a particular favorite. You will learn to dip strawberries, make truffles, and bake a sinful Triple Chocolate Dare You Torte. We also host the **Not So Traditional Thanksgiving** class and the **Super Bowl Snacks** class each year with rave reviews. Watch the Web site for details!

Prices are $40.00 for each adults' class and $15.00 for each children's class. Sign up for classes by calling 555-963-8271 or by emailing us: <u>Sign me up!</u>

See what's cooking this month for the <u>adults' class</u> and <u>children's class</u>.

9. Compare your work to Figure 33 for a possible solution, then save and close the file.

10. Open dw4_12.html from where you store your Data Files, then save it as **children.html**, overwriting the existing file and not updating links. Save the image **cookies_oven.jpg** from the assets folder where you store your Data Files to the website assets folder. Close dw4_12.html.

11. Use your own alignment and formatting settings, compare your work to Figure 34 for a possible solution, then save and close the file.

FIGURE 35

Completed Project Builder 2

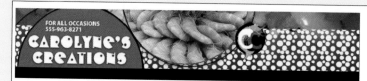

Adult Cooking Class for March: Chinese Cuisine

The class in March will be cooking several traditional Chinese dishes: Peking dumplings, wonton soup, fried rice, Chinese vegetables, and shrimp with lobster sauce. For dessert: banana spring rolls.

This looks easier than it is! Chef Carolyne is demonstrating the first steps in making Chinese dumplings, known as *jiaozi* (pronounced geeow dz). Notice that she is using a traditional wooden rolling pin to roll out the dough. These dumplings were stuffed with pork and then steamed, although other popular fillings are made with chicken and leeks or vegetables with spiced tofu and cellophane noodles. Dumplings can be steamed, boiled, or fried, and have unique names depending on the preparation method.

FIGURE 34

Completed Project Builder 2

Children's Cooking Class for March: Oven Chicken Fingers, Chocolate Chip Cookies

This month we will be baking oven chicken fingers that are dipped in a milk and egg mixture, then coated with breadcrumbs. The chocolate chip cookies are based on a famous recipe that includes chocolate chips, M&Ms, oatmeal, and pecans. Yummy! We will be learning some of the basics like how to cream butter and crack eggs without dropping shells into the batter.

We will provide French fries, green beans, fruit salad, and a beverage to accompany the chicken fingers.

12. Repeat Steps 10 and 11 to open the dw4_13.html file and save it as **adults.html**, overwriting the existing file and saving the files **dumplings1.jpg, dumplings2.jpg,** and **dumplings3.jpg** in the assets folder, then use alignment settings of your choice. Compare your work to Figure 35 for a possible solution, then save and close the file.

13. Open the index page and delete the banner, navigation bar, and horizontal rule.

14. Insert the file **cc_banner_with_text.jpg** from where you store your Data Files in place, of what you just deleted adding appropriate alternate text.

15. Create an image map for each word at the bottom of the navigation bar to be used as a link to that page, as shown in Figure 36. Use **_top** as the target, the names of the "buttons" as the image map names, and appropriate alternate text. Link each image map to its corresponding page.

16. Copy the new banner with the navigation bar to each completed page, deleting existing navigation bars and banners.

17. Save all the pages, then check for broken links and orphaned files. You will see one orphaned file, the original version of the banner.

18. Apply a rule from the style sheet to any text that is not formatted with a style.

19. Preview all the pages in your browser, check to make sure the links work correctly, close your browser, then close all open pages.

FIGURE 36
Completed Project Builder 2

Let Carolyne's Creations be your personal chef, your one stop shop for the latest in kitchen items and fresh ingredients, and your source for new and innovative recipes. We enjoy planning and executing special events for all occasions - from children's birthday parties to corporate retreats. Feel like a guest at your own party. Give us a call or stop by our shop to browse through our selections.

Carolyne's Creations
496 Maple Avenue
Seven Falls, Virginia 52404
555-963-8271
E-mail Carolyne Kate

Copyright 2001 - 2012
Last updated on July 29, 2008

Grace Keiko is a talented young water-color artist who specializes in botanical works. She wants to develop a website to advertise her work, but isn't sure what she would like to include in a website or how to tie the pages together. She decides to spend several hours looking at other artists' websites to help her get started.

1. Connect to the Internet, then navigate to the Kate Nessler website pictured in Figure 37, www.katenessler.com.
2. Spend some time looking at several of the pages in the site to get some ideas.
3. What categories of page content would you include on your website if you were Grace?
4. What external links would you consider including?
5. Describe how you would place external links on the pages and list examples of ones you would use.
6. Would you use text or images for your navigation bar?
7. Would you include rollover effects on the navigation bar elements? If so, describe how they might look.
8. How could you incorporate named anchors on any of the pages?
9. Would you include an image map on a page?
10. Sketch a website plan for Grace, including the pages that you would use as links from the home page.
11. Refer to your website sketch, then create a home page for Grace that includes a navigation bar, a short introductory paragraph about her art, and a few external links.

FIGURE 37
Design Project

Kate Nessler website used with permission from Kate Nessler - www.katenessler.com

In this assignment, you will continue to work on the website that you started in Chapter 1 and developed in the previous chapters.

You will continue building your website by designing and completing a page with a navigation bar. After creating the navigation bar, you will copy it to each completed page in the website. In addition to the navigation bar, you will add several external links and several internal links to other pages as well as to named anchors. You will also link text to a named anchor. After you complete this work, you will check for broken links and orphaned files.

1. Consult your storyboard to decide which page or pages you would like to develop in this chapter. Decide how to design and where to place the navigation bar, named anchors, and any additional page elements you decide to use. Decide which reports should be run on the website to check for accuracy.

2. Research websites that could be included on one or more of your pages as external links of interest to your viewers. Create a list of the external links you want to use. Using your storyboard as a guide, decide where each external link should be placed in the site.

3. Add the external links to existing pages or create any additional pages that contain external links.

4. Create named anchors for key locations on the page, such as the top of the page, then link appropriate text on the page to them.

5. Decide on a design for a navigation bar that will be used on all pages of the website.

6. Create the navigation bar and copy it to all finished pages on the website. If you decided to use graphics for the navigation bar, create the graphics that will be used.

7. Think of a good place to incorporate an image map, then add it to a page.

8. Use the Link Checker panel to check for broken links and orphaned files.

9. Use the checklist in Figure 38 to make sure your website is complete, save your work, then close all open pages.

FIGURE 38
Portfolio Project checklist

Website Checklist

1. Do all pages have a page title?
2. Does the home page have a description and keywords?
3. Does the home page contain contact information?
4. Does every page in the website have consistent navigation links?
5. Does the home page have a last updated statement that will automatically update when the page is saved?
6. Do all paths for links and images work correctly?
7. Do all images have alternate text?
8. Are all colors web-safe?
9. Are there any unnecessary files that you can delete from the assets folder?
10. Is there a style sheet with at least two styles?
11. Did you apply the style sheet to page content?
12. Does at least one page contain links to one or more named anchors?
13. Does at least one page contain an internal link?
14. Do all pages look good using at least two different browsers?

chapter 5

POSITIONING OBJECTS
WITH CSS AND TABLES

1. Create a page using CSS layouts

2. Add content to CSS layout blocks

3. Edit content in CSS layout blocks

4. Create a table

5. Resize, split, and merge cells

6. Insert and align images in table cells

7. Insert text and format cell content

Introduction

To create an organized, attractive web page, you need precise control of the position of text and graphic elements. CSS page layouts can provide this control. **CSS page layouts** consist of containers formatted with CSS styles in which you place web page content. These containers can accommodate images, blocks of text, Flash movies, or any other page element. The appearance and position of the containers are set through the use of HTML tags known as **div tags**. Using div tags, you can position elements next to each other as well as on top of each other in a stack. Another option for controlling the placement of page elements is through the use of tables. **Tables** are placeholders made up of small boxes called cells, into which you can insert text and graphics. Cells in a table are arranged horizontally in **rows** and vertically in **columns**. Using tables on a web page gives you control over the placement of each object on the page, similar to the way CSS blocks control placement. In this chapter, you will use a CSS predefined page layout with div tags to place text and graphics on a page. You will then add a table to one of the CSS blocks on the page to place some of the page elements.

Using Div Tags Versus Tables for Page Layout

Div tags and tables both enable you to control the appearance of content in your web pages. But unlike tables, div tags allow you to stack your information in a vertical pile, allowing for just one piece of information to be visible at a time. Tables are static, which makes it difficult to change them quickly as a need arises. Div tags can be dynamic, changing in response to variables such as a mouse click. You can create dynamic div tags using JavaScript **behaviors**, simple action scripts that let you incorporate interactivity by modifying style or content based on variables like user actions. For example, you could add a JavaScript behavior to a block of text in a div tag to make it become larger or smaller when a viewer places the pointer over it.

There has been much discussion since the inception of CSS about which tool is better—CSS layouts or table layouts. Both have advantages and disadvantages, but designers tend to prefer CSS layouts. In actual practice, many designers use a combination of both tools, choosing the tool that is the best suited to the current design challenge. No matter which tool or tools you plan to use, it is important to complete a rough sketch of a page before you actually begin working on it.

Tools You'll Use

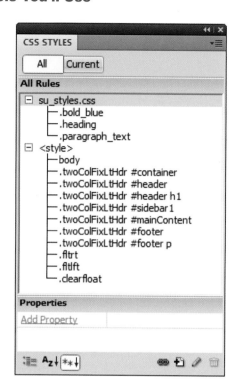

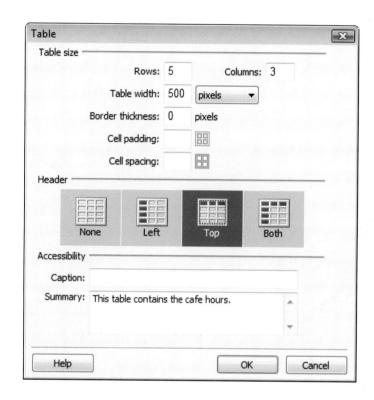

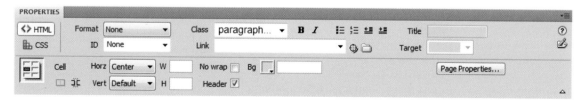

CREATE A PAGE
USING CSS LAYOUTS

What You'll Do

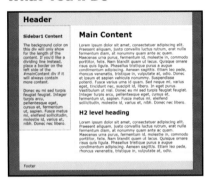

 In this lesson, you will create a new page based on a predefined CSS layout to become the new cafe page for the website.

Understanding Div Tags

Div tags are HTML tags that define how areas of content are formatted or positioned on a web page. For example, when you center an image on a page or inside a table cell, Dreamweaver automatically inserts a div tag in the HTML code. In addition to using div tags to align page elements, designers also use them to assign colors to content blocks, CSS styles to text, and many other properties to page elements. One type of div tag is an **AP** div tag. AP stands for absolutely positioned, so an **AP div tag** creates a container that has a specified, fixed position on a web page. The resulting container that an AP div tag creates on a page is called an **AP element**.

Using CSS Page Layouts

Because building a web page using div tags can be tedious for beginning designers, Dreamweaver provides 32 predesigned layouts in the New Document dialog box, as shown in Figure 1. These layouts contain div tags that control the placement of page content using placeholders. You can

use these layouts to create web pages with attractive and consistent layouts. Placeholder text is displayed in each div tag container until you replace it with your own content. Because div tags use CSS for formatting and positioning, they are the preferred method for building content for web pages. As you become more comfortable using the predesigned layouts, you will begin to build your own CSS-based pages from scratch. You must be careful, however, to test pages with CSS layouts in multiple browsers; some CSS layouts will not render correctly in all browsers. When you use the Dreamweaver predesigned layouts, you can be sure that your pages will appear as you intended in all browsers.

QUICKTIP

The Browser Compatibility Check feature flags code that might present a CSS rendering issue in some browsers by underlining code in green. To see this feature, simply switch to Code view and browse through the code.

Viewing CSS Layout Blocks

As you design web pages using div tags for page layout, you can use Design view to see and adjust CSS content blocks. In Design view, text or images that have been aligned or positioned using div tags have a dotted border, as shown in Figure 2. You can use options on the View/Visual Aids menu to display borders, backgrounds, padding, and margins of various AP elements. In the Visual Aids list on the View menu, you can select options such as CSS Layout Backgrounds, CSS Layout Box Model, CSS Layout Outlines, and AP Element Outlines. The CSS Layout Box Model displays the padding and margins of a block element.

FIGURE 1
New Document dialog box

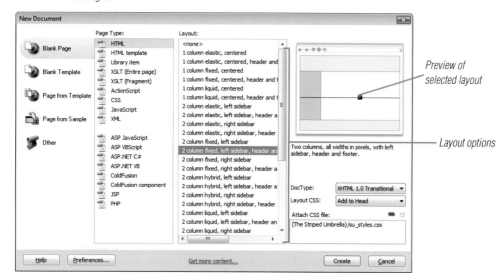

Preview of selected layout

Layout options

FIGURE 2
CSS blocks defined by dotted borders

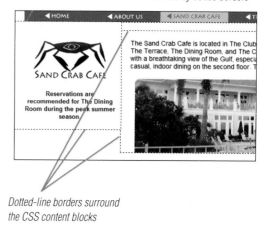

Dotted-line borders surround
the CSS content blocks

Using Tracing Images for Page Design

Another design option for creating a page layout is the use of a tracing image. A **tracing image** is an image that is placed in the background of a document. By adjusting the transparency (opacity) of the image, you can then use it to create page elements on top of it, similar to the way you would place a piece of tracing paper on top of a drawing and trace over it. To insert a tracing image, Use the Modify, Page Properties, Tracing Image text box or the View, Tracing Image, Load command. Browse to select the image you want to use for the tracing image, then adjust the transparency as desired.

Create a page with a CSS layout

1. Open The Striped Umbrella website.

2. Click **File** on the Application bar (Win) or Menu bar (Mac), click **New**, verify that Blank Page is highlighted in the first category of the New Document dialog box, click **HTML** in the Page Type category if necessary, then click **2 column fixed, left sidebar, header and footer** in the Layout category, as shown in Figure 3.

   A fixed layout will remain the same size regardless of the size of the browser window.

   (continued)

FIGURE 3
Pre-defined layout selected for new page

HTML Page Type

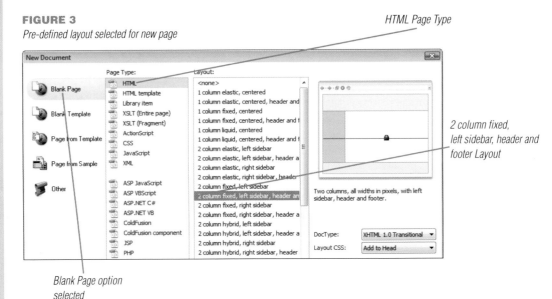

2 column fixed, left sidebar, header and footer Layout

Blank Page option selected

Using XML and XSL to create and format web page content

Another option you have with Dreamweaver is to create containers of information with XML, Extensible Markup Language, and XSL, Extensible Stylesheet Language. **XML** is a language that you use to create the structure of blocks of information, similar to HTML. It uses opening and closing tags and the nested tag structure that is used by HTML documents. However, XML tags do not determine how the information is formatted. This is done through XSL. **XSL** is similar to CSS; the XSL stylesheet information formats the containers created by XML. One more term to learn is **XSLT**, Extensible Stylesheet Language Transformations. XSLT displays the information on a web page and transforms it through the use of the style sheet. XSL transformations can be written as client-side or server-side transformations. To create XML documents, use the XML page type in the New Document dialog box.

Positioning Objects with CSS and Tables

FIGURE 4

The su_styles.css file is attached to the new page

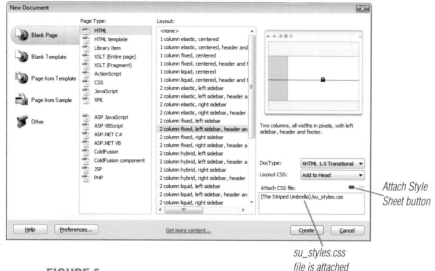

Attach Style Sheet button

su_styles.css file is attached

FIGURE 5

New page based on CSS layout

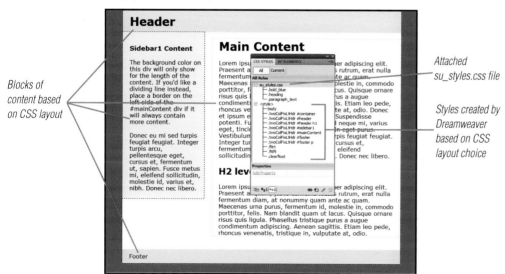

Blocks of content based on CSS layout

Attached su_styles.css file

Styles created by Dreamweaver based on CSS layout choice

3. Click the **Attach Style Sheet button** in the bottom-right corner of the dialog box, then click **Browse** in the Attach External Style Sheet dialog box.

   The Select Style Sheet File dialog box opens.

4. Select the **su_styles.css file** in the Select Style Sheet File dialog box, click **OK**, then click **OK** to close the information box.

   The links will not be relative until the page is saved in the website.

5. Verify that the Link option is selected in the Attach External Style Sheet dialog box, then click **OK** to close the Attach External Style Sheet dialog box.

   The su_styles.css file is attached to the new page, as shown in Figure 4.

6. Click **Create** in the New Document dialog box, open the CSS Styles panel, then expand the styles if necessary.

   A new page is created based on the CSS predefined layout with placeholder text, as shown in Figure 5, that will be replaced with content for The Striped Umbrella website. We will use this new page to create the cafe page.

You created a new page based on a predefined CSS layout, attaching the style sheet for The Striped Umbrella website.

ADD CONTENT
TO CSS LAYOUT BLOCKS

What You'll Do

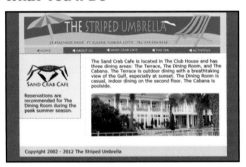

In this lesson, you will copy the text and banner from the index page and paste it into the new page. You will then overwrite the old cafe page with this new one.

Understanding Div Tag Content

As you learned in Lesson 1, a div tag is a container that formats blocks of information on a web page, such as background colors, images, links, tables, and text.

Also, as with formatting text on a web page, you should use CSS styles to format your text when using div tags. You can also add all other properties such as text indent, padding, margins, and background color using CSS styles.

In this lesson, you will use a CSS layout to create a new cafe page that arranges the page content into defined areas on the page.

Using Dreamweaver sample pages

You can use either the Welcome Screen or the New command on the File menu to create several different types of pages. The predesigned CSS page layouts make it very easy to design accessible web pages based on Cascading Style Sheets without an advanced level of expertise in writing HTML code. Predesigned templates are another time-saving feature that promotes consistency across a website. Framesets, CSS Style Sheets, and Starter Pages are a few of the other options. It is worth the time to explore each category to understand what is available to you as a designer. Once you have selected a sample page, you can customize it to suit your client's content and design needs.

Understanding CSS Code

When you view a page based on a predesigned CSS layout in Code view, you will notice helpful comments that explain sections of the code, as shown in Figure 6. The comments are in gray to differentiate them from the rest of the code. The CSS rules reside in the Head section. The code for a CSS container begins with the class, or name of the rule, and is followed by the ID, or the name of the container. A pound sign (#) precedes the ID. For example, in Figure 6, the container described on line 32 begins with the class name .twoColFixLtHdr, which is followed by its ID name, #sidebar. The code that links the rules to the content is located in the body section.

FIGURE 6

Code view for CSS in head content

ID preceded by # sign

Comments in gray text

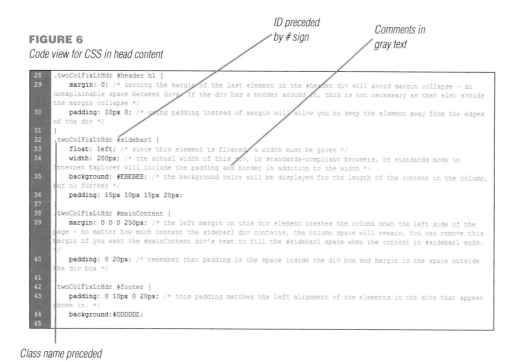

```
28    .twoColFixLtHdr #header h1 {
29        margin: 0; /* zeroing the margin of the last element in the #header div will avoid margin collapse - an
      unexplainable space between divs. If the div has a border around it, this is not necessary as that also avoids
      the margin collapse */
30        padding: 10px 0; /* using padding instead of margin will allow you to keep the element away from the edges
      of the div */
31    }
32    .twoColFixLtHdr #sidebar1 {
33        float: left; /* since this element is floated, a width must be given */
34        width: 200px; /* the actual width of this div, in standards-compliant browsers, or standards mode in
      Internet Explorer will include the padding and border in addition to the width */
35        background: #EBEBEB; /* the background color will be displayed for the length of the content in the column,
      but no further */
36        padding: 15px 10px 15px 20px;
37
38    .twoColFixLtHdr #mainContent {
39        margin: 0 0 0 250px; /* the left margin on this div element creates the column down the left side of the
      page - no matter how much content the sidebar1 div contains, the column space will remain. You can remove this
      margin if you want the #mainContent div's text to fill the #sidebar1 space when the content in #sidebar1 ends.
      */
40        padding: 0 20px; /* remember that padding is the space inside the div box and margin is the space outside
      the div box */
41    }
42    .twoColFixLtHdr #footer {
43        padding: 0 10px 0 20px; /* this padding matches the left alignment of the elements in the divs that appear
      above it. */
44        background:#DDDDDD;
45
```

Class name preceded by period

Add text to a CSS container

1. Select the content between the Header and Footer in the main section of the page, as shown in Figure 7, then press [**Delete**].

2. Import the file **cafe.doc** from the location where you store your Data Files (Win) or copy and paste it (Mac) in the blank container, then delete any extra space after the paragraph.

3. Delete the placeholder content in the left column, delete any extra space at the insertion point, then type **Reservations are recommended for The Dining Room during the peak summer season**.

    > TIP   If your text appears in bold, it is picking up the original placeholder H1 tag. To remove it, select the bold text and change the format setting in the HTML Property inspector from Heading 3 to Paragraph.

4. Delete the word "Footer" in the footer block, then type **Copyright 2002 - 2012 The Striped Umbrella** as shown in Figure 8.

5. Save the page as **cafe.html** in The Striped Umbrella website, overwriting the existing file.

You imported text and typed text in the CSS blocks, replacing the placeholder text, then saved the page as the new cafe.html page.

FIGURE 7
Text selected in main section of new page

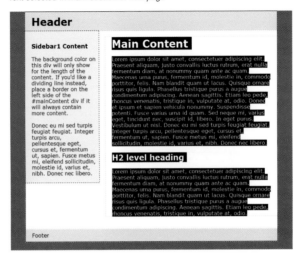

FIGURE 8
Text pasted into mainContent layout block of new page

FIGURE 9

Editing code in the header section

Delete these heading tags

```
132
133   <div id="container">
134     <div id="header">
135       <h1><img src="assets/su_banner.gif" alt="The Striped Umbrella banner" width="735" height="125" /><br />
136       </h1>
137       <table border="0" cellpadding="0" cellspacing="0">
138         <tr>
139           <td><a href="index.html" target="_top" onclick=
    "MM_nbGroup('down','group1','home','assets/home_down.gif',1)" onmouseover=
    "MM_nbGroup('over','home','assets/home_down.gif','assets/home_down.gif',1)" onmouseout="MM_nbGroup('out')"><img
    src="assets/home_down.gif" alt="Navigation bar linking to home page" name="home" border="0" id="home" onload=
    "MM_nbGroup('init','group1','home','assets/home_up.gif',1)" /></a></td>
140           <td><a href="about_us.html" target="_top" onclick=
    "MM_nbGroup('down','group1','about_us','assets/about_us_down.gif',1)" onmouseover=
    "MM_nbGroup('over','about_us','assets/about_us_down.gif','assets/about_us_down.gif',1)" onmouseout=
    "MM_nbGroup('out')"><img src="assets/about_us_up.gif" alt="Navigation button linking to about us page" name=
```

FIGURE 10

Images placed on page

Add images to a CSS container

1. Open the Striped Umbrella index page and copy both the banner and the navigation bar.

2. Switch back to the cafe page, delete the word "Header", and paste the banner and navigation bar into the header section of the page.

   TIP   Press [Ctrl][Tab] (Win) or [⌘][`](Mac) to switch between two open pages.

3. Close the index page.

4. Select the banner, switch to Code View and delete the pair of <H1> tags around the banner, as shown in Figure 9, then switch back to Design view.

   These tags were in the original placeholder text. They are affecting the spacing between the navigation bar and the banner.

   TIP   If you still see a space between the banner and navigation bar, place the insertion point in the space, then press [Delete].

5. Place the insertion point immediately in front of the word "Reservations", insert a paragraph break, press the up arrow on your keyboard, insert **cafe_logo.gif** from where you store your Data Files, then type **Sand Crab Cafe logo** as the alternate text.

6. Place the insertion point after the period after the word "poolside", insert a paragraph break, insert **cafe_photo.jpg** from where you store your Data Files, then type **Sand Crab Cafe photo** as the alternate text.

7. Save your file, then compare your screen to Figure 10.

You copied the banner and navigation bar from the index page, pasted it onto the new cafe page, then added the cafe logo and photo to the page.

EDIT CONTENT
IN CSS LAYOUT BLOCKS

In this lesson, you will center the two images you have added to the page. You will then view the div tag properties and edit the background colors. You will also change the body background color.

Edit Content in CSS Layout Blocks

It is unlikely that you will find a preformatted CSS page layout that is exactly what you have in mind for your website. However, once you have created a page with a predefined CSS layout, it is easy to modify the individual style properties to change content formatting or placement to better fit your needs. You can easily change the properties to fit the color scheme of your website.

During the process of creating a page, you can attach an external style sheet to the page. If you choose to do this, you will see both the external style sheet and any internal styles for the page layout in the CSS Styles panel. Click the plus sign, if necessary, to see the rules listed in each section, and then select the rule you want to

modify. The properties and values for the selected rule appear in the Properties pane, as shown in Figure 11, where you can modify them.

FIGURE 11
Viewing the CSS Styles panel

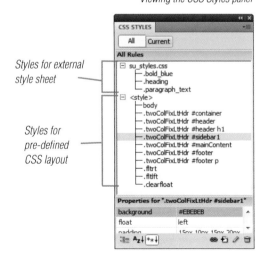

Styles for external style sheet

Styles for pre-defined CSS layout

FIGURE 12

Centering content in layout blocks

Logo and text are centered within CSS blocks

Format content in CSS layout blocks

1. Place the insertion point in front of the cafe logo.

2. Change to the CSS Property inspector if necessary, then click the **Align Center button** 🔳.

   The logo and text are now centered in the left sidebar.

3. Repeat Steps 1 and 2 to center the copyright statement, then compare your page to Figure 12.

   (continued)

Using the Adobe CSS Advisor for cross-browser rendering issues

You can use the Browser Compatibility Check (BCC) feature to check for problems in the HTML code for CSS features that may render differently in multiple browsers. It flags and rates code on three levels: an error that could cause a serious display problem; an error that probably won't cause a serious display problem; or a warning that it has found code that is unsupported, but won't cause a serious display problem. Each bug is linked to the CSS Advisor, a part of the Adobe website, that offers solutions for that particular bug and other helpful information for resolving any issues with your pages. To check for browser compatibility, click File, point to Check Page, and then click Browser Compatibility or click the Check browser compatibility button on the Document toolbar.

4. Move the pointer over the top of the mainContent block (the block containing the cafe description and picture), click the **yellow border** to select the block, (the border turns red after it is selected), then move the pointer on the block border until the floating window shown in Figure 13 appears.

The properties of the div tag are displayed in a floating window. The Property inspector displays the div tag properties.

> TIP You can change the border color of div tags when the mouse is positioned over them in the Preferences dialog box. Select the Highlighting category, then click the Mouse-Over color box and select a different color. You can also disable highlighting by deselecting the Show checkbox for Mouse-Over.

5. Save your work.

You centered the logo, reservations text, and copyright statement. You also viewed the properties of the div tag.

FIGURE 13
Viewing the div tag properties

Border for div block

Properties of div tag

Class assigned to div tag

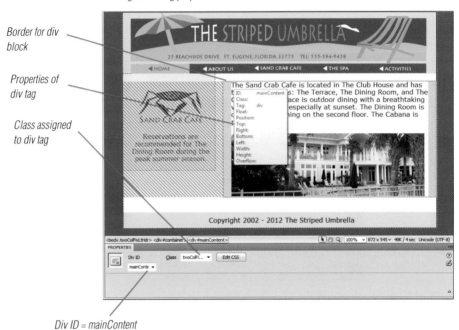

Div ID = mainContent

Viewing options for CSS layout blocks

There are several options for viewing your layout blocks in Design view. You can choose to show or hide outlines, temporarily assign different background colors to each individual layout block, or view the CSS Layout Box Model (padding and margins) of a selected layout. To change these options, use the View/Visual Aids menu, and then select or deselect the CSS Layout Outlines, CSS Layout Backgrounds, or CSS Layout Box Model menu choice. You can also use the Visual Aids button on the Document toolbar.

FIGURE 14

Applying rules from the su_styles.css style sheet

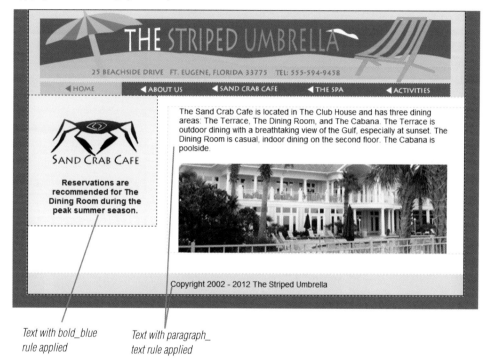

Text with bold_blue
rule applied

Text with paragraph_
text rule applied

Edit styles in CSS layout blocks

1. Place the insertion point at the beginning of the paragraph in front of the words "The Sand Crab Cafe" in the introductory paragraph, press and hold **[Shift]**, then click the space at the end of the paragraph.

2. Click the **Targeted Rule list arrow** in the CSS Property inspector, then click **paragraph_text.**

    The paragraph_text rule is applied to the paragraph.

3. Repeat Steps 1 and 2 to apply the **paragraph_text** rule to the copyright statement and the **bold_blue** rule to the reservation information, as shown in Figure 14.

4. Save your work.

You formatted three text blocks with rules from the style sheet.

Edit CSS layout block properties

1. Click the **twoColFixLtHdr #mainContent rule** in the CSS Styles panel to select it.

    The values of the margin and padding properties are displayed in the Properties pane. The mainContent block has a 250 pixel left margin with 20 px padding on the right and left sides of the block.

(continued)

2. Click the **margin text box** to place the insertion point, replace 250 with **230**, then press **[Enter]** (Win) or **[return]** (Mac) as shown in Figure 15.

   TIP   You can also create more room for content by increasing the width of the container in the CSS Styles panel Properties pane.

   This will give more room for the text in the main paragraph to expand across the page.

3. Select the **cafe photo image**, click the **H space text box** in the Property inspector, type **10** to indent the image in the block, then press **[Tab]**.

4. Click the **twoColFixLtHdr #header** rule in the CSS Styles panel to select it.

5. Click to select the background color #DDDDDD, type **#FFFFFF** as shown in Figure 16, then press **[Enter]** (Win) or **[return]** (Mac).

   The header background color is now white.

   TIP   You only need to use the abbreviated hexadecimal color code, such as #FFF, when specifying colors. However, in the Dreamweaver predesigned CSS layouts, the color codes are shown with the full 6-character codes. Either code will work. You can also specify colors by their names. For example, the color magenta can be specified as "magenta", #FF00FF, or #F0F.

6. Repeat Steps 4 and 5 to change the footer and sidebar1 background colors to **#FFFFFF**.

7. Save your work, then compare your screen to Figure 17.

You changed the margin width of a CSS layout block, indented the cafe photo, then changed the background color of three CSS layout blocks to white.

FIGURE 15

Editing the properties of the twoColFixLtHdr #mainContent rule

Select the twoColFixLtHdr #mainContent rule

Change the margin settings for the block to 0 0 0 230px

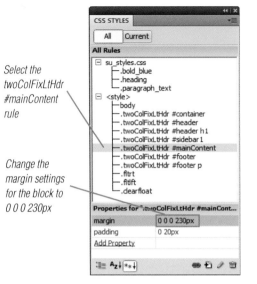

FIGURE 16

Editing the properties of the twoColFixLtHdr #header rule

Select the twoColFixLtHdr #header rule

Change the background color value to #FFFFFF

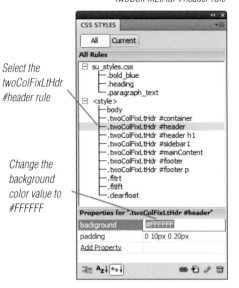

FIGURE 17

The four layout blocks now have a white background

The four blocks have the same background color

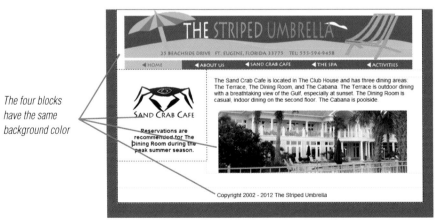

FIGURE 18

Changing the body background value to #FFFFFF

Select the body rule

Change the background
color value to #FFFFFF

Edit page properties

1. Select the **body tag** in the CSS Styles panel.

2. Click to select the background color **#666666**, type **#FFFFFF**, as shown in Figure 18, then press **[Enter]** (Win) or **[return]** (Mac).

   The body tag for the page is now set to display a white background. The body background color is the color of the page behind the CSS container.

3. Save your work, preview the page in your browser, compare your screen to Figure 19, then close the browser.

You changed the value for the background color to white.

FIGURE 19

Viewing the cafe page in the browser

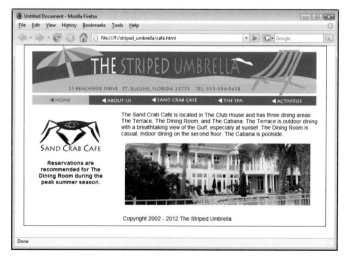

CREATE A TABLE

What You'll Do

 In this lesson, you will create a table for the cafe page in The Striped Umbrella website to provide a grid for the cafe hours.

Understanding Table Modes

Now that you have learned how CSS can act as containers to hold information in place on web pages, let's look at tables as another layout tool. Tables are great when you have a need for a grid layout on a page, such as a chart with text and numbers. Some web pages are based entirely on tables for their page layouts and some pages contain tables inside CSS layout blocks. To create a table, click the Table button on the Insert panel. When the Layout category of the Insert panel is displayed, you can choose Standard mode or Expanded Table mode by clicking the appropriate button on the Insert panel after selecting a table on the page.

Creating a Table

To create a table in Standard mode, click the Table button on the Insert panel to open the Table dialog box. Enter values for the number of rows and columns, the border thickness, table width, cell padding, and cell spacing. The **border** is the outline or frame around the table and the individual cell and is measured in pixels. The table width can be specified in pixels or as a percentage. When the table width is specified as a percentage, the table width will expand to fill up its container (the browser window, a CSS container, or another table). A table placed inside another table is called a **nested table**. Figure 20 could either be a page based on a table set to 100% width (of the browser window or container), or it could be a page that is not based on a table at all. The content spreads across the entire browser window, without a container to set boundaries, such as the pages you created in the first four chapters. When the table width is specified in pixels, the table width stays the same, regardless of the size of the browser window or container. The page in Figure 21 is an example of a page based on a table with a fixed width of 750 pixels. The content will not spread outside the table borders unless it contains images that are wider than the table. **Cell padding** is the distance between the cell content and the **cell walls**, the lines inside the cell borders. **Cell spacing** is the distance between cells.

Using Expanded Tables Mode

Expanded Tables mode is a feature that allows you to change to a table view with expanded table borders and temporary cell padding and cell spacing. This mode makes it much easier to actually see how many rows and columns you have in your table. Often, especially after splitting empty cells, it is difficult to place the insertion point precisely in a table cell. The Expanded Tables mode allows you to see each cell clearly. However, most of the time you will want to work in Standard mode to maintain the WYSIWYG environment. **WYSIWYG** is the acronym for What You See Is What You Get. This

means that your page should look the same in the browser as it does in the web editor. Before you create a table, you should sketch a plan for it that shows its location on the page and the placement of text and graphics in its cells. You should also decide whether to include borders around the tables and cells. Setting the border value to 0 causes the table to appear invisible, so that viewers will not realize that you used a table for the layout unless they look at the code. Figure 22 shows a sketch of the table you will create on The Striped Umbrella cafe page to organize the cafe hours.

Setting Table Accessibility Preferences

You can make a table more accessible to visually handicapped viewers by adding a table caption and a table summary that screen readers can read. The table caption appears on the screen. The table summary does not. These features are especially useful for tables that are used for tabular data. **Table headers** are another way to provide accessibility. Table headers can be placed at the top or sides of a table with data. They are automatically centered and bold and are used by screen readers to help viewers identify the table content. Table captions, summaries, and headers are all created in the Table dialog box.

FIGURE 20

Page shown without using tables or using a table based on a 100% width

Content spreads across the browser window

FIGURE 21

Same page shown using a fixed-width table for layout

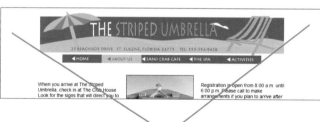

Table confines content; leftover white space displayed outside table borders

FIGURE 22

Sketch of table on cafe page

Cafe Hours

Photo | Hours listed by room

Create a table

1. Click to place the insertion point in the white space between the cafe photo and the footer.

2. Click **Table** in the Common group on the Insert panel.

   The Table dialog box opens.

3. Type **5** in the Rows text box, type **3** in the Columns text box, type **500** in the Table width text box, click the **Table width list arrow**, click **pixels** if necessary, type **0** in the Border thickness text box, then click the **Top** Header.

   > TIP It is better to add more rows than you think you will need when you create your table. After they are filled with content, it is far easier to delete rows than to add rows if you decide later to split or merge cells in the table.

4. In the Summary text box, type **This table contains the cafe hours**, then compare your screen to Figure 23.

5. Click **OK**.

   The table appears on the page, but the table summary is not visible. The summary will not appear in the browser but will be read by screen readers.

   > TIP To edit accessibility preferences for a table, switch to Code view to edit the code directly.

   (continued)

FIGURE 23
Table dialog box

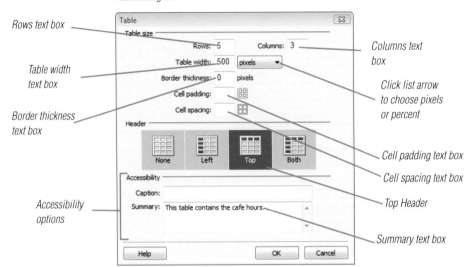

Rows text box

Table width text box

Border thickness text box

Accessibility options

Columns text box

Click list arrow to choose pixels or percent

Cell padding text box

Cell spacing text box

Top Header

Summary text box

DESIGNTIP **Setting table and cell widths when using tables for page layout**

If you use a table to place all the text and graphics contained on a web page, it is wise to set the width of the table in pixels. This ensures that the table will not resize itself proportionately if the browser window size is changed. If you set the width of a table using pixels, the table will remain one size, regardless of the browser window size. For instance, if the width of a table is set to slightly less than 800, the table will stretch across the whole width of a browser window set at a resolution of 800×600. The same table would be the same size on a screen set at 1024×768 and therefore would not stretch across the entire screen. Most designers use a resolution of 800×600 or higher. Be aware, however, that if you set the width of your table at 800 pixels, your table will be too wide to print the entire width of the page, and part of the right side of the page will be cut off. If you are designing a table layout for a page that is likely to be printed by the viewer, you should make your table narrower to fit on a printed page. If you set a table width as a percentage, however, the table would resize itself proportionately in any browser window, regardless of the resolution. You can also set each cell width as either a percentage of the table or as fixed pixels.

FIGURE 24
Expanded Tables mode

Click "exit" to return to Standard mode

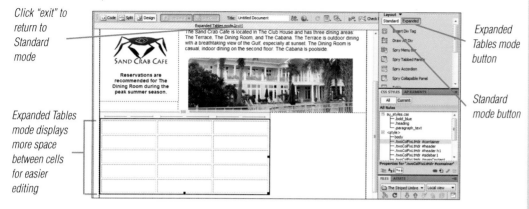

Expanded Tables mode button

Standard mode button

Expanded Tables mode displays more space between cells for easier editing

FIGURE 25
Property inspector showing properties of selected table

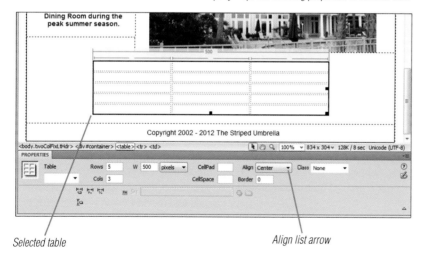

Selected table

Align list arrow

6. Click the **Insert panel list arrow**, click **Layout**, click the **Expanded Tables mode button** Expanded , click **OK** in the Getting Started in Expanded Tables Mode dialog box, then compare your screen to Figure 24.

The Expanded Tables mode makes it easier to select and edit tables.

7. Click the **Standard mode button** Standard to return to Standard mode.

    TIP You can also return to Standard mode by clicking [exit] in the blue bar below the Document toolbar.

You created a table on the cafe page that will display the cafe hours with five rows and three columns and a width of 500 pixels. You used a top header and added a table summary that will be read by screen readers.

Set table properties

1. Move the pointer slowly to the top or bottom edge of the table until you see the pointer change to a Table pointer ⬚⊞ , then click the **table border** to select the table, if necessary.

2. Expand the Property inspector (if necessary) to display the current properties of the new table.

    TIP The Property inspector will display information about the table only when the table is selected.

3. Click the **Align list arrow** in the Property inspector, then click **Center** to center the table on the page, as shown in Figure 25.

    The center alignment formatting will center the table inside the CSS container.

You selected and center-aligned the table.

RESIZE, SPLIT, AND MERGE CELLS

What You'll Do

In this lesson, you will set the width of the table cells to be split across the table in predetermined widths. You will then split one cell. You will also merge some cells to provide space for the table header.

Resizing Table Elements

You can resize the rows or columns of a table manually. To resize a table, row, or column, you must first select the table, then drag one of the table's three selection handles. To change all the columns in a table so that they are the same size, drag the middle-right selection handle. To resize the height of all rows simultaneously, drag the middle-bottom selection handle. To resize the entire table, drag the right-corner selection handle. To resize a row or column individually, drag the interior cell borders up, down, to the left, or to the right. You can also resize selected columns, rows, or individual cells by entering specific measurements in the W and H text boxes in the Property inspector specified either in pixels or as a percentage. Cells whose width or height is specified as a percentage will maintain that percentage in relation to the width or height of the entire table if the table is resized.

Adding or deleting a row

As you add new content to your table, you might find that you have too many or too few rows or columns. You can add or delete one row or column at a time or several at once. You use commands on the Modify menu to add and delete table rows and columns. When you add a new column or row, you must first select the existing column or row to which the new column or row will be adjacent. The Insert Rows or Columns dialog box lets you choose how many rows or columns you want to insert or delete, and where you want them placed in relation to the selected row or column. The new column or row will have the same formatting and number of cells as the selected column or row. After you have split and merged cells, it can be challenging to add or delete rows.

Using the Table button creates a new table with evenly spaced columns and rows. Sometimes you will want to adjust the cells in a table by splitting or merging them. To **split** a cell means to divide it into multiple rows or columns. To **merge** cells means to combine multiple cells into one cell. Using split and merged cells gives you more flexibility and control in placing page elements in a table and can help you create a more visually exciting layout. When you merge cells, the HTML tag used to describe the merged cell changes from a width size tag to a column span or row span tag. For example, <td colspan="2"> is the code for two cells that have been merged into one cell that spans two columns.

DESIGNTIP   **Using nested tables**

A nested table is a table inside a table. To create a nested table, you place the insertion point in the cell where you want to insert the nested table, then click the Table button on the Insert panel. A nested table is a separate table that can be formatted differently from the table in which it is placed. Nested tables are useful when you want part of your table data to have visible borders and part to have invisible borders. For example, you can nest a table with red borders inside a table with invisible borders. You need to plan carefully when you insert nested tables. It is easy to get carried away and insert too many nested tables, which makes it more difficult to apply formatting and rearrange table elements. Before you insert a nested table, consider whether you could achieve the same result by adding rows and columns or by splitting cells.

Resize columns

1. Click inside the **first cell** in the bottom row.

2. Type **30%** in the W text box in the Property inspector, then press **[Enter]** (Win) or **[return]** (Mac) to change the width of the cell to 30 percent of the table width.

   Notice that the column width is shown as a percentage at the top of the first column in the table, along with the table width of 500 pixels.

   | TIP You need to type the % sign next to the number you type in the W text box. Otherwise, the width will be expressed in pixels.

3. Repeat Steps 1 and 2 for the next two cells in the last row, using **30%** for the middle cell and **40%** for the last cell, then compare your screen to Figure 26.

   The combined widths of the three cells add up to 100 percent. As you add content to the table, the columns will remain in this proportion unless you insert an image that is larger than the table cell. If a larger image is inserted, the cell width will expand to display it.

   | TIP Changing the width of a single cell changes the width of the entire column.

You set the width of each of the three cells in the bottom row to set the column sizes for the table. This will keep the table from resizing when you add content.

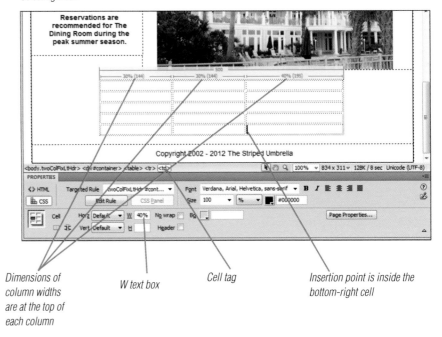

FIGURE 26
Selecting a cell

Dimensions of column widths are at the top of each column

W text box

Cell tag

Insertion point is inside the bottom-right cell

Resetting table widths and heights

After resizing columns and rows in a table, you might want to change the sizes of the columns and rows back to their previous sizes. To reset columns and rows to their previous widths and heights, select the table, click Modify on the Application bar (Win) or Menu bar (Mac), point to Table, then click Clear Cell Heights or Clear Cell Widths. Using the Clear Cell Heights command also forces the cell border to snap to the bottom of any inserted graphics, so you can also use this command to tighten up extra white space in a cell. This menu also has choices for converting table widths and heights from pixels to percents and vice versa.

FIGURE 27

Resizing the height of a row

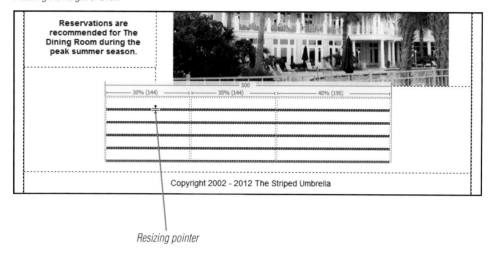

Reservations are
recommended for The
Dining Room during the
peak summer season.

500

|← 30% (144) →|← 30% (144) →|← 40% (195) →|

Copyright 2002 - 2012 The Striped Umbrella

Resizing pointer

Resize rows

1. Place the pointer over the bottom border of the first row until it changes to a resizing pointer ⇕, as shown in Figure 27, then click and drag down about ¼ of an inch to increase the height of the row.

   The border turns darker when you select and drag it.

2. Click **Window** on the menu bar, click **History**, then drag the **slider** in the History panel up one line to the **Set Width**: **40%** mark to return the row to its original height.

3. Close the History panel.

You changed the height of the top row, then used the History panel to change it back to its original height.

HTML table tags

When formatting a table, it is important to understand the basic HTML table tags. The tags used for creating a table are <table> </table>. The tags used to create table rows are <tr></tr>. The tags used to create table cells are <td></td>. Dreamweaver places the   code into each empty table cell at the time it is created. The   code represents a nonbreaking space, or a space that a browser will display on the page. Some browsers will collapse an empty cell, which can ruin the look of a table. The nonbreaking space will hold the cell until content is placed in it, at which time it will be automatically removed.

Split cells

1. Click inside the first cell in the fifth row, then click the **<td>** in the tag selector.

   TIP   You can click the cell tag <td> (the HTML tag for that cell) on the tag selector to select the corresponding cell in the table. To select the entire table, click the <table> tag on the tag selector.

2. Click the **Splits cell into rows or columns button** ⴻⵉⵤ in the Property inspector.

3. Click the **Split cell into Rows option button** (if necessary), type **2** in the Number of rows text box (if necessary), as shown in Figure 28, click **OK**, then click in the cell to deselect it.

   The cell is split, as shown in Figure 29.

   TIP   To create a new row identical to the one above it, place the insertion point in the last cell of a table, then press [Tab].

You split a cell into two rows.

FIGURE 28
Splitting a cell into two rows

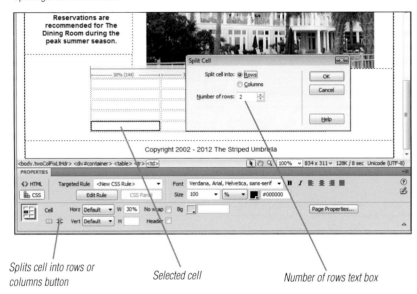

Splits cell into rows or columns button

Selected cell

Number of rows text box

FIGURE 29
Resulting split cells

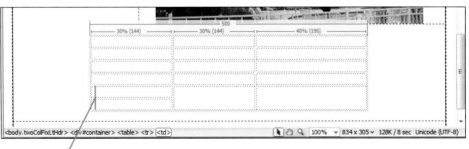

Two cells split from one cell

Positioning Objects with CSS and Tables

FIGURE 30

Merging selected cells into one cell

Resulting merged cell

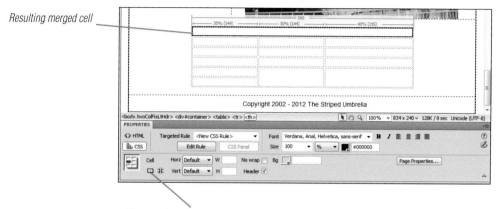

Merges selected cells using spans button

FIGURE 31

Code for merged cells

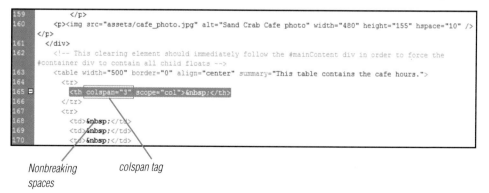

Nonbreaking
spaces

colspan tag

Merge cells

1. Click to set the insertion point in the first cell in the top row, then drag to the right to select the second and third cells in the top row.

2. Click the **Merges selected cells using spans button** ⊞ in the Property inspector.

   The three cells are merged into one cell, as shown in Figure 30. Merged cells are good placeholders for banners or headings.

   > TIP   You can only merge cells that are adjacent to each other.

3. Click the **Show Code view button** ⟨⟩ Code, then view the code for the merged cells, as shown in Figure 31.

   Notice the table tags denoting the column span (th colspan="3") and the nonbreaking spaces ( ) inserted in the empty cells.

   The nonbreaking space is a special character that is inserted automatically in an empty cell to serve as a placeholder until content is added. A nonbreaking space will override automatic word wrap, or prevent a line break from being inserted in HTML code.

4. Click the **Show Design view button** ⬚ Design, select and merge the first cells in rows 2, 3, 4, and 5 in the left column, then save your work.

You merged three cells in the first row to make room for the table header. You then merged four cells in the left column to make room for an image.

INSERT AND ALIGN
IMAGES IN TABLE CELLS

 In this lesson, you will insert an image of a cheesecake in the left column of the table. After placing the image, you will align it within the cell.

Inserting Images in Table Cells

You can insert images in the cells of a table using the Image command in the Images menu on the Insert panel. If you already have images saved in your website that you would like to insert in a table, you can drag them from the Assets panel into the table cells. When you add a large image to a cell, the cell expands to accommodate the inserted image. If you select the Show attributes when inserting Images check box in the Accessibility category of the Preferences dialog box, the Image Tag Accessibility Attributes dialog box will open after you insert an image, prompting you to enter alternate text. Figure 32 shows the John Deere website, which uses several tables for page layout and contains images in its table cells. Notice that some images appear in cells by themselves, and some appear in cells containing text or other graphics. Some cells have a white background, and some have a green background.

Aligning Images in Table Cells

You can align images both horizontally and vertically within a cell. You can align an image horizontally using the Horz (horizontal) alignment options in the Property inspector, as shown in Figure 33. This option is used to align the entire contents of the cell, whether there is one object or several. You can also align an image vertically by the top, middle, bottom, or baseline of a cell. To align an image vertically within a cell, use the Vert (vertical) Align list arrow in the Property inspector, then choose an alignment option. To control spacing between cells, you can use cell padding and cell spacing. **Cell padding** is the space between a cell's border and its contents. **Cell spacing** is the distance between adjacent cells.

FIGURE 32

John Deere website

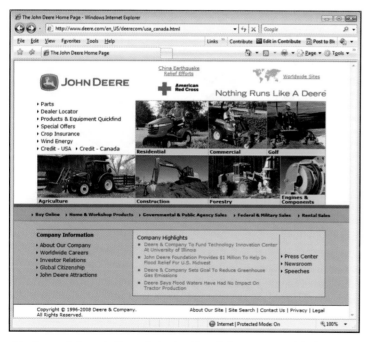

John Deere website used with permission from Deere & Company – www.johndeere.com

FIGURE 33

Horizontally aligning cell contents

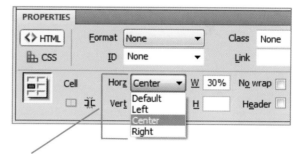

Horizontal alignment options

Insert images in table cells

1. Click in the merged cells in the left column of the table (under the merged cells in the top row) to place the insertion point.

2. Insert **cheesecake.jpg** from where you store your Data Files, then type **Banana Chocolate Cheesecake** for the alternate text.

   | TIP   You may have to click out of the cell if you see extra space around the image.

3. Compare your screen to Figure 34.

4. Refresh the Assets panel to verify that the new image was copied to The Striped Umbrella website assets folder.

5. Save your work, then preview the page in your browser.

6. Close your browser.

You inserted an image into a table cell on the cafe page.

FIGURE 34
Image inserted into table cell

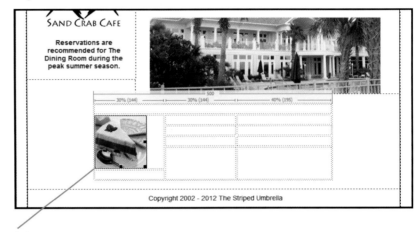

cheesecake.jpg

Using rulers, grids, and guides for positioning page content

There are some other options available to help you position your page content that are available through the View menu. **Grids** provide a graph paper-like view of a page. Horizontal and vertical lines fill the page when this option is turned on. You can edit the line colors, the distance between them, whether they are displayed using lines or dots, and whether or not objects "snap" to them. **Guides** are horizontal or vertical lines that you drag onto the page from the rulers. You can edit both the colors of the guides and the color of the distance, a feature that shows you the distance between two guides. You can lock the guides so you don't accidentally move them and you can set them either to snap to page elements or have page elements snap to them. To display grids or guides, click View on the Application bar (Win) or Menu bar (Mac), point to Grid, then click Show Grid or point to Guides and then click Show Guides.

FIGURE 35
Aligning image in cell

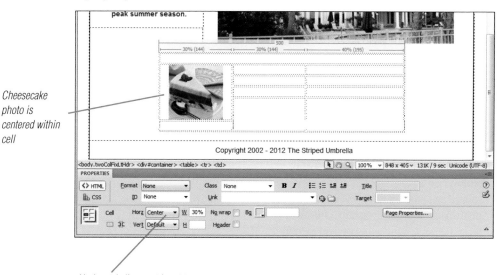

Cheesecake photo is centered within cell

Horizontal alignment is set to center

1. Click to the right side of the **cheesecake image** to place the insertion point.

2. Click the **Horz list arrow** in the Property inspector, then click **Center**. (Both the HTML and CSS Property inspectors have the alignment options.)

   The cheesecake image is centered in the cell. The alignment will be applied to all content inserted into this cell. The effect of the alignment, however, may not be apparent until more content is added to the table.

3. Compare your screen to Figure 35.

4. Save your work.

5. Preview the page in your browser, view the aligned image, then close your browser.

You center-aligned cell content.

Working with div tags

Div tags are used for formatting blocks of content, similar to the way P tags are used to format paragraphs of text. Div tags, however, are more flexible in that they can be used as a container for any type of block content. They are used in various ways, such as centering content on a page or applying color to an area of a web page. One of the benefits of using div tags is that they are combined easily with Cascading Style Sheets for formatting and positioning. When alignment is assigned to a block of content, Dreamweaver will automatically add a div tag. Div tags are frequently used in style sheets to specify formatting attributes.

INSERT TEXT AND FORMAT
CELL CONTENT

What You'll Do

In this lesson, you will type the cafe hours in the table. You will also format the text to enhance its appearance on the page. Last, you will add formatting to some of the cells and cell content.

Inserting Text in a Table

You can enter text in a table either by typing it in a cell, copying it from another source and pasting it into a cell, or importing it from another program. Once you place text in a table cell, you can format it to make it more readable and more visually appealing on the page.

Formatting Cell Content

To format the contents of a cell, select the contents in the cell, then apply formatting to it. For example, you can select an image in a cell and center it, add a border, or add V space. Or, you can select text in a cell and apply a style or use the Text Indent or Text Outdent buttons in the HTML Property inspector to move the text farther away from or closer to the cell walls.

If a cell contains multiple objects of the same type, such as text, you can either format each item individually or select the entire cell and apply formatting that will be applied identically to all items. You can tell whether you have selected the cell contents or the cell by looking to see what options are showing in the Property inspector. Figure 36 shows a selected image in a cell. Notice that the Property inspector displays options for formatting the object, rather than options for formatting the cell.

Formatting Cells

Formatting a cell is different from formatting a cell's contents. Formatting a cell can include setting properties that visually enhance the cell's appearance, such as setting a cell width and assigning a background color. You can also set global alignment properties for the cell content, using the Horz or Vert list arrows on the Property inspector. These options set the alignment for cell content horizontally or vertically. To format a cell, you need to either select the cell or place the insertion point inside the cell you want to format, then choose the cell formatting options you want in the Property inspector. For example, to choose a fill color for a selected cell, click the Background Color button in the Property inspector, then choose a color from the color picker.

QUICKTIP

Cell and table formatting can also be specified through rules in a Cascading Style Sheet. Some options, such as using an image for a cell background, cannot be set using the Property inspector.

To format a cell, you must expand the Property inspector to display the cell formatting options. In Figure 37, notice that the insertion point is positioned in the cheesecake cell, but the image is not selected. The Property inspector displays the formatting options for cells.

FIGURE 36

Property inspector showing options for selected image

Property inspector shows properties
for selected image

Image selected inside
a cell

FIGURE 37

Property inspector showing options for formatting a cell

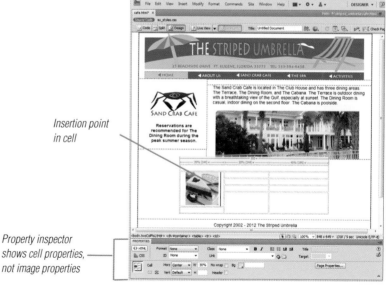

Insertion point
in cell

Property inspector
shows cell properties,
not image properties

Insert text

1. Click in the cell below the cheesecake photo, type **Banana Chocolate**, press **[Shift][Enter]** (Win) or **[shift][return]** (Mac), type **Cheesecake**, press **[Shift][Enter]** (Win) or **[shift][return]** (Mac), then type **Our signature dessert**.

2. Click in the top row of the table to place the insertion point, then type **Sand Crab Cafe Hours**.

   The text is automatically bolded because the top row header was chosen when you created the table.

3. Merge the two bottom-right cells in the last row, then enter the cafe dining area names, hours, and room service information as shown in Figure 38. Use line breaks after the first two lines of text.

   | TIP   If your table cells seem to have extra space in them, click the <table> tag to tighten it up.

   You entered text in the table to provide information about the dining room hours.

FIGURE 38
Typing text into cells

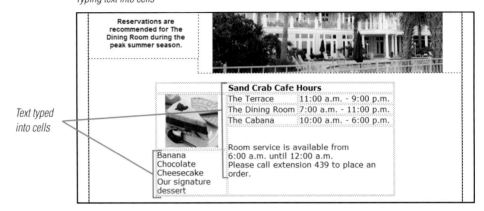

Text typed into cells

Importing and exporting data from tables

You can import and export tabular data into and out of Dreamweaver. Tabular data is data that is arranged in columns and rows and separated by a **delimiter**: a comma, tab, colon, semicolon, or similar character. **Importing** means to bring data created in another software program into Dreamweaver, and **exporting** means to save data created in Dreamweaver in a special file format that can be opened by other programs. Files that are imported into Dreamweaver must be saved as delimited files. **Delimited files** are database or spreadsheet files that have been saved as text files with delimiters such as tabs or commas separating the data. Programs such as Microsoft Access and Microsoft Excel offer many file formats for saving files. To import a delimited file, click File on the Application bar (Win) or Menu bar (Mac), point to Import, then click Tabular Data. The Import Tabular Data dialog box opens, offering you formatting options for the imported table. To export a table that you created in Dreamweaver, click File on the Application bar (Win) or Menu bar (Mac), point to Export, then click Table. The Export Table dialog box opens, letting you choose the type of delimiter you want for the delimited file.

Positioning Objects with CSS and Tables

FIGURE 39

Formatting text using a Cascading Style Sheet

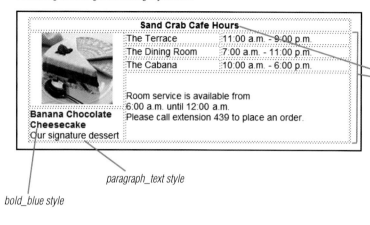

paragraph_text style

paragraph_text style

bold_blue style

Format cell content

1. Select the text "Banana Chocolate Cheesecake," then apply the **bold_blue** rule.

2. Select the text "Our Signature dessert" and apply the **paragraph_text** rule, then select all of the text about the cafe hours and apply the **paragraph_text** rule.

3. Repeat Step 2 to apply the **paragraph_text** rule to the room service text.

   Your screen should resemble Figure 39.

4. Modify the navigation bar to show the cafe button, rather than the home button, in the down state.

You formatted text in table cells using a Cascading Style Sheet, and modified the navigation bar to show the cafe button in the down state.

POWER USER SHORTCUTS

to do this:	use this shortcut:
Insert table	[Ctrl][Alt][T] (Win) or ⌘[option][T] (Mac)
Select a cell	[Ctrl][A] (Win) or ⌘[A] (Mac)
Merge cells	[Ctrl][Alt][M] (Win) or ⌘[option][M] (Mac)
Split cell	[Ctrl][Alt][S] (Win) or ⌘[option][S] (Mac)
Insert row	[Ctrl][M] (Win) or ⌘[M] (Mac)
Insert column	[Ctrl][Shift][A] (Win) or ⌘[Shift][A] (Mac)
Delete row	[Ctrl][Shift][M] (Win) or ⌘[Shift][M] (Mac)
Delete column	[Ctrl][Shift][-] (Win) or ⌘[Shift][-] (Mac)
Increase column span	[Ctrl][Shift][]] (Win) or ⌘[Shift][]] (Mac)
Decrease column span	[Ctrl][Shift][[] (Win) or ⌘[Shift][[] (Mac)

Format cells

1. Click to place the insertion point in the cell with the cheesecake text.

2. Click the **Horz list arrow** in the Property inspector, then click **Center** to center the cell contents.

   You do not need to select the text because you are setting the alignment for all contents in the cell.

3. Repeat Steps 1 and 2 for the cell with the table header and the cell with the room service information.

   | TIP   Click to the right of the nested table to easily select the cell.

4. Click in the cell with the room service text, click the **Vert text box**, then click **Bottom**, as shown in Figure 40.

   | TIP   Setting alignment can be helpful if you need to troubleshoot a page later.

5. Save your work.

You formatted table cells by adding horizontal and vertical alignment.

FIGURE 40

Formatting cells using horizontal and vertical alignment

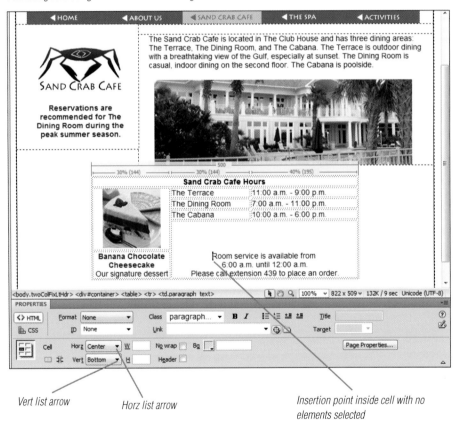

Vert list arrow   Horz list arrow   Insertion point inside cell with no elements selected

FIGURE 41

Hiding visual aids

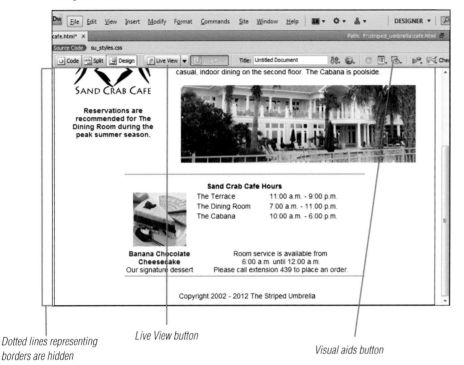

Dotted lines representing
borders are hidden

Live View button

Visual aids button

Using visual aids

Dreamweaver has an option for turning on and off various features, such as table borders, that are displayed in Design view but are not displayed in the browser. This tool is called Visual Aids and can be accessed through the View menu or through the Visual Aids button on the Document toolbar. Most of the time, these features are very helpful while you are editing and formatting a page. However, turning them off is a quick way to see how the page will appear in the browser without having to open it in the browser window.

Modify cell content

1. Click after the word "dessert" in the bottom left cell, then press [Tab].

   Pressing the tab key while the insertion point is in the last cell of the table creates a new row. Even though it looks like the cell with the room service information is the last cell, it is not because of the merged cells.

2. Merge the cells in the new row, click **Insert** on the Application bar (Win) or Menu bar (Mac), point to **HTML**, then click **Horizontal Rule**.

3. Click in front of the table header, then insert another horizontal rule.

4. Save your work.

You added two horizontal rules to the table to set the table off from the rest of the page.

Check layout

1. Click the **Visual Aids button** [icon] on the Document toolbar, then click **Hide All Visual Aids**, as shown in Figure 41.

   The borders around the table, table cells, and CSS blocks are all hidden, allowing you to see more clearly how the page will look in the browser.

2. Repeat Step 1 to show the visual aids again. (*Hint*: You can also click the Live View button on the Document toolbar to see how the page will look in the browser.)

3. Save your work, preview the cafe page in the browser, close the browser, then close Dreamweaver.

You used the Hide All Visual Aids command to hide the table borders and layout block outlines, then showed them again.

Create a page using CSS layouts.

1. Open the blooms & bulbs website, then create a new blank HTML page with the 2 column elastic, left sidebar, header and footer style, linking the blooms_styles.css file to the page.

2. Save the file as **classes.html**, overwriting the existing classes page.

Add content to CSS layout blocks.

1. Open the index page, copy the banner and navigation bar, then close the index page. (*Hint*: If you have space between your banner and navigation bar, place the insertion point between them and press [Delete].)

2. Delete the placeholder text in the header on the classes page (including the <h1> tags), then paste the banner and navigation bar in the header container.

3. Modify the navigation bar to show the classes button as the down image.

4. Delete the footer placeholder text, type **Copyright 2001 - 2012 blooms & bulbs** in the footer container, apply the paragraph_text rule, then center it.

5. Delete the placeholder content from the #mainContent block, including any <h1> tags.

6. Type **Master Gardener Classes Beginning Soon!**, enter a paragraph break, then import the text gardeners.doc.

7. Enter a paragraph break, then insert the flower_bed.jpg from your Data Files folder. Add the alternate text **Flower bed in downtown Alvin** to the image when prompted.

8. Save your work.

Edit content in CSS layout blocks.

1. Select the twoColElsLtHdr #container style in the CSS Styles panel.

2. Edit the rule by changing the width of the container to **48em**, and the float to **Left**. (*Hint*: The Float setting is in the Box category.)

3. Select the twoColElsLtHdr #header style in the CSS panel and change the background color to #FFF.

4. Repeat Step 3 to change the background color of the footer to #FFF and the background color of the sidebar1 to #FFF.

5. Repeat Step 3 to change the body background to #FFF.

6. Place the insertion point in front of the banner, then center the banner.

7. Select the text Master Gardener Classes Beginning Soon! and apply the bold_blue rule.

8. Select the paragraphs of Master Gardener information in the mainContent block and format it with the paragraph_text rule.

9. Save your work.

Create a table.

1. Delete the placeholder text in the left sidebar, then insert a table with the following settings: Rows: **10**, Columns: **2**, Table width: **150 pixels,** Border thickness: **0**, Cell padding: **5**, Cell spacing: **5**, and Header: **Top**. In the Summary text box, enter the text **This table is used to list the class dates and hours.**

2. Center-align the table in the sidebar.

3. Replace the existing page title with the title **Master Gardener classes begin soon!**, then save your work.

Resize, split, and merge cells.

1. Select the first cell in the last row, then set the cell width to **25%**.

2. Select the second cell in the last row, then set the cell width to **75%.**

3. Merge the two cells in the first row.

4. Merge the two cells in the last row.

5. Save your work.

Insert and align images in table cells.

1. Use the Insert panel to insert gardening_gloves.gif in the last row of the table. You can find this image in the assets folder where you store your Data Files. Add the alternate text **Gardening gloves** to the image when prompted, then center the image in the merged cell.

2. Save your work.

Insert text and format cell content.

1. Type **Schedule** in the merged cell in the first row, then center align the cell.

2. Type the dates and times for the classes from Figure 42 in each row of the table.

3. Select Schedule and apply the bold_blue rule.

4. Select the dates and times in the table and apply the paragraph_text rule, then add a horizontal rule under the image at the bottom of the page.

5. Save your work, preview the page in your browser, then close your browser.

6. Close all open pages.

FIGURE 42

Completed Skills Review

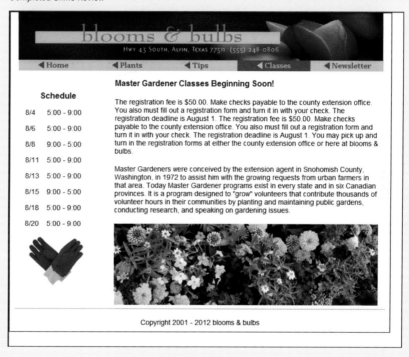

In this exercise, you will continue your work on the TripSmart website that you began in Project Builder 1 in Chapter 1 and developed in the previous chapters. You are ready to begin work on a page that will feature catalog items. You plan to use a CSS layout with a table to place the information on the page.

1. Open the TripSmart website.

2. Create a new page based on the 1 column elastic, centered, header and footer CSS page layout, attaching the tripsmart_styles.css file, then save the file as **catalog.html**, replacing the placeholder catalog page in the website.

3. Open the index page, copy the banner and navigation bar, then close the index page.

4. Paste the banner and navigation bar in the header block, replacing the placeholder text.

5. Edit the oneColElsCtrHdr #container width to **48 em**.

6. Edit the oneColElsCtrHdr #header background to **#FFF**.

7. Edit the oneColElsCtrHdr #footer to have a white background.

8. Save your work.

9. Delete the placeholder content in the oneColElsCtrHdr #mainContent block.

10. Insert a table into the #mainContent block with the following settings: Rows: **5**, Columns: **3**, Table width: **725 pixels**, Border thickness: **0**, Header: **Top**. Enter an appropriate table summary, then center-align the table.

11. Set the cell widths in the bottom row to **33%**, **33%**, and **34%**.

12. Merge the three cells in the first row, type **Our products are backed with a 100% guarantee.**

13. In the three cells in the second row, type **Protection from UV rays; Cool, light-weight, versatile;** and **Pockets for everything** then center the text in each cell.

14. Place the files hat.jpg, pants.jpg, and vest.jpg from the assets folder where you store your Data Files in the three cells in the third row, adding the following alternate text to the images: **Safari hat**, **Kenya convertible pants**, and **Photographer's vest**; center the three images.

15. Type **Safari Hat**, **Kenya Convertible Pants**, and **Photographer's Vest** in the three cells in the fourth row, then center each label.

16. Type **Item number 50501** and **$29.00** with a line break between them in the first cell in the fifth row.

17. Repeat Step 16 to type **Item number 62495** and **$39.50** in the second cell in the fifth row.

18. Repeat Step 16 to type **Item number 52301** and **$54.95** in the third cell in the fifth row, then center each item number and price in the cells.

19. Apply the paragraph_text rule to the three descriptions in the second row.

20. Create a new class rule in the tripsmart_styles.css style sheet named **reverse_text** with the following settings: Font-family, Verdana, Geneva, sans-serif; Font-size, 14 px; Font-style, normal; Font-weight, bold; Color, #FFF. (*Hint*: Be sure to choose Class under Selector Type.)

21. Apply the reverse_text rule to the text "Our products are backed by a 100% guarantee.", then change the cell background color to **#666666**.

22. Apply the reverse_text rule to the three item names under the images, then change the cell background color to **#999**.

23. Create a new rule called **item_numbers** with the following settings: Font: Verdana, Geneva, sans-serif; Size: 10 px; Style: normal; Weight: bold.

24. Apply the item_numbers rule to the three items' numbers and prices.

25. Delete the #footer block placeholder text, then type **TripSmart Copyright 2002 - 2012.**

26. Create a new class rule named **small_ centered_text** with the following settings: Font-family: Verdana, Geneva, sans-serif; Font-size: 12 pixels; Font-style: Normal; Text-align: Center. (*Hint*: the Text-align property is in the Block category.)

27. Apply the small_centered_text rule to the copyright statement.

28. Save your work, view the page in your browser, compare your screen with Figure 43, then close the browser. (*Hint*: You may need to delete the H1 tags from the #mainContent block if you have too much space between the navigation bar and the table.)

29. Save your work, then close all open pages.

FIGURE 43
Sample Project Builder 1

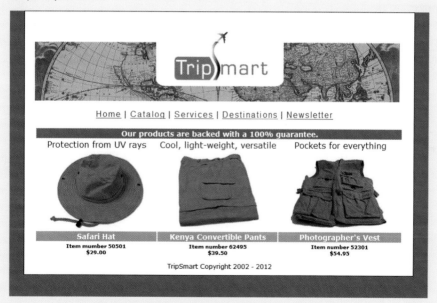

Use Figure 44 as a guide to continue your work on the Carolyne's Creations website that you started in Chapter 1 and developed in the previous chapters. You are now ready to begin work on a page that will showcase the company's catering services. You decide to use CSS with a table for page layout.

1. Open the Carolyne's Creations website, then create a new page based on the 1 column fixed, centered, header and footer layout, attach the cc_styles.css file, and save the page as **catering.html**, overwriting the existing page.

2. Copy the banner that includes the navigation bar from one of the other pages, then paste it on the page, replacing the placeholder content. (*Hint*: If the banner is too wide for the container you're placing it in, edit the width of the container in the CSS styles panel properties to accommodate it.)

3. Edit the container properties with values of your choice to format the page to blend with the existing pages in the website.

4. Use the main area of the page to insert a table that will showcase the catering services, with the following settings: Rows: **10**, Columns: **3**, Table width: **770 pixels**, Border thickness: **0**, Cell padding: **3**, Cell spacing: **0**, adding an appropriate table summary.

5. Center-align the table and set the width of the three cells to **33%**, **33%**, and **34%**.

6. Type **Catering for All Occasions** in the second cell in the second row and **Dinner to Go** in the second cell in the sixth row.

7. Apply the **sub_head** rule to the text you typed in Step 6 and center the text.

8. Merge the cells in the 5th and 9th rows, then Insert rules in the merged cells. (*Hint*: Change the view to Expanded Tables mode to be able to see the cells more easily.)

9. Type **Lunch Boxes**, **Brunch Boxes**, and **Gift Baskets** in the three cells in the third row.

10. Type **Soups**, **Entrees**, and **Desserts** in the three cells in the seventh row.

11. Apply the nav_bar rule to the text you typed in Steps 9 and 10.

12. Use a color of your choice for the background for each cell in the third and seventh rows.

13. Type the text **Call/fax by 9:00 a.m. for lunch orders, Call/fax by 1:00 p.m. for dinner orders, Fax number: 555-963-5938** in the first cell in the last row using a line break to separate each line.

14. Apply the paragraph_text rule to the text you typed in Step 13.

15. Use your word processor to open the file menu items.doc from your Data Files folder. Copy and paste each text block into the cells in the fourth and eighth rows, apply the paragraph_text rule to each text block, then center align each text block in the cells, using Figure 44 as a guide.

16. Merge the last two cells in the last row, then insert the image muffins.jpg with alternate text and any additional formatting of your choice.

17. Delete the footer placeholder text and change the background color of the footer to white.

18. Save your work, preview the page in your browser, make any adjustments that you feel would improve the page appearance, then close all open files.

FIGURE 44
Completed Project Builder 2

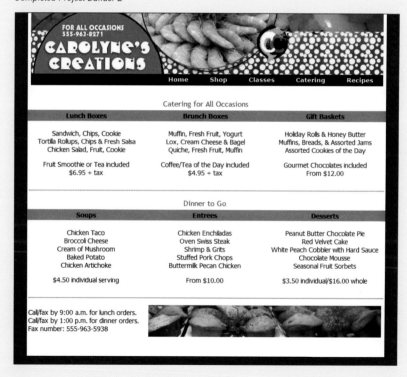

Positioning Objects with CSS and Tables

Jon Bishop is opening a new restaurant and wants to have the restaurant website launched two weeks before his opening. He has hired you to create the site and has asked for several design proposals. You begin by looking at some restaurant sites with pleasing designs.

1. Connect to the Internet, then go to www.jamesatthemill.com, as shown in Figure 45.

2. How are CSS used in this site?

3. How are CSS used to prevent an overload of information in one area of the screen?

4. View the source code for the page and locate the html tags that control the CSS on the page.

5. Use the Reference panel in Dreamweaver to look up the code used in this site to place the content on the page. (To do this, make note of a tag that you don't understand, then open the Reference panel and find that tag the Tag list box in the Reference panel. Select it from the list and read the description in the Reference panel.)

6. Do you see any tables on the page? If so, how are they used?

FIGURE 45
Design Project

James at the Mill website used with permission from Miles James – www.jamesatthemill.com

For this assignment, you will continue to work on the portfolio project that you have been developing since Chapter 1. There will be no Data Files supplied. You are building this website from chapter to chapter, so you must do each Portfolio Project assignment in each chapter to complete your website.

You will continue building your website by designing and completing a page that uses layers rather than tables to control the layout of information.

1. Consult your storyboard to decide which page to create and develop for this chapter. Draw a sketch of the page to show how you will use CSS to lay out the content.

2. Create the new page for the site and set the default preferences for div tags. Add the appropriate number of div tags to the new page and configure them appropriately, making sure to name them and set the properties for each.

3. Add text, background images, and background colors to each container.

4. Create the navigation links that will allow you to add this page to your site.

5. Update the other pages of your site so that each page includes a link to this new page.

6. Add images in the containers (where appropriate), making sure to align them with text so they look good.

7. Review the checklist in Figure 46 and make any necessary modifications.

8. Save your work, preview the page in your browser, make any necessary modifications to improve the page appearance, close your browser, then close all open pages.

FIGURE 46
Portfolio Project checklist

Website Checklist

1. Do all pages have titles?
2. Do all navigation links work correctly?
3. Are all colors in your layers web-safe?
4. Does the use of CSS in your website improve the site navigation?
5. Do your pages look acceptable in at least the two major browsers?
6. Do all images in your CSS containers appear correctly?

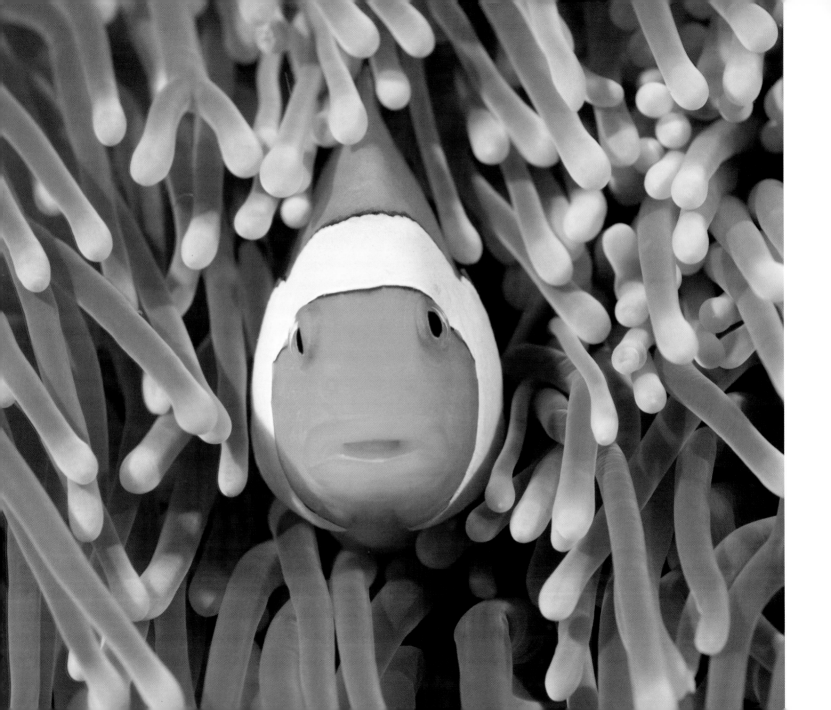

chapter

6

MANAGING A WEB
SERVER AND FILES

1. Perform website maintenance

2. Publish a website and transfer files

3. Check files out and in

4. Cloak files

5. Import and export a site definition

6. Evaluate web content for legal use

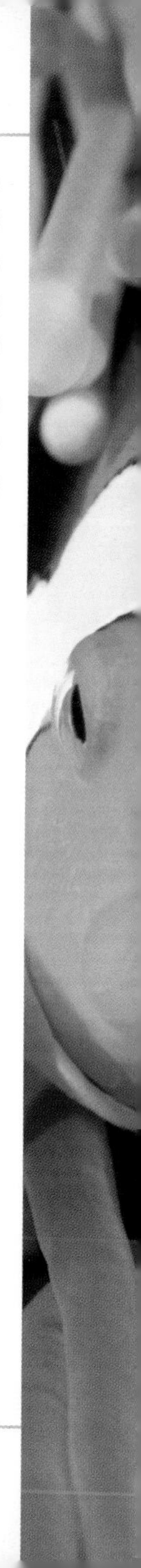

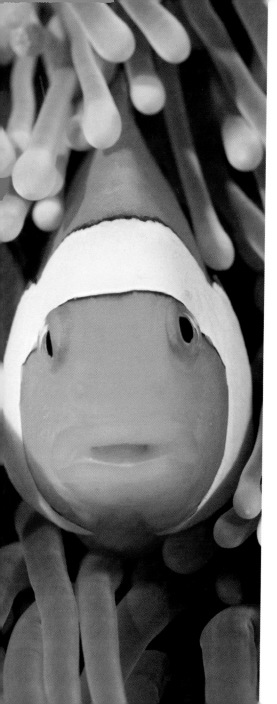

6 MANAGING A WEB
SERVER AND FILES

Introduction

Once you have created all the pages of your website, finalized all the content, and performed site maintenance, you are ready to publish your site to a remote server so the rest of the world can access it. In this chapter, you will start by running some reports to make sure the links in your site work properly, that the colors are web-safe, and that orphaned files are removed. Next, you will set up a connection to the remote site for The Striped Umbrella website. You will then transfer files to the remote site and learn how to keep them up to date. You will also check out a file so that it is not available to other team members while you are editing it and you will learn how to cloak files. When a file is **cloaked**, it is excluded from certain processes, such as being transferred to the remote site. Next, you will export the site definition file from The Striped Umbrella website so that other designers can import the site. Finally, you will research important copyright issues that affect all websites.

Preparing to Publish a Site

Before you publish a site, it is extremely important that you test it regularly to make sure the content is accurate and up to date and that everything is functioning properly. When viewing pages over the Internet, it is very frustrating to click a link that doesn't work or have to wait for pages that load slowly because of large graphics and animations. Remember that the typical viewer has a short attention span and limited patience. Before you publish your site, make sure to use the Link Checker panel to check for broken links and orphaned files. Make sure that all image paths are correct and that all images load quickly and have alternate text. Verify that all pages have titles, and remove all non-web-safe colors. View the pages in at least two different browsers and different versions of the same browser to ensure that everything works correctly. The more frequently you test, the better the chance that your viewers will have a positive experience at your site and want to return. *Before you publish your pages, verify that all content is original to the website, has been obtained legally, and is used properly without violating the copyright of someone else's work.*

Tools You'll Use

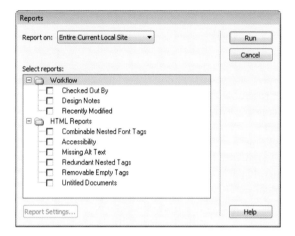

PERFORM WEBSITE
MAINTENANCE

What You'll Do

In this lesson, you will use some Dreamweaver site management tools to check for broken links, orphaned files, and missing alternate text. You will also verify that all colors are web-safe. You will then correct any problems that you find.

Maintaining a Website

As you add pages, links, and content to a website, it can quickly become difficult to manage. It's easier to find and correct errors as you go, rather than waiting until the end of the design phase. It's important to perform maintenance tasks frequently to make sure your website operates smoothly and remains "clean." You have already learned about some of the tools described in the following paragraphs. Although it is important to use them as you create and modify your pages, it is also important to run them at periodic intervals after publishing your website to make sure it is always error-free.

Using the Assets Panel

You should use the Assets panel to check the list of images and colors used in your website. If you see images listed that are not being used, you should move them to a storage folder outside the website until you need them. You should also check to see if all of the colors used in the site are web-safe. If there are non-web-safe colors in the list, locate the elements to which

these colors are applied and apply web-safe colors to them.

Checking Links Sitewide

Before and after you publish your website, you should use the Link Checker panel to make sure all internal links are working. If the Link Checker panel displays any broken links, you should repair them. If the Link Checker panel displays any orphaned files, you should evaluate whether to delete them or link them with existing pages.

Using Site Reports

You can use the Reports command in the Site menu to generate six different HTML reports that can help you maintain your website. You choose the type of report you want to run in the Reports dialog box, shown in Figure 1. You can specify whether to generate the report for the current document, the entire current local site, selected files in the site, or a selected folder. You can also generate workflow reports to see files that have been checked out by others or recently modified or you can view the Design Notes attached to files.

Design Notes are separate files in a website that contain additional information about a page file or a graphic file. In a collaborative situation, designers can record notes to exchange information with other designers. Design Notes can also be used to record sensitive information that would not be included in files that could be viewed on the website. Information about the source files for graphic files, such as Flash files or Fireworks files, are also stored in Design Notes.

Validating Markup

One of the report features in Dreamweaver is the ability to validate markup. This means that Dreamweaver will go through the code to look for errors that could occur with different language versions, such as XHTML or XML. To validate code for a page, click File on the Application bar (Win) or Menu bar (Mac) point to Validate, and then click Markup. The Results tab group displaying the Validation panel opens and lists any pages with errors, the line numbers where the errors occur, and an explanation of the errors. The Validate button on the Validation panel offers the choice of validating a single document, an entire local website, or selected files in a local website.

Testing Pages

Finally, you should test your website using many different types and versions of browsers, platforms, and screen resolutions. You can use the Check Page button on the Document toolbar to check browser

compatibility. This feature lists issues with the pages in your site that may cause problems when the pages are viewed using certain browsers, such as the rendering of square bullets in Mozilla Firefox. If you find such issues, you then have the choice to make changes to your page to eliminate the problems. The Results Tab group's Browser Compatibility window includes a URL that you can visit to find the solutions to problems. You should test every link to make sure it connects to a valid, active website.

Pages that download slowly should be reduced in size to improve performance. You should analyze all user feedback on the website objectively, saving both positive and negative comments for future reference to help you make improvements to the site.

FIGURE 1
Reports dialog box

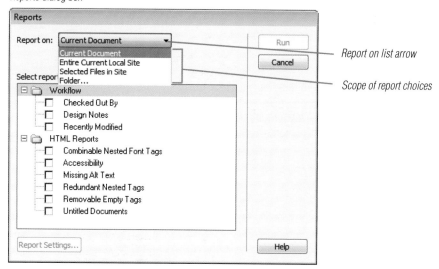

Report on list arrow

Scope of report choices

Check for broken links

1. Open The Striped Umbrella website.

2. Show the Files panel (if necessary).

3. Click **Site** on the Application bar (Win) or Menu bar (Mac), point to **Advanced**, then click **Recreate Site Cache**.

4. Click **Site** on the Application bar (Win) or Menu bar (Mac), then click **Check Links Sitewide**.

   No broken links are listed in the Link Checker panel of the Results tab group, as shown in Figure 2.

You verified that there are no broken links in the website.

Check for orphaned files

1. On the Link Checker panel, click the **Show list arrow**, then click **Orphaned Files**.

   There are no orphaned files, as shown in Figure 3.

2. Close the Results tab group.

You verified that there are no orphaned files in the website.

FIGURE 2

Link Checker panel displaying no broken links

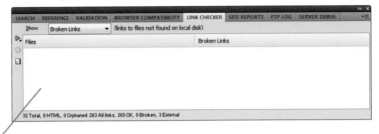

No broken links listed

FIGURE 3

Link Checker panel displaying no orphaned files

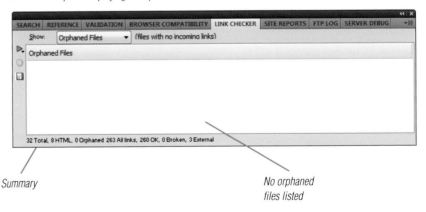

Summary

No orphaned files listed

FIGURE 4

Assets panel displaying web-safe colors

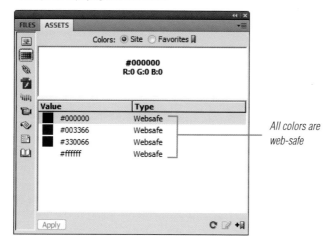

All colors are
web-safe

1. Click the **Assets panel tab**, then click the **Colors button** 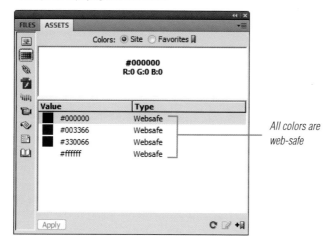 to view the website colors, as shown in Figure 4.

   The Assets panel shows that all colors used in the website are web-safe.

   You verified that the website contains all web-safe colors.

Using Find and Replace to locate non-web-safe colors

As with many software applications, Dreamweaver has a Find and Replace feature that can be used both in Design view and in Code view on the Edit menu. This command can be used to search the current document, selected files, or the entire current local site. If you are looking for a particular non-web-safe color, you will probably save time by using the Find and Replace feature to locate the hexadecimal color code in Code view. If a site has many pages, this will be the fastest way to locate it. The Find and Replace feature can also be used to locate other character combinations, such as a phrase that begins or ends with a particular word or tag. These patterns of character combinations are referred to as **regular expressions**. To find out more, search for "regular expressions" in Dreamweaver Help.

Check for untitled documents

1. Click **Site** on the Application bar (Win) or Menu bar (Mac), then click **Reports** to open the Reports dialog box.

2. Click the **Report on list arrow**, click **Entire Current Local Site**, click the **Untitled Documents check box**, as shown in Figure 5, then click **Run**.

   The Site Reports panel opens in the Results tab group, and shows that the cafe page does not have a page title, as shown in Figure 6.

3. Open the cafe page, replace the current page title "Untitled Document" with the title **The Sand Crab Cafe**, then save the file.

4. Close the cafe page.

5. Run the report again to check the entire site for untitled documents.

   No files should appear in the Site Reports panel.

You ran a report for untitled documents, then added a page title to the cafe page.

FIGURE 5
Reports dialog box with Untitled Documents option selected

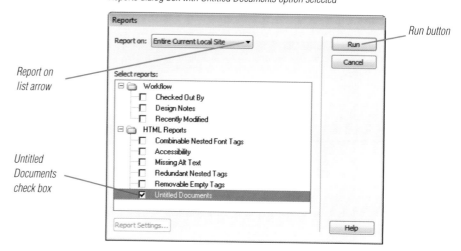

Report on list arrow

Run button

Untitled Documents check box

FIGURE 6
Site Reports panel showing one page without a page title

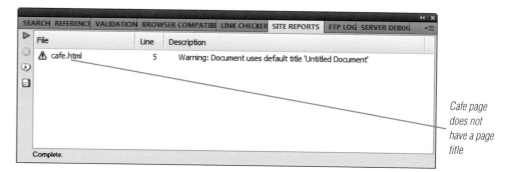

Cafe page does not have a page title

FIGURE 7

Reports dialog box with Missing Alt text option selected

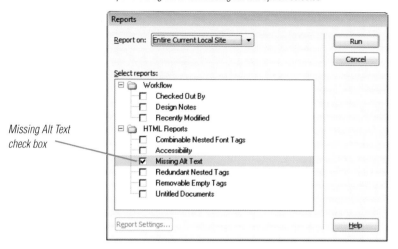

Missing Alt Text check box

1. Using Figure 7 as a guide, run another report that checks the entire current local site for missing alternate text.

   The results show that the spa page contains an image that is missing alternate text, as shown in Figure 8.

2. Open the spa page, then find the image that is missing alternate text.

   TIP The Site Reports panel documents the code line number where the missing alt tag occurs. Sometimes it is faster to locate the errors in Code view, rather than in Design view.

3. Add appropriate alternate text to the image.

4. Save your work, then run the report again to check the entire site for missing alternate text.

   No files should appear in the Site Reports panel.

5. Close the Results tab group, then close all open pages.

You ran a report to check for missing alternate text in the entire site. You then added alternate text for one image and ran the report again.

FIGURE 8

Site Reports panel displaying missing "alt" tag

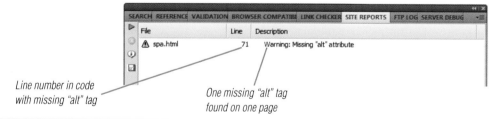

Line number in code with missing "alt" tag

One missing "alt" tag found on one page

Validating Accessibility Standards

There are many accessibility issues to consider to ensure that your website conforms to current accessibility standards. HTML Reports provide an easy way to check for missing alternate text, missing page titles, and other accessibility concerns such as improper markup, deprecated features, or improper use of color or images. HTML Reports can be run on the current document, selected files, or the entire local site. You can also use the Check Page, Accessibility command under the File menu to check for accessibility issues on an open page. After the report is run, a list of issues will open in the Site Reports panel with the line number and description of each problem. If you right-click a description, you will see the option "More Info. . ." Click on this option to read a more detailed description and solutions to correct the issue.

Enable Design Notes

1. Click **Site** on the Application bar (Win) or Menu bar (Mac), click **Manage Sites**, verify that The Striped Umbrella site is selected, click **Edit**, click the **Advanced tab** (if necessary), then click the **Design Notes category**.

2. Click the **Maintain Design Notes check box**, to select it (if necessary), as shown in Figure 9.

   Selecting this option enables the designer to record notes about a page in a separate file linked to the page. For instance, a Design Note for the index.html file would be saved in a file named index.html.mno. This file would be automatically saved in a folder that is created by Dreamweaver named _notes. This folder does not appear in the Files panel, but can be seen using Windows Explorer (Win) or Finder (Mac).

3. Click the **File View Columns category**, then click **Notes** in the File View Columns list.

4. Click the **Options**: **Show check box**, to select it (if necessary).

   The Notes column now displays the word "Show" in the Show column, as shown in Figure 10, indicating that the Notes column will be visible in the Files panel.

5. Click **OK**, then click **Done** in the Manage Sites dialog box.

You set the preference to use Design Notes in the website. You also set the option to display the Notes column in the Files panel.

FIGURE 9

Design Notes category in the Site Definition for The Striped Umbrella

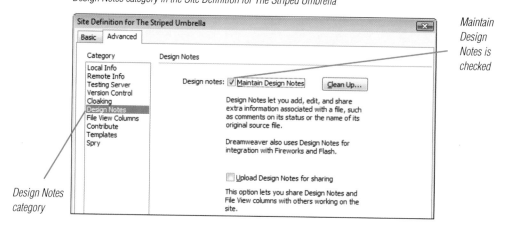

Maintain Design Notes is checked

Design Notes category

FIGURE 10

File View Columns category in the Site Definition for The Striped Umbrella

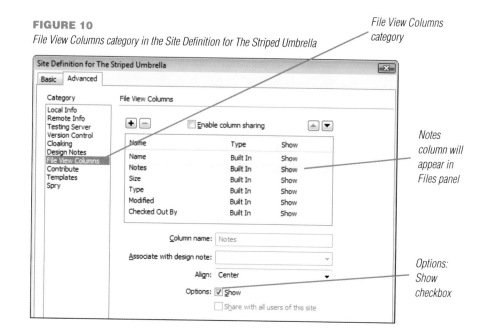

File View Columns category

Notes column will appear in Files panel

Options: Show checkbox

FIGURE 11
Design Notes dialog box

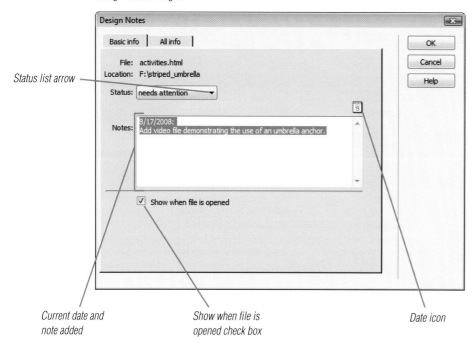

Status list arrow

Current date and
note added

Show when file is
opened check box

Date icon

1. Open the activities page, click **File** on the Application bar (Win) or Menu bar (Mac), click **Design Notes**, then click the **Basic info tab** (if necessary).

   The Design Notes dialog box opens with a text box to record a note related to the open file, the option to display the note each time the file is opened, an option to include the current date, and a status indicator.

2. Click the **Date icon** 📅 above the Notes text box on the right.

   The current date is added to the Notes text box.

3. Type **Add video file demonstrating the use of an umbrella anchor.** in the Notes text box beneath the date.

4. Click the **Status list arrow**, then click **needs attention**.

5. Click the **Show when file is opened** check box to select it, as shown in Figure 11, then click **OK**.

You added a design note to the activities page with the current date and a status indicator. The note will open each time the file is opened.

Using Version Cue to manage assets

Another way to collaborate with team members is through Adobe Version Cue, a workgroup collaboration system that is included in Adobe Creative Suite 4. You can perform such functions such as managing security, backing up data, and using metadata to search files. **Metadata** includes information about a file such as keywords, descriptions, and copyright information. Adobe Bridge also organizes files with metadata.

Edit a Design Note

1. Click **File** on the Application bar (Win) or Menu bar (Mac), then click **Design Notes** to open the Design Note associated with the activities page.

   You can also right-click (Windows) or control-click (Mac) the filename in the Files panel, then click Design Notes, or double-click the yellow Design Notes icon in the Files panel next to the filename to open a Design Note, as shown in Figure 12.

   | TIP   You may have to click the Refresh button [C] to display the Notes icon.

2. Edit the note by adding the sentence **Ask Jane Pinson to send the file.** after the existing text in the Notes section, then click **OK** to close it.

   A file named activities.html.mno has been created in a new folder called _notes. This folder and file will not display in the Files panel unless you have the option to show hidden files and folders selected. However, you can switch to Windows Explorer to see them without selecting this option.

   (continued)

FIGURE 12
Files panel with Notes icon displayed

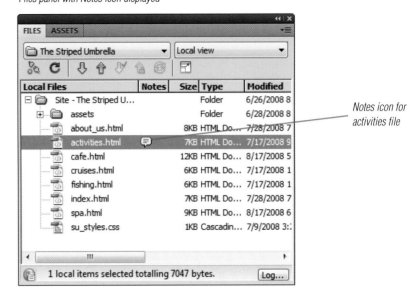

Notes icon for activities file

Deleting a Design Note

There are two steps to deleting a Design Note that you don't need anymore. The first step is to delete the Design Note file. To delete a Design Note, right-click the filename in the Files panel that is associated with the Design Note you want to delete, and then click Explore (Win) or Reveal in Finder (Mac) to open your file management system. Open the _notes folder, then delete the .mno file in the files list, and then close Explorer (Win) or Finder (Mac). The second step is done in Dreamweaver. Click Site on the Application bar (Win) or Menu bar (Mac), click Manage Sites, click Edit, and then select the Design Notes category. Click the Clean Up button. (*Note:* Don't do this if you deselect Maintain Design Notes first or it will delete all of your design notes!) The Design Notes icon will be removed from the Notes column in the Files panel.

FIGURE 13

Windows Explorer displaying the _notes file and folder

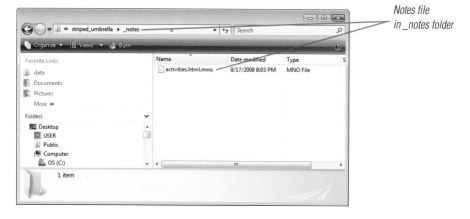

Notes file
in _notes folder

3. Right-click (Win) or control-click (Mac)
   activities.html in the Files panel, then click
   Explore (Win) or **Reveal in Finder** (Mac).

4. Double-click the folder **_notes** to open it, then
   double-click the file **activities.html.mno**,
   shown in Figure 13, to open the file in
   Dreamweaver.

   The notes file opens in Code view in
   Dreamweaver, as shown in Figure 14.

5. Read the file, close it, close Explorer (Win) or
   Finder (Mac), then close the activities page.

*You opened the Design Notes dialog box and
edited the note in the Notes text box. Next, you
viewed the .mno file that Dreamweaver created
when you added the Design Note.*

FIGURE 14

Code for the activities.html.mno file

```
1   <?xml version="1.0" encoding="utf-8" ?>
2   <info>
3       <infoitem key="notes" value="8/17/2008: &#xD;Add video file demonstrating the use of an
    umbrella anchor. Ask Jane Pinson to send the file." />
4       <infoitem key="status" value="needs attention" />
5       <infoitem key="showOnOpen" value="true" />
6   </info>
7
```

PUBLISH A WEBSITE
AND TRANSFER FILES

What You'll Do

In this lesson, you will set up remote access to either an FTP folder or a local/network folder for The Striped Umbrella website. You will also view a website on a remote server, upload files to it, and synchronize the files.

Defining a Remote Site

As you learned in Chapter 1, publishing a site means transferring all the site's files to a web server. A **web server** is a computer that is connected to the Internet with an IP (Internet Protocol) address so that it is available on the Internet. Before you can publish a site to a web server, you must first define the remote site by specifying the Remote Info settings on the Advanced tab of the Site Definition dialog box. You can specify remote settings when you first create a new site and define the root folder (as you did in Chapter 1 when you defined the remote access settings for The Striped Umbrella website), or you can do it after you have completed all of your pages and are confident that your site is ready for public viewing. To specify the remote settings for a site, you must first choose an Access setting, which specifies the type of server you will use. The most common Access setting is FTP (File Transfer Protocol). If you specify FTP, you will need to specify an address for the server and the name of the folder on the FTP site in which your root folder will be stored. You can also use **Secure FTP (SFTP)**, an FTP option that enables you to encrypt file transfers. This option will pro-

tect your files, user names, and passwords. To use SFTP, check the Use Secure FTP (SFTP) check box in the Site Definition dialog box. You will also need to enter login and password information. Figure 15 shows an example of FTP settings in the Remote Info category of the Site Definition dialog box.

QUICKTIP

If you do not have access to an FTP site, you can publish a site to a local/network folder. This is referred to as a **LAN**, or a Local Area Network. Use the alternate steps provided in this lesson to publish your site to a local/network folder.

Viewing a Remote Site

Once you have defined a site to a remote location, you can then view the remote folder in the Files panel by choosing Remote view from the View list. If your remote site is located on an FTP server, Dreamweaver will connect to it. You will see the File Activity dialog box showing the progress of the connection. You can also use the Connects to remote host button on the Files panel toolbar to connect to the remote site. If you defined your site on a local/network folder, then you don't need to use the Connects to remote host button; the root folder and any files and folders it contains will appear in the Files panel when you switch to Remote view.

Transferring Files to and from a Remote Site

After you define a remote site, you will need to transfer or **upload** your files from the local version of your site to the remote host. To do this, view the site in Local view, select the files you want to upload, and then click the Put File(s) button on the Files panel toolbar. Once you click this button, the files will be transferred to the remote site. To view the uploaded files, switch to Remote view, as shown in Figure 16. Or, you can

expand the Files panel to view both the Remote Site and the Local Files panes by clicking the Expand to show local and remote sites button in the Files panel.

If a file you select for uploading requires additional files, such as graphics, a dialog box will open after you click the Put File(s) button and ask if you want those files (known as **dependent files**) to be uploaded. By clicking Yes, all dependent files in the selected page will be uploaded to the appropriate folder in the remote site. If a file that you want to upload is located in a folder in the local site, the folder will be automatically transferred to the remote site.

QUICKTIP

To upload an entire site to a remote host, select the root folder, then click the Put File(s) button.

If you are developing or maintaining a website in a group environment, there might be times when you want to transfer or **download** files that other team members have created from the remote site to your local site. To do this, switch to Remote view, select the files you want to download, then click the Get File(s) button on the Files panel toolbar.

FIGURE 15

FTP settings in the Site Definition for The Striped Umbrella dialog box

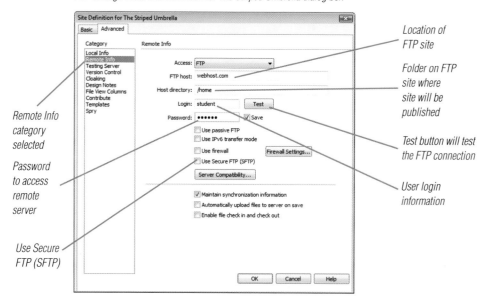

Remote Info category selected

Password to access remote server

Use Secure FTP (SFTP)

Location of FTP site

Folder on FTP site where site will be published

Test button will test the FTP connection

User login information

FIGURE 16

Files panel with Remote view selected

Expand to show local and remote sites button

Remote view

Synchronizing Files

To keep a website up to date—especially one that contains several pages and involves several team members—you will need to update and replace files. Team members might make changes to pages on the local version of the site or make additions to the remote site. If many people are involved in maintaining a site, or if you are constantly making changes to the pages, ensuring that both the local and remote sites have the most up-to-date files could get confusing. Thankfully, you can use the Synchronize command to keep things straight. The Synchronize command instructs Dreamweaver to compare the dates of the saved files in both versions of the site, then transfers only the files that have changed. To synchronize files, use the Synchronize Files dialog box, as shown in Figure 17. You can synchronize an entire site or selected files. You can also specify whether to upload newer files to the remote site, download newer files from the remote site, or both.

FIGURE 17
Synchronize Files dialog box

Specifies to synchronize all files in the site

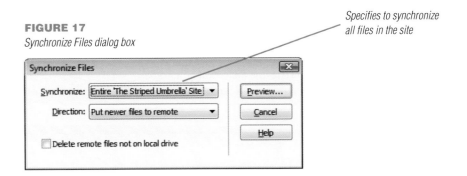

Understanding Dreamweaver connection options
for transferring files

The connection types with which you are probably the most familiar are FTP and Local/Network. Other connection types that you can use with Dreamweaver are Microsoft Visual SafeSource **(VSS)**, WebDav, and RDS. VSS is used only with the Windows operating system with Microsoft Visual SafeSource Client version 6. **WebDav** stands for Web-based Distributed Authoring and Versioning. This type of connection is used with the WebDav protocol. An example would be a website residing on an Apache web server. The **Apache web server** is a public domain, open source web server that is available using several different operating systems including UNIX and Windows. **RDS** stands for Remote Development Services, and is used with web servers using Cold Fusion.

FIGURE 18

FTP settings specified in the Site Definition for The Striped Umbrella dialog box

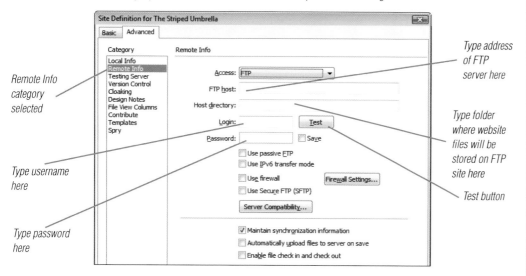

Remote Info category selected

Type username here

Type password here

Type address of FTP server here

Type folder where website files will be stored on FTP site here

Test button

Comparing two files for differences in content

There are situations where it would be helpful to be able to compare the contents of two files, such as a local file and the remote version of the same file; or an original file and the same file that has been saved with a different name. Once the two files are compared and differences are detected, you can merge the information in the files. A good time to compare files is before you upload them to a remote server to prevent accidentally writing over a file with more recent information. To compare files, you must first locate and install a third-party file comparison utility, or "dif" tool, such as Araxis Merge or Beyond Compare. (Dreamweaver does not have a file comparison tool included as part of the software. You will have to download one. If you are not familiar with these tools, find one using your favorite search engine.)

After installing the files comparison utility, use the Preferences command on the Edit menu, and then select the File Compare category. Next, browse to select the application to compare files. After you have set your Preferences, click the Compare with Remote command on the File menu to compare an open file with the remote version.

NOTE: Complete these steps only if you know you can store The Striped Umbrella files on an FTP site and you know the login and password information. If you do not have access to an FTP site, complete the exercise called Set up web server access on a local or network folder on Page 6-18.

1. Click **Site** on the Application bar (Win) or Menu bar (Mac), then click **Manage Sites**.

2. Click **The Striped Umbrella** in the Manage Sites dialog box (if necessary), then click **Edit**.

3. Click the **Advanced tab**, click **Remote Info** in the Category list, click the **Access list arrow**, click **FTP**, then compare your screen to Figure 18.

4. Enter the FTP host, Host directory, Login, and Password information in the dialog box.

   TIP You must have file and folder permissions to use FTP. The server administrator will also tell you the folder name and location to use to publish your files.

5. Click the **Test button** to test the connection to the remote site.

6. If the connection is successful, click **Done** to close the dialog box; if it is not successful, verify that you have the correct settings, then repeat Step 4.

7. Click **OK**, click **OK** to restore the cache, then click **Done** to close the Manage Sites dialog box.

You set up remote access information for The Striped Umbrella website using FTP settings.

Set up web server access on a local or network folder

NOTE: Complete these steps if you do not have the ability to post files to an FTP site and could not complete the previous lesson.

1. Using Windows Explorer (Win) or Finder (Mac), create a new folder on your hard drive or on a shared drive named **su_yourlastname** (e.g., if your last name is Jones, name the folder **su_jones**.)

2. Switch back to Dreamweaver, open The Striped Umbrella website, then open the Manage Sites dialog box.

   TIP   You can also double-click the site name in the Site Name list box in the Files panel to open the Advanced tab in the Site Definition dialog box.

3. Click **The Striped Umbrella**, click **Edit** to open the Site Definition for The Striped Umbrella dialog box, click the **Advanced tab**, then click **Remote Info** in the Category list.

4. Click the **Access list arrow**, then click **Local/Network**.

5. Click the **Browse for File icon** 🗁 next to the Remote folder text box to open the Choose remote root folder for site The Striped Umbrella dialog box, navigate to the folder you created in Step 1, select the folder, click **Open**, then click **Select** (Win) or **Choose** (Mac).

6. Compare your screen to Figure 19, click **OK**, click **OK** in the message window about the site cache, then click **Done**.

You created a new folder and specified it as the remote location for The Striped Umbrella website, then set up remote access to a local or network folder.

FIGURE 19

Local/Network settings specified in the Site Definition for The Striped Umbrella dialog box

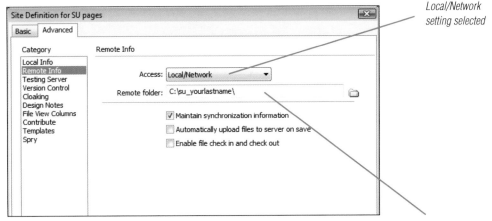

Local/Network setting selected

Local or network drive and folder where remote site will be published (your folder name should end with your last name)

FIGURE 20

Connecting to the remote site

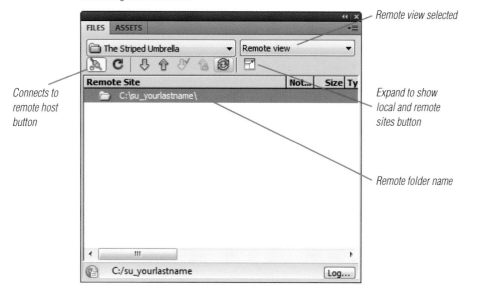

Connects to remote host button

Remote view selected

Expand to show local and remote sites button

Remote folder name

View a website on a remote server

1. Click the **View list arrow** in the Files panel, then click **Remote view**, as shown in Figure 20.

   If you specified your remote access to a local or network folder, then the su_yourlastname folder will now appear in the Files panel. If your remote access is set to an FTP site, Dreamweaver will connect to the host server to see the remote access folder.

2. Click the **Expand to show local and remote sites button** to view both the Remote Site and Local Files panes. The su_yourlast-name folder appears in the Remote Site portion of the expanded Files panel.

   TIP If you don't see your remote site files, click the Connects to remote host button or the Refresh button If you don't see two panes, one with the remote site files and one with the local files, drag the panel border to enlarge the panel.

You used the Files panel to set the view for The Striped Umbrella site to Remote view. You then connected to the remote server to view the contents of the remote folder you specified.

Using a site usability test to test your site

Once you have at least a prototype of the website ready to evaluate, it is a good idea to conduct a site usability test. This is a process that involves asking unbiased people, who are not connected to the design process, to use and evaluate the site. A comprehensive usability test will include pre-test questions, participant tasks, a post-test interview, and a post-test survey. This will provide much-needed information as to how usable the site is to those unfamiliar with it. Typical questions include: "What are your overall impressions?"; "What do you like the best and the least about the site?"; and "How easy is it to navigate inside the site?" For more information, go to www.w3.org and search for "site usability test."

Upload files to a remote server

1. Click the **about_us.html file**, then click the **Put File(s) button** ⬆ on the Files panel toolbar.

   The Dependent Files dialog box opens, asking if you want to include dependent files.

2. Click **Yes**.

   The about_us file, the style sheet file, and the image files used in the about_us page are copied to the remote server. The Background File Activity dialog box appears and flashes the names of each file as they are uploaded.

3. Expand the assets folder in the remote site (if necessary), then compare your screen to Figure 21.

   The remote site now contains the about_us page as well as the images on that page, and the striped_umbrella external style sheet file, all of which are needed by the about_us page.

   | TIP   You might need to expand the su_yourlastname folder in order to view the assets folder.

You used the Put File(s) button to upload the about_us file and all files that are dependent files of the about_us page.

FIGURE 21

Remote view of the site after uploading the about_us page

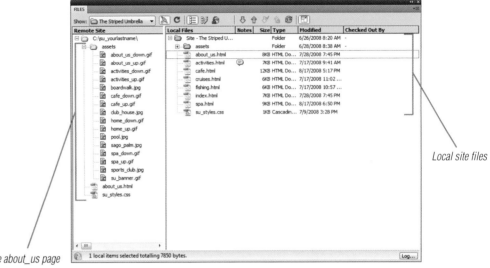

Local site files

The about_us page and its dependent files in remote site

Continuing to work while transferring files to a remote server

During the process of uploading files to a remote server, there are many Dreamweaver functions that you can continue to use while you wait. For example, you can create a new site, create a new page, edit a page, add files and folders, and run reports. However, there are some functions that you cannot use while transferring files, many of which involve accessing files on the remote server or using Check In/Check Out.

FIGURE 22
Synchronize Files dialog box

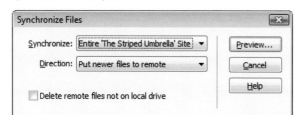

Synchronize files

1. Click the **Synchronize button** 🗓 on the Files panel toolbar to open the Synchronize Files dialog box.

2. Click the **Synchronize list arrow**, then click **Entire 'The Striped Umbrella' Site**.

3. Click the **Direction list arrow**, click **Put newer files to remote** (if necessary), then compare your screen to Figure 22.

4. Click **Preview**.

   The Background File Activity dialog box might appear and flash the names of all the files from the local version of the site that need to be uploaded to the remote site. The Synchronize dialog box shown in Figure 23 then opens and lists all the files that need to be uploaded to the remote site.

5. Click **OK**.

   All the files from the local The Striped Umbrella site are now contained in the remote version of the site. Notice that the remote folders are yellow and the local folders are green.

You synchronized The Striped Umbrella website files to copy all remaining files from the local root folder to the remote root folder.

FIGURE 23

Files that need to be uploaded to the remote site

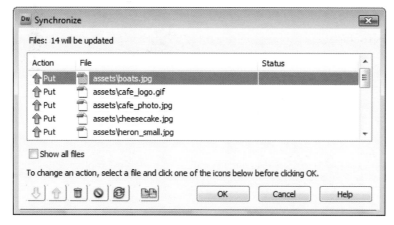

CHECK FILES
OUT AND IN

What You'll Do

In this lesson, you will use the Site Definition dialog box to enable the Check In/Check Out feature. You will then check out the cafe page, make a change to it, and then check it back in.

Managing a Website with a Team

When you work on a large website, chances are that many people will be involved in keeping the site up to date. Different individuals will need to make changes or additions to different pages of the site by adding or deleting content, changing graphics, updating information, and so on. If everyone had access to the pages at the same time, problems could arise. For instance, what if you and another team member both made edits to the same page at the same time? If you post your edited version of the file to the site after the other team member posts his edited version of the same file, the file that you upload will overwrite his version and none of his changes will be incorporated.

Not good! Fortunately, you can avoid this scenario by using Dreamweaver's collaboration tools.

Checking Out and Checking In Files

Checking files in and out is similar to checking library books in and out or video/DVD rentals. No one else can read the same copy that you have checked out. Using Dreamweaver's Check In/Check Out feature ensures that team members cannot overwrite each other's pages. When this feature is enabled, only one person can work on a file at a time. To check out a file, click the file you want to work on in the Files panel, and then click the Check Out File(s) button on the Files panel toolbar. Files that you have checked out are marked with green check marks in the Files panel. Files that have been checked in are marked with padlock icons.

After you finish editing a checked-out file, you need to save and close the file, and then click the Check In button to check the file back in and make it available to other users. When a file is checked in, you cannot make edits to it unless you check it out again. Figure 24 shows the Check Out File(s) and Check In buttons on the Files panel toolbar.

Enabling the Check In/Check Out Feature

To use the Check In/Check Out feature with a team of people, you must first enable it. To turn on this feature, check the Enable file check in and check out check box in the Remote Info settings of the Site Definition dialog box.

FIGURE 24

Check Out File(s) and Check In buttons on the Files Panel toolbar

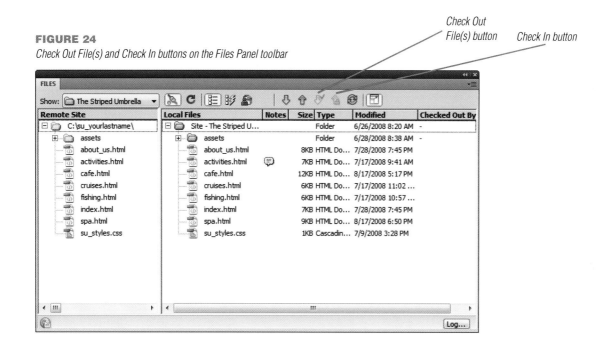

Enable the Check In/Check Out feature

1. Verify that the Site panel is in expanded view, click **Site** on the menu bar, click **Manage Sites** to open the Manage Sites dialog box, click **The Striped Umbrella** in the list, then click **Edit** to open the Site Definition for The Striped Umbrella dialog box.

2. Click **Remote Info** in the Category list, then click the **Enable file check in and check out check box** to select it.

3. Check the **Check out files when opening check box** to select it (if necessary).

4. Type your name using all lowercase letters and no spaces in the Check out name text box.

5. Type your email address in the Email address text box.

6. Compare your screen to Figure 25, click **OK** to close the Site Definition for The Striped Umbrella dialog box, then click **Done** to close the Manage Sites dialog box. Your dialog box will look different if you are using FTP access.

You used the Site Definition for The Striped Umbrella dialog box to enable the Check In/Check Out feature to let team members know when you are working with a file in the site.

Check out a file

1. Click the **cafe page** in the Local Files list in the Files panel to select it.

(continued)

FIGURE 25

Enabling the Check In/Check Out feature

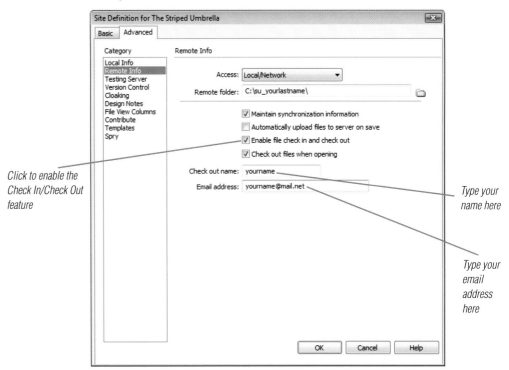

Click to enable the Check In/Check Out feature

Type your name here

Type your email address here

FIGURE 26

Files panel in Local view after checking out cafe page

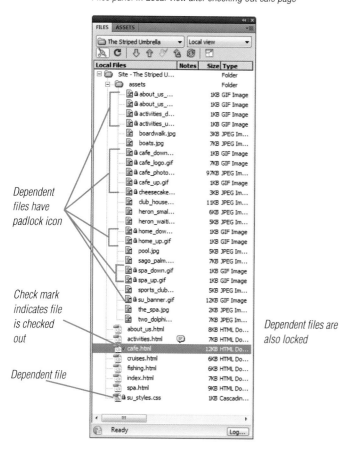

Dependent
files have
padlock icon

Check mark
indicates file
is checked
out

Dependent file

FIGURE 27

Files panel after checking in cafe page

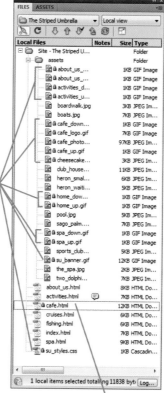

Dependent files are
also locked

Padlock icon indicates file is
read-only and cannot be edited
unless it is checked out

2. Click the **Check Out File(s) button** on the Files panel toolbar.

   The Dependent Files dialog box appears, asking if you want to include all files that are needed for the cafe page.

3. Click **Yes**, expand the assets folder if necessary, collapse the Files panel, click the **View list arrow**, click **Local view**, then compare your screen to Figure 26.

   The cafe file has a check mark next to it indicating you have checked it out. The dependent files have a padlock icon.

   > TIP If a dialog box appears asking "Do you wish to overwrite your local copy of cafe.html?", click Yes.

You checked out the cafe page so that no one else can use it while you work on it.

Check in a file

1. Open the cafe page, change the closing hour for the The Cabana in the table to **7:00 p.m.**, then save your changes.

2. Close the cafe page, then click the **cafe page** in the Files panel to select it.

3. Click the **Check In button** on the Files panel toolbar.

   The Dependent Files dialog box opens, asking if you want to include dependent files.

4. Click **Yes**, click another file in the Files panel to deselect the cafe page, then compare your screen to Figure 27.

   A padlock icon appears instead of a green check mark next to the cafe page on the Files panel.

You made a content change on the cafe page, then checked in the cafe page, making it available for others to check it out.

CLOAK FILES

What You'll Do

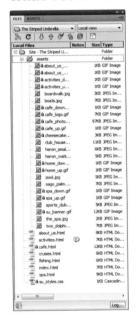

 In this lesson, you will cloak the assets folder so that it is excluded from various operations, such as the Put, Get, Check In, and Check Out commands. You will also use the Site Definition dialog box to cloak all .gif files in the site.

Understanding Cloaking Files

There may be times when you want to exclude a particular file or files from being uploaded to a server. For instance, suppose you have a page that is not quite finished and needs more work before it is ready to be viewed by others. You can exclude such files by **cloaking** them, which marks them for exclusion from several commands, including Put, Get, Synchronize, Check In, and Check Out. Cloaked files are also excluded from site-wide operations, such as checking for links or updating a template or library item. You can cloak a folder or specify a type of file to cloak throughout the site.

QUICKTIP

By default, the cloaking feature is enabled. However, if for some reason it is not turned on, open the Site Definition dialog box, click the Advanced tab, click the Cloaking category, then click the Enable cloaking check box.

Cloaking a Folder

There may be times when you want to cloak an entire folder. For instance, if you are not concerned with replacing outdated image files, you might want to cloak the assets folder of a website to save time when synchronizing files. To cloak a folder, select the folder, click the Options menu button in the Files panel, point to Site, point to Cloaking, and then click Cloak. The folder you cloaked and all the files it contains appear with red slashes across them, as shown in Figure 28. To uncloak a folder, click the Options menu button on the Files panel, point to Site, point to Cloaking, and then click Uncloak.

QUICKTIP

To uncloak all files in a site, click the Files panel Options menu button, point to Site, point to Cloaking, then click Uncloak All.

Cloaking Selected File Types

There may be times when you want to cloak a particular type of file, such as a .jpg file. To cloak a particular file type, open the Site Definition dialog box, click the Cloaking category, click the Cloak files ending with check box, and then type a file extension in the text box below the check box. All files throughout the site that have the specified file extension will be cloaked.

FIGURE 28
Cloaked assets folder in the Files panel

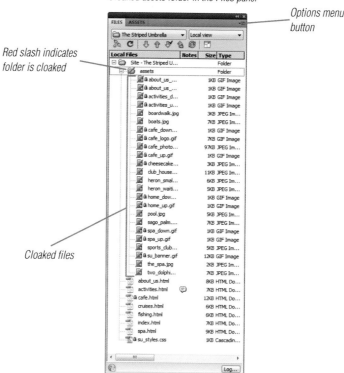

Options menu button

Red slash indicates folder is cloaked

Cloaked files

Cloak and uncloak a folder

1. Verify that Local view is displayed in the Files panel, then open the Manage Sites dialog box.

2. Click **The Striped Umbrella** (if necessary), click **Edit** to open the Site Definition for The Striped Umbrella dialog box, click **Cloaking** in the Category list, verify that the Enable cloaking check box is checked, click **OK**, then click **Done**.

3. Click the **assets folder** in the Files panel, click the **Options menu button** 📑 , point to **Site**, point to **Cloaking**, click **Cloak**, then compare your screen to Figure 29.

   A red slash now appears on top of the assets folder in the Files panel, indicating that all files in the assets folder are cloaked and will be excluded from putting, getting, checking in, checking out, and many other operations.

   > TIP You can also cloak a folder by right-clicking (Win) or [control]-clicking (Mac) the folder, pointing to Cloaking, then clicking Cloak.

4. Right-click (Win) or [control]-click (Mac) the **assets folder**, point to **Cloaking**, then click **Uncloak**.

   The assets folder and all the files it contains no longer appear with red slashes across them, indicating they are no longer cloaked.

   You cloaked the assets folder so that this folder and all the files it contains would be excluded from many operations, including uploading and down-loading files. You then uncloaked the assets folder.

FIGURE 29
Assets folder after cloaking

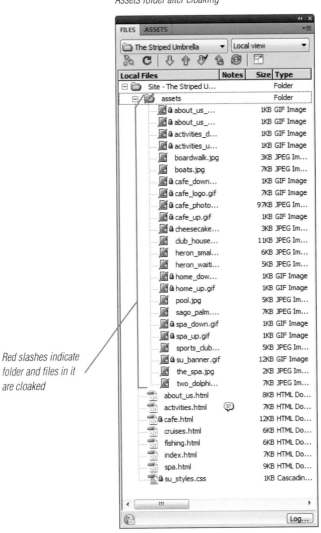

Red slashes indicate folder and files in it are cloaked

FIGURE 30
Specifying a file type to cloak

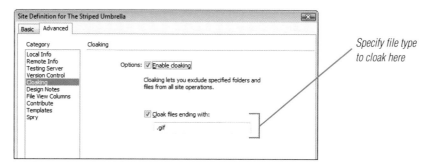

Specify file type
to cloak here

FIGURE 31
Assets folder in Files panel after cloaking .gif files

Assets folder
is not cloaked

All .gif files
are cloaked

Dependent
files for the
cafe page
still show
padlock
icon

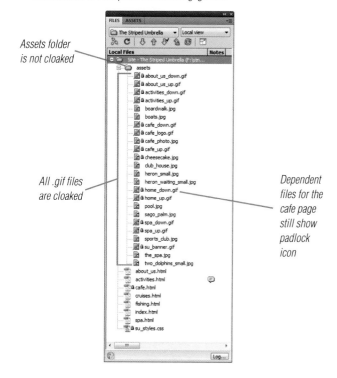

Cloak selected file types

1. Right-click (Win) or [control]-click (Mac) the **assets folder** in the Files panel, point to **Cloaking**, then click **Settings** to open the Site Definition for The Striped Umbrella dialog box with the Cloaking category selected.

2. Click the **Cloak files ending with check box**, select the text in the text box that appears, type **.gif** in the text box, then compare your screen to Figure 30.

3. Click **OK**.

   A dialog box opens, indicating that the site cache will be re-created.

4. Click **OK**, expand the assets folder (if necessary), then compare your screen to Figure 31.

   All of the .gif files in the assets folder appear with red slashes across them, indicating that they are cloaked. Notice that the assets folder is not cloaked.

You cloaked all the .gif files in The Striped Umbrella website.

IMPORT AND EXPORT
A SITE DEFINITION

What You'll Do

In this lesson, you will export the site definition file for The Striped Umbrella website. You will then import The Striped Umbrella website.

Exporting a Site Definition

When you work on a website for a long time, it's likely that at some point you will want to move it to another machine or share it with other collaborators who will help you maintain it. The site definition for a website contains important information about the site, including its URL, preferences that you've specified, and other secure information, such as login and password information. You can use the Export command to export the site definition file to another location. To do this, open the Manage Sites dialog box, click the site you want to export, and then click Export. Because the site definition file contains password information that you will want to keep secret from other site users, you should never save the site definition file in the website. Instead, save it in an external folder.

Importing a Site Definition

If you want to set up another user with a copy of your website, you can import the site definition file. To do this, click Import in the Manage Sites dialog box to open the Import Site dialog box, navigate to the .ste file you want to import, then click Open.

FIGURE 32

Saving The Striped Umbrella.ste file in the su_site_definition folder

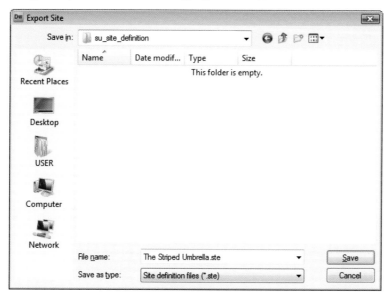

1. Use Windows Explorer (Win) or Finder (Mac) to create a new folder on your hard drive or external drive named **su_site_definition**.

2. Switch back to Dreamweaver, open the Manage Sites dialog box, click **The Striped Umbrella**, then click **Export** to open the Export Site dialog box. If you see a message asking if you are exporting the site to back up your settings or to share your settings with other users, choose the Back up my settings option, then click **OK**.

3. Navigate to and double-click to open the **su_site_definition folder** that you created in Step 1, as shown in Figure 32, click **Save**, then click **Done**.

You used the Export command to create the site definition file and saved it in the su_site_definition folder.

Import a site definition

1. Open the Manage Sites dialog box, click **The Striped Umbrella**, then click **Import** to open the Import Site dialog box.

2. Navigate to the su_site_definition folder, compare your screen to Figure 33, select **The Striped Umbrella.ste**, then click **Open**.

   A dialog box opens and says that a site named The Striped Umbrella already exists. It will name the imported site The Striped Umbrella 2 so that it has a different name.

3. Click **OK**.

4. Click **The Striped Umbrella 2** (if necessary), click **Edit**, then compare your screen to Figure 34.

   The settings show that the The Striped Umbrella 2 site has the same root folder and default images folder as the The Striped Umbrella site. Both of these settings are speci-fied in the The Striped Umbrella.ste file that you imported. Importing a site in this way makes it possible for multiple users with differ-ent computers to work on the same site.

   TIP   Make sure you know who is responsi-ble for which files to keep from overwriting the wrong files when they are published. The Synchronize Files and Check In/Check Out features are good procedures to use with multiple designers.

5. Click **OK**, click **OK** to close the warning mes-sage, then click **Done**.

   TIP   If a dialog box opens warning that the root folder chosen is the same as the folder for the site "The Striped Umbrella," click OK.

You imported The Striped Umbrella.ste file and created a new site, The Striped Umbrella 2.

FIGURE 33
Import Site dialog box

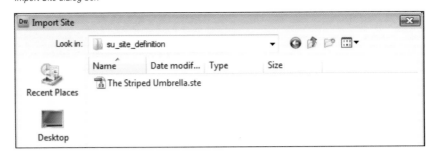

FIGURE 34
Site Definition for the The Striped Umbrella 2 dialog box

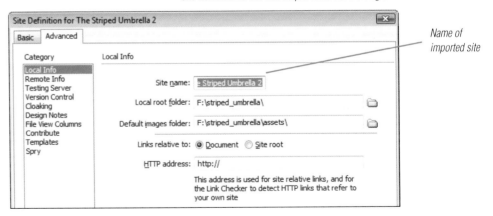

Name of imported site

FIGURE 35

Viewing The Striped Umbrella 2 website files

View the imported site

1. Click the **Expand to show local and remote sites button** on the Files panel toolbar to expand the Files panel.

2. Expand the Site root folder to view the contents (if necessary).

3. Click the **Refresh button** to view the files in the Remote Site pane.

   As shown in Figure 35, the site looks identical to the original The Striped Umbrella site, except the name has been changed to The Striped Umbrella 2.

   TIP If you don't see your remote site files, click the Connects to remote host button.

4. Click the **Collapse to show only local or remote site button** to collapse the Files panel.

5. Open the Manage Sites dialog box, verify that The Striped Umbrella 2 site is selected, click **Remove**, click **Yes** to clear the warning dialog box, then click **Done** to delete The Striped Umbrella 2 website.

6. Close all open pages, then close Dreamweaver.

You viewed the expanded Files panel for The Striped Umbrella 2 website and then deleted The Striped Umbrella 2 website.

POWER USER SHORTCUTS	
to do this:	**use this shortcut:**
Validate Markup	[Shift][F6]
Get	[Ctrl][Shift][D] (Win) or ⌘ [Shift][D] (Mac)
Check Out	[Ctrl][Alt][Shift][D] (Win) or ⌘ [option][Shift][D] (Mac)
Put	[Ctrl][Shift][U] (Win) or ⌘ [Shift][U] (Mac)
Check In	[Ctrl][Alt][Shift][U] (Win) or ⌘ [option][Shift][U] (Mac)
Check Links	[Shift][F8]
Check Links Sitewide	[Ctrl][F8] (Win) or ⌘ [F8] (Mac)

EVALUATE WEB CONTENT FOR LEGAL USE

What You'll Do

In this lesson, you will examine copyright issues in the context of using content gathered from sources such as the Internet.

Can I Use Downloaded Media?

The Internet has made it possible to locate compelling and media-rich content to use in websites. A person who has learned to craft searches can locate a multitude of interesting material, such as graphics, animations, sounds, and text. But just because you can find it easily does not mean that you can use it however you want or under any circumstance. Learning about copyright law can help you decide whether or how to use content created and published by someone other than yourself.

Understanding Intellectual Property

Intellectual property is a product resulting from human creativity. It can include inventions, movies, songs, designs, clothing, and so on.

The purpose of copyright law is to promote progress in society, not expressly to protect the rights of copyright owners. However, the vast majority of work you might want to download and use in a project is protected by either copyright or trademark law.

Copyright protects the particular and tangible *expression* of an idea, not the idea itself. If you wrote a story using the idea of aliens crashing in Roswell, New Mexico, no one could copy or use your story without permission. However, anyone could write a story using a similar plot or characters—the *idea* of aliens crashing in Roswell is not copyright-protected. Generally, copyright lasts for the life of the author plus 70 years.

Trademark protects an image, word, slogan, symbol, or design used to identify goods or services. For example, the Nike swoosh, Disney characters, or the shape of a classic Coca-Cola bottle are works protected by trademark. Trademark protection lasts for 10 years with 10-year renewal terms, lasting indefinitely provided the trademark is in active use.

What Exactly Does the Copyright Owner Own?

Copyright attaches to a work as soon as you create it; you do not have to register it with the U.S. Copyright Office. A copyright owner has a "bundle" of six rights, consisting of:

1) reproduction (including downloading)
2) creation of **derivative works** (for example, a movie version of a book)
3) distribution to the public
4) public performance
5) public display
6) public performance by digital audio transmission of sound recordings

By default, only a copyright holder can create a derivative work of his or her original by transforming or adapting it.

Understanding Fair Use

The law builds in limitations to copyright protection. One limitation to copyright is **fair use**. Fair use allows limited use of copyright-protected work. For example, you could excerpt short passages of a film or song for a class project or parody a television show. Determining if fair use applies to a work depends on the *purpose* of its use, the *nature* of the copyrighted work, *how much* you want to copy, and the *effect* on the market or value of the work. However, there is no clear formula on what constitutes fair use. It is always decided on a case-by-case basis.

How Do I Use Work Properly?

Being a student doesn't mean you can use any amount of any work for class.

On the other hand, the very nature of education means you need to be able to use or reference different work in your studies. There are many situations that allow you to use protected work.

In addition to applying a fair use argument, you can obtain permission, pay a fee, use work that does not have copyright protection, or use work that has a flexible copyright license, where the owner has given the public permission to use the work in certain ways. For more information about open-access licensing, visit www.creativecommons.org. Work that is no longer protected by copyright is in the **public domain**; anyone can use it however

they wish for any purpose. In general, the photos and other media on federal government websites are in the public domain.

Understanding Licensing Agreements

Before you decide whether to use media you find on a website, you must decide whether you can comply with its licensing agreement. A **licensing agreement** is the permission given by a copyright holder that conveys the right to use the copyright holder's work under certain conditions.

Websites have rules that govern how a user may use its text and media, known as **terms of use**. Figures 36, 37, and 38 are great

FIGURE 36
The Library of Congress home page

Link to legal information regarding the use of content on the website

Library of Congress website – www.loc.gov

examples of clear terms of use for the Library of Congress website.

A site's terms of use do not override your right to apply fair use. Also, someone cannot compile public domain images in a website and then claim they own them or dictate how the images can be used. Conversely, someone can erroneously state in their terms of use that you can use work on the site freely, but they may not know the work's copyright status. The burden is on you to research the veracity of anyone claiming you can use work.

Obtaining Permission or a License

The **permissions process** is specific to what you want to use (text, photographs, music, trademarks, merchandise, and so on) and how you want to use it (school term paper, personal website, fabric pattern). How you want to use the work will determine the level and scope of permissions you need to secure. The fundamentals, however, are the same. Your request should contain the following:

- Your full name, address, and complete contact information.
- A specific description of your

intended use. Sometimes including a sketch, storyboard, or link to a website is helpful.
- A signature line for the copyright holder.
- A target date when you would like the copyright holder to respond. This can be important if you're working under deadline.

Posting a Copyright Notice

The familiar © symbol or "Copyright" is no longer required to indicate copyright, nor does it automatically register your work,

Library of Congress website legal page

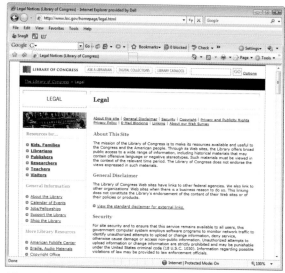

Library of Congress website – www.loc.gov

FIGURE 38
Library of Congress website copyright page

About Copyright and the Collections

Whenever possible, the Library of Congress provides factual information about copyright owners and related matters in the catalog records, finding aids and other texts that accompany collections. As a publicly supported institution, the Library generally does not own rights in its collections. Therefore, it does not charge permission fees for use of such material and generally does not grant or deny permission to publish or otherwise distribute material in its collections. Permission and possible fees may be required from the copyright owner independently of the Library. It is the researcher's obligation to determine and satisfy copyright or other use restrictions when publishing or otherwise distributing materials found in the Library's collections. Transmission or reproduction of protected items beyond that allowed by fair use requires the written permission of the copyright owners. Researchers must make their own assessments of rights in light of their intended use.

If you have any more information about an item you've seen on our website or if you are the copyright owner and believe our website has not properly attributed your work to you or has used it without permission, we want to hear from you. Please contact OGC@loc.gov with your contact information and a link to the relevant content.

but it does serve a useful purpose. When you post or publish it, you are stating clearly to those who may not know anything about copyright law that this work is claimed by you and is not in the public domain. Your case is made even stronger if someone violates your copyright and your notice is clearly visible. That way, violator can never claim ignorance of the law as an excuse for infringing. Common notification styles include:

Copyright 2013
Delmar, Cengage Learning
or
© 2013 Delmar, Cengage Learning

Giving proper attribution for text excerpts is a must; giving attribution for media is excellent practice, but is never a substitute for applying a fair use argument, buying a license, or simply getting permission.

You must provide proper citation for materials you incorporate into your own work, such as the following:

References
Waxer, Barbara M., and Baum, Marsha L. 2006. *Internet Surf and Turf – The Essential Guide to Copyright, Fair Use, and Finding Media.* Boston: Thomson Course Technology.

This expectation applies even to unsigned material and material that does not display the copyright symbol (©). Moreover, the expectation applies just as certainly to ideas you summarize or paraphrase as to words you quote verbatim.

Guidelines have been written by the American Psychological Association (APA) to establish an editorial style to be used to present written material. These guidelines include the way citations are referenced.

Here's a list of the elements that make up an APA-style citation of web-based resources:
- Author's name (if known)
- Date of publication or last revision (if known), in parentheses
- Title of document
- Title of complete work or website (if applicable), underlined
- URL, in angled brackets
- Date of access, in parentheses

Following is an example of how you'd reference the APA Home page on the Reference page of your paper:

APA Style.org. Retrieved August 22, 2012, from APA Online website: http://www.apastyle.org/electext.html

Another set of guidelines used by many schools and university and commercial presses is the Modern Language Association (MLA) style. For more information, go to http://www.mla.org.

Perform website maintenance.

1. Open the blooms & bulbs website, then re-create the site cache.
2. Use the Link Checker panel to check for broken links, then fix any broken links that appear.
3. Use the Link Checker to check for orphaned files. If any orphaned files appear in the report, take steps to link them to appropriate pages or remove them.
4. Use the Assets panel to check for non-web-safe colors. (*Hint*: If you do see any non-web-safe colors, recreate the site cache again, then refresh the Assets panel.)
5. Run an Untitled Documents report for the entire local site. If the report lists any pages that have no titles, add page titles to the untitled pages. Run the report again to verify that all pages have page titles.
6. Run a report to look for missing alternate text. Add alternate text to any graphics that need it, then run the report again to verify that all images contain alternate text.

7. Enable the Design Notes preference and add a Design Note to the classes page as follows: **Shoot a video of the hanging baskets class to add to the page**. Add the status **needs attention** and check the Show when file is opened option.

Publish a website and transfer files.

1. Set up web server access for the blooms & bulbs website on an FTP server or a local/network server (whichever is available to you) using blooms_yourlastname as the remote folder name.
2. View the blooms & bulbs remote site in the Files panel.
3. Upload the iris.jpg file to the remote site, then view the remote site.
4. Synchronize all files in the blooms & bulbs website, so that all files from the local site are uploaded to the remote site.

Check files out and in.

1. Enable the Check In/Check Out feature.
2. Check out the plants page and all dependent pages.
3. Open the plants page, then change the heading style of "Drop by to see our Featured Spring Plants" to bold_blue, then save the file.
4. Check in the plants page and all dependent files.

Cloak files.

1. Verify that cloaking is enabled in the blooms & bulbs website.
2. Cloak the assets folder, then uncloak it.
3. Cloak all the .jpg files in the blooms & bulbs website.

Import and export a site definition.

1. Create a new folder named **blooms_site_definition** on your hard drive or external drive.

2. Export the blooms & bulbs site definition to the blooms_site_definition folder.

3. Import the blooms & bulbs site definition to create a new site called **blooms & bulbs 2**.

4. Make sure that all files from the blooms & bulbs website appear in the Files panel for the imported site, then compare your screen to Figure 39.

5. Remove the blooms & bulbs 2 site.

6. Close all open files.

FIGURE 39
Completed Skills Review

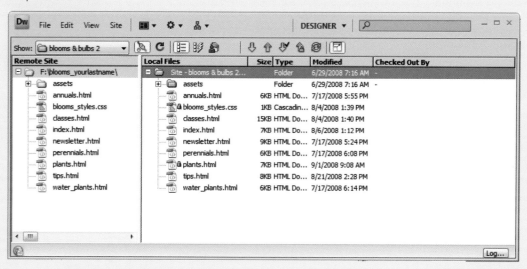

In this Project Builder, you will publish the TripSmart website that you have developed throughout this book to a local/network folder. Mike Andrew, the owner, has asked that you publish the site to a local folder as a backup location. You will first run several reports on the site, specify the remote settings for the site, upload files to the remote site, check files out and in, and cloak files. Finally, you will export and import the site definition.

1. Use the TripSmart website that you began in Project Builder 1 in Chapter 1 and developed in previous chapters.

2. Use the Link Checker panel to check for broken links, then fix any broken links that appear.

3. Use the Link Checker to check for orphaned files. If any orphaned files appear in the report, take steps to link them to appropriate pages or remove them.

4. Use the Assets panel to check for non-web-safe colors.

5. Run an Untitled Documents report for the entire local site. If the report lists any pages that lack titles, add page titles to the untitled pages. Run the report again to verify that all pages have page titles.

6. Run a report to look for missing alternate text. Add alternate text to any graphics that need it, then run the report again to verify that all images contain alternate text.

7. Enable the Design Notes preference, if necessary, and add a design note to the newsletter page as follows: **Add a Flash video showing the river route**. Add the status **needs attention** and check the Show when file is opened option.

8. If you did not do so in Project Builder 1 in Chapter 1, use the Site Definition dialog box to set up web server access for a remote site using a local or network folder.

9. Upload the index page and all dependent files to the remote site.

10. View the remote site to make sure that all files uploaded correctly.

11. Synchronize the files so that all other files on the local TripSmart site are uploaded to the remote site.

12. Enable the Check In/Check Out feature.

13. Check out the index page in the local site and all dependent files.

14. Open the index page, close the index page, then check in the index page and all dependent pages.

15. Cloak all .jpg files in the website.

16. Export the site definition to a new folder named **tripsmart_site_definition**.

17. Import the TripSmart.ste file to create a new site named TripSmart 2.

18. Expand the assets folder in the Files panel (if necessary), then compare your screen to Figure 40.

19. Remove the TripSmart 2 site.

20. Close any open files.

FIGURE 40

Sample Project Builder 1

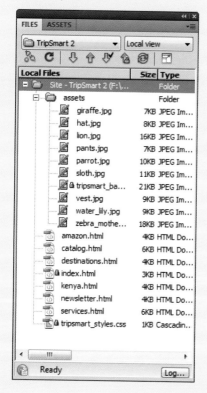

In this Project Builder, you will finish your work on the Carolyne's Creations website. You are ready to publish the website to a remote server and transfer all the files from the local site to the remote site. First, you will run several reports to make sure the website is in good shape. Next, you will enable the Check In/Check Out feature so that other staff members may collaborate on the site. Finally, you will export and import the site definition file.

1. Use the Carolyne's Creations website that you began in Project Builder 1 in Chapter 1 and developed in previous chapters.

2. If you did not do so in Project Builder 2 in Chapter 1, use the Site Definition dialog box to set up web server access for a remote site using either an FTP site or a local or network folder.

3. Run reports for broken links and orphaned files, correcting any errors that you find. The cc_banner.jpg file is no longer needed, so delete the file.

4. Run reports for untitled documents and missing alt text, correcting any errors that you find.

5. Check for non-web-safe colors.

6. Upload the classes.html page and all dependent files to the remote site.

7. View the remote site to make sure that all files uploaded correctly.

8. Synchronize the files so that all other files on the local Carolyne's Creations site are uploaded to the remote site.

9. Enable the Check In/Check Out feature.

10. Check out the classes page and all its dependent files.

11. Open the classes page, then change the price of the adult class to **$45.00**.

12. Save your changes, close the page, then check in the classes page and all dependent pages.

13. Export the site definition to a new folder named **cc_site_definition**.

14. Import the Carolyne's Creations.ste file to create a new site named Carolyne's Creations 2.

15. Expand the root folder in the Files panel (if necessary), compare your screen to Figure 41, then remove the Carolyne's Creations2 site.

FIGURE 41
Completed Project Builder 2

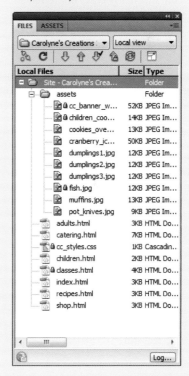

Throughout this book you have used Dreamweaver to create and develop several websites that contain different elements, many of which are found in popular commercial websites. For instance, Figure 42 shows the National Park Service website, which contains photos and information on all the national parks in the United States. This website contains many types of interactive elements, such as image maps and tables—all of which you learned to create in this book.

1. Connect to the Internet, then go to the National Park Service website at www.nps.gov.
2. Spend some time exploring the pages of this site to familiarize yourself with its elements.
3. Type a list of all the elements in this site that you have learned how to create in this book. After each item, write a short description of where and how the element is used in the site.
4. Print the home page and one or two other pages that contain some of the elements you described and attach it to your list.

FIGURE 42
Design Project

National Park Service website – www.nps.gov

In this project, you will finish your work on the website that you created and developed throughout this book.

You will publish your site to a remote server or local or network folder.

1. Before you begin the process of publishing your website to a remote server, make sure that it is ready for public viewing. Use Figure 43 to assist you in making sure your website is complete. If you find problems, make the necessary changes to finalize the site.

2. Decide where to publish your site. The folder where you will publish your site can be either an FTP site or a local/network folder. If you are publishing to an FTP site, be sure to write down all the information you will need to publish to the site, including the URL of the FTP host, the directory on the FTP server where you will publish your site's root folder, and the login and password information.

3. Use the Site Definition dialog box to specify the remote settings for the site using the information that was decided upon in Step 2.

4. Transfer one of the pages and its dependent files to the remote site, then view the remote site to make sure the appropriate files were transferred.

5. Synchronize the files so that all the remaining local pages and dependent files are uploaded to the remote site.

6. Enable the Check In/Check Out feature.

7. Check out one of the pages. Open the checked-out page, make a change to it, save the change, close the page, then check the page back in.

8. Cloak a particular file type.

9. Export the site definition for the site to a new folder on your hard drive or on an external drive.

10. Import the site to create a new version of the site.

11. Close the imported site, save and close all open pages (if necessary), then exit Dreamweaver.

FIGURE 43
Portfolio Project checklist

Website Checklist

1. Are you satisfied with the content and appearance of every page?
2. Are all paths for all links and images correct?
3. Does each page have a title?
4. Do all images appear?
5. Are all colors web-safe?
6. Do all images have appropriate alternate text?
7. Have you eliminated any orphaned files?
8. Have you deleted any unnecessary files?
9. Have you viewed all pages using at least two different browsers?
10. Does the home page have keywords and a description?

1

GETTING STARTED WITH
ADOBE FLASH CS4

1. Understand the Adobe Flash CS4 workspace

2. Open a document and play a movie

3. Create and save a movie

4. Work with the Timeline

5. Distribute an Adobe Flash movie

6. Plan an application or a website

GETTING STARTED WITH
ADOBE FLASH CS4

Introduction

Adobe Flash CS4 Professional is a development tool that allows you to create compelling interactive experiences, often by using animation. You can use Flash to create entire websites, including e-commerce, entertainment, education, and personal use sites. In addition, Flash is an excellent program for developing animations that are used in websites, such as product demonstrations, banner ads, online tutorials, and electronic greeting cards. Also, Flash can be used to create applications, such as games and simulations, that can be delivered over the web and on DVDs. These applications can even be scaled to be displayed on mobile devices, such as cell phones. While it is known as a tool for creating complex animations for the web, Flash also has excellent drawing tools and tools for creating interactive controls, such as navigation buttons and menus. Furthermore, Flash provides the ability to incorporate sounds and video easily into an application.

Flash has become the standard for both professional and casual applications as well as for web developers. Flash is popular because the program is optimized for the web. Web developers need to provide high-impact experiences for the user, which means making sites come alive and turning them from static text and pictures to dynamic, interactive experiences. The problem has been that incorporating high-quality graphics and motion into a website can dramatically increase the download time and frustrate viewers as they wait for an image to appear or for an animation to play. Flash directly addresses this problem by allowing developers to use vector images, which reduce the size of graphic files. Vector images appeal to designers because they are scalable, which means they can be resized and reshaped without distortion. For example, using a vector graphic, you can easily have an object, such as an airplane, become smaller as it moves across the screen without having to create the plane in different sizes.

In addition, Flash provides for streaming content over the Internet. Instead of waiting for the entire contents of a web page to load, the viewer sees a continuous display of images. Another reason Flash has become a standard is that it is made by Adobe. Adobe makes other programs, such as Dreamweaver, Fireworks, Photoshop, and Illustrator. Together these products can be used to create compelling interactive websites and applications. This chapter provides an overview of Flash and presents concepts that are covered in more detail in later chapters.

Tools You'll Use

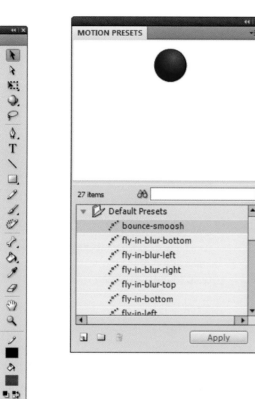

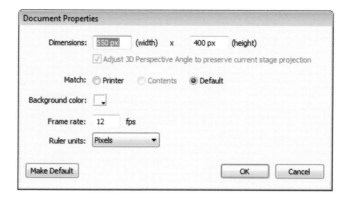

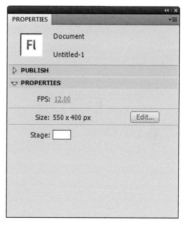

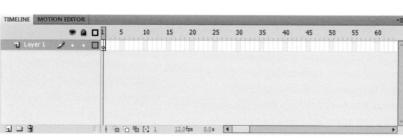

UNDERSTAND THE
ADOBE FLASH CS4
WORKSPACE

What You'll Do

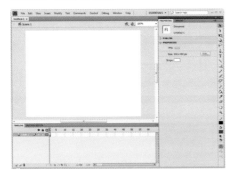

In this lesson, you will learn about the development workspace in Adobe Flash and how to change Flash settings to customize your workspace.

Organizing the Flash Workspace

As a designer, one of the most important things for you to do is to organize your workspace—that is, to decide what to have displayed on the screen and how to arrange the various tools and panels. Because **Flash** is a powerful program with many tools, your workspace may become cluttered. Fortunately, it is easy to customize the workspace to display only the tools needed at any particular time.

The development process in Flash operates according to a movie metaphor: objects placed on the Stage also appear in frames on a Timeline. As you work in Flash, you create a movie by arranging objects (such as graphics and text) on the Stage, and then animating the objects using the Timeline. You can play the movie on the Stage as you are working on it by using the movie controls (start, stop, rewind, and so on). When done the movie can be incorporated into a website or as part of an application, such as a game.

When you start Flash, three basic parts of the workspace are displayed: a menu bar that organizes commands within menus, a Stage where objects are placed, and a Timeline used to organize and control the objects on the Stage. In addition, one or more panels may be displayed. Panels, such as the Tools panel, are used when working with objects and features of the movie. Figure 1 shows a typical Flash workspace.

Stage

The **Stage** contains all of the objects (such as drawings, photos, clip art, and text) that are part of the movie that will be seen by your viewers. It shows how the objects behave within the movie and how they interact with each other. You can resize the Stage and change the background color applied to it. You can draw objects directly on the Stage or drag them from the Library panel to the Stage. You can also import objects developed in another program directly to the Stage. You can specify the size of the Stage (in pixels), which will be the size of the area within your browser window that displays the movie. The gray area surrounding the Stage is the Pasteboard. You can place objects on the Pasteboard as you are creating a movie. However, neither the Pasteboard nor the objects on it will appear when the movie is played in a browser or the Flash Player.

Timeline (Frames and Layers)

The **Timeline** is used to organize and control the movie's contents by specifying when each object appears on the Stage. The Timeline is critical to the creation of movies because a movie is merely a series of still images that appear over time. The images are contained within **frames**, which are segments of the Timeline. Frames in a Flash movie are similar to frames in a motion picture. When a Flash movie is played, a playhead moves from frame to frame on the Timeline, causing the contents of each frame to appear on the Stage in a linear sequence.

The Timeline indicates where you are at any time within the movie and allows you to insert, delete, select, copy, and move frames. It shows the animation in your movie and the layers that contain objects. **Layers** help to organize the objects on the Stage. You can draw and edit objects on one layer without affecting objects on other layers. Layers are a way to stack objects so they can overlap and give a 3D appearance on the Stage.

Panels

Panels are used to view, organize, and modify objects and features in a movie. The most commonly used panels are the Tools panel, the Properties panel (also called the Property inspector), and the Library panel.

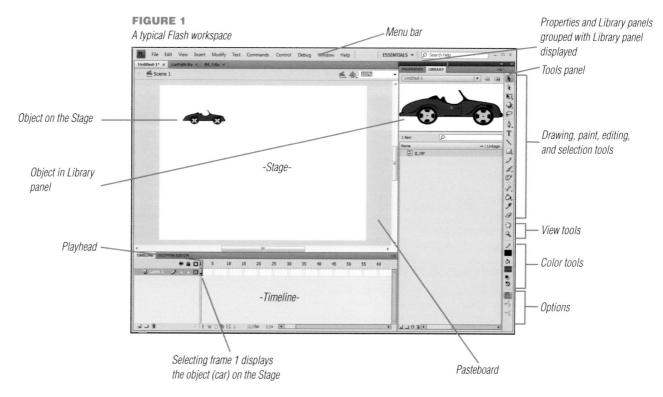

FIGURE 1
A typical Flash workspace

Menu bar

Object on the Stage

Object in Library panel

-Stage-

Playhead

-Timeline-

Selecting frame 1 displays the object (car) on the Stage

Properties and Library panels grouped with Library panel displayed

Tools panel

Drawing, paint, editing, and selection tools

View tools

Color tools

Options

Pasteboard

For example, the Properties panel is used to change the properties of an object, such as the fill color of a circle. The Properties panel is context sensitive, so that if you are working with text it displays the appropriate options, such as font and font size.

You can control which panels are displayed individually or you can choose to display panel sets. Panel sets are groups of the most commonly used panels. For example, the Properties and the Library panels are often grouped together to make a panel set. You use the Window menu on the menu bar to display and hide panels.

Tools Panel

The **Tools panel** contains a set of tools used to draw and edit graphics and text. It is divided into four sections.

The **Tools** section includes draw, paint, text, and selection tools, which are used to create lines, shapes, illustrations, and text. The selection tools are used to select objects so that they can be modified in several ways.

The **Views** section includes the Zoom tool and the Hand tool, which are used to zoom in on and out of parts of the Stage and to pan the Stage window, respectively.

The **Colors** section includes tools and icons used to change the stroke (border of an object) and fill (area inside an object) colors.

The **Options** section includes options for selected tools, such as allowing you to choose the size of the brush when using the Brush tool.

Although several panels open automatically when you start Flash, you may choose to display them only when they are needed. This keeps your workspace from becoming too cluttered. Panels are floating windows, meaning that you can move them around the workspace. This allows you to group (dock) panels together as a way to organize them in the workspace. In addition, you can control how a panel is displayed. That is, you can expand a panel to show all of its features or collapse it to show only the title bar. Collapsing panels reduces the clutter on your workspace, provides a larger area for the Stage, and still provides easy access to often used panels.

If you choose to rearrange panels, first decide if you want a panel to be grouped (docked) with another panel, stacked above or below another panel, a floating panel, or simply a stand-alone panel. An example of each of these is shown in Figure 2.

Arranging panels can be a bit tricky. It's easy to start moving panels around and find that the workspace is cluttered with panels arranged in unintended ways. While you cannot use the Flash Undo feature on the Edit menu to undo a panel move, you can always close a panel or choose the Reset Essentials option from the Workspace command on the Windows

FIGURE 2
Arranging panels

Grouped panels

Floating panel

Stand-alone panel

Stacked panels

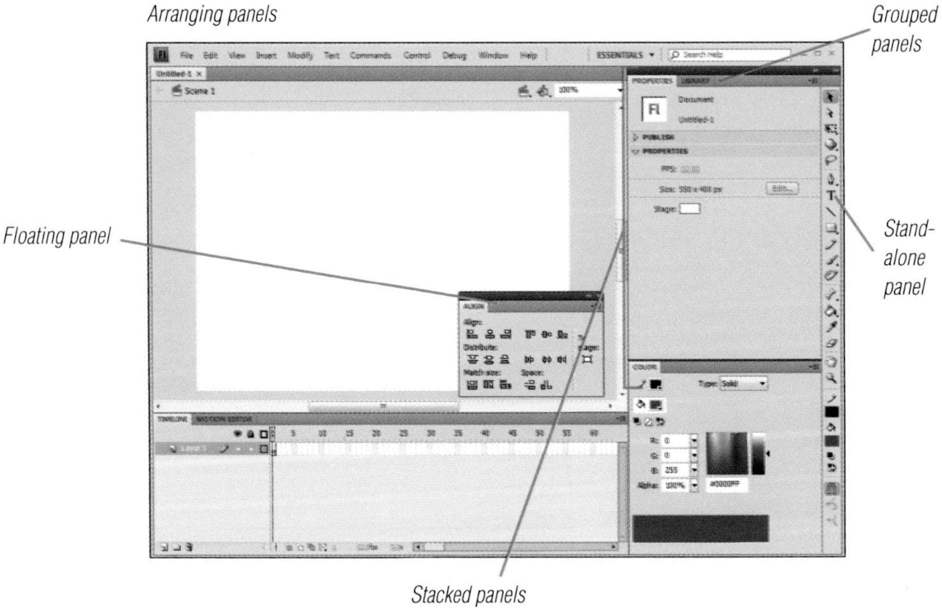

menu. This command displays the default panel arrangement, which is a good starting position when working with Flash.

The key to rearranging panels is the blue drop zone that appears when a panel is being moved. Refer to Figure 3. The drop zone is the area to which the panel can move and is indicated by either a blue line or a rectangle with a blue border. A single blue line indicates the position for stacking a panel above or below another panel. A rectangle with a blue border indicates the position for grouping panels. If you move a panel without using a drop zone, the panel becomes a floating panel and is neither grouped nor stacked with other panels. To move a panel, you drag the panel by its tab until the desired blue drop zone appears, then you release the mouse button. (*Note*: Dragging a panel by its tab moves only that panel. To move a panel set you must drag the group by its title bar.)

Figure 3 shows the Library panel being grouped with the Properties panel. The process is to drag the Library panel tab adjacent to the Properties panel tab. Notice the rectangle with the blue border that surrounds the Properties panel. This indicates the drop zone for the Library panel which groups them together. Figure 4 shows the Library panel after being ungrouped and placed as a floating panel.

FIGURE 3
Grouping the Library panel

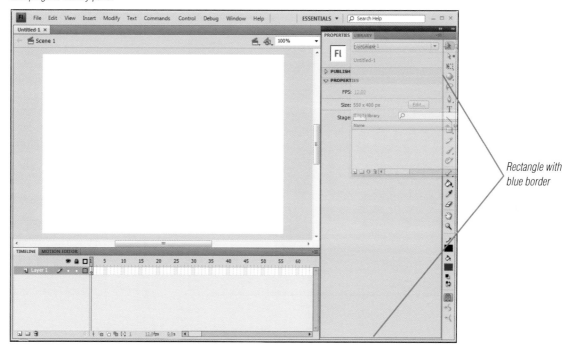

Rectangle with blue border

In addition to moving panels, you can collapse them so that only the title bar appears, and then you can expand them to display the entire panel. The Collapse to Icons button is located in the upper-right corner of each panel, as shown in Figure 4. The Collapse to Icons button is a toggle button, which means it changes or toggles between two states. When clicked, the Collapse to Icons button changes to the Expand Panels button. Finally, if you want to close a panel, you can use the Close option from the drop down menu on the panel title bar, as shown in Figure 4 or you can deselect a panel option on the Windows menu.

Regardless of how you decide to customize your development workspace, the Stage and the menu bar are always displayed. Usually, you display the Timeline, Tools panel, Library panel, Properties panel, and one or more other panels.

Other changes that you can make to the workspace are to change the size of the Stage, move the Stage around the Pasteboard, and change the size of the Timeline panel. To increase the size of the Stage so that the objects on the Stage can be more easily edited, you can change the magnification setting using commands on the View menu or by using the View tools on the Tools panel. The Hand tool on the Tools panel and the scroll bars at the bottom and right of the Stage can be used to reposition the Stage. The Timeline can be resized by dragging the top border. The more complex your Flash movie, the more layers that are used in the Timeline. Increasing the size of the Timeline allows you to view several layers at one time.

FIGURE 4

Ungrouping the Library panel

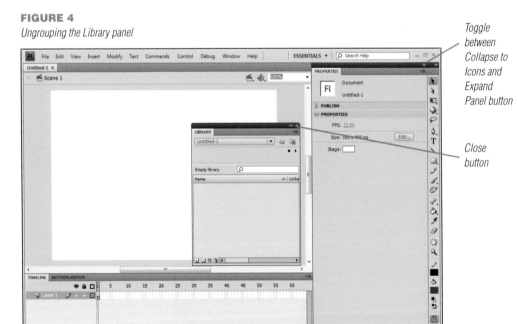

Toggle between Collapse to Icons and Expand Panel button

Close button

QUICKTIP

When working with panels, you can collapse, move, and close them as suits your working style. Settings for an object are not lost if you close or collapse a panel. If, at any time the panels have become confusing, simply return to the Essentials workspace and open panels as needed.

FIGURE 5

The Flash Welcome screen

Start Adobe Flash and work with panels

1. Start the Adobe Flash CS4 program **FL** .

   The Adobe Flash CS4 Welcome screen appears, as shown in Figure 5. This screen allows you to open a recent document or create a new Flash file.

2. Click **Flash File (ActionScript 3.0)** under Create New.

3. Click **Window** on the menu bar, point to **Workspace**, then click **Reset 'Essentials'**.

   TIP As you are rearranging your workspace, you can always select the Reset 'Essentials' option on the Window Workspace submenu to display the default workspace.

4. Click **Window** on the menu bar, then note the panels with check marks. The check marks identify which panels are open.

   TIP The Properties and Library panels may be grouped depending upon the configuration of your Essentials workspace. If so, only the panel that is active (the tab that is selected) will have a check mark.

5. With the Windows menu still open, click **Hide Panels**.

6. Click **Window** on the menu bar, then click **Timeline**.

7. Click **Window** on the menu bar, then click **Tools**.

8. Click **Window** on the menu bar, then click **Library**.

9. Click **Window** on the menu bar, then click **Properties**.

   At this point the Library and Properties panels should be grouped.

10. Click the **Library panel tab** to display the panel.

11. Click the **Properties panel tab** to display the panel.

(continued)

12. Click the **Library panel tab**, then drag the **panel** to the Stage as a floating panel.

13. Click the **Collapse to Icons button** on the Library panel title bar.

14. Click the **Expand Panels button** on the Library panel title bar.

15. Click the **Library panel tab**, drag the **panel** to the right of the Properties panel tab, then when a rectangle with a blue border appears, release the mouse button to group the panels, as shown in Figure 6.

    Note: If the panels do not appear as shown in Figure 6, repeat the step making sure there is a rectangle with a blue border before releasing the mouse button.

16. Click the **Collapse to Icons button** in the upper-right corner of the grouped panels, as shown in Figure 6.

17. Click the **Expand Panels button** delete icon to display the grouped panels.

18. Click **Window** on the menu bar, point to **Workspace**, then click **Reset 'Essentials'**.

    The Essentials workspace appears.

You started Flash and configured the workspace by hiding, moving, and displaying selected panels.

Change the Stage view and display of the Timeline

1. Click **View** on the menu bar, point to **Magnification**, then click **50%**.

2. Click the **Hand tool** 🖑 on the Tools panel, click the middle of the Stage, then drag the **Stage** around the Pasteboard.

(continued)

FIGURE 6
Library panel grouped with the Properties panel

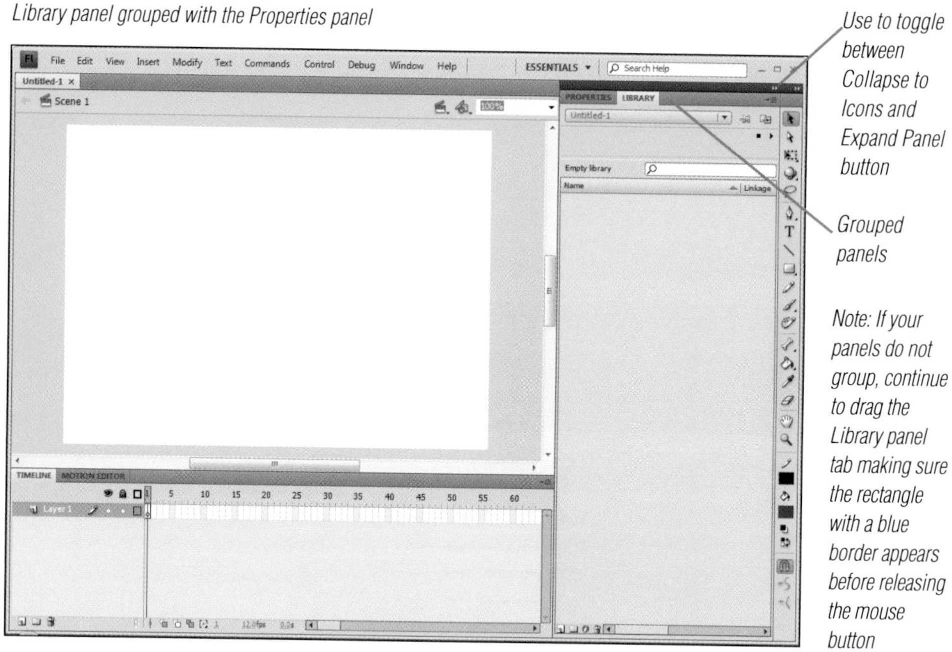

Use to toggle between Collapse to Icons and Expand Panel button

Grouped panels

Note: If your panels do not group, continue to drag the Library panel tab making sure the rectangle with a blue border appears before releasing the mouse button

Understanding your workspace

Organizing the Flash workspace is like organizing your desktop. You may work more efficiently if you have many of the most commonly used items in view and ready to use. Alternately, you may work better if your workspace is relatively uncluttered, giving you more free "desk space." Fortunately, Flash makes it easy for you to decide which items to display and how they are arranged while you work. For example, to toggle the Main toolbar, click Window on the menu bar, point to Toolbars, then click Main. You should become familiar with quickly opening, collapsing, expanding, and closing the various windows, toolbars, and panels in Flash, and experimenting with different layouts and screen resolutions to find the workspace that works best for you.

FIGURE 7

Changing the size of the Timeline panel

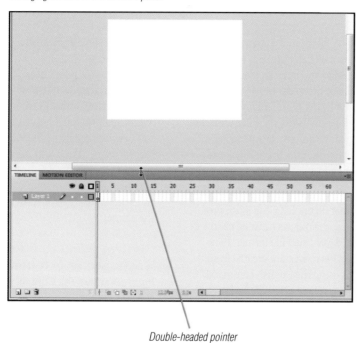

Double-headed pointer

3. Move the pointer to the top of the Timeline title bar, when the pointer changes to a double-headed pointer ↕ , click and drag up to increase the size of the Timeline, as shown in Figure 7.

   Increasing the size of the Timeline panel allows you to view more layers as you add them to the Timeline.

4. Point to the top of the Timeline title bar, when the pointer changes to a double-headed pointer ↕ , click and drag the **title bar** down to decrease the size of the Timeline.

5. Double-click the word **TIMELINE** to collapse the Timeline.

6. Double-click the word **TIMELINE** again to expand the Timeline.

7. Click **View** on the menu bar, point to **Magnification**, then click **100%**.

8. Click **ESSENTIALS** on the menu bar, then click **Reset 'Essentials'**.

   This resets the workspace to the Essentials template.

9. Click the **Selection tool** ↖ on the Tools panel.

10. Click **File** on the menu bar, then click **Save**.

11. Navigate to the drive and folder where your Data Files are stored, type **workspace** for the filename, then click **Save**.

12. Click **File** on the menu bar, then click **Close**.

You used a View command to change the magnification of the Stage; you used the Hand tool to move the Stage around the workspace; you resized, collapsed, and expanded the Timeline panel; then you saved the document.

OPEN A DOCUMENT
AND PLAY A MOVIE

What You'll Do

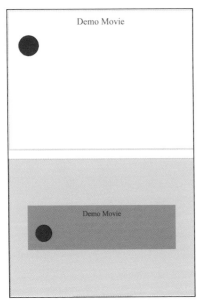

Demo Movie

Demo Movie

 In this lesson, you will open a Flash document (movie); preview, test, and save the movie; then change the movie's document settings.

Opening a Movie in Flash

Flash files are called documents (or movies, interchangeably) and have an .fla file extension. If you have created a movie in Flash and saved it with the name mymovie, the filename will be mymovie.fla. Files with the .fla file extension can only be opened and edited using Flash. After they are opened, you can edit and resave them.

In order for Flash movies to be viewed on computers that do not have the Flash program installed, the movies must be changed to the Flash Player (.swf) file format. Files using the .swf file format are created from Flash movies using the Publish command. Flash .swf movies can be played in a browser without the Flash program, but the Flash Player must be installed on the computer. Flash Players are pre-installed on almost all computers. For those that do not have the player, it can be downloaded free from the Adobe website, *www.adobe.com*. Because .swf files cannot be edited in the Flash program, you should preview the Flash .fla files on the Stage and test them before you publish them as .swf files. Be sure to keep the original .fla

file so that you can make changes if needed at a later date.

Previewing a Movie

After creating a new Flash movie or opening a previously saved movie, you can preview it within the workspace in several ways. When you preview a movie, you play the frames by directing the playhead to move through the Timeline, and you watch the movement on the Stage.

Control Menu Commands (and Keyboard Shortcuts)

Figure 8 shows the Control menu commands, which resemble common DVD-type options:

- Play ([Enter] (Win) or [return] (Mac)) begins playing the movie frame by frame, from the location of the playhead to the end of the movie. For example, if the playhead is on frame 5 and the last frame is frame 40, choosing the Play command will play frames 5–40 of the movie.

When a movie starts, the Play command changes to a Stop command. You can also stop the movie by pressing [Enter] (Win) or [return] (Mac).

- Rewind ([Shift][,] (Win)) or [option] ⌘ [R] (Mac) moves the playhead to frame 1.
- Step Forward One Frame (.) moves the playhead forward one frame at a time.
- Step Backward One Frame (,) moves the playhead backward one frame at a time.

You can turn on the Loop Playback setting to allow the movie to continue playing repeatedly. A check mark next to the Loop Playback command on the Control menu indicates that the feature is active. To turn off this feature, click the Loop Playback command.

Controller

You can also preview a movie using the Controller. To display the Controller, click the Controller option on the Toolbars command of the Window menu.

The decision of which controls to use (the Control menu, keyboard shortcuts, or the Controller) is a matter of personal preference.

Testing a Movie

When you play a movie within the Flash workspace, some interactive functions (such as buttons that are used to jump from one part of the movie to another) do not work. To preview the full functionality of a movie you need to play it using a Flash Player. You can use the Test Movie command on the Control menu to test the movie using a Flash Player.

You can drag the playhead along the Timeline to play frames and display their contents on the Stage. This process, called "scrubbing," provides a quick way to view parts of the movie.

FIGURE 8
Control menu commands

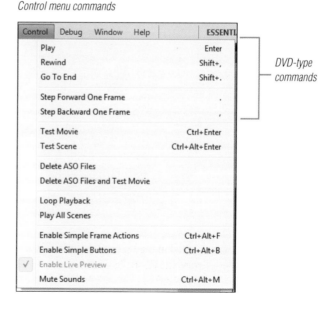

DVD-type commands

Documents, Movies, and Applications

As you work in Flash, you are creating a document. When you save your work as an .fla file, you are saving the document. This is consistent with other Adobe products such as Photoshop that use the word *document* to refer to work created in that progam. In addition, because Flash uses a movie metaphor with a Stage, timeline, frames, animations, and so on, the work done in Flash is often referred to as a movie. So, the phrase *Flash document* and the phrase *Flash movie* are synonymous. Movies can be as small and simple as a ball bouncing across the screen or as complex as a full-length interactive adventure game. Products such as games and educational software, as well as online advertisements and product demonstrations, are referred to as applications (see Figure 9). Applications usually contain multiple Flash documents or movies that are linked.

Using the Flash Player

To view a Flash movie on the web, your computer needs to have the Flash Player installed. An important feature of multimedia players, such as Flash Player, is the ability to decompress a file that has been compressed to give it a small file size that can be delivered more quickly over the Internet. In addition to Adobe, companies such as Apple (QuickTime), Microsoft (Windows Media Player), and RealNetworks (RealPlayer) create players that allow applications, developed with their and other companies' products, to be viewed on the web. The multimedia players are distributed free and can be downloaded from the company's website. The Flash Player is created by Adobe and the latest version is available at *www.adobe.com*.

FIGURE 9
Example of an application

FIGURE 10
Playhead moving across Timeline

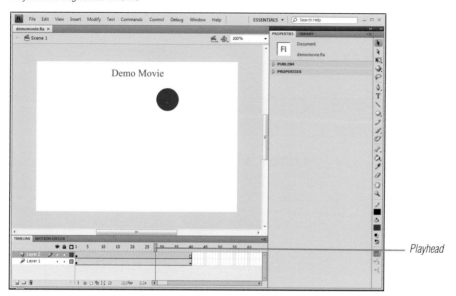

Playhead

Using options and shortcuts

There is often more than one way to complete a particular function when using Flash. For example, if you want to rewind a movie you can use the controls on the controller panel; press [Shift] + [.]; or drag the playhead to frame 1. In addition, Flash provides context menus that are relevant to the current selection. For example, if you point to a graphic and right-click (Win) or [control] click (Mac), a menu opens with graphic-related commands, such as cut and copy. Shortcut keys are also available for many of the most common commands, such as [Ctrl][Z] (Win) or ⌘ [Z] (Mac) for Undo.

Open and play a movie using the Control menu and the Controller

1. Open fl1_1.fla from the drive and folder where your Data Files are stored, then save it as **demomovie.fla**.

2. Click **View** on the menu bar, point to **Magnification**, then click **Fit in Window**.

3. Click **Control** on the menu bar, then click **Play**.

   Notice how the playhead moves across the Timeline as the blue circle moves from the left to the right, as shown in Figure 10.

4. Click **Control** on the menu bar, then click **Rewind**.

5. Press [**Enter**] (Win) or [**return**] (Mac) to play the movie, then press [**Enter**] (Win) or [**return**] (Mac) again to stop the movie before it ends.

6. Click **Window** on the menu bar, point to **Toolbars**, then click **Controller**.

7. Use all the buttons on the Controller to preview the movie, then close the Controller.

8. Point to the **playhead** on the Timeline, then click and drag the **playhead** back and forth to view the contents of the frames and view the movie.

9. Click **frame 1** on the Timeline.

10. Press the **period key** several times, then press the **comma key** several times to move the playhead one frame at a time forward and backward.

You opened a Flash movie and previewed it, using various controls.

Test a movie

1. Click **Control** on the menu bar, then click **Test Movie**.

   The Flash Player window opens, as shown in Figure 11 and the movie starts playing automatically.

2. Click **Control** on the menu bar of the Flash Player window (Win) or application menu bar (Mac), then review the available commands.

3. Click **File** on the menu bar of the Flash Player window (Win) or application menu bar (Mac), then click **Close** to close the Flash Player window.

4. Use your file management program to navigate to the drive and folder where you saved the demomovie.fla file and notice the demomovie.swf file that was created when you tested the movie in the Flash Player window.

   TIP   When you test a movie, Flash automatically creates a file that has an .swf extension in the folder where your movie is stored and then plays the movie in the Flash Player.

5. Return to the Flash program.

You tested a movie in the Flash Player window and viewed the .swf file created as a result of testing the movie.

FIGURE 11
Flash Player window

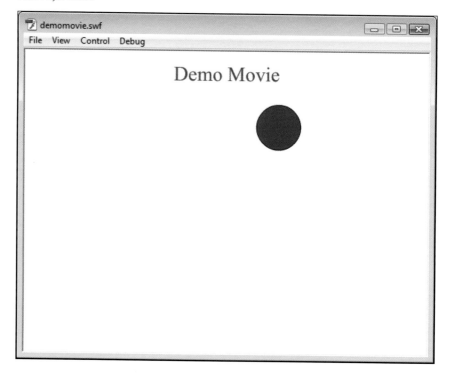

FIGURE 12
Document Properties dialog box

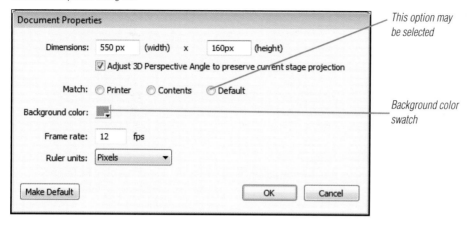

This option may
be selected

Background color
swatch

Change the Document Properties

1. Click **Modify** on the menu bar, then click **Document** to display the Document Properties dialog box.

2. Double-click the number in the **height text box**, then type **160**.

3. Click the **Background color swatch**, then click the **middle gray (#999999) color swatch** in the far-left column of the color palette.

   Note: The Color Swatch palette allows you to click a color to choose it or to enter a number that represents the color.

4. Review the remaining default values shown in Figure 12, then click **OK**.

5. Click **View** on the menu bar, point to **Magnification**, then click **Fit in Window** if it is not already selected. Your screen should resemble Figure 13.

6. Click **File** on the menu bar, then click **Save As**.

7. Navigate to the drive and folder where your Data Files are stored, type **demomovie banner** for the filename, then click **Save** (Win) or **Save As** (Mac).

8. Click **File** on the menu bar, then click **Close**.

You set the document properties including the size of the Stage and background color, then set the magnification and saved the document.

FIGURE 13
Completed changes to document properties

This value might differ

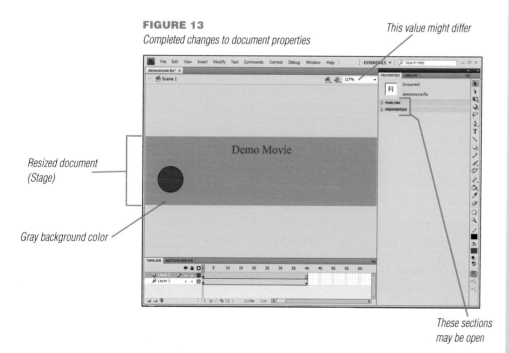

Resized document
(Stage)

Gray background color

These sections
may be open

CREATE AND SAVE
A MOVIE

What You'll Do

 In this lesson, you will create a Flash movie that will include a simple animation, you will add animation effects, and then save the movie.

Creating a Flash Movie

Flash movies are created by placing objects (graphics, text, sounds, photos, and so on) on the Stage, editing these objects (for example, changing their brightness), animating the objects, and adding interactivity with buttons and menus. You can create graphic objects in Flash using the drawing tools, or you can create them in another program, such as Adobe Fireworks, Illustrator, or Photoshop, and then import them into a Flash movie. In addition, you can acquire clip art and stock photographs and import them into a movie. When objects are placed on the Stage, they are automatically placed on a layer and in the currently selected frame of the Timeline.

Figure 14 shows a movie that has an oval object created in Flash. Notice that the playhead is on frame 1 of the movie. The object placed on the Stage appears in frame 1 and appears on the Stage when the playhead is on frame 1. The dot in frame 1

on the Timeline indicates that this frame is a keyframe. The concept of keyframes is critical to understanding how Flash works. A **keyframe** indicates that there is a change in the movie, such as the start or end of an animation, or the playing of a sound. A keyframe is automatically designated in frame 1 of every layer. In addition, you can designate any frame to be a keyframe.

The circle object in Figure 14 was created using the Oval tool. To create an oval or a rectangle, you select the desired tool and then drag the pointer over an area on the Stage. *Note:* Flash groups the Oval and Rectangle tools, along with three other drawing tools, using one button on the Tools panel. To display a menu of these tools, click and hold the rectangle (or oval) button on the Tools panel to display the menu and then click the tool you want to use. If you want to draw a perfect circle or square, press and hold [Shift] after the tool is selected, and then drag the pointer.

If you make a mistake, you can click Edit on the menu bar, and then click Undo. To make changes to an object, such as resizing or changing its color, or to animate an object, you must first select it. You can use the Selection tool to select an entire object or group of objects. You drag the Selection tool pointer around the entire object to make a **marquee**. An object that has been selected displays a dot pattern or a blue border.

Creating an Animation

Figure 15 shows another movie that has 12 frames, as specified in the Timeline. The blue background color on the Timeline indicates a motion animation that starts in frame 1 and ends in frame 12. The dotted line indicates the path the object will follow during the animation. In this case, the object will move from left to right across the Stage. The movement of the object is caused by having the object in different

places on the Stage in different frames of the movie. In this case, frame 6 will display the object midway through the animation. A basic motion animation requires two keyframes. The first keyframe sets the starting position of the object, and the second keyframe sets the ending position of the object. The number of frames between the two keyframes determines the length of the animation. For example, if the starting keyframe is frame 1 and the ending

FIGURE 15
Motion animation

FIGURE 14
Circle object in frame 1

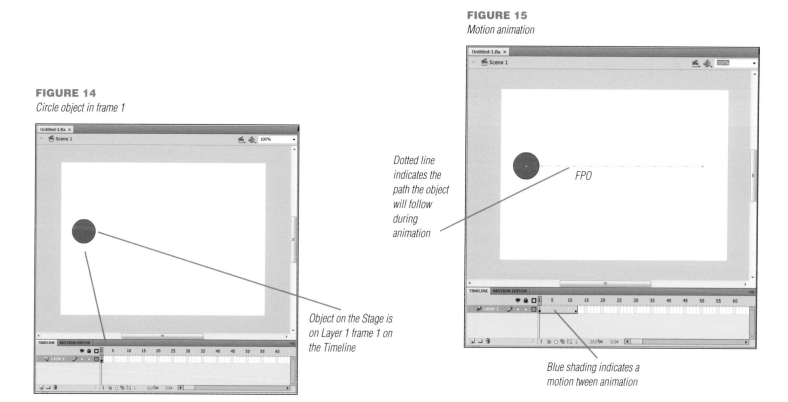

Dotted line indicates the path the object will follow during animation

FPO

Object on the Stage is on Layer 1 frame 1 on the Timeline

Blue shading indicates a motion tween animation

keyframe is frame 12, the object will be animated for 12 frames. As an object is being animated, Flash automatically fills in the frames between them, with a process called **motion tweening**.

The Motion Tween Animation Process

Having an object move around the screen is one of the most common types of animations. Flash provides a process called motion tween that makes it relatively simple to move objects. The process is to select an object on the Stage, then select the Motion Tween command from the Insert menu. If the object is not a symbol, a dialog box opens asking if you want to change the object into a symbol. Creating a symbol allows you to reuse the object for this and other movies, as well as to apply a motion tween. Only symbols can be motion tweened. The final step in the animation process is to select the ending frame for the animation and drag the object to another location on the Stage.

Two important things happen during the animation process. First, the Timeline shows the **tween span** (also called motion span), that is the number of frames in the motion tween. The tween span can be identified on the Timeline by a blue color, which in this case extends for 12 frames. A tween span is equal to one second in duration. The number of frames in a tween span varies and is determined by the number of frames per second setting. In this example, we set the number of frames per second to 12, so the number of frames in a tween for this movie is 12 frames. You can increase or decrease the length of the animation by pointing to either end of the span and dragging it to a new frame. Second, a dotted line, as shown in Figure 16, called the **motion path**, represents the path

FIGURE 16
Line showing the motion path

Blue frame (also called the bounding box) indicates object is a symbol

Motion path line

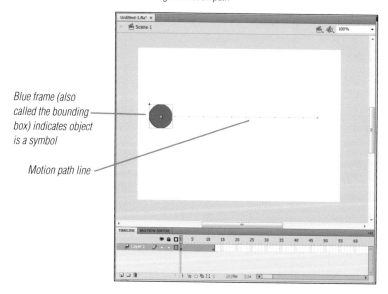

the object takes from the beginning frame to the ending frame. This path can be reshaped to cause the object to travel in a non-linear way. Reshaping a path can be done by using the Selection tool on the Tools panel.

Motion Presets

Flash provides several preconfigured motion tweens that you can apply to an object on the Stage. These allow you to bounce an object across the Stage, fly-in an object from off the Stage, cause an object to pulsate and to spiral in place, as well as many other types of object animations. Figure 17 shows the Motion Presets panel where you choose a preset and apply it to an object. You can preview each preset before applying it and you can easily change to a different preset, if desired.

Adding Effects to an Object

In addition to animating the location of an object (or objects), you can also animate an object's appearance. Objects have proper-ties such as color, brightness, and size. You can alter an object's properties as it is being animated using the motion tween process. For example, you could give the appearance of the object fading in by changing its transparency (alpha setting) or having it grow larger by altering its size over the course of the animation. Another useful effect is applying filters, such as drop shadows or bevels. All of these changes can be made using the Properties panel after selecting the object.

FIGURE 17
Motion Presets panel

Create objects using drawing tools

1. Click **File** on the menu bar, then click **New**.

2. Click **OK** in the New Document window to choose Flash File (ActionScript 3.0) as the new document to create, then save the movie as **tween**.

3. Click **View** on the menu bar, point to **Magnification**, then click **100%**.

4. Click and hold the **Rectangle tool** ▢ (or the Oval tool if it is displayed) on the Tools panel to display the list of tools, as shown in Figure 18, then click the **Oval tool** ○.

5. Verify that the Object Drawing option ▢ in the Options area of the Tools panel is deselected, as shown in Figure 18.

6. Click the **Fill Color tool color swatch** on the Tools panel, then, if necessary, click the **red color swatch** in the left column of the color palette.

7. Click the **Stroke Color tool color swatch** on the Tools panel, then, if necessary, click the **black color swatch** in the left column of the color palette.

8. Press and hold **[Shift]**, drag the **pointer** on the left side of the Stage to draw the circle, as shown in Figure 19, then release the mouse button.

    Pressing and holding [Shift] creates a circle.

9. Click the **Selection tool** on the Tools panel, then drag a **marquee** around the object to select it, as shown in Figure 20, then release the mouse button

    The object appears covered with a dot pattern.

You created an object using the Oval tool and then selected the object using the Selection tool.

FIGURE 18
Drawing tools menu

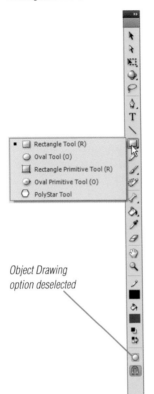

Object Drawing
option deselected

FIGURE 19
Drawing a circle

FIGURE 20
Creating a marquee selection

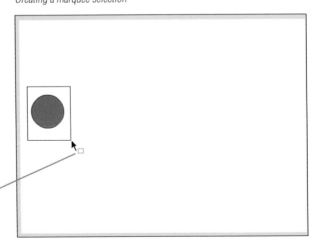

Use the Selection tool to
draw a marquee, which
selects the entire object

Getting Started with Adobe Flash CS4

FIGURE 21
The circle on the right side of the Stage

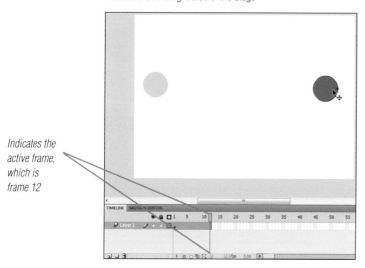

Indicates the
active frame,
which is
frame 12

FIGURE 22
Pointing to the end of the tween span

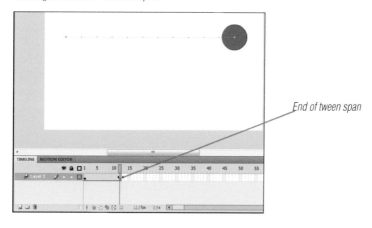

End of tween span

Create a motion tween animation

1. Click **Insert** on the menu bar, then click **Motion Tween**, which opens the Convert selection to symbol for tween dialog box.

2. Click **OK**.

   A blue border surrounds the object indicating that the object is selected. Notice in this case that the playhead automatically moved to frame 12, the last frame in the tween span.

3. Click and then drag the **circle** to the right side of the Stage, as shown in Figure 21.

4. Press **[Enter]**(Win) or **[return]**(Mac) to play the movie.

   The playhead moves through frames 1–12 on the Timeline, and the circle moves across the Stage.

5. Click **frame 6** on Layer 1 on the Timeline.

   Notice that the object is halfway across the screen. This is the result of the tweening process in which the frames between 1 and 12 are filled in with the object in the correct location for each frame.

6. Verify the Selection tool is selected, point to the end of the tween span until the pointer changes to a double-headed arrow ↔, as shown in Figure 22.

7. Click and drag the **tween span** to frame 48.

8. Press **[Enter]**(Win) or **[return]**(Mac) to play the movie.

   Notice it now takes longer (4 seconds, not 1 second) to complete the animation. Also notice that a diamond symbol appears in

   (continued)

frame 48 indicating that a keyframe has been placed in that frame. The diamond symbol indicates a change in the animation. In this case it indicates the end of the animation.

9. Click **frame 24** and notice that the object is still halfway across the screen.

10. Click **File** on the menu bar, then click **Save**.

You created a motion tween animation and changed the length of the tween span.

Reshaping the Motion Path

1. Click **File** on the menu bar, click **Save As**, then save the document with the filename **tween-effects.fla**.

2. Verify the Selection tool ▶ is selected.

3. Click **frame 1** to select it.

   Note: When you see the direction to click a frame, click the frame on the layer not the number on the Timeline.

4. Point to just below the middle of the path until the pointer changes to a pointer with an arc ↳ , as shown in Figure 23.

5. Click and drag the **path** to reshape the path, as shown in Figure 24.

6. Play the movie.

   Note: When you see the direction to play the movie, press [Enter] (Win) or [return] (Mac).

7. Test the movie.

   Note: When you see the direction to test the movie, click Control on the menu bar, then click Test Movie.

8. View the movie, then close the Flash Player window.

(continued)

FIGURE 23
Using the Selection tool to reshape a motion path

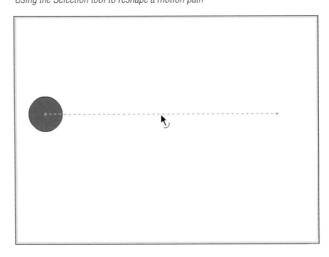

FIGURE 24
Reshaping the motion path

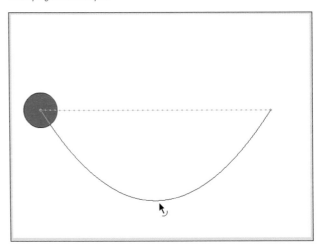

Getting Started with Adobe Flash CS4

FIGURE 25

The Properties panel displayed

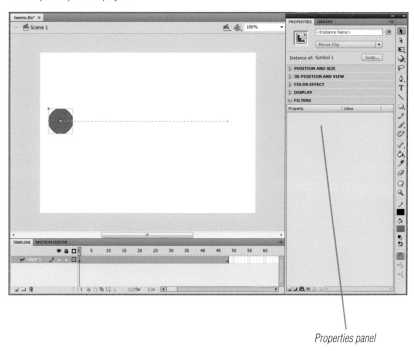

Properties panel

9. Click **Edit** on the menu bar, then click **Undo Reshape**.

You used the Selection tool to reshape a motion path and the Undo command to undo the reshape.

Changing the transparency of an object

1. Click the **Properties panel tab** to display the Properties panel, as shown in Figure 25.

    Note: If the Properties panel is not open, click Window on the menu bar, then click Properties.

2. Verify frame 1 is selected, then click the **object** on the Stage to select it.

    Note: To verify the object is selected, review the available settings in the Properties panel. Make sure POSITION AND SIZE is one of the options.

3. Click **COLOR EFFECT** on the Properties panel, click the **Style list arrow**, then click **Alpha**.

4. Drag the **Alpha slider** to **0**.

    This causes the object to become transparent.

5. Click **frame 48** on the layer to select it.

6. Click **the middle of the bounding box** on the Stage to select the object and check that the object's properties are displayed in the Properties panel.

    Note: To verify the object is selected, review the available settings in the Properties panel. Make sure POSITION AND SIZE is one of the options.

    (continued)

7. Drag the **Alpha slider** 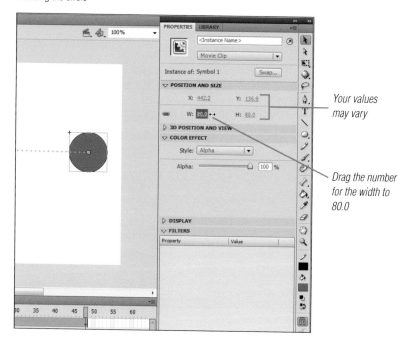 to **100**.

8. Play the movie.

9. Test the movie.

10. View the movie, then close the Flash Player window.

You used the Color Effect option on the Properties panel to change the transparency of an object.

Resize an object

1. Click **frame 1** select it.

2. Click the **object** to select it.

3. Click **POSITION AND SIZE** on the Properties panel if this section is not already open.

4. Review the width (W) and height (H) of the object.

   The width and height are the dimensions of the bounding box around the circle.

5. Click **frame 48** to select it, then click the **object** to select it.

6. Point to the number for the width and when the pointer changes into a double-headed arrow 🔡 , drag the 🔡 **pointer** right to increase the width so that the circle grows in size to 80, as shown in Figure 26.

   Hint: You can also double-click a value in the Properties panel and type the new value.

7. Play the movie.

8. Test the movie.

9. View the movie, then close the Flash Player window.

(continued)

FIGURE 26
Resizing the circle

Your values
may vary

Drag the number
for the width to
80.0

FIGURE 27
The Add filter icon

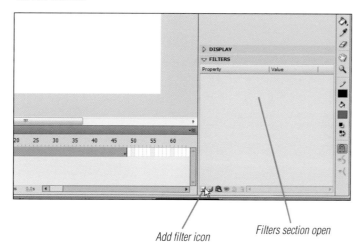

Add filter icon

Filters section open

10. Click **frame 1** to select it, then click the **object** to select it.

11. Drag the **Alpha slider** ⌂ to **100**.

You used the Position and Size option on the Properties panel to change the size of an object.

Add a filter to an object

1. Verify the object is selected by viewing the Properties panel and verifying the object's properties are displayed.

2. Click **FILTERS** on the Properties panel to display the Filters section if it is not already displayed.

3. Click the **Add filter icon** ⬛ at the bottom of the Filters section, as shown in Figure 27.

4. Click **Drop Shadow**, point to the number for the angle, when the pointer changes to a double-headed arrow 🖑, drag the 🖑 **pointer** right to change the number of degrees to **100**.

5. Play the movie.

6. Click **frame 1** to select it, then click the **object** to select it.

7. Click the **Delete Filter icon** ⬛ at the bottom of the Filters section to remove the drop shadow filter.

8. Click the **Add filter icon** ⬛ at the bottom of the panel.

(continued)

9. Click **Bevel**, test the movie, then close the Flash Player window.

10. Point to the number for the Filter distance and when the pointer changes into a double-headed arrow ⟷, drag the ⟷ **pointer** right to increase the setting to **35**.

You used the Filters option in the Properties panel to add and delete filters.

Add a motion preset

1. Verify the playhead is on frame 1 and the object is selected.

2. Click **Window** on the menu bar, then click **Motion Presets**.

3. Drag the **Motion Presets panel** so that it does not obscure the Stage.

4. Click the **list arrow** for the Default Presets, then click **bounce-smoosh** and watch the animation in the preview widow, as shown in Figure 28.

5. Click **Apply**.

   A dialog box opens asking if you want to replace the current motion object with the new selection. You can only apply one motion tween or motion preset to an object at any one time.

6. Click **Yes**.

   The bevel filter is deleted and a new path is displayed.

7. Play the movie, then test the movie.

   Notice the object disappears from the Stage.

   (continued)

FIGURE 28
The Motion Presets panel

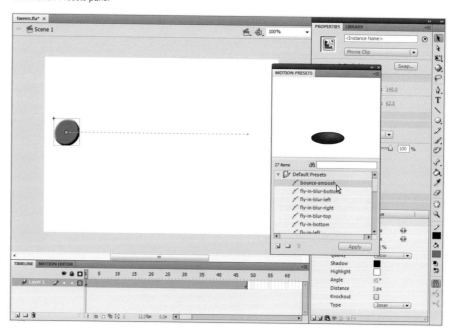

FIGURE 29

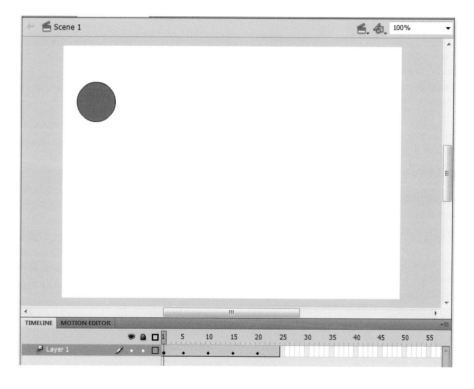

8. Close the Flash Player window.

9. Scroll as needed to see the object, click the **object**, hold **[Shift]**, then click the **path** to select both of them.

10. Press the **up arrow key** [↑] to move the object and the path toward the top of the Stage.

11. Play the movie.

12. Scroll the list of presets, click **pulse**, click **Apply**, then click **Yes**.

13. Play the movie.

    Notice the Timeline has four diamond symbols, as shown in Figure 29. Each one is a keyframe and indicates that there is a change in the motion tween. In this case the change comes each time the ball is resized.

14. Click **frame 1** to select it, then drag the **playhead** from frame 1 to the last frame and notice the change that occurs at each keyframe.

15. Close the Motion Presets panel.

16. Save and close the movie.

You applied motion presets to an object and viewed how keyframes identify changes in the motion tween.

WORK WITH
THE TIMELINE

What You'll Do

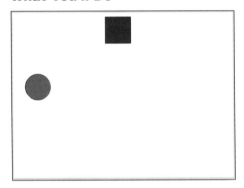

▶ *In this lesson, you will add another layer, allowing you to create an additional animation, and you will use the Timeline to help organize your movie.*

Understanding the Timeline

The Timeline organizes and controls a movie's contents over time. By learning how to read the information provided on the Timeline, you can determine and change what will be happening in a movie, frame by frame. You can determine which objects are animated, what types of animations are being used, when the various objects will appear in a movie, which objects will appear on top of others, and how fast the movie will play. Features of the Timeline are shown in Figure 30 and explained in this lesson.

Using Layers

Each new Flash movie contains one layer, named Layer 1. **Layers** are like transparent sheets of acetate that are stacked on top of each other. This is shown in Figure 31, which also shows how the stacked objects appear on the Stage. Each layer can contain one or more objects. You can add layers using the Layer command on the Insert menu or by clicking the Insert Layer icon on the Timeline. Placing objects on different layers and locking the layers helps

avoid accidentally making changes to one object while editing another.

When you add a new layer, Flash stacks it on top of the other layer(s) in the Timeline. The stacking order of the layers in the Timeline is important because objects on the Stage appear in the same stacking order. For example, if you have two overlapping objects, and the top layer has a drawing of a tree and the bottom layer has a drawing of a house, the tree appears as though it is in front of the house. You can change the stacking order of layers simply by dragging them up or down in the list of layers. You can name layers, hide them so their contents do not appear on the Stage, and lock them so that they cannot be edited.

Using frames

The Timeline is made up of individual segments called **frames**. The content of each layer appears as the playhead moves over the frames while the movie plays so any object in frame 1, no matter which layer it is on, appears on the Stage whenever frame 1 is played. Frames are numbered in increments of five for easy reference, while symbols and colors are used to indicate the type of frame (for example, keyframe (symbol) or motion animation (color)). The upper-right corner of the Timeline contains a Frame View icon. Clicking this icon displays a menu that provides different views of the Timeline, showing more frames or showing a preview (thumbnails) of the objects on a layer, for example. The status bar at the bottom of the Timeline indicates the current frame (the frame that the playhead is currently on), the frame rate (frames per second, also called fps), and the elapsed time from frame 1 to the current frame. Frames per second is the unit of measure for movies.

Using the Playhead

The **playhead** indicates which frame is playing. You can manually move the playhead by dragging it left or right. This makes it easier to locate a frame that you may want to edit. Dragging the playhead also allows you to do a quick check of the movie without having to play it.

Understanding Scenes

When you create a movie, the phrase Scene 1 appears above the Stage. You can add scenes to a movie at any time. Scenes are a way to organize long movies. For example, a movie created for a website could be divided into several scenes: an introduction, a home page,

and content pages. Each scene has its own Timeline. You can insert new scenes by using the Insert menu. Scenes can be given descriptive names, which will help you find them easily if you need to edit a particular scene. The number of scenes is limited only by the computer's memory. There are some drawbacks to using scenes, including potentially larger file sizes and longer download times for the viewer.

FIGURE 30
Elements of the Timeline

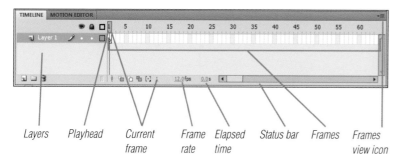

Layers   Playhead   Current   Frame   Elapsed   Status bar   Frames   Frames
                       frame   rate   time   view icon

FIGURE 31
The concept of layers

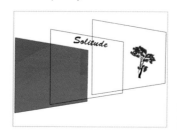

Working with the Timeline

Figure 32 shows the Timeline of a movie created in Lesson 3 with a second object, a square at the top of the Stage. By studying the Timeline, you can learn several things about the square object and this movie. First, the second object (in this example, the square) is placed on its own layer, Layer 2. Second, the layer has a motion animation (indicated by the blue background in the frames and the motion path on the Stage).

Third, the animation runs from frame 1 to frame 48. Fourth, if the objects intersect during the animation, the square will be on top of the circle, because the layer it is placed on (Layer 2) is above the layer that the circle is placed on (Layer 1). Fifth, the frame rate is set to 12, which means that the movie will play 12 frames per second. Sixth, the playhead is at frame 1, which causes the contents of frame 1 for both layers to appear on the Stage.

QUICKTIP

You can adjust the height of the Timeline by positioning the pointer over the top edge of the Timeline title bar until a double-headed pointer appears, and, then dragging the border up or down.

FIGURE 32

The Timeline of a movie with a second object

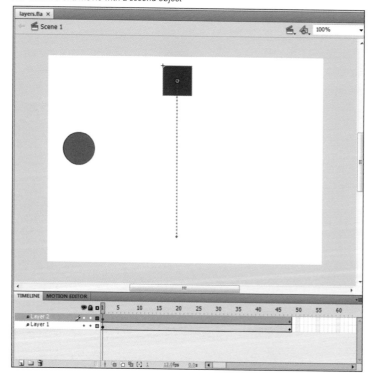

FIGURE 33

Drawing a square

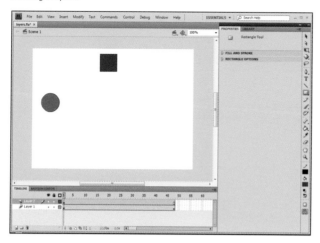

FIGURE 34

Positioning the square at the bottom of the Stage

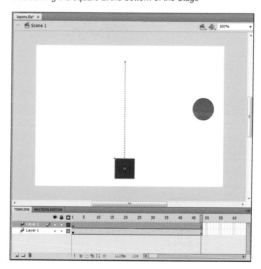

Add a layer

1. Open tween.fla and save it as **layers.fla**.
2. Click **frame 1** on Layer 1.
3. Click **Insert** on the menu bar, point to **Timeline**, then click **Layer**.

   A new layer—Layer 2—appears at the top of the Timeline.

You added a layer to the Timeline.

Create a second animation

1. Click **frame 1** on Layer 2.
2. Select the **Rectangle tool** on the Tools panel.
3. Click the **Fill Color tool color swatch** on the Tools panel, then click the **blue color swatch** in the left column of the color palette.
4. Press and hold [**Shift**], then draw a square resembling the dimensions and position of the square, as shown in Figure 33.
5. Click the **Selection tool** on the Tools panel, then drag a **marquee** around the square to select the object.
6. Click **Insert** on the menu bar, click **Motion Tween**, then click **OK** in the Convert selection to symbol for tween dialog box.
7. Click **frame 48** on Layer 2, then drag the **square** to the bottom of the Stage, as shown in Figure 34.
8. Play the movie.

   The square appears on top if the two objects intersect.

You drew an object and used it to create a second animation.

Work with layers and view Timeline features

1. Click **Layer 2** on the Timeline, then drag it below Layer 1, as shown in Figure 35.

   Layer 2 is now the bottom layer.

2. Play the movie and notice how the square appears beneath the circle if the objects intersect.

3. Click **Layer 2** on the Timeline, then drag it above Layer 1.

4. Play the movie and notice how the square appears above the circle if they intersect.

5. Click the **Frame View icon** ▼≡ on the right corner of the Timeline title bar, as shown in Figure 36, to display the menu.

6. Click **Tiny** to display more frames.

   Notice how more frames appear on the Timeline, but each frame is smaller.

7. Click the **Frame View icon** ▼≡ , then click **Short**.

8. Click the **Frame View icon** ▼≡ , click **Preview**, then note the object thumbnails that appear on the Timeline.

9. Click the **Frame View icon** ▼≡ , then click **Normal**.

You changed the order of the layers, the display of frames, and the way the Timeline is viewed.

FIGURE 35
Changing the stacking order of layers

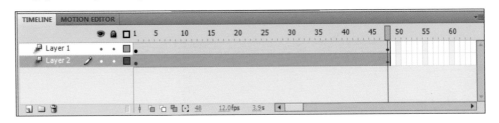

FIGURE 36
Changing the view of the Timeline

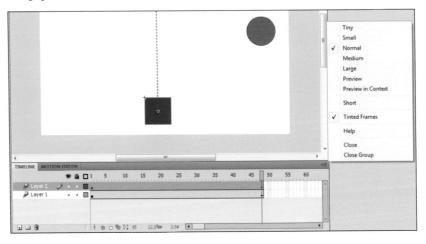

Getting Started with Adobe Flash CS4

FIGURE 37
Changing the frame rate

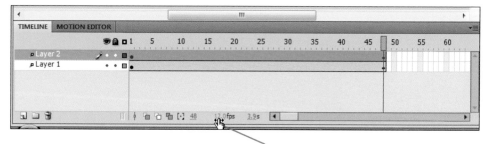

Pointer changes to double-headed arrow

FIGURE 38
Displaying the Properties option

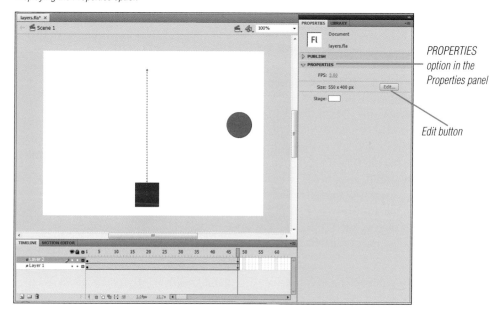

PROPERTIES option in the Properties panel

Edit button

Modify the frame rate

1. Point to the **Frame Rate (fps)** on the bottom of the Timeline so the pointer changes to a double-headed arrow 🐾 in Figure 37.

2. Drag the 🐾 **pointer** to change the frame rate to 3.

   TIP Alternately, you can double-click the frame rate number, then type a new number.

3. Play the movie and notice that the speed of the movie changes.

4. Click a blank area of the Stage, then verify the Properties panel is the active panel. If not, click **Window, Properties**.

5. If the PROPERTIES options are not displayed, click **PROPERTIES** on the Properties panel to display the options, as shown in Figure 38.

   The Properties panel provides information about the Stage, including size and background color.

6. Click the **Edit button** in the PROPERTIES section of the Properties panel to display the Document Properties dialog box.

   TIP Another way to open the Document Properties dialog box is using the Modify menu.

7. Change the frame rate to **18**, click **OK**, then play the movie.

8. Change the frame rate to **12** using the Properties panel.

9. Click **frame 20** on the Timeline and notice the position of the objects on the Stage.

10. Drag the **playhead** left and right to display specific frames.

11. Save your work.

You changed the frame rate of the movie and used the playhead to display the contents of frames.

DISTRIBUTE AN ADOBE
FLASH MOVIE

What You'll Do

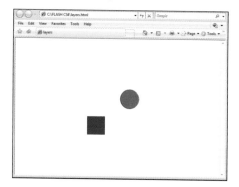

 In this lesson, you will prepare a movie for distribution in various formats.

Distributing Movies

When you develop Flash movies, the program saves them in a file format (.fla) that only users who have the Flash program installed on their computers can view. Usually, Flash movies are viewed on the web as part of a website or directly from a viewer's computer using the Flash Player. Flash files (.fla) cannot be viewed on the web using a web browser. They must be converted into a Flash Player file (.swf) so that the web browser knows the type of file to play (.swf) and the program needed to play the file (Flash Player). In addition, the HTML code needs to be created that instructs the web browser to play the swf file. Fortunately, Flash generates both the swf and HTML files when you use the publish feature of Flash.

The process for publishing a Flash movie is to create and save a movie and then click the Publish command on the File menu. You can specify various settings, such as dimensions for the window in which the movie plays in the browser, before publishing the movie. Publishing a movie creates two files: an HTML file and a Flash Player (.swf) file. Both the HTML and swf files retain the same name as the Flash movie file, but with different file extensions:

- .html—the HTML document
- .swf—the Flash Player file

For example, publishing a movie named layers.fla generates two files–layers.html and layers.swf. The HTML document contains the code that the browser interprets to display the movie on the web. The code also specifies which Flash Player movie the browser should play. Sample HTML code referencing a Flash Player movie is shown in Figure 39. If you are familiar with HTML code, you will recognize this as a complete HTML document. Even if you are not familiar with HTML code, you might recognize the code, as seen in Figure 39, that the browser uses to display the Flash movie. For example, the movie source is set to layers.swf; the background color is set to white (#ffffff is the code for white), and the display dimensions (determined by the size of the Stage) are set to 550 × 400.

Flash provides several other ways to distribute your movies that may or may not involve delivery on the web. You can create a stand-alone movie called a **projector**. Projector files, such as Windows .exe files, maintain the movie's interactivity. Alternately, you can create self-running movies, such as QuickTime .mov files, that are not interactive.

You can play projector and non-interactive files directly from a computer, or you can incorporate them into an application, such as a game, that is downloaded or delivered on a CD or DVD. In addition, Flash provides features for creating movies specifically for mobile devices, such as cell phones.

FIGURE 39
Sample HTML code

```
</head>
<body bgcolor="#ffffff">
<!--url's used in the movie-->
<!--text used in the movie-->
<!-- saved from url=(0013)about:internet -->
<script language="JavaScript" type="text/javascript">
        AC_FL_RunContent(
            'codebase',
'http://download.macromedia.com/pub/shockwave/cabs/flash/swflash.cab#version=10,0,0,0',
            'width', '550',
            'height', '400',
            'src', 'layers',
            'quality', 'high',
            'pluginspage', 'http://www.adobe.com/go/getflashplayer',
            'align', 'middle',
            'play', 'true',
            'loop', 'true',
            'scale', 'showall',
            'wmode', 'window',
            'devicefont', 'false',
            'id', 'layers',
            'bgcolor', '#ffffff',
            'name', 'layers',
            'menu', 'true',
            'allowFullScreen', 'false',
            'allowScriptAccess','sameDomain',
            'movie', 'layers',
            'salign', ''
            ); //end AC code
</script>
<noscript>
        <object classid="clsid:d27cdb6e-ae6d-11cf-96b8-444553540000"
codebase="http://download.macromedia.com/pub/shockwave/cabs/flash/swflash.cab#version=10,0,0,0" width="550"
height="400" id="layers" align="middle">
        <param name="allowScriptAccess" value="sameDomain" />
        <param name="allowFullScreen" value="false" />
        <param name="movie" value="layers.swf" /><param name="quality" value="high" /><param name="bgcolor"
value="#ffffff" />        <embed src="layers.swf" quality="high" bgcolor="#ffffff" width="550" height="400"
name="layers" align="middle" allowScriptAccess="sameDomain" allowFullScreen="false" type="application/x-
shockwave-flash" pluginspage="http://www.adobe.com/go/getflashplayer" />
        </object>
</noscript>
</body>
</html>
```

Publish a movie for distribution on the web

1. Verify layers.fla is open.

2. Click **File** on the menu bar, then click **Publish**.

   The files layers.html and layers.swf are automatically generated and saved in the same folder as the Flash document.

3. Use your file management program to navigate to the drive and folder where you save your work.

4. Notice the three files that begin with "layers," as shown in Figure 40.

   Layers.fla, the Flash movie; layers.html, the HTML document; layers.swf, the Flash Player file.

5. Double-click **layers.html** to play the movie in the browser.

   Note: Depending on your browser, browser settings and version, you may need to complete additional steps to view the layers.html document.

   | TIP   Click the browser button on the taskbar if the movie does not open automatically in your browser.

   Notice the animation takes up only a portion of the browser window, as shown in Figure 41. This is because the Stage size is set to 550 x 440, which is smaller than the browser window.

6. Close the browser.

You used the Publish command to create an HTML document (.html) and a Flash Player file (.swf), then you displayed the HTML document in a web browser.

FIGURE 40
The three layers files after publishing the movie

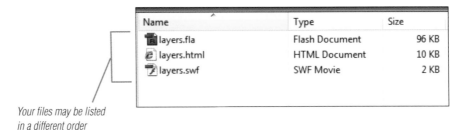

Your files may be listed in a different order

FIGURE 41
The animation played in a browser window

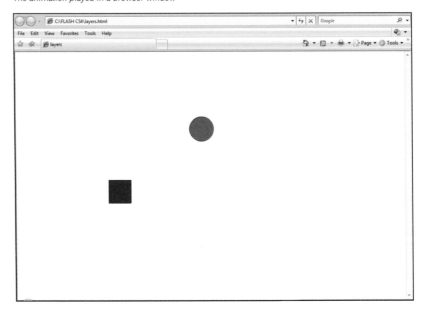

Getting Started with Adobe Flash CS4

FIGURE 42

Publish Settings dialog box with the Formats tab selected

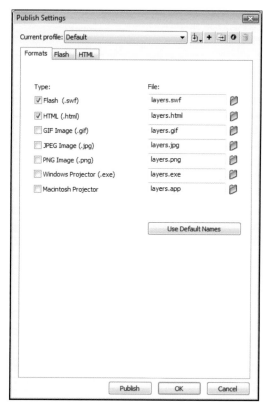

1. Return to Flash, click **File** on the menu bar, then click **Publish Settings** to open the Publish Settings dialog box.

2. Verify the Formats tab is selected, as shown in Figure 42.

    Notice the various file formats (and their file names) that can be generated automatically when you publish a Flash document.

3. Click the **Windows Projector (.exe)** (Win) or **Macintosh Projector** (Mac) **check box**.

4. Click **Publish**, then click **OK**.

5. Use your file management program to navigate to the drive and folder where you save your work.

6. Double-click **layers.exe** (Win), or **layers** (Mac), then notice that the application plays in the Flash Player window.

    In this case, the Flash Player window is sized to the dimensions of the Stage.

    Note: You must have the Flash Player installed to view the movie.

7. Close the Flash Player window.

8. Close layers.fla in Flash, saving your changes if prompted.

You created and displayed a stand-alone projector file.

PLAN AN APPLICATION OR A
WEBSITE

What You'll Do

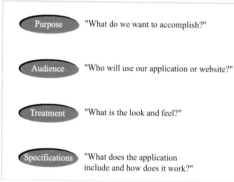

Purpose	"What do we want to accomplish?"
Audience	"Who will use our application or website?"
Treatment	"What is the look and feel?"
Specifications	"What does the application include and how does it work?"

 In this lesson, you will learn how to plan a Flash application. You will also learn about the guidelines for screen design and the interactive design of web pages.

Planning an Application or a Website

Flash can be used to develop animations that are part of a product, such as a game or educational tutorial, and delivered via the internet, a CD, a DVD, or a mobile device. You can use Flash to create enhancements to web pages, such as animated logos and interactive navigation buttons. You can also use Flash to create entire websites. No matter what the application, the first step is planning. Often, the temptation is to jump right into the program and start developing movies. The problem is that this invariably results in a more time-consuming process at best; and wasted effort, resources, and money at worst. The larger and more complex the project is, the more critical the planning process becomes. Planning an application or an entire website should involve the following steps:

Step 1: Stating the Purpose (Goals). "What, specifically, do we want to accomplish?"

Determining the goals is a critical step in planning because goals guide the development process, keep the team members on track, and provide a way to evaluate the application or website, both during and after its development.

Step 2: Identifying the Target Audience. "Who will use our application or website?"

Understanding the potential viewers helps in developing an application or a website that can address their needs. For example, children respond to exploration and surprise, so having a dog wag its tail when the mouse pointer rolls over it might appeal to this audience.

Step 3: Determining the Treatment. "What is the look and feel?"

The treatment is how the application or website will be presented to the user, including the tone, approach, and emphasis.

Tone. Will the application or website be humorous, serious, light, heavy, formal, or informal? The tone of a site can often be used to make a statement—projecting a progressive, high-tech, well-funded corporate image, for instance.

Approach. How much direction will be provided to the user? An interactive game might focus on exploration such as when the user points to an object on the screen and the object becomes animated. While an informational website might provide lots of direction and include lists of options in the form of drop-down menus.

Emphasis. How much emphasis will be placed on the various multimedia elements? For example, a company may want to develop an informational application or website that shows the features of its new product line, including video demonstrations and sound narrations of how each product works. The budget might not allow for the expense of creating the videos, so the emphasis would shift to still pictures with text descriptions.

Step 4: Developing the Specifications and Storyboard. "What precisely does the application or website include and how does it work?"

The specifications state what will be included in each screen, including the arrangement of each element and the functionality of each object (for example, what happens when you click the button labeled Skip Intro). Specifications should include the following:

Playback System. The choice of what configuration to target for playback is critical, especially Internet connection speed, browser versions, screen resolution, screen size especially when targeting mobile devices, and plug-ins.

Elements to Include. The specifications should include details about the various elements that are to be included in the site. What are the dimensions for the animations, and what is the frame rate? What are the sizes of the various objects such as photos, buttons, and so on? What fonts, font sizes, and font formatting will be used? Should video or sound be included?

Functionality. The specifications should include the way the program reacts to an action by the user, such as a mouse click. For example, clicking a door (object) might cause a doorbell to ring (sound), the door

Rich media content and accessibility

Flash provides the tools that allow you to create compelling applications and websites by incorporating rich media content, such as animations, sound, and video. Generally, incorporating rich media enhances the user's experience. However, accessibility becomes an issue for those persons who have visual, hearing, or mobility impairments, or have a cognitive disability. Designers need to utilize techniques that help ensure accessibility, such as providing consistency in navigation and layout, labeling graphics, captioning audio content throughout the applications and website, and providing keyboard access.

to open (an animation), an "exit the program" message to appear (text), or an entirely new screen to be displayed.

The **user interface** involves designing the appearance of objects (how each object is arranged on the screen) and the interactivity (how the user navigates through the site).

A **flowchart** is a visual representation of how the contents in an application or a website are organized and how various screens are linked. It provides a guide for the developer and helps to identify problems with the navigation scheme before work begins. Figure 43 shows a simple flowchart illustrating the site organization and links.

A **storyboard** shows the layout of the various screens. It describes the contents and illustrates how text, graphics, animation, and other screen elements will be positioned. It also indicates the navigation process, such as menus and buttons. Figure 44 shows a storyboard. The exact content (such as a specific photo) does not have to be decided, but it is important to show where text, graphics, photos, buttons, and other elements, will be placed. Thus, the storyboard includes placeholders for the various elements.

Using Screen Design Guidelines

The following screen design guidelines are used by application and web developers.

The implementation of these guidelines is affected by the goals of the application or website, the intended audience, and the content.

Balance in screen design refers to the distribution of optical weight in the layout. Optical weight is the ability of an object to attract the viewer's eye, as determined by the object's size, shape, color, and so on. Figure 44 shows a fairly well-balanced layout, especially if the logo has as much optical weight as the text description. In general, a balanced design is more appealing to a viewer. However, for a game application or entertainment site, a balanced layout may not be desired.

FIGURE 43
Sample Flowchart

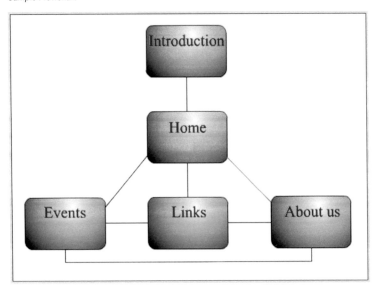

FIGURE 44
Sample Storyboard

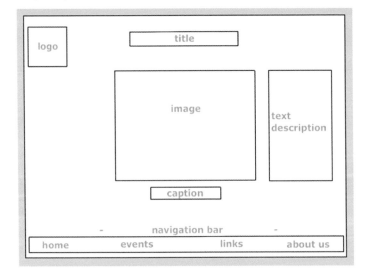

Unity helps the screen objects reinforce each other. **Intra-screen** unity has to do with how the various screen objects relate and how they all fit in. For example, a children's game might only use cartoon characterizations of animals for all the objects—including navigation buttons and sound control buttons, as well as the on-screen characters. **Inter-screen** unity refers to the design that viewers encounter as they navigate from one screen to another, and it provides consistency throughout the application. For example, all navigation buttons are located in the same place on each screen.

Movement refers to the way the viewer's eyes move through the objects on the screen. Different types of objects and various animation techniques can be used to draw the viewer to a location on the screen.

For example, a photo of a waterfall may cause the viewer's eyes to follow the flow of the water down, especially if the waterfall is animated. The designer could then place an object, such as a logo or link, below the waterfall.

Using Interactive Design Guidelines

In addition to screen design guidelines, interactive guidelines determine the interactivity of the application. The following guidelines are not absolute rules but are affected by the goals of the application, the intended audience, and the content:

- Make it simple, easy to understand, and easy to use so that viewers do not have to spend time learning what the application is about and what they need to do.

- Build in consistency in the navigation scheme. Help the users know where they are in the application and help them avoid getting lost.
- Provide feedback. Users need to know when an action, such as clicking a button, has been completed. Changing its color or shape, or adding a sound can indicate this.
- Give the user control. Allow the user to skip long introductions; provide controls for starting, stopping, and rewinding animations, video, and audio; and provide controls for adjusting audio.

Project management

Developing websites or any extensive application, such as a game, involves project management. A project plan needs to be developed that provides the project scope and identifies the milestones, including analyzing, designing, building, testing, and launching. Personnel and resource needs are identified, budgets built, tasks assigned, and schedules developed. Successful projects are a team effort relying on the close collaboration of designers, developers, project managers, graphic artists, programmers, testers, and others. Adobe provides various product suites, such as their Creative Suite 4 (CS4) Web Collection series, that include programs such as Flash, Dreamweaver, Fireworks, Photoshop, and Illustrator. These are the primary tools needed to develop interactive applications and websites. These programs are designed for easy integration. So, a graphic artist can use Photoshop to develop an image that can easily be imported into Flash and used by an animator. In addition, other tools in the suites, such as Adobe Bridge and Adobe Version Cue, help ensure efficient workflow when working in a team environment.

The Flash Workflow Process

After the planning process, you are ready to start work on the Flash documents. The following steps can be used as guidelines in a general workflow process suggested by Adobe.

Step 1: Create and/or acquire the elements to be used in the application. The elements include text, photos, drawings, video, and audio. The elements become the raw material for the graphics, animations, menus, buttons, and content that populate the application and provide the interactivity. You can use the various Flash drawing and text tools to create your own images and text content; or, you can use another program, such as Adobe Photoshop, to develop the elements, and then import them into Flash. Alternately, you can acquire stock clip art and photographs. You can produce video and audio content in-house and import it into Flash or you can acquire these elements from a third party.

Step 2: Arrange the elements and create the animations. Arrange the elements (objects) on the Stage and on the Timeline to define when and how they appear in your application. Once the elements are available, you can create the various animations called for in the specifications.

Step 3: Apply special effects. Flash provides innumerable special effects that can be applied to the various media elements and animations. These include graphic and text filters, such as drop shadows, blurs, glows, and bevels. In addition, there are effects for sounds and animations such as fade-ins and fade-outs, acceleration and deceleration, and morphing.

Step 4: Create the interactivity. Flash provides a scripting feature, ActionScript, which allows you to develop programming code to control how the media elements behave, including how various objects respond to user interactions, such as clicking buttons and rolling over images.

Step 5: Test and publish the application. Testing should be done throughout the development process, including using the Test Movie feature in the Control menu to test the movie using the Flash Player and to publish the movie in order to test it in a browser.

Using the Flash Help feature

Flash provides a comprehensive Help feature that can be very useful when first learning the program. You access the Help feature from the Help menu. The Help feature is organized by categories, including Using Flash CS4 Professional, which have several topics such as Workspace and Managing documents. In addition, the Help feature has a Help Search feature. You use the Help Search feature to search for topics using keywords, such as Timeline. Searching by keywords accesses the Flash Community Help feature, which displays links to content relevant to the search terms. Other resources not affiliated with Adobe are available through the web. You may find some by searching the web for Flash resources.

FIGURE 45
The Flash Help categories

FIGURE 46
The Flash Help Search feature

Search term

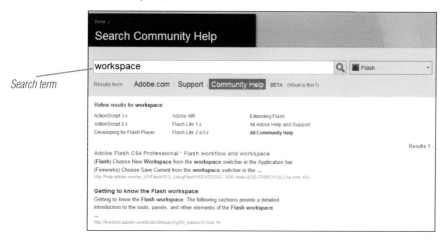

Use Flash Help

1. Start a new Flash document.

2. Click **Help** on the menu bar, then click **Flash Help**.

   Note: If you see a page not found message, be sure you are connected to the Internet.

3. Click the **Expand button** ⊞ next to Workspace to expand the category, as shown in Figure 45.

4. Click **The Timeline**, then click **About the Timeline**.

5. Read through the text in About the Timeline.

6. Scroll to display the top of the Help window.

7. Click in the **Search text box**, then type **workspace**.

8. Press **[Enter]** (Win) or **[return]** (Mac) to access the Community Help site.

9. Study the various links provided on the site.

   Note: Figure 46 shows the results of one search for workspace. New links are added regularly because this is community-based help. Therefore, your results may differ.

10. Close the Community Help site and the Flash Help site, then exit the Flash program.

You used the Flash Help feature to access information on the Timeline and the workspace.

Start Flash, open a movie, set the magnification and make changes to the workspace.

1. Start Flash, open fl1_2.fla, then save it as **skillsdemo1**. This movie has two layers. Layer 1 contains the heading and the line at the top of the Stage. Layer 2 contains an animation that runs for 75 frames.
2. Change the magnification to 50% using the View menu. (*Hint:* Click View, point to Magnification, then click 50%.)
3. Change the magnification to Fit in Window.
4. Change the Timeline view to Small. (*Hint:* Click the Frame View icon in the upper-right corner of the Timeline title bar.)
5. Hide all panels.
6. Display the Tools panel, Timeline panel, Properties panel, and the Library panel.
7. Group the Library and Properties panels if they are not already grouped.
8. Drag the Library panel from the Properties panel and position it on the Stage.
9. Collapse the Library panel.
10. Close the Library panel to remove it from the screen.
11. Reset the Essentials workspace.

Play and test a movie.

1. Drag the playhead to view the contents of each frame. Use the commands on the Control menu to play and rewind the movie.
2. Press [Enter] (Win) or [return] (Mac) to play and stop the movie.

3. Use the Controller to rewind, play, stop, and start the movie.
4. Test the movie in the Flash Player window, then close the Flash Player window.

Change the document size and background color.

1. Use the Properties panel to display the Document Properties dialog box.
2. Change the document height to 380.
3. Change the background color to a medium gray color (#999999).
4. Close the Document Properties dialog box.
5. Play the movie.

Create an object, create a motion tween animation, and apply effects.

1. Insert a new layer above Layer 2, then select frame 1 of the new layer.
2. Draw a green ball in the middle of the left side of the Stage, approximately the same size as the red ball. (*Hint:* The green gradient color can be used to draw the ball. Several gradient colors are found in the bottom row of the color palette when you click on the Fill Color tool in the Tools panel.)
3. Use the Selection tool to draw a marquee around the green ball to select it, then create a motion tween to animate the green ball so that it moves across the screen from left to right.

4. Use the Selection tool to reshape the motion path to an arc by dragging the middle of the path downward.
5. Play the movie.
6. Use the Undo command to undo the reshape. (*Note:* You may need to use the Undo feature twice.)
7. Use the Selection tool to select frame 75 of the new layer, click the green ball if it is not already selected to select it, then use the Properties panel to change the transparency (alpha) from 100% to 20%. (*Hint:* If the Properties panel COLOR EFFECT option is not displayed, make sure the Properties panel is open and click the green ball to make sure it is selected.)
8. Play the movie, then rewind it.
9. Click frame 75 on Layer 3 and click the green ball to select it.
10. Use the Properties panel to increase the width of the ball to 80.
11. Play the movie.
12. Select frame 1 on Layer 3 and click the green ball to select it.
13. Use the Filters option in the Properties panel to add a drop shadow.
14. Play the movie.
15. Select frame 1 on Layer 2 and click the red ball to select it.
16. Open the Motion Presets panel and add a bounce-smoosh preset.
17. Play the movie.
18. Save the movie.

Getting Started with Adobe Flash CS4

Change the frame rate and change the view of the Timeline.

1. Change the frame rate to 8 frames per second, play the movie, then change the frame rate to 12.
2. Change the view of the Timeline to display more frames.
3. Change the view of the Timeline to display a preview of the object thumbnails.
4. Change the view of the Timeline to display the Small view.
5. Click frame 1 on Layer 1, use the playhead to display each frame, then compare your screens to Figure 47.
6. Save the movie.

Publish a movie.

1. Click File on the menu bar, then click Publish.
2. Open your browser, then open skillsdemo1.html.
3. View the movie, then close your browser.

Create a projector file.

1. Display the Publish Settings dialog box.
2. Select the appropriate projector setting for your operating system.
3. Publish the movie, then close the Publish Settings dialog box.
4. Use your file management program to navigate to the drive and folder where yousave your work, then open the skillsdemo1 projector file.

5. View the movie, then close the Flash Player window.

FIGURE 47
Completed Skills Review

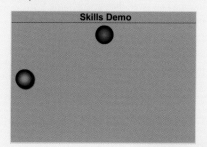
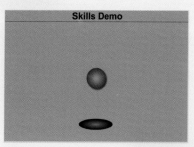

6. Save and close the Flash document.
7. Exit Flash.

Getting Started with Adobe Flash CS4

A friend cannot decide whether to sign up for a class in Flash or Dreamweaver. You help her decide by showing her what you already know about Flash. Since you think she'd enjoy a class in Flash, you decide to show her how easy it is to create a simple animation. You decide to animate three objects. The first object is placed on the center of the Stage and pulsates throughout the movie. The second object enters the Stage from the left side and moves across the middle of the Stage and off the right side of the Stage. The third object enters the Stage from the right side and moves across the middle of the Stage and off the left side of the Stage. The motion paths for the two objects that move across the Stage are reshaped so they go above and below the pulsating object in the middle of the Stage.

1. Open a Flash document, then save it as **demonstration**.
2. Change the view to 50%.
3. Use the tools on the Tools panel to create a circle (or object of your choice) and color of your choice on the middle of the Stage.
4. Draw a marquee around the object to select it and apply a pulse motion preset.
5. Insert a new layer, then select frame 1 on the layer.
6. Create a simple shape or design, and place it off the left side of the Stage and halfway down the Stage.

7. Select the object and insert a motion tween that moves the object directly across the screen and off the right side of the Stage.
8. Reshape the motion path so that the object goes in an arc below the center pulsating object.
9. Insert a new layer, then select frame 1 on the layer.
10. Create an object and place it off the right side of the Stage and halfway down the Stage.

11. Draw a marquee to select the object and insert a motion tween that moves the object directly across the screen and off the left side of the Stage.
12. Reshape the motion path so that the object goes in an arc above the center pulsating object.
13. Play the movie.
14. Add a background color.
15. Play the movie and test it.
16. Save the movie, then compare your movie to the sample provided in Figure 48.

FIGURE 48
Sample completed Project Builder 1

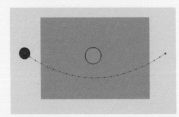

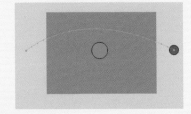

This figure shows the animated objects with outlines of their positions during the animations. Your completed project will not show these outlines.

You've been asked to develop a simple movie about recycling for a day care center. For this project, you will add two animations to an existing movie. You will show three objects that appear on the screen at different times, and then move each object to a recycle bin at different times. You can create the objects using any of the Tools on the Tools panel.

1. Open fl1_3.fla, then save it as **recycle**.
2. Play the movie and study the Timeline to familiarize yourself with the movie's current settings. Currently, there are no animations.

3. Insert a new layer above Layer 2, then draw a small object in the upper-left corner of the Stage.
4. Create a motion tween that moves the object to the recycle bin. (*Hint:* Be sure to select frame 40 on the new layer before creating the motion tween animation.)
5. Reshape the path so that the object moves in an arc to the recycle bin. (*Note:* At this time, the object will appear outside the recycle bin when it is placed in the bin.)
6. Insert a new layer above the top layer, draw a small object in the upper-center of the Stage, then create a motion tween that moves the object to the recycle bin.

7. Insert a new layer above the top layer, draw a small object in the upper-right corner of the Stage, then create a motion tween that moves the object to the recycle bin.
8. Reshape the path so that the object moves in an arc to the recycle bin.
9. Move Layer 1 to the top of all the layers.
10. Play the movie and compare your movie to the sample provided in Figure 49.
11. Save the movie.

FIGURE 49
Sample completed Project Builder 2

This figure shows the animated objects with outlines of their positions during the animations. Your completed project will not show these outlines.

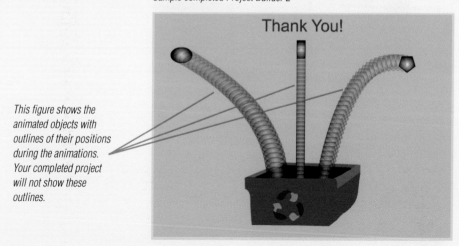

Figure 50 shows the home page of a website. Study the figure and answer the following questions. For each question, indicate how you determined your answer.

1. Connect to the Internet, then go to *www.argosycruises.com*.

2. Open a document in a word processor or open a new Flash document, save the file as **dpc1**, then answer the following questions. (*Hint*: Use the Flash Text tool if you open a Flash document.)

   ■ Whose website is this?
   ■ What is the goal(s) of the site?
   ■ Who is the target audience?
   ■ What treatment (look and feel) is used?
   ■ What are the design layout guidelines being used (balance, movement, etc.)?
   ■ How can animation enhance this page?
   ■ Do you think this is an effective design for the company, its products, and its target audience? Why, or why not?
   ■ What suggestions would you make to improve the design, and why?

FIGURE 50
Design Project

There are numerous companies in the business of developing websites for others. Many of these companies use Flash as one of their primary development tools. These companies promote themselves through their own websites and usually provide online portfolios with samples of their work. Log onto the Internet, then use your favorite search engine and keywords such as Flash developers and Flash animators to locate three of these companies, and generate the following information for each one. A sample website is shown in Figure 51.

1. Company name:
2. Contact information (address, phone, and so on):
3. Website URL:
4. Company mission:
5. Services provided:
6. Sample list of clients:
7. Describe three ways the company seems to have used Flash in its website. Were these effective? Why, or why not?
8. Describe three applications of Flash that the company includes in its portfolio (or showcases or samples). Were these effective? Why, or why not?

9. Would you want to work for this company? Why, or why not?
10. Would you recommend this company to another company that was looking to enhance its website? Why, or why not?

FIGURE 51
Sample website for Portfolio Project

chapter

2

DRAWING OBJECTS IN
ADOBE FLASH

1. Use the Flash drawing tools

2. Select objects and apply colors

3. Work with drawn objects

4. Work with text and text objects

5. Work with layers and objects

chapter **2** DRAWING OBJECTS IN
ADOBE FLASH

Introduction

Computers can display graphics in either a bitmap or a vector format. The difference between these formats is in how they describe an image. Bitmap graphics represent the image as an array of dots, called **pixels**, which are arranged within a grid. Each pixel in an image has an exact position on the screen and a precise color. To make a change in a bitmap graphic, you modify the pixels. When you enlarge a bitmap graphic, the number of pixels remains the same, resulting in jagged edges that decrease the quality of the image. Vector graphics represent the image using lines and curves, which you can resize without losing image quality. Also, the file size of a vector image is generally smaller than the file size of a bitmap image, which makes vector images particularly useful for a website. However, vector graphics are not as effective as bitmap graphics for representing photo-realistic images. One of the most compelling features of Flash is the ability to create and manipulate vector graphics.

Images (objects) created using Flash drawing tools have a stroke (border line), a fill, or both. In addition, the stroke of an object can be segmented into smaller lines. You can modify the size, shape, rotation, and color of each stroke, fill, and segment.

Flash provides two drawing modes, called models. In the Merge Drawing Model, when you draw two shapes and one overlaps the other, a change in the top object may affect the object beneath it. For example, if you draw a circle on top of a rectangle and then move the circle off the rectangle, the portion of the rectangle covered by the circle is removed. The Object Drawing Model allows you to overlap shapes which are then kept separate, so that changes in one object do not affect another object. Another way to avoid having changes in one object affect another is to place them on separate layers on the Timeline as you did in Chapter 1.

Tools You'll Use

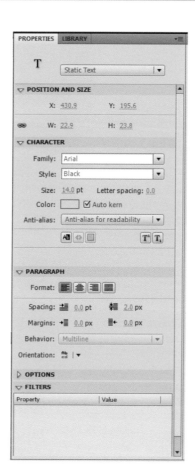

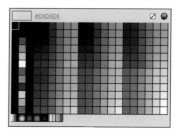

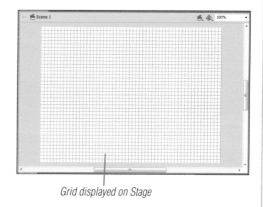

Grid displayed on Stage

USE THE FLASH DRAWING TOOLS

What You'll Do

 In this lesson, you will use several drawing tools to create various vector graphics.

Using Flash Drawing and Editing Tools

When you point to a tool on the Tools panel, its name appears next to the tool. Figure 1 identifies the tools described in the following paragraphs. Several of the tools have options that modify their use. These options are available in the Options area of the Tools panel when the tool is selected.

Selection—Used to select an object or parts of an object, such as the stroke or fill; and to reshape objects. The options for the Selection tool are Snap to Objects (aligns objects), Smooth (smoothes lines), and Straighten (straightens lines).

Subselection—Used to select, drag, and reshape an object. Vector graphics are composed of lines and curves (each of which is a segment) connected by **anchor points**. Selecting an object with this tool displays the anchor points and allows you to use them to edit the object.

Free Transform—Used to rotate, scale, skew, and distort objects.

Gradient Transform—Used to transform a gradient fill by adjusting the size, direction, or center of the fill.

The Free and Gradient Transform tools are grouped within one icon on the Tools panel.

3D Rotation—Used to create 3D effects by rotating movie clips in 3D space on the Stage.

3D Translation—Used to create 3D effects by moving movie clips in 3D space on the Stage.

The 3D Rotation and the 3D Translation tools are grouped within one icon on the Tools panel.

Lasso—Used to select objects or parts of objects. The Polygon Mode option allows you to draw straight lines when selecting an object.

Pen—Used to draw lines and curves by creating a series of dots, known as anchor points, that are automatically connected. Other tools used to add, delete, and convert the anchor points created by the Pen tool are grouped with the Pen tool. To see the menu containing these tools, hold down the Pen tool until the menu opens.

Text—Used to create and edit text.

Line—Used to draw straight lines. You can draw vertical, horizontal, and 45° diagonal lines by pressing and holding [Shift] while drawing the line.

Rectangle—Used to draw rectangular shapes. Press and hold [Shift] to draw a perfect square.

Oval—Used to draw oval shapes. Press and hold [Shift] to draw a perfect circle.

Primitive Rectangle and Oval—Used to draw objects with properties, such as corner radius or inner radius, that can be changed using the Properties panel.

PolyStar—Used to draw polygons and stars.

The Rectangle, Oval, Primitive and PolyStar tools are grouped within one tool on the Tools panel.

Pencil—Used to draw freehand lines and shapes. The Pencil Mode option displays a menu with the following commands: Straighten (draws straight lines), Smooth (draws smooth curved lines), and Ink (draws freehand with no modification).

Brush—Used to draw (paint) with brush-like strokes. Options allow you to set the size and shape of the brush, and to determine the area to be painted, such as inside or behind an object.

Spray Brush—Used to spray colors and patterns onto objects. Dots are the default pattern for the spray. However, you can use a symbol, such as a flag, to create the pattern.

The Brush and Spray Brush tools are grouped together.

Deco—Used to turn graphic shapes into geometric patterns or create kaleidoscopic-like effects.

Bone—Used to animate a set of objects, such as arms and legs, using a series of linked objects to create character animations.

Bind—Used to adjust the relationships between individual bones.

Paint Bucket—Used to fill enclosed areas of a drawing with color. Options allow you to fill areas that have gaps and to make adjustments in a gradient fill.

Ink Bottle—Used to apply line colors and thickness to the stroke of an object.

The Paint Bucket and Ink Bottle are grouped together.

Eyedropper—Used to select stroke, fill, and text attributes so they can be copied from one object to another.

Eraser—Used to erase lines and fills. Options allow you to choose what part of the object to erase, as well as the size and shape of the eraser.

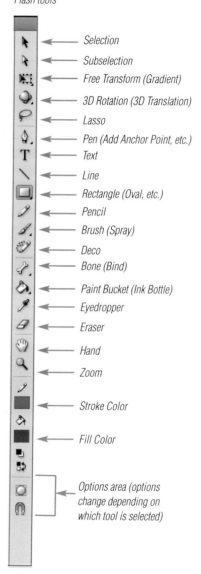

FIGURE 1
Flash tools

Selection
Subselection
Free Transform (Gradient)
3D Rotation (3D Translation)
Lasso
Pen (Add Anchor Point, etc.)
Text
Line
Rectangle (Oval, etc.)
Pencil
Brush (Spray)
Deco
Bone (Bind)
Paint Bucket (Ink Bottle)
Eyedropper
Eraser
Hand
Zoom

Stroke Color

Fill Color

Options area (options change depending on which tool is selected)

Hand—Used to move the Stage around the Pasteboard by dragging the Stage.

Zoom—Used to change the magnification of an area of the Stage. Clicking an area of the Stage zooms in and holding down [Alt] (Win) or [option] ⌘ (Mac) and clicking zooms out.

Stroke Color—Used to set the stroke color of drawn objects.

Fill Color—Used to set the fill color of drawn objects.

Options—Used to select an option for a tool, such as the type of rectangle (object drawn) or size of the brush when using the Brush tool.

Working with Grouped Tools

To display a list of grouped tools, you click the tool and hold the mouse button until the menu opens. For example, if you want to select the Oval tool and the Rectangle tool is displayed, you click and hold the Rectangle tool. Then, when the menu opens, you click the Oval tool option. You know a tool is a grouped tool if you see an arrow in the lower-right corner of the tool icon.

Working with Tool Options

Some tools have additional options that allow you to modify their use. For example, the brush tool has options to set the brush size and to set where the brush fill will be applied. If additional options for a tool are available, they appear at the bottom of the Tools panel in the Options area when the tool is selected. If the option has a menu associated with it, then the option icon will have an arrow in the lower-right corner. Click and hold the option until the menu opens.

Tools for Creating Vector Graphics

The Oval, Rectangle, Pencil, Brush, Line, and Pen tools are used to create vector objects.

Positioning Objects on the Stage

Flash provides several ways to position objects on the Stage including rulers, gridlines, and guides. The Rulers, Grid, and Guides commands, which are found on the View menu, are used to turn on and off these features. Figure 2 shows ruler lines being used to position an object.

FIGURE 2

Using rulers to position an object

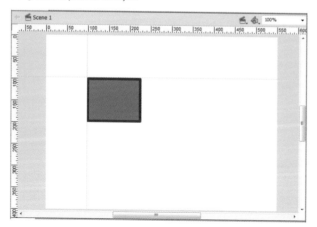

After displaying the rulers, you can drag the lines from the top ruler or the left side ruler to the Stage. To remove a ruler line, you drag the ruler line up to the top ruler or across to the left ruler. You can specify the unit of measure for the rulers.

Figure 3 shows the gridlines displayed and being used to position an object. You can modify the grid size and color. In addition to using rulers and guides to help place objects, you can create a new layer as a Guide layer that you use to position objects on the Stage. When you turn gridlines and guides on, they appear on the Stage. However, they do not appear in the Flash movie when you test or publish it.

Other methods for positioning objects include the align options found on the Align command of the Modify menu, as shown in Figure 4, and the options on the Align panel.

FIGURE 3

Using gridlines to position an object

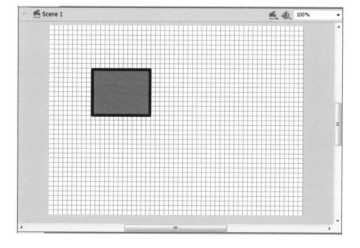

FIGURE 4

The Align command option from the Modify menu

Show gridlines and check settings

1. Open fl2_1.fla from the drive and folder where your Data Files are stored, then save it as **tools**.

2. Click **Window** on the menu bar, point to **Workspace**, then click **Reset 'Essentials'**.

3. Click **View** on the menu bar, point to **Magnification**, then click **Fit in Window**.

4. Click the **Stroke Color tool color swatch** on the Tools panel, then click the **red color swatch** in the left column of the Color palette.

5. Click the **Fill Color tool color swatch** on the Tools panel, then click the **blue color swatch** in the left column of the Color palette.

6. Click **View** on the menu bar, point to **Grid**, then click **Show Grid** to display the gridlines.

   A gray grid appears on the Stage.

7. Point to each tool on the Tools panel, then read its name.

8. Click the **Text tool** T , then click **CHARACTER** to open the area if it is not open already.

   Notice the options in the Properties panel including the CHARACTER area, as shown in Figure 5. The Properties panel options change depending on the tool selected. For the Text tool the properties include the character family and the paragraph family.

You opened a document, saved it, set up the workspace, changed the stroke and fill colors, displayed the grid, viewed tool names on the Tools panel, and then viewed the Text tool options in the Properties panel.

FIGURE 5

Tool name on the Tools panel

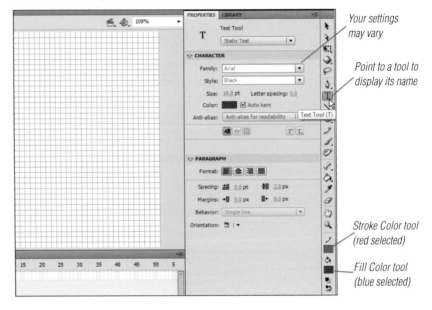

Your settings may vary

Point to a tool to display its name

Stroke Color tool (red selected)

Fill Color tool (blue selected)

FIGURE 6

Objects created with drawing tools

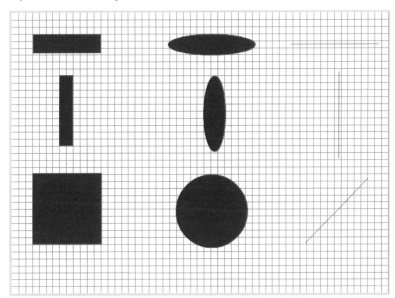

Use the Rectangle, Oval, and Line tools

1. Click the **Rectangle tool** ▣ on the Tools panel.

   Note: If the Rectangle tool is not displayed, click and hold the Oval tool to display the group of tools.

2. Verify that the Object Drawing option ◯ in the Options area of the Tools panel is deselected.

   | TIP   When the Object Drawing option is deselected, the object is drawn so that its stroke and fill can be selected separately.

3. Using Figure 6 as a guide, draw the three rectangle shapes.

   | TIP   Use the grid to approximate shape sizes and hold down [Shift] to draw a square. To undo an action, click the Undo command on the Edit menu.

   Notice the blue color for the fill and the red color for the strokes (border lines).

4. Click and hold down the **Rectangle tool** ▣ on the Tools panel, then click the **Oval tool** ◯ .

5. Using Figure 6 as a guide, draw the three oval shapes.

   | TIP   Hold down [Shift] to draw a perfect circle.

6. Click the **Line tool** ＼ , then, using Figure 6 as a guide, draw the three lines.

   | TIP   Hold down [Shift] to draw a straight line.

You used the Rectangle, Oval, and Line tools to draw objects on the Stage.

Use the Pen, Pencil, and Brush tools

1. Click **Insert** on the menu bar, point to **Timeline**, then click **Layer**.

   A new layer—Layer 2—appears above Layer 1.

2. Click **frame 5** on Layer 2.

3. Click **Insert** on the menu bar, point to **Timeline**, then click **Keyframe**.

   Since the objects were drawn in frame 1 on Layer 1, they are no longer visible when you insert a keyframe in frame 5 on Layer 2. A keyframe allows you to draw in any location on the Stage on the specified frame.

4. Click the **Zoom tool** 🔍 on the Tools panel, click near the upper-left quadrant of the Stage to zoom in, then scroll as needed to see more of the grid.

5. Click the **Pen tool** 🖋 on the Tools panel, position it in the upper-left quadrant of the Stage, as shown in Figure 7, then click to set an anchor point.

6. Using Figure 8 as a guide, click the remaining anchor points to finish drawing an arrow.

   | TIP   To close an object, be sure to re-click the first anchor point as your last action.

7. Click the **Paint Bucket tool** 🪣 , then click inside the arrow.

8. Click **View** on the menu bar, point to **Magnification**, then click **Fit in Window**.

9. Insert a **new layer**, Layer 3, then insert a **keyframe** in frame 10.

10. Click the **Pencil tool** ✏ on the Tools panel.

11. Click **Pencil Mode** in the Options area of the Tools panel, then click the **Smooth option** ⌇ as shown in Figure 9.

(continued)

FIGURE 7
Positioning the Pen tool on the Stage

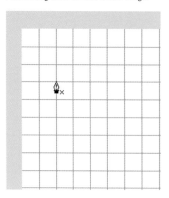

FIGURE 8
Setting anchor points to draw an arrow

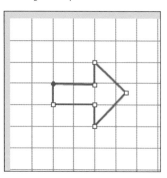

FIGURE 9
Pencil tool options

Click the Pencil Mode Smooth icon to display the 3 options (Note: The Straighten icon might be displayed instead of the Smooth icon.)

Drawing Objects in Adobe Flash

FIGURE 10

Images drawn using drawing tools

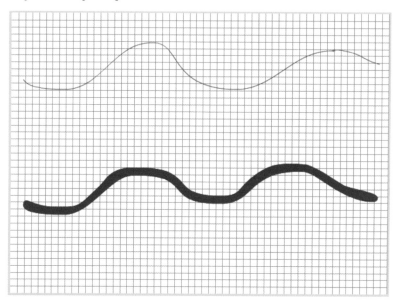

FIGURE 11

The dot pattern indicating the object is selected

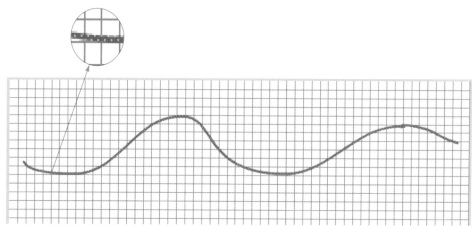

12. Draw the top image, as shown in Figure 10.

13. Click the **Brush tool** ✎ on the Tools panel.

14. Click the **Brush Size Icon** ·. in the Options area of the Tools panel, then click the fifth option from the top.

15. Draw the bottom image, as shown in Figure 10.

    Notice the Pencil tool displays the stroke color and the Brush tool displays the fill color.

You added a layer, inserted a keyframe, then used the Pen tool to draw an arrow; you selected the Smooth option for the Pencil tool and drew an object; you selected a brush size for the Brush tool and drew an object.

Modify an object using tool options

1. Click the **Selection tool** ↖ on the Tools panel, then drag a **marquee** around the top object to select it.

   The line displays a dot pattern, as shown in Figure 11, indicating that it is selected.

2. Click the **Pencil Mode Smooth icon** S. in the Options area of the Tools panel three times. The line becomes smoother.

3. Use the stroke slider △ in the FILL AND STROKE area of the Properties panel to change the stroke size to **20**.

4. Click the **Style list arrow** in the FILL AND STROKE area, then click **Dotted**.

5. Repeat step 4 and change the line style to **Hairline**.

(continued)

6. Click **View** on the menu bar, point to **Grid**, then click **Show Grid** to remove the gridlines.

7. Save your work.

You smoothed objects using the tool options.

Use the Spray tool with a symbol

1. Click **Insert** on the menu bar, point to **Timeline**, then click **Layer**.

2. Click **frame 15** on Layer 4.

3. Click **Insert** on the menu bar, point to **Timeline**, then click **Keyframe**.

4. Click and hold the **Brush tool** on the Tools panel, then click the **Spray Brush tool** .

5. Display the Properties panel if it is not already displayed, then click the **Edit button** in the SYMBOL area of the Properties panel, as shown in Figure 12.

   Note: If the Properties panel does not display the options for the Spray Brush tool, click the Selection tool, then click the Spray Brush tool.

6. Click **Flag** in the Swap Symbol dialog box, then click **OK**.

7. Click the **Random scaling check box** to select it, then click to deselect the **Rotate symbol check box** and the **Random rotation check box** if they are checked.

8. Display the Brush section of the Properties panel, then set the width and height to **9 px**.

(continued)

FIGURE 12
The properties for the Spray Brush tool

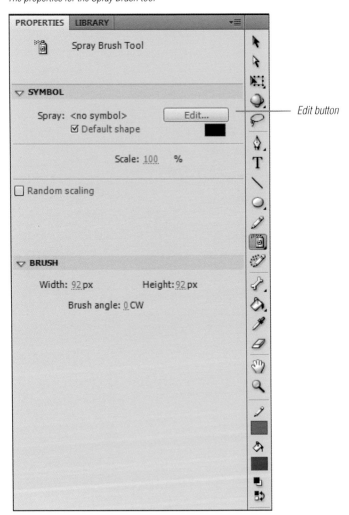

Edit button

Drawing Objects in Adobe Flash

FIGURE 13

A design created using the Spray Brush tool

9. Click the **Spray Brush tool** in the Tools panel, then slowly draw the **U** in USA, as shown in Figure 13.

10. Click the **Selection tool** in the Tools panel, click the **Spray Brush tool** , then draw the **S** in USA.

11. Click the **Selection tool** in the Tools panel, click the **Spray Brush tool** , then draw the **A** in USA.

Hint: If you need to redo the drawing use the Selection tool to draw a marquee around the drawing, then delete the selection.

12. Save your work.

You specified a symbol as a pattern and used the Spray Brush tool to complete a drawing.

SELECT OBJECTS
AND APPLY COLORS

What You'll Do

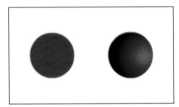

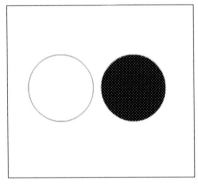

 In this lesson, you will use several techniques to select objects, change the color of strokes and fills, and create a gradient fill.

Selecting Objects

Before you can edit a drawing, you must first select the object, or the part of the object, on which you want to work. Objects are made up of a stroke(s) and a fill. Strokes can have several segments. For example, a rectangle will have four stroke segments, one for each side of the object. These can be selected separately or as a whole. Flash highlights objects that have been selected, as shown in Figure 14. When the stroke of an object is selected, a colored line appears. When the fill of an object is selected, a dot pattern appears; and when objects are grouped, a bounding box appears.

Using the Selection Tool

You can use the Selection tool to select part or all of an object, and to select multiple objects. To select only the fill, click just the fill; to select only the stroke, click just the stroke. To select both the fill and the stroke, double-click the object or draw a marquee around it. To select part of an object, drag a marquee that defines the area you wish to select, as shown in Figure 14. To select multiple objects or combinations of strokes

and fills, press and hold [Shift], then click each item. To deselect an item(s), click a blank area of the Stage.

Using the Lasso Tool

The Lasso tool provides more flexibility than the Selection tool when selecting an object(s) or parts of an object on the Stage. You can use the tool in a freehand manner to draw any shape that then selects the object(s) within the shape. Alternately, you can use the Polygon Mode option to draw straight lines and connect them to form a shape that will select any object(s) within the shape.

Drawing Model Modes

Flash provides two drawing modes, called models. In the Merge Drawing Model mode, the stroke and fill of an object are separate. Thus, as you draw an object such as a circle, the stroke and fill can be selected individually as described earlier. When using the Object Drawing Model mode, the stroke and fill are combined and cannot be selected individually. However, you can use the Break Apart option from the Modify menu to separate the stroke and fill so that they can be selected individually. In addition, you can turn off either the stroke or fill when drawing an object in either mode. You can toggle between the two modes by clicking the Object Drawing option in the Options area of the Tools panel.

Working with Colors

Flash allows you to change the color of the stroke and fill of an object. Figure 15 shows the Colors area of the Tools panel. To change a color, you click the color swatch of the Stroke Color tool or the color swatch of the Fill Color tool, and then select a color swatch on the Color palette. The Color palette, as shown in Figure 16, allows you to select a color from the palette or type in a six-character code that represents the values of three colors (red, green, blue), referred to as

RGB. When these characters are combined in various ways, they can represent virtually any color. The values are in a hexadecimal format (base 16), so they include letters and digits (A–F + 0–9 = 16 options), and they are preceded by a pound sign (#). The first two characters represent the value for red, the next two for green, and the last two for blue. For example, #000000 represents black (lack of color); #FFFFFF represents white; and #FFCC66 represents a shade of gold. You do not have to memorize the codes. There are reference manuals with the codes, and many programs allow you to set the values visually by selecting a color from a palette. You can also use the Properties panel to change the stroke and fill colors.

You can set the desired colors before drawing an object, or you can change a

color of a previously drawn object. You can use the Ink Bottle tool to change the stroke color, and you can use the Paint Bucket tool to change the fill color.

Working with Gradients

A gradient is a color fill that makes a gradual transition from one color to another. Gradients can be very useful for creating a 3D effect, drawing attention to an object, and generally enhancing the appearance of an object. You can apply a gradient fill by using the Paint Bucket tool. The position of the Paint Bucket tool over the object is important because it determines the direction of the gradient fill. The Color palette can be used to create and alter custom gradients.

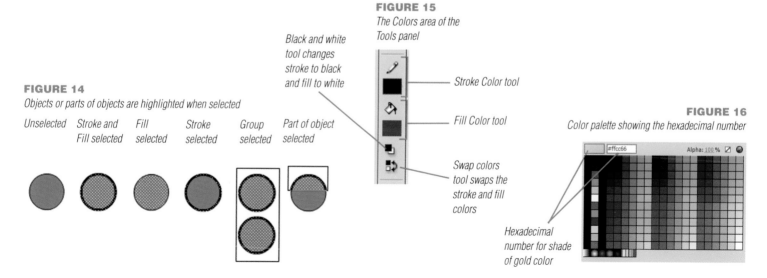

FIGURE 15
The Colors area of the Tools panel

Black and white tool changes stroke to black and fill to white

Stroke Color tool

Fill Color tool

Swap colors tool swaps the stroke and fill colors

FIGURE 14
Objects or parts of objects are highlighted when selected

Unselected | Stroke and Fill selected | Fill selected | Stroke selected | Group selected | Part of object selected

FIGURE 16
Color palette showing the hexadecimal number

#ffcc66   Alpha: 100 %

Hexadecimal number for shade of gold color

Select a drawing using the Selection tool

1. Click **frame 1** on the Timeline.

   > TIP The options available to you in the Properties panel differ depending on whether you click a frame number on the Timeline or a frame within a layer.

2. Click the **Selection tool** ▶ on the Tools panel if it is not already selected, then drag a **marquee** around the circle to select the entire object (both the stroke and the fill).

3. Click anywhere on the Stage to deselect the object.

4. Click inside the circle to select the fill only, then click outside the circle to deselect it.

5. Click the stroke of the circle to select it, as shown in Figure 17, then deselect it.

6. Double-click the **circle** to select it, press and hold **[Shift]**, double-click the **square** to select both objects, then deselect both objects.

7. Click the right border of the square to select it, as shown in Figure 18, then deselect it.

   Objects, such as rectangles, have border segments that can be selected individually.

8. Drag a **marquee** around the square, circle, and diagonal line to select all three objects.

9. Click a blank area of the Stage to deselect the objects.

10. Click inside the oval in row 2 to select the fill, then drag it outside the stroke, as shown in Figure 19.

11. Look at the Properties panel.

    Notice the stroke color is none and the fill color is blue. This is because only the object's

    (continued)

FIGURE 17
Using the Selection tool to select the stroke of the circle

FIGURE 18
Using the Selection tool to select a segment of the stroke of the square

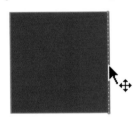

FIGURE 19
Separating the stroke and fill of an object

Drawing Objects in Adobe Flash

FIGURE 20
Circles drawn with the Oval tool

FIGURE 21
Changing the stroke color

fill is selected. You can use the Properties panel to verify what you have selected when working with the Selection tool.

12. Click **Edit** on the menu bar, then click **Undo Move**.

You used the Selection tool to select the stroke and fill of an object, and to select multiple objects.

Change fill and stroke colors

1. Click **Layer 4**, click **Insert** on the menu bar, point to **Timeline**, then click **Layer**.

2. Click **frame 20** of the new layer, click **Insert** on the menu bar, point to **Timeline**, then click **Keyframe**.

3. Select the **Oval tool** on the Tools panel, then draw two circles similar to those shown in Figure 20.

4. Click the **Fill Color tool color swatch** on the Tools panel, then click the **yellow color swatch** in the left column of the Color palette.

5. Click the **Paint Bucket tool** on the Tools panel, then click the fill of the right circle.

6. Click the **Stroke Color tool color swatch** on the Tools panel, then click the **yellow color swatch** in the left column of the color palette.

7. Click and hold the **Paint Bucket tool** on the Tools panel, click the **Ink Bottle tool**, point to the red stroke line of the left circle, as shown in Figure 21, then click to change the stroke color to yellow.

You used the Paint Bucket and Ink Bottle tools to change the fill and stroke colors of an object.

Create a gradient and make changes to the gradient

1. Click the **Fill Color tool color swatch** on the Tools panel, then click the **red gradient color swatch** in the bottom row of the Color palette, as shown in Figure 22.

2. Click and hold the **Ink Bottle tool** on the Tools panel, click the **Paint Bucket tool**, then click the **yellow circle**.

3. Click different parts of the right circle to view how the gradient changes.

4. Click the right side of the circle, as shown in Figure 23.

5. Click and hold the **Free Transform tool** on the Tools panel, then click the **Gradient Transform tool**.

6. Click the **gradient-filled circle**.

7. Drag each of the four handles shown in Figure 24 to determine the effect of each handle on the gradient, then click the **Stage** to deselect the circle.

8. Click the **Selection tool** on the Tools panel, then click inside the left circle.

9. Click the **Fill Color tool color swatch** in the FILL AND STROKE area of the Properties panel, click the **Hex Edit text box**, type **#006637** (two zeros), then press **[Enter]** (Win) or **[return]** (Mac).

   The Fill color swatch and the fill color for the circle change to a shade of green.

10. Save your work.

You applied a gradient fill, you used the Gradient Transform tool to alter the gradient, and you applied a new color using its Hexadecimal number.

FIGURE 22
Selecting the red gradient

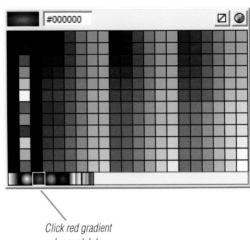

#000000

Click red gradient
color swatch to
select it

FIGURE 23
Clicking the right side of the circle

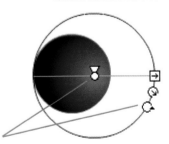

FIGURE 24
Gradient Transform handles

Handles are
used to adjust
the gradient
effect

FIGURE 25
Circle drawn using the Object Drawing Model mode

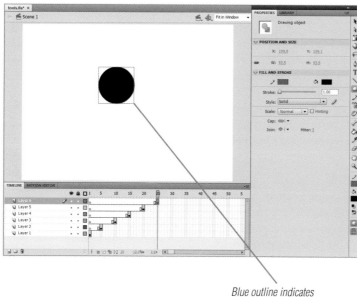

Blue outline indicates
the object is selected

1. Insert a **new layer**, then insert a **keyframe** on frame 25.

2. Select the **Oval tool** , click the **Stroke Color tool color swatch** , then click the **red swatch**.

3. Click the **Fill Color tool color swatch** , then click the **black swatch**.

4. Click the **Object Drawing option** in the Options area of the Tools panel to change the mode to Object Drawing Model.

5. Draw a **circle** as shown in Figure 25.

    Notice that when you use Object Drawing Model mode, objects are automatically selected, and the stroke and fill areas are combined.

6. Click the **Selection tool** on the Tools panel, then click a blank area of the Stage to deselect the object.

7. Click once on the **circle**, then drag the circle around the Stage.

    The entire object is selected, including the stroke and fill areas.

8. Click **Modify** on the menu bar, then click **Break Apart**.

    Breaking apart an object drawn in Object Drawing Model mode allows you to select the strokes and fills individually.

9. Click a blank area of the Stage, click the fill area of the circle, drag to the right, then save your work.

    Notice the fill moves but the stroke stays.

You used the Object Drawing Model mode to draw an object, deselect it, and then break it apart to display and then separate the stroke and fill.

WORK WITH DRAWN OBJECTS

What You'll Do

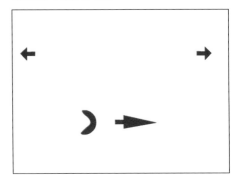

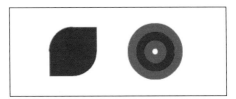

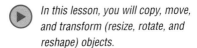 *In this lesson, you will copy, move, and transform (resize, rotate, and reshape) objects.*

Copying and Moving Objects

To copy an object, select it, and then click the Copy command on the Edit menu. To paste the object, click the Paste command on the Edit menu. You can copy an object to another layer by selecting the frame on the layer prior to pasting the object. You can copy and paste more than one object by selecting all the objects before using the Copy or Paste commands.

You move an object by selecting it and dragging it to a new location. You can position an object more precisely by selecting it and then pressing the arrow keys, which move the selection up, down, left, and right in small increments. In addition, you can change the X and Y coordinates in the Properties panel to position an object exactly on the Stage.

Transforming Objects

You use the Free Transform tool and the Transform panel to resize, rotate, skew, and reshape objects. After selecting an object, you click the Free Transform tool to display eight square-shaped handles used to transform the object, and a circle-shaped transformation point located at the center of the object. The transformation point is the point around which the object can be rotated. You can also change its location.

Resizing an Object

You enlarge or reduce the size of an object using the Scale option, which is available when the Free Transform tool is selected. The process is to select the object and click the Free Transform tool, and then click the Scale option in the Options area of the Tools panel. Eight handles appear around the selected object. You drag the corner handles to resize the object without changing its proportions. That is, if the object starts out as a square, dragging a corner handle will change the size of the object, but it will still be a square. On the other hand, if you drag one of the middle handles, the object will be reshaped as taller, shorter, wider, or narrower. In addition, you can change the Width and Height settings in the Properties panel to resize an object in increments of one-tenth of one pixel.

Rotating and Skewing an Object

You use the Rotate and Skew option of the Free Transform tool to rotate an object and to skew it. The process is to select the object, click the Free Transform tool, and then click the Rotate and Skew option in the Options area of the Tools panel. Eight square-shaped handles appear around the object. You drag the corner handles to rotate the object, or you drag the middle handles to skew the object, as shown in Figure 26. The Transform panel can be used to rotate and skew an object in a more precise way; select the object, display the Transform panel (available via the Window menu), enter the desired rotation or skew in degrees, and then press [Enter] (Win) or [return] (Mac).

Distorting an Object

You can use the Distort and Envelope options to reshape an object by dragging its handles. The Distort option allows you to reshape an object by dragging one corner without affecting the other corners of the object. The Envelope option provides more than eight handles to allow more precise distortions. These options are accessed through the Transform command on the Modify menu.

Reshaping a Segment of an Object

You use the Subselection tool to reshape a segment of an object. You click an edge of the object to display handles that can be dragged to reshape the object.

You use the Selection tool to reshape objects. When you point to the edge of an object, the pointer displays an arc symbol. Using the Arc pointer, you drag the edge of the object you want to reshape, as shown in Figure 27. If the Selection tool points to a corner of an object, the pointer changes to an L-shape. You drag the pointer to reshape the corner of the object.

Flipping an Object

You use a Flip option on the Transform menu to flip an object either horizontally or vertically. You select the object, click the Transform command on the Modify menu, and then choose Flip Vertical or Flip Horizontal. Other Transform options allow you to rotate and scale the selected object. The Remove Transform command allows you to restore an object to its original state.

FIGURE 26
Using handles to manipulate an object

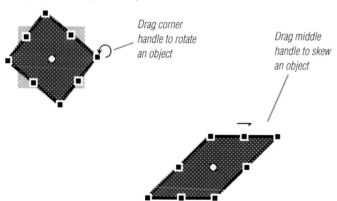

Drag corner handle to rotate an object

Drag middle handle to skew an object

FIGURE 27
Using the Selection tool to distort an object

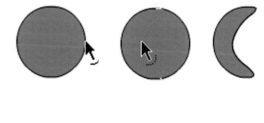

Copy and move an object

1. Click **frame 5** on the Timeline.

2. Click the **Selection tool** ↖ on the Tools panel, then draw a **marquee** around the arrow object to select it.

3. Click **Edit** on the menu bar, click **Copy**, click **Edit** on the menu bar, then click **Paste in Center**.

4. Drag the newly copied **arrow** to the upper-right corner of the Stage, as shown in Figure 28.

5. Verify the right arrow object is selected on the Stage, press the **down arrow key** [↓] on the keyboard to move the object in approximately one-pixel increments, and notice how the Y coordinate in the Properties panel changes.

6. Press the **right arrow key** [→] on the keyboard to move the object in one-pixel increments, and notice how the X coordinate in the Properties panel changes.

7. Select the **number** in the X coordinate box in the Properties panel, type **450**, as shown in Figure 29, then press **[Enter]** (Win) or **[return]** (Mac).

8. Point to the **Y coordinate**, when the pointer changes to a double-headed arrow ⟺ drag the ⟺ **pointer** to change the setting to **30**.

9. Select the **left arrow object**, then set the X and Y coordinates to **36** and **30**, respectively.

10. Click a blank area of the Stage to deselect the object.

You used the Selection tool to select an object, then you copied and moved the object.

FIGURE 28
Moving the copied object

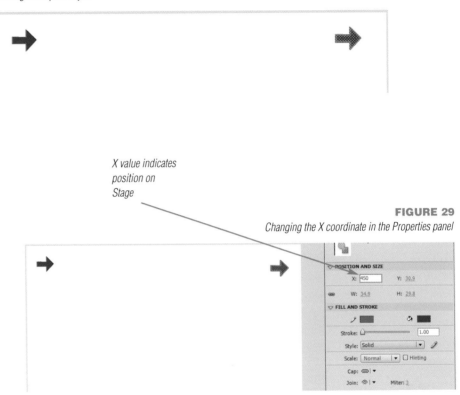

X value indicates position on Stage

FIGURE 29
Changing the X coordinate in the Properties panel

X and Y coordinates

The Stage dimensions are made up of pixels (dots) matching the Stage size. So, a Stage size of 550 × 400 would be 550 pixels wide and 400 pixels high. Each pixel has a location on the Stage designated as the X (across) and Y (down) coordinates. The location of any object is determined by its position from the upper-left corner of the Stage, which is 0,0. So, an object having coordinates of 450,30 would be positioned at 450 pixels across and 30 pixels down the Stage. The registration point of an object is used to align it with the coordinates. The registration point is initially set at the upper-left corner of an object.

FIGURE 30

Resizing an object using the corner handles

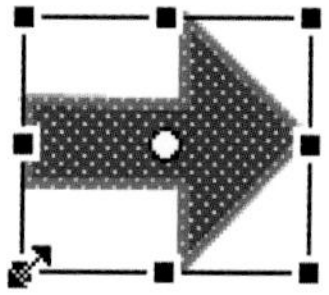

FIGURE 31

Reshaping an object using the middle handles

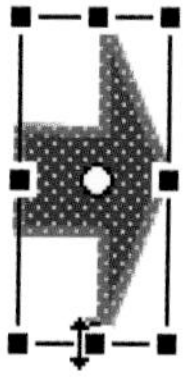

Transform options

Different transform options, such as rotate, skew, and scale, can be accessed through the Options area on the Tools panel when the Free Transform tool is selected, the Transform command on the Modify menu, and the Transform panel via the Transform command on the Window menu.

Resize and reshape an object

1. Draw a **marquee** around the arrow object on the right side of the Stage to select the object.

2. Select the **Free Transform tool** on the Tools panel.

   Note: You may need to click and hold the Gradient tool to display the Free Transform tool.

3. Select the **Scale option** in the Options area of the Tools panel.

4. Drag each **corner handle** toward and then away from the center of the object, as shown in Figure 30.

   As you drag a corner handle, the object's size is changed, but its proportions remain the same.

5. Click **Edit** on the menu bar, then click **Undo Scale**.

6. Repeat Step 5 until the arrow returns to its original size.

   > TIP The object is its original size when the option Undo Scale is no longer available on the Edit menu.

7. Verify the arrow is still selected and the handles are displayed, then select the **Scale option** .

8. Drag each **middle handle** toward and then away from the center of the object, as shown in Figure 31.

   As you drag the middle handles, the object's size and proportions change.

9. Click **Edit** on the menu bar, then click **Undo Scale** as needed to return the arrow to its original size.

You used the Free Transform tool and the Scale option to display an object's handles, and you used the handles to resize and reshape the object.

Rotate, skew, and flip an object

1. Verify that the Free Transform tool and the right arrow are selected (handles displayed), then click the **Rotate and Skew option** in the Options area of the Tools panel.

2. Click the **upper-right corner handle**, then rotate the object clockwise.

3. Click the **upper-middle handle**, then drag it to the right.

   The arrow slants down and to the right.

4. Click **Edit** on the menu bar, click the **Undo Skew** command, then repeat, selecting the Undo Rotate command, until the arrow is in its original shape and orientation.

5. Click the **Selection tool** on the Tools panel, verify that the right arrow is selected, click **Window** on the menu bar, then click **Transform**.

6. Click the **Rotate text box**, type **45**, then press **[Enter]** (Win) or **[return]** (Mac).

   The arrow rotates 45°, as shown in Figure 32.

7. Click **Edit** on the menu bar, then click **Undo Transform**.

8. Close the Transform panel.

9. Draw a **marquee** around the arrow in the upper-left corner of the Stage to select the object.

10. Click **Modify** on the menu bar, point to **Transform**, then click **Flip Horizontal**.

11. Save your work.

You used options on the Tools panel and the Transform panel, as well as commands on the Modify menu to rotate, skew, and flip an object.

FIGURE 32
Using the Transform panel to rotate an object

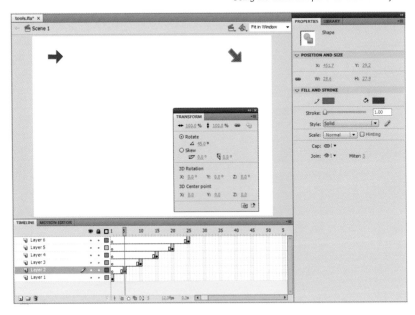

Drawing Objects in Adobe Flash

FIGURE 33

Using the Subselection tool to select an object

Click the tip of the
object to display
the handles

FIGURE 34

Using the Subselection tool to drag a handle to reshape the object

FIGURE 35

Using the Selection tool to drag an edge to reshape the object

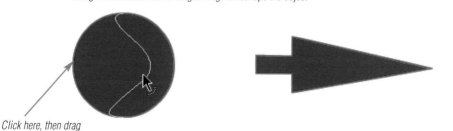

Click here, then drag

Lesson 3   Work with Drawn Objects

Use the Zoom, Subselection, and Selection tools

1. Select the **arrow** in the upper-right corner of the Stage, click **Edit** on the menu bar, click **Copy**, click **Edit** on the menu bar, then click **Paste in Center**.

2. Click the **Zoom tool** 🔍 on the Tools panel, then click the middle of the copied object to enlarge the view.

3. Click the **Subselection tool** ⟨ on the Tools panel, then click the **tip of the arrow** to display the handles, as shown in Figure 33.

   TIP The handles allow you to change any segment of the object.

4. Click the **handle** at the tip of the arrow, then drag it, as shown in Figure 34.

5. Select the **Oval tool** ⌕ on the Tools panel, then deselect the **Object Drawing option** ⬭ in the Options area of the Tools panel.

6. Verify the Fill color is set to blue, then draw a **circle** to the left of the arrow you just modified.

7. Click the **Selection tool** ⟨ on the Tools panel, then point to the left edge of the circle until the Arc pointer ⟨⟩ is displayed.

8. Drag the ⟨⟩ **pointer** to the position shown in Figure 35.

9. Click **View** on the menu bar, point to **Magnification**, then click **100%**.

10. Save your work.

You used the Zoom tool to change the view, and you used the Subselection and Selection tools to reshape objects.

Use the Primitive Rectangle and Oval tools

1. Insert a **new layer** above Layer 6, click **frame 30** on Layer 7, then insert a **Keyframe**.

2. Click and hold down the **Oval tool** ⊙, (or the Rectangle tool if it is displayed) to display the menu.

3. Click the **Rectangle Primitive tool** ⬚, then click the **Reset button** in the Properties panel RECTANGLE OPTIONS area to clear all of the settings.

4. Hold down **[Shift]**, point to the middle of the Stage, then draw the **square** shown in Figure 36.

5. Click the **Selection tool** ▸ in the Tools panel, then drag **the upper-right corner handle** toward the center of the object.
   As you drag the corner, the radius of each of the four corners is changed.

6. Click the **Reset button** in the Properties panel to clear the setting.

7. Slowly drag the **slider** ⌂ in the RECTANGLE OPTIONS area to the right until the radius changes to 100, then slowly drag the **slider** ⌂ to the left until the radius changes to −100.

8. Click the **Reset Button** on the Properties panel to clear the radius settings.

9. Click the **Lock corner radius icon** ⊜ in the Properties panel RECTANGLE OPTIONS area to unlock the individual controls.

10. Type **-60** in the upper-left corner radius text box, then type **-60** in the upper-right corner text box, as shown in Figure 37.

(continued)

FIGURE 36
Drawing an object with the Rectangle Primitive tool

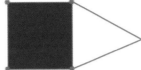

The corner handles can be dragged to change the radius of the corners; in addition, the Properties panel can be used to make changes to the object

FIGURE 37
Setting the corner radius of two corners

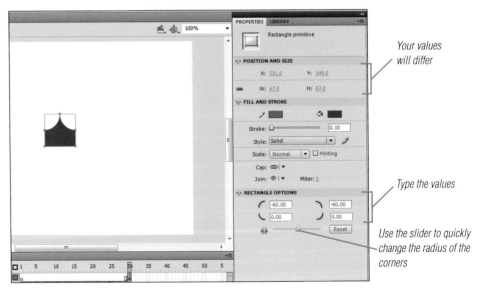

Your values will differ

Type the values

Use the slider to quickly change the radius of the corners

Drawing Objects in Adobe Flash

FIGURE 38

Drawing an object with the Oval Primitive tool

FIGURE 39

Setting the stroke value to 12

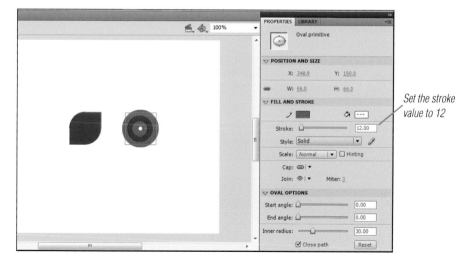

Set the stroke value to 12

11. Click the **Reset button** in the Properties panel to clear the radius settings.

12. Click the **Lock corner radius icon** 🔗 to unlock the individual controls.

13. Set the upper-left corner radius to **60** and the lower-right corner to **60**.

14. Click a blank area of the Stage to deselect the object.

15. Click and hold the **Rectangle Primitive tool** 🔲 , click the **Oval Primitive tool** ⬭ on the Tools panel, then hold down **[Shift]** and draw the **circle** shown in Figure 38.

    TIP Remember some tools are grouped. Click and hold a grouped tool, such as the Oval tool, to see the menu of tools in the group.

16. Click the **Reset button** in the Properties panel OVAL OPTIONS area to clear any settings.

17. Drag the **Start angle slider** 🔘 and the **End angle slider** 🔘 to view their effect on the circle, then drag each **slider** back to 0.

18. Click the **Reset button** to clear the settings.

19. Drag the **Inner radius slider** 🔘 to see the effect on the circle, then set the inner radius to **30**.

20. Display the FILL AND STROKE area of the Properties panel, then set the Stroke value to **12**, as shown in Figure 39.

21. Save your work.

You used the Primitive tools to create objects and the Properties panel to alter them.

WORK WITH TEXT
AND TEXT OBJECTS

What You'll Do

Classic Car Club

Join Us Now

We have great events
each year including a
Car Rally!

 In this lesson, you will enter text using text blocks. You will also resize text blocks, change text attributes, and transform text.

Learning About Text

Flash provides a great deal of flexibility when using text. Among other settings for text, you can specify the typeface (font), size, style (bold, italic), and color (including gradients). You can transform the text by rotating, scaling, skewing, and flipping it. You can even break apart a letter and reshape its segments.

Entering Text and Changing the Text Block

It is important to understand that text is entered into a text block, as shown in Figure 40. You use the Text tool to place a text block on the Stage and to enter and edit text. A text block expands as more text is entered and may even extend beyond the edge of the Stage. You can adjust the size of the text block so that it is a fixed width by dragging the handle in the upper-right corner of the block. Figure 41 shows the process of using the Text tool to enter text and resize the text block. Once you select the Text tool, you click the Stage where you want the text to appear. An insertion point indicates where the next character will appear in the text block when it is typed. You can reshape the text block by dragging the circle handle. After reshaping the text block, the circle handle changes to a square, indicating that the text block now has a fixed width. Then, when you enter more text, it automatically wraps within the text block. You can resize the text block at any time by selecting it with the Selection tool and dragging a handle.

Changing Text Attributes

You can use the Properties panel to change the font, size, and style of a single character or an entire text block. Figure 42 shows the Properties panel when a text object is selected. You select text, display the Properties panel, and make the changes. You use the Selection tool to select the entire text block by drawing a marquee around it. You use the Text tool to select a single character or string of characters by dragging the I-beam pointer over the text you want to select, as shown in Figure 43.

Working with Paragraphs

When working with large bodies of text, such as paragraphs, Flash provides many of the features found in a word processor. You can align paragraphs (left, right, center, justified) within a text block, set margins (space between the border of a text block and the paragraph text), set indents for the first line of a paragraph, and set line spac-ing (distance between paragraphs) using the Properties panel.

Transforming Text

It is important to understand that a text block is an object. Therefore, you can apply filters, such as drop shadows, and you can transform (reshape, rotate, skew, and so on) a text block in the same way you transform other objects. If you want to transform individual characters within a text block, you must first break apart the text block. To do this, you use the Selection tool to select the text block, then you click the Break Apart command on the Modify menu. Each character (or a group of characters) in the text block can now be selected and transformed.

FIGURE 40
A text block

This is a text block used to enter text.

FIGURE 41
Using the Text tool

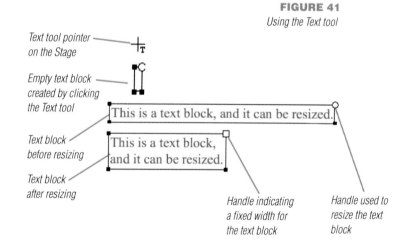

Text tool pointer on the Stage

Empty text block created by clicking the Text tool

This is a text block, and it can be resized.

Text block before resizing

This is a text block, and it can be resized.

Text block after resizing

Handle indicating a fixed width for the text block

Handle used to resize the text block

FIGURE 42
The Properties panel when a text object is selected

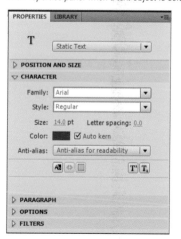

FIGURE 43
Dragging the I-Beam pointer to select text

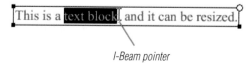

This is a text block, and it can be resized.

I-Beam pointer

Enter text and change text attributes

1. Click **Layer 7**, insert a **new layer**, then insert a **keyframe** in frame 35 of the new layer.

2. Click the **Text tool** T on the Tools panel, click the left-center of the Stage, then type **We have great events each year including a Rally**!

3. Click the **I-Beam pointer** I before the word "Rally," as shown in Figure 44, then type **Car** followed by a space.

4. Verify that the Properties panel is displayed, then drag the I-Beam pointer I across the text to select all the text.

5. Make the following changes in the CHARAC-TER area of the Properties panel: Family: **Arial**; Style: **Black** (Win) or **Bold** (Mac); Size:**16**; Color: **#990000**, then click the **text box**.

   Your Properties panel should resemble Figure 45.

6. Verify the text block is selected, position the **text pointer** ⊹ over the circle handle until the pointer changes to a double arrow ↔, then drag the **handle** to just before the word each, as shown in Figure 46.

7. Select the text using the I-Beam pointer I, then click the **Align center icon** 🔳 in the PARAGRAPH area of the Properties panel.

8. Click the **Selection tool** ⬉ on the Tools panel, click the **text object**, then drag the **object** to the lower-middle of the Stage.

   | TIP   The Selection tool is used to select the text block, and the Text tool is used to select and edit the text within the text block.

You entered text and changed the font, type size, and text color; you also resized the text block and changed the text alignment.

FIGURE 44
Using the Text tool to enter text

We have great events each year including a |Rally!

FIGURE 45
Changes in the CHARACTER area of the Properties panel

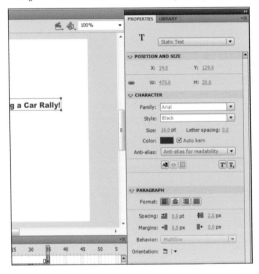

FIGURE 46
Resizing the text block

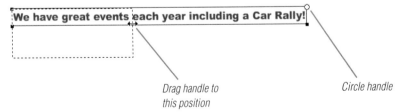

We have great events each year including a Car Rally!

Drag handle to
this position

Circle handle

Drawing Objects in Adobe Flash

FIGURE 47

The Filters options in the Properties panel

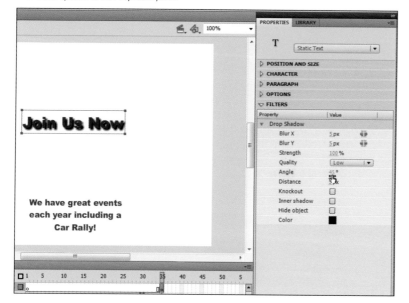

Using filters

You can apply special effects, such as drop shadows, to text using options in the FILTERS area of the Properties panel. The process is to select the desired text, display the FILTERS area of the Properties panel, choose the desired effect, and make any adjustments, such as changing the angle of a drop shadow. You can copy and paste a filter from one object to another using the clipboard icon in the FILTERS area of the Properties panel.

Add a Filter effect to text

1. Click the **Text tool** T on the Tools panel, click the center of the Stage, then type **Join Us Now**. *Hint:* If the text box does not appear, double-click the Stage.

2. Drag the **I-Beam pointer** I across the text to select it, then use the Properties panel to change the Font size to **30** and the Text (fill) color to **#003399**.

3. Click **CHARACTER** on the Properties panel to close the CHARACTER area, then close all areas in the Properties panel except for the FILTERS area.

4. Click the **Selection tool** ↖ on the Tools panel, then verify the text block is selected.

5. Click the **Add filter icon** ⬓ at the bottom of the FILTERS area, then click **Drop Shadow**.

6. Point to the **Angle value** in the FILTERS area of the Properties panel, as shown in Figure 47.

7. When the pointer changes to a double-headed arrow ⇕, drag the ⇕ **pointer** to the right to view the effect on the shadow, then set the Angle to **50**.

8. Click the **Distance value**, when the pointer changes to a double-headed arrow ⇕, drag the ⇕ **pointer** to the right and notice the changes in the drop shadow.

9. Set the Distance to **6**.

10. Use the **Selection tool** ↖ to select the text position and position it as needed to match the placement shown in Figure 47, then save your work.

You used the Filter panel to create a drop shadow and then made changes to it.

Lesson 4   Work with Text and Text Objects

Skew text and align objects

1. Click the **Text tool** T to select it, click the pointer near the top middle of the Stage twice, then type **Classic Car Club**.

2. Click **CHARACTER** in the Properties panel to display the CHARACTER area.

   The attributes of the new text reflect the most recent settings entered in the Properties panel.

3. Drag the **I-Beam pointer** I to select the text, then use the CHARACTER area of the Properties panel to change the font size to **40** and the fill color to **#990000**.

4. Click the **Selection tool** ▶ on the Tools panel to select the text box, then select the **Free Transform tool** 🔣 on the Tools panel.

5. Click the **Rotate and Skew option** ⤸ in the Options area of the Tools panel.

6. Drag the top middle handle to the right, as shown in Figure 48, to skew the text.

7. Click the **Selection tool** ▶ on the Tools panel.

8. Drag a **marquee** around all of the objects on the Stage to select them.

9. Click **Modify** on the menu bar, point to **Align**, verify To Stage has a check mark next to it, then click **Horizontal Center**.

   Note: If the Modify menu closes before you select Horizontal Center, repeat step 9.

10. Click a blank area of the Stage to deselect the objects.

You entered a heading, changed the font size and color, and skewed text using the Free Transform tool, then you aligned the objects on the Stage.

FIGURE 48
Skewing the text

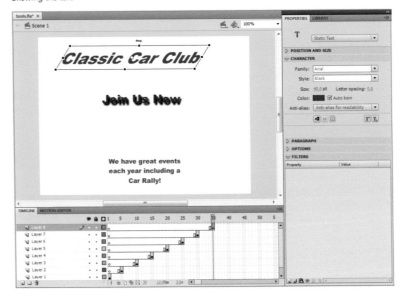

Drawing Objects in Adobe Flash

FIGURE 49
Reshaping a letter

Drag this handle; notice the lines are drawn
from the anchor points on either side of the
anchor point being dragged

FIGURE 50
Applying a gradient fill to each letter

Reshape and apply a gradient to text

1. Click the **Selection tool** , click the **Classic Car Club text block** to select it, click **Modify** on the menu bar, then click **Break Apart**.

   The letters are now individual text blocks.

2. Click **Modify** on the menu bar, then click **Break Apart**.

   The letters are filled with a dot pattern, indicating that they can now be edited.

3. Click the **Zoom tool** on the Tools panel, then click the **"C"** in Classic.

4. Click the **Subselection tool** on the Tools panel, then click the edge of the letter **"C"** to display the object's segment handles.

5. Drag a lower handle on the "C" in Classic, as shown in Figure 49.

6. Click the **Selection tool** , then click a blank area of the Stage to deselect the objects.

7. Click **View** on the menu bar, point to **Magnification**, then click **Fit in Window**.

8. Click the **Fill Color tool color swatch** on the Tools panel, then click the **red gradient color swatch** in the bottom row of the Color palette.

9. Click the **Paint Bucket tool** on the Tools panel, then click the top of each letter to change the fill to a red gradient, as shown in Figure 50.

10. Use the status bar to change the movie frame rate to **3**, click **Control** on the menu bar, click **Test Movie**, watch the movie, then close the Flash Player window.

11. Save your work, then close the movie.

You broke apart a text block, reshaped text, and added a gradient to the text.

WORK WITH LAYERS
AND OBJECTS

What You'll Do

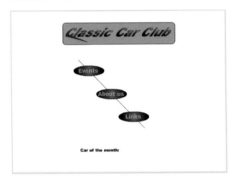

 In this lesson, you will create, rename, reorder, delete, hide, and lock layers. You will also display objects as outlines on layers, use a Guide layer, distribute text to layers, and create a Folder layer.

Learning About Layers

Flash uses two types of spatial organization. First, there is the position of objects on the Stage, and then there is the stacking order of objects that overlap. An example of overlapping objects is text placed on a banner. Layers are used on the Timeline as a way to organize objects. Placing objects on their own layer makes them easier to work with, especially when reshaping them, repositioning them on the Stage, or rearranging their order in relation to other objects. In addition, layers are useful for organizing other elements such as sounds, animations, and ActionScript.

There are five types of layers, as shown in the Layer Properties dialog box displayed in Figure 51 and discussed next.

Normal—The default layer type. All objects on these layers appear in the movie.

Mask—A layer that hides and reveals portions of another layer.

Masked—A layer that contains the objects that are hidden and revealed by a Mask layer.

Folder—A layer that can contain other layers.

Guide (Standard and Motion)—A Standard Guide layer serves as a reference point for positioning objects on the Stage. A Motion Guide layer is used to create a path for animated objects to follow.

Motion Guide, Mask, and Masked layer types are covered in a later chapter.

Working with Layers

The Layer Properties dialog box, accessed through the Timeline command on the Modify menu, allows you to specify the type of layer. It also allows you to name, show (and hide), and lock them. Naming a layer provides a clue to the objects on the layer. For example, naming a layer Logo might indicate that the object on the layer is the company's logo. Hiding a layer(s) may reduce the clutter on the Stage and make it easier to work with selected objects from the layer(s) that are not hidden. Locking a layer(s) prevents the objects from being accidentally edited. Other options in the Layer Properties dialog box allow you to view layers as outlines and change the outline color.

Outlines can be used to help you determine which objects are on a layer. When you turn on this feature, each layer has a colored box that corresponds with the color of the objects on its layer. Icons on the Layers area of the Timeline, as shown in Figure 52, correspond to features in the Layer Properties dialog box.

FIGURE 51
The Layer Properties dialog box

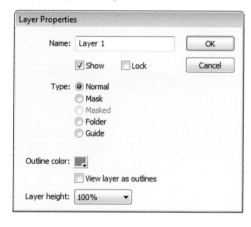

Show or Hide
All Layers

FIGURE 52
The Layers area of the Timeline

Show All Layers
as Outlines

Lock or
Unlock All
Layers

Lock or Unlock
This Layer

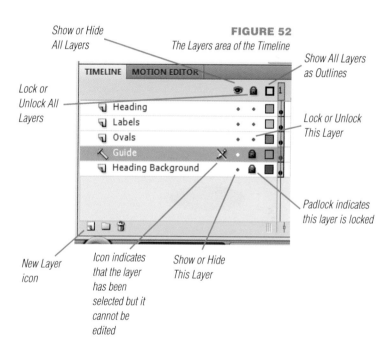

Padlock indicates
this layer is locked

New Layer
icon

Icon indicates
that the layer
has been
selected but it
cannot be
edited

Show or Hide
This Layer

Using a Guide Layer

Guide layers are useful in aligning objects on the Stage. Figure 53 shows a Guide layer that has been used to align three buttons along a diagonal path. The buttons are on one layer and the diagonal line is on another layer, the Guide layer. The process is to insert a new layer above the layer containing the objects to be aligned, you use the Layer Properties command from the Timeline option on the Modify menu to display the Layer Properties dialog box, select Guide as the layer type, and then draw a path that will be used as the guide to align the objects. You then verify the Snap to Guides option from the Snapping command on the View menu is turned on, and drag the desired objects to the Guide line. Objects have a transformation point that is used when snapping to a guide. By default, this point is at the center of the object. Figure 54 shows the process.

FIGURE 53
A Guide layer used to align objects on the Stage

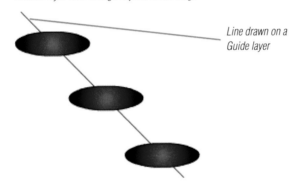

Line drawn on a
Guide layer

FIGURE 54
The transformation point of an object

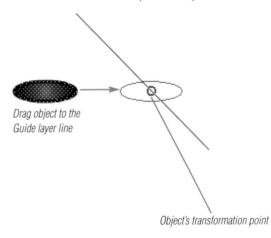

Drag object to the
Guide layer line

Object's transformation point

Distributing Text to Layers

Text blocks are made up of one or more characters. When you break apart a text block, each character becomes an object that can be edited independently of the other characters. You use the Distribute to Layers command from the Timeline option on the Modify menu, which causes each character to automatically be placed on its own layer. Figure 55 shows the seven layers created after the text block containing 55 Chevy has been broken apart and distributed to layers.

Using Folder Layers

As movies become larger and more complex, the number of layers increases. Flash allows you to organize layers by creating folders and grouping other layers in the folders. Figure 56 shows a Folder layer —Layer 4—with seven layers in it. The process is to select the layer that is to become a Folder layer, then use the Layer Properties dialog box to specify a Folder layer. To place other layers in the Folder layer, you drag them from the Timeline to the Folder layer. You click the Folder layer triangle next to Layer 4 to open and close the folder.

FIGURE 55

Distributing text to layers

FIGURE 56

A Folder layer

Create and reorder layers

1. Open fl2_2.fla from the drive and folder where your Data Files are stored, then save it as **layers2.fla**.

2. Click the **Selection tool** ⬉, click **View** on the menu bar, point to **Magnification**, then click **Fit in Window**.

3. Click the **New Layer icon** 🔲 on the bottom of the Timeline (below the layer names) to insert a new layer, Layer 2.

4. Click **Frame 1** of Layer 2.

5. Select the **Rectangle tool** 🔲 on the Tools panel, then set each corner radius to **10** in the RECTANGLE OPTIONS area of the Properties panel, and set the Stroke to **2** in the FILL AND STROKE area.

6. Click the **Fill Color tool color swatch** 🎨 on the Tools panel, click the **Hex Edit text box**, type **#999999**, then press **[Enter]** (Win) or **[return]** (Mac).

7. Click the **Stroke Color tool color swatch** 🖉 on the Tools panel, click the **Hex Edit text box**, type **#000000**, then press **[Enter]** (Win) or **[return]** (Mac).

8. Draw the **rectangle** shown in Figure 57 so it covers the text heading.

9. Drag **Layer 1** above Layer 2 on the Timeline, as shown in Figure 58.

10. Click the **Selection tool** ⬉ on the Tools panel.

11. Click a blank area of the Stage to deselect the objects.

You added a layer, drew an object on the layer, and reordered layers.

FIGURE 57

Drawing a rectangle with a rounded corner

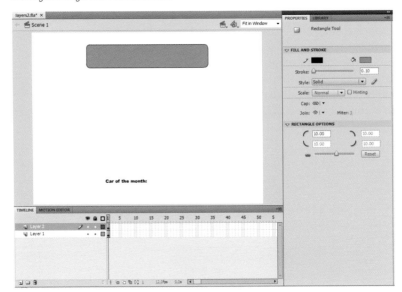

FIGURE 58

Dragging Layer 1 above Layer 2

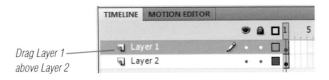

Drag Layer 1 above Layer 2

Drawing Objects in Adobe Flash

FIGURE 59
Renaming layers

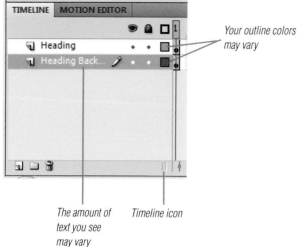

Your outline colors
may vary

The amount of
text you see
may vary

Timeline icon

FIGURE 60
Expanding the layer name area of the Timeline

Drag the
Timeline icon

Rename and delete layers and expand the Timeline

1. Double-click **Layer 1** on the Timeline, type **Heading** in the Layer Name text box, then press **[Enter]** (Win) or **[return]** (Mac).

2. Rename Layer 2 as **Heading Background**.

3. Point to the **Timeline icon** ▓ below the layer names, as shown in Figure 59.

4. When the pointer changes to a double arrow ◂▸ , drag the **icon** to the right to display all the layer names, as shown in Figure 60.

5. Click the **Heading layer**, then click the **Delete icon** 🗑 on the bottom of the Timeline.

6. Click **Edit** on the menu bar, then click **Undo Delete Layer**.

7. Click **Heading Background** to display both layers.

You renamed layers to associate them with objects on the layers, then deleted and restored a layer.

Hide, lock, and display layer outlines

1. Click the **Show or Hide All Layers icon** 👁 to hide all layers, then compare your image to Figure 61.

2. Click the **Show or Hide All Layers icon** 👁 to show all the layers.

3. Click the **Heading Background layer**, then click the **Show or Hide This Layer icon** • twice to hide and then show the layer.

4. Click the **Lock or Unlock All Layers icon** 🔒 to lock all layers.

5. With the layers locked, try to select and edit an object.

6. Click the **Lock or Unlock All Layers icon** 🔒 again to unlock the layers.

7. Click the **Heading Background layer**, then click the **Lock or Unlock This Layer** • to lock the layer.

8. Click the **Show All Layers as Outlines icon** □ to display the outlines of all objects.

   Notice the outlines are color-coded. For example, the two text objects are identified by their color (green) as being on the Heading layer (green).

9. Click the **Show All Layers as Outlines icon** □ to turn off this feature.

You hid and showed layers, you locked and unlocked layers, and you displayed the outlines of objects on a layer.

FIGURE 61
Hiding all the layers

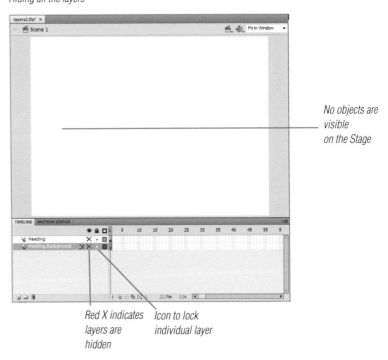

No objects are
visible
on the Stage

Red X indicates
layers are
hidden

Icon to lock
individual layer

FIGURE 62

A diagonal line

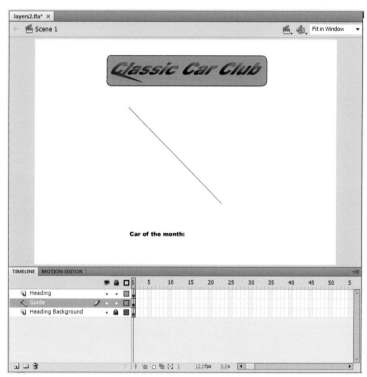

Create a guide for a Guide layer

1. Click the **Heading Background layer**, then click the **New Layer icon** on the bottom of the Timeline to add a new layer, Layer 3.

2. Rename the layer **Guide**.

3. Verify that the Guide layer is selected.

4. Click **Modify** on the menu bar, point to **Timeline**, then click **Layer Properties** to display the Layer Properties dialog box.

5. Click the **Guide option button** in the Type area, then click **OK**.

   A symbol appears next to the word Guide indicating that this is a Guide layer.

6. Click **frame 1** of the Guide layer.

7. Click the **Line tool** on the Tools panel, press and hold **[Shift]**, then draw the diagonal line, as shown in Figure 62.

8. Click the **Lock or Unlock This Layer icon** on the Guide layer to lock it.

You created a guide for a Guide layer and drew a guide line.

Lesson 5   Work with Layers and Objects

FLASH 2-41

Add objects to a Guide layer

1. Add a new layer on the Timeline above the Guide layer, name it **Ovals**, then click **frame 1** of the Ovals layer.

2. Click the **Fill Color tool color swatch** on the Tools panel, then click the **red gradient color swatch** in the bottom row of the Color palette.

3. Select the **Oval tool** on the Tools panel, then verify that the **Object Drawing option** in the Options area of the Tools panel is deselected.

4. Draw the **oval**, as shown in Figure 63.

5. Click the **Selection tool** on the Tools panel, then draw a **marquee** around the oval object to select it.

    | TIP Make sure the entire object (stroke and fill) is selected.

6. Point to the center of the oval, click, then slowly drag it to the Guide layer line, as shown in Figure 64.

7. With the oval object selected, click **Edit** on the menu bar, then click **Copy**.

8. Click **Edit** on the menu bar, click **Paste in Center**, then align the copied object to the Guide layer line beneath the first oval.

9. Click **Edit** on the menu bar, click **Paste in Center**, then align the copied object to the bottom of the Guide layer line.

    | TIP When objects are pasted in the center of the Stage, one object may cover up another object. Move them as needed.

You created a Guide layer and used it to align objects on the Stage.

FIGURE 63
An oval object

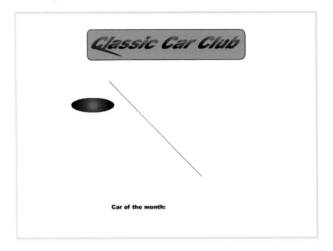

FIGURE 64
Dragging an object to the Guide layer line

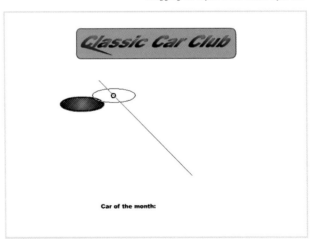

FIGURE 65

Adding text to the oval objects

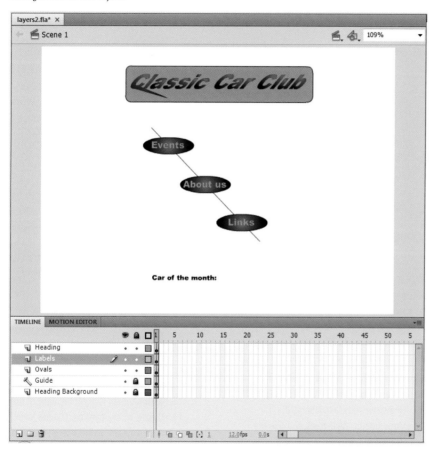

1. Insert a **new layer** on the Timeline above the Ovals layer, then name it **Labels**.

2. Click **frame 1** of the Labels layer.

3. Click the **Text tool** T on the Tools panel, click the **top oval**, then type **Events**.

4. Drag the **I-Beam pointer** I across Events to select the text, then, using the Properties panel set the font to **Arial**, the style to **Black** (Win) or **Bold** (Mac), the font size to **14**, and the fill color to **#999999**.

5. Click the **Selection tool** ↖ on the Tools panel, click the **text box** to select it, then drag the **text box** to center it on the oval, as shown in Figure 65.

   TIP   You can use the arrow keys on the keyboard to nudge the text into place.

6. Repeat Steps 3 through 5, typing **About us** and **Links** text blocks.

7. Test the movie, then close the Flash Player window.

8. Save and then close the document.

9. Exit Flash.

You used the Text tool to create text blocks that were placed on objects.

Use the Flash drawing tools.

1. Start Flash, open fl2_3.fla, then save it as **skillsdemo2**. Refer to Figure 66 as you complete these steps. (*Note:* Figure 66 shows the objects after changes have been made to them. For example, in step 5 you draw a rectangle in the middle of the Stage. Then, in a later step you rotate the rectangle 45 degrees.)

2. Set the view to Fit in Window, then display the Grid.

3. Set the stroke color to black (Hex: **#000000**) and the fill color to blue (Hex: **#0000FF**).

4. Use the Oval tool to draw an oval on the left side of the Stage, then draw a circle beneath the oval. (*Hint:* Use the Undo command as needed.)

5. Use the Rectangle tool to draw a rectangle in the middle of the Stage, then draw a square beneath the rectangle.

6. Use the Line tool to draw a horizontal line on the right side of the Stage, then draw a vertical line beneath the horizontal line and a diagonal line beneath the vertical line.

7. Use the Pen tool to draw an arrow-shaped object above the rectangle. (*Hint:* Use the Zoom tool to enlarge the area of the Stage.)

8. Use the Paint Bucket tool to fill the arrow with the blue color. (*Hint:* If the arrow does not fill, be sure you closed the arrow shape by clicking the first anchor point as your last action.)

9. Use the Pencil tool to draw a freehand line above the oval, then select the line and use the Smooth option to smooth out the line.

10. Use the Rectangle Primitive tool to draw a rectangle below the square and then use the Selection tool to drag a corner to round all the corners.

11. Save your work.

Select objects and apply colors.

1. Use the Selection tool to select the stroke of the circle, then deselect the stroke.

2. Use the Selection tool to select the fill of the circle, then deselect the fill.

3. Use the Ink Bottle tool to change the stroke color of the circle to red (Hex: **#FF0000**).

4. Use the Paint Bucket tool to change the fill color of the square to a red gradient.

5. Change the fill color of the oval to a blue gradient.

6. Save your work.

Work with drawn objects.

1. Copy and paste the arrow object.

2. Move the copied arrow to another location on the Stage.

3. Use the Properties panel to set the height of each arrow to 30.

4. Flip the copied arrow horizontally.

5. Rotate the rectangle to a 45° angle.

6. Skew the square to the right.

7. Copy one of the arrows and use the Subselection tool to reshape it, then delete it.

8. Use the Selection tool to reshape the circle to a crescent shape.

9. Save your work.

Work with text and text objects.

1. Enter the following text in a text block at the top of the Stage: **Gateway to the Pacific**.

2. Select the text, then change the text to font: **Tahoma**, size: **24**, color: **red**.

3. Use the Align option on the Modify menu to horizontally center the text block.

4. Use the up and down arrow keys on the keyboard to align the text block with a gridline.

5. Skew the text block to the right.

6. Save your work.

Work with layers.

1. Insert a layer into the document.

2. Change the name on the new layer to **Heading Bkgnd**.

3. Use the Rectangle Primitive tool to draw a rounded corner rectangle with a blue color that covers the words Gateway to the Pacific.

4. Switch the order of the layers.

5. Lock all layers.

6. Unlock all layers.

7. Hide the Heading Bkgnd layer.

8. Show the Heading Bkgnd layer.

9. Show all layers as outlines.

10. Turn on, then turn off the view of the outlines.

11. Create a new layer as a Guide layer, draw a guildeline on the new layer, lock the layer, then snap the arrows to the guideline.

12. Add a layer and use the Text tool to type **Seattle** below the heading.

13. Save your work.

Drawing Objects in Adobe Flash

Use the Merge Drawing Model mode.

1. Insert a new layer and name it **MergeDraw**.
2. Select the Rectangle tool and verify that the Object Drawing option is deselected.
3. Draw a square in the upper-right of the Stage, then use the Oval tool to draw a circle with a different color that covers approximately half of the square.
4. Verify the stroke and fill of the circle are selected, then using the Selection tool drag the circle off the square. (*Note:* Depending on the size of the circle and where you drew it to overlap the square, your results may vary from what is shown in Figure 66.)

Use the Object Drawing Model mode.

1. Insert a new layer and name it **ObjectDraw**.
2. Select the Rectangle tool and verify that the Object Drawing option is selected.
3. Draw a square with a blue fill color, then use the Oval tool to draw a circle with a different color that covers approximately half of the square.
4. Use the Selection tool to drag the circle off the square. (*Note:* Depending on the size of the circle and where you drew it to overlap the square, your results may vary from what is shown in Figure 66.)
5. Select the Rectangle tool and click the Object Drawing option to deselect it, then repeat step 3 and step 4. Notice how the dragging the circle off the square has a different effect when the Object Drawing option is turned off.

6. Save your work, then compare your image to the example shown in Figure 66.

Use the Spray tool with a symbol.

1. Add a new layer to the Timeline, then add a Keyframe to Frame 5 of the new layer.
2. Name the layer Aces Wild.
3. Select the Spray Brush tool.
4. Click the Edit button in the Symbol section of the Properties panel. (*Note:* If the Properties panel does not display the options for the Spray Brush tool, click the Selection tool, then click the Spray Brush tool.)
5. Select the Ace symbol.
6. Set the Scale width and height to 60.
7. Turn on Rotate symbol and turn off the other options.
8. Set the Brush width and height to 8 px.
9. Draw the W as shown in Figure 66.
10. Click the Selection tool on the Tools panel, then select the Spray Brush tool.
11. Draw the i.
12. Click the Selection tool, select the Spray Brush tool, then draw the n to complete a drawing similar to the one shown in Figure 66. (*Hint:* If you need to redo the drawing, use the Selection tool to draw a marquee around the drawing, then delete the selection.)
13. Test the movie, then save and close the document. (*Note:* If the movie displays too quickly, adjust the frame rate.)
14. Exit Flash.

FIGURE 66
Completed Skills Review

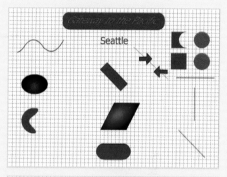

A local travel company, Ultimate Tours, has asked you to design several sample home pages for its new website. The goal of the website is to inform potential customers of its services. The company specializes in exotic treks, tours, and cruises. Thus, while its target audience spans a wide age range, they are all looking for something out of the ordinary.

1. Open a new Flash document and save it as **ultimatetours2**. Refer to Figure 67 as you complete this project.
2. Set the document properties, including the size (your choice) and background color.
3. Create the following on separate layers and name the layers:
   - A text heading; select a font size and font color. Skew the heading, break it apart, then reshape one or more of the characters.
   - A subheading with a different font size and color.
   - At least three objects.
4. Use one or more of the align features (gridlines, rulers, Align command on the Modify menu, arrow keys) to align the objects on the Stage.
5. On another layer, add text to the objects.
6. Lock all layers.
7. Compare your image to the example shown in Figure 67.
8. Save your work.
9. Test the movie, close the Flash Player window, then close the movie.

FIGURE 67
Sample completed Project Builder 1

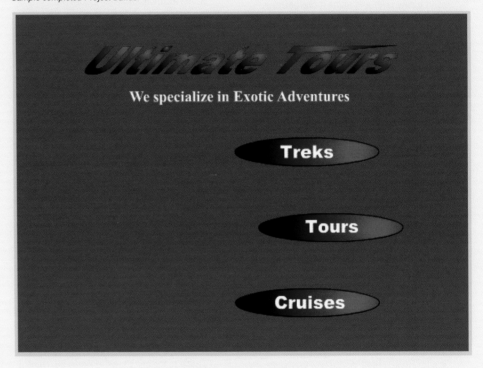

Drawing Objects in Adobe Flash

You have been asked to create several sample designs for the home page of a new organization called The Jazz Club. The club is being organized to bring together music enthusiasts for social events and charitable fundraising activities. The club members plan to sponsor weekly jam sessions and a show once a month. Because the club is just getting started, the organizers are looking to you for help in developing a website.

1. Plan the site by specifying the goal, target audience, treatment ("look and feel"), and elements you want to include (text, graphics, sound, and so on).
2. Sketch out a storyboard that shows the layout of the objects on the various screens and how they are linked together. Be creative in your design.
3. Open a new Flash document and save it as **thejazzclub2**.
4. Set the document properties, including the size and background color, if desired.
5. Display the gridlines and rulers and use them to help align objects on the Stage.
6. Create a heading with a background, text objects, and drawings to be used as links to the categories of information provided on the website. (*Note:* Some of the characters are individual text blocks [e.g. the S in Sessions] allowing you to move the text block without moving the other characters.)

(*Hint:* Use the Oval, Line, and Brush tools to create the notes. After selecting the Brush tool, experiment with the different Brush tool shapes found in the Options area at the bottom of the Tools panel.)
7. Hide the gridlines and rulers.
8. Save your work, then compare your image to the example shown in Figure 68.

FIGURE 68
Sample completed Project Builder 2

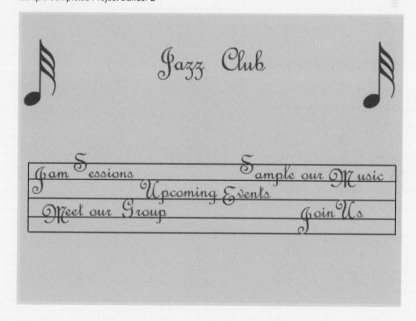

Figure 69 shows the home page of a website. Study the figure and complete the following. For each question indicate how you determined your answer.

1. Connect to the Internet, then go to *www.nps.org*.

2. Open a document in a word processor or open a new Flash document, save the file as **dpc2**, then answer the following questions. (*Hint*: Use the Text tool in Flash.)

    ■ Whose website is this?

    ■ What is the goal(s) of the site?

    ■ Who is the target audience?

    ■ What is the treatment ("look and feel") that is used?

    ■ What are the design layout guidelines being used (balance, movement, and so on)?

    ■ What may be animated on this home page?

    ■ Do you think this is an effective design for the company, its products, and its target audience? Why or why not?

    ■ What suggestions would you make to improve the design and why?

FIGURE 69
Design Project

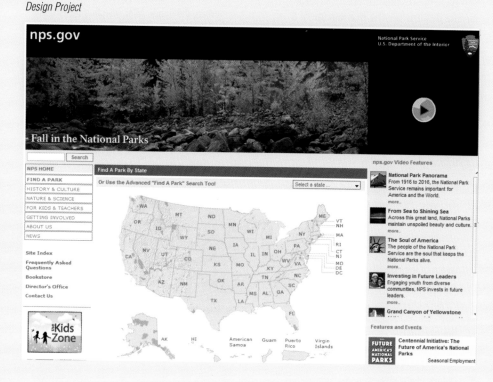

You have decided to create a personal portfolio of your work that you can use when you begin your job search. The portfolio will be a website done completely in Flash.

1. Research what should be included in a portfolio.

2. Plan the site by specifying the goal, target audience, treatment ("look and feel"), and elements you want to include (text, graphics, sound, and so on).

3. Sketch a storyboard that shows the layout of the objects on the various screens and how they are linked together. Be creative in your design.

4. Design the home page to include personal data, contact information, previous employment, education, and samples of your work.

5. Open a new Flash document and save it as **portfolio2**.

6. Set the document properties, including the size and background color, if desired.

7. Display the gridlines and rulers and use them to help align objects on the Stage.

8. Add a border the size of the Stage. (*Hint*: Use the Rectangle tool and set the fill color to none.)

9. Create a heading with its own background, then create other text objects and drawings to be used as links to the categories of information provided on the website. (*Hint*: In the example shown here, the Tahoma font is used. You can replace this font with Impact or any other appropriate font on your computer.)

10. Hide the gridlines and rulers.

11. Save your work, then compare your image to the example shown in Figure 70.

FIGURE 70
Sample Completed Portfolio Project

chapter

3

WORKING WITH SYMBOLS
AND INTERACTIVITY

1. Create symbols and instances

2. Work with libraries

3. Create buttons

4. Assign actions to frames and buttons

5. Importing graphics

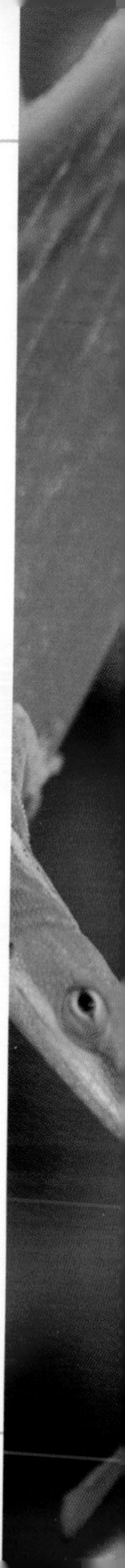

3 WORKING WITH SYMBOLS
AND INTERACTIVITY

Introduction

An important benefit of Flash is its ability to create movies with small file sizes. This allows the movies to be delivered from the web more quickly. One way to keep the file size small is to create reusable graphics, buttons, and movie clips. Flash allows you to create a graphic (drawing) and then make unlimited copies, which you can use throughout the current movie and in other movies. Flash calls the original drawing a **symbol** and the copied drawings **instances**. Flash stores symbols in the Library panel—each time you need a copy of the symbol, you can open the Library panel and drag the symbol to the Stage, which creates an instance (copy) of the symbol. Using instances reduces the movie file size because Flash stores only the symbol's information (size, shape, color), but Flash does not save the instance in the Flash movie. Rather, a link is established between the symbol and an instance so that the instance has the same properties (such as color and shape) as the symbol.

What is especially valuable about this process is that you can change the properties for each instance. For example, if your website is to contain drawings of cars that are similar, you can create just one drawing, convert it to a symbol, insert as many instances of the car as needed, and then change an individual instance as desired.

There are three categories of symbols: graphic, button, and movie clip. A graphic symbol is useful because you can reuse a single image and make changes in each instance of the image. A button symbol is useful because you can create buttons for interactivity, such as starting or stopping a movie. A movie clip symbol is useful for creating complex animations because you can create a movie within a movie. Symbols can be created from objects you draw using the Flash drawing tools. In addition, you can import graphics into a Flash document that can then be converted into symbols.

Tools You'll Use

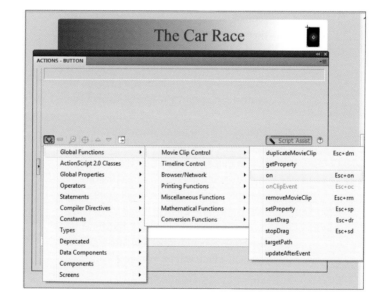

CREATE SYMBOLS
AND INSTANCES

What You'll Do

 In this lesson, you will create graphic symbols, turn them into instances, and then edit the instances.

Creating a Graphic Symbol

You can use the New Symbol command on the Insert menu to create and then draw a symbol. You can also draw an object and then use the Convert to Symbol command on the Modify menu to convert the object to a symbol. The Convert to Symbol dialog box, shown in Figure 1, allows you to name the symbol and specify the type of symbol you want to create (Movie Clip, Button, or Graphic). When naming a symbol, it's a good idea to use a naming convention that allows you to quickly identify the type of symbol and to group like symbols together. For example, you could identify all graphic symbols by naming them g_*name* and all buttons as b_*name*. In Figure 1, the drawing on the Stage is being converted into a graphic symbol, which will be named g_ball.

After you complete the Convert to Symbol dialog box, Flash places the symbol in the Library panel, as shown in Figure 2. In Figure 2, an icon identifying the symbol as a graphic symbol and the symbol name are listed in the Library panel, along with a preview of the selected symbol. To create an instance of the symbol, you simply drag a symbol from the Library panel to the Stage. To edit a symbol, you select it from the Library panel or you use the Edit Symbols command on the Edit menu. This displays the symbol in an edit window, where changes can be made to it. When you edit a symbol, the changes are reflected in all instances of that symbol in your movie. For example, you can draw a car, convert the car to a symbol, and then create several instances of the car. You can uniformly change the size of all the cars by double-clicking the car symbol in the Library panel to open the edit window, and then rescaling it to the desired size.

Working with Instances

You can have as many instances as needed in your movie, and you can edit each one to make it somewhat different from the others. You can rotate, skew (slant), and resize graphic and button instances. In addition, you can change the color, brightness, and transparency. However, there are some limitations. An instance is a single object with no segments or parts, such as a stroke and a fill. You cannot select a part of an instance. Therefore, any changes to the color of the instance are made to the entire object. Of course, you can use layers to stack other objects on top of an instance to change its appearance. In addition, you can use the Break Apart command on the Modify menu to break the link between an instance and a symbol. Once the link is broken, you can make any changes to the object, such as changing its stroke and fill color. However, because the link is broken,

the object is no longer an instance; if you make any changes to the original symbol, then the object is not affected.

The process for creating an instance is to open the Library panel and drag the desired symbol to the Stage. Once the symbol is on the Stage, you select the instance by using the Selection tool to drag a marquee around it. A blue border indicates that the object is selected. Then, you can use the Free Transform tool options (such as Rotate and Skew, or Scale) to modify the

entire image, or you can use the Break Apart command to break apart the instance and edit individual strokes and fills.

QUICKTIP

You need to be careful when editing an instance. Use the Selection tool to drag a marquee around the instance, or click the object once to select it. Do not double-click the instance when it is on the Stage; otherwise, you will open an edit window that is used to edit the symbol, not the instance.

FIGURE 1

Using the Convert to Symbol dialog box to convert an object to a symbol

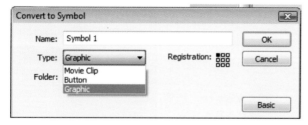

FIGURE 2

A graphic symbol in the Library panel

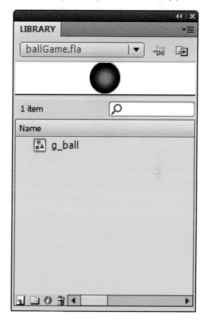

Create a symbol

1. Open fl3_1.fla from the drive and folder where your Data Files are stored, then save it as **coolCar**. This document has one object, a car, that was created using the Flash drawing tools.

2. Verify the Properties panel, the Library panel, and the Tools panel are displayed.

3. Set the magnification to **100%**.

4. Click the **Selection tool** on the Tools panel, then drag a **marquee** around the car to select it.

5. Click **Modify** on the menu bar, then click **Convert to Symbol**.

6. Type **g_car** in the Name text box.

7. Click the **Type list arrow** to display the symbol types, as shown in Figure 3.

8. Click **Graphic**, then click **OK**.

9. Click the **Library panel tab**, then study the Library panel, as shown in Figure 4, and notice it displays the symbol (red car) in the Item Preview window, an icon indicating that this is a graphic symbol, and the name of the symbol (g_car).

The symbol is contained in the library, and the car on the Stage is now an instance of the symbol.

You opened a file with an object, converted the object to a symbol, and displayed the symbol in the Library panel.

FIGURE 3
Options in the Convert to Symbol dialog box

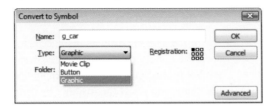

FIGURE 4
Newly created symbol in the Library panel

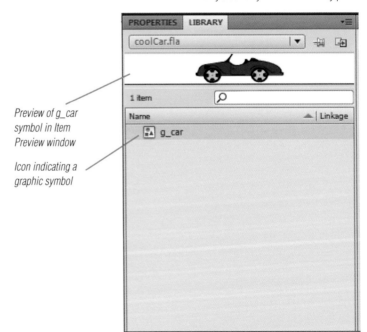

Preview of g_car symbol in Item Preview window

Icon indicating a graphic symbol

FIGURE 5
Creating an instance

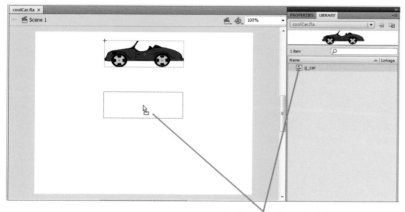

Drag the symbol from the Library
panel to below the original
instance to create a second
instance of the symbol

This area may
not be open

FIGURE 6
The alpha set to 50%

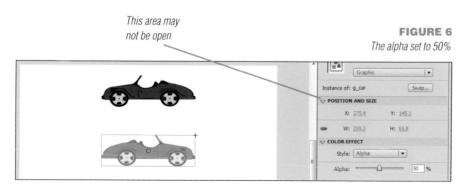

Create and edit an instance

1. Point to the **car image** in the Item Preview
   window of the Library panel, then drag the
   image to the Stage beneath the first car, as
   shown in Figure 5.

   TIP You can also drag the name of the
   symbol from the Library panel to the Stage.
   Both cars on the Stage are instances of the
   graphic symbol in the Library panel.

2. Verify the bottom car is selected, click
   Modify on the menu bar, point to **Transform**,
   then click **Flip Horizontal**.

3. Display the Properties panel, then display
   the COLOR EFFECT area if it is not
   already showing.

4. Click the **Style list arrow**, then click **Alpha**.

5. Drag the **Alpha slider** to 50%.

   Notice how the transparency changes.
   Figure 6 shows the transparency set to 50%.

6. Click a blank area of the Stage to deselect
   the object.

   Changing the alpha setting gives the car
   a more transparent look.

*You created an instance of a symbol and edited the
instance on the Stage.*

Edit a symbol in the edit window

1. Display the Library panel, double-click the **g_car symbol icon** in the Library panel to display the edit window, then compare your screen to Figure 7.

   The g_car symbol appears in the edit window, indicating that you are editing the g_car symbol.

   > TIP You can also edit a symbol by clicking Edit on the menu bar, then clicking Edit Symbols.

2. Click a blank area of the window to deselect the car.

3. Verify the Selection tool is selected, then click the **light gray hubcap** inside the front wheel to select it.

4. Press and hold **[Shift]**, then click the **hubcap** inside the back wheel so both hubcap fills are selected.

5. Set the **Fill Color** to the **blue gradient color swatch** in the bottom row of the color palette, deselect the image, then compare your image to Figure 8.

6. Click **Scene 1** at the top left of the edit window to exit the edit window and return to the main Timeline and main Stage.

   Changes you make to the symbol affect every instance of the symbol on the Stage. The hubcap fill becomes a blue gradient in the Library panel and on the Stage.

   You edited a symbol in the edit window that affected all instances of the symbol.

FIGURE 7
Edit window

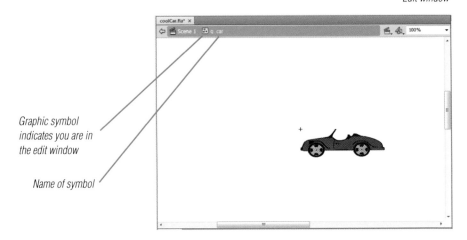

Graphic symbol indicates you are in the edit window

Name of symbol

FIGURE 8
Edited symbol

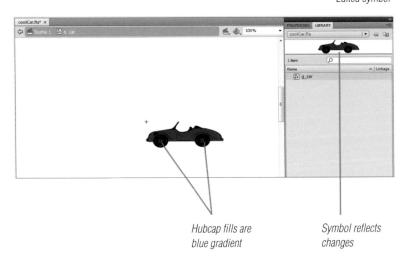

Hubcap fills are blue gradient

Symbol reflects changes

FIGURE 9
The car with the maroon body selected

Break apart an instance

1. Drag a **marquee** around the bottom car to select it if it is not selected.

2. Click **Modify** on the menu bar, then click **Break Apart**.

   The object is no longer linked to the symbol, and its parts (strokes and fills) can now be edited.

3. Click a blank area of the Stage to deselect the object.

4. Click the **blue front hubcap**, press and hold **[Shift]**, then click the **blue back hubcap** so both hubcaps are selected.

5. Set the **Fill Color** to the **light gray color swatch (#999999)** in the left column of the color palette.

6. Double-click the **g_car symbol icon** in the Library panel to display the edit window.

7. Click the **maroon front body** of the car to select it, press and hold **[Shift]**, then click the **maroon back body** of the car, as shown in Figure 9.

8. Set the **Fill Color** to the **red gradient color swatch** in the bottom row of the color palette.

9. Click **Scene 1** at the top left of the edit window, then compare your image to Figure 10.

   The body color of the car in the original instance is a different color, but the body color of the car to which you applied the Break Apart command remains unchanged.

10. Save your work.

You used the Break Apart command to break the link of the instance to its symbol, you edited the object, and then you edited the symbol.

FIGURE 10
Changing the symbol affects only the one instance of the symbol

Instance of the symbol

Object that is no longer an instance of the symbol

WORK WITH
LIBRARIES

What You'll Do

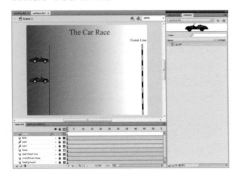

In this lesson, you will use the Library panel to organize the symbols in a movie.

Understanding the Library

The library in a Flash document contains the symbols and other items such as imported graphics, movie clips, and sounds. The Library panel provides a way to view and organize the items, and allows you to change the item name, display item properties, and add and delete items. Figure 11 shows the Library panel for a document. Refer to this figure as you read the following descriptions of the parts of the library.

Title tab—Identifies this as the Library panel.

List box—The list box below the title tab can be used to select an open document and display the Library panel associated with that open document. This allows you to use the items from one movie in another movie. For example, you may have developed a drawing in one Flash movie and need to use it in the movie you

are working on. With both documents open, you simply use the list box to display the library with the desired drawing, and then drag it to the Stage of the current movie. This will automatically place the drawing in the library for the current movie. In addition to the movie libraries, you can create permanent libraries that are available whenever you start Flash. Flash also has sample libraries that contain buttons and other objects. The permanent and sample libraries are accessed through the Common Libraries command on the Window menu. All assets in all of these libraries are available for use in any movie.

Options menu—Shown in Figure 12; provides access to several features used to edit symbols (such as renaming symbols) and organize symbols (such as creating a new folder).

Working with Symbols and Interactivity

Item Preview window—Displays the selected item. If the item is animated or a sound file, a control button appears, allowing you to preview the animation or play the sound.

Toggle Sorting Order icon—Allows you to reorder the list of folders and items within folders.

Name text box—Lists the folder and item names. Each item type has a different icon

associated with it. Clicking an item name or icon displays the item in the Item Preview window.

New Symbol icon—Displays the Create New Symbol dialog box, allowing you to create a new symbol.

New Folder icon—Allows you to create a new folder.

Properties icon—Displays the Properties dialog box for the selected item.

Delete Item icon—Deletes the selected item or folder.

To make changes to an item, you can double-click the item icon in the Library panel to display the edit window.

FIGURE 11
The Library panel

Title tab

Name list box

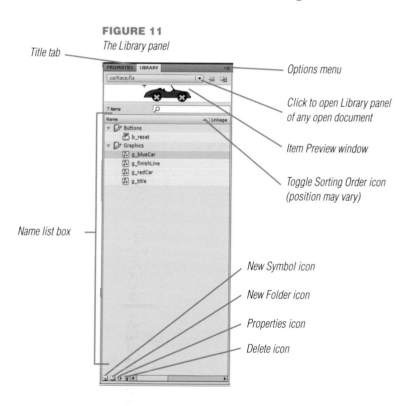

Options menu

Click to open Library panel of any open document

Item Preview window

Toggle Sorting Order icon (position may vary)

New Symbol icon

New Folder icon

Properties icon

Delete icon

FIGURE 12
The Options menu

New Symbol...
New Folder
New Font...
New Video...

Rename
Delete
Duplicate...
Move to...

Edit
Edit with ...
Edit with Soundbooth
Play
Update...

Properties...
Component Definition...
Shared Library Properties...

Select Unused Items

Expand Folder
Collapse Folder
Expand All Folders
Collapse All Folders

Help

Close
Close Group

Create folders in the Library panel

1. Open fl3_2.fla, then save it as **carRace**.

2. Verify the Properties panel, the Library panel, and the **Tools panel** are displayed.

3. Set the magnification to **100%**.

   This movie has eight layers containing various objects such as text blocks, lines, and a background. Two layers contain animations of cars.

4. Test the movie, then close the Flash Player window.

5. Click the **Show or Hide All Layers icon** on the Timeline to hide all of the layers.

6. Click the **Show or Hide This Layer icon** for each layer to show the contents of each layer.

   Note: The reset layer shows an empty Stage. This is because the word Reset is located in frame 65 at the end of the movie and does not appear in frame 1.

7. Click each item in the Library panel to display it in the Item Preview window. Notice that there is one button symbol (b_reset) and five graphic symbols.

   Note: The g_finishLine graphic will look like a black line because the preview window is small.

8. Click the **New Folder icon** in the Library panel, as shown in Figure 13.

9. Type **Graphics** in the Name text box, then press **[Enter]** (Win) or **[return]** (Mac).

   (continued)

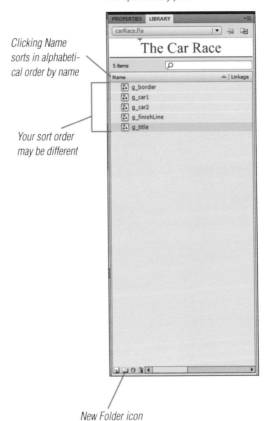

FIGURE 13
The open Library panel

Clicking Name sorts in alphabetical order by name

Your sort order may be different

New Folder icon

FIGURE 14
The Library panel with the folders added

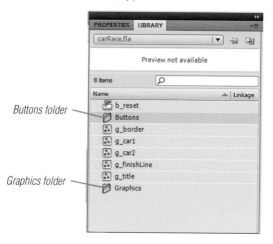

Buttons folder

Graphics folder

FIGURE 15
The Library panel after moving the symbols to the folders

Your folders might be expanded

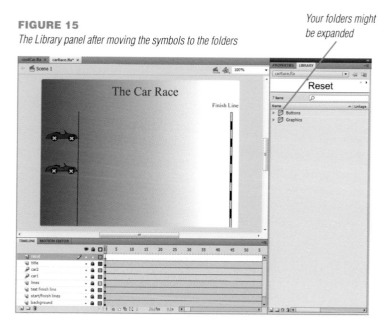

10. Click the **New Folder icon** 📁 on the Library panel.

11. Type **Buttons** in the Name text box, then press [**Enter**] (Win) or [**return**] (Mac).

    Your Library panel should resemble Figure 14.

You opened a Flash movie and created folders in the Library panel.

Organize items within Library panel folders

1. Click **Name** on the Name list box title bar and notice how the items are sorted.

2. Repeat step 1 and notice how the items are sorted.

3. Drag the **g_title symbol** in the Library panel to the Graphics folder.

4. Drag the other graphic symbols to the Graphics folder.

5. Drag the **b_reset symbol** to the Buttons folder, then compare your Library panel to Figure 15.

6. Click the **Graphics folder expand list arrow** ▶ to open it and display the graphic symbols.

7. Click the **Buttons folder expand list arrow** ▶ to open it and display the button symbol.

8. Click the **Graphics folder collapse list arrow** ▼ to close the folder.

9. Click the **Buttons folder collapse list arrow** ▼ to close the folder.

    Note: To remove an item from a folder, drag the item down to a blank area of the Library panel.

You organized the symbols within the folders and opened and closed the folders.

Display the properties of symbols, rename symbols, and delete a symbol

1. Click the **expand list arrow** ▶ for the Graphics folder to display the symbols.

2. Click the **g_car1 symbol**, then click the **Properties icon** 🅘 at the bottom of the Library panel to display the Symbol Properties dialog box.

3. Type **g_redCar** in the Name text box, as shown in Figure 16, then click **OK**.

4. Repeat Steps 2 and 3 renaming the g_car2 symbol to **g_blueCar**.

   TIP Double-click the name to rename it without opening the Symbol Properties dialog box.

5. Click **g_border** in the Library panel to select it.

6. Click the **Delete icon** 🗑 at the bottom of the Library panel.

   TIP You can also select an item and press [Delete], or you can use the Options menu in the Library panel to remove an item from the library. The Undo command in the Edit menu can be used to undelete an item.

You used the Library panel to display the properties of symbols, rename symbols, and delete a symbol.

FIGURE 16
Renaming a symbol

FIGURE 17

The carRace.fla document and the coolCar.fla Library panel

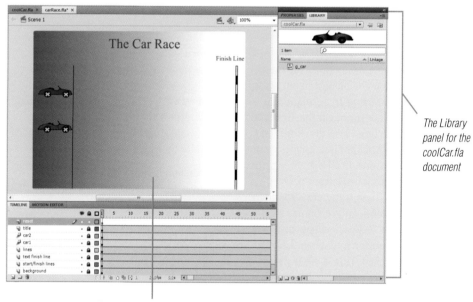

The Library panel for the coolCar.fla document

The carRace.fla document

Use multiple Library panels

1. Click the **Library panel list arrow** near the top of the Library panel to display a list of open documents.

2. Click **coolCar.fla**, then click **g_car**.

   The Library panel for the coolCar document is displayed. However, the carRace document remains open, as shown in Figure 17.

3. Click **frame 1** on the reset layer, then drag the **car** from the Library panel to the center of the Stage.

   The reset layer is the only unlocked layer. Objects cannot be placed on locked layers.

4. Click the **Library panel list arrow** to display the open documents.

5. Click **carRace.fla** to view the carRace document's Library panel.

   Notice the g_car symbol is automatically added to the Library panel of the carRace document.

6. Click the **g_car symbol** in the Library panel.

7. Click the **Delete icon** 🗑 at the bottom of the Library panel.

   You deleted the g_car symbol from the carRace library but it still exists in the coolCar library. The car was also deleted from the Stage.

8. Save your work.

9. Click the **coolCar.fla tab** at the top of the workspace to display the document.

10. Close the coolCar document and save the document if asked.

You used the Library panel to display the contents of another library and added an object from that library to the current document.

CREATE
BUTTONS

What You'll Do

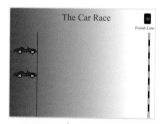

 In this lesson, you will create a button, edit the four button states, and test a button.

Understanding Buttons

Button symbols are used to provide inter-activity. When you click a button, an action occurs, such as starting an animation or jumping to another frame on the Timeline. Any object, including Flash drawings, text blocks, and imported graphic images, can be made into buttons. Unlike graphic symbols, buttons have four states: Up, Over, Down, and Hit. These states correspond to the use of the mouse and recognize that the user requires feedback when the mouse is pointing to a button and when the button has been clicked. This is often shown by a change in the button (such as a differ-ent color or different shape). An example of a button with different colors for the four different states is shown in Figure 18. These four states are explained in the fol-lowing paragraphs.

Up—Represents how the button appears when the mouse pointer is not over it.

Over—Represents how the button appears when the mouse pointer is over it.

Down—Represents how the button appears after the user clicks the mouse.

Hit—Defines the area of the screen that will respond to the click. In most cases, you will want the Hit state to be the same or similar to the Up state in location and size.

When you create a button symbol, Flash automatically creates a new Timeline. The Timeline has only four frames, one for each button state. The Timeline does not play; it merely reacts to the mouse pointer by displaying the appropriate button state and performing an action, such as jumping to a specific frame on the main Timeline.

The process for creating and previewing buttons is as follows:

Create a button symbol—Draw an object or select an object that has already been created and placed on the Stage. Use the Convert to Symbol command on the Modify menu to convert the object to a button symbol and to enter a name for the button.

Edit the button symbol—Select the button and choose the Edit Symbols command on the Edit menu or double-click the button symbol in the Library panel. This displays the button Timeline, shown in Figure 19, which allows you to work with the four button states. The Up state is the original button symbol. Flash automatically places it in frame 1. You need to determine how the original object will change for the other states. To change the button for the Over state, click frame 2 and insert a keyframe. This automatically places a copy of the

button that is in frame 1 into frame 2. Then, alter the button's appearance for the Over state by, for instance, changing the fill color. Use the same process for the Down state. For the Hit state, you insert a keyframe on frame 4 and then specify the area on the screen that will respond to the pointer. If you do not specify a hit area, the image for the Up state is used for the hit area. You add a keyframe to the Hit frame only if you are going to specify the hit area.

Return to the main Timeline—Once you've finished editing a button, you

choose the Edit Document command on the Edit menu, or click Scene 1 above the edit window, to return to the main Timeline.

Preview the button—By default, Flash disables buttons so that you can manipulate them on the Stage. You can preview a button by choosing the Enable Simple Buttons command on the Control menu. You can also choose the Test Movie command on the Control menu to play the movie and test the buttons.

FIGURE 18
The four button states

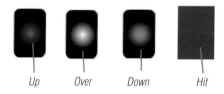

Up   Over   Down   Hit

FIGURE 19
The button Timeline

Create a button

1. Insert a new layer above the top layer in the Timeline, then name the layer **signal**.

2. Select the **Rectangle Primitive tool** ▭ , click the **Stroke Color tool** ✎ on the Tools panel, then click the **No Stroke icon** ☑ in the upper-right corner of the color palette.

3. Set the **Fill Color** ⬚ to the **red gradient Color swatch** in the bottom row of the color palette.

4. Display the Properties panel, click the **Reset button** in the RECTANGLE OPTIONS area, then set the corner radius to **5**.

5. Draw the **rectangle** shown in Figure 20.

6. Click the **Zoom tool** ⚲ on the Tools panel, then click the **rectangle** to enlarge it.

7. Select the **Gradient Transform tool** ⬚ on the Tools panel, then click the **rectangle**.

   You may need to click and hold the Free Transform tool first.

8. Drag the **diagonal arrow** toward the center of the rectangle as shown in Figure 21 to make the red area more round.

9. Click the **Selection tool** ➤ on the Tools panel, then drag a **marquee** around the rectangle to select it.

10. Click **Modify** on the menu bar, then click **Convert to Symbol**.

11. Type **b_signal** in the Name text box, click the **Type list arrow**, click **Button**, then click **OK**.

12. Display the Library panel, drag the **b_signal symbol** to the Buttons folder.

You created a button symbol on the Stage and dragged it to the Buttons folder in the Library panel.

FIGURE 20
The rectangle object

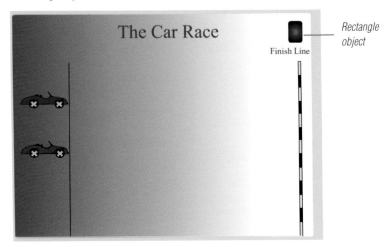

Rectangle object

FIGURE 21
Adjusting the gradient

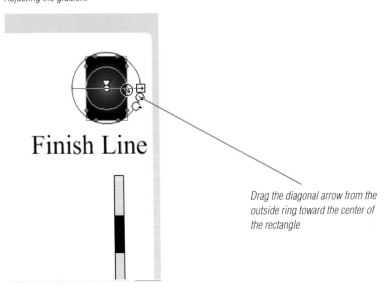

Drag the diagonal arrow from the outside ring toward the center of the rectangle

FIGURE 22

Specifying the hit area

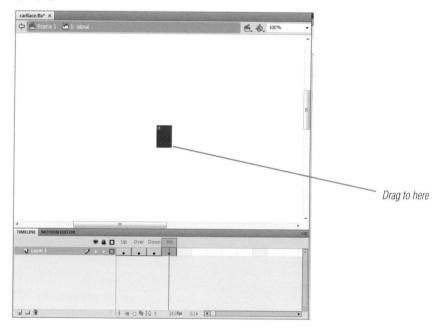

Drag to here

Edit a button and specify a Hit area

1. Open the Buttons folder, right-click (Win) or control-click (Mac) **b_signal** in the Library panel, then click **Edit**.

   Flash displays the edit window showing the Timeline with four button states.

2. Click the blank **Over frame** on Layer 1, then insert a keyframe.

   | TIP The [F6] key inserts a keyframe in the selected frame (Win).

3. Set the **Fill Color** to the **gray gradient color swatch** on the bottom of the color palette.

4. Insert a **keyframe** in the Down frame on Layer 1.

5. Set the **Fill Color** to the **green gradient color swatch** on the bottom of the color palette.

6. Insert a **keyframe** in the Hit frame on Layer 1.

7. Select the **Rectangle tool** on the Tools panel, set the **Fill Color** to the **blue color swatch** in the left column of the color palette.

8. Draw a **rectangle** slightly larger than the button, as shown in Figure 22, then release the mouse button.

   | TIP The Hit area will not be visible on the Stage.

9. Click **Scene 1** above the edit window to return to the main Timeline.

You edited a button by changing the color of its Over and Down states, and you specified the Hit area.

Test a button

1. Click the **Selection tool** ↖ , then click a blank area of the Stage.

2. Click **Control** on the menu bar, then click **Enable Simple Buttons**.

   This command allows you to test buttons on the Stage without viewing the movie in the Flash Player window.

3. Point to the **signal button** on the Stage, then compare your image to Figure 23.

   The pointer changes to a hand 🖑 , indicating that the object is clickable, and the button changes to a gray gradient, the color you selected for the Over State.

4. Press and hold the **mouse button**, then notice that the button changes to a green gradient, the color you selected for the Down state, as shown in Figure 24.

   (continued)

(continued)

FIGURE 23
The button's Over state

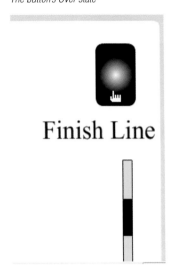

FIGURE 24
The button's Down state

The button Hit area

All buttons have an area that responds to the mouse pointer, including rolling over the button and clicking it. This hit area is usually the same size and shape as the button itself. However, you can specify any area of the button to be the hit area. For example, you could have a button symbol that looks like a target with just the bulls-eye center being the hit area.

FIGURE 25
The button's Up state

5. Release the mouse and notice that the button changes to a gray gradient, the color you selected for the Over state.

6. Move the mouse away from the signal button, and notice that the button returns to a red gradient, the Up state color, as shown in Figure 25.

7. Click **Control** on the menu bar, then click **Enable Simple Buttons** to turn off the command.

8. Click the **View list arrow** above the Stage, as shown in Figure 26, then click **Fit in Window**.

   This shortcut allows you to change the magnification view without using the Magnification command on the View menu or the Zoom tool in the Tools panel.

9. Save your work.

You used the mouse to test a button and view the button states.

FIGURE 26
View options from the View list

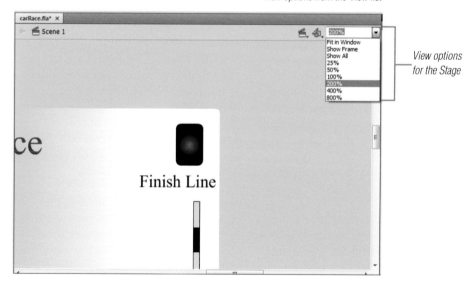

View options for the Stage

ASSIGN ACTIONS
TO FRAMES AND BUTTONS

What You'll Do

In this lesson, you will use ActionScripts to assign actions to frames and buttons.

Understanding Actions

In a basic movie, Flash plays the frames sequentially, repeating the movie without stopping for user input. However, you may often want to provide users with the ability to interact with the movie by allowing them to perform actions, such as starting and stopping the movie or jumping to a specific frame in the movie. One way to provide user interaction is to assign an action to the Down state of a button. Then, whenever the user clicks the button, the action occurs. Flash provides a scripting language, called ActionScript, that allows you to add actions to buttons and frames within a movie. For example, you can place a stop action in a frame that pauses the movie, and then you can assign a play action to a button that starts the movie when the user clicks the button.

Analyzing ActionScript

ActionScript is a powerful scripting language that allows those with even limited programming experience to create complex actions. For example, you can create order

forms that capture user input or volume controls that display when sounds are played. A basic ActionScript involves an event (such as a mouse click) that causes some action to occur by triggering the script. The following is an example of a basic ActionScript:

```
on (release) {
        gotoAndPlay(10);
}
```

In this example, the event is a mouse click (indicated by the word release) that causes the movie's playback head to go to frame 10 and play the frame. This is a simple example of ActionScript code and is easy to follow. Other ActionScript code can be quite complex and may require programming expertise to understand.

ActionScript 2.0 and 3.0

Adobe has identified two types of Flash CS4 users, designers and developers. Designers focus more on the visual features of a Flash movie, including the user interface design, drawing objects, and acquiring and editing additional assets (such as sound clips). Whereas, developers focus more on the programming aspects of a Flash movie, including creation of complex animations and writing the code that specifies how the movie responds to user interactions. In many cases, designers and developers work together to create sophisticated Flash applications. In other cases, designers work without the benefit of a developer's programming expertise. In order to accommodate the varying needs of these two types of uses, Flash CS4 provides two versions of ActionScript, 2.0 and 3.0,

called AS2 and AS3. ActionScript 3.0 is used by developers because it provides a programming environment that is more familiar to them and can be used to create movies that download more quickly. However, the differences between AS2 and AS3 are transparent to designers who do not have programming expertise. AS2 allows the new Flash user to create compelling applications while not having to have a background in programming. At the same time it provides an introduction to ActionScript that can be the basis for learning ActionScript 3.0. ActionScript 2.0 will be used in this chapter. You can

specify ActionScript 2.0 when creating a new document or you can use the Flash section of the Publish Settings command found on the File menu to specify AS2.

An advantage of using AS2 is a feature called Script Assist, which provides an easy way to use ActionScript without having to learn the scripting language. The Script Assist feature within the Actions panel allows you to assign basic actions to frames and objects, such as buttons. Figure 27 shows the Actions panel displaying an ActionScript indicating that when the user clicks the selected object (a button, in this example, b_signal), the movie goes to frame 2.

FIGURE 27

The Actions panel displaying an ActionScript

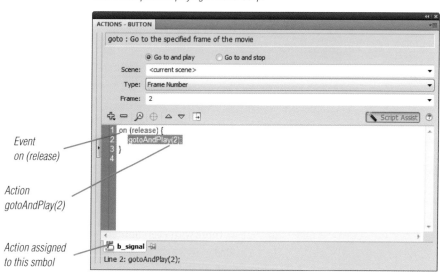

Event
on (release)

Action
gotoAndPlay(2)

Action assigned
to this smbol

The process for assigning actions to buttons, shown in Figure 28, is as follows:

- Select the button on the Stage that you want to assign an action to.
- Display the Actions panel, using the Window menu.
- Select the Script Assist button to display the Script Assist panel within the ActionScript panel.
- Click the Add a new item to the script icon to display a list of Action categories.
- Select the appropriate category from a drop-down list. Flash provides several Action categories. The Timeline Control category within the Global Functions menu allows you to create scripts for controlling movies and navigating within movies. You can use these actions to start and stop movies, jump to specific frames, and respond to user mouse movements and keystrokes.
- Select the desired action, such as goto.
- Specify the event that triggers the action, such as on (release). This step in the process is not shown in Figure 28.

Button actions respond to one or more mouse events, including:

Release—With the pointer inside the button Hit area, the user presses and releases (clicks) the mouse button. This is the default event.

Key Press—With the button displayed, the user presses a predetermined key on the keyboard.

Roll Over—The user moves the pointer into the button Hit area.

Drag Over—The user holds down the mouse button, moves the pointer out of the button Hit area, and then back into the Hit area.

Using Frame Actions—In addition to assigning actions to buttons, you can assign actions to frames. Actions assigned to frames are executed when the playhead reaches the frame. A common frame action is stop, which is often assigned to the first and last frame of a layer on the Timeline.

FIGURE 28
The process for assigning actions to buttons

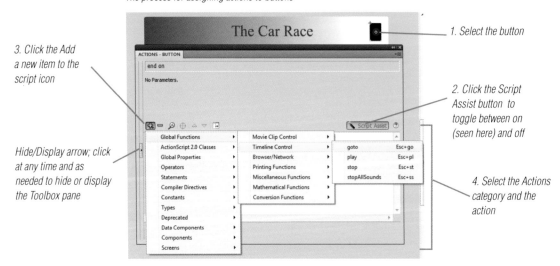

3. Click the Add a new item to the script icon

Hide/Display arrow; click at any time and as needed to hide or display the Toolbox pane

1. Select the button

2. Click the Script Assist button to toggle between on (seen here) and off

4. Select the Actions category and the action

Understanding the Actions panel—The Actions panel has two panes. The left pane (also called the Toolbox pane) uses folders to display the Action categories. The right pane, called the Script pane, is used with the Script Assist feature and it displays the ActionScript code as the code is being generated. When using the Script Assist feature, it is best to close the left pane. This is done by clicking the Hide/Display arrow as shown in Figure 29. The lower-left corner of the Script pane displays the symbol name or the frame to which the action(s)

will apply. Always verify that the desired symbol or frame is displayed.

Using Frame Labels—Buttons are often used to move the playhead to a specific location on the Timeline. For example, clicking a Start button might cause the playhead to jump from frame 1 to frame 10 to start an animation. In addition to referencing frame numbers, like 10, you can reference frame labels in the ActionScript code. Frame labels have an advantage over frame numbers, especially in large and

complex applications, because adding or deleting frames will not disrupt the navigation to a frame reference you already have in actions, since the label remains attached to the frame even if the frame moves. The process is to select a frame and use the Properties panel to specify a name. Then use the name in the ActionScript code instead of the frame number. Figure 30 shows the Timeline with a frame label and the Actions panel with the code that references the label.

FIGURE 29
The Actions panel

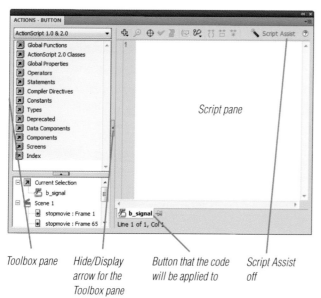

Toolbox pane   Hide/Display arrow for the Toolbox pane   Button that the code will be applied to   Script Assist off

FIGURE 30
The Timeline with a frame label

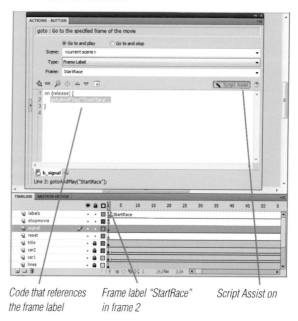

Code that references the frame label   Frame label "StartRace" in frame 2   Script Assist on

Assign a stop action to frames

1. Click **Control** on the menu bar, then click **Test Movie**.

   The movie plays and continues to loop.

2. Close the Flash Player window.

3. Insert a **new layer**, name it **stopmovie**, then click **frame 1** on the layer to select the frame.

4. Click **Window** on the menu bar, then click **Actions** to display the Actions panel.

5. Study the Actions panel. If the Toolbox pane is displayed as shown in Figure 31, then click the **Hide/Display arrow** to hide the pane.

6. Click the **Script Assist button** to turn on the Script Assist feature.

7. Verify stopmovie:1 (indicating the layer and frame to which the action will be applied) is displayed in the lower-left corner of the Script pane.

8. Click the **Add a new item to the script button** 🕂 to display the Script categories, point to **Global Functions**, point to **Timeline Control**, then click **stop**, as shown in Figure 32.

9. Move the Actions panel as needed to see the Timeline, then click **frame 65** on the stopmovie layer.

10. Insert a **keyframe** in frame 65 on the stopmovie layer, then repeat Step 8. Compare your screen to Figure 33. Test the movie.

    The movie does not play because there is a stop action assigned to frame 1.

11. Close the Flash Player window.

You inserted a layer and assigned a stop action to the first and last frames on the layer.

FIGURE 31
The Actions panel Toolbox pane

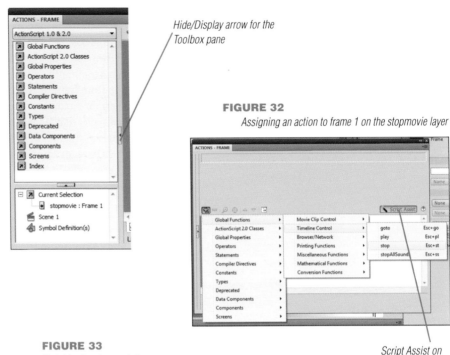

Hide/Display arrow for the Toolbox pane

FIGURE 32
Assigning an action to frame 1 on the stopmovie layer

Script Assist on

FIGURE 33
Script for the stopmovie layer

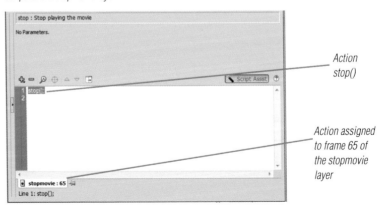

Action
stop()

Action assigned to frame 65 of the stopmovie layer

FIGURE 34

Assigning an event and an action to a button

Button selected

Action assigned
to the button
named b_signal

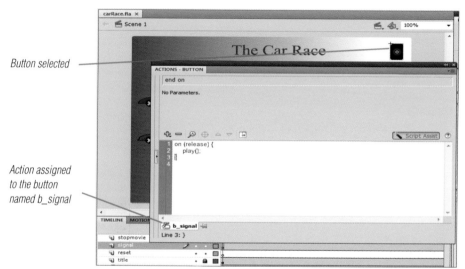

1. Click **frame 1** on the Signal layer.
2. Move the **Actions panel** to view the signal button on the Stage (if necessary).

   TIP   You can collapse the Actions panel to view more of the Stage, then expand the Actions panel when needed. Alternately, you can drag the bottom of the Actions panel up to make the panel smaller.

3. Click the **Selection tool** ▶ on the Tools panel, then click the **button** on the Stage.
4. Verify b_signal is displayed in the lower left of the Actions panel.

   This ensures that the actions specified in the Actions panel will apply to the b_signal button.

5. Click ⚬ to display the Script categories, point to **Global Functions**, point to **Timeline Control**, then click **play**.

   Release is the default event, as shown in Figure 34.

6. Click **Control** on the menu bar, then click **Test Movie**.
7. Click the **signal button** to play the animation.
8. Close the Flash Player window.

You used the Actions panel to assign a play action to a button.

Assign a goto frame action to a button

1. Click **Control** on the menu bar, then click **Test Movie**.

2. Click the **signal button**.

   The movie plays and stops, and the word Reset, which is actually a button, appears.

3. Click the **Reset button** and notice nothing happens because it does not have an action assigned to it.

4. Close the Flash Player window.

5. Click **frame 65** on the reset layer to display the Reset button on the Stage.

   Note: You many need to move the Actions panel to view the Reset button on the Stage.

6. Click the **Reset button** on the Stage to select it.

7. Verify b_reset is displayed in the lower left of the Actions panel.

8. Verify Script Assist is active, click ⊕, point to **Global Functions**, point to **Timeline Control**, click goto, then verify Frame 1 is specified, as shown in Figure 35.

9. Click **Control** on the menu bar, then click **Test Movie**.

10. Click the **signal button** to start the movie, then when the movie stops, click the **Reset button**.

11. Close the Flash Player window.

You used the Actions panel to assign an action to a button.

FIGURE 35

Assigning a goto action to a button

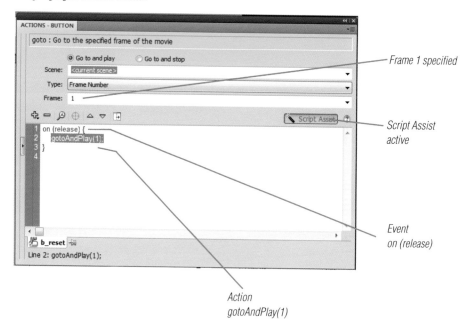

Frame 1 specified

Script Assist active

Event on (release)

Action gotoAndPlay(1)

FIGURE 36

Assigning a keypress action to a button

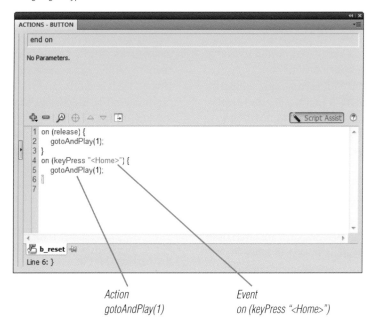

Action
gotoAndPlay(1)

Event
on (keyPress "<Home>")

1. Click the **right curly bracket** (}) in the Actions panel to highlight the bracket in Step 3 of the ActionScript.

2. Click ⊕ in the Script Assist window, point to **Global Functions**, point to **Movie Clip Control**, then click **on**.

   The Script Assist window displays several event options. Release is selected.

3. Click the **Release check box** to deselect the option.

4. Click the **Key Press check box** to select it, then press the **[Home] key** on the keyboard.

   TIP   If your keyboard does not have a [Home] key, use [fn]+[←] (Mac) or one of the function keys (Win) to complete the steps.

5. Click ⊕ in the Script Assist window, point to **Global Functions**, point to **Timeline Control**, then click **goto**.

   The ActionScript now indicates that pressing the [Home] key will cause the playhead to go to frame 1, as shown in Figure 36.

   The Reset button can now be activated by clicking it or by pressing the [Home] key.

6. Click **File** on the menu bar, point to **Publish Preview**, then click **Default – (HTML)**.

   The movie opens in your default browser.

   Note: If a warning message opens, follow the messages to allow blocked content.

7. Click the **signal button** to start the movie, then when the movie stops, press the **[Home] key**.

8. Close the browser window.

9. Close the Actions panel, then save and close the movie.

You added an event that triggers a goto frame action.

LESSON 5

IMPORTING
GRAPHICS

What You'll Do

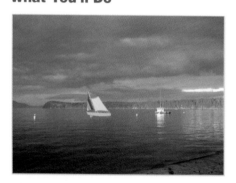

In this lesson, you will import and work with bitmap and vector graphics.

Understanding Graphic Types

Flash provides excellent drawing tools that allow you to create various objects that can be changed into symbols. In addition, you can import graphics and other assets, such as photographs and sounds. There are two types of graphic files, bitmap graphics and vector graphics. They are distinguished by the way in which the image is represented.

Bitmap images are made up of a group of tiny dots of color called **pixels** (picture elements). Bitmap graphics are often used with photographic images because they can represent subtle gradients in color. However, one disadvantage of bitmap graphics is the inability to enlarge the graphic without distorting the image. This is because both the computer screen's resolution (pixels per inch) and the number of pixels making up the image are a fixed number. So, when you enlarge an image each pixel must increase in size to fill the larger image dimensions. This causes the pixels to display jagged edges as shown in Figure 37.

Vector graphics represent an image as a geometric shape made up of lines and arcs that are combined to create various shapes, such as circles and rectangles. This is similar to Flash drawings that include strokes and fills. Flash drawing tools create vector graphics. An advantage of vector graphics is that they can be resized without distorting the image. The reason is that the geometric shapes are based on mathematical models that are recalculated when the image is resized. Figure 38 shows an example of a vector graphic before and after resizing. Vector graphics are best used for drawings rather than for images requiring photographic quality.

There are several programs that allow you to create and edit graphics including Adobe Illustrator, Fireworks, and Photoshop. There are also clip art and stock photograph collections that are available online. Filename extensions identify the file type. For example, .jpg, .tif, .bmp, and .gif are file formats for bitmap graphics; while .ai is a vector file format.

Importing and Editing Graphics

Once you have identified the graphic you would like to include in a Flash document, you can use the Import feature to bring the graphic into Flash. The process for importing is to select the Import command from the File menu and specify where to import (Stage or library). Then you navigate to the location where the file is stored and select it. After importing a vector graphic you can work with it as you would any graphic. Because bitmap graphics are not easy to edit in Flash, you may want to use another program, like Photoshop, to obtain the desired size, color, and other enhancements before importing the graphic.

FIGURE 37
Bitmap graphic enlarged

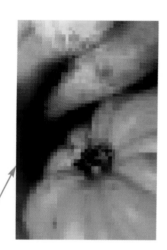

FIGURE 38
Vector graphic enlarged

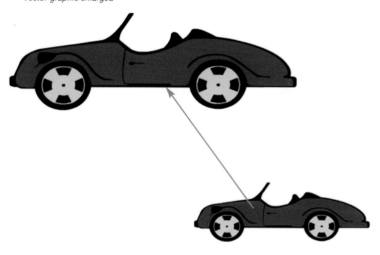

Importing graphics

1. Start a new Flash document, then save it as **sailing.fla**.

2. Click **File** on the menu bar, point to **Import**, then click **Import to Library**.

3. Navigate to the folder where your Data Files are stored, click **islandview.jpg**, then click **Open** (Win) or **Import to Library** (Mac).

   Islandview.jpg is a digital photo that was edited in Photoshop and saved as a .jpg file.

4. Display the Library panel and notice the icon used for bitmap graphics.

5. Drag the **islandview icon** to the Stage, then lock the layer.

6. Click **File** on the menu bar, point to **Import**, then click **Import to Library**.

7. Navigate to the folder where your Data Files are stored, then click **sailboat.ai**.

   This graphic was created using Adobe Illustrator and is made up of several layers.

8. Click **Open** (Win) or **Import to Library** (Mac).

   A dialog box appears asking you to choose the layers to import. All layers are selected by default.

9. Click **OK**.

   The graphic is added to the Library panel as a symbol.

10. Add a new layer to the Timeline, click **frame 1** on the layer, then drag the **sailboat icon** to the Stage, as shown in Figure 39.

   (continued)

FIGURE 39

Positioning the sailboat image on the Stage

Working with Symbols and Interactivity

FIGURE 40

Changing the color of the sail

FIGURE 41

Rotating and skewing the sailboat image

11. Click **Modify** on the menu bar, click **Break apart**, then repeat this step until the dotted pattern that indicates the image is no longer a symbol appears.

12. Click the **Selection tool** ▸ , then click a blank area of the Pasteboard.

13. Click the **left sail**, then change the color to a rainbow pattern, as shown in Figure 40.

    Hint: The rainbow color is found at the bottom of the palette for the Fill Color tool.

14. Use the **Selection tool** ▸ to drag a **marquee** around the entire sailboat to select it, then convert the image to a graphic symbol named **sailboat**.

15. Change the width of the boat to **60** on the Properties panel.

16. Click the **Zoom tool** ⚲ on the Tools panel, click the **sailboat** twice, then scroll as needed to view both sailboats.

    Notice how the bitmap photograph becomes distorted, while the vector sailboat does not.

17. Change the magnification to **Fit in Window**.

18. Use the **Free Transform tool** ▨ to rotate and skew the sailboat slightly to the left as shown in Figure 41.

19. Test the movie, close the Flash Player window, then save your work and exit Flash.

You imported bitmap and vector graphics, and edited the vector graphic.

Create a symbol.

1. Start Flash, open fl3_3.fla, then save it as **skillsdemo3**. This document consists of a single object that was created using the Flash drawing tools.
2. Use the Selection tool to drag a marquee around the ball to select it.
3. Convert the ball to a graphic symbol with the name g_beachball.
4. Double-click the g_beachball symbol on the Library panel to open the edit window, change the fill color to a rainbow gradient, add a text block that sits on top of the ball with the words **BEACH BALL** (see Figure 42), change the font color to white, then click Scene 1 to return to the main Timeline.
5. With the ball selected, create a motion tween animation that moves the ball from the left edge of the Stage to the right edge of the Stage.
6. Use the Selection tool to drag the middle of the motion path up to near the middle of the Stage to create an arc.
7. Select the last frame of the animation on the Timeline and set Rotate to 1 time in the Rotation area of the Properties panel.
8. Play the movie.
   The ball should move across the Stage in an arc and spin at the same time.
9. Lock the beachball-spin layer.

Create and edit an instance.

1. Insert a new layer and name it **redBall**.

2. Click frame 1 on the redBall layer, then drag the g_beachball symbol from the Library panel so it is on top of the ball on the Stage.
3. Use the arrow keys to align the ball so that it covers the ball on the Stage.
4. With the ball selected, break apart the object.
5. Change the fill color of the ball to a red gradient and change the text to **RED BALL**.
6. Insert a new layer and name it **greenBall**.
7. Click frame 12 on the greenBall layer, then insert a keyframe.
8. Drag the g_beachball symbol from the Library panel so it is on top of the ball that is near the middle of the Stage. (*Note:* Align only the balls, not the text.)
9. With the ball selected, break apart the object and change the fill color of the ball to a green gradient and the text to **GREEN BALL**.
10. Move the beachball-spin layer to above the other layers.
11. Insert a new layer and name it **title**.
12. Click frame 1 on the title layer, create a text block at the top middle of the Stage with the words **Beachball Spin** using Arial as the font, blue as the color, and 20 as the font size.
13. Insert a new layer above the title layer and name it **titlebkgnd**.
14. Draw a primitive rectangle with a corner radius of 10, a medium gray fill (#999999) and no stroke that covers the Beachball Spin title text.
15. Verify the rectangle is selected, convert it to a graphic symbol, then name it **g_bkgnd**.

16. Move the title layer so it is above the title-bkgnd layer.
17. Play the movie, then save your work.

Create a folder in the Library panel.

1. Click the New Folder button at the bottom of the Library panel to create a new folder.
2. Name the folder **Graphics**.
3. Move the two graphic symbols to the Graphics folder.
4. Expand the Graphics folder.
5. Save your work.

Work with the Library panel.

1. Rename the g_bkgnd symbol to **g_title-bkgnd** in the Library panel.
2. Collapse and expand the folder.
3. Save your work.

Create a button.

1. Insert a new layer above the title layer and name it **startButton**.
2. Drag the g_title-bkgnd symbol from the Library panel to the bottom center of the Stage.
3. Create a text block with the word **Start** formatted with white, bold, 22-pt Arial, then position the text block on top of the g_title-bkgnd object. Center the text block on top of the g_title-bkgnd object.
4. Select the rectangle and the text. (*Hint*: Drag a marquee around both objects or click the Selection tool, press and hold [Shift], then click each object.)

5. Convert the selected objects to a button symbol and name it **b_start**.
6. Create a new folder named **Buttons** in the Library panel and move the b_start button symbol to the folder.
7. Display the edit window for the b_start button.
8. Insert a keyframe in the Over frame.
9. Select the text and change the color to gray.
10. Insert a keyframe in the Down frame.
11. Select the text and change the color to blue.
12. Insert a keyframe in the Hit frame.
13. Draw a rectangular object that covers the button area for the Hit state.
14. Click Scene 1 to exit the edit window and return to the main Timeline.
15. Save your work.

Test a button.

1. Turn on Enable Simple Buttons.
2. Point to the button and notice the color change.
3. Click the button and notice the other color change.

Stop a movie.

1. Insert a new layer and name it **stopmovie**.
2. Insert a keyframe in frame 24 on the new layer.
3. With frame 24 selected, display the Actions panel.
4. Assign a stop action to the frame.
5. Click frame 1 on the stopmovie layer.
6. Assign a stop action to frame 1.
7. Save your work.

Assign a goto action to a button.

1. Click Control on the menu bar, then click Enable Simple Buttons to turn off this feature.
2. Use the Selection tool to select the Start button on the Stage.
3. Use Script Assist in the Actions panel to assign an event and a goto action to the button. (*Hint*: Refer to the section on assigning a goto action as needed.)
4. Test the movie.

FIGURE 42
Completed Skills Review

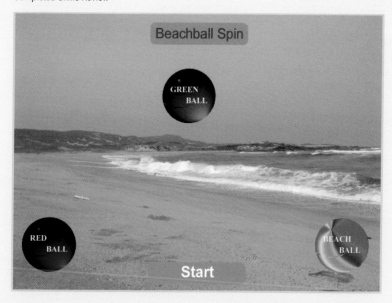

Import a graphic.

1. Import BeachScene.jpg from the drive and folder where your Data Files are stored to the Library panel.
2. Insert a new layer and name the layer **background**.
3. Select frame 1 on the background layer, then drag the BeachScene image to the Stage.
4. Move the background layer to the bottom of the Timeline.
5. Test the movie.
6. Save your work, then compare your image to Figure 42.
7. Exit Flash.

Working with Symbols and Interactivity

The Ultimate Tours travel company has asked you to design a sample navigation scheme for its website. The company wants to see how its home page will link with one of its main categories (Treks). Figure 43 shows a sample home page and Treks screen. Using the figures or the home page you created in Chapter 2 as a guide, you will add a Treks screen and link it to the home page. (*Hint*: Assume that all of the drawings on the home page are on frame 1, unless noted.)

1. Open ultimatetours2.fla (the file you created in Chapter 2 Project Builder 1), then save it as **ultimatetours3**.
2. Insert a layer above the Subheading layer and name it **logo**.
3. Import the UTLogo.jpg file from the drive and folder where your Data Files are stored to the Library panel.
4. Select frame 1 on the logo layer and drag the logo image to the upper-left corner of the Stage.
5. Select the logo and convert it to a graphic symbol with the name **g_utlogo**.
6. Lock the **logo layer**.
7. Select the layer that the Ultimate Tours text block is on, then insert a keyframe on a frame at least five frames farther along the Timeline.
8. Insert a new layer, name it **treks headings**, insert a keyframe on the last frame of the movie, then create the Treks screen shown in Figure 43, except for the home graphic. (*Note:* The underline was created using the Line tool.)
9. Convert the Treks graphic on the home page to a button symbol named **b_treks**, then edit the symbol so that different colors appear for the different states.
10. Assign a goto action that jumps the playhead to the Treks screen when the Treks button is clicked. (*Hint:* You need to use ActionScript 2.0 to complete the steps that follow. You can set the ActionScript version by selecting Publish Settings from the File menu, clicking the Flash tab and specifying ActionScript 2.0.)
11. Insert a new layer and name it **stopmovie**. Add stop actions that cause the movie to stop after displaying the home page and after displaying the Treks page. Make sure there is a keyframe in the last frame of the stopmovie layer.
12. Insert a new layer and name it **homeButton**, insert a keyframe on the last frame of the movie, then draw the home button image with the Home text.
13. Convert the image to a button symbol named **b_home**, then edit the symbol so that different colors appear for the different states. Assign a goto action for the button that jumps the movie to frame 1.
14. Select the last frame of the movie on the **logo layer** and insert a keyframe. (*Note:* You do this so that the logo appears on the home page and on the Treks page.)
15. Test the movie.
16. Save your work, then compare your web pages to the samples shown in Figure 43.

FIGURE 43
Sample completed Project Builder 1

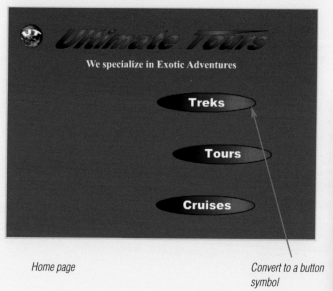

Home page

Convert to a button symbol

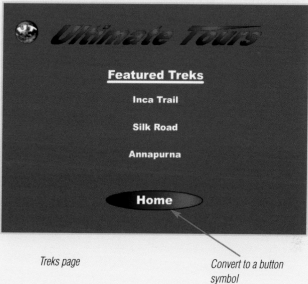

Treks page

Convert to a button symbol

You have been asked to assist the International Student Association (ISA). The association sponsors a series of monthly events, each focusing on a different culture from around the world. The events are led by a guest speaker who makes a presentation, followed by a discussion. The events are free and they are open to everyone. ISA would like you to design a Flash movie that will be used with its website. The movie starts by providing information about the series, and then provides a link to the upcoming event.

1. Open a new Flash ActionScript 2.0 document and save it as **isa3**.
2. Create an initial Information screen with general information about the association's series.
3. Assign an action to frame 1 that stops the movie.
4. Create two more screens: a next event screen that presents information about the next event and a series screen that lists the series (all nine events for the school year—September through May).
5. Add a button on the general information screen that jumps the movie to the next event screen, and add a second button on the information screen that jumps the movie to the series screen.
6. On the next event and series screens, add a Return button that jumps the movie back to the general information screen.
7. On the next event screen, create a second button that jumps the movie to the series screen.
8. On the series screen, create a second button that jumps the movie to the event screen.
9. For each button you create, specify different colors for each state of each button.
10. Add an action that stops the movie on the next event screen, and another action that stops the movie on the series screen. (*Hint:* Place the stop actions on the same layer as the stop action created in step 3.)
11. Test the movie.
12. Save your work, then compare your movie to the sample shown in Figure 44.

FIGURE 44
Sample completed Project Builder 2

*Sample general
information screen*

*Sample next
event screen*

*Sample series
screen*

Figure 45 shows the home page of a website. Study the figure and complete the following questions. For each question, indicate how you determined your answer.

1. Connect to the Internet and go to *www.zoo.org*. Notice that this website has images that change as you visit the website.
2. Open a document in a word processor or open a new Flash document, save the file as **dpc3**, then answer the following questions. (*Hint*: Use the Text tool in Flash.)
   - Whose website is this?
   - What is the goal(s) of the site?
   - Who is the target audience?
   - What treatment ("look and feel") is used?
   - What are the design layout guidelines being used (balance, movement, and so on)?
   - What may be animated in this home page?
   - Do you think this is an effective design for the company, its products, and its target audience? Why or why not?
   - What suggestions would you make to improve the design, and why?

FIGURE 45
Design Project

This is a continuation of the Chapter 2 Portfolio Project, which is the development of a personal portfolio. The home page has several categories, including the following:

- Personal data
- Contact information
- Previous employment
- Education
- Samples of your work

In this project, you will create a button that will be used to link the home page of your portfolio to the animations page. Next, you will create another button to start the animation.

1. Open portfolio2.fla (the file you created in Portfolio Project, Chapter 2), then save it as **portfolio3**. (*Hint*: When you open the file, you may receive a warning message that the font is missing. You can replace this font with the default, or with any other appropriate font on your computer.)
2. Unlock the layers as needed.
3. Insert a new layer, name it **sampleAnimations**, then insert a keyframe on frame 2.
4. Create a Sample Animations screen that has a text block with an oval background and the words **Sample Animations** at the top of the Stage, then add another text block and oval background with the word **Tweened**. (*Note*: This screen will have several animation samples added to it later.)

5. Insert a new layer, name it **home button**, then insert a keyframe on frame 2.
6. Add another text block with an oval background that says **Home** at the bottom of the Stage.
7. Insert a new layer, name it **tweened Animation**, then insert a keyframe on frame 3.
8. Create an animation(s) of your choice using objects you draw or import, or objects from the Library panel of another document. (*Note:* To create a motion tween animation when starting in a frame other than frame 1, you need to specify the ending frame of the animation by inserting a keyframe before repositioning the object on the Stage.) (*Hint:* To create more than one animation that plays at the same time, put each animation on its own layer.)
9. Insert a new layer, name it **animationHeading**, then insert a keyframe on frame 3.
10. Add a heading to the screen used for the animation(s).
11. On the Sample Animations screen, convert the Tweened and Home text blocks into button symbols, then edit each symbol so that different colors appear for the different states. For the Tweened button, assign an action that jumps to the frame that plays an animation. For the Home button, assign an action to the Home button that jumps to the frame that displays My Portfolio. (*Hint*: You need to use ActionScript 2.0. You can set the ActionsScript version by selecting Publish

Settings from the File menu, clicking the Flash tab and specifying ActionScript 2.0.)
12. Change the Animations graphic on the home page to a button, then edit the symbol so that different colors appear for the different states. Assign an action to the Animations button that jumps to the Sample Animations screen.
13. Insert a new layer, then name it **stopmovie**. Insert keyframes and assign stop actions to the appropriate frames.
14. Test the movie.
15. Save your work, then compare your movie to the sample shown in Figure 46.

FIGURE 46
Sample completed Portfolio Project

Click to run the animation

chapter

4 CREATING ANIMATIONS

1. Create motion tween animations

2. Create classic tween animations

3. Create frame-by-frame animations

4. Create shape tween animations

5. Create movie clips

6. Animate text

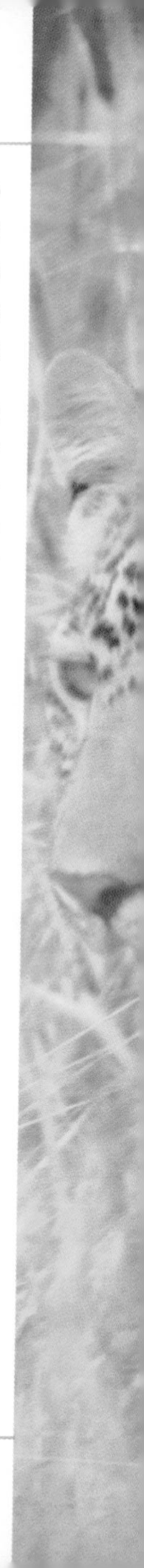

chapter

4 CREATING ANIMATIONS

Introduction

Animation can be an important part of your application or website, whether the focus is on e-commerce (attracts attention and provides product demonstrations), education (simulates complex processes such as DNA replication), or entertainment (provides interactive games).

How Does Animation Work?

The perception of motion in an animation is actually an illusion. Animation is like a motion picture in that it is made up of a series of still images. Research has found that our eye captures and holds an image for one-tenth of a second before processing another image. By retaining each impression for one-tenth of a second, we perceive a series of rapidly displayed still images as a single, moving image. This phenomenon is known as persistence of vision and provides the basis for the frame rate in animations. Frame rates of 10–12 frames-per-second (fps) generally provide

an acceptably smooth computer-based animation. Lower frame rates result in a jerky image, while higher frame rates may result in a blurred image. Flash uses a default frame rate of 12 fps.

Flash Animation

Creating animation is one of the most powerful features of Flash, yet developing basic animations is a simple process. Flash allows you to create animations that can move and rotate an object around the Stage, and change its size, shape, or color. You can also use the animation features in Flash to create special effects, such as an object zooming or fading in and out. You can combine animation effects so that an object changes shape and color as it moves across the Stage. Animations are created by changing the content of successive frames. Flash provides two animation methods: frame-by-frame animation and tweened animation. Tweened animations can be motion, classic, or shape tweens.

Tools You'll Use

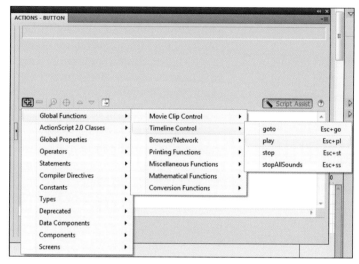

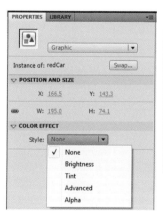

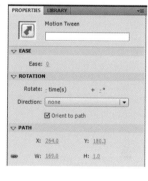

CREATE MOTION TWEEN
ANIMATIONS

What You'll Do

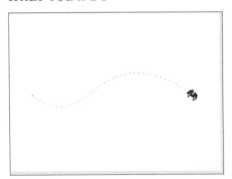

In this lesson, you will create and edit motion tween animations.

Understanding Motion Tween Animations

An animation implies some sort of movement in an object. However, the concept of animation is quite a bit more broad. Objects have specific properties such as position, size, color, and shape. Any change in a property of an object over time (i.e., across frames in the Timeline) can be considered an animation. So, having an object start at the left of the screen in frame 1 and then having it move across the screen and end up at the right side in frame 10 would be a change in the position property of the object. Each of the in-between frames (2-9) would show the position of the object as it moves across the screen. In a motion tween animation, you specify the position of the object in the beginning and ending frames and Flash fills in the in-between frames, a process known as tweening. Fortunately, you can change several properties with one motion tween. For example, you could have a car move

across the screen and, at the same time, you could have the size of the car change to give the impression of the car moving away from the viewer. Motion tweens are new to Flash CS4.

The process for creating a motion tween animation is to select the frame and layer where the animation will start. If necessary, insert a keyframe (by default, frame 1 of each layer has a keyframe). Select the object on the Stage, then select the Motion Tween command from the Insert menu. If the object is not already a symbol, you will be asked if you want to convert it to a symbol. You must convert the object to a symbol if prompted, because only symbols can have a motion tween applied. Then you select the ending frame and make any changes to the object, such as moving it to another location or resizing it. When you create a motion tween, a tween span appears on the Timeline.

Tween Spans

Figure 1 shows a motion tween animation of a car that starts in frame 1 and ends in frame 30. The Onion Skin feature is enabled so that outlines of the car are displayed for each frame of the animation in the figure. Notice a blue highlight appears on the Timeline for the frames of the animation. The blue highlighted area is called the tween or motion span. By default the number of frames in a tween span is equal to the number of frames in one second of the movie. So, if the frame rate is 12 frames per second, then the span is 12 frames. You can increase or decrease the number of frames in the span by dragging the end of the span. In addition, you can move the span to a different location on the Timeline, and you can copy the span to have it apply to another object.

Motion Path

The animation shown in Figure 2 includes a position change (from frame 1 to frame 30); a motion path showing the position change is displayed on the Stage. Each symbol on the path corresponds to a frame on the Timeline and indicates the location of the object (in this example, the car) when the frame is played. A motion path can be altered by dragging a point on the path

FIGURE 1

Sample motion tween animation

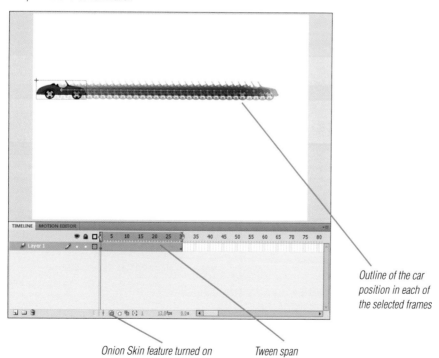

Outline of the car position in each of the selected frames

Onion Skin feature turned on   *Tween span*

using the Selection and Subselection tools or by manipulating Bezier handles as shown in Figure 3. Entire paths can be moved around the Stage and reshaped using the Free Transform tool.

Property Keyframes

A keyframe indicates a change in a Flash movie, such as the start or ending of an animation. Motion tween animations use property keyframes that are specific to each property such as a position keyframe, color keyframe, or rotation keyframe. In most cases these are automatically placed on the Timeline as the motion tween animation is created.

Keep in mind:
- Only one object on the Stage can be animated in each tween span.
- You can have multiple motion tween animations playing at the same time, if they are on different layers.
- A motion tween is, in essence, an object animation because while several changes can be made in the object's properties, only one object is animated for each motion tween.
- The types of objects that can be tweened include graphic, button, and movie clip symbols, as well as text fields.
- You can remove a motion tween animation by clicking the tween span on the Timeline and choosing Remove Tween from the Insert menu.

FIGURE 2
The motion path

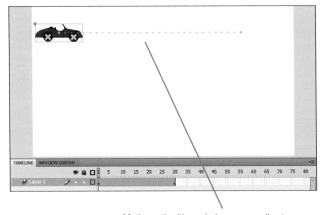

Motion path with symbols corresponding to a frame in the Timeline and showing the location of the car when the frame is played

FIGURE 3
Bezier handles used to alter the path

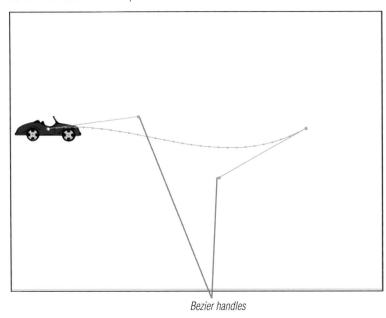

Bezier handles

FIGURE 4
Positioning the car object

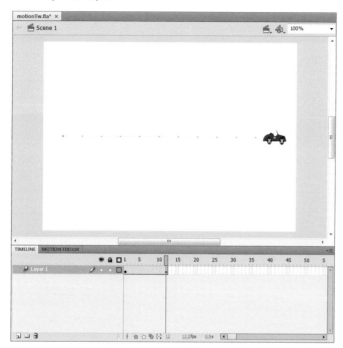

FIGURE 5
Change the end of the tween span

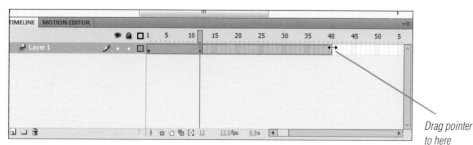

Drag pointer
to here

Create a motion tween animation

1. Open fl4_1.fla from the drive and folder where your Data Files are stored, then save it as **motionTw**.

   This document has one drawn object—a car that has been converted to a symbol.

2. Click the **Selection tool** ▸ on the Tools panel, then click the **car** to select it.

3. Click **Insert** on the menu bar, then click **Motion Tween**.

   Notice the tween span appears on the Timeline. The number of frames in the span equals the frames per second for the movie.

4. Verify the playhead is on the last frame of the tween span, then drag the **car** to the right side of the Stage, as shown in Figure 4.

   A motion path appears on the Stage with dots indicating the position of the object for each frame. A diamond symbol appears in frame 12. This is a position keyframe automatically inserted at the end of the motion path. This assumes the document frame rate is set to 12.

   Note: To see the diamond symbol more clearly, move the playhead.

5. Point to the end of the tween span, when the pointer changes to a double arrow ↔, drag the **tween span** to frame 40, as shown in Figure 5.

6. Click **frame 1** on the Timeline, then press the **period key** to move the playhead one frame at a time and notice the position of the car for each frame.

7. Play the movie, then save your work.

You created a motion tween animation, extended the length of the animation, and viewed the position of the animated object in each frame of the animation.

Edit a motion path

1. Click the **Selection tool** ↖ on the Tools panel, then click a blank area of the Stage.

2. Click **frame 1** on Layer 1.

3. Point to the middle of the motion path, as shown in Figure 6.

4. When the pointer changes to a pointer with an arc ↖⌒, drag the ↖⌒ **pointer** down, as shown in Figure 7.

(continued)

FIGURE 6
Pointing to the middle of the path

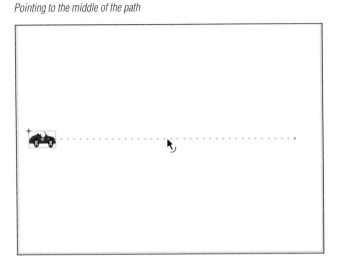

FIGURE 7
Dragging the motion path down

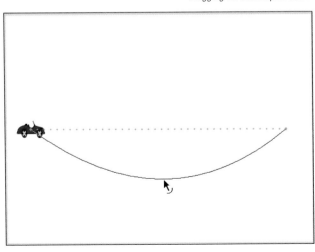

Creating Animations

FIGURE 8
Displaying the Bezier handles

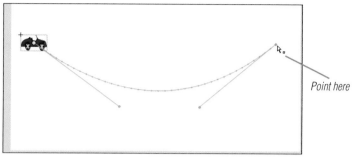

Point here

*Drag pointer
to here*

FIGURE 9
Using the handles to alter the shape of the path

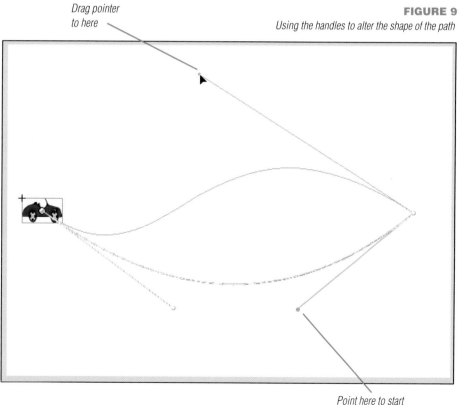

Point here to start

5. Play the movie, then click **frame 1** on Layer 1.

6. Click the **Subselection tool** on the Tools panel, point to the end of the motion path, when the pointer changes into an arrow with a small square, click the end of path to display Bezier handles, as shown in Figure 8.

7. Point to the **lower right handle**, when the pointer changes into a delta symbol, drag the handle up and toward the center of the Stage to form a horizontal S shape, as shown in Figure 9.

8. Play the movie, then save your work.

You edited a motion path by using the Selection tool to drag the path and by using the Subselection tool to display and reposition Bezier handles.

Change the ease value of an animation

1. Play the movie and notice that the car moves at a constant speed.

2. Display the **Properties panel**, then click **frame 1** on Layer 1.

3. Point to the **Ease value**, when the pointer changes to a hand with a double arrow 🖑, drag the 🖑 **pointer** to the right to set the value at **100**, as shown in Figure 10.

4. Play the movie.

   The car starts moving fast and slows down near the end of the animation. Notice the word "out" is displayed next to the ease value in the Properties panel indicating that the object will ease out, slow down, at the end of the animation.

5. Click **frame 1** on Layer 1.

6. Point to the **Ease value** in the Properties panel, then drag the 🖑 **pointer** to the left to set the value to **–100**.

7. Play the movie.

   The car starts moving slowly and speeds up near the end of the animation. Notice the word "in" is displayed next to the ease value in the Properties panel. Also, notice the dots are grouped closer together at the beginning of the motion path indicating that the object does not move very far in that section of the path.

8. Set the ease value to **0**.

9. Save your work.

You changed the ease out and ease in values of the animation.

FIGURE 10
Changing the ease value

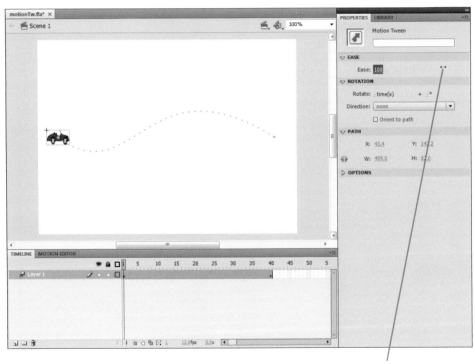

Drag the pointer to the right

FIGURE 11

Changing the width of the object

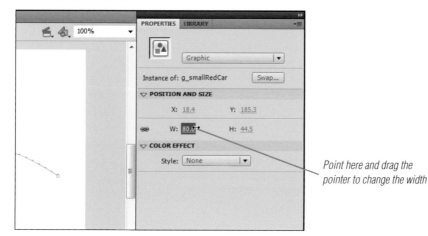

Point here and drag the
pointer to change the width

FIGURE 12

Using the Free Transform tool to skew the object

Point to the middle handle and
drag the pointer to the right

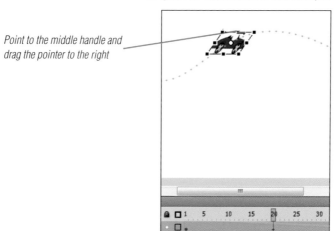

Resize and reshape an object

1. Click **frame 1** on Layer 1.

2. Click the **Selection tool** ⬆ , then click
   the **car**.

3. Point to the **width (W:)** value in the Properties
   panel, when the pointer changes to a hand
   with a double arrow 🖑 , drag the 🖑
   pointer to the right to set the value to **80**,
   as shown in Figure 11.

4. Play the movie.

5. Click **frame 40** on Layer 1, then click the **car**.

6. Point to the **width (W:)** value in the
   Properties panel, when the pointer changes
   to a hand with a double arrow 🖑 , drag the
   🖑 **pointer** to the left to set the value to **30**.

7. Play the movie.

   The car starts out large and ends up small.

8. Click **frame 20** on Layer 1.

9. Click the **Free Transform tool** 🔧 in the
   Tools panel, then verify the Rotate and Skew
   option ↺ is selected.

10. Point to the **top middle handle**, when the
    pointer changes to a double line ⇌ , drag
    the ⇌ **pointer** to the right to skew the
    object, as shown in Figure 12.

    A skew keyframe appears in frame 20.

11. Play the movie, use the Undo command on
    the Edit menu to undo the skew, then save
    the movie.

    Note: You may have to click the Undo com-
    mand more than one time to undo the skew.

    The skew keyframe is removed from frame 20.

You resized and skewed a motion tween object.

Create a color effect

1. Click the **Selection tool** ▶ in the Tools panel.

2. Click **frame 40** on Layer 1.

3. Click the **car** to select it.

4. Click the **Style list arrow** in the COLOR EFFECTS area of the Properties panel.

5. Click **Alpha**, then drag the **slider** △ to set the value to **0%**, as shown in Figure 13.

6. Play the movie.

   Notice the car slowly becomes transparent.

7. Reset the Alpha to **100%**.

8. Click **frame 40** on Layer 1.

9. Click the **car** to select it.

10. Click the **Style list arrow** in the COLOR EFFECT area of the Properties panel.

11. Click **Advanced**, then set the x R + value for Red to **100**, as shown in Figure 14.

12. Play the movie.

    Notice the car slowly changes to a shade of red. Because the car is a symbol, it is one part (not a composite of pieces). As a result changes made to the color value affect the entire car.

13. Set the x R + value back to **0**, then save your work.

You changed the alpha and advanced color option for an object.

FIGURE 13
Setting the Alpha (transparency) value

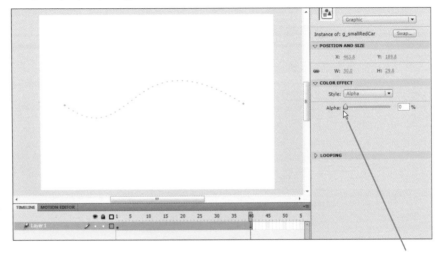

Drag the slider to the left

FIGURE 14
Changing a color value for the object

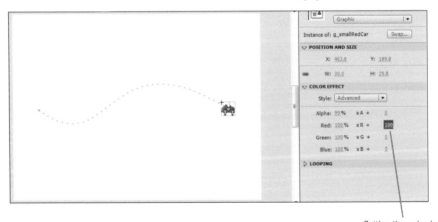

Setting the red value

FIGURE 15
Aligning the car to the path

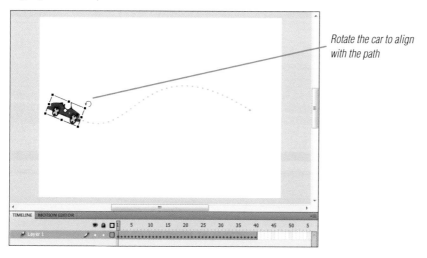

Rotate the car to align
with the path

FIGURE 16
Aligning the car to the end of the motion path

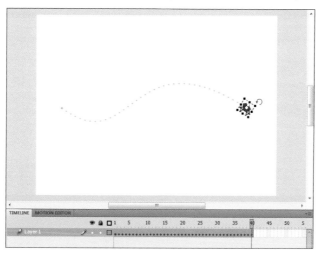

Orient an object to a path

1. Play the movie.

   Notice the car follows the path but it is not oriented to the path.

2. Click **frame 1** on Layer 1.

3. Click the **Orient to path check box** in the ROTATION area of the Properties panel.

4. Click the **Free Transform tool** ⤧ on the Tools panel, then verify the Rotate and Skew option ⟳ near the bottom of the Tools panel is selected.

5. Point to the upper-right corner of the car, when the pointer changes into a circular arrow ⟳, rotate the front of the car so that it aligns with the path, as shown in Figure 15.

6. Click **frame 40** on Layer 1, then rotate the back of the car so that it aligns with the path, as shown in Figure 16.

7. Play the movie.

   The car is oriented to the path.

   Notice the diamond symbol in each Layer 1 frame. These are rotation keyframes that indicate the object will change in each frame as it rotates to stay oriented to the path.

8. Save your work, then close the document.

You oriented an object to a motion path and aligned the object with the path in the first and last frames of the motion tween.

Copy a motion path

1. Open fl4_2.fla, save it as **tweenEdits**, then play the movie.

2. Insert a **new layer** and name it **biker2**, then click **frame 1** on the biker2 layer.

3. Verify the Selection tool ▸ is selected, drag the **g_biker symbol** from the Library panel to the Stage, as shown in Figure 17.

4. Click any frame on the tween span on the biker layer.

5. Click **Edit** on the menu bar, point to **Timeline**, then click **Copy Motion**.

6. Click the new instance of the biker, click **Edit** on the menu bar, point to **Timeline**, then click **Paste Motion**.

7. Play the movie, then hide the biker layer.

8. Click **frame 1** on the biker2 layer, click the **Free Transform tool** ⊠ on the Tools panel, then click the **path** to select it, as shown in Figure 18.

(continued)

FIGURE 17
Dragging the biker symbol to the Stage

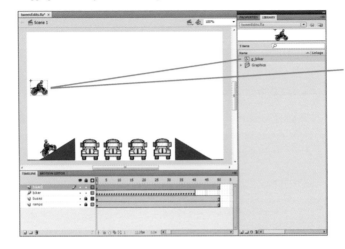

Drag g_biker symbol from the Library panel and position it on the Stage

FIGURE 18
Selecting the path with the Free Transform tool

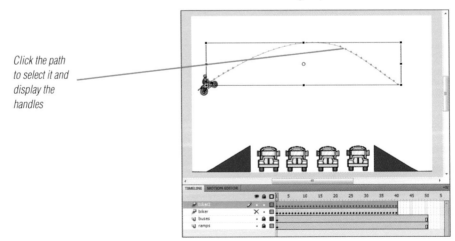

Click the path to select it and display the handles

FIGURE 19

Positioning the path

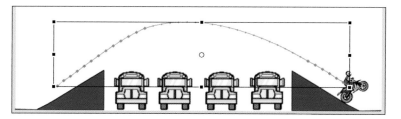

FIGURE 20

Aligning the biker to the path

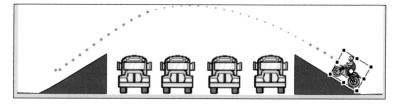

9. Click **Modify** on the menu bar, point to **Transform**, then click **Flip Horizontal**.

10. Use the arrow keys on the keyboard to position the path, as shown in Figure 19.

11. Click the **biker object**, click **Modify** on the menu bar, point to **Transform**, then click **Flip Horizontal**.

12. Use the Free Transform tool 🔧 and the arrow keys to align the biker, as shown in Figure 20.

13. Play the movie, then save your work.

You copied a motion path to another object.

Rotate an object

1. Click **frame 1** on the biker2 layer, then display the Properties panel.

2. Point to the **Rotate times value** in the ROTATION area of the Properties panel, when the pointer changes to a hand with a double arrow 🖐, drag the 🖐 **pointer** to the right to set the count to **1**, as shown in Figure 21.

3. Verify the Direction is set to **CW (Clockwise)**, then play the movie.

   The biker object rotates one time in a clockwise direction. Look at the Timeline. Notice some of the keyframes have been removed from the motion tween span. This is because, as the biker rotates, he is no longer oriented to the path. Motion tweens do not allow an object to be rotated and oriented to a path simultaneously since orienting an object to a path rotates the object in each frame along the path. You can use a classic tween to rotate and orient an object to a path at the same time. The remaining keyframes at the beginning and ending of the tween span were used to align the original biker to the ramp.

4. Click **frame 1** on the biker2 layer, set the rotation count to **2**, click the **Direction list arrow**, click **CCW** (Counter Clockwise), then play the movie.

5. Click **Orient to path** to select it.

   The rotate value is automatically set to no times (indicated by a -), as shown in Figure 22.

6. Play the movie, then save your work.

You caused an object to rotate by setting the rotate value and specifying a rotation direction.

FIGURE 21
Changing the rotate value

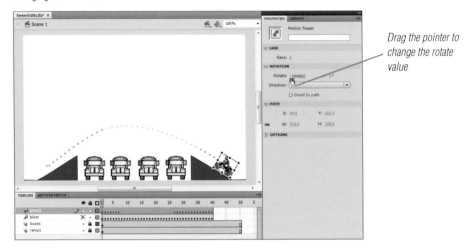

Drag the pointer to change the rotate value

FIGURE 22
The Properties panel showing that the rotate value is set to no times

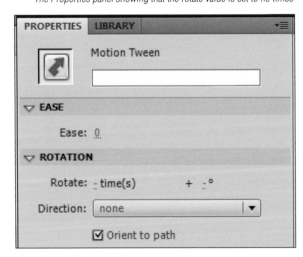

FIGURE 23
Timeline showing the motion tween removed

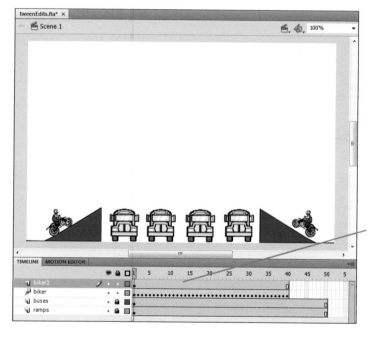

Removal of motion tween in the biker2 layer removes the blue highlight in the Timeline

Remove a motion tween

1. Unhide the **biker layer**, then play the movie.
2. Click anywhere on the tween span on the biker2 layer to select the path.
3. Click **Insert** on the menu bar, then click **Remove Tween**.
4. Click a blank area of the Stage, then notice that the blue highlight on the biker2 layer is gone, as shown in Figure 23.
5. Play the movie and notice that the biker on the biker2 layer is visible but it does not move.
6. Use the Undo command in the Edit menu to undo the Remove Tween process.

   Note: You may need to select the Undo command more than one time.
7. Click **biker2** on the Timeline to select the layer.
8. Click the **Delete icon** at the bottom of the Timeline to delete the biker2 layer that includes the motion tween.
9. Test the movie, then close the Flash Player window.
10. Save your work.

You removed an object's motion tween, undid the action, then deleted a layer containing a motion tween and undid the action.

Work with multiple motion tweens

1. Click **frame 40** on the biker layer, then click the **biker** on the Stage.

2. Lock the **biker layer**, then add a **new layer** above the biker layer and name it **bikeOffStage**.

3. Click **frame 40** on the bikeOffStage layer.

4. Click **Insert** on the menu bar, point to **Timeline**, then click **Keyframe**.

5. Drag an instance of the **g_biker symbol** from the Library panel so it is on top of the biker on the Stage, as shown in Figure 24.

6. Use the the Free Transform tool and the arrow keys on the keyboard to align the two biker objects.

7. Click **frame 41** on the **bikeOffStage** layer, then insert a **keyframe**.

8. Use the **arrow keys** on the keyboard and the **Free Transform tool** to align the biker with the bottom of the ramp, as shown in Figure 25.

(continued)

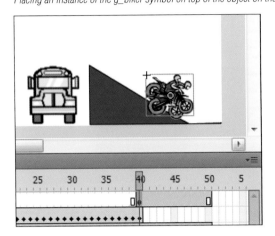

FIGURE 24

Placing an instance of the g_biker symbol on top of the object on the Stage

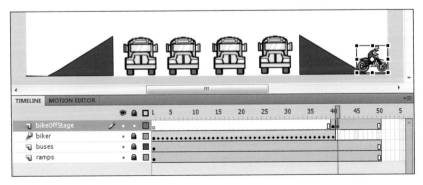

FIGURE 25

Aligning the biker with the ramp

Creating Animations

FIGURE 26

Dragging the biker object off the Stage

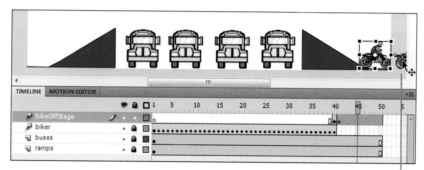

Drag the object off
the Stage

9. Click the **Selection tool**, then click the **biker**.

10. Click the **View list arrow**, then click **100%**.

11. Click **Insert** on the menu bar, then click **Motion Tween**.

12. Click **frame 45** on the bikeOffStage layer, then drag the **biker** off the Stage, as shown in Figure 26.

13. Test the movie, close the Flash Player window, save your work, then close the document.

You created a second motion tween for the movie.

CREATE CLASSIC TWEEN
ANIMATIONS

What You'll Do

In this lesson, you will create a motion guide and attach an animation to it.

Understanding Classic Tweens

Classic tweens are similar to motion tweens in that you can create animations that change the properties of an object over time. Motion tweens are easier to use and allow the greatest degree of control over tweened animations. Classic tweens are a bit more complex to create, however, they provide certain capabilities that some developers desire. For example, with a motion tween, you can alter the ease value so that an object starts out fast and ends slow, but with a classic tween, you can alter the ease value so that an object starts out fast, slows down, and then speeds up again. You can do this because a motion tween consists of one object over the tween span, but a classic tween can have more than one instance of the object over the tween span. The process for creating a classic tween animation that moves an object is to select the starting frame and, if necessary, insert a keyframe. Next, insert a keyframe at the ending frame, and click anywhere on the layer between the keyframes. Then select classic tween from the Insert menu, select the ending frame, and move the object to the position you want it to be in the ending frame. While all prior versions of Flash used classic tweening only, you now have a choice between classic tweens and motion tweens.

Understanding Motion Guides

When you use motion tweening to generate an animation that moves an object, a motion path that shows the movement is automatically created on the Stage. When you use classic tweening, the object moves in a straight line from the beginning location to the ending location on the Stage. There is no path displayed. You can draw a path, called a **motion guide**, that can be used to alter the path of a classic tween animation as shown in Figure 27. A motion guide is drawn on the motion guide layer with the classic tween animation placed on its own layer beneath the motion guide layer, as shown in Figure 28. The process for creating a motion guide and attaching it to a classic tween animation is:

- Create a classic tween animation.
- Insert a new layer above the classic tween animation layer and change the

Creating Animations

layer properties to a Guide layer. Drag the classic tween animation layer to the guide layer so that it indents, as shown in Figure 28. This indicates that the classic tween animation layer is associated with the motion guide layer.

- Draw a path using the Pen, Pencil, Line, Circle, Rectangle, or Brush tools.
- Attach the object to the path by clicking the first keyframe of the layer that contains the animation, and then dragging the object by its transformation point to the beginning of the path. Select the end keyframe and then repeat the steps to attach the object to the end of the path.

Depending on the type of object you are animating and the path, you may need to orient the object to the path.

The advantages of using a motion guide are that you can have an object move along any path, including a path that intersects itself, and you can easily change the shape of the path, allowing you to experiment with different motions. A consideration when using a motion guide is that, in some instances, orienting the object along the path may result in an unnatural-looking animation. You can fix this by stepping through the animation one frame at a time until you reach the frame where the object is positioned poorly. You can then insert a keyframe and adjust the object as desired.

Transformation Point and Registration Point

Each symbol has a transformation point in the form of a circle (O) that is used to orient the object when it is being animated. For example, when you rotate a symbol, the transformation point is the pivot point around which the object rotates. The transformation point is also the point that snaps to a motion guide, as shown in Figure 27. When attaching an object to a path, you can drag the transformation point to the path. The default position for a transformation point is the center of the object. You can reposition the transformation point while in the symbol edit mode by dragging the transformation point to a different location in the object. Objects also have a registration point (+) that is used to position the object on the Stage using ActionScript code. The transformation and registration points can overlap—this is displayed as a plus sign within a circle ⊕.

FIGURE 27
A motion guide with an object (motorbike) attached

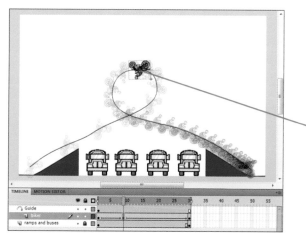

Transformation
point ⊕

FIGURE 28
A motion guide layer

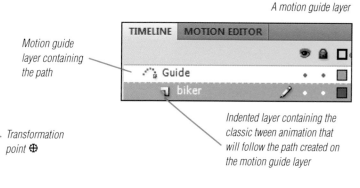

Motion guide
layer containing
the path

Indented layer containing the
classic tween animation that
will follow the path created on
the motion guide layer

Create a classic tween animation

1. Open fl4_3.fla, then save it as **cTween**.

2. Insert a **new layer**, then name it **biker**.

3. Click **frame 1** on the biker layer, then drag the **biker symbol** from the Library panel to the Stage, as shown in Figure 29.

4. Click **frame 30** on the biker layer, click **Insert** on the menu bar, point to **Timeline**, then click **Keyframe**.

5. Drag the **biker** to the position shown in Figure 30.

6. Click **frame 2** on the biker layer, click **Insert** on the menu bar, then click **Classic Tween**.

   An arrow appears on the Timeline indicating that this is a classic tween.

7. Play the movie.

You created an animation using a classic tween.

Add a motion guide and orient the object to the guide

1. Insert a **new layer**, then name it **Guide**.

2. Click **Modify** on the menu bar, point to **Timeline**, then click **Layer Properties**.

3. Click the **Guide option button**, click **OK**, then drag the **biker layer** up to the Guide layer, as shown in Figure 31.

   The biker layer indents below the Guide layer.

4. Click **frame 1** on the Guide layer, click the **Pencil tool** on the Tools panel, then set the stroke color to **black**.

   (continued)

FIGURE 29
Dragging the biker symbol to the Stage

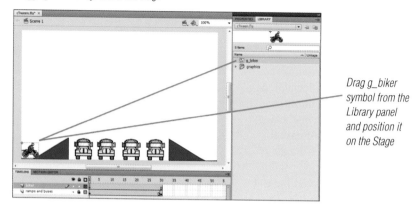

Drag g_biker symbol from the Library panel and position it on the Stage

FIGURE 30
Repositioning the biker

FIGURE 31
Dragging the biker layer up to the Guide layer

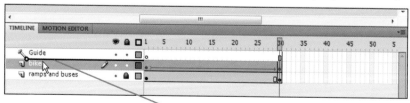

Drag biker layer up to but not above the Guide layer

FIGURE 32

Drawing a guide path on a Guide layer

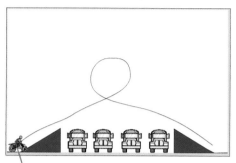

Point to the middle of the biker object

FIGURE 33

Aligning the object with the guide path

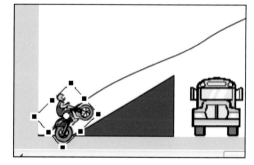

FIGURE 34

Aligning the object with the end of the guide path

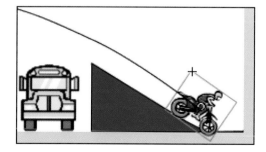

Lesson 2   Create Classic Tween Animations

5. Point to the middle of the biker, then draw a line with a loop similar to the one shown in Figure 32.

6. Click **frame 30** on the biker layer, click the **Selection tool** ▸ , then drag the **biker** so that it snaps to the end of the line.

   Hint: Use the Zoom tool to zoom in on the biker to make it easier to see you have placed the transformation point on the path.

7. Play the movie.

8. Click **frame 1** on the biker layer, then click the **biker** to select the object.

9. Click the **Free Transform tool** ▦ on the Tools panel, then rotate the **biker**, as shown in Figure 33.

10. Click **frame 30** on the biker layer, then rotate the **biker**, as shown in Figure 34.

11. Click the **Selection tool** ▸ , then click **frame 1** on the biker layer.

12. Display the Properties panel, then click the **Orient to path check box**.

13. Play the movie.

14. Click **frame 1** on the biker layer, then set the Ease value in the Properties panel to **100**.

15. Insert a **keyframe** on the frame on the biker layer that displays the highest point in the animation, then set the ease value to **100**.

16. Test the movie, save your work, then close the document.

You added a motion guide, oriented the animated object to the guide, and set an ease value.

CREATE FRAME-BY-FRAME ANIMATIONS

What You'll Do

In this lesson, you will create frame-by-frame animations.

Understanding Frame-by-Frame Animations

A frame-by-frame animation (also called a frame animation) is created by specifying the object that is to appear in each frame of a sequence of frames. Figure 35 shows three images that are variations of a cartoon character. In this example, the head and body remain the same, but the arms and legs change to represent a walking motion. If these individual images are placed into succeeding frames (with keyframes), an animation is created.

Frame-by-frame animations are useful when you want to change individual parts of an image. The images in Figure 35 are simple—only three images are needed for the animation. However, depending on the complexity of the image and the desired movements, the time needed to display each change can be substantial. When creating a frame-by-frame animation, you need to consider the following points:

- The number of different images. The more images there are, the more effort is needed to create them. However, the greater the number of images, the less change you need to make in each image and the more realistic the movement in the animation may seem.
- The number of frames in which each image will appear. Changing the number of frames in which the object appears may change the effect of the animation. If each image appears in only one frame, the animation may appear rather jerky, since the frames change very rapidly. However, in some cases, you may want to give the impression of a rapid change in an object, such as rapidly blinking colors. If so, you could make changes in the color of an object from one frame to another.
- The movie frame rate. Frame rates below 10 may appear jerky, while those above 30 may appear blurred. The frame rate is easy to change, and you should experiment with different rates until you get the desired effect.

Keyframes are critical to the development of frame animations because they signify a change in the object. Because frame animations are created by changing the object, each frame in a frame animation may need to be a keyframe. The exception is when you want an object displayed in several frames before it changes.

Creating a Frame-by-Frame Animation

To create a frame animation, select the frame on the layer where you want the animation to begin, insert a keyframe, and then place the object on the Stage. Next, select the frame where you want the change to occur, insert a keyframe, and then change the object. You can also add a new object in place of the original one. Figure 36 shows the first three frames of an animation in which three different objects are placed one on top of the other in succeeding frames. In the figure, the movement is shown as shadows. These shadows are visible because the Onion Skin feature is turned on. In this movie, the objects stay in place during the animation. However, a frame animation can also involve movement of the object around the Stage.

Using the Onion Skin Feature

Normally, Flash displays one frame of an animation sequence at a time on the Stage. Turning on the Onion Skin feature allows you to view an outline of the object(s) in any number of frames. This can help in positioning animated objects on the Stage.

FIGURE 35
Three images used in an animation

FIGURE 36
A frame-by-frame animation of 3 figures appearing to walk in place

Onion Skin feature is turned on so that all of the objects in frames 1-3 are viewable even though the playhead is on frame 1

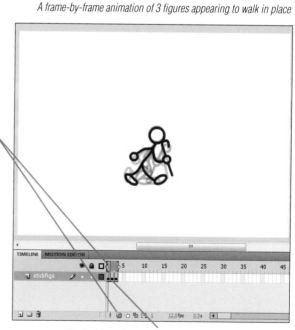

The 3 objects placed on top of each other on the Stage, each in its own frame on the Timeline

Create an in-place frame-by-frame animation

1. Open fl4_4.fla, then save it as **frameAn**.

2. Insert a **new layer**, name it **stickfigs**, click **frame 1** of the stickfigs layer, then drag **stickfig1** from the Library panel to the center of the Stage so it touches the white walkway.

3. Click **frame 2** of the stickfigs layer to select it, click **Insert** on the menu bar, point to **Timeline**, then click **Keyframe**.

4. Drag **stickfig2** so it is on top of stickfig1, as shown in Figure 37, use the arrow keys on the keyboard to align the heads, then click a blank area of the Stage to deselect stickfig2.

5. Select **stickfig1** by clicking the foot that points up, as shown in Figure 38, then press **[Delete]**.

6. Click **frame 3** on Layer 1 to select it, insert a **keyframe**, drag **stickfig3** so it is on top of stickfig2, then use the **arrow keys** on the keyboard to align the heads.

7. Click a blank area of the Stage to deselect stickfig3.

8. Select **stickfig2** by clicking the foot that points down, as shown in Figure 39, then press **[Delete]**.

9. Play the movie.

You created a frame-by-frame animation.

FIGURE 37
Dragging stickfig2 on top of stickfig1

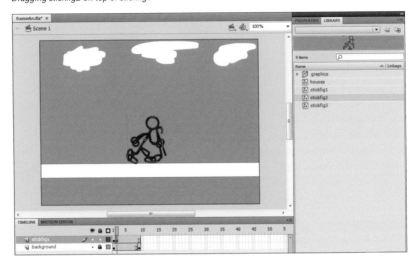

FIGURE 38
Selecting stickfig1

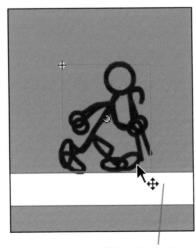

Click foot that points up

FIGURE 39
Selecting stickfig2

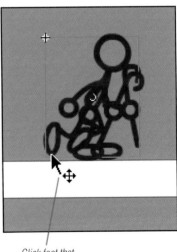

Click foot that points down

Creating Animations

FIGURE 40

Moving the houses layer to below the stickfigs layer

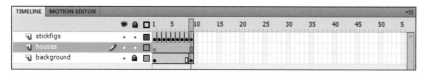

FIGURE 41

Positioning the houses symbol on the Stage

FIGURE 42

Repositioning the houses object

Copy frames and add a moving background

1. Click **frame 1** of the stickfigs layer, hold down **[Shift]**, then click **frame 3**.

2. Click **Edit** on the menu bar, point to **Timeline**, then click **Copy Frames**.

3. Click **frame 4** of the stickfigs layer, click **Edit** on the menu bar, point to **Timeline**, then click **Paste Frames**.

4. Click **frame 7**, then repeat step 3.

5. Click **frame 10** of the stickfigs layer, hold down **[Shift]**, then click **frame 13**.

6. Click **Edit** on the menu bar, point to **Timeline**, then click **Remove Frames**.

7. Insert a **new layer**, name the layer **houses**, then drag the **houses layer** below the stickfigs layer, as shown in Figure 40.

8. Click **frame 1** of the houses layer, then drag the **houses symbol** from the Library panel to the Stage, position the house, as shown in Figure 41.

9. Play the movie.

10. Click **frame 1** of the houses layer, click **Insert** on the menu bar, then click **Motion Tween**.

11. Click **frame 9** on the houses layer, then drag the **houses object** to the left, as shown in Figure 42.

12. Test the movie, close the Flash Player window, save your work, then close the document.

You copied frames and added a motion tween to a movie with an in-place frame-by-frame animation.

Create a frame-by-frame animation of a moving object

1. Open fl4_5.fla, then save it as **frameM**.

   This document has a background layer that contains a row of houses and clouds.

2. Insert a **new layer**, then name it **stickfigs**.

3. Click **View** on the menu bar, point to **Magnification**, then click **50%**.

4. Click **frame 5** on the stickfigs layer, then insert a **keyframe**.

5. Drag **stickfig1** from the Library panel to the left edge of the Stage, as shown in Figure 43.

6. Click **frame 6** on the stickfigs layer, then click **Insert** on the menu bar, point to **Timeline**, then click **Blank Keyframe**.

   A blank keyframe keeps the object in the previous frame from appearing in the current frame.

7. Click the **Edit Multiple Frames button** on the Timeline status bar to turn it on.

   This allows you to view the contents of more than one frame at a time.

8. Drag **stickfig2** to the right of stickfig1, as shown in Figure 44.

9. Click **frame 7** on the stickfigs layer, then insert a **Blank Keyframe**.

10. Drag **stickfig3** to the right of stickfig2, as shown in Figure 45.

   (continued)

FIGURE 43
Positioning stickfig1 on the Stage

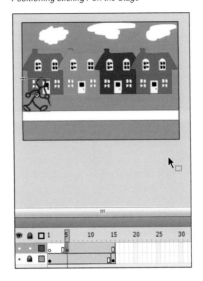

FIGURE 44
Positioning stickfig2 on the Stage

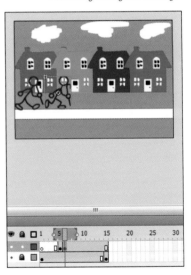

FIGURE 45
Positioning stickfig3 on the Stage

FIGURE 46

Adding stickfig3 as the final object

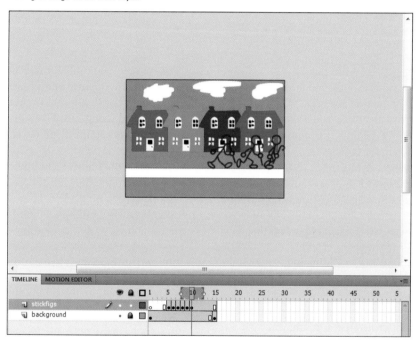

11. Click **frame 8** on the stickfigs layer, insert a **Blank Keyframe**, then drag **stickfig1** from the Library panel to the right of stickfig3.

12. Click **frame 9** on the stickfigs layer, insert a **Blank Keyframe**, then drag **stickfig2** to the right of stickfig1.

13. Click **frame 10** on the stickfigs layer, insert a **Blank Keyframe**, then drag **stickfig3** to the right of stickfig2.

    Your screen should resemble Figure 46.

14. Click **frame 11** on the stickfigs layer, then insert a **Blank Keyframe**.

15. Click the **Edit Multiple Frames button** on the Timeline status bar to turn it off.

16. Test the movie, then close the Flash Player window.

17. Change the frame rate to **6** fps.

18. Test the movie, then close the Flash Player window.

19. Save the movie, then close the document.

You created a frame-by-frame animation that causes objects to appear to move across the screen.

CREATE SHAPE TWEEN
ANIMATIONS

What You'll Do

 In this lesson, you will create a shape tween animation and specify shape hints.

Shape Tweening

In previous lessons, you learned that you can use motion tweening to change the shape of an object. You accomplish this by selecting the Free Transform tool and then dragging the handles to resize and skew the object. While this is easy and allows you to include motion along with the change in shape, there are two drawbacks. First, you are limited in the type of changes (resizing and skewing) that can be made to the shape of an object. Second, you must work with the same object throughout the animation. When you use **shape tweening**, however, you can have an animation change the shape of an object to any form you desire, and you can include two objects in the animation with two different shapes. As with motion tweening, you can use shape tweening to change other properties of an object, such as the color, location, and size.

Using Shape Tweening to Create a Morphing Effect

Morphing involves changing one object into another, sometimes unrelated, object.

For example, you could turn a robot into a man, or turn a football into a basketball. The viewer sees the transformation as a series of incremental changes. In Flash, the first object appears on the Stage and changes into the second object as the movie plays. The number of frames included from the beginning to the end of this shape tween animation determines how quickly the morphing effect takes place. The first frame in the animation displays the first object and the last frame displays the second object. The in-between frames display the different shapes that are created as the first object changes into the second object.

When working with shape tweening, you need to keep the following points in mind:

- Shape tweening can be applied only to editable graphics. To apply shape tweening to instances, groups, symbols, text blocks, or bitmaps, you must break apart the object to make it editable. To do this, you use the Break Apart command on the Modify menu. When you break apart an instance of a symbol, it is no longer linked to the original symbol.

- You can shape tween more than one object at a time as long as all the objects are on the same layer. However, if the shapes are complex and/or if they involve movement in which the objects cross paths, the results may be unpredictable.
- You can use shape tweening to move an object in a straight line, but other options, such as rotating an object, are not available.
- You can use the settings in the Properties panel to set options (such as the ease value, which causes acceleration or deceleration) for a shape tween.
- Shape hints can be used to control more complex shape changes.

Properties Panel Options

Figure 47 shows the Properties panel options for a shape tween. The options allow you to adjust several aspects of the animation, as described in the following:

- Adjust the rate of change between frames to create a more natural appearance during the transition by setting an ease value. Setting the value between -1 and -100 will begin the shape tween gradually and accelerate it toward the end of the animation. Setting the value between 1 and 100 will begin the shape tween rapidly and decelerate it toward the end of the animation. By default, the rate of change is set to 0, which causes a constant rate of change between frames.
- Choose a blend option. The Distributive option creates an animation in which the in-between shapes are smoother and more irregular. The Angular option preserves the corners and straight lines and works only with objects that have these features. If the objects do not have corners, Flash defaults to the Distributive option.

Shape Hints

You can use shape hints to control the shape's transition appearance during animation. Shape hints allow you to specify a location on the beginning object that corresponds to a location on the ending object. Figure 48 shows two shape animations of the same objects, one using shape hints and the other not using shape hints. The figure also shows how the object being reshaped appears in one of the in-between frames. Notice that with the shape hints, the object in the in-between frame is more recognizable.

FIGURE 47
The Properties panel options for a shape tween

FIGURE 48
Two shape animations with and without shape hints

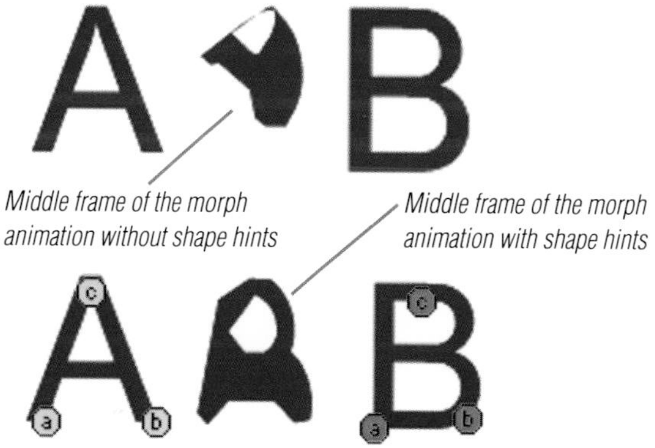

Middle frame of the morph animation without shape hints

Middle frame of the morph animation with shape hints

Create a shape tween animation

1. Open fl4_6.fla, then save it as **antiqueCar**.

2. Set the view to **Fit in Window**.

   | TIP This chapter assumes you always set the magnification to Fit in Window.

3. Click **frame 30** on the shape layer, then insert a **keyframe**.

4. Click the **Selection tool** ▶ on the Tools panel, then click a blank area of the pasteboard to deselect the car.

5. Point to the right side of the top of the car, then use the arc pointer ▷ to drag the **car top** to create the shape shown in Figure 49.

6. Click anywhere on the shape layer between frames 1 and 30.

7. Click **Insert** on the menu bar, then click **Shape Tween**.

8. Click **frame 1** on the shape layer, then play the movie.

9. Click **frame 30** on the shape layer.

10. Click the **Selection tool** ▶ on the Tools panel, then drag a **marquee** around the car to select it if it is not already selected.

11. Drag the **car** to the right side of the Stage.

12. Play the movie, then save and close it.

You created a shape tween animation, causing an object to change shape as it moves over several frames.

FIGURE 49
The reshaped object

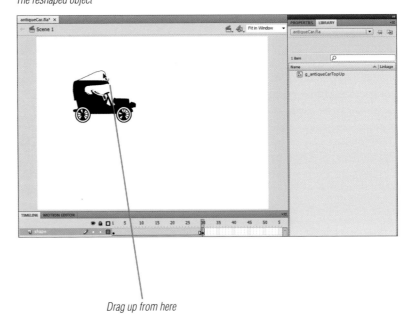

Drag up from here

Create a morphing effect

1. Open fl4_7.fla, then save it as **morphCar**.
2. Click **frame 40** on the morph layer.
3. Click **Insert** on the menu bar, point to **Timeline**, then click **Blank Keyframe**.

   | TIP Inserting a blank keyframe prevents the object in the preceding keyframe from automatically being inserted into the blank keyframe.

4. Click the **Edit Multiple Frames button** on the Timeline.

   Turning on the Edit Multiple Frames feature allows you to align the two objects to be morphed.

5. Display the Library panel.
6. Drag the **g_antiqueCarTopDown graphic** symbol from the Library panel directly on top of the car on the Stage, as shown in Figure 50.

   | TIP Use the arrow keys to move the object in small increments as needed.

7. Make sure the **g_antiqueCarTopDown** object is selected, click **Modify** on the menu bar, then click **Break Apart**.
8. Click the **Edit Multiple Frames button** to turn off the feature.
9. Click anywhere between frames 1 and 40 on the morph layer, click **Insert** on the menu bar, then click **Shape Tween**.
10. Click **frame 1** on the Timeline, then play the movie.

    The first car morphs into the second car.

11. Save the movie.

You created a morphing effect, causing one object to change into another.

FIGURE 50
Positioning the car instance on the Stage

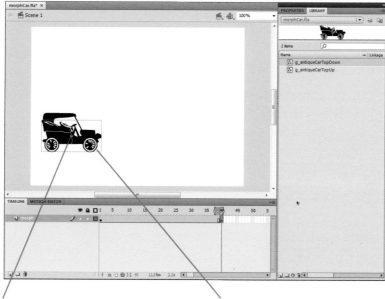

Transformation point appears when the mouse is released

Line up both cars so it appears that there is only one car; use the spokes on the wheels to help you know when the two objects are aligned

Adjust the rate of change in a shape tween animation

1. Click **frame 40** on the morph layer.

2. Click the **Selection tool** ⭢ on the Tools panel, then drag a **marquee** around the car to select it (if necessary).

3. Drag the **car** to the right side of the Stage.

4. Click **frame 1** on the morph layer.

5. Set the ease value on the Properties panel to **−100**, as shown in Figure 51.

6. Click the **Stage**, then play the movie.

   The car starts out slow and speeds up as the morphing process is completed.

7. Repeat Steps 4 and 5, but change the ease value to **100**.

8. Click **frame 1** on the Timeline, then play the movie.

   The car starts out fast and slows down as the morphing process is completed.

9. Save your work, then close the movie.

You added motion to a shape tween animation and changed the ease value.

FIGURE 51

Setting the ease value of the morph

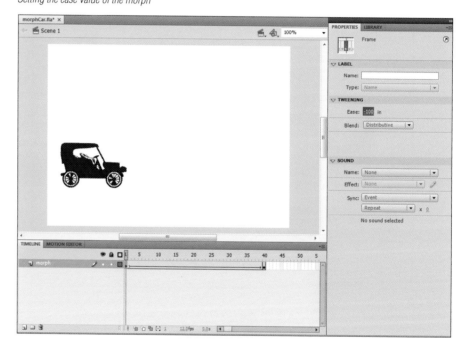

Creating Animations

FIGURE 52
Positioning a shape hint

FIGURE 53
Adding shape hints

FIGURE 54
Matching shape hints

Use shape hints

1. Open fl4_8.fla, then save it as **shapeHints**.

2. Play the movie and notice how the L morphs into a Z.

3. Click **frame 15** on the Timeline, the midpoint of the animation, then notice the shape.

4. Click **frame 1** on the hints layer to display the first object.

5. Make sure the object is selected, click **Modify** on the menu bar, point to **Shape**, then click **Add Shape Hint**.

6. Drag the **Shape Hint icon** 🅰 to the location shown in Figure 52.

7. Repeat Steps 5 and 6 to set a second and third Shape Hint icon, as shown in Figure 53.

8. Click **frame 30** on the hints layer.

   The shape hints are stacked on top of each other.

9. Drag the **Shape Hint icons** to match Figure 54.

10. Click **frame 15** on the hints layer, then notice how the object is more recognizable now that the shape hints have been added.

11. Click **frame 1** on the Timeline, then play the movie.

12. Save your work, then close the movie.

You added shape hints to a morph animation.

CREATE MOVIE
CLIPS

What You'll Do

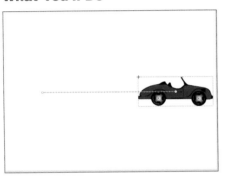

 In this lesson, you will create, edit, and animate a movie clip.

Understanding Movie Clip Symbols

Until now you have been working with two kinds of symbols, graphic and button. A third type is a **movie clip symbol**, which provides a way to create more complex types of animations. A movie clip is essentially a movie within a movie. Each movie clip has its own Timeline, which is independent of the main Timeline. This allows you to nest a movie clip that is running one animation within another animation or in a scene on the main Timeline. Because a movie clip retains its own Timeline, when you insert an instance of the movie clip symbol into a Flash document, the movie clip continues in an endless loop even if the main Timeline stops.

The wheels on a car rotating while the car is moving across the screen is an example of a movie clip with an animation that is nested in another animation. To create the animated movie clip, a drawing of a wheel separate from the car is converted into a movie clip symbol. Then the movie clip symbol is opened in the edit window, which includes a Timeline that is unique to the movie clip. In the edit window, an animation is created that causes the wheel to rotate. After exiting the edit window and returning to the main Timeline, an instance of the movie clip symbol is placed on each wheel of the car. Finally, the car, including the wheels, is animated on the main Timeline. As the car is moving across the screen, the wheels are rotating according to their own Timeline. This process is shown in Figure 55.

In addition to allowing you to create more complex animations, movie clips help to organize the different reusable pieces of a movie and provide for smaller movie file sizes. This is because only one movie clip symbol needs to be stored in the Library panel while an unlimited number of instances of the symbol can be used in the Flash document. An animated movie clip can be viewed in the edit window that is displayed when you double-click on the movie clip symbol in the Library panel; and it can be viewed when you test or publish the movie that contains the movie clip. It is important to note that an animated movie clip cannot be viewed simply by playing the movie on the main Timeline.

In this lesson, you will learn how to create a movie clip symbol from a drawn object, edit the movie clip to create an animation, and nest the movie clip in another animation.

FIGURE 55

The process of nesting a movie clip within an animation

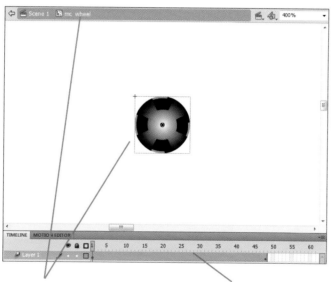

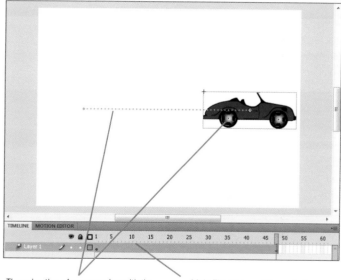

The movie clip of a wheel that has been animated to rotate shown in the edit window

Timeline in the edit window used to create the animation of the rotating wheel

The animation of a car moving with the wheels placed on the car

Main Timeline used to create the animation of the moving car

Break apart a graphic symbol and select parts of the object to separate from the graphic

1. Open fl4_9.fla, then save it as **mClip**.

   This document has one graphic symbol—a car that has been placed on the Stage.

2. Click the **Selection tool** ↖ on the Tools panel, then click the **car** to select it.

3. Click **Modify** on the menu bar, then click **Break Apart**.

4. Click a blank area of the Stage to deselect the object.

5. Click the **Zoom tool** 🔍 on the Tools panel, then click the **front wheel** two times to zoom in on the wheel.

6. Click the **Selection tool** ↖ on the Tools panel.

7. Click the **gray hubcap**, hold down **[Shift]**, then click the rest of the wheel, as shown in Figure 56.

   Hint: There are several small parts to the wheel, so click until a dot pattern covers the entire wheel, but do not select the tire. Use the Undo command if you select the tire.

8. Drag the **selected area** down below the car, as shown in Figure 57.

9. Compare your selected wheel to Figure 57, if your wheel does not match the figure, use the Undo command to move the wheel back to its original position, and repeat step 7.

You broke apart a graphic symbol and selected parts of the object to separate from the graphic.

FIGURE 56
Selecting the wheel

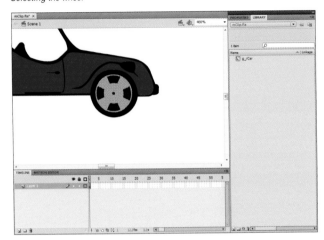

FIGURE 57
Separating the wheel from the car

Creating Animations

FIGURE 58
Selecting the gray area of the wheel

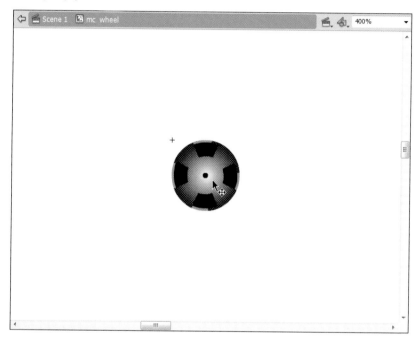

Create and edit a movie clip

1. Verify the wheel is selected, click **Modify** on the menu bar, then click **Convert to Symbol**.

2. Type **mc_wheel** for the name, select **Movie Clip** for the Type, then click **OK**.

   The mc_wheel movie clip appears in the Library panel.

3. Double-click the **mc_wheel icon** in the Library panel to display the edit window.

4. Click the **Zoom tool** 🔍 on the Tools panel, then click the **wheel** twice to zoom in on the wheel.

   The movie clip has been broken apart as indicated by the dot pattern.

5. Click the **Selection tool** ▶, click a blank area of the Stage to deselect the object, then click the **gray area** of the wheel to select it, as shown in Figure 58.

6. Click the **Fill color tool color swatch** 🔲 on the Tools panel, then click the **gray gradient color swatch** in the bottom row of the palette.

You created a movie clip symbol and edited it to change the color of the object.

Animate a movie clip

1. Use the Selection tool ![pointer] to drag a marquee around the entire wheel to select it.

2. Click **Insert** on the menu bar, click **Motion Tween**, then click **OK** for the Convert selection to symbol for tween dialog box.

3. Point to the end of the tween span on Layer 1 of the Timeline, when the pointer changes to a double-headed arrow ↔, drag the span to **frame 48**, as shown in Figure 59.

4. Click **frame 1** on Layer 1.

5. Display the Properties panel.

6. Change the rotate value to **4** times and verify the Direction is **CW (Clockwise)**, as shown in Figure 60.
   Hint: If you don't see the Rotate option, click the Selection tool, then drag a marquee around the object.

7. Verify the frame rate in the Timeline status bar is **12**, test the movie, then close the Flash Player window.

8. Click **Scene 1** near the top left side of the edit widow to exit the edit window.

9. Drag the **wheel** on the Stage and position it so it is on top of the front wheel of the car.

10. Click **View** on the menu bar, point to **Magnification**, then click **Fit in Window**.

11. Drag the **mc_wheel movie clip** from the Library panel and position it using the arrow keys as needed so it is on the back wheel.
    Hint: Use the Zoom tool as needed to zoom in on the wheel.

(continued)

FIGURE 59
Increasing the tween span on the Timeline

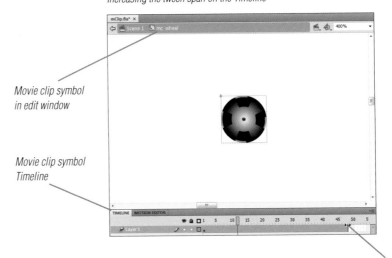

Movie clip symbol
in edit window

Movie clip symbol
Timeline

Drag the tween
span to frame 48

FIGURE 60
Changing the rotate value

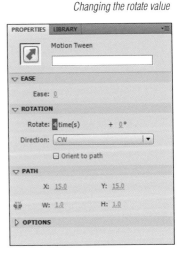

Creating Animations

FIGURE 61
Repositioning the car

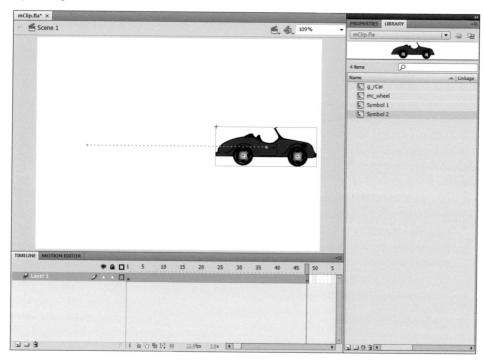

12. Test the movie and notice how the wheels turn, then close the Flash Player window.

13. Use the Selection tool ▶ to drag a marquee around the car to select it and the wheels.

14. Click **Insert** on the menu bar, click **Motion Tween**, then click **OK**.

15. Drag the tween span on Layer 1 to **frame 48**.

16. Click **frame 48** on Layer 1, then drag the **car** to the right side of the Stage, as shown in Figure 61.

17. Test the movie, then close the Flash Player window.

18. Save your work, then close the document.

You edited a movie clip to create an animation, then nested the movie clip in an animation on the main Timeline.

ANIMATE
TEXT

What You'll Do

 In this lesson, you will animate text by scrolling, rotating, zooming, and resizing it.

Animating Text

You can motion tween text block objects just as you do graphic objects. You can resize, rotate, reposition, and change their colors. Figure 62 shows three examples of animated text with the Onion Skin feature turned on. When the movie starts, each of the following occurs one after the other:

- The Classic Car Club text block scrolls in from the left side to the top center of the Stage. This is done by creating the text block, positioning it off the Stage, and creating a motion-tweened animation that moves it to the Stage.
- The Annual text block appears and rotates five times. This occurs after you create the Annual text block,

position it in the middle of the Stage under the heading, and use the Properties panel to specify a clockwise rotation that repeats five times.

- The ROAD RALLY text block slowly zooms out and appears in the middle of the Stage. This occurs after you create the text block and use the Free Transform tool handles to resize it to a small block at the beginning of the animation. Then, you resize the text block to a larger size at the end of the animation.

Once you create a motion animation using a text block, the text block becomes a symbol and you are unable to edit individual characters within the text block. You can, however, edit the symbol as a whole.

Creating Animations

FIGURE 62
Three examples of animated text

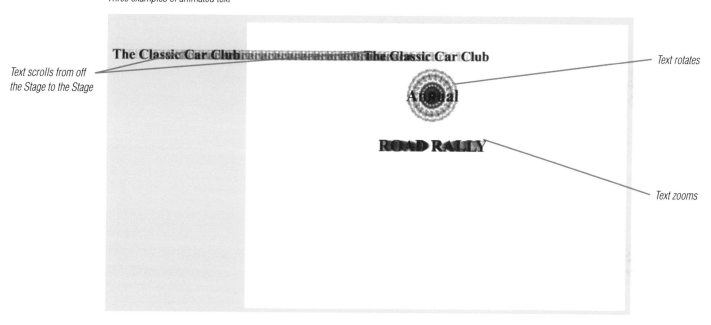

Text scrolls from off
the Stage to the Stage

Text rotates

Text zooms

Select, copy, and paste frames

1. Open fl4_10.fla, then save the movie as **textAn**.

   This document has a frame-by-frame animation of a car where the front end rotates up and down, and then the car moves off the screen.

2. Play the movie, then click **frame 1** on the Timeline.

3. Press the **period [.] key** to move through the animation one frame at a time and notice the changes to the object in each frame.

4. Change the view to **Fit in Window**.

5. Click **frame 9** on the carGo layer, press and hold **[Shift]**, then click **frame 1** to select all the frames, as shown in Figure 63.

6. Click **Edit** on the menu bar, point to **Timeline**, then click **Cut Frames**.

7. Click the **Frame View icon** ▾≣ near the upper right of the Timeline, then click **Small**.

8. Click **frame 71** on the carGo layer.

9. Click **Edit** on the menu bar, point to **Timeline**, then click **Paste Frames**.

10. Click **frame 1** on the carGo layer.

11. Point to the **vertical line** on the Timeline until the ↔ appears, then drag it to the left until frame 80 appears on the Timeline, as shown in Figure 64 (if necessary).

12. Change the view to **100%**.

13. Play the movie, then save your work.

You selected frames and moved them from one location on the Timeline to another location on the Timeline.

FIGURE 63
Selecting a range of frames

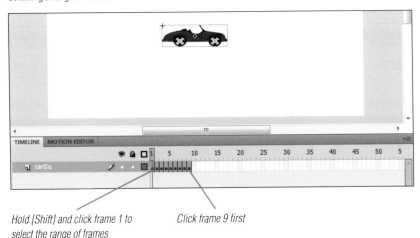

Hold [Shift] and click frame 1 to select the range of frames   Click frame 9 first

FIGURE 64
Expanding the view of the Timeline

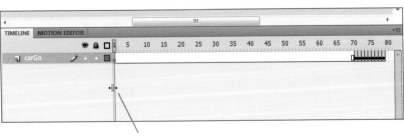

Drag the pointer to the left

Creating Animations

FIGURE 65
Positioning the Text tool pointer outside the Stage

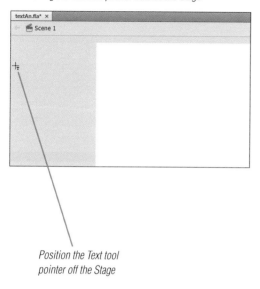

Position the Text tool
pointer off the Stage

FIGURE 66
Positioning the text block

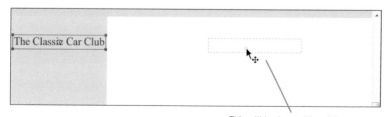

This will be the position of the text
block at the end of the animation

Create animated text

1. Insert a **new layer**, then name it **scrollText**.

2. Click **frame 1** on the scrollText layer.

3. Click the **Text tool** T on the Tools panel, click the ⊥⊤ **pointer** outside the Stage in the upper-left corner of the pasteboard, as shown in Figure 65, then click to display a text box.

   TIP You may need to scroll the Stage to make room for the text box.

4. Click the **Family list arrow** in the Properties panel, then click **Times New Roman** if it is not already selected.

5. Change the Character size to **20**.

6. Click the **Text (fill) color swatch** ▮, then click the **blue color swatch** on the left column of the color palette.

7. Type **The Classic Car Club**.

8. Click the **Selection tool** ▸, click **Insert** on the menu bar, then click **Motion Tween**.

9. Click **frame 20** on the scrollText layer, then insert a **keyframe**.

10. Drag the **text block** horizontally to the top center of the Stage, as shown in Figure 66.

11. Click **frame 1** on the Timeline, then play the movie.

    The text moves to center Stage from offstage left.

You created a text block object and applied a motion tween animation to it.

Create rotating text

1. Insert a **new layer**, then name it **rotateText**.

2. Insert a **keyframe** in frame 21 on the rotateText layer.

3. Click the **Text tool** T on the Tools panel, position the pointer beneath the "a" in "Classic," then click to display a blank text box.

4. Change the Character size in the Properties panel to **24**, type **Annual**, then compare your image to Figure 67.

5. Click the **Selection tool** ⟍ on the Tools panel, verify Annual is selected, click **Insert** on the menu bar, then click **Motion Tween**.

6. Set the Rotate value in the Properties panel to **2** times with a **CW** (clockwise) direction.

   ┃ TIP You may need to click the frame in the Timeline to have the rotate setting appear.

7. Point to the end of the tween span (frame 79) until the pointer changes to ↔ , then drag the ↔ **pointer** to frame 30, as shown in Figure 68.

8. Click **frame 79** on the rotateText layer, then insert a **keyframe**.

9. Click **frame 1** on the Timeline, then play the movie.

   The Annual text rotates clockwise two times.

You inserted a new layer, created a rotating text block, applied a motion tween to text, and used the Properties panel to rotate the text box.

FIGURE 67
Positioning the Annual text block

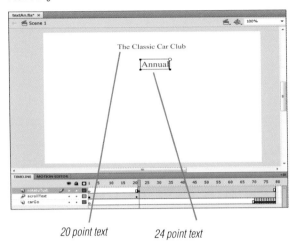

20 point text   24 point text

FIGURE 68
Resizing the tween span from frame 79 to frame 30

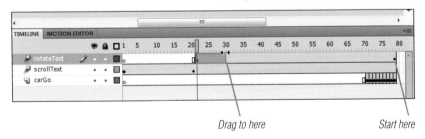

Drag to here   Start here

FIGURE 69
Using the Text tool to type ROAD RALLY

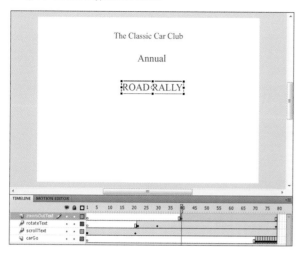

FIGURE 70
Resizing the Text block

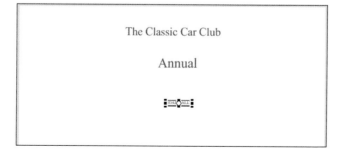

1. Insert a **new layer**, name it **zoomOutText**, then insert a **keyframe** in frame 40 on the layer.

2. Click the **Text tool** T, position the pointer beneath the Annual text box, aligning it with the "h" in "The," then type **ROAD RALLY**, as shown in Figure 69.

3. Click the **Selection tool**, click **frame 40** on the zoomOutText layer, click **Insert** on the menu bar, then click **Motion Tween**.

4. Click **frame 40** on the zoomOutText layer, click the **Free Transform tool**, then click the **Scale button** in the Options area of the Tools panel.

5. Drag the upper-left corner handle inward to resize the text block, as shown in Figure 70.

6. Click **frame 79** on the ZoomOutText layer, verify the Scale option in the Options area of the Tools panel is selected, then drag the upper-left corner handle outward to resize the text block to its original size.

7. Test the movie, then close the Flash Player window.

You created a motion animation that caused a text block to zoom out.

Lesson 6 Animate Text

Make a text block into a button

1. Insert a **new layer**, then name it **continue**.

2. Insert a **keyframe** in frame 71 on the continue layer.

3. Click the **Text tool** T on the Tools panel, position the **Text tool pointer** ⊥ₜ beneath the back wheel of the car, then type **Click to continue**.

4. Drag the **pointer** over the text to select it, change the character size in the Properties panel to **12**, click the **Selection tool** ⤢ on the Tools panel, then compare your image to Figure 71.

5. Verify that the text box is selected, click **Modify** on the menu bar, click **Convert to Symbol**, type **b_continue** in the Name text box, set the Type to **Button**, then click **OK**.

6. Double-click the **text block** to edit the button.

7. Insert a **keyframe** in the Over frame, set the fill color to the **black color swatch** in the left column of the color palette.

8. Insert a **keyframe** in the Down frame, set the fill color to the **bright green color swatch** in the left column of the color palette.

9. Insert a **keyframe** in the Hit frame, select the **Rectangle tool** ⬚ on the Tools panel, then draw a **rectangle** that covers the text block, as shown in Figure 72.

10. Click **Scene 1** at the top left of the edit window to return to the main Timeline.

You made the text block into a button.

FIGURE 71
Adding a button

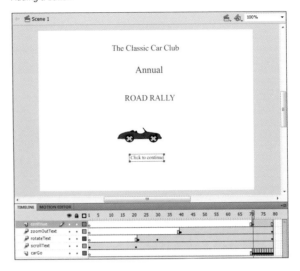

FIGURE 72
The rectangle that defines the hit area

Creating Animations

FIGURE 73

Adding a play action

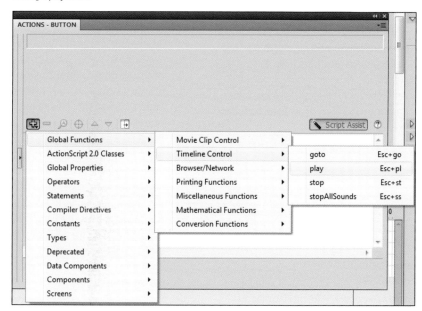

1. Display the Actions panel.

2. Click the **Selection tool** ▸ on the Tools panel, then click the **Click to continue button** on the Stage.

3. Verify the Script Assist button is turned on, then verify the button symbol and b_continue are displayed in the lower-left corner of the Actions panel.

   Note: You need to have ActionScript 2.0 active. You can check your ActionScript version by choosing Publish Settings on the Edit menu, then selecting the Flash tab.

4. Click the **Add a new item to the script button** ⊕ in the Script Assist window, point to **Global Functions**, point to **Timeline Control**, then click **play**, as shown in Figure 73.

5. Insert a **new layer**, name it **stopmovie**, then insert a **keyframe** in frame 71 on that layer.

6. Verify that stopmovie:71 is displayed in the lower-left corner of the Actions panel.

7. Click the **Add a new item to the script button** ⊕ in the Script Assist window, point to **Global Functions**, point to **Timeline Control**, then click **stop**.

8. Click **Control** on the menu bar, click **Test Movie**, then click the **Click to continue button** when it appears.

   The movie plays the animated text blocks, then plays the animated car when you click the Click to continue button.

9. Close the Flash Player movie window, save and close the movie, then exit Flash.

You inserted a play button and added a play action to it, then inserted a stop action on another layer.

Create a motion tween animation.

1. Start Flash, open fl4_11.fla, then save it as **skillsdemo4**.
2. Insert a keyframe in frame 20 on the ballAn layer.
3. Display the Library panel, then drag the g_vball graphic symbol to the lower-left corner of the Stage.
4. Click frame 20 on the ballAn layer, then insert a motion tween.
5. Point to the end of frame 20, when the pointer changes to a double-headed arrow, drag the pointer to frame 40 to set the tween span from frames 20 to 40.
6. With frame 40 selected, drag the object to the lower-right corner of the Stage.
7. Change the view of the Timeline to Small so more frames are in view.
8. Insert a blank keyframe in frame 41.
9. Play the movie, then save your work.

Edit a motion tween.

1. Click frame 20, use the Selection tool to alter the motion path to form an arc, then play the movie.
2. Use the Subsection tool to display the Bezier handles, use them to form a curved path, then play the movie.
3. Select frame 20, use the Properties panel to change the ease value to **100**, then play the movie.
4. Select frame 20, change the ease value to **-100**, then play the movie.

5. Select frame 40, select the object, use the Properties panel to change the width of the object to **30**, then play the movie. (*Hint:* Verify the Lock width and height values together chain is unbroken. This will ensure that when one value is changed, the other value changes proportionally.)
6. Select frame 35, select the object, use the Free transform tool to skew the object, then play the movie.
7. Select frame 40, select the object, use the Properties panel to change the alpha setting to **0**, then play the movie.
8. Change the alpha setting back to **100**.
9. Select frame 40, select the object, then use the Advanced Style option in the COLOR EFFECT area of the Properties panel to create a red color.
10. Lock the ballAn layer.
11. Play the movie, then save your work.

Create a classic tween.

1. Insert a new layer and name it **v-ball**.
2. Insert a keyframe in frame 76 on the v-ball layer.
3. Insert a keyframe in frame 41 on the v-ball layer.
4. Drag an instance of the g_vball symbol from the Library panel to the lower-left corner of the Stage.
5. Insert a keyframe in frame 50 on the v-ball layer and drag the ball to the lower-right corner of the Stage.

6. Click on any frame between 41 and 50 on the v-ball layer and insert a Classic tween.
7. Insert a blank keyframe at frame 51 on the v-ball layer.
8. Play the movie, then save your work.

Create a motion guide.

1. Insert a new layer above the v-ball layer and name it **path**.
2. Insert a keyframe in frame 76 on the path layer.
3. Change the path layer to a Guide layer.
4. Insert a keyframe at frame 41 on the path layer.
5. Select the pencil tool, point to the middle of the ball and draw a path with a loop.
6. Insert a keyframe in frame 50 on the path layer.
7. Drag the v-ball layer up to the path layer so that it indents below the path layer.
8. Click frame 41 on the v-ball layer and attach the ball to the path.
9. Click frame 50 on the v-ball layer and attach the ball to the path.
10. Click frame 41 on the v-ball layer and use the Properties panel to orient the ball to the path.
11. Lock the v-ball and path layers.
12. Hide the path layer.
13. Play the movie, then save the movie.

Create a frame animation.

1. Insert a new layer and name it **corner-ball**.
2. Insert a keyframe in frame 76 on the corner-ball layer.

3. Insert a keyframe in frame 51 on the corner-ball layer, then drag the g_vball graphic from the Library panel to the lower-left corner of the Stage.

4. Insert a blank keyframe in frame 55 on the corner-ball layer, then drag g_vball graphic from the Library panel to the upper-left corner of the Stage.

5. Insert a blank keyframe in frame 59 on the corner-ball layer, then drag the g_vball graphic from the Library panel to the upper-right corner of the Stage.

6. Insert a blank keyframe in the frame 63 on the corner-ball layer, then drag the g_vball graphic from the Library panel to the lower-right corner of the Stage.

7. Insert a blank keyframe in frame 66 on the corner-ball layer.

8. Lock the corner-ball layer.

9. Change the movie frame rate to 3 frames per second, then play the movie.

10. Change the movie frame rate to 12 frames per second, play the movie, then save your work.

Create a movie clip.

1. Insert a new layer and name it **spin-ball**.

2. Insert a keyframe at frame 76 on the spin-ball layer.

3. Insert a keyframe at frame 51 on the spin-ball layer.

4. Drag an instance of the g_vball symbol from the Library panel to the center of the Stage.

5. Select the ball and convert it to a movie clip with the name **mc_ball**.

6. Display the edit window for the mc_ball movie clip.

7. Create a motion tween that rotates the ball 6 times counterclockwise in 12 frames.

8. Exit the edit window.

9. Insert a blank keyframe in frame 66 of the spin-ball layer.

10. Lock the spin-ball layer.

11. Test the movie, close the Flash Player window, then save your work.

Animate text.

1. Insert a new layer above the spin-ball layer and name it **heading**.

2. Insert a keyframe in frame 76 on the heading layer.

3. Click frame 1 on the heading layer.

4. Use the Text tool to type **Having fun with a** in a location off the top-left of the Stage.

5. Change the text to Arial, 20 point, light gray (#CCCCCC), and boldface.

6. Select frame 1 on the heading layer and insert a motion tween.

7. Click frame 10 on the heading layer, insert a keyframe, then use the Selection tool to drag the text to the top-center of the Stage.

8. Play the movie and save your work.

9. Lock the heading layer.

10. Insert a new layer and name it **zoom**.

11. Insert a keyframe in frame 76 on the zoom layer.

12. Insert a keyframe in frame 11 on the zoom layer.

13. Use the Text tool to type **Volleyball** below the heading, then center it as needed.

14. Select frame 11 on the zoom layer and create a motion tween.

15. Insert a keyframe in frame 20 on the zoom layer.

16. Click frame 11 on the zoom layer and select the text block.

17. Use the Free Transform tool to resize the text block to approximately one-fourth its original size.

18. Select frame 20 on the zoom layer, and resize the text block to approximately the size shown in Figure 74.

19. Lock the zoom layer.

20. Test the movie, close the Flash Player window, save your work.

Morph text.

1. Insert a new layer above the heading layer and name it **morph**.

2. Insert a keyframe in frame 66 on the morph layer.

3. Drag the g_vball symbol to the center of the Stage.

4. Use the Properties panel to resize the width to **60** px. (*Hint*: Verify the Lock width and height values together chain is unbroken. This will ensure that when one value is changed, the other value changes proportionally.)

Creating Animations

5. Break apart the object.
6. Insert a blank keyframe in frame 76 on the morph layer.
7. Turn on the Edit Multiple Frames feature.
8. Drag the g_vball symbol to the Stage and use the Properties panel to resize the width to **60** px. *(Hint:* Verify the Lock width and height values together chain is unbroken.

This will ensure that when one value is changed, the other value changes proportionally).
9. Center the football on top of the volleyball.
10. Break apart the football object.
11. Turn off the Edit Multiple Frames feature.
12. Click frame 66 on the morph layer and insert a shape tween.

13. Test the movie, then close the Flash Player window.
14. Add shape hints to the volleyball and the football.
15. Lock the morph layer.
16. Test the movie, close the Flash Player window, then save your work.
17. Exit Flash.

FIGURE 74
Completed Skills Review

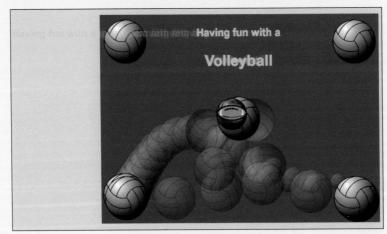

The Ultimate Tours travel company has asked you to design several sample animations for its website. Figure 75 shows a sample home page and the Cruises screen. Using these (or one of the home pages you created in Chapter 3) as a guide, complete the following:

(Tip: If you need to insert frames, select the frame where the inserted frame is to go and press [F5] (Win) or use the Timeline command from the Insert menu (Win) (Mac). To insert several frames, select a range of frames and press [F5] (Win), or use the Timeline command from the Insert menu (Win) (Mac). To move the contents of a frame, you can select the frames you want to move, then use the Cut and Paste commands from the Edit menu to move the contents.)

1. Open ultimatetours3.fla (the file you created in Chapter 3 Project Builder 1) and save it as **ultimatetours4**.

2. Animate the heading Ultimate Tours on the home page so that it zooms out from a transparent text block.

3. Have the logo appear next.

4. After the heading and logo appear, make the subheading We Specialize in Exotic Adventures appear.

5. Make each of the buttons (Treks, Tours, Cruises) scroll from the bottom of the Stage to its position on the Stage. Stagger the buttons so they scroll onto the Stage one after the other.

6. Assign a stop action after the home page appears.

7. Add a new layer, name it **cruises headings**, then add the text blocks shown in Figure 75 (Featured Cruises, Panama Canal, Caribbean, Galapagos).

8. Insert keyframes in the ending frames for the Ultimate Tours title, logo, and home button so that they appear on the cruises screen.

9. Import the graphic file ship.gif from the drive and folder where your Data Files are stored to the Library panel, then rename the graphic file **g_ship**. (*Hint*: To import a graphic to the Library panel, click File on the menu bar, point to Import, then click Import to Library. Navigate to the drive and folder where your Data Files are stored, then select the desired file and click Open (Win) or Import to Library (Mac).)

10. Create a motion tween animation that moves the ship across the screen, then alter the motion path to cause a dip in it, similar to the path shown in Figure 75.

11. Orient the boat to the motion path.

12. Assign a goto action to the Cruises button so it jumps to the frame that has the Cruises screen.

13. Test the movie, then compare your movie to the example shown in Figure 75.

FIGURE 75

Sample completed Project Builder 1

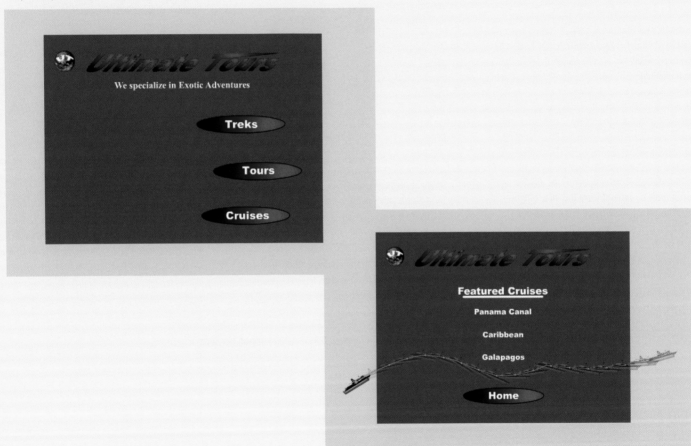

Creating Animations

You have been asked to demonstrate some of the animation features of Flash. You have decided to create a movie clip that includes a frame-by-frame animation and then use the movie clip in a motion tween animation. Figure 76 shows the stick figure that will walk across the screen and jump up at each line on the sidewalk. The movement across the screen is a motion tween. The jumping up is a movie clip.

To complete this project, do the following:

1. Start a new Flash document and name it **jumper4**.

2. Add a background color, sidewalk with lines, and houses or other graphics of your choice, adding layers as needed and naming them appropriately. (*Note:* You can open a previous movie that used the stick figures, such as frameAn, then with your movie open, click the list arrow under the Library panel tab. This displays a list of all open documents. Click the name of the file that has the stick figures to display its Library panel. Then drag the symbols you need to the Stage of your movie. This will place the objects in the jumper4 Library panel.)

3. Create a new movie clip. (*Note:* You can create a new movie clip by selecting New Symbol from the Insert menu, then you can drag objects from the Library panel to the movie clip edit window.)

4. Edit the clip to create a frame-by-frame animation of the stick figures walking in place. In the movie clip, place the stick figures one after the other, but have one of the stick figures in the sequence placed above the others to create a jumping effect. You will use each stick figure two times in the sequence.

5. Exit the edit window and place the movie clip on the Stage, then create a motion tween that moves the movie clip from the left side to the right side of the Stage.

6. Test the movie. (*Note:* Movie clips do not play from the Stage, you must use the Test Movie command.)

7. Close the Flash Player movie, then save the movie.

FIGURE 76
Sample completed Project Builder 2

Figure 77 shows a website for kids. Study the figure and complete the following. For each question, indicate how you determined your answer.

1. Connect to the Internet, then go to *www.smokeybear.com/kids*.
2. Open a document in a word processor or open a new Flash document, save the file as **dpc4**, then answer the following questions. (*Hint*: Use the Text tool in Flash.)
   - What seems to be the purpose of this site?
   - Who would be the target audience?
   - How might a frame animation be used in this site?
   - How might a motion tween animation be used?
   - How might a motion guide be used?
   - How might motion animation effects be used?
   - How might the text be animated?

FIGURE 77
Design Project

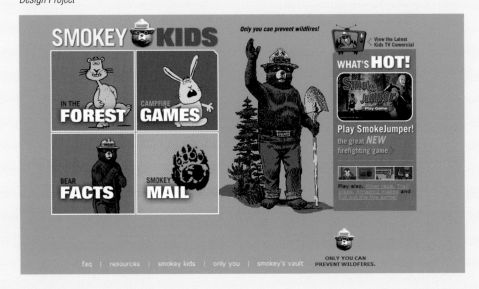

Creating Animations

This is a continuation of the Portfolio Project in Chapter 3, which is the development of a personal portfolio. The home page has several categories, including the following:

- Personal data
- Contact information
- Previous employment
- Education
- Samples of your work

In this project, you will create several buttons for the sample animations screen and link them to the animations.

1. Open portfolio3.fla (the file you created in Portfolio Project, Chapter 3) and save it as **portfolio4**. (*Hint*: When you open the file, you may receive a missing font message, meaning a font used in this document is not available on your computer. You can choose a substitute font or use a default font. If you have to use a default font or if you substitute a font, the resulting text may not look as intended.)

2. Display the Sample Animation screen and change the heading to Sample Animations.

3. Add layers and create buttons with labels, as shown in Figure 78, for the tweened animation, frame-by-frame animation, motion path animation, and animated text.

4. Create a tween animation or use the passing cars animation from Chapter 3, and link it to the appropriate button on the Sample

Animations screen by assigning a go to action to the button.

5. Create a frame-by-frame animation, and link it to the appropriate button on the Sample Animations screen.

6. Create a motion path animation, and link it to the appropriate button on the Sample Animations screen.

FIGURE 78
Sample completed Portfolio Project

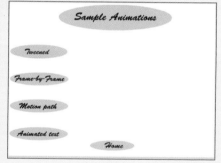

7. Create several text animations, using scrolling, rotating, and zooming; then link them to the appropriate button on the Sample Animations screen.

8. Add a layer and create a Home button that links the Sample Animations screen to the Home screen.

9. Create frame actions that cause the movie to return to the Sample Animations screen after each animation has been played.

10. Test the movie.

11. Save your work, then compare sample pages from your movie to the example shown for two of the screens in Figure 78.

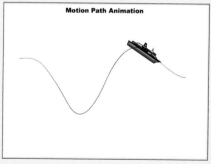

Creating Animations

chapter

5

CREATING SPECIAL
EFFECTS

1. Create a mask effect

2. Add sound

3. Add video

4. Create an animated navigation bar

5. Create character animations using inverse kinematics

6. Create 3D effects

ADOBE FLASH CS4

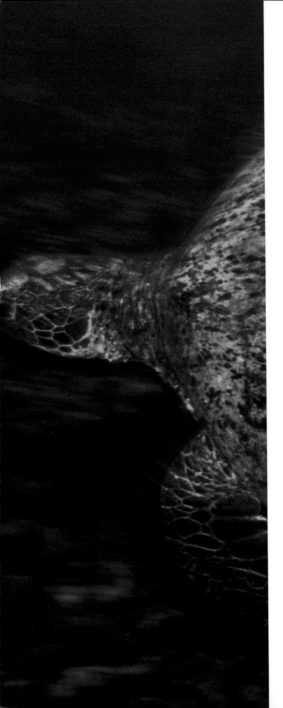

5 CREATING SPECIAL EFFECTS

Introduction

Now that you are familiar with the basics of Flash, you can begin to apply some of the special features that can enhance a movie. Special effects can provide variety and add interest to a movie, as well as draw the viewer's attention to a location or event in the movie. One type of special effect is a spotlight that highlights an area(s) of the movie or reveals selected content on the Stage. You can use sound effects to enhance a movie by creating moods and dramatizing events. In addition, you can add sound to a button to provide feedback to the viewer when the button is clicked. Video can be incorporated into a Flash movie and effects such as fading in and out can be applied to the display of the video.

Another type of special effect is an animated navigation bar, for example, one that causes a drop-down menu when the user rolls over a button. This effect can be created using masks and invisible buttons.

Two new features of Adobe Flash CS4 are Inverse Kinematics and 3D Effects. Inverse Kinematics allows you to easily create character animations and even allows users to interact with the character when viewing the Flash movie. The 3D tools allow you to create 3D effects such as objects moving and rotating through 3D space.

Tools You'll Use

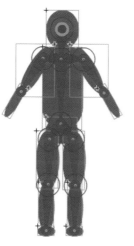

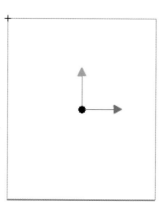

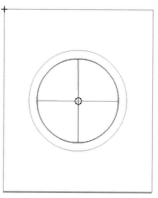

CREATE A
MASK EFFECT

What You'll Do

Cla ssic Car lub

 In this lesson, you will apply a mask effect.

Understanding Mask Layers

A **mask layer** allows you to cover up the objects on one or more layers and, at the same time, create a window through which you can view objects on those layer(s). You can determine the size and shape of the window and specify whether it moves around the Stage. Moving the window around the Stage can create effects such as a spotlight that highlights certain content on the Stage, drawing the viewer's attention to a specific location. Because the window can move around the Stage, you can use a mask layer to reveal only the area of the Stage and the objects you want the viewer to see.

You need at least two layers on the Timeline when you are working with a mask layer. One layer, called the mask layer, contains the window object through which you view the objects on the second layer below. The second layer, called the masked layer, contains the object(s) that are viewed through the window. Figure 1 shows how a mask layer works: The top part of the figure shows the mask layer with the window in the shape of a circle. The next part of the figure shows the layer to be masked. The last part of the figure shows the result of applying the mask. Figure 1 illustrates the simplest use of a mask layer. In most cases, you want to have other objects appear on the Stage and have the mask layer affect only a certain portion of the Stage.

The process for using a mask layer follows:
- Select an original layer that will become the masked layer—it contains the objects that you want to display through the mask layer window.
- Insert a new layer above the masked layer that will become the mask layer. A mask layer always masks the layer(s) immediately below it.
- Draw a filled shape, such as a circle, or create an instance of a symbol that will become the window on the mask layer. Flash will ignore bitmaps, gradients, transparency colors, and line styles on a mask layer. On a mask layer, filled areas become transparent and non-filled areas become opaque when viewed over a masked layer.

- Select the new layer and open the Layer Properties dialog box using the Timeline option from the Modify menu, then select Mask. Flash converts the layer to the mask layer.
- Select the original layer and open the Layer Properties dialog box using the Layer command on the Modify menu, and then choosing Masked. Flash converts the layer to the masked layer.
- Lock both the mask and masked layers.
- To mask additional layers: Drag an existing layer beneath the mask layer, or create a new layer beneath the mask layer and use the Layer Properties dialog box to convert it to a masked layer.
- To unlink a masked layer: Drag it above the mask layer, or select it and select Normal from the Layer Properties dialog box.

FIGURE 1
A mask layer with a window

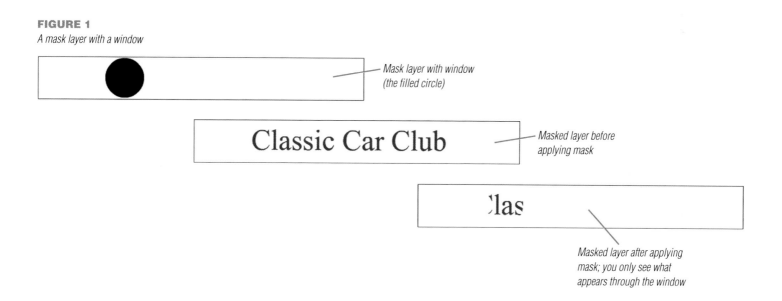

Mask layer with window
(the filled circle)

Masked layer before
applying mask

Masked layer after applying
mask; you only see what
appears through the window

Create a mask layer

1. Open fl5_1.fla, then save it as **classicCC**.

2. Insert a **new layer**, name it **mask**, then click **frame 1** on the mask layer.

3. Select the **Oval tool** on the Tools panel, set the **Stroke Color** to **No Stroke** on the top row of the color palette.

4. Set the **Fill Color** to the **black color swatch** in the left column of the color palette.

5. Draw the **circle** shown in Figure 2, click the **Selection tool** on the Tools panel, then drag a **marquee** around the circle to select it.

6. Click **Insert** on the menu bar, click **Motion Tween**, then click **OK** to convert the drawing into a symbol so that it can be tweened.

7. Click **frame 40** on the mask layer, then drag the **circle** to the position shown in Figure 3.

8. Click **mask** on the Timeline to select the mask layer, click **Modify** on the menu bar, point to **Timeline**, then click **Layer Properties**.

9. Verify that the Show check box is selected in the Name section, click the **Lock check box** to select it, click the **Mask option button** in the Type section, then click **OK**.

   The mask layer has a shaded mask icon next to it on the Timeline.

10. Play the movie from frame 1 and notice how the circle object covers the text on the heading layer as it moves across the Stage.

    Note: The circle object will not become transparent until a masked layer is created beneath it.

You created a mask layer containing a circle object that moves across the Stage.

FIGURE 2
Object to be used as the window on a mask layer

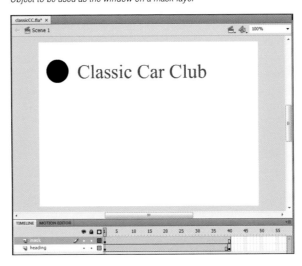

FIGURE 3
Repositioning the circle

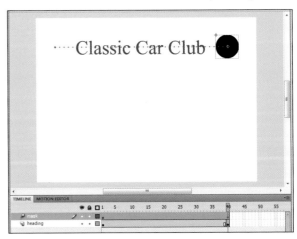

FIGURE 4

The completed Layer Properties dialog box

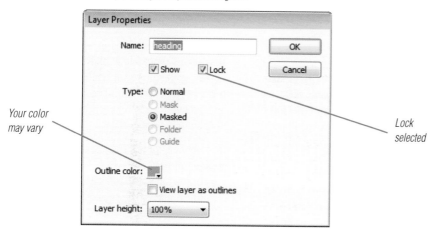

*Your color
may vary*

*Lock
selected*

Create a masked layer

1. Click **heading** on the Timeline to select the heading layer, click **Modify** on the menu bar, point to **Timeline**, then click **Layer Properties** to open the Layer Properties dialog box.

2. Verify that the Show check box is selected in the Name section, click the **Lock check box** to select it, click the **Masked option button** in the Type section, compare your dialog box to Figure 4, then click **OK**.

    The text on the Stage seems to disappear. The heading layer title appears indented and has a shaded masked icon next to it on the Timeline.

3. Play the movie and notice how the circle object acts as a window to display the text on the heading layer.

4. Click **Control** on the menu bar, then click **Test Movie**.

5. View the movie, then close the Flash Player window.

6. Save your work, then close the movie.

You used the Layer Properties dialog box to create a masked layer.

ADD
SOUND

What You'll Do

 In this lesson, you will add sound to an animation.

Incorporating Animation and Sound

Sound can be extremely useful in a Flash movie. Sounds are often the only effective way to convey an idea, elicit an emotion, dramatize a point, and provide feedback to a user's action, such as clicking a button. How would you describe in words or show in an animation the sound a whale makes? Think about how chilling it is to hear the footsteps on the stairway of a haunted house. Consider how useful it is to hear the pronunciation of "buenos dias" as you are studying Spanish. All types of sounds can be incorporated into a Flash movie: for example, CD-quality music that might

be used as background for a movie; narrations that help explain what the user is seeing; various sound effects, such as a car horn beeping; and recordings of special events, such as a presidential speech or a rock concert.

The process for adding a sound to a movie follows:
- Import a sound file into a Flash movie; Flash places the sound file into the movie's library.
- Create a new layer.
- Select the desired frame on the new layer where you want the sound to play and drag the sound symbol to the Stage.

You can place more than one sound file on a layer, and you can place sounds on layers with other objects. However, it is recommended that you place each sound on a separate layer so that it is easier to identify and edit. In Figure 5, the sound layer shows a wave pattern that extends from frame 1 to frame 24. The wave pattern gives some indication of the volume of the sound at any particular frame. The higher spikes in the pattern indicate a louder sound. The wave pattern also gives some indication of the pitch. The denser the wave pattern,

the lower the pitch. You can alter the sound by adding or removing frames. However, removing frames may create undesired effects. It is best to make changes to a sound file using a sound-editing program.

You can use options in the Properties panel, as shown in Figure 6, to synchronize a sound to an event (such as clicking a button) and to specify special effects (such as fade in and fade out). You can import the following sound file formats into Flash:

- ASND (Windows or Macintosh)
- WAV (Windows only)
- AIFF (Macintosh only)
- MP3 (Windows or Macintosh)

If you have QuickTime 4 or later installed on your computer, you can import these additional sound file formats:

- AIFF (Windows or Macintosh)
- Sound Designer II (Macintosh only)
- Sound Only QuickTime Movies (Windows or Macintosh)
- Sun AU (Windows or Macintosh)
- System 7 Sounds (Macintosh only)
- WAV (Windows or Macintosh)

FIGURE 5
A wave pattern displayed on a sound layer

FIGURE 6
Sound Effect options in the Properties panel

Add sound to a movie

1. Open fl5_2.fla, then save it as **rallySnd**.

2. Play the movie and notice that there is no sound.

3. Click the **stopmovie layer**, insert a **new layer**, then name it **carSnd**.

4. Insert a **keyframe** in frame 72 on the carSnd layer.

5. Click **File** on the menu bar, point to **Import**, then click **Import to Library**.

6. Use the Import to Library dialog box to navigate to the drive and folder where your Data Files are stored, click the **CarSnd.wav file**, then click **Open** (Win) or **Import to Library** (Mac).

7. Display the Library Panel if it is not displayed.

8. Click **frame 72** on the CarSnd layer.

9. Drag the **CarSnd sound symbol** 🔊 to the Stage, as shown in Figure 7.

   After releasing the mouse button, notice the wave pattern that has been placed on the carSnd layer starting in frame 72.

   | TIP The wave pattern may not appear on the layer until the movie is played one time.

10. Click **Control** on the menu bar, then click **Test Movie**.

11. Click the **Click to continue button** to test the sound.

12. Close the Flash Player window.

You imported a sound and added it to a movie.

FIGURE 7
Dragging the CarSnd symbol to the Stage

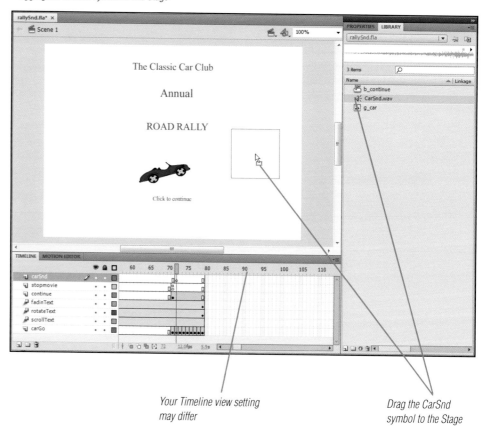

Your Timeline view setting
may differ

Drag the CarSnd
symbol to the Stage

FIGURE 8

The Timeline for the button with the sound layer

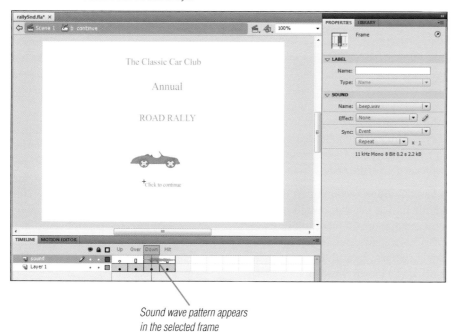

*Sound wave pattern appears
in the selected frame*

Add sound to a button

1. Click **frame 71** on the carSnd layer.
2. Click the **Selection tool** ▸ on the Tools panel, drag a **marquee** around "Click to continue" to select the button, then double-click the **selection** to display the button's Timeline.
3. Insert a **new layer** above Layer 1, then name it **sound**.
4. Click the **Down frame** on the sound layer, click **Insert** on the menu bar, point to **Timeline**, then click **Blank Keyframe**.
5. Click **File** on the menu bar, point to **Import**, then click **Import to Library**.
6. Use the Import to Library dialog box to navigate to the drive and folder where your Data Files are stored, click the **beep.wav file**, then click **Open** (Win) or **Import to Library** (Mac).
7. Display the Properties panel, click the **Name list arrow** in the SOUND area, then click **beep.wav**.
8. Click the **Sync list arrow** in the Properties panel, click **Event**, then compare your screen to Figure 8.
9. Click **Scene 1** on the upper left of the edit window title bar to display the main Timeline.
10. Test the movie.
11. Click the **Click to continue button** and listen to the sounds, then close the Flash Player window.
12. Save your work, then close the movie.

You added a sound layer to a button, imported a sound, then attached the sound to the button.

ADD
VIDEO

What You'll Do

In this lesson, you will import a video, add actions to video control buttons, and then synchronize sound to a video clip.

Incorporating Video

Adobe Flash allows you to import FLV (Flash video) files that then can be used in a Flash document. Flash provides several ways to add video to a movie, depending on the application and, especially, file size. Video content can be embedded directly into a Flash document, progressively downloaded, or streamed.

Embedded video becomes part of the SWF file similar to other objects, such as sound and graphics. A placeholder appears on the Stage and is used to display the video during playback. If the video is imported as a movie clip symbol, then the placeholder can be edited, including rotating, resizing, and even animating it. Because embedded video becomes part of the SWF file, the technique of embedding video is best used for small video clips in order to keep the file size small. The process for embedding video is to import a video file using the Import Video Wizard. Then, you place the video on the Stage and add controls as desired. Figure 9

shows a video placeholder for an embedded video. The video file (fireworks.mov) is in the Library panel and the video layer in the Timeline contains the video object.

Progressive downloading allows you to use ActionScript to load an external FLV file into a SWF file; the video then plays when the SWF file is played. With progressive downloading, the FLV file resides outside the SWF file. Therefore, the SWF file size can be kept smaller than when the video is embedded in the Flash document. The video begins playing soon after the first part of the file has been downloaded.

Streaming video provides a constant connection between the user and the video delivery. Streaming has several advantages over the other methods of delivering video, including starting the video quicker and allowing for live video delivery. However, streaming video requires the Flash Media Server, an Adobe software product designed specifically for streaming video content.

Using the Adobe Media Encoder

The Adobe Media Encoder is an application used by Flash to convert various video file formats, such as .mov, .avi, and .mpeg, to the FLV (Flash Video) format so the videos can be used with Flash. The Encoder allows you to, among other things, choose the size of the placeholder the video will play in, to edit the video, and to insert cue points that can be used to synchronize the video with animations and sound. Figure 10 shows the Encoder ready to convert the fireworks.mov video (Source Name) to fireworks.flv (Output File). The Start Queue button is used to start the process. When the conversion is complete, a green check mark is displayed in the Status column. The Adobe Media Encoder can be accessed through the Import Video Wizard.

Using the Import Video Wizard

The Import Video Wizard is used to import FLV files into Flash documents. The Wizard, in a step-by-step process, leads you through a series of windows that allows you to select the file to be imported and the deployment method (embed, progressive, streaming). In addition, you can specify whether or not to have the video converted to a movie clip symbol which allows you to animate the placeholder. The Wizard appears when you choose the Import Video command from the Import option on the File menu.

FIGURE 9

An embedded video

FIGURE 10

The Adobe Media Encoder

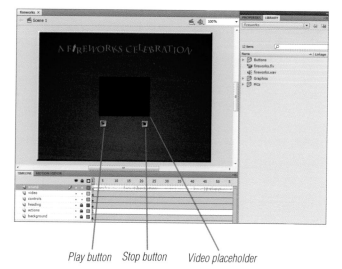

Play button   Stop button   Video placeholder

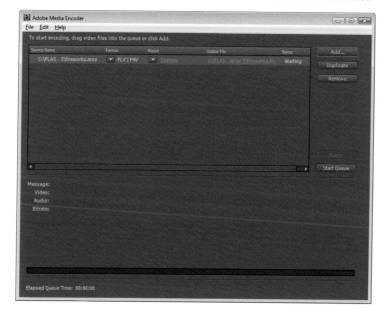

Import a video

1. Open fl5_3.fla, then save it as **fireworks**.

   Note: If the Missing Font Warning message appears, click Use Default.

   The movie has four layers and 85 frames. The actions layer has a stop action in frame 1. The heading layer contains the text object. The controls layer contains start and stop buttons that will be used to control the video. The background layer contains a blue gradient background object. The Library panel contains the two button symbols and a sound file as well as graphics and movie clip files.

2. Insert a **new layer** above the controls layer, name it **video**, then click **frame 1** on the video layer.

3. Click **File** on the menu bar, point to **Import**, then click **Import Video**.

   The Import Video Wizard begins by asking for the path to the video file and the desired method for importing the file, as shown in Figure 11.

4. Click the **Embed FLV in SWF and play in timeline option button**.

5. Click **Browse**, navigate to the drive and folder where your Data Files are stored, click **fireworks.mov**, then click **Open**.

   A message appears indicating that the video format is not valid for embedding video. You must convert the file to the FLV format.

   (continued)

FIGURE 11
The Import Video Wizard

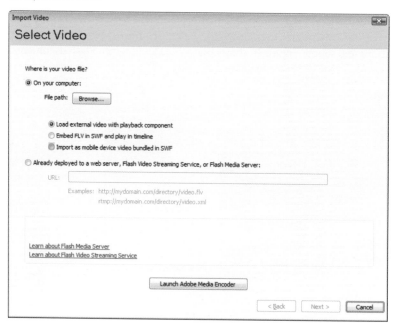

FIGURE 12

The embed video options

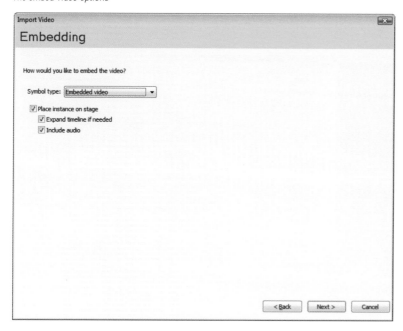

6. Click **OK**, then click the **Launch Adobe Media Encoder button**.

   Note: If a message about browsing to the file after it is converted opens, click OK.

   After several moments the encoder opens.

   Note: Click the Adobe Media Encoder button on the taskbar if the encoder does not open automatically in its own window.

7. Click **Start Queue**, when the process is done as indicated by a green check mark, close the encoder window.

8. Click **OK** to close the message window if one opens, then click the **Browse button**.

9. Click **fireworks.flv**, then click **Open**.

   Note: If you do not see fireworks.flv, navigate to the drive and folder where your solution file is stored.

   The Select Video screen now displays the path to the fireworks.flv file.

10. Click **Next** (Win) or **Continue** (Mac) in the Wizard.

    The Embedding window opens, which allows you to specify how you would like to embed the video.

11. Verify your settings match those in Figure 12.

12. Click **Next** (Win) or **Continue** (Mac).

13. Read the Finish Video Import screen, then click **Finish**.

    The video is encoded and placed on the Stage and in the Library panel.

You imported a video and then *specified the embed and encoding type.*

Attach actions to video control buttons

1. Test the movie, then click the **control buttons**.

   Nothing happens because there is a stop action in frame 1 and no actions have been assigned to the buttons.

2. Close the Flash Player window.

3. Open the Actions panel.

4. Click the **play button** on the Stage, then verify the playback – play button symbol appears at the lower left of the Script pane.

5. Turn on Script Assist if it is off.

6. Click the **Add a new item to the script button**, point to **Global Functions**, point to **Timeline Control**, then click **play** as shown in Figure 13.

7. Click the **Stop button** on the Stage, then verify the playback - stop button symbol appears at the lower left of the Script pane.

8. Click the **Add a new item to the script button**, point to **Global Functions**, point to **Timeline Control**, then click **stop**.

9. Close the Actions panel.

10. Test the movie, click the **play button**, then click the **stop button**.

    The video plays, however there is no sound.

11. Close the Flash Player window.

You assigned play and stop actions to video control buttons.

FIGURE 13
Using Script Assist to assign a play action to a button

Script Assist on

Play button selected

FIGURE 14

The completed Properties panel

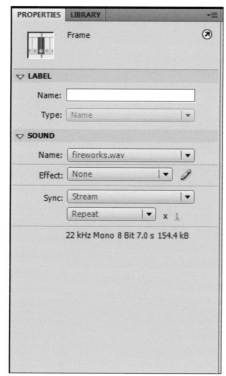

1. Insert a **new layer** above the video layer, then name it **sound**.
2. Click **frame 1** on the sound layer.
3. Display the Properties panel, then display the SOUND area options.
4. Click the **Name list arrow** in the SOUND area, then click **fireworks.wav**.
5. Click the **Sync sound list arrow** in the SOUND area, click **Stream**, then compare your screen to Figure 14.
6. Test the movie, click the **play button**, then click the **stop button**.
7. Close the Flash Player window, save your work, then close the file.

You inserted a layer, then you synchronized a sound to the video clip.

CREATE AN ANIMATED
NAVIGATION BAR

What You'll Do

In this lesson, you will work through the process to create one drop-down menu. A navigation bar has been provided as well as the necessary buttons.

Understanding Animated Navigation Bars

A common navigation scheme for a website is a navigation bar with drop-down menus, such as the one shown in Figure 15. Using a navigation bar has several advantages. First, it allows the developer to provide several menu options to the user without cluttering the screen, thereby providing more screen space for the website content. Second, it allows the user to go quickly to a location on the site without having to navigate several screens to find the desired content. Third, it provides consistency in function and appearance, making it easy for users to learn and work with the navigation scheme.

There are various ways to create drop-down menus using the animation capabilities of Flash and ActionScript. One common technique allows you to give the illusion of a drop-down menu by using masks that reveal the menu. When the user points to (rolls over) an option in the navigation bar, a list or "menu" of buttons is displayed ("drops down"). Then the user can click a button to go to another location in the website or trig-

ger some other action. The dropping down of the list is actually an illusion created by using a mask to "uncover" the menu options.

The process is as follows:
- Create a navigation bar. This could be as basic as a background graphic in the shape of a rectangle with navigation bar buttons.
- Position the drop-down buttons. Add a layer beneath the navigation bar layer. Next, select an empty frame adjacent to the frame containing the navigation bar. Place the buttons on the Stage below their respective menu items on the navigation bar. If the navigation bar has an Events button with two choices, Road Rally and Auction, that you want to appear as buttons on a drop-down menu, position these two buttons below the Events button on the drop-down buttons layer.
- Add the animated mask. Add a mask layer above the drop-down buttons layer and create an animation of an object that starts above the drop-down buttons

and moves down to reveal them. Then change the layer to a mask layer and the drop-down buttons layer to a masked layer.

- Assign actions to the drop-down buttons. Select each drop-down button and assign an action, such as "on (release) gotoAndPlay."
- Assign a roll over action to the navigation bar button. The desired effect is to have the drop-down buttons appear when the user points to a navigation bar button. Therefore, you need to assign an "on rollOver" action to the navigation bar button that causes the playhead to go to the frame that plays the animation on the mask layer. This can be done using the Script Assist feature.
- Create an invisible button. When the user points to a navigation bar button,

the drop-down menu appears showing the drop-down buttons. There needs to be a way to have the menu disappear when the user points away from the navigation bar button. This can be done by creating a button on a layer below the masked layer. This button is slightly larger than the drop-down buttons and their navigation bar button, as shown in Figure 16. A rollOver action is assigned to this button so that when the user rolls off the drop-down or navigation bar buttons, he or she rolls onto this button and the action is carried out. This button should be made transparent so the user does not see it.

Using Frame Labels

Until now, you have worked with frame numbers in ActionScript code when creat-

ing a goto action. Frame labels can also be used in the code. You can assign a label to a frame as an identifier. For example, you could assign the label home to frame 10 and then create a goto home action that will cause the playhead to jump to frame 10. One advantage of using frame labels is that if you insert frames in the Timeline, the label adjusts for the added frames. So, you do not have to change the ActionScript that uses the frame label. Another advantage is that the descriptive labels help you identify parts of the movie as you work with the Timeline. You assign a frame label by selecting the desired frame and typing a label in the Frame text box in the Properties panel.

FIGURE 15
A website with a navigation bar with drop-down menus

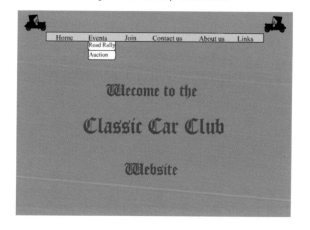

FIGURE 16
A button that will be assigned a rollOver action

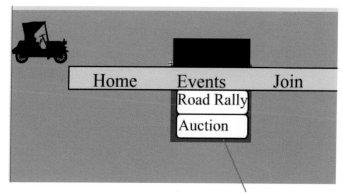

When the user rolls over the blue button with the pointer, a script is executed that causes the drop-down menu to disappear

Position the drop-down buttons

1. Open fl5_4.fla, then save it as **navBar**.

2. Click the **homeBkgrnd layer**, insert a **new layer**, then name it **roadRally**.

3. Click **frame 2** on the roadRally layer, then insert a **keyframe**.

4. Display the Library panel, open the Buttons folder, then drag the **b_roadRally button** to the position just below the Events button on the Navigation bar, as shown in Figure 17.

5. Insert a **new layer** above the homeBkgrnd layer, then name it **auction**.

6. Click **frame 2** on the auction layer, then insert a **keyframe**.

7. Drag the **b_auction button** from the Library panel and position it below the b_roadRally button.

8. Click the **Zoom tool** 🔍 on the Tools panel, then click the **Events button** on the Stage to enlarge the view.

9. Click the **Selection tool** ▶ on the Tools panel, then click each button and use the arrow keys to position them, as shown in Figure 18.

   The top line of the Road Rally button must overlap the bottom border of the navigation bar, and the bottom border of the Road Rally button must overlap the top border of the Auction button.

You placed the drop-down buttons on the Stage and repositioned them.

FIGURE 17
Positioning the b_roadRally button

The expand icon indicates that this is a folder layer. In this case, all of navigation bar buttons are within this folder. Clicking the arrow reveals the contents of the folder.

Drag from library to here

FIGURE 18
Positioning the buttons

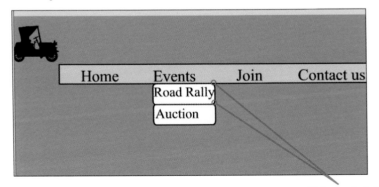

Make sure the button borders overlap

FIGURE 19
The drawn rectangle that covers the buttons

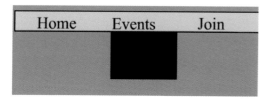

FIGURE 20
Dragging the rectangle above the buttons

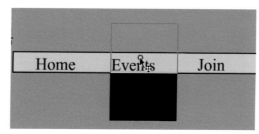

FIGURE 21
The rectangle positioned over the buttons

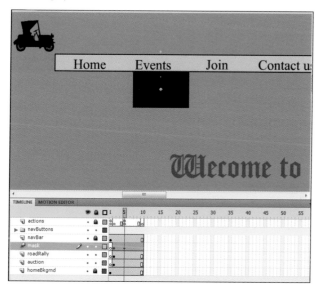

Lesson 4 Create an Animated Navigation Bar

1. Click the **roadRally layer**, insert a **new layer** above the roadRally layer, then name it **mask**.

2. Click **frame 2** on the mask layer, then insert a **keyframe**.

3. Select the **Rectangle tool** ▭. on the Tools panel, set the **Stroke Color** to **none** ☑ , then set the **Fill Color** to **black**.

4. Draw a **rectangle** that covers the buttons, as shown in Figure 19.

5. Click the **Selection tool** ▸ on the Tools panel, then drag the **rectangle** to above the buttons, as shown in Figure 20.

6. Verify the rectangle is selected, click **Insert** on the menu bar, click **Motion Tween**, then click **OK**.

7. Click **frame 5** on the mask layer, then insert a **keyframe**.

8. Use the **Selection tool** ▸ to move the **rectangle**, as shown in Figure 21.

9. Click **mask** on the Timeline, click **Modify** on the menu bar, point to **Timeline**, click **Layer Properties**, click the **Mask option button**, then click **OK**.

10. Click **roadRally** on the Timeline.

11. Click **Modify** on the menu bar, point to **Timeline**, click **Layer Properties**, click the **Masked option button**, then click **OK**.

12. Click **auction** on the Timeline, then repeat step 11.

13. Drag the **playhead** along the Timeline, notice how the mask hides and reveals the buttons.

You added a mask that animates to hide and reveal the menu buttons.

Assign an action to a drop-down button

1. Click **frame 2** on the roadRally layer, then click the **Road Rally button** to select it.

2. Open the **Actions panel** and verify the Script Assist button is selected and b_roadRally is displayed, as shown in Figure 22.

   b_roadRally in the lower-left corner of the Script pane indicates that the b_roadRally button symbol is selected on the Stage and that the ActionScript you create will apply to this object.

3. Click the **Add a new item to the script icon** ⊕ , point to **Global Functions**, point to **Timeline Control**, then click **goto**.

4. Click the **Scene list arrow**, point to **Scene 2** as shown in Figure 23, then click.

   Scenes are a way to organize large movies. In this case Scene 2 contains the Road Rally screen for the website.

5. Verify the Type is set to Frame Number and the Frame is set to 1.

6. Collapse the Actions panel.

You used the Script Assist window to assign a goto action to a menu button.

FIGURE 22
The Actions panel with the b_roadRally button selected

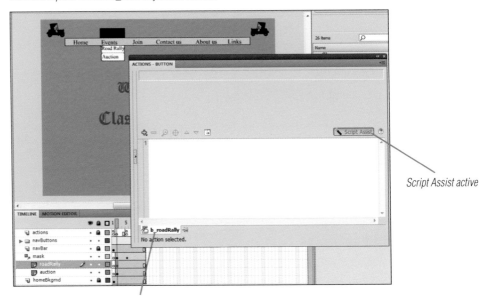

Script Assist active

b_roadRally button indicating the action to be created will be assigned to the button

FIGURE 23
Selecting the scene to go to

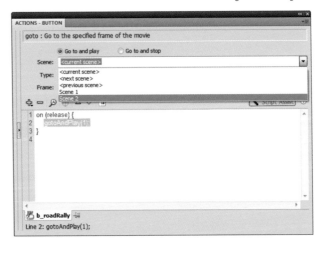

FIGURE 24
Specifying a frame label

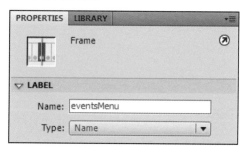

FIGURE 25
The completed Actions panel

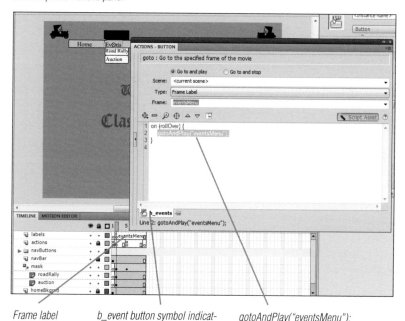

Frame label

b_event button symbol indicating the action will be assigned to the button

gotoAndPlay("eventsMenu");

Add a frame label and assign a rollover action

1. Insert a **new layer** at the top of the Timeline, name it **labels**, then insert a **keyframe** in frame 2 on the labels layer.

2. Display the Properties panel, click inside the **Name text box** in the LABEL area, then type **eventsMenu**, as shown in Figure 24.

3. Click the **Events button** on the Stage to select it.

4. Expand the Actions panel, then verify b_events is displayed in the lower-left corner of the Script pane.

5. Click the **Add a new item to the script icon** ⌖, point to **Global Functions**, point to **Movie Clip Control**, then click **on**.

6. Click the **Release check box** to deselect it, then click the **Roll Over check box** to select it.

7. Click the **Add a new item to the script icon** ⌖, point to **Global Functions**, point to **Timeline Control**, then click **goto**.

8. Click the **Type list arrow**, then click **Frame Label**.

9. Click the **Frame list arrow**, then click **eventsMenu**.

   Your screen should resemble Figure 25.

10. Click **Control** on the menu bar, then click **Test Movie**.

11. Point to **Events**, then click **Road Rally**.

12. Close the Flash Player window, collapse the Actions panel, then save your work.

You added a frame label and assigned a rollOver action using the frame label.

Lesson 4   Create an Animated Navigation Bar

FLASH 5-23

Add an invisible button

1. Click **Control** on the menu bar, click **Test Movie**, move the pointer over Events on the navigation bar, then move the pointer away from Events.

   Notice that when you point to Events, the drop-down menu appears. However, when you move the pointer away from the menu, it does not disappear.

2. Close the Flash Player window.

3. Insert a **new layer** above the homeBkgrnd layer, then name it **rollOver**.

4. Insert a **keyframe** in frame 2 on the rollOver layer.

5. Select the **Rectangle tool** on the Tools panel, verify that the Stroke Color is set to **none**, then set the **Fill Color** to **blue**.

6. Draw a **rectangle**, as shown in Figure 26.

7. Click the **Selection tool** on the Tools panel, then click the **blue rectangle** to select it.

8. Click **Modify** on the menu bar, then click **Convert to Symbol**.

9. Type **b_rollOver** for the name, click the **Type list arrow**, click **Button**, then click **OK**.

10. Expand the Actions panel.

(continued)

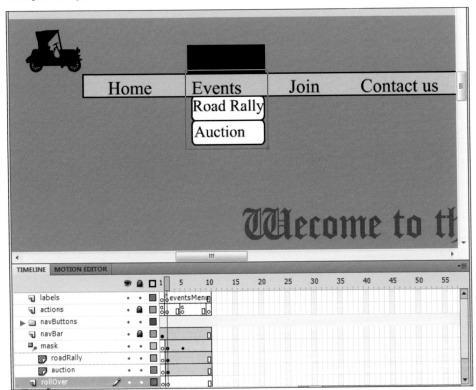

FIGURE 26
Drawing the rectangle

FIGURE 27

The Actions panel displaying Actionscript assigned to the b_rollOver button symbol

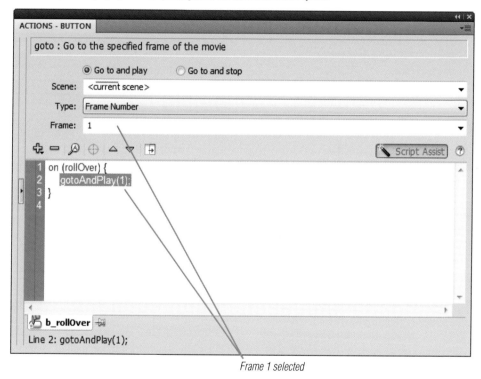

Frame 1 selected

11. Verify the rollOver button is selected and b_rollOver is displayed in the lower-left corner of the Script pane.

12. Click the **Add a new item to the script icon** ⚙, point to **Global Functions**, point to **Movie Clip Control**, then click **on**.

13. Click the **Release check box** to deselect it, then click the **Roll Over check box** to select it.

14. Click the **Add a new item to the script icon** ⚙, point to **Global Functions**, point to **Timeline Control**, then click **goto**.

15. Verify Frame 1 is specified, as shown in Figure 27.

16. Close the Actions panel.

17. Click the **Style list arrow** in the COLOR EFFECT area of the Properties panel, click **Alpha**, then set the percentage to **0**.

18. Click **Control** on the menu bar, then click **Test Movie**.

19. Point to **Events** to display the drop-down menu, then move the pointer away from Events.

The drop-down menu disappears.

20. Close the Flash Player window, then save and close the movie.

21. Exit Flash.

You added a button and assigned a rollOver action to it, then made the button transparent.

CREATE CHARACTER ANIMATIONS
USING INVERSE KINEMATICS

What You'll Do

In this lesson, you will use the bone tool to create a character animation and create a movie clip that can be manipulated by the viewer.

Understanding Inverse Kinematics

One way to create character animations is to use the frame-by-frame process in which you place individually drawn objects into a series of successive frames. You did this with the stick figure graphics in an earlier chapter. Those graphics were simple to draw. However, if you have more complex drawings, such as fill shapes that are more realistic, and if you want to create animations that show an unlimited number of poses, the time required to develop all of the necessary drawings would be considerable.

Flash provides a process that allows you to create a single image and add a structure to the image that can be used to animate the various parts of the image. The process is called **Inverse Kinematics (IK)** and involves creating an articulated structure of bones that allow you to link the parts of an image. Once the bone structure is created, you can animate the image by changing the position of any of

its parts. The bone structure causes the related parts to animate in a natural way. For example, if you draw an image of a person, create the bone structure, and then move the person's right foot, then all parts of the leg (lower leg, knee, upper leg) respond. This makes it easy to animate various movements.

Figure 28 shows a drawing of a character before and after the bone structure is added. Figure 29 shows how moving the right foot moves the entire leg. The image is made up of several small drawings, each one converted to a graphic symbol. These include a head, torso, upper and lower arms, upper and lower legs, hips, and feet.

Creating the Bone Structure

The bone structure can be applied to a single drawn shape, such as an oval created with the Flash drawing tools. More often it is applied to an image, such as a character, made up of several drawings. When this is the case, each drawing is converted to a graphic symbol or a movie clip symbol and then assembled to form the desired image. If you import a graphic, it needs to be broken apart using the Modify menu and the individual parts of the imported graphic converted to graphic symbols or movie clip symbols. If the imported graphic has only one part (such as a bitmap), it needs to be broken apart and treated as a single drawn shape.

Once the image is ready, you use the Bone tool to create the bone structure, called the armature, by clicking and dragging the Bone tool pointer to link one part of the image to another. You continue adding bones to the structure until all parts of the image are linked. For a human form you would link the head to the torso and the torso to the upper left arm and the upper left arm to the lower left arm, and so on. The bones in an armature are connected to each other in a parent-child hierarchy, so that adjusting the child adjusts the parent.

Animating the IK Object

As you are creating the bone structure, a layer named Armature_1 is added to the Timeline, and the image with the bone structure is placed in frame 1 on the layer. This new layer is called a **pose layer**. Each pose layer can contain only one armature and its associated image. Animating the image is done on this layer. When animating using inverse kinematics, you simply specify the start and end positions of the image. Flash interpolates the position of the parts of the image for the in-between frames. So, you can insert a keyframe in any frame after frame 1 on the Armature_1 layer and then change the position of one or more of the bones. This is referred to as creating a pose. When one bone moves, the other connected bones move in relation to it. Additional poses can be set along the Timeline by inserting keyframes and adjusting the bone structure. Animations of IK objects, other than those within movie clips, only allow you to change the shape, position, and ease in the animation.

FIGURE 28
Drawings showing before and after the bone structure is added

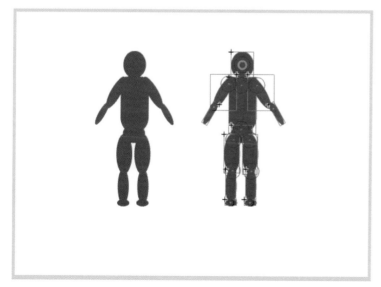

FIGURE 29
Moving the foot moves the other parts of the leg

Creating a Movie Clip with an IK Object

Movie clips provide a great deal of flexibility when animating IK objects. You can change properties such as the color effect and you can nest one movie clip within another. So, you could have a movie clip of a character walking and nest another movie clip within it to have its mouth move. In addition, you can apply a motion tween to a movie clip. So, you could have a movie clip of a character walking and have it play within a motion tween which causes the character (movie clip) to jump over an obstacle.

Runtime Feature

Flash provides a runtime feature for manipulation of an IK object. That is, you can allow the user to click on the object and adjust the image. This is useful if you are creating a game or just wanting to provide some interaction on a website. The process is to click a frame on the Armature layer, then use the Properties panel to set the Type to Runtime. The runtime feature only works with IK structures connected to drawn shapes or movie clip symbols, not graphic or button symbols. In addition, only one pose can used. At the time this book was published, some browsers, such as Firefox, supported the runtime feature, but other browsers did not.

IK Objects

As you are working with IK objects, keep in mind the following:

- The Undo feature can be used to undo a series of actions such as undoing a mistake made when creating the bone structure.
- The bone structure may disappear as you are working on it. This could be caused by going outside the image as you are connecting the parts of the image. If the bone structure disappears, use the Undo feature to Undo your last action.
- To delete an individual bone and all of its children, click the bone and press [Delete]. You can select multiple bones to delete by holding down [Shift] and clicking each bone.
- To delete all bones, select the image and choose the Break Apart command from the Modify menu.
- To create IK animations, ActionScript 3.0 and Flash Player 10 need to be specified in the Publish Settings dialog box, which is displayed by choosing Publish Settings from the File menu.

FIGURE 30
Connecting the head and torso

FIGURE 31
Connecting the torso and the upper arm

FIGURE 32
Connecting the upper and lower arms

Note: If the bone structure disappears as you are working on it, use the Undo feature to undo your last action.

FIGURE 33
The completed bone structure

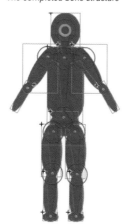

Create the bone structure

1. Open fl5_5.fla, then save it as **kicker**.

   This document has a graphic symbol made up of 13 individual drawings to form a character shape.

2. Use the **Selection tool** ⊾ to drag a marquee around the image to select it.

   Notice the separate objects.

3. Click a blank area of the Stage to deselect the image.

4. Click the **Zoom tool** ⚲ , then click the image to zoom in on it.

5. Scroll the Stage to view the head, then click the **Bone tool** 🦴 on the Tools panel.

6. Point to the middle of the head, when the pointer changes to a bone with a cross 🦴, drag the 🦴 **pointer** down to the torso as shown in Figure 30, then release the mouse button.

7. Point to the bottom of the bone, when the pointer changes to a bone with a cross 🦴, drag the 🦴 **pointer** to the left as shown in Figure 31.

8. Point to the left end of the bone, when the pointer changes to a bone with a cross 🦴, drag the 🦴 **pointer** down as shown in Figure 32.

   Notice that a bone connects two overlapping objects, such as the bone used to connect the upper arm and lower arm.

9. Using Figure 33 as a guide, complete the drawing of the other bones.

   Hint: Use the Undo command as needed if your connections do not match Figure 33.

10. Save your work.

You created a bone structure by connecting objects on the Stage with the Bone tool.

Animate the character

1. Change the view to **Fit in Window**.

2. Click **frame 10** on the Armature_1 layer, then insert a **keyframe**.

3. Click the **Selection tool**, then click a blank area of the Stage to deselect the object if it is selected.

4. Point to the **right foot**, when the pointer changes to a bone with a delta symbol, drag the pointer to position the foot as shown in Figure 34.

5. Point to the **right arm**, then use the pointer to position it as shown in Figure 35.

6. Use the pointer to position the left arm and left foot as shown in Figure 36.

   Hint: To position the left foot, move the left knee first, then move the left foot.

7. Click **frame 20** on the Armature_1 layer, then insert a **keyframe**.

8. Adjust the arms and legs as shown in Figure 37.

   Hint: Move the right leg to the position shown to create a kicking motion.

9. Click the **Free Transform tool** on the Tools panel, then drag a **marquee** around the image to select it.

10. Point to the **upper-right handle**, when the pointer changes to an arc, drag the pointer to the left as shown in Figure 38.

11. Test the movie, close the Flash Player window, then save the movie.

You animated the character by adjusting the armatures of the various bones.

FIGURE 34
Positioning the right foot

FIGURE 35
Positioning the right arm

FIGURE 36
Positioning the left arm and left foot

right leg

FIGURE 37
Positioning the left arm and left leg

right leg

FIGURE 38
Rotating the object

FIGURE 39

Increasing the length of the tween span

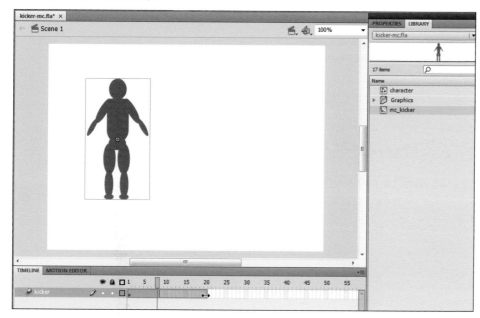

1. Click **File** on the menu bar, click **Save as**, type **kicker-mc**, then click **OK** [Win] or **Save as** [Mac].

2. Click **frame 1** on the Armature_1 layer.

3. Use the **Selection tool** to drag a marquee around the entire image to select it.

4. Click **Modify** on the menu bar, then click **Convert to Symbol**.

5. Type **mc_kicker** for the name, select **Movie Clip** for the Type, then click **OK**.

6. Click **Armature_1** on the Timeline, then click the **Delete icon**.

7. Click **frame 1** on the kicker layer, display the Library panel, then drag the **mc_kicker** symbol to the Stage.

8. Insert a **Motion Tween**.

9. Drag the **tween span** on the Timeline to **frame 20**, as shown in Figure 39.

10. Click **frame 10** on the kicker layer.

11. Verify the object is selected, then press the **up arrow** [↑] on the keyboard 10 times.

12. Click **frame 20**, then press the **down arrow** [↓] on the keyboard 10 times.

13. Test the movie, close the Flash Player window, then save your work.

You created a movie clip and applied a motion tween to it.

Apply an ease value

1. Double-click the **mc_kicker symbol** in the Library panel to display the edit window, then scroll as needed to see the entire object.

2. Display the Properties panel.

3. Click **frame 10** on the Armature_2 layer.

4. Set the Ease Strength to **−100**.

5. Click the **Type list arrow** in the EASE area, then click **Simple (Fastest)**, as shown in Figure 40.

   Frame 10 is the start of the motion tween where the right leg begins to kick downward. Setting the ease value to −100 will cause the leg motion to start out slow and accelerate as the leg follows through to the end of the kicking motion. This is a more natural way to represent the kick than to have the leg speed constant throughout the downward motion and follow through.

6. Click **Scene 1** on the edit window title bar to return to the main Timeline.

7. Test the movie, close the Flash Player window, save your work, then close the file.

You added an ease value to the movie clip.

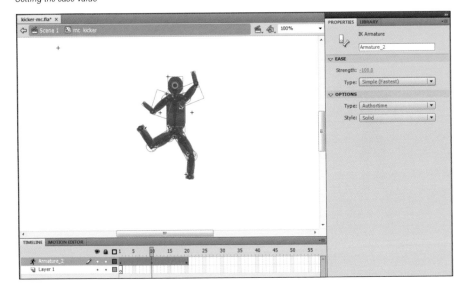

FIGURE 40
Setting the ease value

Creating Special Effects

FIGURE 41
The completed armature structure

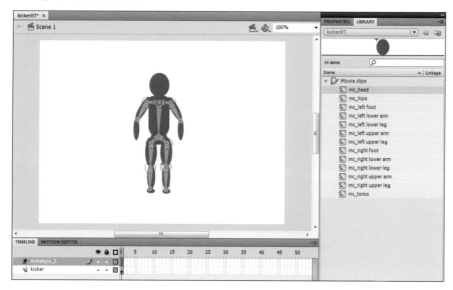

1. Open fl5_6.fla, then save it as **kickerRT**.

   This is the same character used in the kicker movie, however it has been created using movie clips instead of graphic symbols. Also, only one pose is used.

2. Use the **Bone tool** ✐, to create the armature structure as shown in Figure 41.

3. Click **frame 1** on the Armature_3 layer, click the **Type list arrow** in the OPTIONS area of the Properties panel, then click **Runtime**.

4. Click **File**, point to **Publish Preview**, then click **Default -(HTML)** to display the movie in a browser, then drag the parts of the character, such as an arm or a leg.

   Hint: Press [F12] (Win) to display the movie in a browser.

5. Close your browser.

6. Save your work, then close the document.

You created an animated character, set the play to runtime and manipulated the character in a browser.

CREATE 3D
EFFECTS

What You'll Do

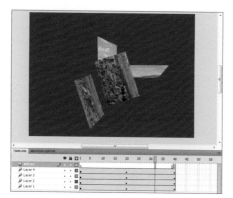

In this lesson, you will create a movie with 3D effects.

Flash allows you to create 3D effects by manipulating objects in 3D space on the Stage. Until now you have been working in two dimensions, width and height. The default settings for the Stage are 550 pixels wide and 400 pixels high. These are represented by an x axis (across) and a y axis (down). Any position on the Stage can be specified by x and y coordinates. The upper-left corner of the Stage has an x value of 0 and a y value of 0, and the lower-right corner has an x value of 550 and a y value of 400, as shown in Figure 42. In 3D space there is also a z axis that represents depth. Flash provides two tools, 3D Translation and 3D Rotation that can be used to move and rotate objects using all three axes. In addition, Flash provides two other properties that can be adjusted to control the view of an object. The Perspective Angle property controls the angle of the object and can be used to create a zooming in and out effect. The Vanishing Point property more precisely controls the direction of an object as it moves away from the viewer.

The Perspective Angle and the Vanishing Point settings are found in the Properties panel.

The 3D Tools

The 3D tools are available on the Tools panel. By default the 3D Rotation tool is displayed on the Tools panel. To access the 3D Translation tool, click and hold the 3D Rotation tool to open the menu. Toggle between these two 3D tools as needed.

The process for creating 3D effects is to create a movie clip (only movie clips can have 3D effects applied to them), place the movie clip on the Stage and then click it with either of the 3D tools. When you click an object with the 3D Translation tool, the three axes, X, Y, and Z appear on top of the object, as shown in Figure 43. Each has its own color: red (X), green (Y), and blue (Z). The X and Y axes have arrows and the Z axis is represented by a dot. You point to an arrow or the black dot and drag it to reposition the object.

When you click the object with the 3D Rotation tool, the three axes, X, Y, and Z appear on top of the object, as shown in Figure 44. Dragging the X axis (red) will flip the object horizontally. Dragging the Y axis (green) will flip the object vertically. Dragging the Z axis (blue) will spin the object. A forth option, the orange circle, rotates the object around the X and Y axes at the same time.

Using a Motion Tween with a 3D Effect

Creating 3D effects requires a change in the position of an object. A motion tween is used to specify where on the Timeline the effect will take place. This allows you to create more than one effect by selecting various frames in the tween span and making adjustments as desired. If you are animating more than one object, each object should be on its own layer.

FIGURE 42
The x and y coordinates on the Stage

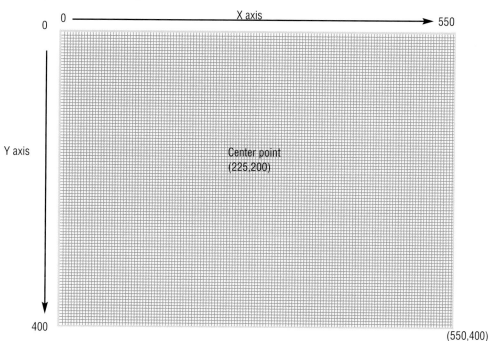

FIGURE 43
The 3D Translation tool

FIGURE 44
The 3D Rotation tool

Create a 3D animation

1. Open fl5_7.fla, then save it as **puzzle**.

   Note: The document opens with the ruler feature turned on and showing the vertical and horizontal lines that intersect at the center of the Stage.

2. Click **frame 1** on Layer 1, insert a **motion tween**, then drag the tween span to **frame 40**.

3. Click **frame 20** on Layer 1, then select the **3D Translation tool** ⅄ from the Tools panel.

4. Click the image in the upper-right corner of the Stage, point to the **green arrow**, then use the ➤ **pointer** to drag the image down to the horizontal ruler line.

5. Click the **red arrow**, then use the ➤ **pointer** to drag the image to the left, as shown in Figure 45.

6. Select the **3D Rotation tool** ⊙, point to the **green line Y axis** on the right side of the object, then drag the ➤ **pointer** down and to the left to flip the image horizontally.

7. Click **frame 40** on Layer 1, then use the **3D Translation tool** ⅄ to move the image to the position shown in Figure 46.

8. Use the **3D Rotation tool** ⊙ to drag the solid green line down and to the right, which flips the image again.

9. Click **frame 1** on Layer 2, insert a **motion tween**, then drag the tween span to **frame 40**.

10. Click **frame 20** on Layer 2, select the **3D Translation tool** ⅄, then drag the image to the position shown in Figure 47.

(continued)

FIGURE 45
Using the 3D Translation tool to position an object

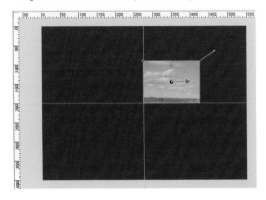

FIGURE 46
Using the 3D Translation tool to position the object again

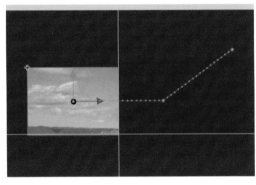

FIGURE 47
Using the 3D Translation tool to position a second object

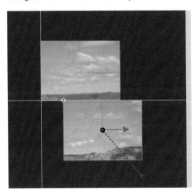

FIGURE 48

Using the 3D Translation tool to position the second object again

FIGURE 49

Using the 3D Translation tool to position a third object

FIGURE 50

Using the 3D Translation tool to position the third object again

FIGURE 51

The completed 3D effects movie

11. Select the **3D Rotation tool** 🔄, then point to the **bottom red line X axis** and drag the line to the left and up to flip the image vertically.

12. Click **frame 40** on Layer 2, then use the **3D Translation tool** 🔧 to position the image as shown in Figure 48.

13. Use the **3D Rotation tool** 🔄 to flip the image vertically again.

14. Click **frame 1** on Layer 3, insert a **motion tween**, then increase the tween span to **frame 40**.

15. Click **frame 20** on Layer 3, select the **3D Translation tool** 🔧, then use the arrows to drag the image to the position shown in Figure 49.

16. Select the **3D Rotation tool** 🔄, then point to the **blue line Z axis** and drag the line to rotate the image clockwise 180 degrees.

17. Click **frame 40** on Layer 3, use the **3D Translation tool** 🔧 to position the image as shown in Figure 50, then use the **3D Rotation tool** 🔄 to rotate the image again.

18. Repeat steps 14–17 for Layer 4, making adjustments as needed such as
    * moving the image into the upper-right corner of the lower-left quadrant

    * using the orange circle and the 3D Rotation tool 🔄 two different times in two different frames, to rotate the X and Y axis simultaneously.

19. Use the 3D tools to make adjustments as needed so your screen resembles Figure 51.

20. Play the movie, close the Flash Player window, then save your work.

You created a movie with 3D effects.

Create a mask effect.

1. Start Flash, open fl5_8.fla, then save it as **skills demo5**.
2. Verify the frame rate is set to 12 and the Flash Publish Settings (accessed from the File menu) are set to Flash Player 10 and ActionScript 3.0.
3. Insert a new layer above the table layer, then name it **heading**.
4. Select frame 1 on the heading layer, then use the Text tool to create the Aces Wild heading with the following characteristics: size 48, color #006633, and Byington (or similar) font.
5. Use the Align command in the Modify menu to center the heading on the Stage.
6. Use the Selection tool to select the heading and then convert it to a graphic symbol with the name **g_heading**.
7. Insert a keyframe in frame 40 on the heading layer.
8. Insert a new layer above the heading layer, then name it **ending-heading**.
9. Insert a keyframe in frame 40 on the ending-heading layer.
10. Drag the g_heading symbol from the Library panel and position it on top of the heading on the Stage. Use the keyboard arrow keys as needed to position the g_heading symbol.
11. Lock the ending-heading layer.
12. Insert a new layer above the heading layer, then name it **circle**.
13. Select frame 1 on the circle layer, then use the Oval tool to create a black-filled circle that is slightly larger in height than the heading text.
14. Place the circle to the left of the heading.
15. Convert the circle to a graphic symbol with the name **g_mask**.
16. Create a motion tween that moves the circle across and to the right side of the heading.
17. Extend the tween span in the Timeline to frame 40 (if necessary).
18. Change the circle layer to a mask layer and lock the layer.
19. Change the heading layer to a masked layer and lock the layer.
20. Insert keyframes in frame 40 on the table and the head and body layers.
21. Insert a new layer above the table layer, name it **stopmovie**, move the stopmovie layer below the table layer, then insert a keyframe in frame 40. (*Note:* You want to add a stop action to this frame. Because ActionScript 3.0 is needed when working with Inverse Kinematics and with the 3D feature, you cannot use the Script Assist feature of Flash. Rather, you must type the code directly into the Actions panel.)
22. Open the Actions panel, verify Script Assist is turned off and stopmovie: 40 is displayed in the lower left of the panel, then type **stop( );** for the code.
23. Test the movie, then save your work.

Create a character animation.

1. Select frame 1 on the Timeline, then use the Zoom tool to enlarge the view of the character.
2. Use the Bone tool to join the body with the upper and lower left arm, and the upper and lower right arm. (*Note:* The bone structure stops at the elbow on each arm.)
3. Select frame 6 on the Armature_1 layer.
4. Use the Selection tool to move the ends of the arms so that the lower left and lower right arms are horizontal and touch at the chest. This will cause the elbows to point out away from the body.
5. Select frame 12 on the Armature_1 layer.
6. Use the Selection tool to move the end of the right arm so that it is straight and pointing to the upper-left corner of the Stage.
7. Extend the Armature_1 layer to frame 40 (if necessary).
8. Select frame 40 on the Armature_1 layer.
9. Use the Selection tool to reposition the arms to their original positions, that is, so the arms are touching the table.
10. Change the view to Fit in Window.
11. Test the movie, then save your work.

Create a frame-by-frame animation.

1. Select frame 4 on the card layer, then insert a keyframe.
2. Use the arrow keys on the keyboard as needed to reposition the card so that it is at the end of the right arm.
3. Select frame 5 on the card layer, then insert a keyframe.
4. Use the arrow keys on the keyboard to reposition the card so that it is at the end of the right arm.

Creating Special Effects

5. Repeat steps 3 and 4 in frame 6 through frame 12 on the card layer.
6. Select frame 13 on the card layer, then insert a blank keyframe.
7. Test the movie, close the Flash Player window, then save your work.

Create a 3D effect.

1. Insert a new layer above the card layer, then name it **ace3D**.
2. Select frame 12 on the ace3D layer, then insert a keyframe.
3. Drag the mc_aceD movie clip from the Library panel to the Stage, display the Properties panel, verify the Lock width and height values together icon is not a broken link, then resize the width to 10.6.
4. Reposition the ace to on top of the card held by the character.
5. Verify frame 12 on the ace3D layer is selected, then create a motion tween.
6. Verify the tween span on the Timeline extends from frame 12 through frame 40.
7. Select frame 40 on the ace3D layer.
8. Use the 3D Translation tool to reposition the card to the upper-left corner of the Stage in a diagonal line that extends from the character's right shoulder. (*Hint:* Use both the red and green arrows to move the card to create a diagonal line.)
9. Use the Free Transform tool and the Scale option at the bottom of the Tools panel to resize the card to a width of between 80 and 90.

10. Select frame 26 on the ace3D layer.
11. Use the 3D Rotation tool to add a 3D effect.
12. Select frame 40 on the ace3D layer.
13. Use the 3D Rotation tool to add a 3D effect that causes the card to display right side up, as seen in Figure 52.
14. Test the movie, close the Flash Player window, then save your work.

FIGURE 52
Completed Skills Review

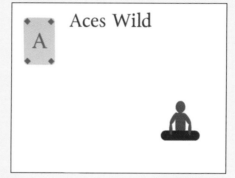

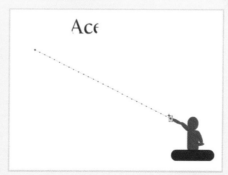

Add sound to a movie.

1. Insert a new layer at the top of the Timeline, then name it **sound**.
2. Insert a keyframe in frame 5 on the sound layer.
3. Drag introSound.wav from the Library panel to the Stage.
4. Insert a keyframe in frame 40 on the sound layer.
5. Test the movie, compare your movie to the images in Figure 52, close the Flash Player window, save your work, then close the file.

Creating Special Effects

Work with video.

1. Open fl5_9.fla, then save it as **skillsdemo5-video**.
2. Add a new layer above the headings layer, then name it **video**.
3. Import tour-video.mov from the drive and folder where you store your Data Files to the Library, using the Import Video command, as an embedded video. (*Note:* You will need to use the Adobe Media Encoder to convert the file to the flv format, then you will need to browse to the drive and folder where you save your Solution Files to open the converted file.)
4. Verify that the video is in the Library panel and on the center of the Stage, note the number of frames needed to display the entire video. (*Hint*: Be sure to position the video placeholder, if necessary, to prevent overlapping the text subheading.)
5. Add a new layer, name it **controls**, then select frame 1 on the layer.
6. Use the Text tool to create a text box with the word **Play** beneath and to the left side of the video. Set the text characteristics to the following: family **Arial**, style **Narrow** (Win) or **Regular** (Mac), size **20** pt, and color **White**.
7. Convert the text to a button symbol with the name **b_play**.
8. Edit three stages of the button symbol, for example, make the color of the letters change when the mouse pointer is over the word Play.
9. Use the Actions panel and Script Assist to assign a play action to the button that plays the movie when the mouse is released.
10. Use the Text tool to create a text box with the word **Pause** beneath and to the right side of the video. Use the same text characteristics used for the Play button.
11. Convert the text to a button symbol with the name **b_pause**.
12. Edit the button symbol so that the color of the letters changes when the mouse pointer is over the word Pause.
13. Use the Actions panel to assign a stop action to the button when it is released.
14. Add a new layer, then name it **stopMovie**.
15. Add a stop action to frame 1 on the stopMovie layer.
16. Add a keyframe at the end of the movie on the headings layer.
17. Test the movie, compare your screen to Figure 53, close the Flash Player window, then save your work.
18. Exit Flash.

FIGURE 53
Completed Skills Review - video

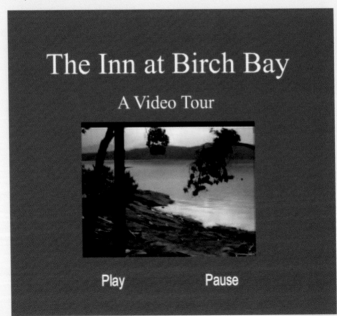

Creating Special Effects

The Ultimate Tours travel company has asked you to design several sample animations for its website. Figure 54 shows a sample Cruises screen with a mask effect, as the spotlight rotates across the screen and highlights different ships. Complete the following for the Cruises screen of the Ultimate Tours website:

Add objects to the ultimatetours5 document.

1. Open fl5_10.fla, then save it as **assets**.
2. Open ultimatetours4.fla (the file you created in Chapter 4 Project Builder 1), and save it as **ultimatetours5**.
3. Insert a new layer at the top of the Timeline and select frame 1 on the layer.
4. Display the Library panel, then click the list arrow below the Library tab to display the list of open documents.
5. Select assets and drag each of the symbols in the Library panel to the Stage, delete the layer, click the assets tab, then close the assets file. (*Note*: This will add the objects from the assets file to the ultimatetours5 Library panel.)
6. Display the Library panel for ultimatetours5.

Add layers and objects to the Stage.

1. Insert a new layer at the top of the Timeline, then name it **background**.
2. Insert a keyframe in a frame that is higher than the last frame in the current movie (such as frame 100) on the background layer, then draw a dark gray rectangle (#333333) that covers the Stage.
3. Insert a keyframe that is at least 30 frames higher on the background layer (such as frame 130), then lock the layer. *(Note:* All of the subsequent layers will use the same frames (such as 100 to 130), so be sure to add keyframes to these frames as needed.)
4. Insert a new layer, name it **heading**, and create the Mystery Ships heading.
5. Insert a new layer, name it **lighthouse**, then place the g_lighthouse symbol on the Stage.

Add a motion tween and mask effect.

1. Insert a new layer, name it **searchlight**, and place the g_searchlight symbol to the left of the lighthouse.
2. Use the Free Transform tool to create a motion tween that causes the searchlight to rotate from the left to the right of the lighthouse.

(Hint: The searchlight will rotate (pivot) around the transformation point (small circle) of the graphic. You need to move the transformation point so it is at the narrow end of the graphic. To do this, select the graphic with the Free Transform tool to display the transformation point, then drag the point to the desired location (narrow end) on the graphic.)

3. Create a new layer for each of the three ships, name each layer appropriately (**ship1**, **ship2**, and **ship3**), and place them on the Stage so that the searchlight highlights them as it moves from left to right across the Stage.
4. Insert a new layer above the ship layers, name it **searchlight mask**, and using the g_searchlight symbol, add a motion tween that duplicates the one created in step 2.
5. Create a mask effect that has a searchlight as the mask and reveals the ships when the searchlight is over them. (*Note*: The two searchlight motion tweens are needed on different layers because one will become a mask and will not be visible in the movie.)

Add a sound and interactivity.

1. Insert a new layer, name it **sound**, insert a keyframe in frame 100 (or the appropriate frame) on the layer, then drag the sound file to the Stage.

2. Insert a new layer, name it **home button**, insert a keyframe in the last frame of the movie, then add the b_home button to the bottom center of the Stage.

3. Add an action to the home button to have the playhead go to frame 1 of the movie when the button is clicked.

4. Insert a new layer, name it **stopaction**, and add a stop action at the end of the movie.

5. Drag (scrub) the playhead on the Timeline to locate the Galapagos text (cruise heading layer for example), unlock the cruise heading layer (or layer that has the Galapogos text).

6. Change the Galapagos text to **Mystery Ships**, then create a button that changes color for the different phases and that jumps to frame 100 (or the appropriate frame) when the user clicks the Mystery Ships text.

7. Test the movie, then compare your image to the example shown in Figure 54.

8. Close the Flash Player window, then save your work.

FIGURE 54

Sample completed Project Builder 1

You have been asked to develop a website illustrating the signs of the zodiac. The introductory screen should have a heading with a mask effect and 12 zodiac signs, each of which could become a button. Clicking a sign button displays an information screen with a different graphic to represent the sign and information about the sign, as well as special effects such as sound, mask effect, and character animation (inverse kinematics). Each information screen would be linked to the introductory screen. (*Note:* Using the inverse kinematics feature requires ActionScript 3.0, therefore, you will start with a movie that has the ActionScript for the buttons and stop actions already developed.)

1. Open fl5_11.fla, save it as **zodiac5**, then change the frame rate to **12 fps**.
2. Test the movie and then study the Timeline to understand how the movie works.
3. Refer to Figure 55 as you complete the introductory screen with the following:
   - A new layer above the signs layer named **heading** with the heading, **Signs of the** that appears from frame 1 through frame 31
   - A new layer named **masked** that contains the word **Zodiac** and that appears from frame 1 through frame 31
   - A mask layer that passes across the heading Zodiac

(*Notes:* Use a fill color that can be seen on the black background. After creating the motion tween, drag the end of the tween span on the Timeline to frame 31. Be sure to set the Layer Properties for the mask and masked layers.)
   - A new layer that displays the word **Zodiac** in frame 31 only
(*Note:* Remove frames 32–80 from the layer by using the Remove Frames option from the Timeline command of the Edit menu.)
   - A new layer with a sound that plays from frame 1 through frame 31 as the mask is revealing the contents of the masked layer
4. Refer to Figure 55 as you complete the scorpio screen with the following:
(*Notes:* The scorpio screen starts in frame 51. Remove frames in other layers containing content that you do not want displayed after frame 31, such as the Zodiac heading.)
   - A new layer with the three-line heading
   - An inverse kinematics animation that moves the tail (*Note:* Be sure to connect the head to the tail.)
5. Test the movie, then save it.
6. Save the movie as **zodiac5-mc**.
7. Select frame 51 on the Armature1 layer and convert the IK animation to a movie clip.
8. Delete the Armature1 layer, then select frame 51 on the scorpio layer and drag the movie clip to the Stage.
9. Create a motion tween to animate the movie clip so the scorpion moves across the screen.

10. Test the movie, compare your screens to Figure 55, close the Flash Player window, then save the movie.

FIGURE 55
Sample completed Project Builder 2

View of screen at frame 31

Figure 56 shows the home page of a website. Study the figure and complete the following questions. For each question, indicate how you determined your answer.

1. Connect to the Internet, then go to *www.nikeid.com*.

   TIP: Use Figure 56 to answer the questions. Go to the site and explore several links to get a feeling for how the site is constructed.

2. Open a document in a word processor or open a new Flash document, save the file as **dpc5**, then answer the following questions. (*Hint*: Use the Text tool in Flash.)

   ■ Who's site is this and what seems to be the purpose of this site?

   ■ Who would be the target audience?

   ■ How might a character animation using inverse kinematics be used?

   ■ How might video be used?

   ■ How might a mask effect be used?

   ■ How might sound be used? How might 3D be used?

   ■ What suggestions would you make to improve the design and why?

FIGURE 56
Design Project

This is a continuation of the Portfolio Project in Chapter 4, which is the development of a personal portfolio. The home page has several categories, including the following:

- Personal data
- Contact information
- Previous employment
- Education
- Samples of your work

In this project, you will create several buttons for the Sample Animations screen and link them to their respective animations.

1. Open portfolio4.fla (the file you created in Portfolio Project, Chapter 4) and save it as **portfolio5**. (*Hint*: When you open the file, you may receive a missing font message, meaning a font used in this document is not available on your computer. You can choose a substitute font or use a default font.)

2. Display the Sample Animations screen. You will be adding buttons to this screen that play various animations. In each case, have the animation return to the Sample Animations screen at the end of the animation.

3. Add a button for a character animation so it appears on the Sample Animations screen, add a new layer and create a character animation (inverse kinematics) on that layer,

then link the character animation button to the character animation.

4. Add a button for a mask effect so it appears on the Sample Animations screen, add new layers to create a mask effect (such as to the words My Portfolio) on that layer, add a sound that plays as the mask is revealing the contents of the masked layer, then link the mask effect button to the mask effect animation.

5. Add a button for an animated navigation bar so it appears on the Sample Animations screen, add a new layer and create an animated navigation bar on that layer, then link

the navigation bar button to the animated navigation bar.

6. Test the movie, then compare your Sample Animation screen to the example shown in Figure 57.

7. Close the Flash Player window, then save your work.

FIGURE 57
Sample completed Portfolio Project

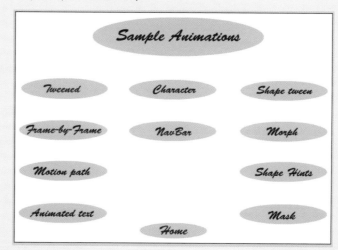

chapter

1

GETTING STARTED WITH
ADOBE
PHOTOSHOP CS4

1. Start Adobe Photoshop CS4

2. Learn how to open and save an image

3. Use organizational and management features

4. Examine the Photoshop window

5. Use the Layers and History panels

6. Learn about Photoshop by using Help

7. View and print an image

8. Close a file and exit Photoshop

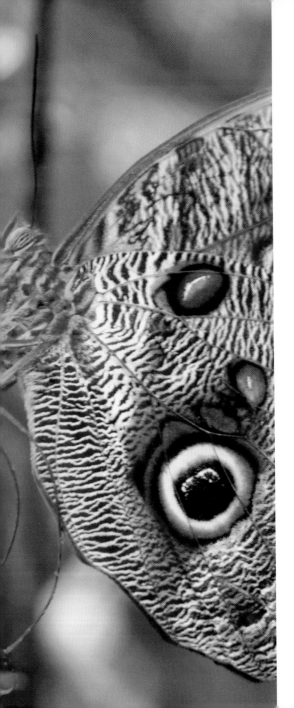

1 GETTING STARTED WITH
ADOBE
PHOTOSHOP CS4

Using Photoshop

Adobe Photoshop CS4 is an image-editing program that lets you create and modify digital images. 'CS' stands for Creative Suite, a complete design environment. Although Adobe makes Photoshop available as a standalone product, it also comes bundled with all of their Creative Suite options, whether your interests lie with print design, web design, or multimedia production. A **digital image** is a picture in electronic form. Using Photoshop, you can create original artwork, manipulate color images, and retouch photographs. In addition to being a robust application popular with graphics professionals, Photoshop is practical for anyone who wants to enhance existing artwork or create new masterpieces. For example, you can repair and restore damaged areas within an image, combine images, and create graphics and special effects for the web.

> **QUICK**TIP
>
> In Photoshop, a digital image may be referred to as a file, document, graphic, picture, or image.

Understanding Platform User Interfaces

Photoshop is available for both Windows and Macintosh platforms. Regardless of which platform you use, the features and commands are very similar. Some of the Windows and Macintosh keyboard commands differ in name, but they have equivalent functions. For example, the [Ctrl] and [Alt] keys are used in Windows, and the [⌘] and [option] keys are used on Macintosh computers. There are also visual differences between the Windows and Macintosh versions of Photoshop due to the user interface differences found in each platform.

Understanding Sources

Photoshop allows you to work with images from a variety of sources. You can create your own original artwork in Photoshop, use images downloaded from the web, or use images that have been scanned or created using a digital camera. Whether you create Photoshop images to print in high resolution or optimize them for multimedia presentations, web-based functions, or animation projects, Photoshop is a powerful tool for communicating your ideas visually.

Tools You'll Use

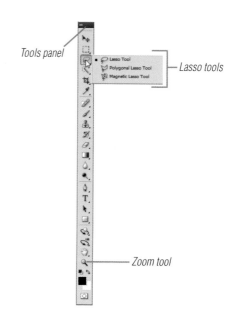

Tools panel

Lasso tools

Zoom tool

Options bar

START ADOBE
PHOTOSHOP CS4

What You'll Do

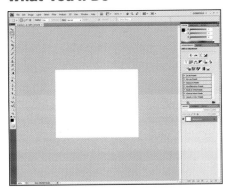

 In this lesson, you'll start Photoshop for Windows or Macintosh, then create a file.

Defining Image-Editing Software

Photoshop is an image-editing program. An **image-editing** program allows you to manipulate graphic images so that they can be reproduced by professional printers using full-color processes. Using panels, tools, menus, and a variety of techniques, you can modify a Photoshop image by rotating it, resizing it, changing its colors, or adding text to it. You can also use Photoshop to create and open different kinds of file formats, which enables you to create your own images, import them from a digital camera or scanner, or use files (in other formats) purchased from outside sources. Table 1 lists some of the graphics file formats that Photoshop can open and create.

Understanding Images

Every image is made up of very small squares, which are called **pixels**, and each pixel represents a color or shade. Pixels within an image can be added, deleted, or modified.

QUICKTIP

Photoshop files can become quite large. After a file is complete, you might want to **flatten** it, an irreversible process that combines all layers and reduces the file size.

Using Photoshop Features

Photoshop includes many tools that you can use to manipulate images and text. Within an image, you can add new items and modify existing elements, change colors, and draw shapes. For example, using the Lasso tool, you can outline a section of an image and drag the section onto another area of the image. You can also isolate a foreground or background image. You can extract all or part of a complex image from nearly any background and use it elsewhere.

QUICKTIP

You can create logos in Photoshop. A **logo** is a distinctive image that you can create by combining symbols, shapes, colors, and text. Logos give graphic identity to organizations, such as corporations, universities, and retail stores.

You can also create and format text, called **type**, in Photoshop. You can apply a variety of special effects to type; for example, you can change the appearance of type and increase or decrease the distance between characters. You can also edit type after it has been created and formatted.

Adobe Dreamweaver CS4, a web production software program included in the Design Suite, allows you to optimize, preview, and animate images. Because Dreamweaver is part of the same suite as Photoshop, you can jump seamlessly between the two programs.

Using these two programs, you can also quickly turn any graphics image into a gif animation. Photoshop and Dreamweaver let you compress file size (while optimizing image quality) to ensure that your files download quickly from a web page. Using Photoshop optimization features, you can view multiple versions of an image and select the one that best suits your needs.

Starting Photoshop and Creating a File

The specific way you start Photoshop depends on which computer platform you are using. However, when you start Photoshop in either platform, the computer displays a **splash screen**, a window that contains information about the software, and then the Photoshop window opens.

After you start Photoshop, you can create a file from scratch. You use the New dialog box to create a file. You can also use the New dialog box to set the size of the image you're about to create by typing dimensions in the Width and Height text boxes.

TABLE 1: Some Supported Graphic File Formats

file format	filename extension	file format	filename extension
3D Studio	.3ds	Photoshop PDF	.pdf
Bitmap	.bmp	PICT file	.pct, .pic, or .pict
Cineon	.cin		
Dicom	.dcm	Pixar	.pxr
Filmstrip	.flm	QuickTime	.mov or .mp4
Google Earth	.kmz		
Graphics Interchange Format	.gif	Radiance	.hdr
		RAW	varies
JPEG Picture Format	.jpg, .jpe, or .jpeg	Scitex CT	.sct
		Tagged Image Format	.tif or .tiff
PC Paintbrush	.pcx		
Photoshop	.psd	Targa	.tga or .vda
Photoshop Encapsulated PostScript	.eps	U3D	.u3d
		Wavefront	.obj

Start Photoshop (Windows)

1. Click the **Start button** 🌐 on the taskbar.

2. Point to **All Programs**, point to **Adobe Photoshop CS4**, as shown in Figure 1, then click **Adobe Photoshop CS4**.

    TIP   The Adobe Photoshop CS4 program might be found in the Start menu (in the left pane) or in the Adobe folder, which is in the Program Files folder on the hard drive (Win).

3. Click **File** on the Application bar, then click **New** to open the New dialog box.

4. Double-click the number in the Width text box, type **500**, click the **Width list arrow**, then click **pixels** (if it is not already selected).

5. Double-click the number in the Height text box, type **400**, then specify a resolution of **72** pixels/inch (if necessary).

6. Click **OK**.

    TIP   By default, the document window (the background of the active image) is gray. This color can be changed by right-clicking the background and then making a color selection.

7. Click the **arrow** ▶ at the bottom of the image window, point to **Show**, then click **Document Sizes** (if it is not already displayed).

You started Photoshop in Windows, then created a file with custom dimensions. Setting custom dimensions lets you specify the exact size of the image you are creating. You changed the display at the bottom of the image window so the document size is visible.

FIGURE 1
Starting Photoshop CS4 (Windows)

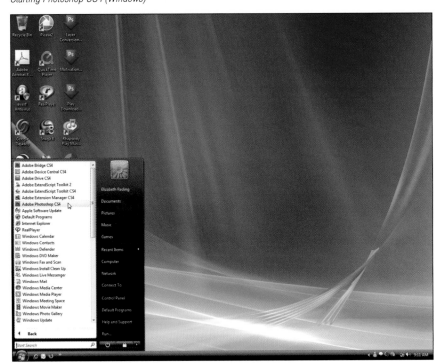

Understanding hardware requirements (Windows)

Adobe Photoshop CS4 has the following minimum system requirements:

- Processor: Intel Xeon, Xeon Dual, Centrino, or Pentium 4 processor
- Operating System: Microsoft® Windows XP SP2 or higher, or Windows Vista
- Memory: 320 MB of RAM
- Storage space: 650 MB of available hard-disk space
- Video RAM: 64 MB; Monitor with 1024 × 768 resolution
- 16-bit video card and Quick Time 7 for Multimedia features

FIGURE 2

Starting Photoshop CS4 (Macintosh)   *Items as icons view*

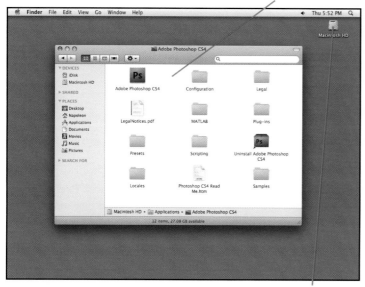

Hard drive icon

Understanding hardware requirements (Macintosh)

Adobe Photoshop CS4 has the following minimum system requirements:

- Processor: G4, G5, or Intel-based
- Operating System: Mac OS X version 10.3 through 10.5
- Memory: 320 MB of RAM (384 MB recommended)
- Storage space: 1.5 GB of available hard-disk space
- Monitor: 1024 × 768 or greater monitor resolution with 16-bit color or greater video card
- PostScript Printer PostScript Level 2, Adobe PostScript 3
- Video RAM: 64 MB
- CD-ROM Drive: CD-ROM Drive required

Start Photoshop (Macintosh)

1. Double-click the **hard drive icon** on the desktop, double-click the **Applications folder**, then double-click the **Adobe Photoshop CS4 folder**. Compare your screen to Figure 2.

2. Double-click the **Adobe Photoshop CS4 program icon**.

3. Click **File** on the Application bar, then click **New**.

    TIP   If the Color Settings dialog box opens, click No. If a Welcome screen opens, click Close.

4. Double-click the number in the Width text box, type **500**, click the **Width list arrow**, then click **pixels** (if necessary).

5. Double-click the number in the Height text box, type **400**, click the **Height list arrow**, click **pixels** (if necessary), then verify a resolution of **72** pixels/inch.

6. Click **OK**.

    TIP   The gray document window background can be turned on by clicking Window on the Application bar, then clicking Application frame.

7. Click the **arrow** ▶ at the bottom of the image window, point to **Show**, then click **Document Sizes** (if it is not already checked).

You started Photoshop for Macintosh, then created a file with custom dimensions. You verified that the document size is visible at the bottom of the image window.

LEARN HOW TO OPEN AND
SAVE AN IMAGE

What You'll Do

 In this lesson, you'll locate and open files using the File menu and Adobe Bridge, flag and sort files, then save a file with a new name.

Opening and Saving Files

Photoshop provides several options for opening and saving a file. Often, the project you're working on determines the techniques you use for opening and saving files. For example, you might want to preserve the original version of a file while you modify a copy. You can open a file, then immediately save it with a different filename, as well as open and save files in many different file formats. When working with graphic images you can open a Photoshop file that has been saved as a bitmap (.bmp) file, then save it as a JPEG (.jpg) file to use on a web page.

Customizing How You Open Files

You can customize how you open your files by setting preferences. **Preferences** are options you can set that are based on your work habits. For example, you can use the Open Recent command on the File menu to instantly locate and open the files that you recently worked on, or you can allow others to preview your files as thumbnails. Figure 3 shows the Preferences dialog box options for handling your files.

TIP   In cases when the correct file format is not automatically determined, you can use the Open As command on the File menu (Win) or Open as Smart Object (Mac).

FIGURE 3
Preferences dialog box

Option for thumbnail preview

Number of files to appear in Open Recent list

Browsing Through Files

You can easily find the files you're looking for by using **Adobe Bridge**, a stand-alone application that serves as the hub for the Adobe Creative Suite. See the magnifying loupe tool in the Filmstrip view in Figure 4. You can open Adobe Bridge (or just Bridge) by clicking the Launch Bridge button on the Application bar. You can also open Bridge using the File menu in Photoshop.

When you open Bridge, a series of panels allows you to view the files on your hard drive as hierarchical files and folders. In addition to the Favorites and Folders panels in the upper-left corner of the Bridge window, there are other important areas. Directly beneath the Favorites and Folders panels is the Filter panel which allows you to review properties of images in the Content panel. In the (default) Essentials view, the Preview panel displays a window containing the Metadata and Keywords panels, which stores information about a selected file (such as keywords) that can then be used as search parameters. You can use this tree structure to find the file you are seeking. When you locate a file, you can click its thumbnail to see information about its size, format, and creation and modification dates. (Clicking a thumbnail selects the image. You can select multiple non-contiguous images by pressing and holding [Ctrl] (Win) or ⌘ (Mac) each time you click an image.) You can select contiguous images by clicking the first image, then pressing

TIP   Click a thumbnail while in Filmstrip view and the pointer changes to a Loupe tool that magnifies content. Drag the loupe over the filmstrip image to enlarge select areas. The arrowhead in the upper-left corner of the window points to the area to be magnified. Clicking the arrowhead closes the loupe.

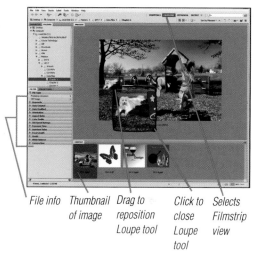

FIGURE 4
Adobe Bridge window

File info   Thumbnail   Drag to   Click to   Selects
            of image   reposition   close   Filmstrip
                        Loupe tool   Loupe   view
                                       tool

Type information to
be printed here

FIGURE 5
File Info dialog box

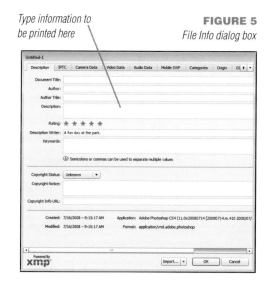

Using the Photoshop File Info dialog box

You can use the File Info dialog box to identify a file, add a caption or other text, or add a copyright notice. The Description section allows you to enter printable text, as shown in Figure 5. For example, to add your name to an image, click File on the Application bar, click File Info, then click in the Description text box. (You can move from field to field by pressing [Tab] or by clicking in individual text boxes.) Type your name, course number, or other identifying information in the Description text box, or click stars to assign a rating. You can enter additional information in the other text boxes, then save all the File Info data as a separate file that has an .xmp extension. To print selected data from the File Info dialog box, click File on the Application bar, then click Print. Click the Color Management list arrow, then click Output. Available options are listed in the right panel. To print the filename, select the Labels check box. You can also select check boxes that let you print crop marks and registration marks. If you choose, you can even add a background color or border to your image. After you select the items you want to print, click Print.

and holding [Shift] and clicking the last image in the group. You can open a file using Bridge by double-clicking its thumbnail, and find out information such as the file's format, and when it was created and edited. You can close Bridge by clicking File (Win) or Bridge CS4 (Mac) on the (Bridge) Application bar, then clicking Exit (Win) or Quit Adobe Bridge CS4 (Mac) or by clicking the window's Close button.

Understanding the Power of Bridge

In addition to allowing you to see all your images, Bridge can be used to rate (assign importance), sort (organize by name, rating, and other criteria), and label your images. Figure 4, on the previous page, contains images that are assigned a rating and shown in Filmstrip view. There are three views in Bridge (Essentials, Filmstrip, and Metadata) that are controlled by tabs to the left of the search text box. To assist in organizing your images, you can assign a color label or rating to one or more images regardless of your current view. Any number of selected images can be assigned a color label by clicking Label on the Application bar, then clicking one of the six options.

Creating a PDF Presentation

Using Bridge you can create a PDF Presentation (a presentation in the PDF file format). Such a presentation can be viewed full-screen on any computer monitor, or in Adobe Acrobat Reader as a PDF file. You can create such a presentation by opening Bridge, locating and selecting images using the file hierarchy, then clicking the Output button on the Bridge Application bar. The Output panel, shown in Figure 6, opens and displays the images you have selected. You can add images by pressing [Ctrl] (Win) or ⌘ (Mac) while clicking additional images.

FIGURE 6
Output panel in Bridge

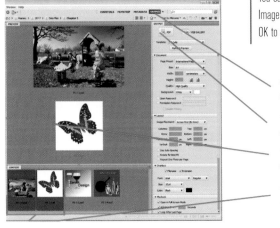

Click to create output

Click to create PDF

Output preview

Selected thumbnails

Using Save As Versus Save

Sometimes it's more efficient to create a new image by modifying an existing one, especially if it contains elements and special effects that you want to use again. The Save As command on the File menu (in Photoshop) creates a copy of the file, prompts you to give the duplicate file a new name, and then displays the new filename in the image's title bar. You use the Save As command to name an unnamed file or to save an existing file with a new name. For example, throughout this book, you will be instructed to open your Data Files and use the Save As command. Saving your Data Files with new names keeps the original files intact in case you have to start the lesson over again or you want to repeat an exercise. When you use the Save command, you save the changes you made to the open file.

Getting Started with Adobe Photoshop CS4

FIGURE 7
Open dialog box for Windows

Look in list arrow
displays list of
available drives

FIGURE 7
Open dialog box for Macintosh

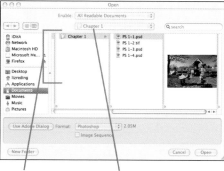

Available folders
and files may differ
from your list

Selected filename

Available folders
and files

Current file location
list arrow

FIGURE 8
Adobe Bridge window

Essentials button

Preview of selected file
displays here

Your list may
be different

Click the Keywords
panel tab to assign
keywords to a selected
file, then click any of the
displayed keywords

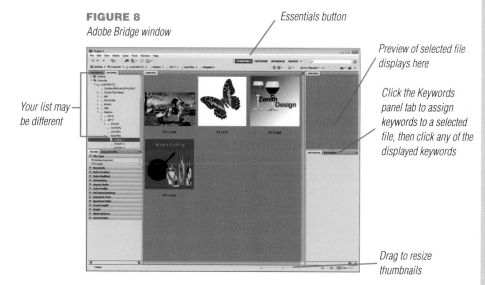

Drag to resize
thumbnails

Lesson 2   Learn How to Open and Save an Image

Open a file using the Application bar

1. Click **File** on the Application bar, then click **Open**.

2. Click the **Look in list arrow** (Win) or the **Current file location list arrow** (Mac), then navigate to the drive and folder where you store your Data Files.

3. Click **PS 1-1.psd**, as shown in Figure 7, then click **Open**.

   TIP   Click Update, if you receive a message stating that some text layers need to be updated.

You used the Open command on the File menu to locate and open a file.

Open a file using the Folders panel in Adobe Bridge

1. Click the **Launch Bridge button** ▶Br on the Application bar, then click the **Folders panel tab** FOLDERS (if necessary).

2. Navigate through the hierarchical tree to the drive and folder where you store your Chapter 1 Data Files, then click the **Essentials button** if it is not already selected.

3. Drag the **slider** (at the bottom of the Bridge window) a third of the way between the Smaller thumbnail size button ▫ and the Larger thumbnail size button ▫. Compare your screen to Figure 8.

4. Double-click the **image of a butterfly** (PS 1-2.tif). Bridge is no longer visible.

5. Close the butterfly image in Photoshop.

You used the Folders panel tab in Adobe Bridge to locate and open a file. This feature makes it easy to see which file you want to use.

Use the Save As command

1. Verify that the **PS 1-1.psd window** is active.

2. Click **File** on the Application bar, click **Save As**, then compare your Save As dialog box to Figure 9.

3. If the drive containing your Data Files is not displayed, click the **Save in list arrow** (Win) or the **Where list arrow** (Mac), then navigate to the drive and folder where you store your Chapter 1 Data Files.

4. Select the current filename in the File name text box (Win) or Save As text box (Mac) (if necessary); type **Playground**, then click **Save**.

   TIP Click OK to close the Maximize Compatibility dialog box (if necessary).

You used the Save As command on the File menu to save the file with a new name. This command makes it possible for you to save a changed version of an image while keeping the original file intact.

Change from Tabbed to Floating Documents

1. Click the **Arrange Documents button** ▦ ▾ on the Application bar, then click **2 Up**.

   TIP The Arrange Documents button is a temporary change to the workspace that will be in effect for the current Photoshop session.

2. Click ▦ ▾ , then click **Float All in Windows**. Compare your Playground image to Figure 10.

You changed the arrangement of open documents from consolidation to a 2 Up format to each image displaying in its own window.

FIGURE 9
Save As dialog box

Your list of files
might be different

New filename

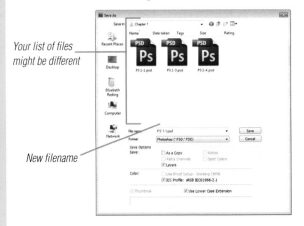

FIGURE 10
Playground image

Duplicate file has
new name

Changing file formats

In addition to using the Save As command to duplicate an existing file, it is a handy way of changing one format into another. For example, you can open an image you created in a digital camera, then make modifications in the Photoshop format. To do this, open the .jpg file in Photoshop, click File on the Application bar, then click Save As. Name the file, click the Format list arrow, click Photoshop (*.psd, *.pdd) (Win) or Photoshop (Mac), then click Save. You can also change formats using Bridge by selecting the file, clicking Tools on the Application bar, pointing to Photoshop, then clicking Image Processor. Section 3 of the Image Processor dialog box lets you determine the new file format.

Rated and
Approved file

FIGURE 11
Images in Adobe Bridge

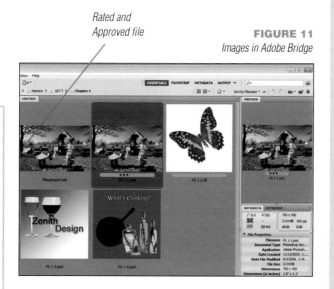

Getting photos from your camera

You can use Bridge to move photos from your camera into your computer by plugging your camera into your computer, opening Adobe Bridge, clicking File on the (Bridge) Application bar, then clicking Get Photos from Camera. Once you do this, the Adobe Bridge CS4 Photo Downloader dialog box opens. This dialog box lets you decide from which device you'll download images, where you want to store them, and whether or not you want to rename them, among other options.

FIGURE 12
Sorted files

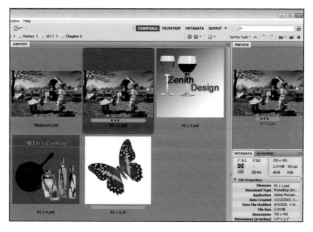

Rate and filter with Bridge

1. Click the **Launch Bridge button** ▶Br on the Application bar.

2. Click the **Folders panel tab** FOLDERS if it is not already selected, then click the drive and folder where you store your Chapter 1 Data Files on the File Hierarchy tree (if necessary).

3. Click the butterfly image, file **PS 1-2.tif** to select it.

4. Press and hold **[Ctrl]** (Win) or ⌘ (Mac), click **PS 1-1.psd** (the image of the playground), then release **[Ctrl]** (Win) or ⌘ (Mac).

5. Click **Label** on the Application bar, then click **Approved**.

6. Click **PS 1-1.psd**, click **Label** on the Application bar, then click **★★★**. See Figure 11.

7. Click **View** on the Application bar, point to **Sort**, then click **By Type**. Compare your screen to Figure 12.

   The order of the files is changed.

   TIP You can also change the order of files (in the Content panel) using the Sort by Filename list arrow in the Filter panel. When you click the Sort by Filename list arrow, you'll see a list of sorting options. Click the option you want and the files in the Content panel will be rearranged.

8. Click **View** on the Application bar, point to **Sort**, then click **Manually**.

   TIP You can change the Bridge view at any time, depending on the type of information you need to see.

9. Click **File** (Win) or **Adobe Bridge CS4** (Mac) on the (Bridge) Application bar, then click **Exit** or **Quit Adobe Bridge CS4** (Mac).

You labeled files using Bridge, sorted the files in a folder, then changed the sort order. When finished, you closed Bridge.

Lesson 2   Learn How to Open and Save an Image

USE ORGANIZATIONAL AND
MANAGEMENT FEATURES

What You'll Do

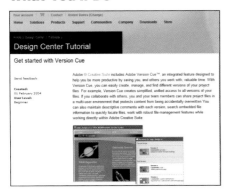

In this lesson, you'll learn how to use Version Cue and Bridge.

Learning about Version Cue

Version Cue is a file versioning and management feature of the Adobe Creative Suite that can be used to organize your work whether you work in groups or by yourself. Version Cue is accessed through Bridge. You can see Version Cue in Bridge in two different locations: the Favorites tab and the Folders tab. Figure 13 shows Version Cue in the Favorites tab of Bridge. You can also view Version Cue in the Folders tab by collapsing the Desktop, as shown in Figure 14.

Understanding Version Cue Workspaces

Regardless of where in Bridge you access it (the Favorites or Folders tab), Version Cue installs a **workspace** in which it stores projects and project files, and keeps track of file versions. The Version Cue workspace can be installed locally on your own computer and can be made public or kept private. It can also be installed on a server and can be used by many users through a network.

FIGURE 13
Favorites tab in Adobe Bridge

Your list of Favorites may differ

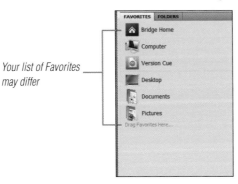

FIGURE 14
Folders tab in Adobe Bridge

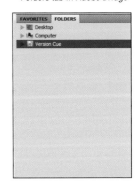

Getting Started with Adobe Photoshop CS4

Using Version Cue's Administrative Functions

Once you log into Version Cue using Adobe Drive (shown in Figure 15), you can control who uses the workspace and how it is used with the tabs at the top of the screen. Adobe Drive, which you use to connect to Version Cue, lets you open your server, browse projects and other servers, and perform advanced tasks.

Making Use of Bridge

You've already seen how you can use Bridge to find, identify, and sort files. But did you know that you can use Bridge Center to organize, label, and open files as a group? First you select one or more files, right-click the selection (Win) or [control]-click the selection (Mac), then click Open, or Open With, to display the files in your favorite CS4 program. You can apply labels, and ratings, or sort the selected files.

QUICKTIP

You can use Bridge to stitch together panoramic photos, rename images in batches, or automate image conversions with the Tools menu. Select the file(s) in Bridge you want to modify, click Tools on the Application bar, point to Photoshop, then click a command and make option modifications.

FIGURE 15
Adobe Drive and Version Cue

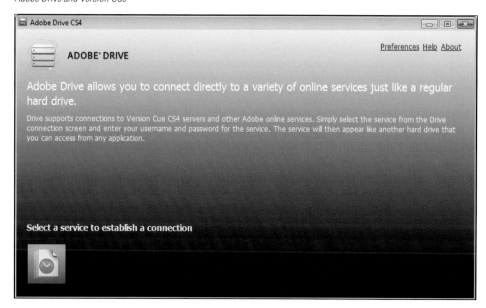

EXAMINE THE
PHOTOSHOP WINDOW

What You'll Do

 In this lesson, you'll arrange documents and change the default display, select a tool on the Tools panel, use a shortcut key to cycle through the hidden tools, select and add a tool to the Tool Preset picker, use the Window menu to show and hide panels in the workspace, and create a customized workspace.

Learning About the Workspace

The Photoshop **workspace** is the area within the Photoshop program window that includes the entire window, from the command menus at the top of your screen to the status bar (Win) at the bottom. Desktop items are visible in this area (Mac). The (Windows) workspace is shown in Figure 16.

In Windows, the area containing the menu bar (containing Photoshop commands) and the title bar (displaying the program name) is called the **Application bar**. These two areas have been combined to use space more efficiently. On the Mac, the main menus are at the top of the screen, but not on the Application bar. If the active image window is maximized, the filename of the open unnamed file is **Untitled-1**, because it has not been named. The Application bar also contains the **workspace switcher**, a Close button, and Minimize/Maximize, and Restore buttons (Win).

You can choose a menu command by clicking it or by pressing [Alt] plus the underlined letter in the menu name (Win). Some commands display shortcut keys on the right side of the menu. Shortcut keys provide an alternative way to activate menu commands. Some commands might appear dimmed, which means they are not currently available. An ellipsis after a command indicates additional choices.

DESIGNTIP **Overcoming information overload**

One of the most common experiences shared by first-time Photoshop users is information overload. There are just too many places and things to look at! When you feel your brain overheating, take a moment and sit back. Remind yourself that the active image area is the central area where you can see a composite of your work. All the tools and panels are there to help you, not to add to the confusion. The tools and features in Photoshop CS4 are designed to be easier to find and use, making any given task faster to complete.

Finding Tools Everywhere

The **Tools panel** contains tools associated with frequently used Photoshop commands. The face of a tool contains a graphical representation of its function; for example, the Zoom tool shows a magnifying glass. You can place the pointer over each tool to display a tool tip, which tells you the name or function of that tool. Some tools have additional hidden tools, indicated by a small black triangle in the lower-right corner of the tool.

The **options bar**, located directly under the Application bar, displays the current settings for each tool. For example, when you click the Type tool, the default font and font size appear on the options bar, which can be changed if desired. You can move the options bar anywhere in the workspace for easier access. The options bar also contains the Tool Preset picker. This is the left-most tool on the options bar and displays the active tool. You can click the list arrow on this tool to select another tool without having to use the Tools panel. The options bar also contains the panel well, an area where you can assemble panels for quick access.

Panels, sometimes called palettes, are small windows used to verify settings and modify images. By default, panels appear in stacked groups at the right side of the window.

FIGURE 16
Workspace

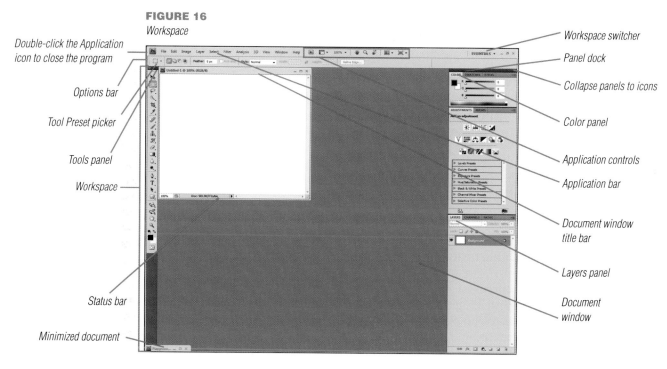

Double-click the Application icon to close the program

Options bar

Tool Preset picker

Tools panel

Workspace

Status bar

Minimized document

Workspace switcher

Panel dock

Collapse panels to icons

Color panel

Application controls

Application bar

Document window title bar

Layers panel

Document window

A collection of panels usually in a vertical orientation is called a **dock**. The dock is the dark gray bar above the collection of panels. The arrows in the dock are used to maximize and minimize the panels. You can display a panel by simply clicking the panel tab, making it the active panel. Panels can be separated and moved anywhere in the workspace by dragging their tabs to new locations. You can dock a panel by dragging its tab in or out of a dock. As you move a panel, you'll see a blue highlighted drop zone. A **drop zone** is an area where you can move a panel. You can also change the order of tabs by dragging a tab to a new location within its panel. Each panel contains a menu that you can view by clicking the list arrow in its upper-right corner.

The **status bar** is located at the bottom of the program window (Win) or work area (Mac). It displays information, such as the file size of the active window and a description of the active tool. You can display other informa-tion on the status bar, such as the current tool, by clicking the black triangle to view a pull-down menu with more options.

Rulers can help you precisely measure and position an object in the workspace. The rulers do not appear the first time you use Photoshop, but you can display them by clicking Rulers on the View menu.

Using Tool Shortcut Keys
Each tool has a corresponding shortcut key. For example, the shortcut key for the Type tool is T. After you know a tool's shortcut key, you can select the tool on the Tools panel by pressing its shortcut key. To select and cycle through a tool's hidden tools, you press and hold [Shift], then press the tool's shortcut key until the desired tool appears.

Customizing Your Environment
Photoshop makes it easy for you to position elements you work with just where you want them. If you move elements around to make your environment more convenient, you can always return your workspace to its original appearance by resetting the default panel locations. Once you have your work area arranged the way you want it, you can create a customized workspace by clicking the workspace switcher on the Application bar, then clicking Save Workspace. If you want to open a named workspace, click the workspace switcher, then click the name of the workspace you want to use. In addition, Photoshop comes with many customized workspaces that are designed for specific tasks.

FIGURE 17
Keyboard Shortcuts and Menus dialog box

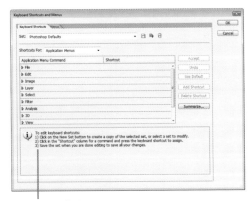

Instructions to edit shortcuts

Creating customized keyboard shortcuts
Keyboard shortcuts can make your work with Photoshop images faster and easier. In fact, once you discover the power of keyboard shortcuts, you may never use menus again. In addition to the keyboard shortcuts that are preprogrammed in Photoshop, you can create your own. To do this, click Edit on the Application bar, then click Keyboard Shortcuts. The Keyboard Shortcuts and Menus dialog box opens, as shown in Figure 17.

Getting Started with Adobe Photoshop CS4

DESIGNTIP Composition 101

What makes one image merely okay and another terrific? While any such judgement is subjective, there are some rules governing image composition. It goes without saying that, as the artist, you have a message you're trying to deliver ... something you're trying to say to the viewer. This is true whether the medium is oil painting, photography, or Photoshop imagery.

Elements under your control in your composition are tone, sharpness, scale, and arrangement. (You may see these items classified differently elsewhere, but they amount to the same concepts.)

Tone is the brightness and contrast within an image. Using light and shadows you can shift the focus of the viewer's eye and control the mood.

Sharpness is used to direct the viewer's eye to a specific area of an image. **Scale** is the size relationship of objects to one another, and **arrangement** is how objects are positioned to one another.

Are objects in your image contributing to clarity or clutter? Are similarly-sized objects confusing the viewer? Would blurring one area of an image change the viewer's focus?

These are tools you have to influence your artistic expression. Make sure the viewer understands what you want seen.

FIGURE 18
Hidden tools

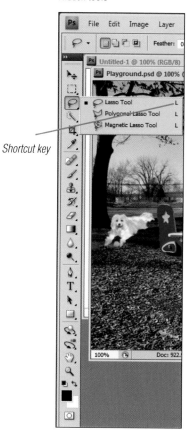

Shortcut key

Select a tool

1. Click the **Lasso tool** 🔍 on the Tools panel, press and hold the mouse button until a list of hidden tools appears, then release the mouse button. See Figure 18. Note the shortcut key, L, next to the tool name.

2. Click the **Polygonal Lasso tool** 🔍 on the Tools panel.

3. Press and hold **[Shift]**, press **[L]** three times to cycle through the Lasso tools, then release **[Shift]**. Did you notice how the options bar changes for each selected Lasso tool?

> TIP You can return the tools to their default setting by clicking the Click to open the Tool Preset picker list arrow on the options bar, clicking the list arrow, then clicking Reset All Tools.

You selected the Lasso tool on the Tools panel and used its shortcut key to cycle through the Lasso tools. Becoming familiar with shortcut keys can speed up your work and make you more efficient.

Learning shortcut keys

Don't worry about learning shortcut keys. As you become more familiar with Photoshop, you'll gradually pick up shortcuts for menu commands, such as saving a file, or Tools panel tools, such as the Move tool. You'll notice that as you learn to use shortcut keys, your speed while working with Photoshop will increase and you'll complete tasks with fewer mouse clicks.

Select a tool from the Tool Preset picker

1. Click the **Click to open the Tool Preset picker list arrow** ✂☐ on the options bar.

   The name of a button is displayed in a tool tip, the descriptive text that appears when you point to the button. Your Tool Preset picker list will differ, and may contain no entries at all. This list can be customized by each user.

2. Deselect the **Current Tool Only check box** (if necessary). See Figure 19.

3. Double-click **Magnetic Lasso 24 pixels** in the list.

You selected the Magnetic Lasso tool using the Tool Preset picker. The Tool Preset picker makes it easy to access frequently used tools and their settings.

FIGURE 19
Using the Tool Preset picker

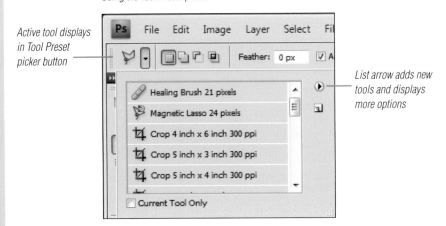

Active tool displays in Tool Preset picker button

List arrow adds new tools and displays more options

FIGURE 20
Full screen mode with Application bar

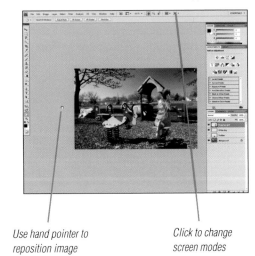

Use hand pointer to reposition image

Click to change screen modes

Using the Full Screen Mode

By default, Photoshop displays images in consolidated tabs. This means that each image is displayed within its own tab. You can choose from three other modes: Maximized Screen Mode, Full Screen Mode with Application Bar, and Full Screen Mode. And why would you want to stray from the familiar Standard Screen Mode? Perhaps your image is so large that it's difficult to see it all in Standard Mode, or perhaps you want a less cluttered screen. Maybe you just want to try something different. You can switch between modes by clicking the Change Screen Mode button (located in the Application controls area of the Application bar) or by pressing the keyboard shortcut F. When you click this button, the screen displays changes. Click the Hand tool (or press the keyboard shortcut H), and you can reposition the active image, as shown in Figure 20.

DESIGNTIP Arranging elements

The appearance of elements in an image is important, but of equal importance is the way in which the elements are arranged. The components of any image should form a cohesive unit so that the reader is unaware of all the different parts, yet influenced by the way they work together to emphasize a message or reveal information. For example, if a large image is used, it should be easy for the reader to connect the image with any descriptive text. There should be an easily understood connection between the text and the artwork, and the reader should be able to seamlessly connect them.

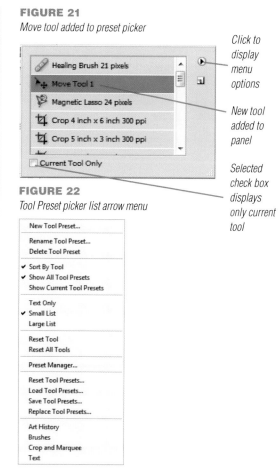

FIGURE 21
Move tool added to preset picker

Click to display menu options

New tool added to panel

Selected check box displays only current tool

FIGURE 22
Tool Preset picker list arrow menu

Modifying a tool preset

Once you've created tool presets, you'll probably want to know how they can be deleted and renamed. To delete any tool preset, select it on the Tool Preset picker panel. Click the list arrow on the Tool Preset picker panel to view the menu, shown in Figure 22, then click Delete Tool Preset. To rename a tool preset, click the same list arrow, then click Rename Tool Preset.

Add a tool to the Tool Preset picker

1. Click the **Move tool** on the Tools panel.
2. Click the **Click to open the Tool Preset picker list arrow** on the options bar.
3. Click the **list arrow** on the Tool Preset picker.
4. Click **New Tool Preset**, then click **OK** to accept the default name (Move Tool 1). Compare your list to Figure 21.

   TIP You can display the currently selected tool alone by selecting the Current Tool Only check box.

You added the Move tool to the Tool Preset picker. Once you know how to add tools to the Tool Preset picker, you can quickly and easily customize your work environment.

Change the default display

1. Click **Edit** (Win) or **Photoshop** (Mac) on the Application bar, then click **Preferences** (Win) or point to **Preferences**, then click **Interface** (Mac).
2. Click **Interface** in the left panel (Win), click the **Open Documents in Tabs check box** to deselect it, then click **OK**.

You changed the default display so that each time you open Photoshop, each image will display in its own window rather than in tabs.

Show and hide panels

1. Click **Window** on the Application bar, then verify that **Color** has a check mark next to it, then close the menu.

2. Click the **Swatches tab** next to the Color tab to make the Swatches panel active, as shown in Figure 23.

3. Click the **Collapse to Icons arrow** to collapse the panels.

4. Click the **Expand Panels arrow** to expand the panels.

5. Click **Window** on the Application bar, then click **Swatches** to deselect it.

   TIP   You can hide all open panels by pressing [Shift], then [Tab], then show them by pressing [Shift], then [Tab] again. To hide all open panels, the options bar, and the Tools panel, press [Tab], then show them by pressing [Tab] again.

6. Click **Window** on the Application bar, then click **Swatches** to redisplay the Swatches panel.

You collapsed and expanded the panels, then used the Window menu to show and hide the Swatches panel. You might want to hide panels at times in order to enlarge your work area.

FIGURE 23
Active Swatches panel

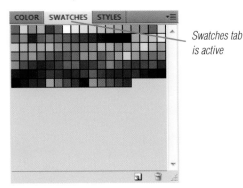

Swatches tab
is active

DESIGNTIP   Balancing objects

The **optical center** occurs approximately three-eighths from the top of the page and is the point around which objects on the page are balanced. Once the optical center is located, objects can be positioned around it. A page can have a symmetrical or asymmetrical balance relative to an imaginary vertical line in the center of the page. In a **symmetrical balance**, objects are placed equally on either side of the vertical line. This type of layout tends toward a restful, formal design. In an **asymmetrical balance,** objects are placed unequally relative to the vertical line. Asymmetrical balance uses white space to balance the positioned objects, and is more dynamic and informal. A page with objects arranged asymmetrically tends to provide more visual interest because it is more surprising in appearance.

DESIGNTIP   Considering ethical implications

Because Photoshop enables you to make so many dramatic changes to images, you should consider the ethical ramifications and implications of altering images. Is it proper or appropriate to alter an image just because you have the technical expertise to do so? Are there any legal responsibilities or liabilities involved in making these alterations? Because the general public is more aware about the topic of **intellectual property** (an image or idea that is owned and retained by legal control) with the increased availability of information and content, you should make sure you have the legal right to alter an image, especially if you plan on displaying or distributing the image to others. Know who retains the rights to an image, and if necessary, make sure you have written permission for its use, alteration, and/or distribution. Not taking these precautions could be costly.

FIGURE 24
Save Workspace dialog box

FIGURE 25
Image Size dialog box

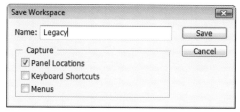

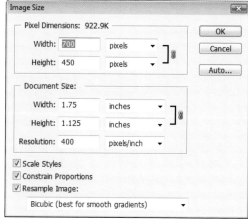

Resizing an image

You may have created the perfect image, but the size may not be correct for your print format. Document size is a combination of the printed dimensions and pixel resolution. An image designed for a website, for example, might be too small for an image that will be printed in a newsletter. You can easily resize an image using the Image Size command on the Image menu. To use this feature, open the file you want to resize, click Image on the Application bar, then click Image Size. The Image Size dialog box, shown in Figure 25, opens. By changing the dimensions in the text boxes, you'll have your image resized in no time. Note the check mark next to Resample Image. With resampling checked, you can change the total number of pixels in the image and the print dimensions independently. With resampling off, you can change either the dimensions or the resolution; Photoshop will automatically adjust whichever value you ignore.

Create a customized workspace

1. Click **Window** on the Application bar, click **History**, then drag the newly displayed panel in the gray space beneath the Swatches panel. (*Hint:* When you drag one panel into another, you'll see a light blue line, indicating that the new panel will dock with the existing panels.)

2. Click **Window** on the Application bar, point to **Workspace**, then click **Save Workspace**.

3. Type **Legacy** in the Name text box, then verify that only **Panel Locations** has a check mark beside it, as shown in Figure 24.

4. Click **Save**.

5. Click **Window** on the Application bar, then point to **Workspace**.

   The name of the new workspace appears on the Window menu.

   TIP   You can use the Rotate View tool on the Application bar to *non-destructively* change the orientation of the image canvas. Click the Reset View button on the options bar to restore the canvas to its original angle.

6. Click **Essentials (Default)**.

7. Click the **workspace switcher** on the Application bar, then click **Legacy**.

8. Click the **workspace switcher** on the Application bar, then click **Essentials**.

You created a customized workspace, reset the panel locations, tested the new workspace, then reset the panel locations to the default setting. Customized workspaces provide you with a work area that is always tailored to your needs.

USE THE LAYERS AND HISTORY PANELS

What You'll Do

 In this lesson, you'll hide and display a layer, move a layer on the Layers panel, and then undo the move by deleting the Layer Order state on the History panel.

Learning About Layers

A **layer** is a section within an image that can be manipulated independently. Layers allow you to control individual elements within an image and create great dramatic effects and variations of the same image. Layers enable you to easily manipulate individual characteristics within an image. Each Photoshop file has at least one layer, and can contain many individual layers, or groups of layers.

You can think of layers in a Photoshop image as individual sheets of clear plastic that are in a stack. It's possible for your file to quickly accumulate dozens of layers. The **Layers panel** displays all the layers in an open file. You can use the Layers panel to create, copy, delete, display, hide, merge, lock, group or reposition layers.

QUICKTIP

In Photoshop, using and understanding layers is the key to success.

Setting preferences

The Preferences dialog box contains several topics, each with its own settings: General; Interface; File Handling; Performance; Cursors; Transparency & Gamut; Units & Rulers; Guides, Grid, & Slices; Plug-Ins; Type; and Camera Raw. To open the Preferences dialog box, click Edit (Win) or Photoshop (Mac) on the Application bar, point to Preferences, then click a topic that represents the settings you want to change. If you move panels around the workspace, or make other changes to them, you can choose to retain those changes the next time you start the program. To always start a new session with default panels, click Interface on the Preferences menu, deselect the Remember Panel Locations check box, then click OK. Each time you start Photoshop, the panels will be reset to their default locations and values.

Understanding the Layers Panel

The order in which the layers appear on the Layers panel matches the order in which they appear in the image; the topmost layer in the Layers panel is the topmost layer on the image. You can make a layer active by clicking its name on the Layers panel. When a layer is active, it is highlighted on the Layers panel, and the name of the layer appears in parentheses in the image title bar. Only one layer can be active at a time. Figure 26 shows an image with its Layers panel. Do you see that this image contains six layers? Each layer can be moved or modified individually on the panel to give a different effect to the overall image. If you look at the Layers panel, you'll see that the Finger Painting text layer is dark, indicating that it is currently active.

Displaying and Hiding Layers

You can use the Layers panel to control which layers are visible in an image. You can show or hide a layer by clicking the Indicates layer visibility button next to the layer thumbnail. When a layer is hidden, you are not able to merge it with another, select it, or print it. Hiding some layers can make it easier to focus on particular areas of an image.

Using the History Panel

Photoshop records each task you complete in an image on the **History panel**. This record of events, called states, makes it easy to see what changes occurred and the tools or commands that you used to make the modifications. The History panel, shown in Figure 26, displays up to 20 states and automatically updates the list to display the most recently performed tasks. The list contains the name of the tool or command used to change the image. You can delete a state on the History panel by selecting it and dragging it to the Delete current state button. Deleting a state is equivalent to using the Undo command. You can also use the History panel to create a new image from any state.

FIGURE 26
Layers and History panels

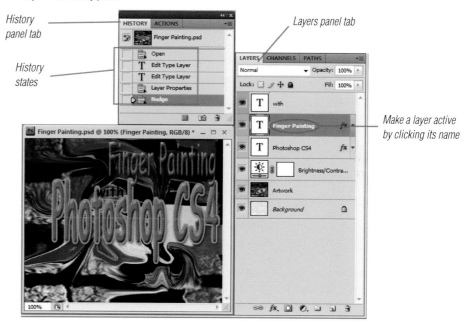

History panel tab

History states

Layers panel tab

Make a layer active by clicking its name

Hide and display a layer

1. Click the **Toddler layer** on the Layers panel.

   TIP Depending on the size of the window, you might only be able to see the initial characters of the layer name.

2. Verify that the **Show Transform Controls check box** on the options bar is not checked, then click the **Indicates layer visibility button** ☐ on the Toddler layer to display the image, as shown in Figure 27.

   TIP By default, transparent areas of an image have a checkerboard display on the Layers panel.

3. Click the **Indicates layer visibility button** 👁 on the Toddler layer to hide the layer.

You made the Toddler layer active on the Layers panel, then clicked the Indicates layer visibility button to display and hide a layer. Hiding layers is an important skill that can be used to remove distracting elements. Once you've finished working on a specific layer, you can display the additional layers.

FIGURE 27
Playground image

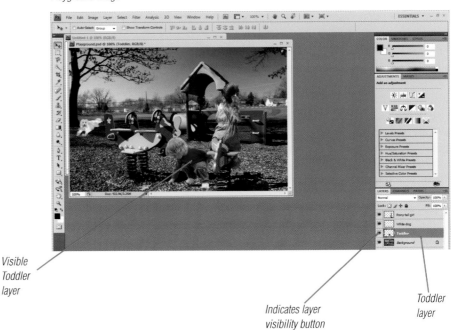

Visible Toddler layer

Indicates layer visibility button

Toddler layer

DESIGNTIP **Overcoming the fear of white space**

One design element that is often overlooked is *white space*. It's there on every page, and it doesn't seem to be doing much, does it? Take a look at a typical page in this book. Is every inch of space filled with either text or graphics? Of course not. If it were it would be impossible to read and it would be horribly ugly. The best example of the use of white space are the margins surrounding a page. This white space acts as a visual barrier—a resting place for the eyes. Without white space, the words on a page would crowd into each other, and the effect would be a cramped, cluttered, and hard to read page. Thoughtful use of white space makes it possible for you to guide the reader's eye from one location on the page to another. For many, one of the first design hurdles that must be overcome is the irresistible urge to put too much *stuff* on a page. When you are new to design, you may want to fill each page completely. Remember, less is more. Think of white space as a beautiful frame setting off an equally beautiful image.

FIGURE 28
Layer moved in Layers panel

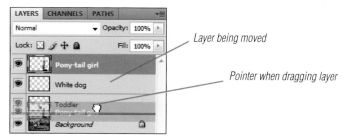

Layer being moved

Pointer when dragging layer

FIGURE 29
Result of moved layer

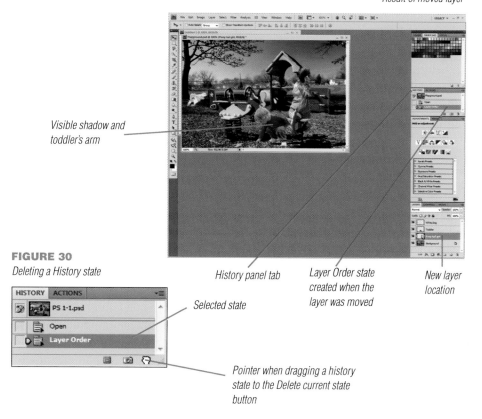

Visible shadow and toddler's arm

FIGURE 30
Deleting a History state

History panel tab

Selected state

Layer Order state created when the layer was moved

New layer location

Pointer when dragging a history state to the Delete current state button

Move a layer on the Layers panel and delete a state on the History panel

1. Click the **Indicates layer visibility button** on the Toddler layer on the Layers panel.

2. Click the **workspace switcher list arrow** on the Application bar, then click **Legacy**.

3. Click and drag the **Pony-tail girl layer** on the Layers panel, beneath the Toddler layer in the panel, as shown in Figure 28.

   The shadow of the toddler is now visible. See Figure 29.

4. Click **Layer Order** on the History panel, then drag it to the **Delete current state button** on the History panel, as shown in Figure 30.

   TIP   Each time you close and reopen an image, the History panel is cleared.

   The shadow of the toddler is now less visible.

5. Click **File** on the Application bar, then click **Save**.

You moved the Pony-tail girl layer so it was behind the Toddler layer, then returned it to its original position by dragging the Layer Order state to the Delete current state button on the History panel. You can easily use the History panel to undo what you've done.

LEARN ABOUT PHOTOSHOP
BY USING HELP

What You'll Do

 In this lesson, you'll open Help, then view and find information from the list of topics and the Search feature.

Understanding the Power of Help

Photoshop features an extensive Help system that you can use to access definitions, explanations, and useful tips. Help information is displayed in a browser window, so you must have web browser software installed on your computer to view the information; however, you do not need an Internet connection to use Photoshop Help.

Using Help Topics

The Home page of the Help window has links in the right pane that you can use to retrieve information about Photoshop commands and features. In the left pane is a list of topics from which you can choose. Help items have a plus sign (+) to the left of the

topic name. The plus sign (+) indicates that there are subtopics found within. To see the subtopics, click the plus sign (+). Topics and subtopics are links, meaning that the text is clickable. When you click any of the links, the right pane will display information (which may also contain links). The Search feature is located in a tab on the toolbar (above the left and right panes) in the form of a text box. You can search the Photoshop Help System by typing in the text box, then pressing [Enter] (Win) or [return] (Mac).

FIGURE 31
Topics in the Help window

Help links

FIGURE 32

Contents section of the Help window

Choosing
Colors topic in
Contents

Subtopic

1. Click **Help** on the Application bar, then click **Photoshop Help**.

   TIP   You can also open the Help window by pressing **[F1]** (Win) or ⌘ **[/]** (Mac).

2. Click the **plus sign (+)** to the left of the word **Color**.

3. Click **the plus sign (+)** to the left of **Choosing colors**, then click **Adobe Color Picker overview** in the left pane. See Figure 32.

   TIP   You can maximize the window (if you want to take advantage of the full screen display).

   Bear in mind that Help is web-driven and, like any web site, can change as errors and inconsistencies are found.

You used the Photoshop Help command on the Help menu to open the Help window and view a topic in Contents.

Understanding the differences between monitor, images, and device resolution

Image resolution is determined by the number of pixels per inch (ppi) that are printed on a page. Pixel dimensions (the number of pixels along the height and width of a bitmap image) determine the amount of detail in an image, while image resolution controls the amount of space over which the pixels are printed. High resolution images show greater detail and more subtle color transitions than low resolution images. Device resolution or printer resolution is measured by the ink dots per inch (dpi) produced by printers. You can set the resolution of your computer monitor to determine the detail with which images will be displayed. Each monitor should be calibrated to describe how the monitor reproduces colors. Monitor calibration is one of the first things you should do because it determines whether your colors are being accurately represented, which in turn determines how accurately your output will match your design intentions.

Get help and support

1. Click **Help** on the Application bar, then click **Photoshop Help**.

2. Click the **link** beneath the Community Help icon (*http://www.adobe.com/go/lr_ Photoshop_community*). Compare your Help window to Figure 33.

You accessed the Community Help feature.

FIGURE 33
Community Help window

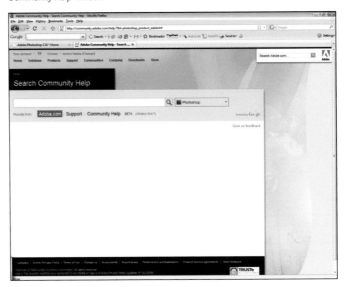

FIGURE 34
How-To Help topics

Using How-To Help features

Using Help would always be easy if you knew the name of the feature you wanted up look up. To help you find out how to complete common tasks, Photoshop has a listing of "How-To's" in the Help menu. Click Help on the Application bar, point to the How-To you'd like to read, as shown in Figure 34, then click the item about which you want more information.

Getting Started with Adobe Photoshop CS4

FIGURE 35
Search text box in Help

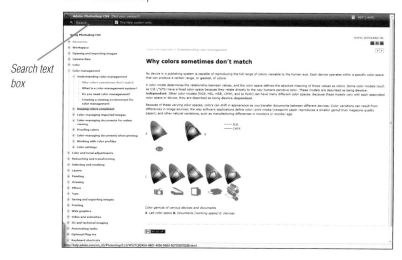

Search text
box

FIGURE 36
Additional keyboard shortcuts

Keys for using panels

This is not a complete list of keyboard shortcuts. This table lists only those shortcuts that are not displayed in menu commands or tool tips.

Result	Windows	Mac OS
Set options (except for Actions, Animation, Styles, Brushes, Tool Presets, and Layer Comps panels)	Alt-click New button	Option-click New button
Delete without confirmation (except for the Brushes panel)	Alt-click Delete button	Option-click Delete button
Apply value and keep text box active	Shift + Enter	Shift + Return
Load as a selection	Control-click channel, layer, or path thumbnail.	Command-click channel, layer, or path thumbnail.
Add to current selection	Control + Shift-click channel, layer, or path thumbnail.	Command + Shift-click channel, layer, or path thumbnail.
Subtract from current selection	Control + Alt-click channel, path, or layer thumbnail.	Command + Option-click channel, path, or layer thumbnail.
Intersect with current selection	Control + Shift + Alt-click channel, path, or layer thumbnail.	Command + Shift + Option-click channel, path, or layer thumbnail.
Show/Hide all panels	Tab	Tab
Show/Hide all panels except the toolbox and options bar	Shift + Tab	Shift + Tab
Highlight options bar	Select tool and press Enter	Select tool and press Return
Increase/decrease units by 10 in a pop-up menu	Shift + Up Arrow/Down Arrow	Shift + Up Arrow/Down Arrow

Find information using Search

1. Click the **Search text box** in the Help window.
2. Type **print quality**, then press **[Enter]** (Win) or **[return]** (Mac).

   TIP   You can search for multiple words by inserting a space; do not use punctuation in the text box.

3. Scroll down the left pane (if necessary), click **2** or **Next** to go to the next page, scroll down (if necessary), click **Why colors sometimes don't match**, then compare your Help screen to Figure 35.
4. Click the **Close box** on your browser window or tab when you are finished reading the topic.

You entered a search term, viewed search results, then closed the Help window.

Finding hidden keyboard shortcuts

There are oodles of keyboard shortcuts in Photoshop, and not all of them are listed in menus. Figure 36 contains a table of additional keyboard shortcuts that are not available on menus or ScreenTips. You can find this help topic by searching on keyboard shortcuts.

VIEW AND PRINT
AN IMAGE

What You'll Do

 In this lesson, you'll use the Zoom tool on the Application bar and Tools panel to increase and decrease your views of the image. You'll also change the page orientation settings in the Page Setup dialog box, and print the image.

Getting a Closer Look

When you edit an image in Photoshop, it is important that you have a good view of the area that you are focusing on. Photoshop has a variety of methods that allow you to enlarge or reduce your current view. You can use the Zoom tool by clicking the image to zoom in on (magnify the view) or zoom out of (reduce the view) areas of your image. Zooming in or out enlarges or reduces your *view*, not the actual image. The maximum zoom factor is 1600%. The current zoom percentage appears in the document's title bar, on the Navigator panel, on the status bar, and on the Application bar. When the Zoom tool is selected, the options bar provides additional choices for changing your view, as shown in Figure 37. For example, the Resize Windows To Fit check box automatically resizes the window whenever you magnify or reduce the view. You can also change the zoom percentage using the Navigator panel and the status bar by typing a new value in the zoom text box.

Printing Your Image

In many cases, a professional print shop might be the best option for printing a Photoshop image to get the highest quality. Lacking a professional print shop, you can print a Photoshop image using a standard black-and-white or color printer from within Photoshop, or you can switch to Bridge and then choose to send output to a PDF or Web Gallery. The printed image will be a composite of all visible layers. The quality of your printer and paper will affect the appearance of your output. The Page Setup dialog box displays options for printing, such as paper orientation. **Orientation** is the direction in which an image appears on the page. In **portrait orientation**, the image is printed with the shorter edges of the paper at the top and bottom. In **landscape orientation**, the image is printed with the longer edges of the paper at the top and bottom.

Use the Print command when you want to print multiple copies of an image. Use the Print One Copy command to print a single copy without making dialog box selections, and use the Print dialog box when you want to handle color values using color management.

Understanding Color Handling in Printing

The Print dialog box that opens when you click Print on the File menu lets you determine how colors are output. You can click the Color Handling list arrow to choose whether to use color management, and whether Photoshop or the printing device should control this process. If you let Photoshop determine the colors, Photoshop performs any necessary conversions to color values appropriate for the selected printer. If you choose to let the printer determine the colors, the printer will convert document color values to the corresponding printer color values. In this scenario, Photoshop does not alter the color values. If no color management is selected, no color values will be changed when the image is printed.

Viewing an Image in Multiple Views

You can use the New Window command (accessed by pointing to Arrange on the Window menu) to open multiple views of the same image. You can change the zoom percentage in each view so you can spotlight the areas you want to modify, and then modify the specific area of the image in each view. Because you are working on the same image in multiple views, not in multiple versions, Photoshop automatically applies the changes you make in one view to all views. Although you can close the views you no longer need at any time, Photoshop will not save any changes until you save the file.

FIGURE 37
Zoom tool options bar

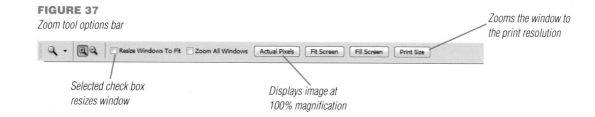

Zooms the window to the print resolution

Selected check box resizes window

Displays image at 100% magnification

Choosing a Photoshop version

You may have noticed that the title bar on the images in this book say 'Adobe Photoshop CS4 Extended'. What's that about? Well, the release of the Adobe Creative Suite 4 offers two versions of Photoshop: Adobe Photoshop CS4 and Adobe Photoshop CS4 Extended. The Extended version has additional animation and measurement features and is ideal for multimedia creative professionals, film and video creative professionals, graphic and web designers who push the limits of 3D and motion, as well as those professionals in the fields of manufacturing, medicine, architecture, engineering and construction, and science and research. Photoshop CS4 is ideal for professional photographers, serious amateur photographers, graphic and web designers, and print service providers.

Use the Zoom tool

1. Click the **Indicates layer visibility button** 👁 on the Layers panel for the Toddler layer so the layer is no longer displayed.

2. Click the **Zoom tool** 🔍 on the Application bar.

   TIP   You can also click the Zoom tool on the Tools panel.

3. Select the **Resize Windows To Fit check box** (if it is not already selected) on the options bar.

4. Position the **Zoom In pointer** ⊕ over the center of the image, then click the **image**.

   TIP   Position the pointer over the part of the image you want to keep in view.

5. Press **[Alt]** (Win) or **[option]** (Mac), then when the Zoom Out pointer appears, click the center of the image twice with the **Zoom Out pointer** ⊖.

6. Release **[Alt]** (Win) or **[option]** (Mac), then compare your image to Figure 38.

   The zoom factor for the image is 66.7%. Your zoom factor may differ.

You selected the Zoom tool on the Tools panel and used it to zoom in to and out of the image. The Zoom tool makes it possible to see the detail in specific areas of an image, or to see the whole image at once, depending on your needs.

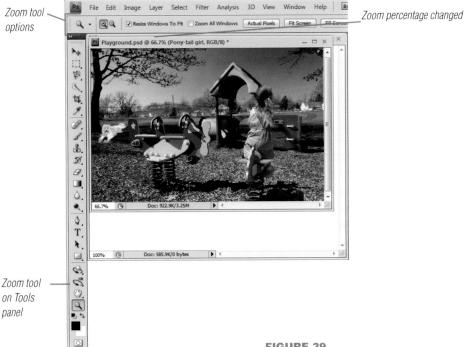

FIGURE 38
Reduced image

Zoom tool options

Zoom percentage changed

Zoom tool on Tools panel

FIGURE 39
Navigator panel

Viewed area of image

Using the Navigator panel

You can change the magnification factor of an image using the Navigator panel or the Zoom tool on the Tools panel. You can open the Navigator panel by clicking Window on the Application bar, then clicking Navigator. By double-clicking the Zoom text box on the Navigator panel, you can enter a new magnification factor, then press [Enter] (Win) or [return] (Mac). The magnification factor—shown as a percentage—is displayed in the lower-left corner of the Navigator panel, as shown in Figure 39. The red border in the panel, called the Proxy Preview Area, defines the area of the image that is magnified. You can drag the Proxy Preview Area inside the Navigator panel to view other areas of the image at the current magnification factor.

Getting Started with Adobe Photoshop CS4

FIGURE 40

Page Setup dialog box

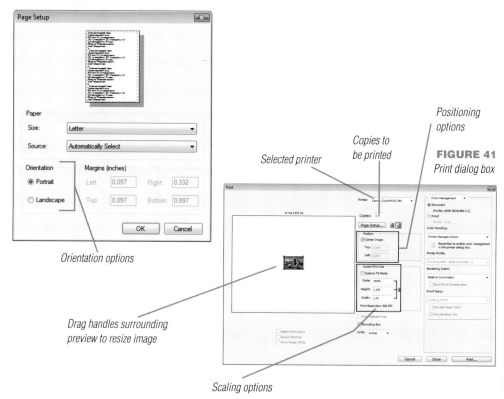

Orientation options

Copies to be printed

Selected printer

Positioning options

FIGURE 41

Print dialog box

Drag handles surrounding preview to resize image

Scaling options

1. Click **File** on the Application bar, then click **Page Setup** to open the Page Setup dialog box, as shown in Figure 40.

   TIP If you have not selected a printer using the Print Center, a warning box might appear (Mac).

   Page setup and print settings vary slightly in Macintosh.

2. Click the **Landscape option button** in the Orientation section (Win) or **Click the Landscape icon** (Mac), then click **OK**.

   TIP Choose either Landscape option (Mac).

3. Click **File** on the Application bar, click **Print**, then click **Proceed** in the message box that opens. If a PostScript dialog box opens, click **OK** (Mac).

4. Make sure that **1** appears in the Copies text box, then click **Print**. See Figure 41.

   TIP You can use the handles surrounding the image preview in the Print dialog box to scale the print size.

You used the Page Setup command on the File menu to open the Page Setup dialog box, changed the page orientation, then printed the image. Changing the page orientation can make an image fit better on a printed page.

Previewing and creating a Proof Setup

You can create and save a Proof Setup, which lets you preview your image to see how it will look when printed on a specific device. This feature lets you see how colors can be interpreted by different devices. By using this feature, you can decrease the chance that the colors on the printed copy of the image will vary from what you viewed on your monitor. Create a custom proof by clicking View on the Application bar, pointing to Proof Setup, then clicking Custom. Specify the conditions in the Customize Proof Condition dialog box, then click OK. Each proof setup has the .psf extension and can be loaded by clicking View on the Application bar, pointing to Proof Setup, clicking Custom, then clicking Load.

Create a PDF with Bridge

1. Click the **Launch Bridge button** ▶Br on the Application bar.

2. Click the **Folders tab** (if necessary), then click **Chapter 1** in the location where your Data Files are stored in the Folders tab (if necessary).

3. Click the **Output button** in the Bridge options bar.

4. Click the **PDF button** in the Output tab.

5. Click **Playground.psd,** hold **[Shift]**, click **PS 1-4.psd** in the Content tab, then release **[Shift]**.

6. Click the **Template list arrow**, click ***5 Contact Sheet**, click **Refresh Preview**, then compare your screen to Figure 1-42.

7. Scroll down the Output panel, click **Save**, locate the folder where your Data Files are stored, type **your name Chapter 1 files** in the text box, then click **Save.** You may need to click OK to close a warning box.

You launched Adobe Bridge, then generated a PDF which was printed using Adobe Acrobat.

FIGURE 42

PDF Output options in Bridge

PDF option

Click to refresh preview screen

DESIGNTIP **Using contrast to add emphasis**

Contrast is an important design principle that uses opposing elements, such as colors or lines, to produce an intensified effect in an image, page, or publication. Just as you can use a font attribute to make some text stand out from the rest, you can use contrasting elements to make certain graphic objects stand out. You can create contrast in many ways: by changing the sizes of objects; by varying object weights, such as making a line heavier surrounding an image; by altering the position of an object, such as changing the location on the page, or rotating the image so it is positioned on an angle; by drawing attention-getting shapes or a colorful box behind an object that makes it stand out (called a **matte**); or by adding carefully selected colors that emphasize an object.

FIGURE 43

Web Gallery options in Bridge

Web Gallery
button

Create a Web Gallery with Bridge

1. Verify that Bridge is open.

2. Click the **Web Gallery button** in the Output tab, click **Refresh Preview**, then compare your screen to Figure 43.

3. Click the **View Slideshow button** in the Output Preview window, then click the **Play Slideshow button**.

4. Scroll down the Output panel, click the **Save to Disk option button**, click the **Browse button**, locate the folder where your Data Files are stored, then click **OK** (Win) or **Choose** (Mac).

5. Click **Save** in the Create Gallery section of the Output panel, then click **OK** when the Gallery has been created.

6. Click **File** on the Bridge menu, then click **Exit** (Win) or click **Adobe Bridge CS4**, then click **Quit Adobe Bridge CS4** (Mac).

You launched Adobe Bridge, then generated a Web Gallery.

CLOSE A FILE
AND EXIT PHOTOSHOP

What You'll Do

 In this lesson, you'll use the Close and Exit (Win) or Quit (Mac) commands to close a file and exit Photoshop.

Concluding Your Work Session

At the end of your work session, you might have opened several files; you now need to decide which ones you want to save.

QUICKTIP

If you share a computer with other people, it's a good idea to reset Photoshop's preferences back to their default settings. You can do so when you start Photoshop by clicking Window on the Application bar, pointing to Workspace, then clicking Essentials (Default).

Closing Versus Exiting

When you are finished working on an image, you need to save and close it. You can close one file at a time, or close all open files at the same time by exiting the program. Closing a file leaves Photoshop open, which allows you to open or create another file. Exiting Photoshop closes the file, closes Photoshop, and returns you to the desktop, where you can choose to open another program or shut down the computer. Photoshop will prompt you to save any changes before it closes the files. If you do not modify a new or existing file, Photoshop will close it automatically when you exit.

QUICKTIP

To close all open files, click File on the Application bar, then click Close All.

Using Adobe online

Periodically, when you start Photoshop, an Update dialog box might appear, prompting you to search for updates or new information on the Adobe website. If you click Yes, Photoshop will automatically notify you that a download is available; however, you do not have to select it. You can also obtain information about Photoshop from the Adobe Photoshop website (*www.adobe.com/products/photoshop/main.html*), where you can link to downloads, tips, training, galleries, examples, and other support topics.

Getting Started with Adobe Photoshop CS4

FIGURE 44
Closing a file using the File menu

Workspace
switcher

Close command

Exit command

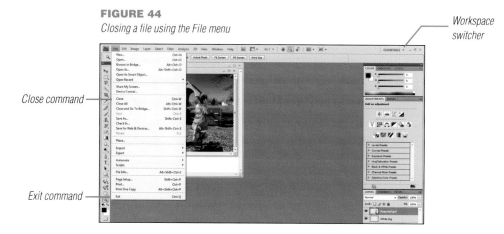

Close a file and exit Photoshop

1. Click the **workspace switcher**, then click **Essentials**.

2. Click **File** on the Application bar, then compare your screen to Figure 44.

3. Click **Close**.

   TIP You can close an open file (without closing Photoshop) by clicking the Close button in the image window. Photoshop will prompt you to save any unsaved changes before closing the file.

4. If asked to save your work, click **Yes** (Win) or **Save** (Mac).

5. Click **File** on the Application bar, then click **Exit** (Win) or click **Photoshop** on the Application bar, then click **Quit Photoshop** (Mac).

   TIP To exit Photoshop and close an open file, click the Close button in the program window. Photoshop will prompt you to save any unsaved changes before closing.

6. If asked to save your work (the untitled file), click **No**.

You closed the current file and exited the program by using the Close and Exit (Win) or Quit (Mac) commands.

DESIGNTIP **Using a scanner and a digital camera**

If you have a scanner, you can import print images, such as those taken from photographs, magazines, or line drawings, into Photoshop. Remember that images taken from magazines are owned by others, and that you need permission to distribute them. There are many types of scanners, including flatbed or single-sheet feed. You can also use a digital camera to create your own images. A digital camera captures images as digital files and stores them on some form of electronic medium, such as a SmartMedia card or memory stick. After you upload the images from your camera to your computer, you can work with images in Photoshop.

You can open a scanned or uploaded image (which usually has a .jpg extension or another graphics file format) by clicking File on the Application bar, then clicking Open. All Formats is the default file type, so you should be able to see all available image files in the Open dialog box. Locate the folder containing your scanned or digital camera images, click the file you want to open, then click Open. A scanned or digital camera image contains all its imagery in a single layer. You can add layers to the image, but you can only save these new layers if you save the image as a Photoshop image (with the extension .psd).

Power User Shortcuts

to do this:	use this method:
Close a file	[Ctrl][W] (Win) ⌘[W] (Mac)
Create a new file	[Ctrl][N] (Win), ⌘[N] (Mac)
Create a workspace	Window ➤ Workspace ➤ Save Workspace
Drag a layer	✋
Exit Photoshop	[Ctrl][Q] (Win), ⌘[Q] (Mac)
Hide a layer	👁
Lasso tool	⬭ or L
Modify workspace display	ESSENTIALS ▾
Open a file	[Ctrl][O] (Win), ⌘[O] (Mac)
Launch Bridge	▸Br
Open Help	[F1] (Win), ⌘ [/] (Mac)
Open Preferences dialog box	[Ctrl][K] (Win) ⌘[K] (Mac)
Page Setup	[Shift][Ctrl][P] (Win) [Shift]⌘[P] (Mac)
Print File	File ➤ Print or, [Ctrl][P] (Win) ⌘[P] (Mac)

to do this:	use this method:
Reset preferences to default settings	[Shift][Alt][Ctrl] (Win) [Shift] option ⌘ (Mac)
Save a file	[Ctrl][S] (Win) ⌘[S] (Mac)
Show a layer	☐
Show hidden lasso tools	[Shift] L
Show History panel	🕘
Show or hide all open panels	[Shift][Tab]
Show or hide all open panels, the options bar, and the Tools panel	[Tab]
Show or hide Swatches panel	Window ➤ Swatches
Use Save As	[Shift][Ctrl][S] (Win) [Shift]⌘[S] (Mac)
Zoom in	🔍 [Ctrl][+] (Win), ⌘[+] (Mac)
Zoom out	[Alt] 🔍 (Win) [Ctrl][-] (Win), ⌘[−] (Mac)
Zoom tool	🔍 or Z

Getting Started with Adobe Photoshop CS4

Start Adobe Photoshop CS4.

1. Start Photoshop.
2. Create a new image that is 500 × 500 pixels, accept the default resolution, then name and save it as **Review**.

Open and save an image.

1. Open PS 1-3.psd from the drive and folder where you store your Data Files, and if prompted, update the text layers.
2. Save it as **Zenith Design Logo**.

Use organizational and management features.

1. Open Adobe Bridge.
2. Click the Folders tab, then locate the folder that contains your Data Files.
3. Close Adobe Bridge.

Examine the Photoshop window.

1. Locate the image title bar and the current zoom percentage.
2. Locate the menu you use to open an image.
3. View the Tools panel, the options bar, and the panels that are showing.
4. Click the Move tool on the Tools panel, then view the Move tool options on the options bar.
5. Create, save and display a customized workspace (based on Essentials) called History and Layers that captures panel locations and displays the History panel above the Layers panel.

Use the Layers and History panels.

1. Drag the Wine Glasses layer so it is above the Zenith layer, then use the History panel to undo the state.

2. Drag the Wine Glasses layer above the Zenith layer again.
3. Use the Indicates layer visibility button to hide the Wine Glasses layer.
4. Make the Wine Glasses layer visible again.
5. Hide the Zenith layer.
6. Show the Zenith layer.
7. Show the Tag Line layer.

Learn about Photoshop by using Help.

1. Open the Adobe Photoshop CS4 Help window.
2. Using the Index, find information about resetting to the default workspace.

3. Print the information you find.

4. Close the Help window.

View and print an image.

1. Make sure that all the layers are visible in the Layers panel.

2. Click the Zoom tool, then make sure the setting is selected to resize the window to fit.

3. Zoom in on the wine glasses twice.

4. Zoom out to the original perspective.

5. Print one copy of the image.

6. Save your work.

Close a file and exit Photoshop.

1. Compare your screen to Figure 45, then close the Zenith Design Logo file.

2. Close the Review file.

3. Exit (Win) or Quit (Mac) Photoshop.

FIGURE 45
Completed Skills Review

Getting Started with Adobe Photoshop CS4

As a new Photoshop user, you are comforted knowing that Photoshop's Help system provides definitions, explanations, procedures, and other helpful information. It also includes examples and demonstrations to show how Photoshop features work. You use the Help system to learn about image size and resolution.

1. Open the Photoshop Help window.
2. Click the Workspace topic in the topics list.
3. Click the Panels and menus subtopic, in the left pane, then click Enter values in panels, dialog boxes, and the options bar topic.
4. Click the Display context menus topic, then read this topic.
5. Click the Opening and importing images topic in the left pane.
6. Click the Image size and resolution topic in the left pane, then click About monitor resolution. Print out this topic, then compare your screen to the sample shown in Figure 46.

FIGURE 46
Sample Project Builder 1

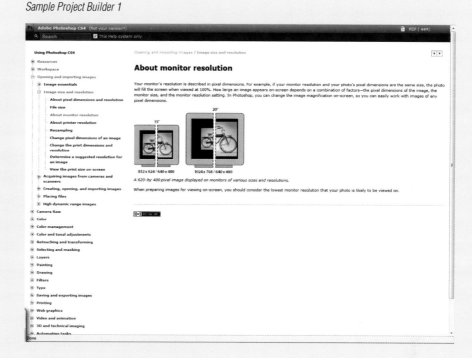

Kitchen Experience, your local specialty cooking shop, has just added herb-infused oils to its product line. They have hired you to draft a flyer that features these new products. You use Photoshop to create this flyer.

1. Open PS 1-4.psd, then save it as **Cooking**.
2. Display the Essentials workspace (if necessary).
3. Make the Measuring Spoons layer visible.
4. Drag the Oils layer so the content appears behind the Skillet layer content.
5. Drag the Measuring Spoons layer above the Skillet layer.
6. Save the file, then compare your image to the sample shown in Figure 47.

FIGURE 47
Sample Project Builder 2

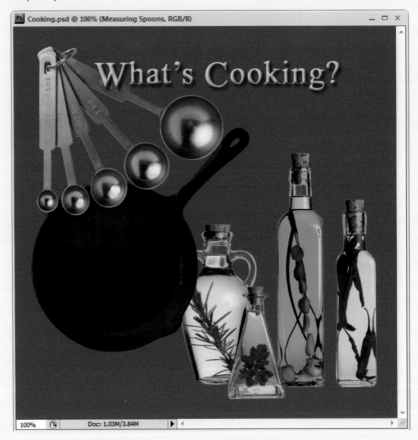

Getting Started with Adobe Photoshop CS4

DESIGN PROJECT

As an avid, albeit novice Photoshop user, you have grasped the importance of how layers affect your image. With a little practice, you can examine a single-layer image and guess which objects might display on their own layers. Now, you're ready to examine the images created by Photoshop experts and critique them on their use of layers.

1. Connect to the Internet, and use your browser to find interesting artwork located on at least two websites.
2. Download a single-layer image (in its native format) from each website.
3. Start Photoshop, then open the downloaded images.
4. Save one image as **Critique-1** and the other as **Critique-2** in the Photoshop format (use the .psd extension).
5. Analyze each image for its potential use of layers.

6. Open the File Info dialog box for Critique-1.psd, then type in the Description section your speculation as to the number of layers there might be in the image, their possible order on the Layers panel, and how moving the layers would affect the image.

7. Close the dialog box.

8. Compare your image to the sample shown in Figure 48, then close the files.

FIGURE 48
Sample Design Project

Getting Started with Adobe Photoshop CS4

You are preparing to work on a series of design projects to enhance your portfolio. You decide to see what information on digital imaging is available on the Adobe website. You also want to increase your familiarity with the Adobe website so that you can take advantage of product information and support, user tips and feedback, and become a more skilled Photoshop user.

1. Connect to the Internet and go to the Adobe website at *www.adobe.com*.
2. Point to Products, then find the link for the Photoshop family, as shown in Figure 49.
3. Use the links on the web page to search for information about digital imaging options.
4. Print the relevant page(s).
5. Start Photoshop and open the Photoshop Help window.

6. Search for information about Adjusting the Monitor Display, then print the relevant page(s).

FIGURE 49
Completed Portfolio Project

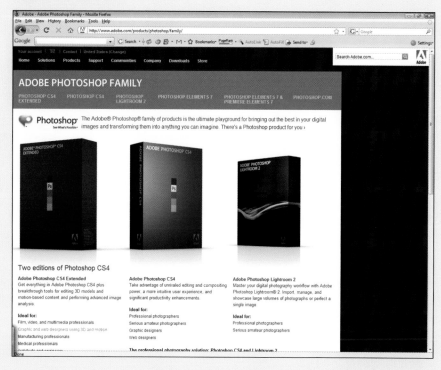

7. Evaluate the information in the documents, and then compare any significant differences.

chapter

2

WORKING
WITH LAYERS

1. Examine and convert layers

2. Add and delete layers

3. Add a selection from one image to another

4. Organize layers with layer groups and colors

2 WORKING
WITH LAYERS

Layers Are Everything

You can use Photoshop to create sophisticated images in part because a Photoshop image can contain multiple layers. Each object created in Photoshop can exist on its own individual layer, making it easy to control the position and quality of each layer in the stack. Depending on your computer's resources, you can have a maximum of 8000 layers in each Photoshop image with each layer containing as much or as little detail as necessary.

QUICKTIP

The transparent areas in a layer do not increase file size.

Understanding the Importance of Layers

Layers make it possible to manipulate the tiniest detail within your image, which gives you tremendous flexibility when you make changes. By placing objects, effects, styles, and type on separate layers, you can modify them individually *without* affecting other layers. The advantage to using multiple layers is that you can isolate effects and images on one layer without affecting the others. The disadvantage of using multiple layers is that your file size might become very large. However, once your image is finished, you can dramatically reduce its file size by combining all the layers into one.

Using Layers to Modify an Image

You can add, delete, and move layers in your image. You can also drag a portion of an image, called a **selection**, from one Photoshop image to another. When you do this, a new layer is automatically created. Copying layers from one image to another makes it easy to transfer a complicated effect, a simple image, or a piece of type. You can also hide and display each layer, or change its opacity. **Opacity** is the ability to see through a layer so that layers beneath it are visible. The more opacity a layer has, the less see-through (transparent) it is. You can continuously change the overall appearance of your image by changing the order of your layers, until you achieve just the look you want.

Tools You'll Use

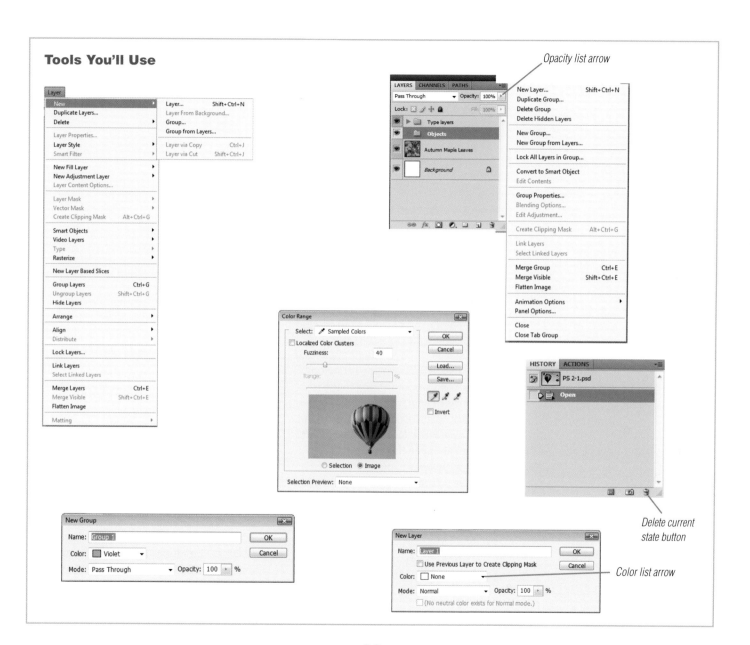

EXAMINE AND
CONVERT LAYERS

What You'll Do

In this lesson, you'll use the Layers panel to delete a Background layer and the Layer menu to create a Background layer from an image layer.

Learning About the Layers Panel

The **Layers panel** lists all the layers within a Photoshop file and makes it possible for you to manipulate one or more layers. By default, this panel is located in the lower-right corner of the screen, but it can be moved to a new location by dragging the panel's tab. In some cases, the entire name of the layer might not appear on the panel. If a layer name is too long, an ellipsis appears, indicating that part of the name is hidden from view. You can view a layer's entire name by holding the pointer over the name until the full name appears. The **layer thumbnail** appears to the left of the layer name and contains a miniature picture of the layer's content, as shown in Figure 1. To the left of the layer thumbnail, you can add color, which you can use to easily identify layers. The Layers panel also contains common buttons, such as the Delete layer button and the Create new layer button.

QUICKTIP
You can hide or resize Layers panel thumbnails to improve your computer's performance. To remove or change the size of layer thumbnails, click the Layers panel list arrow, then click Panel Options to open the Layers Panel Options dialog box. Click the option button next to the desired thumbnail size, or click the None option button to remove thumbnails, then click OK. An icon of the selected thumbnail size or a paintbrush icon appears.

Recognizing Layer Types

The Layers panel includes several types of layers: Background, type, adjustment, and image (non-type). The Background layer—whose name appears in italics—is always at the bottom of the stack. Type layers—layers that contain text—contain the type layer icon in the layer thumbnail, and image layers display a thumbnail of their contents. Adjustment layers, which make changes to layers, have a variety of thumbnails, depending on the kind of adjustment. Along with dragging selections from one Photoshop image to another, you can also drag objects created in other applications, such as Adobe

Dreamweaver, Adobe InDesign, or Adobe Flash, onto a Photoshop image, which creates a layer containing the object you dragged from the other program window.

Organizing Layers

One of the benefits of using layers is that you can create different design effects by rearranging their order. Figure 2 contains the same layers as Figure 1, but they are arranged differently. Did you notice that the yellow-striped balloon is partially obscured by the black-striped balloon and the lighthouse balloon? This reorganization was created by dragging the layer containing the yellow balloon below the Black striped balloon layer and by dragging the Lighthouse balloon layer above Layer 2 on the Layers panel. When organizing layers, you may find it helpful to resize the Layers panel so you can see more layers within the image.

FIGURE 1
Image with multiple layers

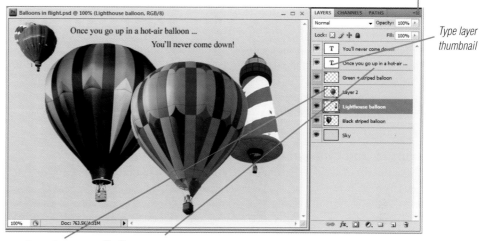

Layers panel list arrow

Type layer thumbnail

Image layer thumbnail

Position mouse over layer name to display full title

Guide

FIGURE 2
Layers rearranged

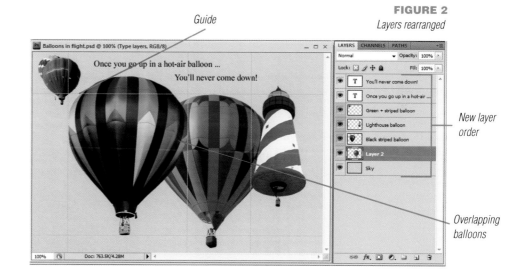

New layer order

Overlapping balloons

Converting Layers

When you open an image created with a digital camera, you'll notice that the entire image appears in the Background layer. The Background layer of any image is the initial layer and is always located at the bottom of the stack. You cannot change its position in the stack, nor can you change its opacity or lighten or darken its colors. You can, however, convert a Background layer into an image layer (non-type layer), and you can convert an image layer into a Background layer. You need to modify the image layer *before* converting it to a Background layer. You might want to convert a Background layer into an image layer so that you can use the full range of editing tools on the layer content. You might want to convert an image layer into a Background layer after you have made all your changes and want it to be the bottom layer in the stack.

QUICKTIP

Before converting an image layer to a Background layer, you must first delete the existing Background layer. You can delete a Background layer by selecting it on the Layers panel, then dragging it to the Delete layer button on the Layers panel.

Using rulers and changing units of measurement

You can display horizontal and vertical rulers to help you better position elements. To display or hide rulers, click View on the Application bar, then click Rulers. (A check mark to the left of the Rulers command indicates that the rulers are displayed.) In addition to displaying or hiding rulers, you can also choose from various units of measurement. Your choices include pixels, inches, centimeters, millimeters, points, picas, and percentages. Pixels, for example, display more tick marks and can make it easier to make tiny adjustments. You can change the units of measurement by clicking Edit [Win] or Photoshop [Mac] on the Application bar, pointing to Preferences, then clicking Units & Rulers. In the Preferences dialog box, click the Rulers list arrow, click the units you want to use, then click OK. The easiest way to change units of measurement, however, is shown in Figure 3. Once the rulers are displayed, right-click (Win) or [Ctrl]-click (Mac) either the vertical or horizontal ruler, then click the unit of measurement you want. When displayed, the Info panel, displays the current coordinates in your image. Regardless of the units of measurement in use, the X/Y coordinates are displayed in the Info panel.

FIGURE 3
Changing units of measurement

Right-click (Win) or [Ctrl]-click (Mac) to display measurement choices

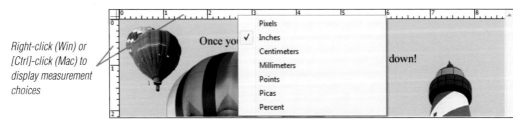

FIGURE 4

Warning box

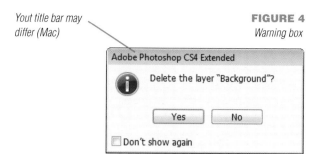

Yout title bar may differ (Mac)

FIGURE 5

Background layer deleted

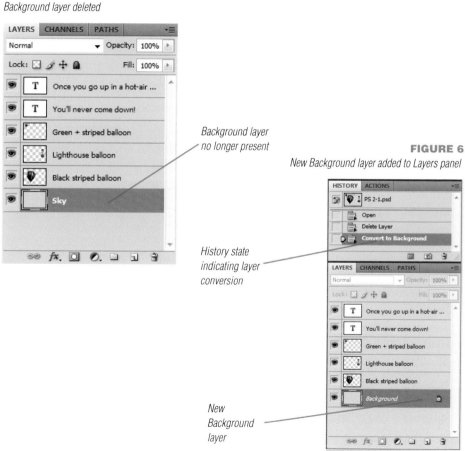

Background layer no longer present

FIGURE 6

New Background layer added to Layers panel

History state indicating layer conversion

New Background layer

Convert an image layer into a Background layer

1. Open PS 2-1.psd from the drive and folder where you store your Data Files, then save it as **Balloons in flight**.

   TIP If you receive a warning box about maximum compatibility, or a message stating that some of the text layers need to be updated before they can be used for vector-based output, and/or a warning box about maximum compatibility, click Update and/or click OK.

2. Click **View** on the Application bar, click **Rulers** if your rulers are not visible, then make sure that the rulers are displayed in pixels.

   TIP If you are unsure which units of measurement are used, right-click (Win) or [Ctrl]-click (Mac) one of the rulers, then verify that Pixels is selected, or click Pixels (if necessary).

3. Click the **workspace switcher** on the Application bar, then click **History and Layers** (created in the Skills Review in Chapter 1).

4. On the Layers panel, scroll down, click the **Background layer**, then click the **Delete layer button** 🗑 .

5. Click **Yes** in the dialog box, as shown in Figure 4, then compare your Layers panel to Figure 5.

6. Click **Layer** on the Application bar, point to **New**, then click **Background From Layer**.

   The Sky layer has been converted into the Background layer. Did you notice that in addition to the image layer being converted to the Background layer that a state now appears on the History panel that says Convert to Background? See Figure 6.

7. Save your work.

You displayed the rulers and switched to a previously created workspace, deleted the Background layer of an image, then converted an image layer into the Background layer. You can convert any layer into the Background layer, as long as you first delete the existing Background layer.

ADD AND
DELETE LAYERS

What You'll Do

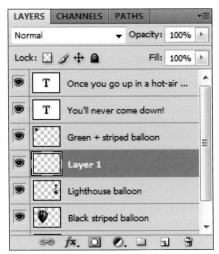

In this lesson, you'll create a new layer using the New command on the Layer menu, delete a layer, and create a new layer using buttons on the Layers panel.

Adding Layers to an Image

Because it's so important to make use of multiple layers, Photoshop makes it easy to add and delete layers. You can create layers in three ways:

- Use the New command on the Layer menu.
- Use the New Layer command on the Layers panel menu.
- Click the Create a new layer button on the Layers panel.

QUICKTIP

See Table 1 for tips on navigating the Layers panel.

Objects on new layers have a default opacity setting of 100%, which means that objects on lower layers are not visible. Each layer

Merging layers

You can combine multiple image layers into a single layer using the merging process. Merging layers is useful when you want to combine multiple layers in order to make specific edits permanent. (This merging process is different from flattening in that it's selective. Flattening merges *all* visible layers.) In order for layers to be merged, they must be visible and next to each other on the Layers panel. You can merge all visible layers within an image, or just the ones you select. Type layers cannot be merged until they are **rasterized** (turned into a bitmapped image layer), or converted into uneditable text. To merge two layers, make sure that they are next to each other and that the Indicates layer visibility button is visible on each layer, then click the layer in the higher position on the Layers panel. Click Layer on the Application bar, then click Merge Down. The active layer and the layer immediately beneath it will be combined into a single layer. To merge all visible layers, click the Layers panel list arrow, then click Merge Visible. Most layer commands that are available on the Layer menu, such as Merge Down, are also available using the Layers panel list arrow.

Working with Layers

has the Normal (default) blending mode applied to it. (A **blending mode** is a feature that affects a layer's underlying pixels, and is used to lighten or darken colors.)

Naming a Layer

Photoshop automatically assigns a sequential number to each new layer name, but you can rename a layer at any time. So, if you have four named layers and add a new layer, the default name of the new layer will be Layer 1. Although calling a layer "Layer 12" is fine, you might want to use a more descriptive name so it is easier to distinguish one layer from another. If you use the New command on the Layer menu, you can name the layer when you create it. You can rename a layer at any time by using either of these methods:

- Click the Layers panel list arrow, click Layer Properties, type the name in the Name text box, then click OK.
- Double-click the name on the Layers panel, type the new name, then press [Enter] (Win) or [return] (Mac).

Deleting Layers from an Image

You might want to delete an unused or unnecessary layer. You can use any of four methods to delete a layer:

- Click the name on the Layers panel, click the Layers panel list arrow, then click Delete Layer, as shown in Figure 7.
- Click the name on the Layers panel, click the Delete layer button on the Layers panel, then click Yes in the warning box.
- Click the name on the Layers panel, press and hold [Alt] (Win) or [option] (Mac), then click the Delete layer button on the Layers panel.
- Drag the layer name on the Layers panel to the Delete layer button on the Layers panel.
- Right-click a layer (Win) or [Ctrl]-click a layer (Mac).

You should be certain that you no longer need a layer before you delete it. If you delete a layer by accident, you can restore it during the current editing session by deleting the Delete Layer state on the History panel.

QUICKTIP

Photoshop always numbers layers sequentially, no matter how many layers you add or delete.

TABLE 1: Shortcuts for Navigating the Layers Panel

Use the combination:	to navigate:
[Alt][[] (Win) or [option][[] (Mac)	down the Layers panel
[Alt][]] (Win) or [option][]] (Mac)	up the Layers panel
[Ctrl][[] (Win) or ⌘[[] (Mac)	down one layer*
[Ctrl][]] (Win) or ⌘[]] (Mac)	up one layer*
[Ctrl][Shift] [[] (Win) or ⌘[Shift] [[] (Mac)	to bottom of stack*
[Ctrl][Shift] []] (Win) or ⌘[Shift] []] (Mac)	to top of stack*
	*Excluding the Background layer

Layers panel list arrow

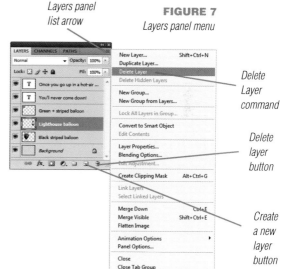

FIGURE 7
Layers panel menu

Delete Layer command

Delete layer button

Create a new layer button

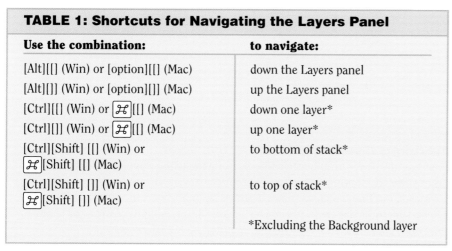

Add a layer using the Layer menu

1. Click the **Lighthouse balloon layer** on the Layers panel.

2. Click **Layer** on the Application bar, point to **New**, then click **Layer** to open the New Layer dialog box, as shown in Figure 8.

   A new layer will be added above the active layer.

   | TIP You can change the layer name in the New Layer dialog box before it appears on the Layers panel.

3. Click **OK**.

   The New Layer dialog box closes and the new layer appears above the Lighthouse balloon layer on the Layers panel. The New Layer state is added to the History panel. See Figure 9.

   You created a new layer above the Lighthouse balloon layer using the New command on the Layer menu. The layer does not yet contain any content.

FIGURE 8
New Layer dialog box

FIGURE 9
New layer in Layers panel

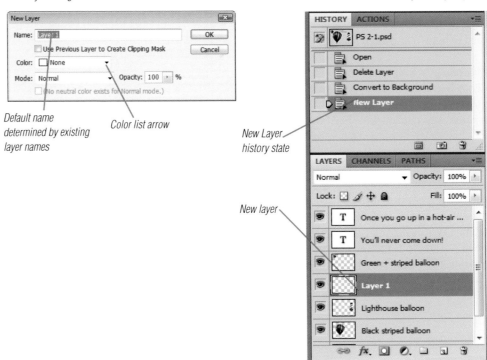

Default name determined by existing layer names

Color list arrow

New Layer history state

New layer

Inserting a layer beneath the active layer

When you add a layer to an image either by using the Layer menu or clicking the Create a new layer button on the Layers panel, the new layer is inserted above the active layer. But there might be times when you want to insert the new layer beneath, or in back of, the active layer. You can do so easily, by pressing [Ctrl] (Win) or ⌘ (Mac) while clicking the Create a new layer button on the Layers panel.

FIGURE 10
New layer with default settings

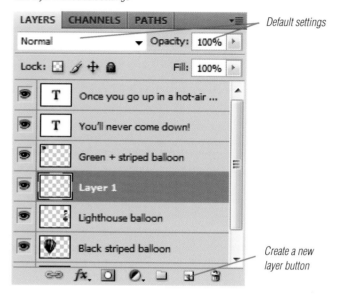

Default settings

Create a new
layer button

Delete a layer

1. Position the **Layer selection pointer** 🖑 over Layer 1 on the Layers panel.

2. Drag **Layer 1** to the **Delete layer button** 🗑 on the Layers panel.

   TIP You can also delete the layer by dragging the New Layer state on the History panel to the Delete current state button.

3. If the Delete the layer "Layer 1" dialog box opens, click the **Don't show again check box**, then click **Yes**.

   TIP Many dialog boxes let you turn off this reminder feature by selecting the Don't show again check box. Selecting these check boxes can improve your efficiency.

You used the Delete layer button on the Layers panel to delete a layer.

Add a layer using the Layers panel

1. Click the **Lightouse balloon layer** on the Layers panel, if it is not already selected.

2. Click the **Create a new layer button** 🔲 on the Layers panel, then compare your Layers panel to Figure 10.

3. Save your work.

You used the Create a new layer button on the Layers panel to add a new layer.

Right-clicking for everyone (Mac)

Mac users, are you feeling left out because you can't right-click? If so, you'll welcome this news: anyone (yes, even Mac users!) can right-click simply by replacing the mouse that came with your computer with any two-button mouse that uses a USB connector. OS X was designed to recognize secondary clicks without having to add software. Once you've switched mice, just plug and play! You can then right-click using the (Win) instructions in the steps.

ADD A SELECTION FROM ONE IMAGE TO ANOTHER

What You'll Do

 In this lesson, you'll use the Invert check box in the Color Range dialog box to make a selection, drag the selection to another image, and remove the fringe from a selection using the Defringe command.

Understanding Selections

Often the Photoshop file you want to create involves using an image or part of an image from another file. To use an image or part of an image, you must first select it. Photoshop refers to this as "making a selection." A selection is an area of an image surrounded by a **marquee**, a dashed line that encloses the area you want to edit or move to another image, as shown in Figure 11. You can drag a marquee around a selection using four marquee tools: Rectangular Marquee, Elliptical Marquee, Single Row Marquee, and Single Column Marquee. Table 2 displays the four marquee tools and other selection tools. You can set options for

each tool on the options bar when the tool you want to use is active.

Understanding the Extract and Color Range Commands

In addition to using selection tools, Photoshop provides other methods for incorporating imagery from other files. The **Extract command**, located on the Filter menu, separates an image from a background or surrounding imagery. You can use the **Color Range command**, located on the Select menu, to select a particular color contained in an existing image. Depending on the area you want, you can use the Color Range dialog box to extract a portion of an image.

Cropping an image

You might find an image that you really like, except that it contains a particular portion that you don't need. You can exclude, or **crop**, certain parts of an image by using the Crop tool on the Tools panel. Cropping hides areas of an image from view *without* decreasing resolution quality. To crop an image, click the Crop tool on the Tools panel, drag the pointer around the area you *want to keep*, then press [Enter] (Win) or [return] (Mac).

For example, you can select the Invert check box to choose one color and then select the portion of the image that is every color *except* that one. After you select all the imagery you want from another image, you can drag it into your open file.

Making a Selection and Moving a Selection

You can use a variety of methods and tools to make a selection, which can then be used as a specific part of a layer or as the entire layer. You use selections to isolate an area you want to alter. For example, you can use the Magnetic Lasso tool to select complex shapes by clicking the starting point, tracing an approximate outline, then clicking the ending point. Later, you can use the Crop tool to trim areas from a selection. When you use the Move tool to drag a selection to the destination image, Photoshop places the selection in a new layer above the previously active layer.

Defringing Layer Contents

Sometimes when you make a selection, then move it into another image, the newly selected image can contain unwanted pixels that give the appearance of a fringe, or halo. You can remove this effect using a Matting command called Defringe. This command is available on the Layer menu and allows you to replace fringe pixels with the colors of other nearby pixels. You can determine a width for replacement pixels between 1 and 200. It's magic!

FIGURE 11
Marquee selections

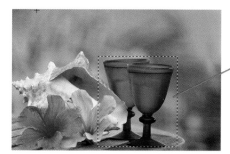

Area selected using the Rectangular Marquee tool

Specific element selected using the Magnetic Lasso tool

TABLE 2: Selection Tools

tool	tool name	tool	tool name
⬚	Rectangular Marquee tool	⚲	Lasso tool
◯	Elliptical Marquee tool	⋈	Polygonal Lasso tool
⋯	Single Row Marquee tool	🖉	Magnetic Lasso tool
⋮	Single Column Marquee tool	◭	Eraser tool
🔲	Crop tool	🖊	Background Eraser tool
✳	Magic Wand tool	🖊	Magic Eraser tool

Make a color range selection

1. Open PS 2-2.psd from the drive and folder where you store your Data Files, save it as **Yellow striped balloon**, click the **title bar**, then drag the **window** to an empty area of the workspace so that you can see both images.

   | TIP When more than one file is open, each has its own set of rulers. The ruler on the inactive file appears dimmed.

2. With the Yellow striped balloon image selected, click **Select** on the Application bar, then click **Color Range**.

   | TIP If the background color is solid, you can select the Invert check box to pick only the pixels in the image area.

3. Click the **Image option button**, then type **150** in the Fuzziness text box (or drag the **slider** all the way to the right until you see **150**).

4. Position the **Eyedropper pointer** 🖋 in the **blue background** of the image in the Color Range dialog box, then click the **background**.

5. Select the **Invert check box**. Compare the settings in your dialog box to Figure 12.

6. Click **OK**, then compare your Yellow striped balloon.psd image to Figure 13.

You opened a file and used the Color Range dialog box to select the image pixels by selecting the image's inverted colors. Selecting the inverse is an important skill in making selections.

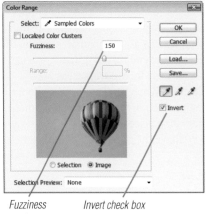

FIGURE 12
Color Range dialog box

Fuzziness
text box   Invert check box

FIGURE 13
Marquee surrounding selection

Marquee surrounds
everything that is the
inverse of the blue
background

Using the Place command

You can add an image from another image to a layer using the Place command. Place an image in a Photoshop layer by clicking File on the Application bar, then clicking Place. The placed artwork appears *flattened* inside a bounding box at the center of the Photoshop image. The artwork maintains its original aspect ratio; however, if the artwork is larger than the Photoshop image, it is resized to fit. The Place command works well if you want to insert a multi-layered image in another image. (If all you want is a specific layer from an image, you should just drag the layer you want into an image and not use the Place command.)

FIGURE 14
Yellow striped balloon image dragged to Balloons in flight image

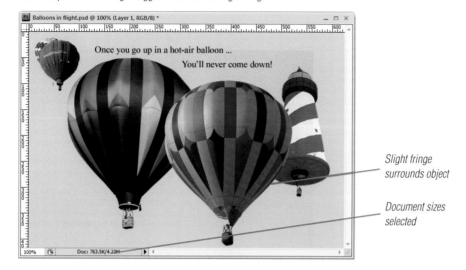

Slight fringe
surrounds object

Document sizes
selected

FIGURE 15
New layer defringed

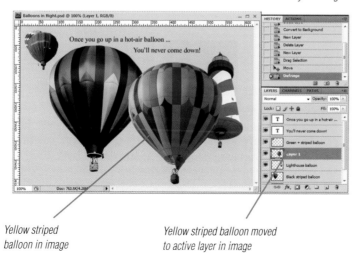

Yellow striped
balloon in image

Yellow striped balloon moved
to active layer in image

Move a selection to another image

1. Click the **Move tool** ⊹ on the Tools panel.
2. Position the **Move tool pointer** ⊱ anywhere over the selection in the Yellow striped balloon image.
3. Drag the **selection** to the Balloons in flight image, then release the mouse button.

   The Yellow striped balloon image moves to the Balloons in flight file appearing on Layer 1.
4. If necessary, use the **Move tool pointer** ⊹ to drag the yellow-striped balloon to the approximate location shown in Figure 14.
5. Click the **triangle** ▶ in the document window status bar, point to **Show**, then verify that Document Sizes is selected.

You dragged a selection from one image to another. You verified that the document size is displayed in the window.

Defringe the selection

1. With Layer 1 selected, click **Layer** on the Application bar, point to **Matting** then click **Defringe**. Defringing a selection gets rid of the halo effect that sometimes occurs when objects are dragged from one image to another.
2. Type **2** in the Width text box, then click **OK**.
3. Save your work.
4. Close **Yellow striped ballon.psd**, then compare the Balloons in flight image to Figure 15.

You removed the fringe from a selection.

ORGANIZE LAYERS WITH
LAYER GROUPS AND COLORS

What You'll Do

 In this lesson, you'll use the Layers panel menu to create, name, and color a layer group, and then add layers to it. You'll add finishing touches to the image, save it as a copy, then flatten it.

Understanding Layer Groups

A **layer group** is a Photoshop feature that allows you to organize your layers on the Layers panel. A layer group contains individual layers. For example, you can create a layer group that contains all the type layers in your image. To create a layer group, you click the Layers panel list arrow, then click New Group. As with layers, it is helpful to choose a descriptive name for a layer group.

QUICKTIP

You can press [Ctrl][G] (Win) or ⌘ [G] (Mac) to place the selected layer in a layer group.

Organizing Layers into Groups

After you create a layer group, you simply drag layers on the Layers panel directly on top of the layer group. You can remove layers from a layer group by dragging them out of the layer group to a new location on the Layers panel or by deleting them. Some changes made to a layer group, such as blending mode or opacity changes, affect every layer in the layer group. You can choose to expand or collapse layer groups, depending on the amount of information you need to see. Expanding a layer group

Duplicating a layer

When you add a new layer by clicking the Create a new layer button on the Layers panel, the new layer contains default settings. However, you might want to create a new layer that has the same settings as an existing layer. You can do so by duplicating an existing layer to create a copy of that layer and its settings. Duplicating a layer is also a good way to preserve your modifications, because you can modify the duplicate layer and not worry about losing your original work. To create a duplicate layer, select the layer you want to copy, click the Layers panel list arrow, click Duplicate Layer, then click OK. The new layer will appear above the original.

shows all of the layers in the layer group, and collapsing a layer group hides all of the layers in a layer group. You can expand or collapse a layer group by clicking the triangle to the left of the layer group icon. Figure 16 shows one expanded layer group and one collapsed layer group.

Adding Color to a Layer

If your image has relatively few layers, it's easy to locate the layers. However, if your image contains many layers, you might need some help in organizing them. You can organize layers by color-coding them, which makes it easy to find the layer or the group

you want, regardless of its location on the Layers panel. For example, you can put all type layers in red or put the layers associated with a particular portion of an image in blue. To color the Background layer, you must first convert it to a regular layer.

QUICKTIP

You can also color-code a layer group without losing the color-coding you applied to individual layers.

Flattening an Image

After you make all the necessary modifications to your image, you can greatly reduce

the file size by flattening the image.

Flattening merges all visible layers into a single Background layer and discards all hidden layers. Make sure that all layers that you want to display are visible before you flatten the image. Because flattening removes an image's individual layers, it's a good idea to make a copy of the original image *before* it is flattened. The status bar displays the file's current size and the size it will be when flattened. If you work on a Macintosh, you'll find this information in the lower-left corner of the document window.

FIGURE 16
Layer groups

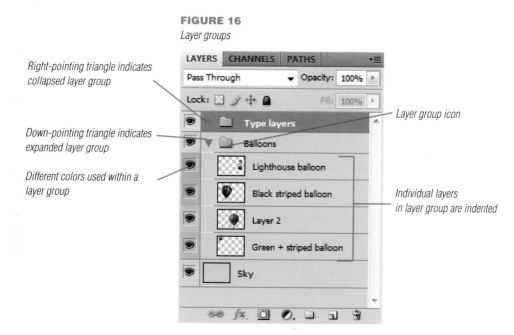

Right-pointing triangle indicates collapsed layer group

Down-pointing triangle indicates expanded layer group

Different colors used within a layer group

Layer group icon

Individual layers in layer group are indented

Understanding Layer Comps

The ability to create a **layer comp**, a variation on the arrangement and visibility of existing layers, is a powerful tool that can make your work more organized. You can create a layer comp by clicking the Layer Comps button on the vertical dock (if it's visible), or by clicking Window on the Application bar, then clicking Layer Comps. Clicking the Create New Layer Comp button on the panel opens the New Layer Comp dialog box, shown in Figure 17, which allows you to name the layer comp and set parameters.

Using Layer Comps

Multiple layer comps, shown in Figure 18, make it easy to switch back and forth between variations on an image theme. Say, for example, that you want to show a client multiple arrangements of layers. The layer comp is an ideal tool for this.

FIGURE 17
New Layer Comp dialog box

Type new comp name

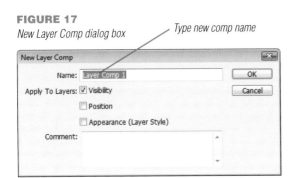

FIGURE 18
Multiple Layer Comps in image

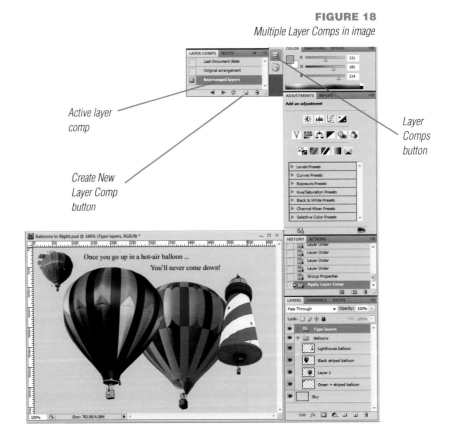

Active layer comp

Create New Layer Comp button

Layer Comps button

FIGURE 19
New Group dialog box

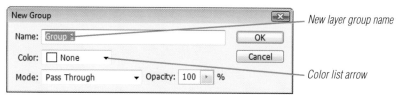

New layer group name

Color list arrow

FIGURE 20
New layer group in Layers panel

New layer group

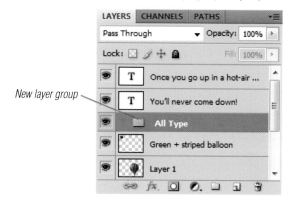

FIGURE 21
Layers added to the All Type layer group

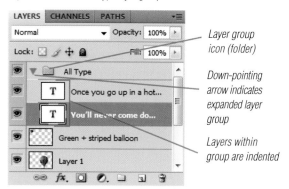

Layer group icon (folder)

Down-pointing arrow indicates expanded layer group

Layers within group are indented

Create a layer group

1. Click the **Green + striped balloon layer**, click the **Layers panel list arrow** ▾☰, then click **New Group**.

   The New Group dialog box opens, as shown in Figure 19.

   > TIP Photoshop automatically places a new layer group above the active layer.

2. Type **All Type** in the Name text box.

3. Click the **Color list arrow**, click **Green**, then click **OK.**

   The New Group dialog box closes. Compare your Layers panel to Figure 20.

You used the Layers panel menu to create a layer group, then named and applied a color to it. This new group will contain all the type layers in the image.

Move layers to the layer group

1. Click the **Once you go up in a hot-air balloon layer** on the Layers panel, then drag it on to the **All Type layer group**.

2. Click the **You'll never come down! layer**, drag it on to the **All Type layer group**, then compare your Layers panel to Figure 21.

   > TIP If the You'll never come down! layer is not below the Once you go up in a hot-air balloon layer, move the layers to match Figure 21.

3. Click the **triangle** ▽ to the left of the layer group icon (folder) to collapse the layer group.

You created a layer group, then moved two layers into that layer group. Creating layer groups is a great organization tool, especially in complex images with many layers.

Lesson 4 Organize Layers with Layer Groups and Colors

PHOTOSHOP 2-19

Rename a layer and adjust opacity

1. Double-click **Layer 1**, type **Yellow striped balloon**, then press **[Enter]** (Win) or **[return]** (Mac).

2. Double-click the **Opacity text box** on the Layers panel, type **85**, then press **[Enter]** (Win) or **[return]** (Mac).

3. Drag the **Yellow striped balloon layer** beneath the Lighthouse balloon layer, then compare your image to Figure 22.

4. Save your work.

You renamed the new layer, adjusted opacity, and rearranged layers.

Create layer comps

1. Click **Window** on the Application bar, then click **Layer Comps**.

2. Click the **Create New Layer Comp button** 🔲 on the Layer Comps panel.

3. Type **Green off/Yellow off** in the Name text box, as shown in Figure 23, then click **OK**.

4. Click the **Indicates layer visibility button** 👁 on the Green + striped balloon layer and the Yellow striped balloon layer.

5. Click the **Update Layer Comp button** 🔄 on the Layer Comps panel. Compare your Layer Comps panel to Figure 24.

6. Save your work, then click the **Layer Comps button** on the vertical dock to close the Layer Comps panel.

You created a Layer Comp in an existing image.

FIGURE 22
Finished image

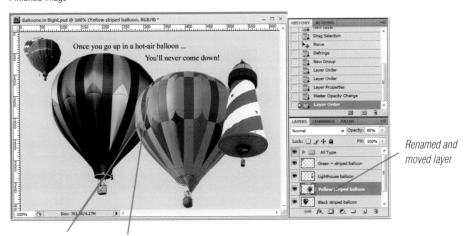

Overlapping balloon layers

Lower opacity allows pixels on lower layers to show through

Renamed and moved layer

FIGURE 23
New Layer Comp dialog box

New Layer Comp name

FIGURE 24
Layer Comps panel

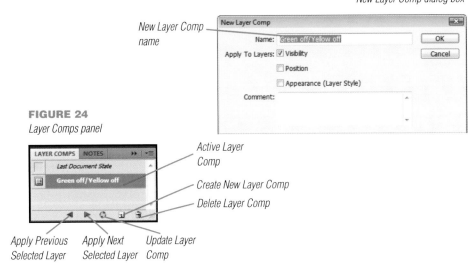

Active Layer Comp

Create New Layer Comp

Delete Layer Comp

Apply Previous Selected Layer Comp

Apply Next Selected Layer Comp

Update Layer Comp

FIGURE 25

Save As dialog box

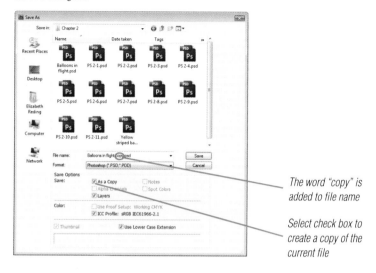

The word "copy" is added to file name

Select check box to create a copy of the current file

Flatten an image

1. Click **File** on the Application bar, then click **Save As**.

2. Click the **As a Copy check box** to add a check mark, then compare your dialog box to Figure 25.

   TIP If "copy" does not display in the File name text box, click this text box and type copy to add it to the name.

3. Click **Save**.

   Photoshop saves and closes a copy of the file containing all the layers and effects.

4. Click **Layer** on the Application bar, then click **Flatten Image**.

5. Click **OK** in the warning box, if necessary, then save your work.

6. Compare your Layers panel to Figure 26.

7. Click the **workspace switcher** on the Application bar, then click **Essentials**.

8. Close all open images, then exit Photoshop.

You saved the file as a copy, and then flattened the image. The image now has a single layer.

FIGURE 26

Flattened image layer

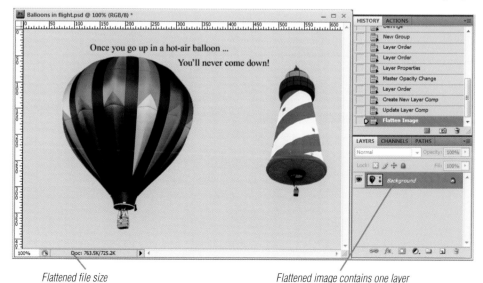

Flattened file size

Flattened image contains one layer

Power User Shortcuts

to do this:	use this method:
Adjust layer opacity	Click Opacity list arrow on Layers panel, drag opacity slider or Double-click Opacity text box, type a percentage
Change measurements	Right-click (Win) or [Ctrl]-click (Mac) ruler
Color a layer	Click Layers panel list arrow, Layer Properties, Color list arrow
Create a layer comp	Click Create New Layer Comps button on the Layer Comps panel 🔲
Create a layer group	▾≣ , New Group
Delete a layer	🗑
Defringe a selection	Layer ➤ Matting ➤ Defringe

to do this:	use this method:
Flatten an image	Layer ➤ Flatten Image
Use the Move tool	🔀 or V
Make a New Background layer from existing layer	Layer ➤ New ➤ Background From Layer
Make a New layer	Layer ➤ New ➤ Layer or 🔲
Rename a layer	Double-click layer name, type new name
Select color range	Select ➤ Color Range
Show/Hide Rulers	View ➤ Rulers [Ctrl][R] (Win) ⌘[R] (Mac)
Update a layer comp	🔄

Key: Menu items are indicated by ➤ between the menu name and its command. Blue bold letters are shortcuts for selecting tools on the Tools panel.

Examine and convert layers.

1. Start Photoshop.
2. Open PS 2-3.psd from the drive and folder where you store your Data Files, update any text layers if necessary, then save it as **Music Store**.
3. Make sure the rulers appear and that pixels are the unit of measurement.
4. Delete the Background layer.
5. Verify that the Rainbow blend layer is active, then convert the image layer to a Background layer.
6. Save your work.

Add and delete layers.

1. Make Layer 2 active.
2. Create a new layer above this layer using the Layer menu.
3. Accept the default name (Layer 4), and change the color of the layer to Red.
4. Delete Layer 4.
5. Make Layer 2 active (if it is not already the active layer), then create a new layer using the Create a new layer button on the Layers panel.
6. Save your work.

Add a selection from one image to another.

1. Open PS 2-4.psd.
2. Reposition this image of a horn by dragging the window to the right of the Music Store image.
3. Open the Color Range dialog box. (*Hint*: Use the Select menu.)
4. Verify that the Image option button is selected, the Invert check box is selected, then set the Fuzziness to 0.
5. Sample the white background in the preview window in the dialog box, then close the dialog box.
6. Use the Move tool to drag the selection into the Music Store image.
7. Position the selection so that the upper-left edge of the instrument matches the sample shown in Figure 27.
8. Defringe the horn selection (in the Music Store image) using a 3 pixel width.
9. Close PS 2-4.psd.
10. Drag Layer 4 above Layer 3.
11. Rename Layer 4 **Horn**.
12. Change the opacity for the Horn layer to 55%.
13. Drag the Horn layer so it is beneath Layer 2.
14. Hide Layer 1.
15. Hide the rulers.
16. Save your work.

Working with Layers

Organize layers with layer groups and colors.

1. Create a Layer Group called **Type Layers** and assign the color yellow to the group.
2. Drag the following layers into the Type Layers folder: Allegro, Music Store, Layer 2.
3. Delete Layer 2, then collapse the Layer Group folder.
4. Move the Notes layer beneath the Horn layer.
5. Create a layer comp called **Notes layer on**.
6. Update the layer comp.
7. Hide the Notes layer.
8. Create a new layer comp called **Notes layer off**, then update the layer comp.
9. Display the previous layer comp, save your work, then close the tab group. (*Hint:* Click the Layer Comps list arrow, then click Close Tab Group.)
10. Save a copy of the Music Store file using the default naming scheme (add 'copy' to the end of the existing filename).
11. Flatten the original image. (*Hint:* Be sure to discard hidden layers.)
12. Save your work, then compare your image to Figure 27.

FIGURE 27
Completed Skills Review

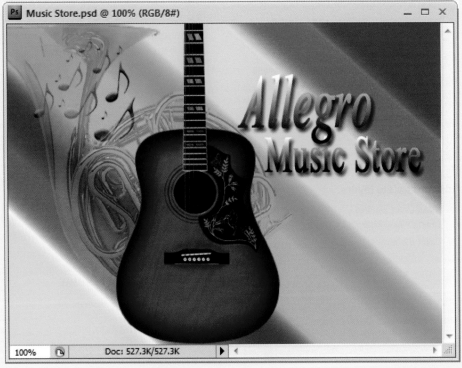

A credit union is developing a hotline for members to use to help abate credit card fraud as soon as it occurs. They're going to distribute ten thousand refrigerator magnets over the next three weeks. As part of their effort to build community awareness of the project, they've sponsored a contest for the magnet design. You decide to enter the contest.

1. Open PS 2-5.psd, then save it as **Combat Fraud**. The Palatino Linotype font is used in this file. Please make a substitution if this font is not available on your computer.
2. Open PS 2-6.psd, use the Color Range dialog box or any selection tool on the Tools panel to select the cell phone image, then drag it to the Outlaw Fraud image.
3. Rename the newly created layer **Cell Phone** if necessary, then apply a color to the layer on the Layers panel. Make sure the Cell Phone layer is beneath the type layers.
4. Convert the Background layer to an image layer, then rename it **Banner**.
5. Change the opacity of the Banner layer to any setting you like.
6. Defringe the Cell Phone layer using the pixel width of your choice.
7. Save your work, close PS 2-6.psd, then compare your image to the sample shown in Figure 28.

FIGURE 28
Completed Project Builder 1

Working with Layers

Your local 4-H chapter wants to promote its upcoming fair and has hired you to create a promotional billboard commemorating this event. The Board of Directors decides that the billboard should be humorous.

1. Open PS 2-7.psd, then save it as **4H Billboard**. Substitute any missing fonts.
2. Open PS 2-8.psd, use the Color Range dialog box or any selection tool on the Tools panel to create a marquee around the llama, then drag the selection to the 4-H Billboard image.
3. Name the new layer **Llama**.
4. Change the opacity of the Llama layer to 90% and defringe the layer containing the llama.
5. Save your work, then compare your image to the sample shown in Figure 29.

FIGURE 29
Completed Project Builder 2

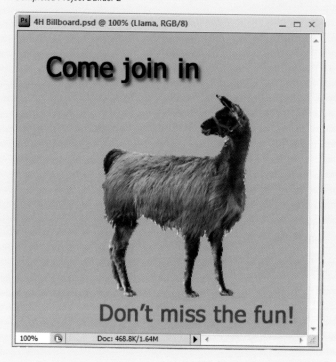

Working with Layers

A friend of yours has designed a new heat-absorbing coffee cup for take-out orders. She is going to present the prototype to a prospective vendor, but first needs to print a brochure. She's asked you to design an eye-catching cover.

1. Open PS 2-9.psd, update the text layers if necessary, then save it as **Coffee Cover**. The Garamond font is used in this file. Please make a substitution if this font is not available on your computer.
2. Open PS 2-10.psd, then drag the entire image to Coffee Cover.
3. Close PS 2-10.psd.
4. Rename Layer 1 with the name **Mocha**.
5. Delete the Background layer and convert the Mocha layer into a new Background layer.
6. Reposition the layer objects so they look like the sample. (*Hint*: You might have to reorganize the layers in the stack so all layers are visible.)
7. Create a layer group above Layer 2, name it **Hot Shot Text**, apply a color of your choice to the layer group, then drag the type layers to it.
8. Save your work, then compare your image to Figure 30.

FIGURE 30
Completed Design Project

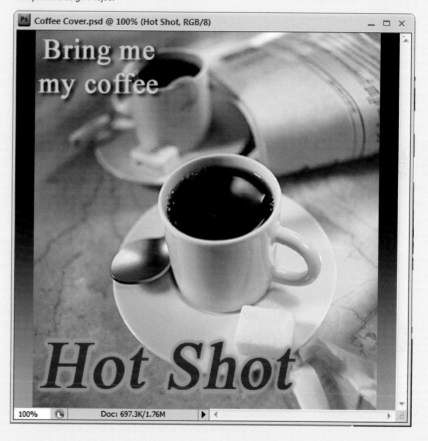

Harvest Market, a line of natural food stores, and the trucking associations in your state have formed a coalition to deliver fresh fruit and vegetables to food banks and other food distribution programs. The truckers want to promote the project by displaying a sign on their trucks. Your task is to create a design that will become the Harvest Market logo. Keep in mind that the design will be seen from a distance.

1. Open PS 2-11.psd, then save it as **Harvest Market**. Update the text layers as necessary.

2. Obtain at least two images of different-sized produce. You can obtain images by using what is available on your computer, scanning print media, or connecting to the Internet and downloading images.

3. Open one of the produce files, select it, then drag or copy it to the Harvest Market image. (*Hint*: Experiment with some of the other selection tools. Note that some tools require you to copy and paste the image after you select it.)

4. Repeat step 3, then close the two produce image files.

5. Set the opacity of the Market layer to 80%.

6. Arrange the layers so that smaller images appear on top of the larger ones. (You can move layers to any location in the image you choose.)

7. Create a layer group for the type layers, and apply a color to it.

Working with Layers

8. You can delete any layers you feel do not add to the image. (In the sample image, the Veggies layer has been deleted.)

9. Save your work, then compare your image to Figure 31.

10. What are the advantages and disadvantages of using multiple images? How would you assess the ease and efficiency of the selection techniques you've learned? Which styles did you apply to the type layers, and why?

FIGURE 31
Completed Portfolio Project

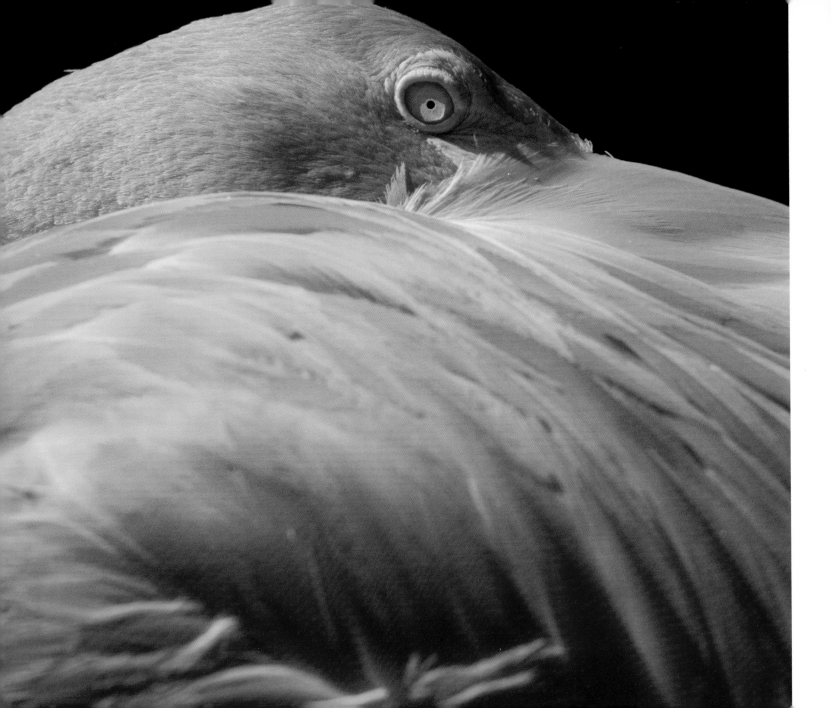

MAKING
SELECTIONS

1. Make a selection using shapes

2. Modify a marquee

3. Select using color and modify a selection

4. Add a vignette effect to a selection

Combining Images

Most Photoshop images are created using a technique called **compositing**—combining images from different sources. These sources include other Photoshop images, royalty-free images, pictures taken with digital cameras, and scanned artwork. How you get all those images into your Photoshop images is an art unto itself. You can include additional images by using tools on the Tools panel and menu commands. And to work with all these images, you need to know how to select them—or exactly the parts you want to work with.

Understanding Selection Tools

The two basic methods you can use to make selections are using a tool or using color. You can use three free-form tools to create your own unique selections, four fixed area tools to create circular or rectangular selections, and a wand tool to make selections using color. In addition, you can use menu commands to increase

or decrease selections that you made with these tools, or make selections based on color.

Understanding Which Selection Tool to Use

With so many tools available, how do you know which one to use? After you become familiar with the different selection options, you'll learn how to look at images and evaluate selection opportunities. With experience, you'll learn how to identify edges that can be used to isolate imagery, and how to spot colors that can be used to isolate a specific object.

Combining Imagery

After you decide on an object that you want to place in a Photoshop image, you can add the object to another image by cutting, copying, and pasting, dragging and dropping objects using the Move tool, or using the **Clipboard**, the temporary storage area provided by your operating system.

Tools You'll Use

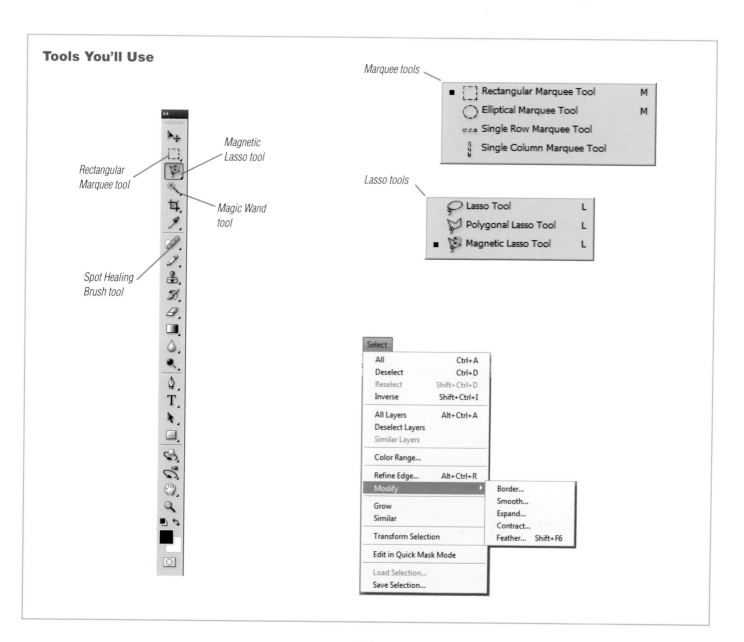

Marquee tools

- ■ ⬚ Rectangular Marquee Tool   M
- ◯ Elliptical Marquee Tool   M
- ⚏ Single Row Marquee Tool
- ⁞ Single Column Marquee Tool

Magnetic Lasso tool

Rectangular Marquee tool

Magic Wand tool

Spot Healing Brush tool

Lasso tools

- ◯ Lasso Tool   L
- ◺ Polygonal Lasso Tool   L
- ■ ◺ Magnetic Lasso Tool   L

Select	
All	Ctrl+A
Deselect	Ctrl+D
Reselect	Shift+Ctrl+D
Inverse	Shift+Ctrl+I
All Layers	Alt+Ctrl+A
Deselect Layers	
Similar Layers	
Color Range...	
Refine Edge...	Alt+Ctrl+R
Modify ▶	
Grow	
Similar	
Transform Selection	
Edit in Quick Mask Mode	
Load Selection...	
Save Selection...	

Modify ▶
- Border...
- Smooth...
- Expand...
- Contract...
- Feather...   Shift+F6

MAKE A SELECTION
USING SHAPES

What You'll Do

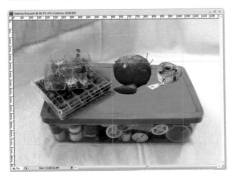

 In this lesson, you'll make selections using a marquee tool and a lasso tool, position a selection with the Move tool, deselect a selection, and drag a complex selection into another image.

Selecting by Shape

The Photoshop selection tools make it easy to select objects that are rectangular or elliptical in nature. It would be a boring world if every image we wanted fell into one of those categories, so fortunately, they don't. While some objects are round or square, most are unusual in shape. Making selections can sometimes be a painstaking process because many objects don't have clearly defined edges. To select an object by shape, you need to click the appropriate tool on the Tools panel, then drag the pointer around the object. The selected area is defined by a **marquee**, or series of dotted lines, as shown in Figure 1.

Creating a Selection

Drawing a rectangular marquee is easier than drawing an elliptical marquee, but with practice, you'll be able to create both types of marquees easily. Table 1 lists the tools you can use to make selections using

shapes. Figure 2 shows a marquee surrounding an irregular shape.

> QUICKTIP
>
> A marquee is sometimes referred to as *marching ants* because the dots within the marquee appear to be moving.

Using Fastening Points

Each time you click one of the marquee tools, a fastening point is added to the image. A **fastening point** is an anchor within the marquee. When the marquee pointer reaches the initial fastening point (after making its way around the image), a very small circle appears on the pointer, indicating that you have reached the starting point. Clicking the pointer when this circle appears closes the marquee. Some fastening points, such as those in a circular marquee, are not visible, while others, such as those created by the Polygonal or Magnetic Lasso tools, are visible.

Making Selections

Selecting, Deselecting, and Reselecting

After a selection is made, you can move, copy, transform, or make adjustments to it. A selection stays selected until you unselect, or **deselect**, it. You can deselect a selection by clicking Select on the Application bar, then clicking Deselect. You can reselect a deselected object by clicking Select on the Application bar, then clicking Reselect.

QUICKTIP

You can select the entire image by clicking Select on the Application bar, then clicking All.

FIGURE 1
Elliptical Marquee tool used to create marquee

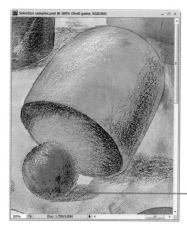

Elliptical Marquee
tool surrounds
object

QUICKTIP

Correcting a Selection Error

At some point, you'll spend a lot of time making a complex selection only to realize that the wrong layer was active. Remember the History panel? Every action you do is automatically recorded, and you can use the selection state to retrace your steps and recoup the time spent. Your fix may be as simple as selecting the proper History state and changing the active layer in the Layers panel.

FIGURE 2
Marquee surrounding irregular shape

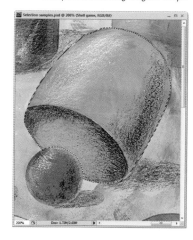

TABLE 1: Selection Tools by Shape

tool	button	effect
Rectangular Marquee tool		Creates a rectangular selection. Press [Shift] while dragging to create a square.
Elliptical Marquee tool		Creates an elliptical selection. Press [Shift] while dragging to create a circle.
Single Row Marquee tool		Creates a 1-pixel-wide row selection.
Single Column Marquee tool		Creates a 1-pixel-wide column selection.
Lasso tool		Creates a freehand selection.
Polygonal Lasso tool		Creates straight line selections. Press [Alt] (Win) or [option] (Mac) to create freehand segments.
Magnetic Lasso tool		Creates selections that snap to an edge of an object. Press [Alt] (Win) or [option] (Mac) to alternate between freehand and magnetic line segments.

Placing a Selection

You can place a selection in a Photoshop image in many ways. You can copy or cut a selection, then paste it to a different location in the same image or to a different image. You can also use the Move tool to drag a selection to a new location.

Using Guides

Guides are non-printing horizontal and vertical lines that you can display on top of an image to help you position a selection. You can create an unlimited number of horizontal and vertical guides. You create a guide by displaying the rulers, positioning the pointer on either ruler, then clicking and dragging the guide into position. Figure 3 shows the creation of a horizontal guide in a file that contains two existing guides. You delete a guide by selecting the Move tool on the Tools panel, positioning the pointer over the guide, then clicking and dragging it back

to its ruler. If the Snap feature is enabled, as you drag an object toward a guide, the object will be pulled toward the guide. To turn on the Snap feature, click View on the Application bar, then click Snap. A check mark appears to the left of the command if the feature is enabled.

FIGURE 3
Creating guides in image

Dragging a guide to a new location

FIGURE 4

Rectangular Marquee tool selection

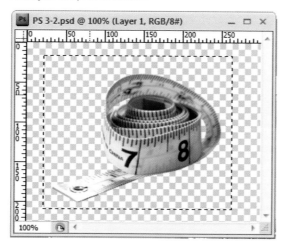

TABLE 2: Working with a Selection

if you want to:	then do this:
Move a selection (an image) using the mouse	Position the ⊹ over the selection, then drag the marquee and its contents
Copy a selection to the Clipboard	Activate image containing the selection, click Edit ➢ Copy
Cut a selection to the Clipboard	Activate image containing the selection, click Edit ➢ Cut
Paste a selection from the Clipboard	Activate image where you want the selection, click Edit ➢ Paste
Delete a selection	Make selection, then press [Delete] (Win) or [delete] (Mac)
Deselect a selection	Press [Ctrl][D] (Win) or ⌘[D] (Mac)

Lesson 1 Make a Selection Using Shapes

Create a selection with the Rectangular Marquee tool

1. Start Photoshop, open PS 3-1.psd from the drive and folder where you store your Data Files, save it as **Sewing Box**, then click **OK** if the Maximize compatibility dialog box displays.
2. Click the **workspace switcher** on the Application bar, click **Analysis**, click the **Layers tab**, then display the rulers (if necessary) in pixels.
3. Open PS 3-2.psd, then display the rulers in pixels for this image (if necessary).
4. Click the **Rectangular Marquee tool** ⬚ on the Tools panel.
5. Make sure the value in the Feather text box on the options bar is **0 px**.

   Feathering determines the amount of blur between the selection and the pixels surrounding it.
6. Drag the **Marquee pointer** ╋ to select the tape measure from approximately **20 H/20 V** to **260 H/210 V**. See Figure 4.

   The first measurement refers to the horizontal ruler (H); the second measurement refers to the vertical ruler (V).

   TIP You can also use the X/Y coordinates displayed in the Info panel.
7. Click the **Move tool** ⊹ on the Tools panel, then drag the selection to any location in the Sewing Box image.

   The selection now appears in the Sewing Box image on a new layer (Layer 1).

   TIP Table 2 describes methods you can use to work with selections in an image.

Using the Rectangular Marquee tool, you created a selection in an image, then you dragged that selection into another image. This left the original image intact, and created a copy of the selection in the destination image.

PHOTOSHOP 3-7

Position a selection with the Move tool

1. Verify that the **Move tool** ⊹ is selected on the Tools panel, and display the rulers (if necessary).

2. If you do not see guides in the Sewing Box image, click **View** on the Application bar, point to **Show**, then click **Guides**.

3. Drag the **tape measure** so that the top-right corner snaps to the ruler guides at approximately **1030 H/250 V**. Compare your image to Figure 5.

   Did you feel the snap to effect as you positioned the selection within the guides? This feature makes it easy to properly position objects within an image.

   > TIP If you didn't feel the image snap to the guides, click View on the Application bar, point to Snap To, then click Guides.

4. Rename Layer 1 **Tape Measure**.

You used the Move tool to reposition a selection in an existing image, then you renamed the layer.

FIGURE 5
Rectangular selection in image

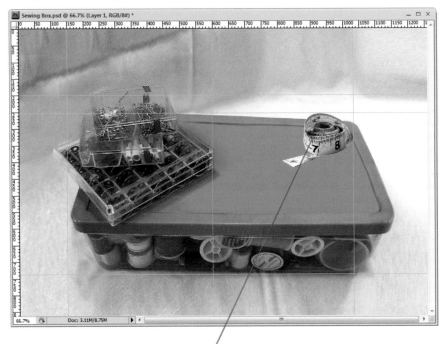

Tape measure

Using Smart Guides

Wouldn't it be great to be able to see a vertical or horizontal guide as you move an object? Using Smart Guides, you can do just that. Smart Guides are turned on by clicking View on the Application bar, pointing to Show, then clicking Smart Guides. Once this feature is turned on, horizontal and vertical purple guidelines appear automatically when you draw a shape or move an object. This feature allows you to align layer content as you move it.

FIGURE 6
Deselect command

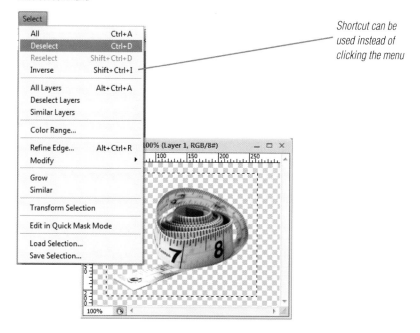

Shortcut can be used instead of clicking the menu

Deselect a selection

1. Click **Window** on the Application bar, then click **PS 3-2.psd**.

   TIP   If you can see the window of the image you want anywhere on the screen, you can just click it to make it active instead of using the Window menu.

2. Click **Select** on the Application bar, then click **Deselect**, as shown in Figure 6.

You hid the active layer, then used the Deselect command on the Select menu to deselect the object you had moved into this image. When you deselect a selection, the marquee no longer surrounds it.

FIGURE 7
Save Selection dialog box

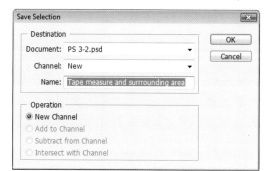

Saving and loading a selection

Any selection can be saved independently of the surrounding image, so that if you want to use it again in the image, you can do so without having to retrace it using one of the marquee tools. Once a selection is made, you can save it in the image by clicking Select on the Application bar, then clicking Save Selection. The Save Selection dialog box opens, as shown in Figure 7; be sure to give the selection a meaningful name. When you want to load a saved selection, click Select on the Application bar, then click Load Selection. Click the Channel list arrow, click the named selection, then click OK.

Lesson 1   Make a Selection Using Shapes

Create a selection with the Magnetic Lasso tool

1. Click the **Magnetic Lasso tool** 🔲 on the Tools panel, then change the settings on the options bar so that they are the same as those shown in Figure 8. Table 3 describes Magnetic Lasso tool settings.

2. Open PS 3-3.psd from the drive and folder where you store your Data Files.

3. Click the **Magnetic Lasso tool pointer** 🔲 once anywhere on the edge of the pin cushion, to create your first fastening point.

   TIP   If you click a spot that is not at the edge of the pin cushion, press [Esc] (Win) or ⌘ [Z] (Mac) to undo the action, then start again.

4. Drag the **Magnetic Lasso tool pointer** 🔲 slowly around the pin cushion (clicking at the top of each pin may be helpful) until it is almost entirely selected, then click directly over the initial fastening point. See Figure 9.

   Don't worry about all the nooks and crannies surrounding the pin cushion: the Magnetic Lasso tool will select those automatically. You will see a small circle next to the pointer when it is directly over the initial fastening point, indicating that you are closing the selection. The individual segments turn into a marquee.

   TIP   If you feel that the Magnetic Lasso tool is missing some major details while you're tracing, you can insert additional fastening points by clicking the pointer while dragging. For example, click the mouse button at a location where you want to change the selection shape.

You created a selection with the Magnetic Lasso tool.

FIGURE 8
Options for the Magnetic Lasso tool

FIGURE 9
Creating a selection with the Magnetic Lasso tool

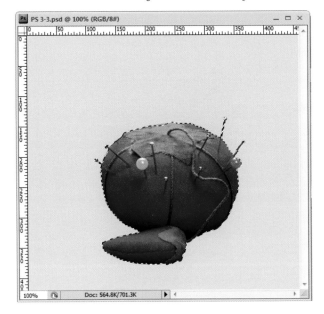

Mastering the art of selections

You might feel that it is difficult when you first start making selections. Making selections is a skill, and like most skills, it takes a lot of practice to become proficient. In addition to practice, make sure that you're comfortable in your work area, that your hands are steady, and that your mouse is working well. A non-optical mouse that is dirty will make selecting an onerous task, so make sure your mouse is well cared for and is functioning correctly.

FIGURE 10

Selection copied into image

Defringing the layer
reduces the amount
of the original
background that
appears; your results
will vary

Complex selection
includes only object,
no background

TABLE 3: Magnetic Lasso Tool Settings

setting	description
Feather	The amount of blur between the selection and the pixels surrounding it. This setting is measured in pixels and can be a value between 0 and 250.
Anti-alias	The smoothness of the selection, achieved by softening the color transition between edge and background pixels.
Width	The interior width by detecting an edge from the pointer. This setting is measured in pixels and can have a value from 1 to 40.
Contrast	The tool's sensitivity. This setting can be a value between 1 percent and 100 percent: higher values detect high-contrast edges.
Frequency	The rate at which fastening points are applied. This setting can be a value between 0 and 100: higher values insert more fastening points.

Move a complex selection to an existing image

1. Click the **Move tool** ⊹ on the Tools panel.

   TIP   You can also click the Click to open the Tool Preset picker list arrow on the options bar, then double-click the Move tool.

2. Use the **Move tool pointer** ⊹ to drag the pin cushion selection to the Sewing Box image.

   The selection appears on a new layer (Layer 1).

3. Drag the object so that the left edge of the pin cushion snaps to the guide at approximately **600 Y** and the top of the pin cushion snaps to the guide at **200 X** using the coordinates on the info panel.

4. Use the Layer menu to defringe the new Layer 1 at a width of **1** pixel.

5. Close the PS 3-3.psd image without saving your changes.

6. Rename the new layer **Pin Cushion** in the Sewing Box image.

7. Save your work, then compare your image to Figure 10.

8. Click **Window** on the Application bar, then click **PS 3-2.psd.**

9. Close the PS 3-2.psd image without saving your changes.

You dragged a complex selection into an existing Photoshop image. You positioned the object using ruler guides and renamed a layer. You also defringed a selection to eliminate its white border.

MODIFY A
MARQUEE

What You'll Do

 In this lesson, you'll move and enlarge a marquee, drag a selection into a Photoshop image, then position a selection using ruler guides.

Changing the Size of a Marquee

Not all objects are easy to select. Sometimes, when you make a selection, you might need to change the size or shape of the marquee.

The options bar contains selection buttons that help you add to and subtract from a marquee, or intersect with a selection. The marquee in Figure 11 was modified into the one shown in Figure 12 by clicking the Add to selection button. After the Add to selection button is active, you can draw an additional marquee (directly adjacent to the selection), and it will be added to the current marquee.

One method you can use to increase the size of a marquee is the Grow command. After you make a selection, you can increase the marquee size by clicking Select on the Application bar, then by clicking Grow. The Grow command selects pixels adjacent to the marquee that have colors similar to those specified by the Magic Wand tool. The Similar command selects both adjacent and non-adjacent pixels.

QUICKTIP

While the Grow command selects adjacent pixels that have similar colors, the Expand command increases a selection by a specific number of pixels.

Modifying a Marquee

While a selection is active, you can modify the marquee by expanding or contracting it, smoothing out its edges, or enlarging it to add a border around the selection. These four commands, Expand, Contract, Smooth, and Border, are submenus of the Modify command, which is found on the Select menu. For example, you might want to enlarge your selection. Using the Expand command, you can increase the size of the selection, as shown in Figure 13.

Making Selections

Moving a Marquee

After you create a marquee, you can move the marquee to another location in the same image or to another image entirely. You might want to move a marquee if you've drawn it in the wrong image or the wrong location. Sometimes it's easier to draw a marquee elsewhere on the page, and then move it to the desired location.

QUICKTIP

You can always hide and display layers as necessary to facilitate making a selection.

FIGURE 12
Selection with additions

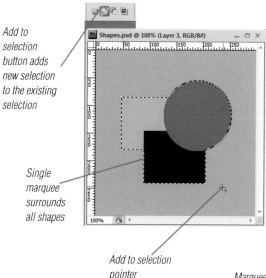

Add to selection button adds new selection to the existing selection

Single marquee surrounds all shapes

Add to selection pointer

FIGURE 11
New selection

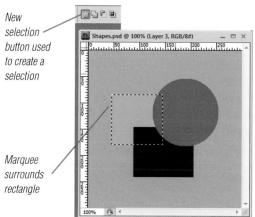

New selection button used to create a selection

Marquee surrounds rectangle

Using the Quick Selection Tool

The Quick Selection tool lets you paint-to-select an object from the interior using a resizeable brush. As you paint the object, the selection grows. Using the Auto-Enhance check box, rough edges and blockiness are automatically reduced to give you a perfect selection. As with other selection tools, the Quick Selection tool has options to add and subtract from your selection.

FIGURE 13
Expanded selection

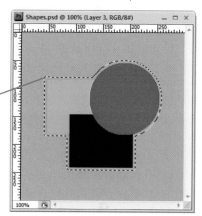

Marquee expanded by 5 pixels

Adding and subtracting from a selection

Of course knowing how to make a selection is important, but it's just as important to know how to make alterations in an existing selection. Sometimes it's almost impossible to create that perfect marquee on the first try. Perhaps your hand moved while you were tracing, or you just got distracted. Using the Add to selection, Subtract from selection, and Intersect with selection buttons (which appear with all selection tools), you can alter an existing marquee without having to start from scratch.

Move and enlarge a marquee

1. Open PS 3-4.psd from the drive and folder where you store your Data Files. Change the zoom factor to **200%**.

2. Click the **Elliptical Marquee tool** ◯ on the Tools panel.

   | TIP The Elliptical Marquee tool might be hidden under the Rectangular Marquee tool.

3. Click the **New selection button** ▢ on the options bar (if it is not already selected).

4. Drag the **Marquee pointer** ╋ to select the area from approximately **150 X/50 Y** to **200 X/130 Y**. Compare your image to Figure 14.

5. Position the **pointer** ▷⋮⋮ in the center of the selection.

6. Drag the **Move pointer** ▶ so the marquee covers the thimble, at approximately **100 X/100 Y**, as shown in Figure 15.

   | TIP You can also nudge a selection to move it, by pressing the arrow keys. Each time you press an arrow key, the selection moves one pixel in the direction of the arrow.

7. Click the **Magic Wand tool** ⚲ on the Tools panel, then enter a Tolerance of **16,** and select the **Anti-alias** and **Contiguous checkboxes**.

8. Click **Select** on the Application bar, then click **Similar**.

9. Click **Select** on the Application bar, point to **Modify**, then click **Expand**.

10. Type **1** in the Expand By text box of the Expand Selection dialog box, then click **OK**.

11. Deselect the selection.

You created a marquee, then dragged the marquee to reposition it. You then enlarged a selection marquee by using the Similar and Expand commands.

FIGURE 14
Selection in image

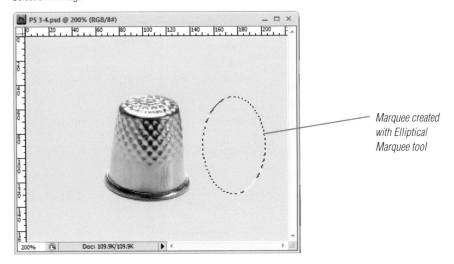

Marquee created with Elliptical Marquee tool

FIGURE 15
Moved selection

New marquee location

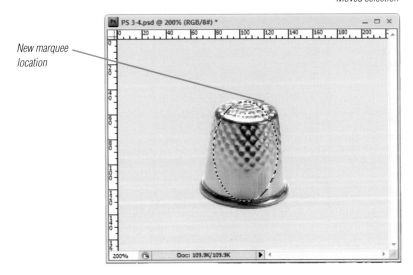

FIGURE 16

Quick Selection tool settings

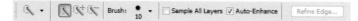

FIGURE 17

Selection in file

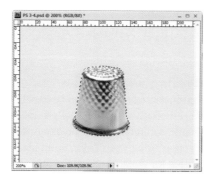

FIGURE 18

Selection moved to the Sewing Box image

Use the Quick Selection tool

1. Click the **Quick Selection tool** ![icon] on the Tools panel, then adjust your settings using Figure 16.

   TIP If you need to change the Brush settings, click Brush list arrow on the options bar, then drag the sliders so the settings are 10 px diameter, 0% hardness, 1% spacing, 0° angle, 100% roundness, and Pen Pressure size.

2. Position the pointer in the **center of the thimble,** then slowly drag the pointer to the outer edges until the object is selected. See Figure 17.

   TIP Sometimes making a selection is easy, sometimes . . . not so much. Time and practice will hone your selection skills. It will get easier.

3. Click the **Move tool** ![icon] on the Tools panel.

4. Position the **Move pointer** ![icon] over the selection, then drag the **thimble** to the Sewing Box image.

5. Drag the **thimble** so that it is to the left of the pin cushion and snaps to the vertical guide at approximately **600 X/550Y**.

6. Defringe the thimble using a setting of **1** pixel.

7. Rename the new layer **Thimble**.

8. Save your work on the sewing box image, then compare your image to Figure 18.

9. Make **PS 3-4.psd** active.

10. Close PS 3-4.psd without saving your changes.

You selected an object using the Quick Selection tool, then you dragged the selection into an existing image.

SELECT USING COLOR AND
MODIFY A SELECTION

What You'll Do

In this lesson, you'll make selections using both the Color Range command and the Magic Wand tool. You'll also flip a selection, then fix an image using the Healing Brush tool.

Selecting with Color

Selections based on color can be easy to make, especially when the background of an image is different from the image itself. High contrast between colors is an ideal condition for making selections based on color. You can make selections using color with the Color Range command on the Select menu, or you can use the Magic Wand tool on the Tools panel.

Using the Magic Wand Tool

When you select the Magic Wand tool, the following options are available on the options bar, as shown in Figure 19:

- The four selection buttons.
- The Tolerance setting, which allows you to specify whether similar pixels will be selected. This setting has a value from 0 to 255, and the lower the value, the closer in color the selected pixels will be.
- The Anti-alias check box, which softens the selection's appearance.
- The Contiguous check box, which lets you select pixels that are next to one another.
- The Sample All Layers check box, which lets you select pixels from multiple layers at once.

Knowing which selection tool to use

The hardest part of making a selection might be determining which selection tool to use. How are you supposed to know if you should use a marquee tool or a lasso tool? The first question you need to ask yourself is, "What do I want to select?" Becoming proficient in making selections means that you need to assess the qualities of the object you want to select, and then decide which method to use. Ask yourself: Does the object have a definable shape? Does it have an identifiable edge? Are there common colors that can be used to create a selection?

Using the Color Range Command

You can use the Color Range command to make the same selections as with the Magic Wand tool. When you use the Color Range command, the Color Range dialog box opens. This dialog box lets you use the pointer to identify which colors you want to use to make a selection. You can also select the Invert check box to *exclude* the chosen color from the selection. The **fuzziness** setting is similar to tolerance, in that the lower the value, the closer in color pixels must be to be selected.

QUICKTIP

Unlike the Magic Wand tool, the Color Range command does not give you the option of excluding contiguous pixels.

Transforming a Selection

After you place a selection in a Photoshop image, you can change its size and other qualities by clicking Edit on the Application bar, pointing to Transform, then clicking any of the commands on the submenu. After you select certain commands, small squares called **handles** surround the selection. To complete the command, you drag a handle until the image has the look you want, then press [Enter] (Win) or [return] (Mac). You can also use the Transform submenu to flip a selection horizontally or vertically.

Understanding the Healing Brush Tool

If you place a selection then notice that the image has a few imperfections, you can fix the image. You can fix imperfections such as dirt, scratches, bulging veins on skin, or wrinkles on a face using the Healing Brush tool on the Tools panel.

QUICKTIP

When correcting someone's portrait, make sure your subject looks the way he or she *thinks* they look. That's not always possible, but strive to get as close as you can to their ideal!

Using the Healing Brush Tool

This tool lets you sample an area, then paint over the imperfections. What is the result? The less-than-desirable pixels seem to disappear into the surrounding image. In addition to matching the sampled pixels, the Healing Brush tool also matches the texture, lighting, and shading of the sample. This is why the painted pixels blend so effortlessly into the existing image. Corrections can be painted using broad strokes, or using clicks of the mouse.

QUICKTIP

To take a sample, press and hold [Alt] (Win) or [option] (Mac) while dragging the pointer over the area you want to duplicate.

FIGURE 19
Options for the Magic Wand tool

Lesson 3   Select Using Color and Modify a Selection

Select using color range

1. Open PS 3-5.psd from the drive and folder where you store your Data Files.
2. Click **Select** on the Application bar, then click **Color Range**.
3. Click the **Image option button** (if it is not already selected).
4. Click the **Invert check box** to add a check mark (if necessary).
5. Verify that your settings match those shown in Figure 20, click anywhere in the background area surrounding the sample image, then click **OK**.

   The Color Range dialog box closes and the spool of thread in the image is selected.
6. Click the **Move tool** ⊹ on the Tools panel.
7. Drag the selection into Sewing Box.psd, then position the selection as shown in Figure 21.
8. Rename the new layer **Thread**.
9. Defringe the spool of thread using a setting of **1** pixel.
10. Activate **PS 3-5.psd**, then close this file without saving any changes.

You made a selection within an image using the Color Range command on the Select menu, and dragged the selection to an existing image.

FIGURE 20
Completed Color Range dialog box

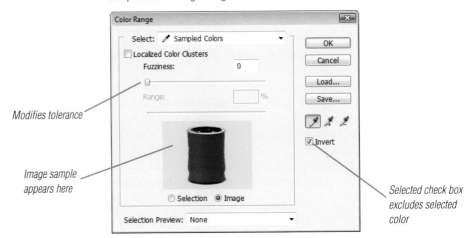

Modifies tolerance

Image sample appears here

Selected check box excludes selected color

FIGURE 21
Selection in image

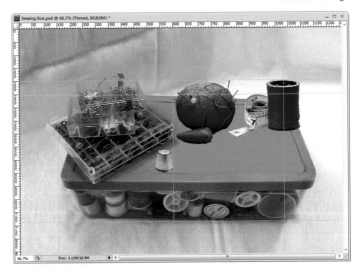

Making Selections

FIGURE 22
Magic Wand tool settings

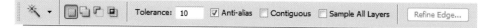

FIGURE 23
Selected area

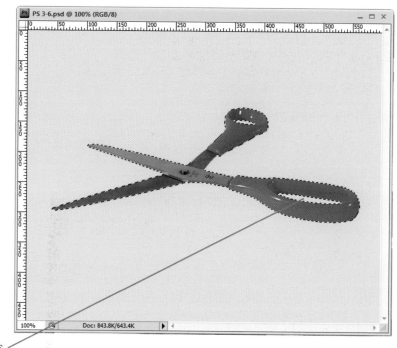

Selection excludes background color

1. Open PS 3-6.psd from the drive and folder where you store your Data Files.

2. Click the **Magic Wand tool** on the Tools panel.

3. Change the settings on the options bar to match those shown in Figure 22.

4. Click anywhere in the background area of the image (such as **50 X/50 Y**).

   TIP Had you selected the Contiguous check box, the pixels within the handles *would not* have been selected. The Contiguous check box is a powerful feature of the Magic Wand tool.

5. Click **Select** on the Application bar, then click **Inverse**. Compare your selection to Figure 23.

6. Click the **Move tool** on the Tools panel, then drag the selection into Sewing Box.psd.

You made a selection using the Magic Wand tool, then dragged it into an existing image. The Magic Wand tool is just one more way you can make a selection. One advantage of using the Magic Wand tool (versus the Color Range tool) is the Contiguous check box, which lets you choose pixels that are next to one another.

Flip a selection

1. Click **Edit** on the Application bar, point to **Transform**, then click **Flip Horizontal**.

2. Rename Layer 1 as **Scissors**.

3. Defringe **Scissors** using a **1** pixel setting.

4. Drag the flipped selection with the **Move tool pointer** ▶⊕ so it is positioned as shown in Figure 24.

5. Make **PS 3-6.psd** the active file, then close PS 3-6.psd without saving your changes.

6. Save your work.

You flipped and repositioned a selection. Sometimes it's helpful to flip an object to help direct the viewer's eye to a desired focal point.

FIGURE 24
Flipped and positioned selection

Getting rid of red eye

When digital photos of your favorite people have that annoying red eye, what do you do? You use the Red Eye tool to eliminate this effect. To do this, select the Red Eye tool (which is grouped on the Tools panel with the Spot Healing Brush tool, the Healing Brush tool, and the Patch tool), then either click a red area of an eye or draw a selection over a red eye. When you release the mouse button, the red eye effect is removed.

Making Selections

FIGURE 25
Healing Brush tool options

FIGURE 26
Healed area

Crack removed
from image

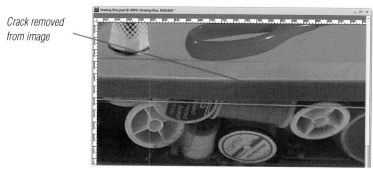

FIGURE 27
Image after using the Healing Brush

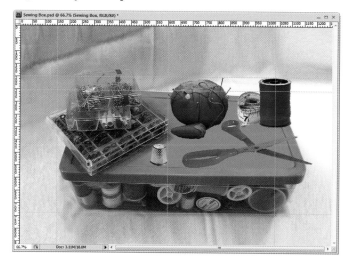

Lesson 3 Select Using Color and Modify a Selection

Fix imperfections with the Healing Brush tool

1. Click the **Sewing Box layer** on the Layers panel, then click the **Zoom tool** on the Tools panel.

2. Click the image with the **Zoom tool pointer** above the pink spool of thread (in the box) at **750 X/600 Y** until the zoom factor is **200%** and you can see the crack in the lid of the box.

3. Click the **Healing Brush tool** on the Tools panel. Change the settings on the options bar to match those shown in Figure 25.

   TIP If you need to change the Brush settings, click the Brush list arrow on the options bar, then drag the sliders so the settings are 10 px diameter, 0% hardness, 1% spacing, 0° angle, 100% roundness, and Pen Pressure size.

4. Press and hold **[Alt]** (Win) or **[option]** (Mac), click next to the crack at any location on the green lid, such as **700 X/580 Y**, then release **[Alt]** (Win) or **[option]** (Mac).

   You sampled an area of the box that is not cracked so that you can use the Healing Brush tool to paint a damaged area with the sample.

5. Click the crack (at approximately **720 X/580 Y**).

6. Repeat steps 4 and 5, each time choosing a new source location, then clicking at a parallel location on the crack.

   Compare the repaired area to Figure 26.

7. Click the **Zoom tool** on the Tools panel press and hold **[Alt]** (Win) or **[option]** (Mac), click the center of the image with the **Zoom tool pointer** until the zoom factor is **66.67%**, then release **[Alt]** (Win) or **[option]** (Mac).

8. Save your work, then compare your image to Figure 27.

You used the Healing Brush tool to fix an imperfection in an image.

ADD A VIGNETTE EFFECT
TO A SELECTION

What You'll Do

In this lesson, you'll create a vignette
effect, using a layer mask and feathering.

Understanding Vignettes

Traditionally, a **vignette** is a picture or
portrait whose border fades into the surrounding color at its edges. You can use a
vignette effect to give an image an old-
world appearance. You can also use a
vignette effect to tone down an overwhelming background. You can create a
vignette effect in Photoshop by creating a
mask with a blurred edge. A **mask** lets you
protect or modify a particular area and is
created using a marquee.

Creating a Vignette

A **vignette effect** uses feathering to fade a
marquee shape. The **feather** setting blurs
the area between the selection and the
surrounding pixels, which creates a distinctive fade at the edge of the selection.
You can create a vignette effect by using a
marquee or lasso tool to create a marquee
in an image layer. After the selection is
created, you can modify the feather setting
(a 10- or 20-pixel setting creates a nice
fade) to increase the blur effect on the outside edge of the selection.

Getting that Healing feeling

The Spot Healing Brush tool works in much the same way as the Healing Brush tool in
that it removes blemishes and other imperfections. Unlike the Healing Brush tool, the
Spot Healing Brush tool does not require you to take a sample. When using the Spot
Healing Brush tool, you must choose whether you want to use a proximity match type
(which uses pixels around the edge of the selection as a patch) or a create texture type
(which uses all the pixels in the selection to create a texture that is used to fix the area).
You also have the option of sampling all the visible layers or only the active layer.

FIGURE 28
Marquee in image

FIGURE 29
Layers panel

Feathered mask creates
vignette effect

FIGURE 30
Vignette in image

Vignette effect
fades border

Lesson 4   Add a Vignette Effect to a Selection

Create a vignette

1. Verify that the **Sewing Box layer** is selected.

2. Click the **Rectangular Marquee tool** ⬚, on the Tools panel.

3. Change the **Feather setting** on the options bar to **20px**.

4. Create a selection with the **Marquee pointer** ┼ from **50 X/50 Y** to **1200 X/800 Y**, as shown in Figure 28.

5. Click **Layer** on the Application bar, point to **Layer Mask**, then click **Reveal Selection**.

   The vignette effect is added to the layer.

   Compare your Layers panel to Figure 29.

6. Click **View** on the Application bar, then click **Rulers** to hide them.

7. Click **View** on the Application bar, then click **Clear Guides**.

8. Save your work, then compare your image to Figure 30.

9. Close the Sewing Box image, select **Essentials** from the workspace switcher, then exit Photoshop.

You created a vignette effect by adding a feathered layer mask. You also rearranged layers and defringed a selection. Once the image was finished, you hid the rulers and cleared the guides.

Power User Shortcuts

to do this:	use this method:
Copy selection	Click Edit ➢ Copy or [Ctrl][C] (Win) or ⌘[C] (Mac)
Create vignette effect	Marquee or Lasso tool, create selection, click Layer ➢ Layer Mask ➢ Reveal Selection
Cut selection	Click Edit ➢ Cut or [Ctrl][X] (Win) or ⌘[X] (Mac)
Deselect object	Select ➢ Deselect or [Ctrl][D] (Win) or ⌘[D] (Mac)
Elliptical Marquee tool	⬭ or [Shift] M
Flip image	Edit ➢ Transform ➢ Flip Horizontal
Grow selection	Select ➢ Grow
Increase selection	Select ➢ Similar
Lasso tool	⬭ or [Shift] L
Magnetic Lasso tool	⬭ or [Shift] L
Move tool	⬭ or V

to do this:	use this method:
Move selection marquee	Position pointer in selection, drag ⬭ to new location
Paste selection	Edit ➢ Paste or [Ctrl][V] (Win) or ⌘[V] (Mac)
Polygonal Lasso tool	⬭ or [Shift] L
Rectangular Marquee tool	⬭ or [Shift] M
Reselect a deselected object	Select ➢ Reselect, or [Shift][Ctrl][D] (Win) or [Shift]⌘[D] (Mac)
Select all objects	Select ➢ All, or [Ctrl][A] (Win) or ⌘[A] (Mac)
Select using color range	Select ➢ Color Range, click sample area
Select using Magic Wand tool	⬭ or W, then click image
Select using Quick Selection tool	⬭ or [Shift] W, then drag pointer over image
Single Column Marquee tool	⬭
Single Row Marquee tool	⬭

Key: Menu items are indicated by ➢ between the menu name and its command. Blue bold letters are shortcuts for selecting tools on the Tools panel.

Make a selection using shapes.

1. Open PS 3-7.psd from the drive and folder where you store your Data Files, substitute any missing fonts, then save it as **Cool cats**.
2. Open PS 3-8.tif.
3. Display the rulers in each image window (if necessary), switch to the Analysis workspace, then display the Layers panel.
4. Use the Rectangular Marquee tool to select the entire image in PS 3-8.tif. (*Hint*: Reset the Feather setting to 0 pixels, if necessary.)
5. Deselect the selection.
6. Use the Magnetic Lasso tool to create a selection surrounding only the Block cat in the image. (*Hint*: You can use the Zoom tool to make the image larger.)
7. Drag the selection into the Cool cats image, positioning it so the right side of the cat is at 490 X, and the bottom of the right paw is at 450 Y.
8. Save your work.
9. Close PS 3-8.tif without saving any changes.

Modify a marquee.

1. Open PS 3-9.tif.
2. Change the settings on the Magic Wand tool to Tolerance = 5, and make sure that the Contiguous check box is selected.
3. Use the Elliptical Marquee tool to create a marquee from 100 X/50 Y to 200 X/100 Y, using a setting of 0 in the Feather text box.
4. Use the Grow command on the Select menu.
5. Use the Inverse command on the Select menu.

6. Drag the selection into the Cool cats image, positioning it so the upper-left corner of the selection is near 0 X/0 Y.
7. Defringe the new layer using a width of 2 pixels.
8. Save your work.
9. Close PS 3-9.tif without saving any changes.

Select using color and modify a selection.

1. Open PS 3-10.tif.
2. Use the Color Range dialog box to select only the kitten.
3. Drag the selection into the Cool cats image.
4. Flip the kitten image (in the Cool cats image) horizontally.

FIGURE 31
Completed Skills Review project

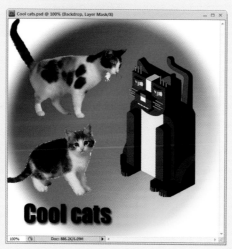

5. Position the kitten image so the bottom right snaps to the ruler guides at 230 X/450 Y.
6. Defringe the kitten using a width of 2 pixels.
7. Save your work.
8. Close PS 3-10.tif without saving any changes.

Add a vignette effect to a selection.

1. Use a 15-pixel feather setting and the Backdrop layer to create an elliptical selection surrounding the contents of the Cool cats image.
2. Add a layer mask that reveals the selection.
3. Hide the rulers and guides, then switch to the Essentials workspace.
4. Save your work.
5. Compare your image to Figure 31.

Making Selections

As a professional photographer, you often take photos of people for use in various publications. You recently took a photograph of a woman that will be used in a marketing brochure. The client is happy with the overall picture, but wants the facial lines smoothed out. You decide to use the Healing Brush tool to ensure that the client is happy with the final product.

1. Open PS 3-11.psd, then save it as **Portrait**.
2. Make a copy of the Original layer using the default name, or the name of your choice.
3. Use the Original copy layer and the Healing Brush tool to smooth the appearance of facial lines in this image. (*Hint*: You may have greater success if you use short strokes with the Healing Brush tool than if you paint long strokes.)
4. Create a vignette effect on the Original copy layer that reveals the selection using an elliptical marquee.
5. Reorder the layers (if necessary), so that the vignette effect is visible.
6. Save your work, then compare your image to the sample shown in Figure 32.

FIGURE 32
Completed Project Builder 1

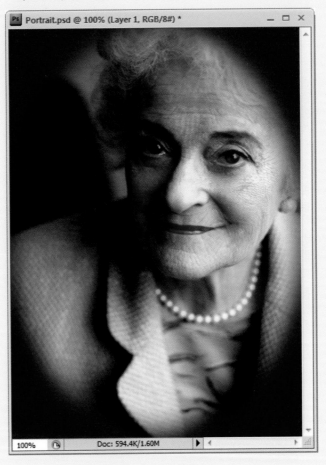

Making Selections

The St. Louis Athletic Association, which sponsors the St. Louis Marathon, is holding a contest for artwork to announce the upcoming race. Submissions can be created on paper or computer-generated. You feel you have a good chance at winning this contest, using Photoshop as your tool.

1. Open PS 3-12.psd, then save it as **Marathon Contest**.
2. Locate at least two pieces of appropriate artwork—either on your hard disk, in a royalty-free collection, or from scanned images—that you can use in this file.
3. Use any appropriate methods to select imagery from the artwork.
4. After the selections have been made, copy each selection into Marathon Contest.
5. Arrange the images into a design that you think will be eye-catching and attractive.
6. Deselect the selections in the files you are no longer using, and close them without saving the changes.
7. Add a vignette effect to the Backdrop layer.
8. Display the type layers if they are hidden.
9. Defringe any layers, as necessary.
10. Save your work, then compare your screen to the sample shown in Figure 33.

FIGURE 33
Completed Project Builder 2

Making Selections

You are aware that there will be an opening in your firm's design department. Before you can be considered for the job, you need to increase your Photoshop compositing knowledge and experience. You have decided to teach yourself, using informational sources on the Internet and images that can be scanned or purchased.

1. Connect to the Internet and use your browser and favorite search engine to find information on image compositing. (Make a record of the site you found so you can use it for future reference, if necessary.)

2. Create a new Photoshop image, using the dimensions of your choice, then save it as **Sample Compositing**.

3. Locate at least two pieces of artwork—either on your hard disk, in a royalty-free collection, or from scanned images—that you can use. (The images can contain people, plants, animals, or inanimate objects.)

4. Select the images in the artwork, then copy each into the Sample Compositing image, using the method of your choice.

5. Rename each of the layers using meaningful names.

6. Apply a color to each new layer.

7. Arrange the images in a pleasing design. (*Hint*: Remember that you can flip any image, if necessary.)

8. Deselect the selections in the artwork, then close the files without saving the changes.

9. If desired, create a background layer for the image.

10. If necessary, add a vignette effect to a layer.

11. Defringe any images as you see necessary.

12. Save your work, then compare your screen to the sample shown in Figure 34.

FIGURE 34
Completed Design Project

At your design firm, a Fortune 500 client plans to start a 24-hour cable sports network called Total Sportz that will cover any nonprofessional sporting event. You have been asked to create some preliminary designs for the network, using images from multiple sources.

1. Open PS 3-13.psd, then save it as **Total Sportz**. (*Hint*: Click Update to close the warning box regarding missing fonts, if necessary.)

2. Locate several pieces of sports-related artwork—either on your hard disk, in a royalty-free collection, or from scanned images. Remember that the images should not show professional sports figures, if possible.

3. Select imagery from the artwork and move it into the Total Sportz image.

4. Arrange the images in an interesting design. (*Hint*: Remember that you can flip any image, if necessary.)

5. Change each layer name to describe the sport in the layer image.

6. Deselect the selections in the files that you used, then close the files without saving the changes.

7. If necessary, add a vignette effect to a layer and/or adjust opacity.

8. Defringe any images (if necessary).

9. Save your work, then compare your image to the sample shown in Figure 35.

FIGURE 35
Completed Portfolio Project

Making Selections

chapter

4

INCORPORATING COLOR
TECHNIQUES

1. Work with color to transform an image

2. Use the Color Picker and the Swatches panel

3. Place a border around an image

4. Blend colors using the Gradient tool

5. Add color to a grayscale image

6. Use filters, opacity, and blending modes

7. Match colors

Using Color

Color can make or break an image. Sometimes colors can draw us into an image; other times they can repel us. We all know which colors we like, but when it comes to creating an image, it is helpful to have some knowledge of color theory and be familiar with color terminology.

Understanding how Photoshop measures, displays, and prints color can be valuable when you create new images or modify existing images. Some colors you choose might be difficult for a professional printer to reproduce or might look muddy when printed. As you become more experienced using color, you will learn which colors reproduce well and which ones do not.

Understanding Color Modes and Color Models

Photoshop displays and prints images using specific color modes. A **mode** is the amount of color data that can be stored in a given file format, based on an established model. A **model** determines how pigments combine to produce resulting colors. This is the way your computer or printer associates a name or number with colors. Photoshop uses standard color models as the basis for its color modes.

Displaying and Printing Images

An image displayed on your monitor, such as an icon on your desktop, is a **bitmap**, a geometric arrangement of different color dots on a rectangular grid. Each dot, called a **pixel**, represents a color or shade. Bitmapped images are *resolution-dependent* and can lose detail—often demonstrated by a jagged appearance—when highly magnified. When printed, images with high resolutions tend to show more detail and subtler color transitions than low-resolution images.

Tools You'll Use

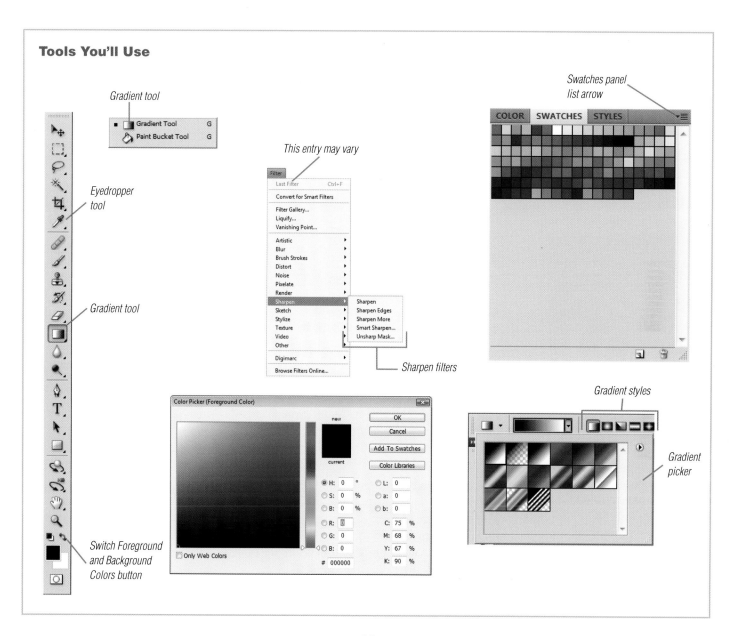

Gradient tool

Swatches panel list arrow

Eyedropper tool

This entry may vary

Gradient tool

Sharpen filters

Switch Foreground and Background Colors button

Gradient styles

Gradient picker

WORK WITH COLOR TO
TRANSFORM AN IMAGE

What You'll Do

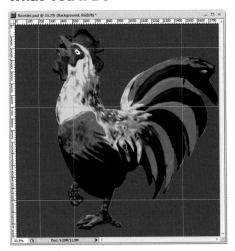

 In this lesson, you'll use the Color panel, the Paint Bucket tool, and the Eyedropper tool to change the background color of an image.

Learning About Color Models

Photoshop reproduces colors using models of color modes. The range of displayed colors, or **gamut**, for each model available in Photoshop is shown in Figure 1. The shape of each color gamut indicates the range of colors it can display. If a color is out of gamut, it is beyond the color space that your monitor can display or that your printer can print. You select the color mode from the Mode command on the Image menu. The available Photoshop color models include Lab, HSB, RGB, CMYK, Bitmap, and Grayscale.

QUICKTIP

A color mode is used to determine which color model will be used to display and print an image.

DESIGNTIP **Understanding the psychology of color**

Have you ever wondered why some colors make you react a certain way? You might have noticed that some colors affect you differently than others. Color is such an important part of our lives, and in Photoshop, it's key. Specific colors are often used in print and web pages to evoke the following responses:

- Blue tends to instill a feeling of safety and stability and is often used by financial services.
- Certain shades of green can generate a soft, calming feeling, while others suggest youthfulness and growth.
- Red commands attention and can be used as a call to action; it can also distract a reader's attention from other content.
- White evokes the feeling of purity and innocence, looks cool and fresh, and is often used to suggest luxury.
- Black conveys feelings of power and strength, but can also suggest darkness and negativity.

Lab Model

The Lab model is based on one luminance (lightness) component and two chromatic components (from green to red, and from blue to yellow). Using the Lab model has distinct advantages: you have the largest number of colors available to you and the greatest precision with which to create them. You can also create all the colors contained by other color models, which are limited in their respective color ranges. The Lab model is device-independent—the colors will not vary, regardless of the hardware. Use this model when working with photo CD images so that you can independently edit the luminance and color values.

HSB Model

Based on the human perception of color, the HSB (Hue, Saturation, Brightness) model has three fundamental characteristics: hue, saturation, and brightness. The color reflected from or transmitted through an object is called **hue**. Expressed as a degree (between 0° and 360°), each hue is identified by a color name (such as red or green). **Saturation** (or *chroma*) is the strength or purity of the color, representing the amount of gray in proportion to hue. Saturation is measured as a percentage from 0% (gray) to 100% (fully saturated). **Brightness** is the measurement of relative lightness or darkness of a color and is measured as a percentage from 0% (black) to 100% (white). Although you can use the HSB model to define a color on the Color panel or in the Color Picker dialog box, Photoshop *does not* offer HSB mode as a choice for creating or editing images.

RGB Mode

Photoshop uses color modes to determine how to display and print an image. Each mode is based on established models used in color reproduction. Most colors in the visible spectrum can be represented by mixing various proportions and intensities of red, green, and blue (RGB) colored light. RGB colors are additive colors. **Additive colors** are used for lighting, video, and computer monitors; color is created by light passing through red, green, and blue phosphors. When the values of red, green, and blue are zero, the result is black; when the values are all 255, the result is white. Photoshop assigns each component of the RGB mode an intensity value. Your colors can vary from monitor to monitor even if you are using the exact RGB values on different computers.

FIGURE 1
Photoshop color gamuts

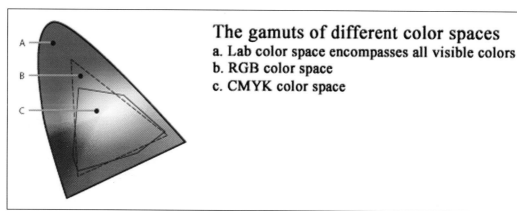

The gamuts of different color spaces
a. Lab color space encompasses all visible colors
b. RGB color space
c. CMYK color space

CMYK Mode

The light-absorbing quality of ink printed on paper is the basis of the CMYK (Cyan, Magenta, Yellow, Black) mode. Unlike the RGB mode—in which components are *combined* to create new colors—the CMYK mode is based on colors being partially *absorbed* as the ink hits the paper and being partially *reflected* back to your eyes. CMYK colors are **subtractive colors**—the *absence* of cyan, magenta, yellow, and black creates white. Subtractive (CMYK) and additive (RGB) colors are complementary colors; a pair from one model creates a color in the other. When combined, cyan, magenta, and yellow absorb all color and produce black. The CMYK mode—in which the lightest colors are assigned the highest percentages of ink colors—is used in four-color process printing. Converting an RGB image into a CMYK image produces a **color separation** (the commercial printing process of separating colors for use with different inks). Note, however, that because your monitor uses RGB mode, you will not see the exact colors until you print the image, and even then the colors can vary depending on the printer and offset press.

Understanding the Bitmap and Grayscale Modes

In addition to the RGB and CMYK modes, Photoshop provides two specialized color modes: bitmap and grayscale. The **bitmap mode** uses black or white color values to represent image pixels, and is a good choice for images with subtle color gradations, such as photographs or painted images. The **grayscale mode** uses up to 256 shades of gray, assigning a brightness value from 0 (black) to 255 (white) to each pixel. Displayed colors can vary from monitor to monitor even if you use identical color settings on different computers.

Changing Foreground and Background Colors

In Photoshop, the **foreground color** is black by default and is used to paint, fill, and apply a border to a selection. The **background color** is white by default and is used to make **gradient fills** (gradual blends of multiple colors) and fill in areas of an image that have been erased. You can change foreground and background colors using the Color panel, the Swatches panel, the Color Picker, or the Eyedropper tool. One method of changing foreground and background colors is **sampling**, in which an existing color is used. You can restore the default colors by clicking the Default Foreground and Background Colors button on the Tools panel, shown in Figure 2. You can apply a color to the background of a layer using the Paint Bucket tool. When you click an image with the Paint Bucket Tool, the current foreground color on the Tools panel fills the active layer.

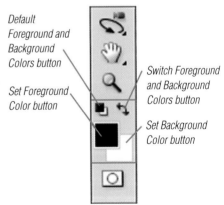

FIGURE 2
Foreground and background color buttons

Default Foreground and Background Colors button

Set Foreground Color button

Switch Foreground and Background Colors button

Set Background Color button

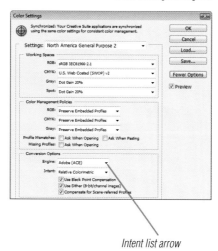

Intent list arrow

Creating a rendering intent

The use of a **rendering intent** determines how colors are converted by a color management system. A **color management system** is used to keep colors looking consistent as they move between devices. Colors are defined and interpreted using a **profile**. You can create a rendering intent by clicking Edit on the Application bar, then clicking Color Settings. Click the More Options button in the Color Settings dialog box, click the Intent list arrow shown in Figure 4, then click one of the four options. Since a gamut is the range of color that a color system can display or print, the rendering intent is constantly evaluating the color gamut and deciding whether or not the colors need adjusting. So, colors that fall inside the destination gamut may not be changed, or they may be adjusted when translated to a smaller color gamut.

Set the default foreground and background colors

1. Start Photoshop, open PS 4-1.psd from the drive and folder where you save your Data Files, then save it as **Rooster**.

   TIP Whenever the Photoshop Format Options dialog box appears, click OK to maximize compatibility.

2. Click the **Default Foreground and Background Colors button** ▪ on the Tools panel.

   TIP If you accidently click the Set foreground color button, the Color Picker (Foreground Color) dialog box opens.

3. Change the status bar so the document sizes display (if necessary).

   TIP Document sizes will not display in the status bar if the image window is too small. Drag the lower-right corner of the image window to expand the window and display the menu button and document sizes.

4. Display the rulers in pixels (if necessary), show the guides (if necessary), then compare your screen to Figure 3.

   TIP You can right-click (Win) or [control]-click (Mac) one of the rulers to choose Pixels, Inches, Centimeters, Millimeters, Points, Picas, or Percent as a unit of measurement, instead of using the Rulers and Units Preferences dialog box.

You set the default foreground and background colors and displayed rulers in pixels.

Change the background color using the Color panel

1. Click the **Background layer** on the Layers panel.

2. Display the History and Layers workspace.

3. Click the **Color panel tab** COLOR (if necessary).

4. Drag each color slider on the Color panel until you reach the values shown in Figure 5.

   The active color changes to the new color. Did you notice that this image is using the RGB mode?

   TIP   You can also double-click each component's text box on the Color panel and type the color values.

5. Click the **Paint Bucket tool** 🖎 on the Tools panel.

   TIP   If the Paint Bucket tool is not visible on the Tools panel, click the Gradient tool on the Tools panel, press and hold the mouse button until the list of hidden tools opens, then click the Paint Bucket tool.

6. Click the image with the **Paint Bucket pointer** 🖎.

7. Drag the **Paint Bucket state** on the History panel onto the **Delete current state button** 🗑.

   TIP   You can also undo the last action by clicking Edit on the menu bar, then clicking Undo Paint Bucket.

You set new values in the Color panel, used the Paint Bucket tool to change the background to that color, then undid the change. You can change colors on the Color panel by dragging the sliders or by typing values in the color text boxes.

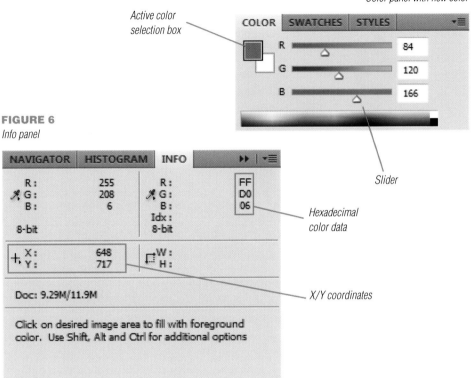

FIGURE 5
Color panel with new color

Active color selection box

Slider

FIGURE 6
Info panel

Hexadecimal color data

X/Y coordinates

Using ruler coordinates

Photoshop rulers run along the top and left sides of the document window. Each point on an image has a horizontal and vertical location. These two numbers, called X and Y coordinates, appear on the Info panel (which is located in the tab group with the Navigator and Histogram panels) as shown in Figure 6. The X coordinate refers to the horizontal location, and the Y coordinate refers to the vertical location. You can use one or both sets of guides to identify coordinates of a location, such as a color you want to sample. If you have difficulty seeing the ruler markings, you can increase the size of the image; the greater the zoom factor, the more detailed the measurement hashes.

FIGURE 7
New foreground color applied to Background layer

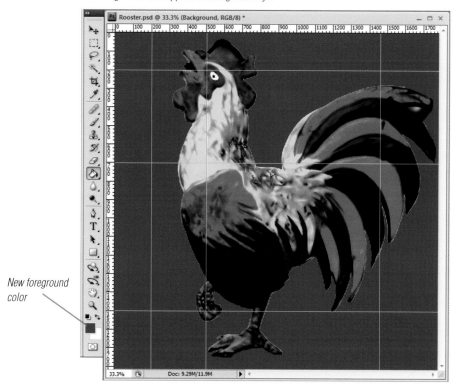

New foreground
color

Change the background color using the Eyedropper tool

1. Click the **Background layer** on the Layers panel.

2. Click the **Eyedropper tool** 🖋. on the Tools panel.

3. Click the **red part of the rooster's crown** in the image with the **Eyedropper pointer** 🖋, using the Info panel and the blue guides to help ensure accuracy.

   The Set foreground color button displays the red color that you clicked (or sampled).

   | TIP   Don't worry if you see a warning sign on the Color panel.

4. Click the **Paint Bucket tool** 🪣 on the Tools panel.

5. Click the image, then compare your screen to Figure 7.

   You might have noticed that in this instance, it doesn't matter where on the layer you click, as long as the correct layer is selected.

6. Save your work.

You used the Eyedropper tool to sample a color as the foreground color, then used the Paint Bucket tool to change the background color to the color you sampled. Using the Eyedropper tool is a convenient way of sampling a color in any Photoshop image.

Using hexadecimal values in the Info panel

Colors can be expressed in a **hexadecimal value**, three pairs of letters or numbers that define the R, G, and B components of a color. The three pairs of letters/numbers are expressed in values from 00 (minimum luminance) to ff (maximum luminance). 000000 represents the value of black, ffffff is white, and ff0000 is red. To view hexadecimal values in the Info panel, click the Info panel list arrow, then click Panel Options. Click Web Color from either the First Color Readout or Second Color Readout Mode list arrow, then click OK. This is just one more way you can exactly determine a specific color in an image.

USE THE COLOR PICKER AND
THE SWATCHES PANEL

What You'll Do

In this lesson, you'll use the Color Picker and the Swatches panel to select new colors, then you'll add a new color to the background and to the Swatches panel. You'll also learn how to access and download color themes from kuler.

Making Selections from the Color Picker

Depending on the color model you are using, you can select colors using the **Color Picker**, a feature that lets you choose a color from a color spectrum or numerically define a custom color. You can change colors in the Color Picker dialog box by using the following methods:

- Drag the sliders along the vertical color bar.
- Click inside the vertical color bar.
- Click a color in the Color field.
- Enter a value in any of the text boxes.

Figure 8 shows a color in the Color Picker dialog box. A circular marker indicates the active color. The color slider displays the range of color levels available for the active color component. The adjustments you make by dragging or clicking a new color are reflected in the text boxes; when you choose a new color, the previous color appears below the new color in the preview area.

Using kuler to coordinate colors

Kuler, by Adobe Labs, is a web-hosted application from which you can download pre-coordinated color themes or design your own. These collections can be saved in your own Mykuler space or shared with others. Use kuler as a fast, effective way of ensuring that your use of color is consistent and harmonious. If you decide to select an existing kuler theme, you'll find that there are thousands from which to choose. Kuler themes can be seen by clicking the Window menu, pointing to Extensions, then clicking Kuler. You can also access kuler through your browser at *kuler.adobe.com*, using the kuler desktop (which requires the installation of Adobe AIR), or from Adobe Illustrator (CS4 or higher). When you pass the mouse over any paint chip in the kuler website, the colors in the theme expand. Click the theme name, and the colors display in the paint chips at the top of the window.

Using the Swatches Panel

You can also change colors using the Swatches panel. The **Swatches panel** is a visual display of colors you can choose from, as shown in Figure 9. You can add your own colors to the panel by sampling a color from an image, and you can also delete colors. When you add a swatch to the Swatches panel, Photoshop assigns a default name that has a sequential number, or you can name the swatch whatever you like. Photoshop places new swatches in the first available space at the end of the panel. You can view swatch names by clicking the Swatches panel list arrow, then clicking Small List. You can restore the default Swatches panel by clicking the Swatches panel list arrow, clicking Reset Swatches, then clicking OK.

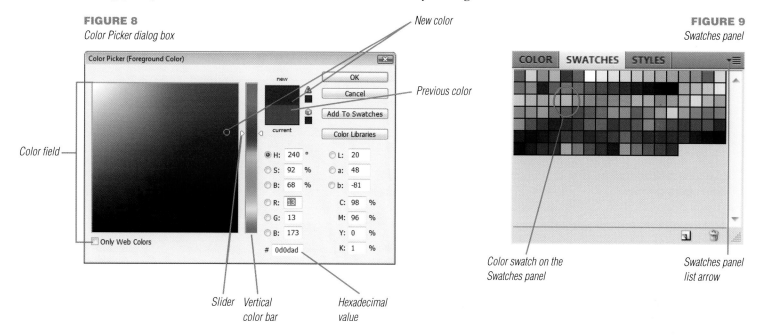

FIGURE 8
Color Picker dialog box

New color

Previous color

Color field

Only Web Colors

Slider Vertical
color bar

Hexadecimal
value

FIGURE 9
Swatches panel

Color swatch on the
Swatches panel

Swatches panel
list arrow

Downloading a kuler theme

Once you've logged into kuler, you can download a theme as an Adobe Swatch Exchange (ASE) file. Click the download button, select a name and location for the downloaded file, then click Save. You can add a kuler theme to your color panel by clicking the Swatches panel option button, then clicking Load Swatches. The new colors will display at the end of the Swatches panel.

Lesson 2   Use the Color Picker and the Swatches Panel

Select a color using the Color Picker dialog box

1. Click the **Set foreground color button** on the Tools panel, then verify that the H: option button is selected in the Color Picker dialog box.

2. Click the **R: option button**.

3. Click the **bottom-right corner** of the Color field (purple), as shown in Figure 10.

   TIP   If the Warning: out-of-gamut for printing indicator appears next to the color, then this color exceeds the printable range.

4. Click **OK**.

You opened the Color Picker dialog box, selected a different color mode, and then selected a new color.

Select a color using the Swatches panel

1. Click the **Swatches panel tab** SWATCHES .

2. Click the **second swatch from the left in the first row** (RGB Yellow), as shown in Figure 11.

   Did you notice that the foreground color on the Tools panel changed to a light, bright yellow?

3. Click the **Paint Bucket tool** 🪣 on the Tools panel (if it is not already selected).

4. Click the image with the **Paint Bucket pointer** 🪣, then compare your screen to Figure 12.

You opened the Swatches panel, selected a color, and then used the Paint Bucket tool to change the background to that color.

FIGURE 10
Color Picker dialog box

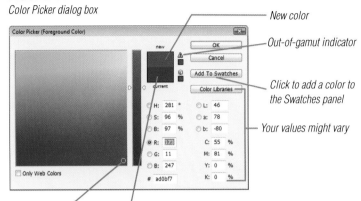

New color

Out-of-gamut indicator

Click to add a color to the Swatches panel

Your values might vary

Click here for new color   Previous color

FIGURE 11
Swatches panel

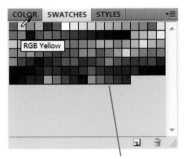

Your swatches on the last row might vary

FIGURE 12
New foreground color applied to Background layer

1. Click the **Eyedropper tool** 🖋 on the
   Tools panel.

2. Click **above and to the left of the rooster's eye**
   at coordinates **500 X/200 Y**.

   > TIP Use the Zoom tool whenever necessary
   > to enlarge/decrease your workspace so you
   > can better see what you're working on.

3. Click the **empty area to the right of the last
   swatch** in the bottom row of the Swatches
   panel with the **Paint Bucket pointer** 🪣.

4. Type **Rooster eye surround** in the Name
   text box.

5. Click **OK** in the Color Swatch Name dialog box.

   > TIP To delete a color from the Swatches
   > panel, press [Alt] (Win) or [option] (Mac),
   > position the pointer over a swatch, then click
   > the swatch.

6. Save your work, then compare the
   new swatch on your Swatches panel to
   Figure 13.

*You used the Eyedropper tool to sample a color,
and then added the color to the Swatches panel,
and gave it a descriptive name. Adding swatches
to the Swatches panel makes it easy to reuse
frequently used colors.*

FIGURE 13
Swatch added to Swatches panel

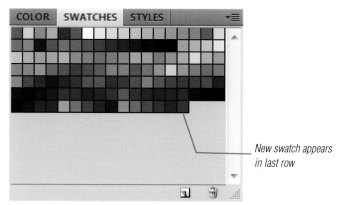

New swatch appears
in last row

Maintaining your focus

Adobe Photoshop is probably unlike any other program you've used before. In other
programs, there's a central area on the screen where you focus your attention. In
Photoshop, there's the workspace containing your document, but you've probably
already figured out that if you don't have the correct layer selected in the Layer's
panel, things won't quite work out as you expected. In addition, you have to make sure
you've got the right tool selected in the Tools panel. You also need to keep an eye on
the History panel. As you work on your image, it might feel a lot like negotiating a
shopping mall parking lot on the day before a holiday: you've got to be looking in a lot
of places at once.

Use kuler from a web browser

1. Open your favorite browser, then type **kuler.adobe.com** in the URL text box.

2. Click the **Sign In link**, then type your **Adobe ID** and **password**. (If you don't have an Adobe ID, click the Register link and follow the instructions.)

3. Click the **Newest link**, then compare your results with Figure 14. (Your color results will be different.)

4. Type **wine olives** in the Search text box, press **[Enter]** (Win) or **[return]** (Mac). The swatch shown in Figure 15 will display.

5. Click the **Download this theme as an Adobe Swatch Exchange file button** , find the location where you save your Data Files in the Select location for download by kuler.adobe.com dialog box, then click **Save**.

6. Sign Out from kuler, then activate Photoshop.

7. Click the **Swatches list arrow**, then click **Load Swatches**.

8. Find the location where you save your Data Files, click the **Files of type list arrow** (Win), click **Swatch Exchange (*.ASE)**, click **Wine, Olives and Cheese**, then click **Load**.

You searched the kuler website and downloaded a color theme to your Photoshop Swatches panel.

FIGURE 14

Kuler website

Color chip for active theme: the displayed theme will vary

Active color theme is expanded

Indicates the current user

Click to download the active theme

Hover pointer over a theme to expand it

FIGURE 15

Theme in kuler

FIGURE 16
Kuler panel

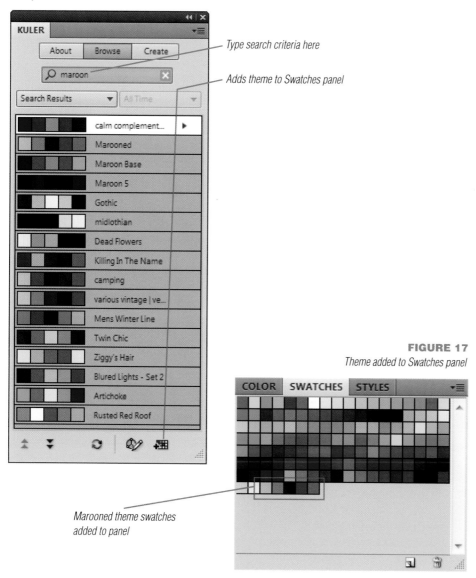

Type search criteria here

Adds theme to Swatches panel

Marooned theme swatches
added to panel

FIGURE 17
Theme added to Swatches panel

1. Click **Window** on the Application bar, point to **Extensions**, then click **Kuler**.

2. Click the **Search text box**, type **maroon**, then press **[Enter]** (Win) or **[return]** (Mac). Compare your kuler panel to Figure 16.

   TIP Your kuler panel may differ as themes change frequently.

3. Click the **Marooned** theme, then click the **Add selected theme to swatches button**. Compare your Swatches panel to Figure 17.

4. Close the kuler panel.

You opened kuler in Photoshop, then added a color theme to the Swatches panel.

PLACE A BORDER AROUND
AN IMAGE

What You'll Do

In this lesson, you'll apply a downloaded color and add a border to an image.

Emphasizing an Image

You can emphasize an image by placing a border around its edges. This process is called **stroking the edges**. The default color of the border is the current foreground color on the Tools panel. You can change the width, color, location, and blending mode of a border using the Stroke dialog box. The default stroke width is the setting last applied; you can apply a width from 1 to 16 pixels. The location option buttons in the dialog box determine where the border will be placed. If you want to change the location of the stroke, you must first delete the previously applied stroke, or Photoshop will apply the new border over the existing one.

Locking Transparent Pixels

As you modify layers, you can lock some properties to protect their contents. The ability to lock—or protect—elements within a layer is controlled from within the Layers panel, as shown in Figure 18. It's a good idea to lock transparent pixels when you add borders so that stray marks will

not be included in the stroke. You can lock the following layer properties:

- Transparency: Limits editing capabilities to areas in a layer that are opaque.
- Image: Makes it impossible to modify layer pixels using painting tools.
- Position: Prevents pixels within a layer from being moved.

QUICKTIP

You can lock transparency or image pixels only in a layer containing an image, not in one containing type.

FIGURE 18
Layers panel locking options

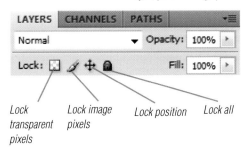

Incorporating Color Techniques

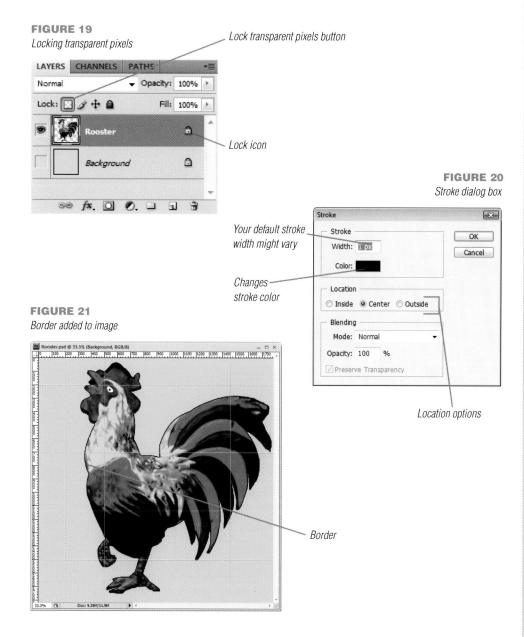

FIGURE 19
Locking transparent pixels

Lock transparent pixels button

Lock icon

FIGURE 20
Stroke dialog box

Your default stroke
width might vary

Changes
stroke color

Location options

FIGURE 21
Border added to image

Border

Create a border

1. Click the **Indicates layer visibility button** 👁
    on the Background layer on the Layers panel.

    TIP You can click the Indicates layer visibil-
    ity button to hide distracting layers.

2. Click the **Default Foreground and Background
    Colors button** ▪️.

    The foreground color will become the default
    border color.

3. Click the **Rooster layer** on the Layers panel.

4. Click the **Lock transparent pixels button** ☒
    on the Layers panel. See Figure 19.

    The border will be applied only to the pixels
    on the edge of the rooster.

5. Click **Edit** on the menu bar, then click **Stroke** to
    open the Stroke dialog box. See Figure 20.

6. Type **5** in the Width text box, click the **Inside
    option button**, then click **OK**.

    TIP Determining the correct border location
    can be confusing. Try different settings until
    you achieve the look you want.

7. Click the **Indicates layer visibility button** ▢
    on the Background layer on the Layers panel.

8. Activate the Background layer on the Layers
    panel, click the newly-added tan-colored box
    in the Swatches panel (255 R, 211 G, 114 B),
    click the **Paint Bucket tool** ◇ on the Tools
    panel, then click the image.

9. Save your work, then compare your image to
    Figure 21.

*You hid a layer, changed the foreground color to
black, locked transparent pixels, then used the
Stroke dialog box to apply a border to the image.*

BLEND COLORS USING THE
GRADIENT TOOL

What You'll Do

In this lesson, you'll create a gradient fill from a sampled color and a swatch, then apply it to the background.

Understanding Gradients

A **gradient fill**, or simply **gradient**, is a blend of colors used to fill a selection of a layer or an entire layer. A gradient's appearance is determined by its beginning and ending points, and its length, direction, and angle. Gradients allow you to create dramatic effects, using existing color combinations or your own colors. The Gradient picker, as shown in Figure 22, offers multi-color gradient fills and a few that use the current foreground or background colors on the Tools panel.

FIGURE 22
Gradient picker

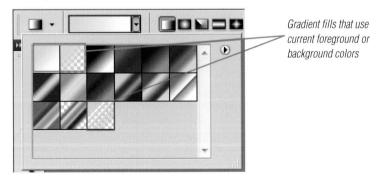

Gradient fills that use current foreground or background colors

Using the Gradient Tool

You use the Gradient tool to create gradients in images. When you choose the Gradient tool, five gradient styles become available on the options bar. These styles—Linear, Radial, Angle, Reflected, and Diamond—are shown in Figure 23. In each example, the gradient was drawn from 50 X/50 Y to 100 X/100 Y.

Customizing Gradients

Using the **gradient presets**—predesigned gradient fills that are displayed in the Gradient picker—is a great way to learn how to use gradients. But as you become more familiar with Photoshop, you might want to venture into the world of the unknown and create your own gradient designs. You can create your own designs by modifying an existing gradient using the Gradient Editor. You can open the Gradient Editor, shown in Figure 24, by clicking the selected gradient pattern that appears on the options bar. After it's open, you can use it to make the following modifications:

- Create a new gradient from an existing gradient.
- Modify an existing gradient.
- Add intermediate colors to a gradient.
- Create a blend between more than two colors.
- Adjust the opacity values.
- Determine the placement of the midpoint.

FIGURE 23
Sample gradients

FIGURE 24
Gradient Editor dialog box

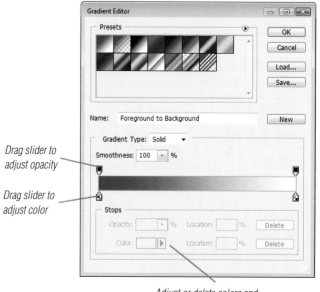

Drag slider to adjust opacity

Drag slider to adjust color

Adjust or delete colors and opacity values

Create a gradient from a sample color

1. Verify that the **Eyedropper tool** 🖊 is selected.

2. Click the **yellow neck** in the image at coordinates **500 X/600 Y**.

   TIP To accurately select the coordinates, adjust the zoom factor as necessary.

3. Click the **Switch Foreground and Background Colors button** ⤵ on the Tools panel.

4. Click the **Maroon swatch** (R=180 G=25 B=29) on the Swatches panel (one of the new swatches you added) with the **Eyedropper pointer** 🖊.

5. Click the **Indicates layer visibility button** 👁 on the Rooster layer, as shown in Figure 25.

6. Click the **Paint Bucket tool** 🖌 on the Tools panel, then press and hold the mouse button until the list of hidden tools opens.

7. Click the **Gradient tool** 🖌 on the Tools panel, then click the **Angle Gradient button** 🖌 on the options bar (if it is not already selected).

8. Click the **Click to open Gradient picker list arrow** on the options bar, then click **Foreground to Background** (the first gradient fill in the first row), as shown in Figure 26.

You sampled a color on the image to set the background color, changed the foreground color using an existing swatch, selected the Gradient tool, and then chose a gradient fill and style.

FIGURE 25
Rooster layer hidden

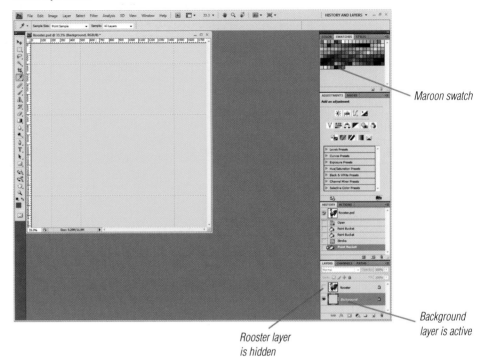

Maroon swatch

Background layer is active

Rooster layer is hidden

Click to open Gradient picker list arrow

FIGURE 26
Gradient picker

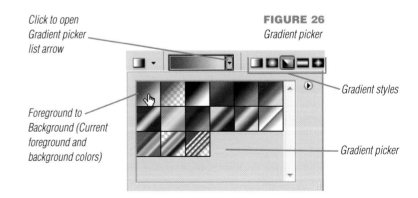

Foreground to Background (Current foreground and background colors)

Gradient styles

Gradient picker

FIGURE 27

Gradient fill applied to Background layer

Apply a gradient fill

1. Click the **Click to open Gradient picker list arrow** to close the Gradient picker.

    TIP   You can also close the Gradient picker by pressing [Esc] (Win) or [esc] (Mac).

2. Drag the **Gradient pointer** -+- from **1430 X/200 Y** to **200 X/1500 Y** using the Info panel and the guides to help you create the gradient in the work area.

3. Click the **Indicates layer visibility button** on the Rooster layer.

    The Rooster layer appears against the new background, as shown in Figure 27.

    TIP   It is a good practice to save your work early and often in the creation process, especially before making significant changes or printing.

4. Save your work.

You applied the gradient fill to the background. You can create dramatic effects using the gradient fill in combination with foreground and background colors.

Collaborating with ConnectNow

Adobe has created a tool to help you collaborate with others: ConnectNow. This online tool lets you share information and collaborate with others. Using screen sharing, chat, shared notes, audio, and video, you can more effectively manage your workflow and get your work done. Open ConnectNow from within Photoshop by clicking File on the Application bar, then clicking Share My Screen or type *www.adobe.com/acom/connect-now* in your favorite browser. Once you have logged into Adobe ConnectNow, you can invite participants, share your computer screen, and upload files. ConnectNow uses the metaphor of a meeting, into which you invite participants and use pod tools to interact. When you are finished, you click the End Meeting command from the Meeting menu. You can use the Connections panel in Photoshop by clicking Window on the Application bar, pointing to Extensions, then clicking Connections to log in and check for updates.

ADD COLOR TO A
GRAYSCALE IMAGE

What You'll Do

In this lesson, you'll convert an image to grayscale, change the color mode, then colorize a grayscale image using the Hue/Saturation dialog box.

Colorizing Options

Grayscale images can contain up to 256 shades of gray, assigning a brightness value from 0 (black) to 255 (white) to each pixel. Since the earliest days of photography, people have been tinting grayscale images with color to create a certain mood or emphasize an image in a way that purely realistic colors could not. To capture this effect in Photoshop, you convert an image to the Grayscale mode, then choose the color mode you want to work in before you continue. When you apply a color to a grayscale image, each pixel becomes a shade of that particular color instead of gray.

Converting Grayscale and Color Modes

When you convert a color image to grayscale, the light and dark values—called the **luminosity**—remain, while the color information is deleted. When you change from grayscale to a color mode, the foreground and background colors on the Tools panel change from black and white to the previously selected colors.

Converting a color image to black and white

Using the Black & White command, you can easily convert a color image to black and white. This feature lets you quickly make the color to black and white conversion while maintaining full control over how individual colors are converted. Tones can also be applied to the grayscale by applying color tones (the numeric values for each color). To use this feature, click Image on the menu bar, point to Adjustments, then click Black & White. The Black & White command can also be applied as an Adjustment layer.

Tweaking Adjustments

Once you have made your color mode conversion to grayscale, you may want to make some adjustments. You can fine-tune the Brightness/Contrast, filters, and blending modes in a grayscale image.

Colorizing a Grayscale Image

In order for a grayscale image to be colorized, you must change the color mode to one that accommodates color. After you change the color mode, and then adjust settings in the Hue/Saturation dialog box, Photoshop determines the colorization range based on the hue of the currently selected foreground color. If you want a different colorization range, you need to change the foreground color.

FIGURE 28
Gradient Map dialog box

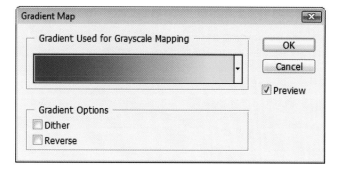

Applying a gradient effect

You can also use the Gradient Map to apply a colored gradient effect to a grayscale image. The Gradient Map uses gradient fills (the same ones displayed in the Gradient picker) to colorize the image, which can produce some stunning effects. You use the Gradient Map dialog box, shown in Figure 28, to apply a gradient effect to a grayscale image. You can access the Gradient Map dialog box using the Adjustments command on the Image menu.

Change the color mode

1. Open PS 4-2.psd from the drive and folder where you store your Data Files, save it as **Rooster Colorized**, then turn off the rulers if they are displayed.

2. Click **Image** on the Application bar, point to **Mode**, then click **Grayscale**.

3. Click **Flatten** in the warning box, then click **Discard**.

   The color mode of the image is changed to grayscale, and the image is flattened so there is only a single layer. All the color information in the image has been discarded.

4. Click **Image** on the Application bar, point to **Mode**, then click **RGB Color**.

   The color mode is changed back to RGB color, although there is still no color in the image. Compare your screen to Figure 29.

   You converted the image to Grayscale, which discarded the existing color information. Then you changed the color mode to RGB color.

FIGURE 29
Image with RGB mode

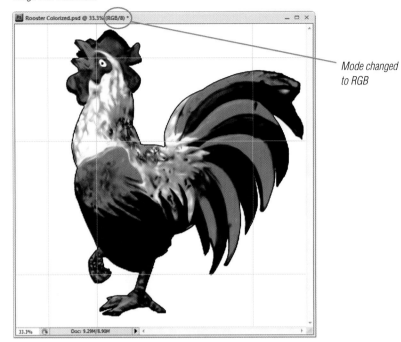

Mode changed
to RGB

Rooster Colorized.psd @ 33.3% (RGB/8) *

33.3%   Doc: 9.29M/8.90M

Converting color images to grayscale

Like everything else in Photoshop, there is more than one way of converting a color image into one that is black and white. Changing the color mode to grayscale is the quickest method. You can also make this conversion through desaturation by clicking Image on the menu bar, pointing to Adjustments, then clicking Black & White, or Desaturate. Converting to Grayscale mode generally results in losing contrast, as does the desaturation method, while using the Black & White method retains the contrast of the original image.

FIGURE 30
Hue/Saturation dialog box

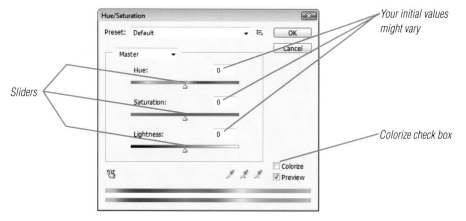

Your initial values might vary

Sliders

Colorize check box

FIGURE 31
Colorized image

Colorize a grayscale image

1. Click **Image** on the Application bar, point to **Adjustments**, then click **Hue/Saturation** to open the Hue/Saturation dialog box, as shown in Figure 30.

2. Click the **Colorize check box** in the Hue/Saturation dialog box to add a check mark.

3. Drag the **Hue slider** until the text box displays **240**.

   TIP You can also type values in the text boxes in the Hue/Saturation dialog box. Negative numbers must be preceded by a minus sign or a hyphen. Positive numbers can be preceded by an optional plus sign (+).

4. Drag the **Saturation slider** until the text box displays **55**.

5. Drag the **Lightness slider** until the text box displays **-15**.

6. Click **OK**.

7. Save your work, then compare your screen to Figure 31.

You colorized a grayscale image by adjusting settings in the Hue/Saturation dialog box.

Understanding the Hue/Saturation dialog box

The Hue/Saturation dialog box is an important tool in the world of color enhancement. Useful for both color and grayscale images, the saturation slider can be used to boost a range of colors. By clicking the Edit list arrow, you can isolate which colors (all, cyan, blue, magenta, red, yellow, or green) you want to modify. Using this tool requires patience and experimentation, but gives you great control over the colors in your image.

Lesson 5   Add Color to a Grayscale Image

USE FILTERS, OPACITY,
AND BLENDING MODES

What You'll Do

 In this lesson, you'll adjust the brightness and contrast in the Rooster colorized image, apply a Sharpen filter, and adjust the opacity of the lines applied by the filter. You'll also adjust the color balance of the Rooster image.

Manipulating an Image

As you work in Photoshop, you might realize that some images have fundamental problems that need correcting, while others just need to be further enhanced. For example, you might need to adjust an image's contrast and sharpness, or you might want to colorize an otherwise dull image. You can use a variety of techniques to change the way an image looks. For example, you have learned how to use the Adjustments command on the Image menu to modify hue and saturation, but you can also use this command to adjust brightness and contrast, color balance, and a host of other visual effects.

Understanding Filters

Filters are Photoshop commands that can significantly alter an image's appearance. Experimenting with Photoshop's filters is a fun way to completely change the look of an image. For example, the Watercolor filter gives the illusion that your image was

Fixing blurry scanned images

An unfortunate result of scanning a picture is that the image can become blurry. You can fix this, however, using the Unsharp Mask filter. This filter both sharpens and smoothes the image by increasing the contrast along element edges. Here's how it works: the smoothing effect removes stray marks, and the sharpening effect emphasizes contrasting neighboring pixels. Most scanners come with their own Unsharp Masks built into the TWAIN driver, but using Photoshop, you have access to a more powerful version of this filter. You can use Photoshop's Unsharp Mask to control the sharpening process by adjusting key settings. In most cases, your scanner's Unsharp Mask might not give you this flexibility. Regardless of the technical aspects, the result is a sharper image. You can apply the Unsharp Mask by clicking Filter on the menu bar, pointing to Sharpen, then clicking Unsharp Mask.

painted using traditional watercolors. Sharpen filters can appear to add definition to the entire image, or just the edges. Compare the different Sharpen filters applied in Figure 32. The **Sharpen More filter** increases the contrast of adjacent pixels and can focus a blurry image. Be careful not to overuse sharpening tools (or any filter), because you can create high-contrast lines or add graininess in color or brightness.

Choosing Blending Modes

A **blending mode** controls how pixels are made either darker or lighter based on underlying colors. Photoshop provides a variety of blending modes, listed in Table 1, to combine the color of the pixels in the current layer with those in layer(s) beneath it. You can see a list of blending modes by clicking the Add a layer style button on the Layers panel.

Understanding Blending Mode Components

You should consider the following underlying colors when planning a blending mode: **base color**, which is the original color of the image; **blend color**, which is the color you apply with a paint or edit tool; and **resulting color**, which is the color that is created as a result of applying the blend color.

Softening Filter Effects

Opacity can soften the line that the filter creates, but it doesn't affect the opacity of the entire layer. After a filter has been applied, you can modify the opacity and apply a blending mode using the Layers panel or the Fade dialog box. You can open the Fade dialog box by clicking Edit on the menu bar, then clicking the Fade command.

QUICKTIP

The Fade command appears only after a filter has been applied. When available, the command name includes the name of the applied filter.

Balancing Colors

As you adjust settings, such as hue and saturation, you might create unwanted imbalances in your image. You can adjust colors to correct or improve an image's appearance. For example, you can decrease a color by increasing the amount of its opposite color. You use the Color Balance dialog box to balance the color in an image.

FIGURE 32
Sharpen filters

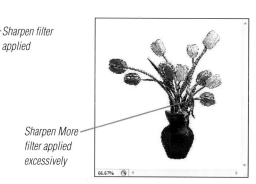

Original image

Sharpen filter applied

Sharpen More filter applied excessively

TABLE 1: Blending Modes

blending mode	description
Dissolve, Behind, and Clear modes	Dissolve mode creates a grainy, mottled appearance. The Behind mode paints on the transparent part of the layer—the lower the opacity, the grainier the image. The Clear mode paints individual pixels. All modes are available only when the Lock transparent pixels check box is *not* selected.
Multiply and Screen modes	Multiply mode creates semitransparent shadow effects. This mode assesses the information in each channel, then multiplies the value of the base color by the blend color. The resulting color is always *darker* than the base color. The Screen mode multiplies the value of the inverse of the blend and base colors. After it is applied, the resulting color is always *lighter* than the base color.
Overlay mode	Dark and light values (luminosity) are preserved, dark base colors are multiplied (darkened), and light areas are screened (lightened).
Soft Light and Hard Light modes	Soft Light lightens a light base color and darkens a dark base color. The Hard Light blending mode creates a similar effect, but provides greater contrast between the base and blend colors.
Color Dodge and Color Burn modes	Color Dodge mode brightens the base color to reflect the blend color. The Color Burn mode darkens the base color to reflect the blend color.
Darken and Lighten modes	Darken mode selects a new resulting color based on whichever color is darker—the base color or the blend color. The Lighten mode selects a new resulting color based on the lighter of the two colors.
Difference and Exclusion modes	The Difference mode subtracts the value of the blend color from the value of the base color, or vice versa, depending on which color has the greater brightness value. The Exclusion mode creates an effect similar to that of the Difference mode, but with less contrast between the blend and base colors.
Color and Luminosity modes	The Color mode creates a resulting color with the luminance of the base color, and the hue and saturation of the blend color. The Luminosity mode creates a resulting color with the hue and saturation of the base color, and the luminance of the blend color.
Hue and Saturation modes	The Hue mode creates a resulting color with the luminance of the base color and the hue of the blend color. The Saturation mode creates a resulting color with the luminance of the base color and the saturation of the blend color.

FIGURE 33
Brightness/Contrast dialog box

FIGURE 34
Shadows/Highlights dialog box

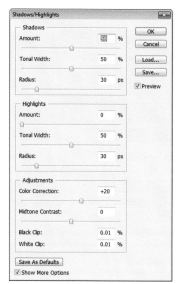

Adjust brightness and contrast

1. Click **Image** on the Application bar, point to **Adjustments**, then click **Brightness/Contrast** to open the Brightness/Contrast dialog box.

2. Drag the **Brightness slider** until **15** appears in the Brightness text box.

3. Drag the **Contrast slider** until **25** appears in the Contrast text box. Compare your screen to Figure 33.

4. Click **OK**.

You adjusted settings in the Brightness/Contrast dialog box. The image now looks much brighter, with a higher degree of contrast, which obscures some of the finer detail in the image.

Correcting shadows and highlights
The ability to correct shadows and highlights will delight photographers everywhere. This image correction feature (opened by clicking Image on the Application bar, pointing to Adjustments, then clicking Shadows/Highlights) lets you modify overall lighting and make subtle adjustments. Figure 34 shows the Shadows/Highlights dialog box with the Show More Options check box selected. Check out this one-stop shopping for shadow and highlight adjustments!

Lesson 6   Use Filters, Opacity, and Blending Modes

Work with a filter, a blending mode, and an opacity setting

1. Click **Filter** on the Application bar, point to **Sharpen**, then click **Sharpen More**.

   The border and other features of the image are intensified.

2. Click **Edit** on the Application bar, then click **Fade Sharpen More** to open the Fade dialog box, as shown in Figure 35.

3. Drag the **Opacity slider** until **45** appears in the Opacity text box.

   The opacity setting softened the lines applied by the Sharpen More filter.

4. Click the **Mode list arrow**, then click **Dissolve**.

   The Dissolve setting blends the surrounding pixels.

5. Click **OK**.

6. Save your work, then compare your image to Figure 36.

You applied the Sharpen More filter, then adjusted the opacity and changed the color mode in the Fade dialog box. The border in the image looks crisper than before, with a greater level of detail.

FIGURE 35
Fade dialog box

FIGURE 36
Image settings adjusted

FIGURE 37
Color Balance dialog box

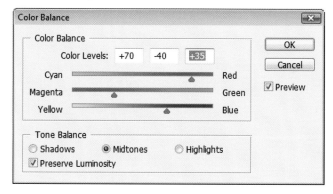

FIGURE 38

Image with colors balanced

Adjust color balance

1. Switch to the Rooster image, with the Background layer active.

   The image you worked with earlier in this chapter becomes active.

2. Click **Image** on the Application bar, point to **Adjustments**, then click **Color Balance**.

3. Drag the **Cyan-Red slider** until **+70** appears in the first text box.

4. Drag the **Magenta-Green slider** until **–40** appears in the middle text box.

5. Drag the **Yellow-Blue slider** until **+35** appears in the last text box, as shown in Figure 37.

   Subtle changes were made in the color balance in the image.

6. Click **OK**.

7. Save your work, then compare your image to Figure 38.

You balanced the colors in the Rooster image by adjusting settings in the Color Balance dialog box.

MATCH COLORS

What You'll Do

In this lesson, you'll make selections in source and target images, then use the Match Color command to replace the target color.

Finding the Right Color

If it hasn't happened already, at some point you'll be working on an image and wish you could grab a color from another image to use in this one. Just as you can use the Eyedropper tool to sample any color in the current image for the foreground and background, you can sample a color from any other image to use in the current one. Perhaps the skin tones in one image look washed out: you can use the Match Color command to replace those tones with skin tone colors from another image. Or maybe the jacket color in one image would look better using a color in another image.

Using Selections to Match Colors

Remember that this is Photoshop, where everything is about layers and selections.

To replace a color in one image with one you've matched from another, you work with—you guessed it—layers and selections.

Suppose you've located the perfect color in another image. The image you are working with is the **target**, and the image that contains your perfect color is the **source**. By activating the layer on which the color lies in the source image, and making a selection around the color, you can have Photoshop match the color in the source and replace a color in the target. To accomplish this, you use the Match Color command, which is available by pointing to Adjustments on the Image menu.

FIGURE 39
Selection in source image

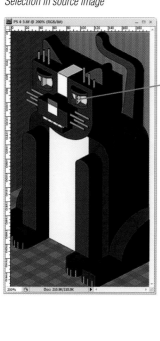

Selected area

FIGURE 40
Match Color dialog box

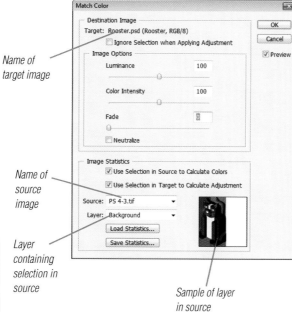

Name of
target image

Name of
source
image

FIGURE 41
Image with matched colors

Layer
containing
selection in
source

Sample of layer
in source

Modified selection

Match a color

1. Click the **Rooster layer** on the Layers panel, then zoom (once) into the eye of the rooster.

2. Click the **Magic Wand tool** ✨ on the Tools panel.

3. Verify that the **Anti-alias** and **Contiguous check boxes** on the options bar are selected, then set the **Tolerance** to **10**.

4. Click the image with the **Magic Wand pointer** ✨ on the white of the eye at approximately **550 X/210 Y**.

5. Open PS 4-3.tif from the drive and folder where you store your Data Files, zoom into the image (if necessary), change the tolerance to **40**, then click the **light green part of the cat's eye (**at **100 X/95 Y)** with the **Magic Wand pointer** ✨. Compare your selection to Figure 39.

6. Activate the **Rooster image**, click **Image** on the Application bar, point to **Adjustments**, then click **Match Color**.

7. Click the **Source list arrow**, then click **PS 4-3.tif**. Compare your settings to Figure 40.

8. Click **OK**.

9. Deselect the selection, turn off the rulers and the guides, save your work, then compare your image to Figure 41.

10. Close all open images, display the Essentials workspace then exit Photoshop.

You used the Match Color dialog box to replace a color in one image with a color from another image. The Match Color dialog box makes it easy to sample colors from other images, giving you even more options for incorporating color into an image.

Power User Shortcuts

to do this:	use this method:
Apply a sharpen filter	Filter ➤ Sharpen
Balance colors	Image ➤ Adjustments ➤ Color Balance
Change color mode	Image ➤ Mode
Choose a background color from the Swatches panel	[Ctrl]Color swatch (Win) [⌘]Color swatch (Mac)
Delete a swatch from the Swatches panel	[Alt], click swatch (Win) [option], click swatch (Mac)
Eyedropper tool	✐. or I
Fill with background color	[Shift][Backspace] (Win) [⌘][delete] (Mac)
Fill with foreground color	[Alt][Backspace] (Win) option [delete] (Mac)
Gradient tool	▣
Guide pointer	✛ or ╪
Hide a layer	👁

to do this:	use this method:
Hide or show rulers	[Ctrl][R] (Win) [⌘][R] (Mac)
Hide or show the Color panel	[F6] (Win) COLOR
Lock transparent pixels check box on/off	[/]
Make Swatches panel active	SWATCHES
Paint Bucket tool	◇ or G
Return background and foreground colors to default	▣ or D
Show a layer	☐
Show hidden Paint Bucket/ Gradient tools	[Shift] G
Switch between open files	[Ctrl][Tab] (Win) [control][tab] (Mac)
Switch foreground and background colors	↰ or X

Key: Menu items are indicated by ➤ between the menu name and its command. Blue bold letters are shortcuts for selecting tools on the Tools panel.

Work with color to transform an image.

1. Start Photoshop.
2. Open PS 4-4.psd from the drive and folder where you store your Data Files, then save it as **Firetruck**.
3. Make sure the rulers display in pixels, and that the default foreground and background colors display.
4. Use the Eyedropper tool to sample the red color at 90 X/165 Y using the guides to help.
5. Use the Paint Bucket tool to apply the new foreground color to the Background layer.
6. Undo your last step using either the Edit menu or the History panel. (*Hint:* You can switch to another workspace that displays the necessary panels.)
7. Switch the foreground and background colors.
8. Save your work.

Use the Color Picker and the Swatches panel.

1. Use the Set foreground color button to open the Color Picker dialog box.
2. Click the R:, G:, and B: option buttons, one at a time. Note how the color panel changes.
3. With the B: option button selected, click the panel in the upper-left corner, then click OK.
4. Switch the foreground and background colors.
5. Add the foreground color (red) to the Swatches panel using a meaningful name of your choice.

Place a border around an image.

1. Make Layer 1 active (if it is not already active).
2. Revert to the default foreground and background colors.
3. Create a border by applying a 2-pixel outside stroke to the firetruck.
4. Save your work.

Blend colors using the Gradient tool.

1. Change the foreground color to the sixth swatch from the right in the top row of the Swatches panel (35% Gray). (Your swatch location may vary.)
2. Switch foreground and background colors.
3. Use the new red swatch that you added previously as the foreground color.
4. Make the Background layer active.
5. Use the Gradient tool, apply the Angle Gradient with its default settings, then using the guides to help, drag the pointer from 145 X/70 Y to 35 X/165 Y.
6. Save your work, and turn off the rulers display.

Add color to a grayscale image.

1. Open PS 4–5.psd, then save it as **Firetruck Colorized**.
2. Change the color mode to RGB Color.
3. Open the Hue/Saturation dialog box, then select the Colorize check box.
4. Drag the sliders so the text boxes show the following values: 155, 56, and –30, then click OK.
5. Save your work.

Use filters, opacity, and blending modes.

1. Use the Sharpen filter to sharpen the image.
2. Open the Fade Sharpen dialog box by using the Edit menu, change the opacity to 40%, change the mode to Hard Light, then save your work.
3. Open the Color Balance dialog box.
4. Change the color level settings so the text boxes show the following values: +61, –15, and +20.
5. Turn off the rulers display (if necessary).
6. Save your work.

Match colors.

1. Open PS 4-6.tif, then use the Magic Wand tool to select the light yellow in the cat's eye.
2. Select the white areas of the firetruck cab in Firetruck.psd. (*Hint:* You can press [Shift] and click on multiple areas using the Magic Wand tool.)
3. Use the Match Color dialog box to change the white in Layer 1 of the firetruck image to yellow (in the cat's eye). Compare your images to Figure 42. (The brightness of your colors may vary.)
4. Save your work.
5. Exit Photoshop.

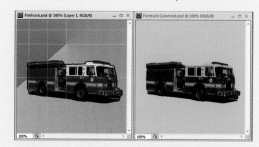

FIGURE 42
Completed Skills Review

You are finally able to leave your current job and pursue your lifelong dream of opening a furniture repair and restoration business. While you're waiting for the laser stripper and refinisher to arrive, you start to work on a sign design.

1. Open PS 4-7.psd, substitute any missing fonts, then save it as **Furniture Fixer**.
2. Move the objects to any location to achieve a layout you think looks attractive and eye-catching.
3. Sample the blue pliers in the tool belt, then switch the foreground and background colors.
4. Sample the red tape measure in the tool belt.
5. Use any Gradient tool to create an interesting effect on the Background layer.
6. Save the image, then compare your screen to the sample shown in Figure 43.

FIGURE 43
Completed Project Builder 1

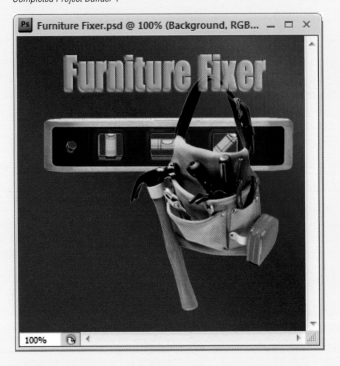

Incorporating Color Techniques

You're painting the swing set at the PB&J Preschool, when you notice a staff member struggling to create a flyer for the school. Although the basic flyer is complete, it doesn't convey the high energy of the school. You offer to help, and soon find yourself in charge of creating an exciting background for the image.

1. Open PS 4-8.psd, update layers as needed, then save it as **Preschool**.
2. Apply a foreground color of your choice to the Background layer.
3. Add a new layer above the Background layer, then select a background color and apply a gradient you have not used before to the layer. (*Hint*: Remember that you can immediately undo a gradient that you don't want.)
4. Add the foreground and background colors to the Swatches panel.
5. Apply a Sharpen filter to the Boy at blackboard layer and adjust the opacity of the filter.
6. Save your work.
7. Compare your screen to the sample shown in Figure 44.

FIGURE 44
Completed Project Builder 2

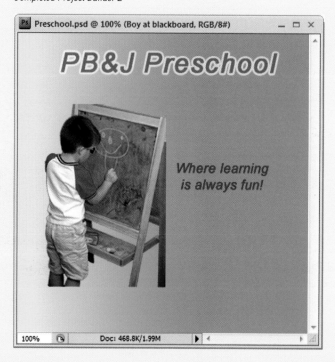

A local Top 40 morning radio show recently conducted a survey about chocolate, and discovered that only one in seven people knew about its health benefits. Now everyone is talking about chocolate. An interior designer wants to incorporate chocolates into her fall decorating theme, and has asked you to create a poster. You decide to highlight as many varieties as possible.

1. Open PS 4-9.psd, then save it as **Chocolate**.
2. If you choose, you can add any appropriate images that have been scanned or captured using a digital camera.
3. Activate the Background layer, then sample colors from the image for foreground and background colors. (*Hint*: Try to sample unusual colors, to widen your design horizons.)
4. Add the sampled colors to the Swatches panel.
5. Display the rulers, then move the existing guides to indicate the coordinates of the colors you sampled.
6. Create a gradient fill by using both the foreground and background colors and the gradient style of your choice.
7. Defringe the Chocolate layer, if necessary.
8. Hide the rulers, save your work, then compare your image to the sample shown in Figure 45.

FIGURE 45
Completed Design Project

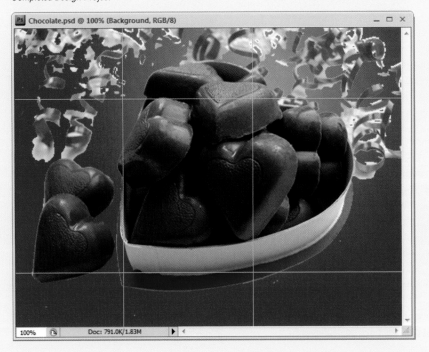

PORTFOLIO PROJECT

An educational toy and game store has hired you to design a poster announcing this year's Most Unusual Hobby contest. After reviewing the photos from last year's awards ceremony, you decide to build a poster using the winner of the Handicrafts Award. You'll use your knowledge of Photoshop color modes to convert the color mode, adjust color in the image, and add an interesting background.

1. Open PS 4-10.psd, then save it as **Rubberband**.
2. Convert the image to Grayscale mode. (*Hint*: When Photoshop prompts you to flatten the layers, click Don't Flatten.)
3. Convert the image to RGB Color mode. (*Hint*: When Photoshop prompts you to flatten the layers, click Don't Flatten.)
4. Colorize the image and adjust the Hue, Saturation, and Lightness settings as desired.
5. Adjust Brightness/Contrast settings as desired.
6. Adjust Color Balance settings as desired.
7. Sample the image to create a new foreground color, then add a color of your choice as the background color.
8. Apply any two Sharpen filters and adjust the opacity for one of them.
9. Add a reflected gradient to the Background layer that follows the path of one of the main bands on the ball.
10. Save your work, then compare your image to the sample shown in Figure 46.
11. Be prepared to discuss the color-correcting methods you used and why you chose them.

FIGURE 46
Completed Portfolio Project

chapter

5 PLACING TYPE IN
AN IMAGE

1. Learn about type and how it is created

2. Change spacing and adjust baseline shift

3. Use the Drop Shadow style

4. Apply anti-aliasing to type

5. Modify type with the Bevel and Emboss style

6. Apply special effects to type using filters

7. Create text on a path

Learning About Type

Text plays an important design role when combined with images for posters, magazine and newspaper advertisements, and other graphics materials that need to communicate detailed information. In Photoshop, text is referred to as **type**. You can use type to express the ideas conveyed in a file's imagery or to deliver an additional message. You can manipulate type in many ways to reflect or reinforce the meaning behind an image. As in other programs, type has its own unique characteristics in Photoshop. For example, you can change its appearance by using different fonts (also called typefaces) and colors.

Understanding the Purpose of Type

Type is typically used along with imagery to deliver a message quickly and with flare. Because type is used sparingly (often there's not a lot of room for it), its appearance is very important; color and imagery are frequently used to *complement* or *reinforce* the message within the text. Type should be limited, direct, and to the point. It should be large enough for easy reading, but should not overwhelm or distract from the central image. For example, a vibrant and daring advertisement should contain just enough type to interest the reader, without demanding too much reading.

Getting the Most Out of Type

Words can express an idea, but the appearance of the type is what drives the point home. After you decide on the content you want to use and create the type, you can experiment with its appearance by changing its **font** (characters with a similar appearance), size, and color. You can also apply special effects that make it stand out, or appear to pop off the page.

Tools You'll Use

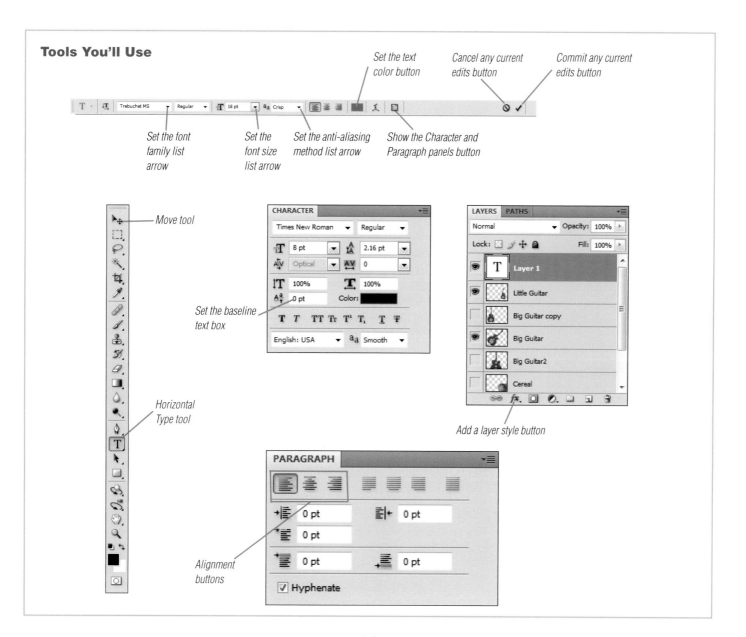

Set the text color button

Cancel any current edits button

Commit any current edits button

Set the font family list arrow

Set the font size list arrow

Set the anti-aliasing method list arrow

Show the Character and Paragraph panels button

Move tool

CHARACTER

Times New Roman   Regular

8 pt   2.16 pt

Optical   0

100%   100%

0 pt   Color:

T T TT Tr T' T, T ‡

English: USA   Smooth

LAYERS   PATHS

Normal   Opacity: 100%

Lock: Fill: 100%

T   Layer 1

Little Guitar

Big Guitar copy

Big Guitar

Big Guitar2

Cereal

Set the baseline text box

Horizontal Type tool

Add a layer style button

PARAGRAPH

0 pt   0 pt

0 pt

0 pt   0 pt

☑ Hyphenate

Alignment buttons

LEARN ABOUT TYPE AND
HOW IT IS CREATED

What You'll Do

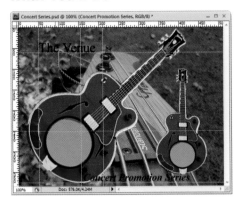

 In this lesson, you'll create a type layer, then change the alignment, font family, size, and color of the type.

Introducing Type Types

Outline type is mathematically defined, which means that it can be scaled to any size without losing its sharp, smooth edges. Some programs, such as Adobe Illustrator, create outline type, also known as **vector fonts**. **Bitmap type** is composed of pixels, and, like images, can develop jagged edges when enlarged. The type you create in Photoshop is initially outline type, but it is converted into bitmap type when you apply special filters. Using the type tools and the options bar, you can create horizontal or vertical type and modify font size and alignment. You use the Color Picker dialog box to change type color. When you create type in Photoshop, it is automatically placed on a new type layer on the Layers panel.

QUICKTIP
Keeping type on separate layers makes it much easier to modify and change positions within the image.

Getting to Know Font Families

Each **font family** represents a complete set of characters, letters, and symbols for a particular typeface. Font families are generally divided into three categories: serif, sans serif, and symbol. Characters in **serif fonts** have a tail, or stroke, at the end of some characters. These tails make it easier for the eye to recognize words. For this reason, serif fonts are generally used in text passages. **Sans serif fonts** do not have tails and are commonly used in headlines.

TIP The Verdana typeface was designed primarily for use on a computer screen.

Symbol fonts are used to display unique characters (such as $, ÷, or ™). Table 1 lists some commonly used serif and sans serif fonts. After you select the Horizontal Type tool, you can change font families using the options bar.

Measuring Type Size

The size of each character within a font is measured in **points**. **PostScript**, a programming language that optimizes printed text and graphics, was introduced by Adobe in 1985. In PostScript measurement, one inch is equivalent to 72 points or six picas. Therefore, one pica is equivalent to 12 points. In traditional measurement, one inch is equivalent to 72.27 points. The default Photoshop type size is 12 points. In Photoshop, you have the option of using PostScript or traditional character measurement.

Acquiring Fonts

Your computer has many fonts installed on it, but no matter how many fonts you have, you probably can use more. Fonts can be purchased from private companies, individual designers, computer stores, or catalog companies. Fonts are delivered on CD, DVD, or over the Internet. Using your browser and your favorite search engine, you can locate websites where you can purchase or download fonts. Many websites offer specialty fonts, such as the website shown in Figure 1. Other websites offer these fonts free of charge or for a nominal fee.

TABLE 1: Commonly Used Serif and Sans Serif Fonts

serif fonts	sample	sans serif fonts	sample
Lucida Handwriting	*Adobe Photoshop*	Arial	Adobe Photoshop
Rockwell	Adobe Photoshop	Bauhaus	Adobe Photoshop
Times New Roman	Adobe Photoshop	Century Gothic	Adobe Photoshop

FIGURE 1
Font website

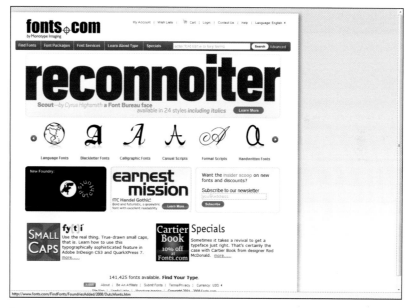

Courtesy of Fonts.com - http://fonts.com/

Create and modify type

1. Start Photoshop, open PS 5-1.psd from the drive and folder where you store your Data Files, update the layers (if necessary), then save the file as **Concert Series**.

2. Display the document size in the status bar, the rulers in pixels (if they are not already displayed), and change the workspace to **Typography**.

   TIP   You can quickly toggle the rulers on and off by pressing [Ctrl][R] (Win) or ⌘[R] (Mac).

3. Click the **Default Foreground and Background Colors button** ■◻ on the Tools panel.

4. Click the **Horizontal Type tool** T on the Tools panel.

5. Click the **Set the font family list arrow** on the options bar, click **Arial** (a sans serif font), click the **Set the font style list arrow**, then click **Italic**.

   TIP   If Arial is not available, make a reasonable substitution.

6. Click the **Set the font size list arrow** on the options bar, then click **6 pt** (if it is not already selected).

7. Click the image with the **Horizontal Type pointer** ⌖ at approximately **155 X/375 Y**, then type **Concert Promotion Series** as shown in Figure 2.

You created a type layer by using the Horizontal Type tool on the Tools panel and modified the font family and font size.

FIGURE 2
New type in image

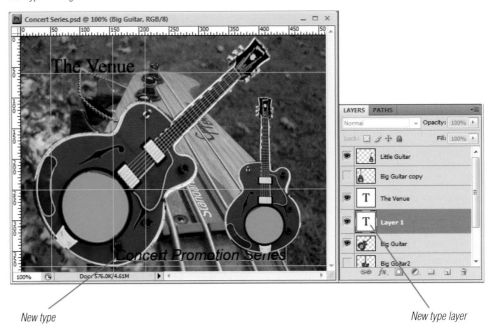

New type

New type layer

Using the active layer panel background (Macintosh)
Icons used in Macintosh to identify type layers are similar to those found in Windows. In Macintosh, the active layer has the same Type and Layer style buttons. The active layer's background color is the same color as the color used to highlight a selected item. (In Windows, the active layer's background color is a dark cyan blue.)

FIGURE 3
Type with new color

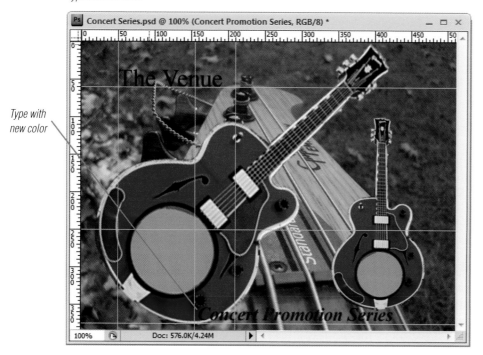

Type with new color

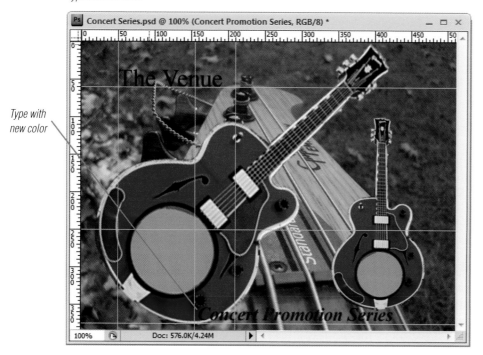

Using the Swatches panel to change type color

You can also use the Swatches panel to change type color. Select the type, then click a color on the Swatches panel. The new color that you click will appear in the Set foreground color button on the Tools panel and will be applied to type that is currently selected.

Change type color using an existing image color

1. Press **[Ctrl][A]** (Win) or **⌘[A]** (Mac) to select all the text.
2. Click the **Set the font family list arrow** on the options bar, scroll down, then click **Times New Roman**.
   > TIP Click in the Set the font family text box and you can select a different font by typing the first few characters of the font name. Scroll through the fonts by clicking in the Set the font family text box, then pressing the [UpArrow] or [DownArrow].
3. Click the **Set the font style list arrow**, then click **Bold Italic**.
4. Click the **Set the text color button** ▬ on the options bar.
   > TIP Drag the Set text color dialog box out of the way if it blocks your view of the image.

   As you position the pointer over the image, the pointer automatically becomes an Eyedropper pointer.
5. Click the image with the **Eyedropper pointer** 🖉 anywhere in the blue area at the top of the large guitar at approximately **155 X/175 Y**.

   The new color is now the active color in the Set text color dialog box.
6. Click **OK** in the Select text color dialog box.
7. Click the **Commit any current edits button** ✓ on the options bar.

   Clicking the Commit any current edits button accepts your changes and makes them permanent in the image.
8. Save your work, then compare your image to Figure 3.

You changed the font family, modified the color of the type by using an existing image color, and committed the current edits.

CHANGE SPACING AND
ADJUST BASELINE SHIFT

What You'll Do

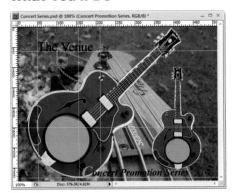

 In this lesson, you'll adjust the spacing between characters and change the baseline of type.

Adjusting Spacing

Competition for readers on the visual landscape is fierce. To get and maintain an edge over other designers, Photoshop provides tools that let you make adjustments to your type, offering you the opportunity to make your type more distinctive. These adjustments might not be very dramatic, but they can influence readers in subtle ways. For example, type that is too small and difficult to read might make the reader impatient (at the very least), and he or she might not even look at the image (at the very worst). You can make finite adjustments, called **type spacing**, to the space between characters and between lines of type. Adjusting type spacing affects the ease with which words are read.

Understanding Character and Line Spacing

Fonts in desktop publishing and word processing programs use proportional spacing, whereas typewriters use monotype spacing. In **monotype spacing**, each character occupies the same amount of space. This means that wide characters such as "o" and "w" take up the same real estate on the page as narrow ones such as "i" and "l". In **proportional spacing**, each character can take up a different amount of space, depending on its width. **Kerning** controls the amount of space between characters and can affect several characters, a word, or an entire paragraph. **Tracking** inserts a *uniform* amount of space between selected characters. Figure 4 shows an example of type before and after it has been kerned.

The second line of text takes up less room and has less space between its characters, making it easier to read. You can also change the amount of space, called **leading**, between lines of type, to add or decrease the distance between lines of text.

Using the Character Panel

The **Character panel**, shown in Figure 5, helps you manually or automatically control type properties such as kerning, tracking, and leading. You open the Character panel from the options bar and the Dock.

Adjusting the Baseline Shift

Type rests on an invisible line called a **baseline**. Using the Character panel, you can adjust the **baseline shift**, the vertical distance that type moves from its baseline. You can add interest to type by changing the baseline shift. Negative adjustments to the baseline move characters *below* the baseline, while positive adjustments move characters *above* the baseline.

QUICKTIP

Clicking the Set the text color button on either the options bar or the Character panel opens the Select text color dialog box.

FIGURE 4
Kerned characters

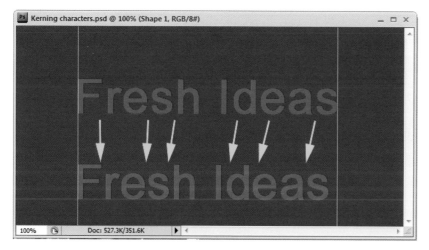

FIGURE 5
Character panel

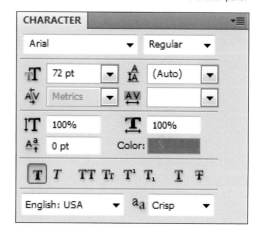

Kern characters

1. Click the **Concert Promotion Series type layer** on the Layers panel (if it is not already selected).

2. Click the **Horizontal Type tool** T. on the Tools panel.

3. Click between "r" and "i" in the word "Series."

4. Click the **Set the kerning between two characters list arrow** 𝔸𝕍 on the Character panel, then click **–25**.

   The spacing between the two characters decreases.

   > TIP   You can close the Character panel by clicking the list arrow in the upper-right corner of its title bar then clicking the Close command. You can also open and close the Character panel by clicking the Character button on the vertical dock.

5. Click between "i" and "o" in the word "Promotion."

6. Click 𝔸𝕍 , then click **–25**, as shown in Figure 6.

7. Click the **Commit any current edits button** ✔ on the options bar.

You modified the kerning between characters by using the Character panel.

FIGURE 6
Kerned type

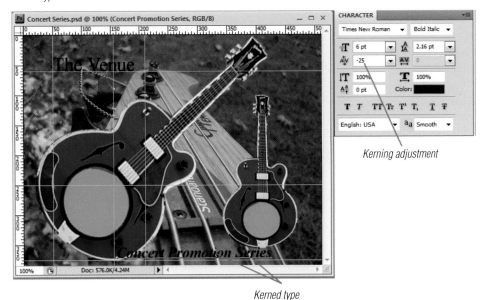

Kerning adjustment

Kerned type

Correcting spelling errors

Are you concerned that your gorgeous image will be ruined by misspelled words? Photoshop understands your pain and has included a spelling checker to make sure you are never plagued by incorrect spellings. If you want, the spelling checker will check the type on the current layer, or all the layers in the image. First, make sure the correct dictionary for your language is selected. English: USA is the default, but you can choose another language by clicking the Set the language on selected characters for hyphenation and spelling list arrow at the bottom of the Character panel. To check spelling, click Edit on the Application bar, then click Check Spelling. The spelling checker will automatically stop at each word not already appearing in the dictionary. One or more suggestions might be offered, which you can either accept or reject.

FIGURE 7
Select text color dialog box

Your color field may differ (Mac)

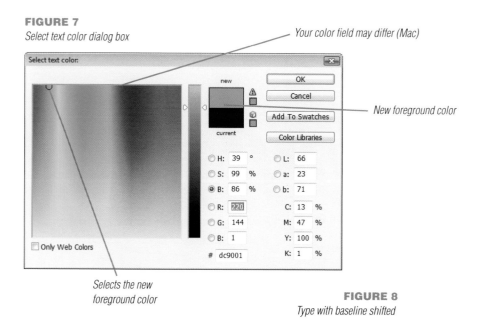

Selects the new foreground color

New foreground color

FIGURE 8
Type with baseline shifted

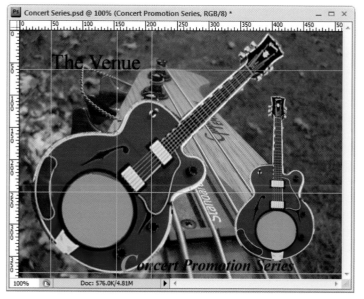

Shift the baseline

1. Use the **Horizontal Type pointer** [I] to select the "C" in "Concert".

2. Click the **Set the text color button** ▬ on the options bar.

3. Click anywhere in the gold area in the center of either guitar, such as **100 X/250 Y**, compare your Select text color dialog box to Figure 7, then click **OK**.

4. Double-click **6** in the Set the font size text box on the Character panel, type **10**, double-click **0** in the Set the baseline shift text box on the Character panel, then type **–1**.

5. Click the **Commit any current edits button** ✔ on the options bar.

6. Save your work, then compare your screen to Figure 8.

You changed the type color, then adjusted the baseline of the first character in a word, to make the first character stand out.

USE THE DROP
SHADOW STYLE

What You'll Do

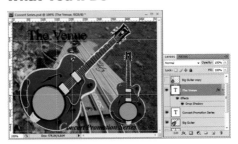

In this lesson, you'll apply the drop shadow style to a type layer, then modify drop shadow settings.

Adding Effects to Type

Layer styles (effects which can be applied to a type or image layer) can greatly enhance the appearance of type and improve its effectiveness. A type layer is indicated by the appearance of the T icon in the layer's thumbnail box. When a layer style is applied to any layer, the Indicates layer effects icon (*f x*) appears in that layer when it is active. The Layers panel is a great source of information. You can see which effects have been applied to a layer by clicking the arrow to the left of the Indicates layer effects icon on the Layers panel if the layer is active or inactive. Figure 9 shows a layer that has two type layer styles applied to it. Layer styles are linked to the contents of a layer, which means that if a type layer is moved or modified, the layer's style will still be applied to the type.

QUICKTIP

Type layer icons in the Macintosh version of Photoshop are similar though not identical to those in the Windows version.

Using the Drop Shadow

One method of placing emphasis on type is to add a drop shadow to it. A **drop shadow** creates an illusion that another colored layer of identical text is behind the selected type. The drop shadow default color is black, but it can be changed to another color using the Color Picker dialog box, or any of the other methods for changing color.

Applying a Style

You can apply a style, such as a drop shadow, to the active layer, by clicking Layer on the Application bar, pointing to Layer Style, then clicking a style.

The settings in the Layer Style dialog box are "sticky," meaning that they display the settings that you last used. An alternative method to using the Application bar is to select the layer that you want to apply the style to, click the Add a layer style button on the Layers panel, then click a style. Regardless of which method you use, the Layer Style dialog box opens. You use this dialog box to add all kinds of effects to type. Depending on which style you've chosen, the Layer Style dialog box displays options appropriate to that style.

QUICKTIP
You can apply styles to objects as well as to type.

Controlling a Drop Shadow

You can control many aspects of a drop shadow's appearance, including its angle, its distance behind the type, and the amount of blur it contains. The **angle** determines where the shadow falls relative to the text, and the **distance** determines how far the shadow falls from the text. The **spread** determines the width of the shadow text,

and the **size** determines the clarity of the shadow. Figure 10 shows samples of two different drop shadow effects. The first line of type uses the default background color (black), has an angle of 160 degrees, a distance of 10 pixels, a spread of 0%, and a size of five pixels. The second line of type uses a purple background color, has an angle of 120 degrees, a distance of 20 pixels, a spread of 10%, and a size of five pixels. As you modify the drop shadow, the preview window displays the changes.

FIGURE 9
Effects in a type layer

Layer style applied

Indicates effect(s) applied in layer

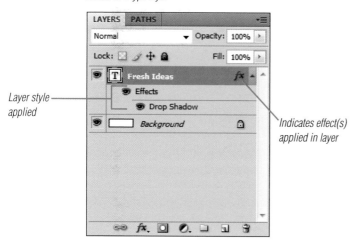

FIGURE 10
Sample drop shadows

Add a drop shadow

1. Click the **layer thumbnail** on The Venue type layer.

2. Double-click **8** in the Set the font size text box in the Character panel, type **12**, then press **[Enter]** (Win) or **[return]** (Mac).

3. Click the **Add a layer style button** *fx.* on the Layers panel.

   > TIP You can make your life easier by creating your own styles. Do you apply the stroke effect often? You can create your own stroke style by clicking the Add a layer style button on the Layers panel, clicking Stroke, entering your settings, then clicking New Style.

4. Click **Drop Shadow**.

5. Compare your Layer Style dialog box to Figure 11.

   The default drop shadow settings are applied to the type. Table 2 describes the drop shadow settings.

   > TIP You can also open the Layer Style dialog box by double-clicking a layer on the Layers panel.

You created a drop shadow by using the Add a layer style button on the Layers panel and the Layer Style dialog box.

FIGURE 11
Drop shadow settings

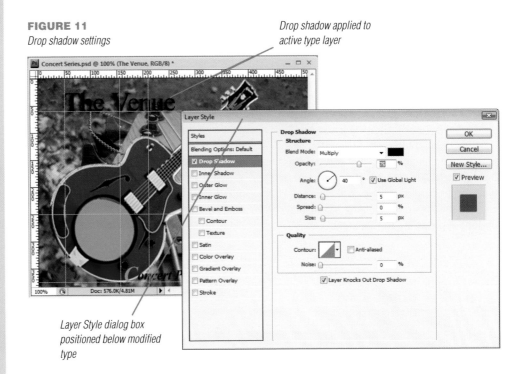

Drop shadow applied to active type layer

Layer Style dialog box positioned below modified type

TABLE 2: Drop Shadow Settings

setting	scale	explanation
Angle	0–360 degrees	At 0 degrees, the shadow appears on the baseline of the original text. At 90 degrees, the shadow appears directly below the original text.
Distance	0–30,000 pixels	A larger pixel size increases the distance from which the shadow text falls relative to the original text.
Spread	0–100%	A larger percentage increases the width of the shadow text.
Size	0–250 pixels	A larger pixel size increases the blur of the shadow text.

Placing Type in an Image

FIGURE 12
Layer Style dialog box

Angle text box —

Distance text box —

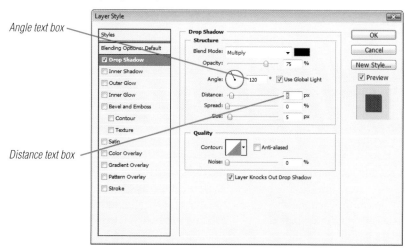

FIGURE 13
Drop shadow added to type layer

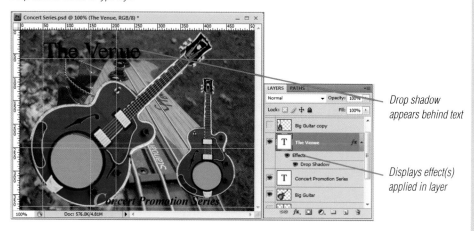

Drop shadow
appears behind text

Displays effect(s)
applied in layer

Modify drop shadow settings

1. Double-click the number in the Angle text box, then type **120**.

   Each style in the Layer Style dialog box shows different options in the center section. These options are displayed as you click each style (in the Styles pane).

   TIP You can also set the angle by dragging the dial slider in the Layer Style dialog box.

2. Double-click the number in the Distance text box, then type **8**. See Figure 12.

   TIP You can create your own layer style in the Layer Style dialog box, by selecting style settings, clicking New Style, typing a new name or accepting the default, then clicking OK. The new style appears as a preset in the Styles list of the Layer Style dialog box.

3. Click **OK**, then compare your screen to Figure 13.

4. Click the **list arrow to the right of the Indicates layer effects icon** on The Venue layer to collapse the list.

5. Save your work.

You used the Layer Style dialog box to modify the settings for the drop shadow.

APPLY ANTI-ALIASING
TO TYPE

What You'll Do

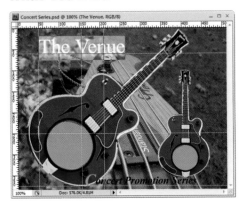

In this lesson, you'll view the effects of the anti-aliasing feature, then use the History panel to return the type to its original state.

Eliminating the "Jaggies"

In the good old days of dot-matrix printers, jagged edges were obvious in many print ads. You can still see these jagged edges in designs produced on less sophisticated printers. To prevent the jagged edges (sometimes called "jaggies") that often accompany bitmap type, Photoshop offers an anti-aliasing feature. **Anti-aliasing** partially fills in pixel edges with additional colors, resulting in smooth-edge type and an increased number of colors in the image. Anti-aliasing is useful for improving the display of large type in print media; however, this can cause a file to become large.

Knowing When to Apply Anti-Aliasing

As a rule, type that has a point size greater than 12 should have some anti-aliasing method applied. Sometimes, smaller type sizes can become blurry or muddy when anti-aliasing is used. As part of the process, anti-aliasing adds intermediate colors to your image in an effort to reduce the jagged edges. As a designer, you need to weigh these three factors (type size, file size, and image quality) when determining if you should apply anti-aliasing.

Understanding Anti-Aliasing

Anti-aliasing improves the display of type against the background. You can use five anti-aliasing methods: None, Sharp, Crisp, Strong, and Smooth. An example of each method is shown in Figure 14. The **None** setting applies no anti-aliasing, and can result in type that has jagged edges.

The **Sharp** setting displays type with the best possible resolution. The **Crisp** setting gives type more definition and makes type appear sharper. The **Strong** setting makes type appear heavier, much like the bold attribute. The **Smooth** setting gives type more rounded edges.

QUICKTIP

Generally, the type used in your image should be the messenger, not the message. As you work with type, keep in mind that using more than two fonts in one image might be distracting or make the overall appearance unprofessional.

FIGURE 14
Anti-aliasing effects

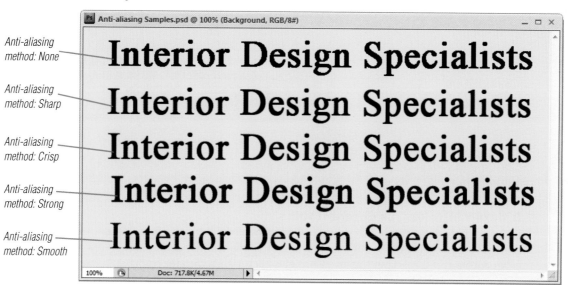

Anti-aliasing method: None

Anti-aliasing method: Sharp

Anti-aliasing method: Crisp

Anti-aliasing method: Strong

Anti-aliasing method: Smooth

Apply anti-aliasing

1. Double-click the **layer thumbnail** on The Venue layer.

2. Click the **Set the anti-aliasing method list arrow** aa Sharp ▾ on the options bar.

   > TIP   You've probably noticed that some items, such as the Set the anti-aliasing method list arrow, the Set the text color button, and the Set the kerning between two characters list arrow are duplicated on the options bar and the Character panel. So which should you use? Whichever one you feel most comfortable using. These tasks are performed identically regardless of the feature's origin.

3. Click **Strong**, then compare your work to Figure 15.

4. Click the **Commit any current edits button** ✔ on the options bar.

You applied the Strong anti-aliasing setting to see how the setting affected the appearance of type.

FIGURE 15
Effect of Strong anti-aliasing

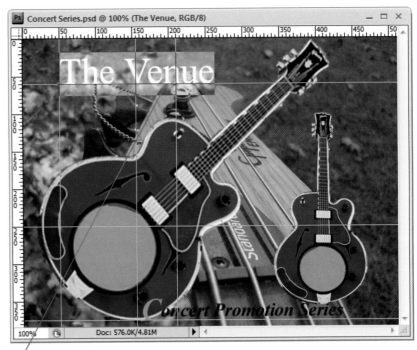

Type appearance altered

Different strokes for different folks

You're probably already aware that you can use different methods to achieve the same goals in Photoshop. For instance, if you want to see the type options bar, you can either double-click a type layer thumbnail or single-click it, then click the Horizontal Type tool. The method you use determines what you'll see in the History panel. Using the double-clicking method, a change in the anti-aliasing method will result in the following history state 'Edit Type Layer'. Using the single-clicking method to change to the anti-alias method to Crisp results in an 'Anti Alias Crisp' history state.

FIGURE 16

Deleting a state from the History panel

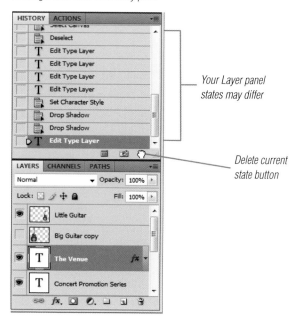

Your Layer panel
states may differ

Delete current
state button

1. Click the **workspace switcher** on the Application bar, then click **History and Layers**.

   The History panel is now visible.

2. Click the **Edit Type Layer state** listed at the bottom of the History panel, then drag it to the **Delete current state button** 🗑 , as shown in Figure 16.

   | TIP   Various methods of undoing actions are reviewed in Table 3.

3. Return the display to the **Typography** workspace.

4. Save your work.

You deleted a state in the History panel to return the type to its original appearance. The History panel offers an easy way of undoing previous steps.

TABLE 3: Undoing Actions

method	description	keyboard shortcut
Undo	Edit ➢ Undo	[Ctrl][Z] (Win) ⌘[Z] (Mac)
Step Backward	Click Edit on the Application bar, then click Step Backward	[Alt][Ctrl][Z] (Win) [option] ⌘[Z] (Mac)
History panel	Drag state to the Delete current state button on the History panel, or click the Delete current state button on the History panel	[Alt] 🗑 (Win) [option] 🗑 (Mac) 🗑

MODIFY TYPE WITH THE
BEVEL AND EMBOSS STYLE

What You'll Do

 In this lesson, you'll apply the Bevel and Emboss style, then modify the Bevel and Emboss settings.

Using the Bevel and Emboss Style

You use the Bevel and Emboss style to add combinations of shadows and highlights to a layer and make type appear to have dimension and shine. You can use the Layer menu or the Layers panel to apply the Bevel and Emboss style to the active layer. Like all Layer styles, the Bevel and Emboss style is linked to the type layer to which it is applied.

Understanding Bevel and Emboss Settings

You can use two categories of Bevel and Emboss settings: structure and shading. **Structure** determines the size and physical properties of the object, and **shading** determines the lighting effects. Figure 17 contains several variations of Bevel and Emboss structure settings, while additional Bevel and Emboss structure settings are listed in Table 4. The shading

Filling type with imagery

You can use the imagery from a layer in one file as the fill pattern for another image's type layer. To create this effect, open a multi-layer file that contains the imagery you want to use (the source), then open the file that contains the type you want to fill (the target). In the source file, activate the layer containing the imagery you want to use, use the Select menu to select all, then use the Edit menu to copy the selection. In the target file, press [Ctrl] (Win) or ⌘ (Mac) while clicking the type layer to which the imagery will be applied, then click Paste Into on the Edit menu. The imagery will appear within the type.

used in the Bevel and Emboss style determines how and where light is projected on the type. You can control a variety of settings, including the angle, altitude, and gloss contour, to create a unique appearance. The **Angle** setting determines where the shadow falls relative to the text, and the **Altitude** setting affects the amount of visible dimension. For example, an altitude of 0 degrees looks flat, while a setting of 90 degrees has a more three-dimensional appearance. The **Gloss Contour** setting determines the pattern with which light is reflected, and the **Highlight Mode** and **Shadow Mode** settings determine how pigments are combined. When the Use Global Light check box is selected, *all the type* in the image will be affected by your changes.

FIGURE 17
Bevel and Emboss style samples

TABLE 4: Bevel and Emboss Structure Settings

sample	style	technique	direction	size	soften
1	Inner Bevel	Smooth	Up	5	1
2	Outer Bevel	Chisel Hard	Up	5	8
3	Emboss	Smooth	Down	10	3
4	Pillow Emboss	Chisel Soft	Up	10	3

Lesson 5 Modify Type with the Bevel and Emboss Style

Add the Bevel and Emboss style with the Layer menu

1. Verify that **The Venue layer** is the active layer, then use any Zoom tool so the image is viewed at a zoom level of 200%.

2. Click the **Set the text color button** ▬ on the options bar, click the silver area in the large guitar (at approximately **70 X/330 Y**), then click **OK**.

3. Click **Layer** on the Application bar, point to **Layer Style**, click **Bevel and Emboss**, then click **Bevel and Emboss** in the Styles column (if it is not already selected).

4. Review the Layer Style dialog box shown in Figure 18, then move the Layer Style dialog box (if necessary), so you can see "The Venue" type.

You applied the Bevel and Emboss style by using the Layer menu. This gave the text a more three-dimensional look.

FIGURE 18
Layer Style dialog box

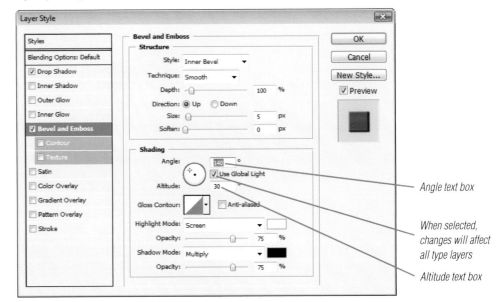

Angle text box

When selected, changes will affect all type layers

Altitude text box

Warping type

You can add dimension and style to your type by using the Warp Text feature. After you select the type layer you want to warp, click the Horizontal Type tool on the Tools panel. Click the Create warped text button on the options bar to open the Warp Text dialog box. If a warning box opens telling you that your request cannot be completed because the type layer uses a faux bold style, click the Toggle the Character and Paragraph panels button on the options bar, click the Character panel list arrow, click Faux Bold to deselect it, then click the Create warped text button again. You can click the Style list arrow to select from 15 available styles. After you select a style, you can modify its appearance by dragging the Bend, Horizontal Distortion, and Vertical Distortion sliders.

Placing Type in an Image

FIGURE 19
Bevel and Emboss style applied to type

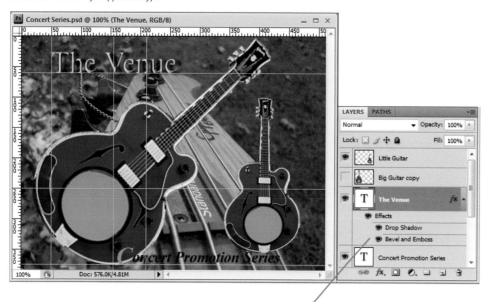

*Bevel and Emboss
style applied to layer*

1. Double-click the number in the Angle text box, then type **165**.

   You can use the Layer Style dialog box to change the structure by adjusting style, technique, direction, size, and soften settings.

2. Double-click the **Altitude text box**, then type **20**.

3. Click **OK**, reduce the zoom level to 100%, expand The Venue layer in the Layers panel, then compare your type to Figure 19.

4. Save your work.

You modified the default settings for the Bevel and Emboss style. Experimenting with different settings is crucial to achieve the effect you want.

APPLY SPECIAL EFFECTS TO
TYPE USING FILTERS

What You'll Do

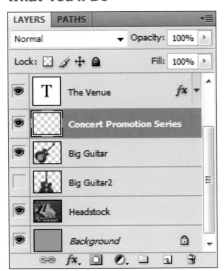

 In this lesson, you'll rasterize a type layer, then apply a filter to it to change its appearance.

Understanding Filters

Like an image layer, a type layer can have one or more filters applied to it to achieve special effects and make your text look unique. Some filter dialog boxes have preview windows that let you see the results of the particular filter before it is applied to the layer. Other filters must be applied to the layer before you can see the results. Before a filter can be applied to a type layer, the type layer must first be **rasterized**, or converted to an image layer. After it is rasterized, the type characters *can no longer be edited* because it is composed of pixels, just like artwork. When a type layer is rasterized, the T icon in the layer thumbnail becomes an image thumbnail while the Effects icons remain on the type layer.

Creating Special Effects

Filters enable you to apply a variety of special effects to type, as shown in Figure 20. Notice that none of the original type layers on the Layers panel in Figure 20 display the T icon in the layer thumbnail because the layers have all been rasterized.

> **QUICK**TIP
>
> Because you cannot edit type after it has been rasterized, you should save your original type by making a copy of the layer *before* you rasterize it, then hide it from view.

Producing Distortions

Distort filters let you create waves or curves in type. Some of the types of distortions you can produce include Glass, Pinch, Ripple, Shear, Spherize, Twirl, Wave, and Zigzag. These effects are sometimes used as the basis of a corporate logo. The Twirl dialog box, shown in Figure 21, lets you determine the amount of twirl effect you want to apply. By dragging the Angle slider, you control how much twirl effect is added to a layer. Most filter dialog boxes have Zoom In and Zoom Out buttons that make it easy to see the effects of the filter.

Using Textures and Relief

Many filters let you create the appearance of textures and **relief** (the height of ridges within an object). One of the Stylize filters, Wind, applies lines throughout the type, making it appear shredded. The Wind dialog box, shown in Figure 22, lets you determine the kind of wind and its direction. The Texture filter lets you choose the type of texture you want to apply to a layer: Brick, Burlap, Canvas, or Sandstone.

Blurring Imagery

The Gaussian Blur filter softens the appearance of type by blurring its edge pixels. You can control the amount of blur applied to the type by entering high or low values in the Gaussian Blur dialog box. The higher the blur value, the blurrier the effect.

QUICKTIP

Be careful: too much blur applied to type can make it unreadable.

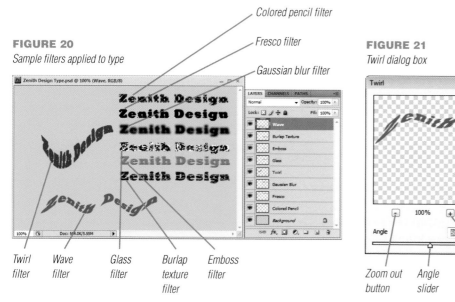

FIGURE 20
Sample filters applied to type

Colored pencil filter

Fresco filter

Gaussian blur filter

Twirl filter
Wave filter
Glass filter
Burlap texture filter
Emboss filter

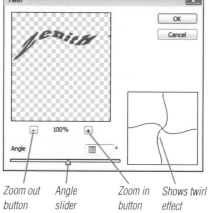

FIGURE 21
Twirl dialog box

Zoom out button
Angle slider
Zoom in button
Shows twirl effect

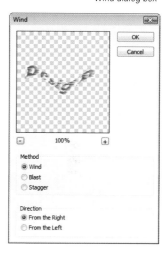

FIGURE 22
Wind dialog box

Rasterize a type layer

1. Click the **Concert Promotion Series** layer on the Layers panel.

2. Click **Filter** on the Application bar, point to **Noise**, then click **Dust & Scratches**.

3. Click **OK** to rasterize the type and close the warning box shown in Figure 23.

   | TIP You can also rasterize a type layer by clicking Layer on the Application bar, pointing to Rasterize, then clicking Type.

   The Dust & Scratches dialog box opens.

You rasterized a type layer in preparation for filter application.

FIGURE 23
Warning box

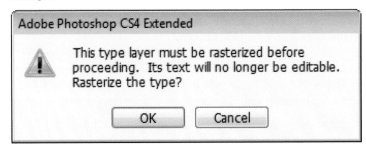

Adobe Photoshop CS4 Extended

This type layer must be rasterized before proceeding. Its text will no longer be editable. Rasterize the type?

OK   Cancel

DESIGNTIP **Using multiple filters**

Sometimes, adding one filter doesn't achieve the effect you had in mind. You can use multiple filters to create a unique effect. Before you try your hand at filters, though, it's a good idea to make a copy of the original layer. That way, if things don't turn out as you planned, you can always start over. You don't even have to write down which filters you used, because you can always look at the History panel to review which filters you applied.

FIGURE 24

Dust & Scratches dialog box

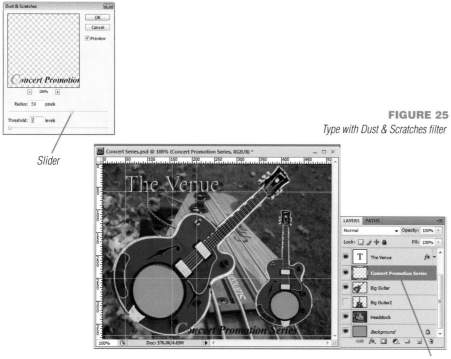

FIGURE 25
Type with Dust & Scratches filter

Slider

No longer a type layer

Modify filter settings

1. Drag the default background patterns in the preview window of the dialog box to position the type so at least part of the type is visible.

2. Drag the sliders in the Dust & Scratches dialog box until **50** appears in the Radius pixels text box, and **0** appears in the Threshold levels text box, as shown in Figure 24.

3. Click **OK**.

4. Save your work. Compare your modified type to Figure 25.

You modified the Dust & Scratches filter settings to modify the appearance of the layer.

Creating a neon glow

Want to create a really cool effect that takes absolutely no time at all, and works on both type and objects? You can create a neon glow that appears to surround an object. You can apply the Neon Glow filter (one of the Artistic filters) to any flattened image. This effect works best by starting with any imagery—either type or objects—that has a solid color background. Flatten the image so there's only a Background layer. Click the Magic Wand tool on the Tools panel, then click the solid color (in the background). Click Filter on the Application bar, point to Artistic, then click Neon Glow. Adjust the glow size, the glow brightness, and color, if you wish, then click OK. (An example of this technique is used in the Design Project at the end of this chapter.)

CREATE TEXT
ON A PATH

What You'll Do

In this lesson, you'll create a shape, then add type to it.

Understanding Text on a Path

Although it is possible to create some cool type effects by adding layer styles such as bevel, emboss, and drop shadow, you can also create some awesome warped text. Suppose you want type to conform to a shape, such as an oval or a free-form you've drawn? No problem—just create the shape and add the text!

Creating Text on a Path

You start by creating a shape using one of the Photoshop shape tools on the Tools panel, and then adding type to that shape (which is called a path). Add type to a shape by clicking the Horizontal Type tool. When the pointer nears the path, you'll see that it changes to the Type tool pointer. Click the path when the Type tool pointer displays and begin typing. You can change fonts, font sizes, add styles, and any other interesting effects you've learned to apply with type. As you will see, the type is on a path!

QUICKTIP

Don't worry when you see the outline of the path on the screen. The path won't print, only the type will.

FIGURE 26
Type on a path

Path does
not display
when image
is printed

Create a path and add type

1. Click the **Rectangle tool** ▣ on the Tools panel.
2. Click the **Ellipse tool** ◯ on the options bar.
3. Click the **Paths button** ▨ on the options bar.
4. Drag the **Paths pointer** ╀⊗ to create a circular path within the gold circle on the large guitar from **100 X/250 Y** while holding [Shift].
5. Click the **Horizontal Type tool** T, on the Tools panel.
6. Change the font to **Arial**, use the Bold font style, set the font size to **8** pt, then verify that the **Left align text button** is selected.

   TIP You can change to any point size by typing the number in the Set the font size text box.

7. Click the **Horizontal Type pointer** ꞇ at approximately **90 X/270 Y** on the left edge of the ellipse.
8. Change the font color by sampling the blue at the top of the large guitar then type **The Venue**.
9. Commit any current edits.
10. Hide the rulers and guides, return to the **Essentials** workspace, and save your work. Compare your image to Figure 26.
11. Close the Concert Series.psd file and exit Photoshop.

You created a path using a shape tool, then added type to it.

Power User Shortcuts

to do this:	use this method:
Apply anti-alias method	aₐ Sharp ▼
Apply Bevel and Emboss style	fx., Bevel and Emboss
Apply blur filter to type	Filter ➢ Blur ➢ Gaussian Blur
Apply Drop Shadow style	fx., Drop Shadow
Cancel any current edits	⊘
Change font family	Times New Roman ▼
Change font size	T 6 pt ▼
Change type color	▬
Close type effects	▽
Commit current edits	✓
Display/hide rulers	[Ctrl][R] (Win) or ⌘[R] (Mac)
Erase a History state	Select state, drag to 🗑

to do this:	use this method:
Horizontal Type tool	T. or T
Kern characters	A̲V Metrics ▼
Move tool	►₊ or V
Open Character panel	🗐
Save image changes	[Ctrl][S] (Win) or ⌘[S] (Mac)
See type effects (active layer)	▼
See type effects (inactive layer)	▼
Select all text	[Ctrl][A] (Win) or ⌘[A] (Mac)
Shift baseline of type	ᵀT 100%
Warp type	⊥

Key: Menu items are indicated by ➢ between the menu name and its command. Blue bold letters are shortcuts for selecting tools on the Tools panel.

Learn about type and how it is created.

1. Open PS 5-2.psd from the drive and folder where you store your Data Files, then save it as **ZD-Logo**.
2. Display the rulers with pixels.
3. Use the Horizontal Type tool to create a type layer that starts at 45 X/95 Y.
4. Use a black 35 pt Lucida Sans font or substitute another font.
5. Type **Zenith**.
6. Use the Horizontal Type tool and a 16 pt type size to create a type layer at 70 X/180 Y, then type **Always the best**.
7. Save your work.

Change spacing and adjust baseline shift.

1. Use the Horizontal Type tool to create a new type layer at 205 X/95 Y.
2. Use a 35 pt Myriad font.
3. Type **Design**.
4. Select the Design type.
5. Change the type color to the color used in the lower-left background.
6. Change the type size of the Z and D to 50 pts.
7. Adjust the baseline shift of the Z and D to –5.
8. Save your work.

Use the Drop Shadow style.

1. Activate the Zenith type layer.
2. Apply the Drop Shadow style.
3. In the Layer Style dialog box, set the angle to 150°, then close the Layer Style dialog box.
4. Save your work.

Apply anti-aliasing to type.

1. Activate the Zenith type layer.
2. Change the Anti-Alias method to Smooth (if necessary).
3. Save your work.

Modify type with the Bevel and Emboss style.

1. Activate the Design type layer.
2. Apply the Bevel and Emboss style.
3. In the Layer Style dialog box, set the style to Inner Bevel.
4. Set the angle to 150° and the altitude to 30°.
5. Close the Layer Style dialog box.
6. Activate the Zenith type layer.
7. Apply the Bevel and Emboss style.
8. Set the style to Inner Bevel.
9. Verify that the angle is set to 150° and the altitude is set to 30°.
10. Close the Layer Style dialog box.
11. Save your work.

Apply special effects to type using filters.

1. Apply a 1.0 pixel Gaussian Blur effect to the "Always the best" layer.
2. Save your work.

Create text on a path.

1. Use the Ellipse tool to draw an ellipse from approximately 200 X/120 Y to 370 X/185 Y.
2. Click the line with the Horizontal Type tool at 210 X/130 Y.
3. Type **Founded in 1957** using the second color swatch in the first row of the Swatches panel (RGB Yellow), in a 16 pt Arial font.
4. Change the anti-aliasing method to Crisp.
5. Change the opacity of the type (using the Opacity slider in the Layers panel) on the path to 45%.
6. Turn off the ruler display.
7. Save your work, then compare your image to Figure 27.

FIGURE 27
Completed Skills Review Project

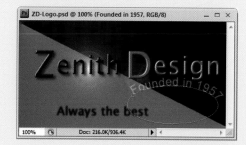

A local flower shop, Beautiful Blooms, asks you to design its color advertisement for the trade magazine, *Florists United*. You have already started on the image, and need to add some type.

1. Open PS 5-3.psd, then save it as **Beautiful Blooms Ad**.
2. Click the Horizontal Type tool, then type **Beautiful Blooms** using a 55 pt Impact font in black.
3. Create a catchy phrase of your choice, using a 24 pt Verdana font.
4. Apply a drop shadow style to the name of the flower shop using the following settings: Multiply blend mode, 75% Opacity, 30%, 5 pixel distance, 0° spread, and 5 pixel size.
5. Apply a Bevel and Emboss style to the catch phrase using the following settings: Inner Bevel style, Smooth technique, 100% depth, Up direction, 5 pixel size, 0 pixel soften, 30° angle, 30° altitude, and using global light.
6. Compare your image to the sample in Figure 28.
7. Save your work.

FIGURE 28
Sample Project Builder 1

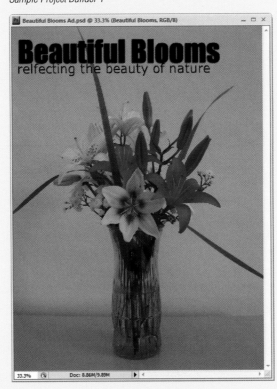

Placing Type in an Image

You are a junior art director for an advertising agency. You have been working on an ad that promotes milk and milk products. You have started the project, but still have a few details to finish up before it is complete.

1. Open PS 5-4.psd, then save it as **Milk Promotion**.
2. Create a shape using any shape tool, then use the shape as a text path and type a snappy phrase of your choosing on the shape.
3. Use a 24 pt Arial font in the style and color of your choice for the catch phrase type layer. (If necessary, substitute another font.)
4. Create a Bevel and Emboss style on the type layer, setting the angle to 100° and the altitude to 30°.
5. Compare your image to the sample in Figure 29.
6. Save your work.

FIGURE 29
Sample Project Builder 2

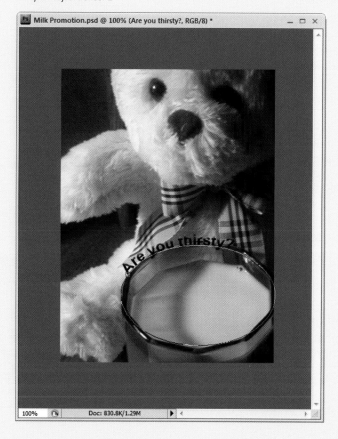

Placing Type in an Image

You are a freelance designer. A local clothing store, Attitude, is expanding and has hired you to work on an advertisement. You have already created the file, and inserted the necessary type layers. Before you proceed, you decide to explore the Internet to find information on using type to create an effective design.

1. Connect to the Internet and use your browser to find information about typography. (Make a record of the site you found so you can use it for future reference, if necessary.)
2. Find information about using type as an effective design element.
3. Open PS 5-5.psd, update the layers (if necessary), then save the file as **Attitude**.
4. Modify the existing type by changing fonts, font colors, and font sizes.
5. Edit the type, if necessary, to make it shorter and clearer.
6. Rearrange the position of the type to create an effective design.
7. Add a Bevel and Emboss style using your choice of settings, then compare your image to the sample in Figure 30. (The fonts Mistral and Trebuchet MS are used in this image. Make substitutions if you don't have these fonts on your computer.)
8. Save your work.

FIGURE 30
Sample Design Project

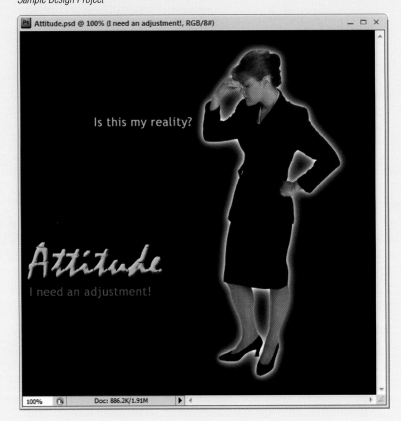

Placing Type in an Image

You have been hired by your community to create an advertising campaign that promotes tourism. Decide what aspect of the community you want to emphasize. Locate appropriate imagery (already existing on your hard drive, on the web, your own creation, or using a scanner), then add type to create a meaningful Photoshop image.

1. Create an image with the dimensions 550 pixels × 550 pixels.
2. Save this file as **Community Promotion**.
3. Locate appropriate imagery of your community on your hard drive, from a digital camera, or a scanner.
4. Add at least two layers of type in the image, using multiple font sizes. (Use any fonts available on your computer. You can use multiple fonts if you want.)
5. Add a Bevel and Emboss style to at least one type layer, and add a drop shadow to at least one layer. (*Hint*: You can add both effects to the same layer.)
6. Position type layers to create an effective design.
7. Compare your image to the sample in Figure 31.
8. Save your work.

FIGURE 31
Sample Portfolio Project

INTEGRATING
ADOBE CS4 WEB PREMIUM

1. Insert a Photoshop image into a Dreamweaver document

2. Create a Photoshop document and import it into Flash

3. Insert and edit a Flash movie in Dreamweaver

1 INTEGRATING
ADOBE CS4 WEB PREMIUM

Introduction

The Adobe Creative Suite 4 Web Premium of integrated web development products includes Dreamweaver, Flash, and Photoshop. Used together, these tools allow you to create websites that include compelling graphics, animations, and interactivity. Recognizing that developing a website often involves team members with varying expertise (graphic designers, animators, programmers, and so on), Adobe has designed these products so that they integrate easily. This integration allows you to move from one product to another as you bring together the elements of a website. For example, you can create a graphic image using Photoshop, import the image into Dreamweaver, and then edit the image starting from the Dreamweaver environment. While each of the products can stand alone, they have a similar look and feel, with common features and interface elements, such as the Properties panel that allow you to transfer your skills from one product to another. Adobe provides two other products that you can use when working with these web development tools. Adobe Bridge CS4 provides a quick way to organize, locate, and display the elements used to create websites and applications (such as Photoshop images, Flash movies, and Dreamweaver documents). Adobe Version Cue CS4 is used in a workgroup process where team members need access to the latest versions of a file. Using Version Cue, you set up a project, add users and assign permissions, and add files to the project. Then, users can "check out" a file and work on it. The check out process ensures that only one person is working on a file at a time. When the file is saved, a new version is created while the previous versions are maintained. Version Cue is accessed through Adobe Bridge and requires a connection to a server.

Tools You'll Use

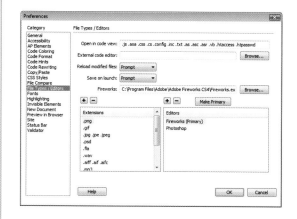

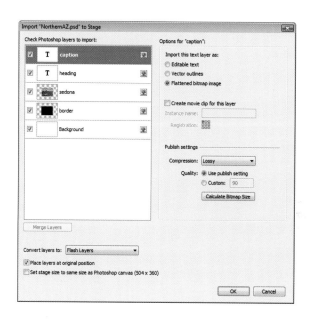

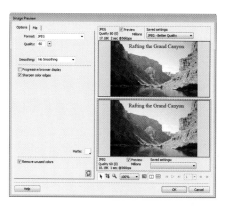

INSERT A PHOTOSHOP IMAGE INTO
A DREAMWEAVER DOCUMENT

What You'll Do

In this lesson, you will integrate a Photoshop image into a Dreamweaver document and edit the image from Dreamweaver.

Inserting a Photoshop Image into Dreamweaver

The process for inserting a Photoshop image into a Dreamweaver document is to create the image in Photoshop and save it in the PSD file format. Then, start Dreamweaver and open an existing HTML document or start a new one. Next, select the location in the page where you want the image to appear and insert the PSD file. The Image Preview dialog box opens, as shown in Figure 1. This dialog box allows you to convert the PSD file to one of the web-ready file types (PNG, JPEG, or GIF). You can also use the dialog box to change the optimization settings in order to reduce the file size while maintaining the desired quality. For example, a JPEG format would usually result in higher quality for a photograph than a GIF format. However, the GIF format might have a smaller file size. The Image Preview dialog box allows you to display two or four images at a time and compare the quality of images as the settings are changed.

After completing the Image Preview dialog box, the image appears on the

Dreamweaver document with a green icon, as shown in Figure 2. This icon indicates that the image is a **Smart Object**, that is, an object that contains a link to the source file. To edit the source file, you select the image in the Dreamweaver document and then click the Photoshop Edit button on the Properties panel. This launches Photoshop, displays the image, and allows you to edit and save the PSD file. Dreamweaver recognizes when the file has been updated and changes the icon to red and green. This alerts you that the source file has been changed and allows you to update the image in the Dreamweaver document without having to reinsert the image. All of the optimization settings that were originally specified are kept. In addition, all instances of the image within the website are automatically updated.

Another process for inserting Photoshop images into a Dreamweaver document is to copy and paste the image from one application to the other. When you copy and paste a PSD file from Photoshop to Dreamweaver, the Image Preview dialog box opens, allowing you convert the PSD file to a PNG, JPG, or GIF format. In addition, you can change the optimization settings. A copied image does not appear in Dreamweaver as a Smart Object. However, Dreamweaver keeps track of the source file and if you want to edit the image you can select the image on the page and click the Photoshop Edit button on the Properties panel to display the image in Photoshop. After editing the image, you choose the Copy Merged command (assuming you have added a layer or layers). Next, you return to Dreamweaver and paste the edited image over the old one.

The previously set file type (PNG, JPG, GIF) and optimization settings would be applied to the edited image.

The advantages of creating a Smart Object are that you are alerted when a source file has been changed, the update process is very easy, and all instances of the image within the website are updated automatically. The advantage of the copy/paste process is that you can copy a portion of the image, a single layer, a group of layers, or a slice of an image.

Setting Photoshop as the Primary External Image Editor

You can import a Photoshop image into a Dreamweaver document. Later on, when desired, you can edit the graphic by launching the Photoshop program from within Dreamweaver. This requires that in Dreamweaver you set Photoshop as the primary external image editor for PSD, GIF, JPEG, and PNG files. You can set the external image editor using settings in the Preferences dialog box in Dreamweaver.

FIGURE 1
The Image Preview dialog box

FIGURE 2
The inserted image with the green icon

Green icon indicates a Smart Object

Setting up the Folder Structure for the Files

Figure 3 shows the folder structure and files you will be developing in this chapter. You will use the Southwest folder as the destination folder when you save an HTML document or SWF file. You will use the assets folder as the destination folder when you save a Photoshop image. As you work through the chapter, you will integrate Photoshop images and a Flash movie into Dreamweaver documents.

Using Design Notes

When you insert an image or file created in Photoshop or Flash in Dreamweaver, information about the original source file (PSD or FLA) is saved in a Design Notes file (MNO). For example, if in Dreamweaver you import a file named airplane.jpg whose source file is airplane.psd, Dreamweaver creates a Design Notes file named airplane.jpg.mno. The Design Notes file contains references to the source PSD file, which allows you to edit it by opening

Photoshop from Dreamweaver. You should save your Photoshop source PSD file and exported files in the Dreamweaver site. Saving in this location ensures that any developer sharing the site can also access the source PSD file. A Design Notes file also contains the optimization settings you specify in the Image Preview dialog box.

FIGURE 3

Structure of the website

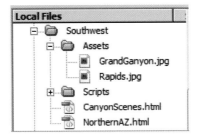

FIGURE 4

The CanyonScenes.html document

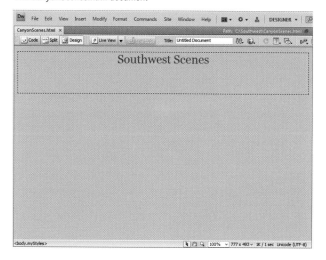

FIGURE 5

Dreamweaver Preferences dialog box (Win)

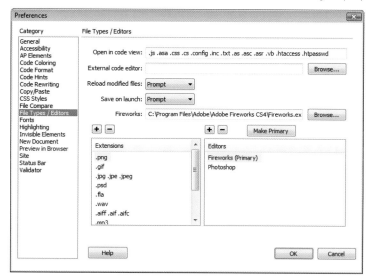

This lesson requires that you have Dreamweaver CS4 and Photoshop CS4 installed on your computer.

1. Use your operating system's file management tool to navigate to where you store your Data Files, then create a folder named **Southwest**.

2. Create a folder in the Southwest folder, then name it **Assets**.

3. Start Dreamweaver, **open ic_1.html**, save it to the Southwest folder as **CanyonScenes.html**, then update links, if prompted.

   Your screen should resemble Figure 4.

4. Click **Edit** (Win) or **Dreamweaver** (Mac) on the menu bar, then click **Preferences**.

5. Click **File Types / Editors** to display the options shown in Figure 5.

   | TIP Each file type has a default editor.

6. Scroll down the Extensions column, click **.psd**, then verify that Photoshop (Primary) (Win) or Adobe Photoshop CS4 (Primary) (Mac) appears in the Editors column.

7. Click **.png** in the Extensions column, click **Photoshop** (Win) or **Adobe Photoshop CS4** (Mac) in the Editors column, then click **Make Primary** (if necessary).

8. Repeat Step 5 for **.gif** and **.jpg .jpe .jpeg** file types in the Extensions column (if necessary).

9. Click **OK** to close the Preferences dialog box.

You opened and saved an HTML document, then used the Preferences dialog box to verify that Photoshop is the primary external editor for .psd, .png, .gif, and .jpg files.

Lesson 1   Insert a Photoshop Image into a Dreamweaver Document

Edit a Photoshop document

1. Start Photoshop.

2. Open **ic_1.psd** from where you store your Data Files, then save it as **GrandCanyon.psd**.

   This document has a single image, a photo of the Grand Canyon.

3. Click the **Text tool** T on the Tools panel, then change the font to **Times New Roman**, the size to **18pt**, and the color to **#293bc5**.

4. Click the **top-left corner** of the sky to create an insertion point, type **Rafting the Grand Canyon**, then position the text as shown in Figure 6.

5. Save your document, specifying Maximize compatibility (if necessary).

6. Exit Photoshop.

You opened a Photoshop PSD file, added a text layer, inserted text, saved the file, and exited Photoshop.

FIGURE 6
Positioning the text

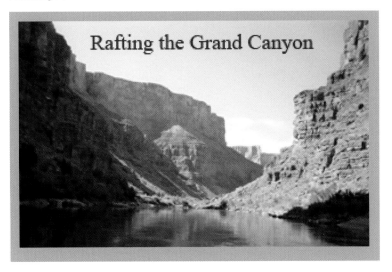

FIGURE 7

The Image Preview dialog box with two preview windows

Quality set to 60

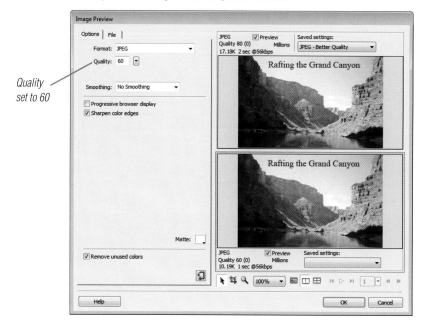

Insert a Photoshop image into a Dreamweaver document

1. Display Dreamweaver, then position the insertion point below the heading.

2. Click **Insert** on the Application bar, then click **Image**.

3. Use the Select Image Source dialog box to select the **GrandCanyon.psd** file, then click **OK** (Win) or **Choose** (Mac).

   The Image Preview dialog box appears, where you can change various attributes, including Format and Quality.

4. Verify that JPEG is specified for the Format and 80 is specified for the Quality.

5. Click the **2 preview windows icon** ⊞ .

6. Click the **Quality list arrow** ⊡ , use the slider to set the Quality to **60**, click away from the Quality list arrow, then compare your dialog box to Figure 7.

   Notice reducing the quality setting does not affect the quality of the image, but the file size has been reduced from its original size.

7. Click **OK** to apply the changes.

8. Navigate to the **Assets folder** in the Southwest folder in the Save Web Image dialog box, then click **Save**.

9. Type **A photo of the Grand Canyon** for the Alternate text in the Image Tag Accessibility Attributes dialog box, then click **OK**.

   The image appears in Dreamweaver with the Smart Object green icon displayed.

10. Save your work.

You changed the optimization settings for a Photoshop image and inserted it into a Dreamweaver document.

Edit a Photoshop image from a Dreamweaver document

1. Verify that the **image** is selected, then click the **Photoshop Edit button** 🆇 in the Properties panel.

   The GrandCanyon.psd image opens in Photoshop.

2. Verify that the text layer is selected in the Layers panel, click the **Add a layer style icon** 🆇, then click **Drop Shadow**.

3. Click **OK** in the Layer Style dialog box to accept the default values.

   Your image should resemble Figure 8.

4. Save the document.

5. Exit Photoshop and display Dreamweaver.

   Notice the icon has changed to red and green, indicating that the source image has been updated.

6. Point to the image, **right-click** (Win) or **[control]-click** (Mac), then click **Update From Original**.

You used Photoshop to edit an image in Dreamweaver and then updated the image.

FIGURE 8
The edited Photoshop image

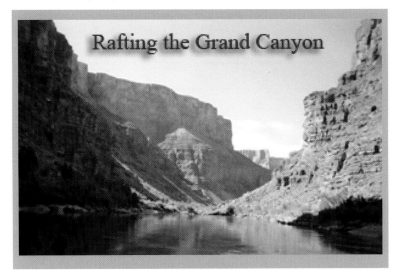

FIGURE 9

Image placed in the document with no Smart Object icon

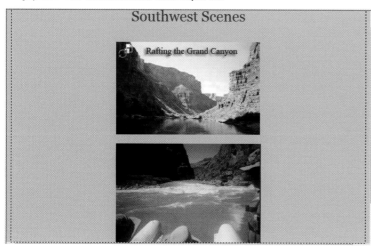

FIGURE 10

Selecting part of the image

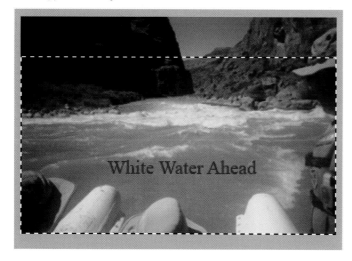

Copy and paste a Photoshop image to a Dreamweaver document

1. Start Photoshop, open **ic_2.psd**, then save it as **Rapids.psd**.
2. Click **Select** on the Application bar, then click **All**.
3. Click **Edit** on the Application bar, click **Copy**, then close the document.
4. Display Dreamweaver, set an insertion point below the Grand Canyon image, click **Edit** on the Application bar, then click **Paste**.
5. Click **OK** in the Image Preview dialog box, save the file to the Assets folder, then type **Photo of rapids** as the alternate text.

   Figure 9 shows that the image is placed in the document, but not as a Smart Object.
6. With the image selected, click the **Photoshop Edit button** in the Properties panel.
7. Use the **Text tool** T to type **White Water Ahead** and place it just in front of the raft.
8. Use the **Rectangular Marquee tool** to select the part of the image shown in Figure 10.
9. Click **Edit** on the Application bar, click **Copy Merged**, then save the document and exit Photoshop.
10. Display Dreamweaver, verify that the lower image in selected, click **Edit** on the Application bar, then click **Paste**.
11. Save your work, close all documents, then exit Dreamweaver.

You copied and pasted a Photoshop image into a Dreamweaver document, edited the image in Photoshop, then repasted the image.

CREATE A PHOTOSHOP DOCUMENT
AND IMPORT IT INTO FLASH

What You'll Do

Northern Arizona Scenic Sites

SEDONA, ARIZONA

In this lesson, you will create a Photoshop document, import it into Flash, and create an animation.

Importing a Photoshop Document into Flash

Flash allows you to import Photoshop PSD files directly into a Flash document. An advantage of using Photoshop to create graphics and enhance photographs is that the drawing and selection tools, as well as the photo retouching features, allow you to produce more creative and complex images. A key feature of importing PSD files is that you can choose to have the Photoshop layers imported as Flash layers. This allows you to edit individual parts of an image, such as animating text or using a photograph to create a button.

The process for importing Photoshop files into Flash is to open a Flash document and select the Import option from the File menu. Then, choose to import to the Stage or to the Library panel and specify which PSD file to import. The Import dialog box appears, as shown in Figure 11, with the following options:

- Check Photoshop layers to import. Allows you to specify which layers to import.
- Options for "Layer . . .". Allows you to specify how the selected layer will be imported. Here you decide whether or not you want to be able to edit the contents (text, image, background, etc.) of the layer. If you choose not to make it editable, the content is flattened as a bitmap image. If you choose to make an image editable, a movie clip symbol is created using the image. The movie clip has its own Timeline, making it easy to animate the image separately from other content in the Flash document.
- Publish settings. Allows you to specify the degree of compression and document quality to apply to the image when it is published as a SWF file. This has no effect on the image that is imported into the Flash document.

- Convert layers to. Allows you to have the content of Photoshop layers be imported as Flash layers or as keyframes.

- Place layers at original position. Allows you to specify that the contents of the PSD file retain the same relative position they had in Photoshop.

- Set stage to same size as Photoshop canvas. Allows you have the Flash Stage resize to the same size as the Photoshop document.

FIGURE 11
Import dialog box

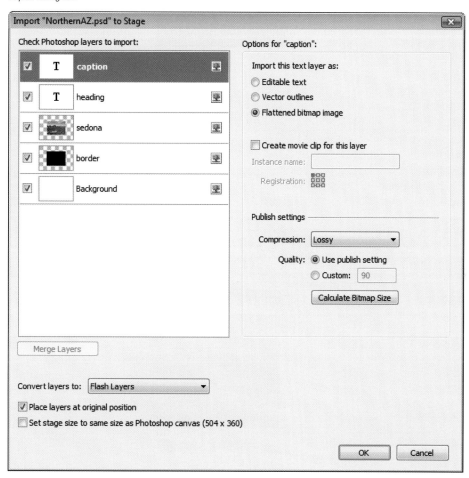

Create a Photoshop image with several layers

1. Start Photoshop.
2. Open **ic_3.psd** from where you store your Data Files, then save it as **NorthernAZ.psd**.

   This document has a single image and a white background.
3. Click the **Background layer** in the Layers panel, then click the **Create a new layer icon** 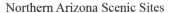 at the bottom of the Layers panel.
4. Change the layer name to **border**.
5. Select the **Rectangle tool** 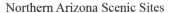, on the Tools panel, change the fill color to **black**, then draw a rectangle slightly larger than the image, as shown in Figure 12.
6. Click the **sedona layer** in the Layers panel, then click the **Create a new layer icon** 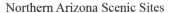 .
7. Change the layer name to **heading**.
8. Click the **Text tool** T on the Tools panel, then change the font to **Times New Roman**, the font size to **30pt**, and the color to **#293bc5**.
9. Type **Northern Arizona Scenic Sites**, then position the text as shown in Figure 13.
10. Insert a new layer above the heading layer, then name it **caption**.
11. Select the **Text tool** T , then change the font to **Rosewood Std**, the size to **24pt**, and the color to **#993300**.

    | TIP If this font is not available, select a different font.
12. Type **SEDONA, ARIZONA**, then position the text as shown in Figure 14.
13. Save your work, close the document, then exit Photoshop.

You opened a Photoshop file, added layers with a shape and text, and positioned the text.

FIGURE 12
The completed rectangle

FIGURE 13
Positioning the heading

FIGURE 14
Positioning the caption

FIGURE 15
Selecting the Editable text option

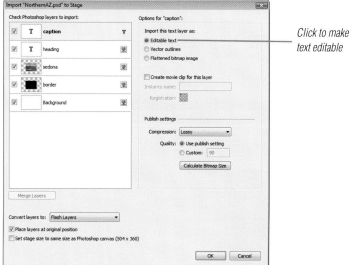

Click to make text editable

FIGURE 16
The completed Import dialog box

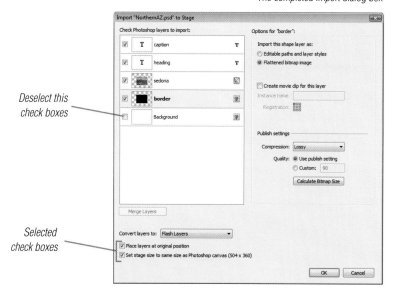

Deselect this check boxes

Selected check boxes

Import a Photoshop document into Flash

1. Start Flash, then click **Flash File (ActionScript 2.0)** in the Create New category.

2. Save the document to where you store your Data Files, with the filename **AZScenes.fla**.

3. Change the frame rate to **30 fps**.

4. Change the view to **Fit in Window**.

5. Click **File** on the menu bar, point to **Import**, then click **Import to Stage**.

6. Navigate to where you store your Data Files, click **NorthernAZ.psd**, then click **Open** (Win) or **Import** (Mac).

   The Import dialog box opens.

7. Click the **caption layer**, then click **Editable text**, as shown in Figure 15.

8. Click the **heading layer**, then click **Editable text**.

9. Click the **sedona layer**, then click **Bitmap image with editable layer styles**.

10. Click **border**, then verify that **Flattened bitmap image** is selected.

11. Click the **check box** for the Background layer to deselect the layer so it will not be imported.

12. Verify that the Convert layers to: option is set to Flash Layers and the **Place layers at original position check box** is selected.

13. Click the **Set stage size to same size as Photoshop canvas (504 x 360) check box** to select it.

    Your dialog box should resemble Figure 16.

14. Click **OK**.

You selected a Photoshop file to import, selected which layers to import, and specified whether or not the content could be edited.

Edit a Photoshop image that has been imported into Flash

1. Study the Flash Timeline and notice the four new layers that were created.

   Layer 1 is the default layer that appears when a new document is opened. It does not have any content.

2. Click Layer 1, then click the **Delete Layer icon** 🗑 to delete the layer.

3. Click the **Show or Hide All Layers icon** 👁 to hide all of the objects on the Stage.

4. Starting with the border layer, unhide each layer one by one to view its contents.

5. Double-click the **NorthernAZ.psd** Assets folder in the Library panel.

6. Click **border** to display the bitmap image, then click **sedona** to view the movie clip image.

7. Double-click the **Assets folder**, then click **sedona** to view the sedona bitmap image.

   The bitmap image is used to create the sedona movie clip.

8. Click the **Selection tool** ↖ on the Tools panel, if necessary, click **frame 1** of the heading layer, then verify that the heading is selected.

9. Click the **Text tool** T on the Tools panel, then drag the I-beam pointer I across the text to select it.

10. Click the **Fill Color tool** 🖍 on the Tools panel, then type **#336600** for the color.

11. Click the **Selection tool** ↖ on the Tools panel, then click a blank area of the Stage to deselect the heading, as shown in Figure 17.

(continued)

FIGURE 17
The completed edits

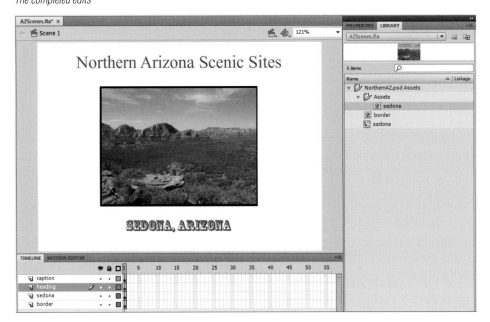

FIGURE 18

The Timeline with keyframes inserted

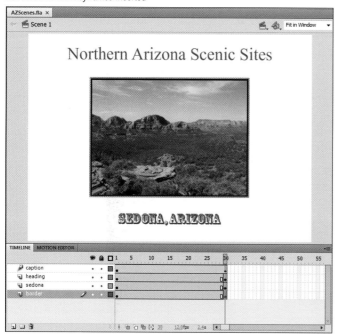

12. Save your work.

Your viewed the contents of the layers that were created when a Photoshop file was imported into Flash, and changed the color of the text heading.

Create an animation using the Photoshop-created text

1. Click the **Sedona, Arizona text** on the Stage to select it, then convert it to a Graphic symbol with the name **g_sedona caption**.

2. Click **Insert** on the menu bar, then click **Motion Tween**.

3. Click **frame 1** on the caption layer, then click the **text** to select it.

4. Click the **Color Effect Style list arrow** on the Properties panel, then click **Alpha**.

5. Change the alpha setting to **0**.

6. Click **frame 30** on the caption layer, click the **blank text block** on the Stage, then change the alpha setting to **100**.

7. Set the frame rate to **12**.

8. Insert keyframes in Frame 30 of the remaining layers, as shown in Figure 18.

9. Click **Control** on the menu bar, then click **Test Movie**.

10. Close the test movie window.

11. Click **File** on the menu bar, click **Publish Settings**, deselect the HTML option, click **Publish**, then click **OK**.

12. Save your work, close the document, then exit Flash.

You created an animation using Photoshop-imported text.

INSERT AND EDIT
A FLASH MOVIE
IN DREAMWEAVER

What You'll Do

Northern Arizona Scenic Sites

SEDONA, ARIZONA

In this lesson, you will insert a Flash movie into a Dreamweaver document and edit the movie within Dreamweaver.

Inserting a Flash Movie into a Dreamweaver Document

You can easily insert a Flash movie (.swf) into a Dreamweaver document. To do this, set the insertion point where you want the movie to appear, and then use the Media command on the Insert menu to select SWF as the media to insert. If the file is not in the root folder for the website, you are asked whether you would like to copy it into the root folder. It is recommended that you copy the file to the root folder, so that it is accessible when you publish the site. When the insert process is completed, a placeholder appears at the insertion point in the document.

Using the Properties Panel with the Movie

When you click the placeholder to select it, the Properties panel displays information about the movie, including the filename, as shown in Figure 19.

You can use the Properties panel to complete the following:

- Edit the Flash movie
- Play and stop the Flash movie
- Set width and height dimensions
- Cause the movie to loop
- Reposition the placeholder in the document window

To edit the Flash movie, you select the placeholder, click the Edit button on the Properties panel, and specify the source file (FLA). This opens Flash and displays the source file. After making changes to the document, you re-export it to Dreamweaver by selecting the Done button at the upper-left corner of the Flash window or by choosing the Update for Dreamweaver command on the File menu. Choosing Done will close the document, while choosing Update for Dreamweaver will keep the document open. Both processes will automatically save the document. (*Hint*: Before starting the editing process from Dreamweaver, you should close Flash.)

FIGURE 19

The Properties panel with a selected

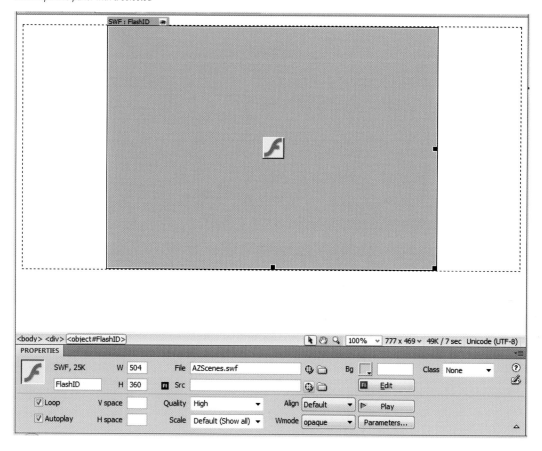

Insert a Flash movie into Dreamweaver

1. Start Dreamweaver.

2. Create a new Blank Page HTML document with no layout, then save it as **NorthernAZ.html** to the Southwest folder.

3. Click **Insert** on the Application bar, point to **Media**, then click **SWF**.

4. Navigate to where you store your Data Files, click **AZScenes.swf**, then click **OK** (Win) or **Choose** (Mac).

5. If a "This file is outside of the root folder..." message appears, click **Yes**, then click **Save** when the Copy File As dialog box appears.

6. Type **Photo of Sedona Arizona** for the title in the Object Tag Accessibility Attributes dialog box, then click **OK**.

   A Flash movie placeholder is inserted at the location of the insertion line, as shown in Figure 20.

7. Verify that the placeholder is selected, click **Format** on the Application bar, point to **Align**, then click **Center**.

8. Save your work.

   If a Copy Dependent Files message box appears, click OK.

You inserted a Flash movie into a Dreamweaver document and copied the Flash movie to the root folder of the website.

FIGURE 20
The Flash movie placeholder

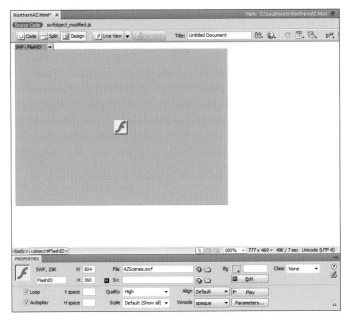

Integrating Adobe CS4 Web Premium

FIGURE 21
Changing the movie height

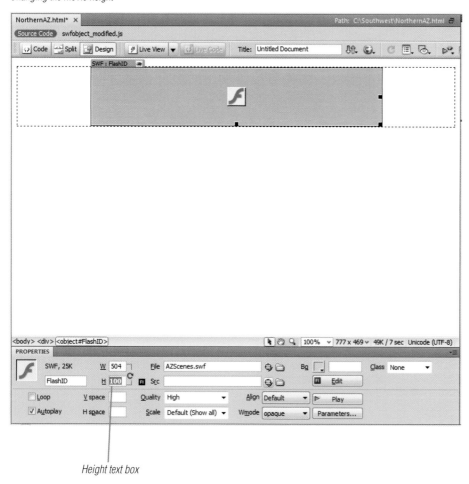

Height text box

1. Click the **Flash movie placeholder** to select it (if necessary).

2. Click **Play** in the Properties panel.

3. Click **Stop** in the Properties panel.

4. Click the **Loop check box** in the Properties panel to deselect it.

5. Double-click the **height box (H)**, type **100**, then press **[Enter]** (Win) or **[return]** (Mac).

   Your screen should resemble Figure 21.

6. Click the **Play button** in the Properties panel.

7. View the resized movie, then click the **Stop button**.

8. Click the **Reset size icon** ↻ in the Properties panel to restore the previous setting.

9. Save your work.

You played a Flash movie and changed its settings in Dreamweaver by turning off the Loop option, and then changing and resetting the movie height.

Edit a Flash movie from Dreamweaver

1. Click the **Flash placeholder** to select it, then click **Edit** in the Properties panel.

2. Navigate to where you store your Data Files, click **AZScenes.fla**, then click **Open**.

3. Insert a new layer above the caption layer, then name it **stopmovie**.

4. Click **frame 1** of the stopmovie layer.

5. Display the **Actions panel**, verify that the **Script Assist button** is on, then verify that **stopmovie 1:** is displayed at the lower-left corner of the script pane, as shown in Figure 22.

6. Click the **Add a new item to the script button** , point to **Global Functions**, point to **Timeline Control**, then click **stop**.

7. Click **frame 1** on the sedona layer, then click the image to select it.

8. Click **Modify** on the menu bar, then click **Convert to Symbol**.

9. Type **b_sedona** for the name, click **Button** for the Type, then click **OK**.

10. Display the Actions panel, if necessary, then verify that **b_sedona** is displayed at the lower-left corner of the script pane.

11. Click the **Add a new item to the script button** , point to **Global Functions**, point to **Movie Clip Control**, then click **on**.

(continued)

FIGURE 22
Verifying the settings in the Script pane

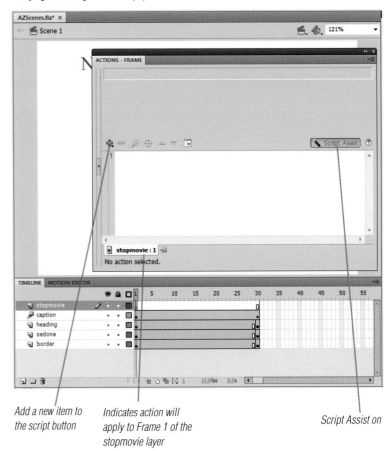

Add a new item to the script button

Indicates action will apply to Frame 1 of the stopmovie layer

Script Assist on

FIGURE 23

Specifying the frame to go to

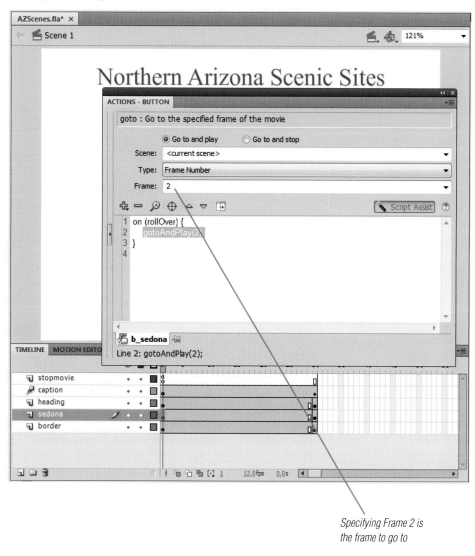

Specifying Frame 2 is
the frame to go to

12. Click the **Release check box** to deselect it,
    then click the **Roll Over check box** to select it.

13. Click the **Add a new item to the script
    button** ⊕ , point to **Global Functions**, point
    to **Timeline Control**, then click **goto**.

14. Change the Frame to **2**, as shown in Figure 23.

15. Click **Control** on the menu bar, then click
    Test Movie.

16. Point to the image to view the animation, then
    close the test movie window.

17. Click the **Done button** above the upper-left
    corner to return to Dreamweaver and
    close Flash.

18. In Dreamweaver, verify that the Flash
    placeholder is selected, then click **Play** in
    the Properties panel.

19. Point to the image to play the animation.

20. Click **File** on the menu bar, point to **Preview
    in Browser**, click **IExplore** (Win) or **Safari**
    (Mac), then save your work if prompted.

    ❙ TIP   Your default browser may vary.

21. View the movie, close the browser, save
    your work, then close the document and
    exit Flash.

*You edited a Flash movie from Dreamweaver by
creating a rollover action that plays an animation.*

Designate the primary external image editor.

1. Start Dreamweaver CS4.
2. Display the Preferences dialog box and display the File Types / Editors option.
3. Verify that Photoshop is set as the default image editor for . psd, .png, .gif, and .jpg files.

Set up the Dreamweaver site.

1. Create a folder where you store your Data Files and name it **Foods**.
2. Add a folder within the Foods folder named **Assets**.
3. Create a new Dreamweaver site named **Foods-for-Thought**, using the Foods folder as the root folder and the Assets folder as the default images folder.

Edit a Photoshop file.

1. Open bread-heading.psd in Photoshop CS4.
2. Add a layer below the text layer, name it **background**, then draw a white rectangle for the background.
3. Save the file with the name **bread-headingRev.psd**.
4. Close the file.

Insert a Photoshop image into a Dreamweaver document.

1. Open the Foods-for-Thought site in Dreamweaver, if necessary.
2. Create a new Blank Page HTML document and save it as **food-home.html** in the root folder.

3. Insert the bread-headingRev.psd file into the document as a .jpeg file saved to the Assets folder and with **The Staff of Life heading** for the alternate text.
4. Use the Align option from the Format menu to center-align the heading across the document, then save your work.

Edit a Photoshop image from Dreamweaver.

1. Select the bread-headingRev.jpg image and click the Photoshop Edit button in the Properties panel.
2. Change the text formatting to italic.
3. Save the document, then close it.
4. Display the food-home.html file in Dreamweaver, right-click (Win) or [control]-click (Mac), then choose Update From Original.
5. Save the Dreamweaver document.

Import a Photoshop image to Flash.

1. Display Photoshop, open bread-photo.psd, then save it as **bread-photoRev.psd**.
2. Add a layer below the photo layer and name it **border**.
3. Draw a black rectangle slightly larger than the photo.
4. Save the document and then close the document.
5. Start Flash CS4 and create a new Flash File (ActionScript2).

6. Change the frame rate to 30 fps.
7. Save the document with the filename **bread-An.fla**.
8. Import the bread-photoRev.psd file to the Stage, making each layer except the background editable and setting the Stage size to the same size as the Photoshop canvas.
9. Delete Layer 1 in the timeline.
10. Publish the document to create the SWF file.
11. Save your work and close the document.
12. Exit Flash.

Insert a Flash movie into a Dreamweaver document.

1. Display Dreamweaver and set an insertion point below the heading.
2. Insert the bread-An.swf file below the photo image, and save the file to the Assets folder.
3. Enter **Animation of the word Bread** for the title.
4. Save your work.

Play a Flash movie and change the movie settings from Dreamweaver.

1. Select the Flash movie placeholder.
2. Click Play, then click Stop.
3. Deselect the Loop feature.
4. Change the movie window height to **250**, play the movie, then stop the movie.
5. Reset the size.
6. Save your work.

Edit a Flash movie from Dreamweaver.

1. Select the movie placeholder, then click Edit.
2. Select the bread-An.fla file in the Locate FLA file dialog box, then click Open.
3. Create a motion animation that causes the word Bread to scroll in from off the left side of the Stage.
4. Add a layer, name it **stopmovie**, then create a stop action in frame 1 of the layer.
5. Insert a keyframe in the last frame of the stopmovie layer, then create a stop action in the frame.
6. Select the photo and convert it to a button symbol with the name **b_photo**.
7. Create a rollover action for the button that causes the animation to play when the pointer rolls over the photo.
8. Enter keyframes into the last frame of the movie for the other layers.
9. Test the movie.
10. Click Done to return to the document in Dreamweaver.
11. Play the Flash movie in Dreamweaver, then stop the movie.
12. Save your work.
13. Display the web page in a browser, then compare your screen to Figure 24.

FIGURE 24
Completed Skills Review

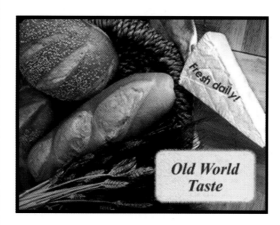

Ultimate Tours has asked you to develop a Dreamweaver website for their travel company. The site will include graphics exported from Photoshop and the Flash animations that were developed in Flash Chapter 5 for the Ultimate Tours website.

1. Create a folder on your hard drive and name it **ULTours**, then create a folder within the ULTours folder named **Assets**.
2. In Dreamweaver, create a new site named **Ultimate_Tours**, using the ULTours folder as the local root folder and the Assets folder as the default images folder.
3. Open ULTours_home.html and save it as **ULTours_homeRev.html** to the root folder for the ULTours folder.
4. Start Photoshop and open ULTours-heading.psd, updating the links if prompted.
5. Change the text formatting to italic and save the document with the filename **ULTours-headingRev.psd**.
6. Display Dreamweaver and insert the UlTours-headingRev.psd image into the ULTours_homeRev.html file as a .jpg file, stored in the Assets folder with alternate text of **The Trip of a Lifetime heading**.

7. Edit the heading in Photoshop from Dreamweaver and change the text to white.
8. Save the image in Photoshop.
9. Display Dreamweaver and update the image.
10. Open ULTours-photo.psd in Photoshop and type **The Islands** as a heading above the mountain, on its own layer.
11. Save the document as **ULTours-photoRev.psd**.
12. Create a new Flash File (ActionScript 2.0) and save it as **ULTours-photoAn.fla**.
13. Change the frame rate to 40 fps.
14. Import the ULTours-photoRev.psd to the Stage with all layers being editable and the Set stage size to same size as Photoshop canvas checked.
15. Rename Layer 1 **Gray border**, then draw a gray border around the edge of the photo. (*Hint*: Increase the size of the Stage a few pixels to accommodate the border and center the border on the Stage.)
16. Display the Publish Settings dialog box, deselect the HTML option, publish and save the movie, then exit Flash.
17. Display Dreamweaver and insert the ULTours-photoAn.swf file to the right of the heading, saving the file to the Assets folder and providing alternate text.

18. Center the heading and photo across the page.
19. Play the Flash movie in Dreamweaver, then stop the movie.
20. Edit the movie from Dreamweaver. If a Copy Dependent Files message box appears, click OK.
21. Create an animation that zooms in the text.
22. Convert the photo to a button and add ActionScript so that when the pointer rolls over the image, the movie plays.
23. Insert a new layer named **stopmovie**, then add stop actions to the first and last frames of the movie.
24. Add keyframes to the end movie for each of the other layers.
25. Test the movie.
26. Use the Done button to return to the Dreamweaver document.
27. Play the movie in Dreamweaver, then save your work.
28. Insert the ultimatetours5.swf file below the heading and provide a title.
29. Save your work, view the document in a browser, then compare your image to the sample in Figure 25.

FIGURE 25
Sample Completed Project Builder 1

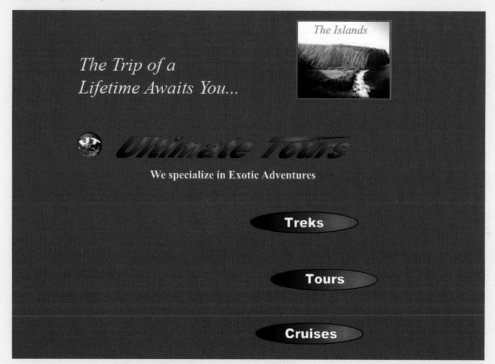

This project begins with the Striped Umbrella site created in Dreamweaver Chapter 5.

You have been asked to enhance the Striped Umbrella site by adding a Flash movie and changing a graphic image on the cafe page. Figure 26 shows the completed page for this part of the website. The idea is to replace the static crab logo image with a Flash animation that plays in the same space on the page.

1. In Photoshop, open the crab_logo.psd file.

2. Turn the visibility off and on for each layer to see the image is constructed.

3. In Flash, start a new Flash File (ActionScript 2.0) and import the crab_logo.psd file to the Stage, specifying that each layer is editable and setting the Stage size to the same size as the Photoshop canvas.

4. In Flash, create an animation using the crab_logo.psd image. You decide on the type of animation, which could be a zoom or fade in; the entire crab moving; the crab claws moving; and so forth. (*Hint*: The crab image is made up of a body and left and right claws. If you want to animate these as one object, you can press and hold [Shift] to select all three, then convert them to a graphic symbol. Include a rollover effect or some other form of user interaction.) Save

the movie as **crab_Anim.fla**. Display the Publish Settings dialog box, deselect the HTML option and publish the document.

5. In Dreamweaver, open the Striped Umbrella site on the Files panel.

6. Open the cafe.html page and delete the cafe_logo graphic on the page.

7. Insert the crab_Anim.swf file in the cell where the cafe_logo graphic had been.

8. Select the Flash movie placeholder and use the Properties panel to play and stop the animation.

9. Save your work.

10. View the web page in your browser.

FIGURE 26
Sample Completed Project Builder 2

Crab is animated
on mouse over

Figure 27 shows the home page of a website. Study the figure and complete the following questions. For each question, indicate how you determined your answer.

1. Connect to the Internet, and go to *www.memphiszoo.org*.
2. Open a document in a word processor or in Flash, save the file as **dpcIntegration**, then answer the following questions.

- What seems to be the purpose of this site?
- Who would be the target audience?
- Identify three elements within the web page that could have been created or enhanced using Photoshop.
- Identify two elements on the page and indicate how you would use Photoshop to enhance them.
- Identify an animation that could have been developed by Flash.

- Indicate how you would use Flash to enhance the page.
- What would be the value of using Flash, Dreamweaver, and Photoshop to create the website?
- What suggestions would you make to improve on the design, and why?

FIGURE 27
Design Project

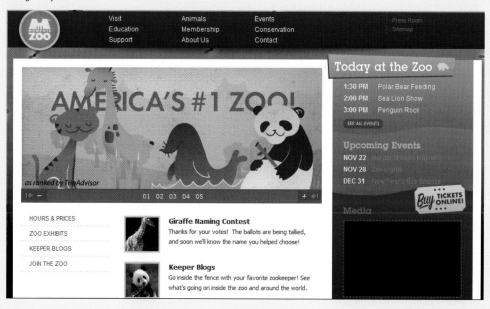

PORTFOLIO PROJECT

This is a continuation of the Portfolio Project in Flash Chapter 5. You will create a website in Dreamweaver, import graphic files from Photoshop, and import portfolio5.swf into the site. The home page of the website will include a heading and photo image (of your choice), as shown in Figure 28.

1. Create a folder on your hard drive and name it **Portfoliowebsite**, then create a folder within the Portfoliowebsite folder named **Assets**.
2. In Dreamweaver, create a new site named **PortfolioWeb**, using the Portfoliowebsite folder as the local root folder.
3. Open portfoliohome.html and save it as **portfoliohomeRev.html** to the Portfoliowebsite site.
4. Copy the files portfolio-heading.psd and portfolio-photo.psd to the Portfoliowebsite folder, rename them portfolio-headingRev.psd and portfolio-photoRev.psd, respectively.

5. Insert the portfolio-headingRev.psd image as a .jpg file in the Assets folder, and provide alternate text.
6. Insert the portfolio-photoRev.psd image to the right of the heading as a .jpg file in the Assets folder, and provide alternate text.
7. Center the heading and photo across the page. (*Hint*: You can use a photo of your choice, if desired.)
8. Insert portfolio5.swf below the heading and center it across the page.
9. Select the movie, then play and stop it.
10. Select the heading and edit it in Photoshop to apply a drop shadow, then save it, return to the Dreamweaver document and update the image.
11. Select the photo, choose to edit it in Photoshop, and add an inner glow effect, then save it, return to the Dreamweaver document and update the image.

12. From Dreamweaver choose to edit the Flash movie.
13. In Photoshop, create a graphic that resembles a portfolio case and name it **portfolioCase.psd**.
14. In Flash, import portfolioCase.psd to the Stage, specifying all the layers to be editable and not importing the background layer.
15. Center the portfolioCase image on the Stage.
16. Remove all of the frames in all of the layers for the newly imported image, except for frame 1 of each layer.
    (*Hint*: Use the Selection tool to select the frames, click Edit on the menu bar, point to Timeline, then click Remove frames.)
17. Use the Done button to update the Flash movie and return to Dreamweaver.
18. In Dreamweaver, save your work, display the document in a browser, then compare your image to the sample in Figure 28.

FIGURE 28

Sample Completed Portfolio Project

Read the following information carefully!!

Find out from your instructor the location where you will store your files.

- To complete many of the chapters in this book, you need to use the Data Files on the CD at the back of this book.

- All of the Data Files are organized in folders named after the chapter in which they are used. You should leave all the Data Files in these folders; do not move any Data File out of the folder in which it is originally stored.

- Your instructor will tell you whether you will be working from the CD or copying the files to a drive on your computer or on a server. Your instructor will also tell you where you will store the files you create and modify.

Copy and organize your Data Files.

- Use the Data Files List to organize your files to a USB storage device, network folder, hard drive, or other storage device.

- Create a subfolder for each chapter in the location where you are storing your files, and name it according to the chapter title (e.g., Flash Chapter 1).

- For each chapter you are assigned, copy the files listed in the **Data File Supplied** column into that chapter's folder.

- If you are working from the CD, you should store the files you modify or create in each chapter in the chapter folder. (Note that you cannot work from the CD for the Dreamweaver and integration chapters. The files need to be saved to a storage device.)

Find and keep track of your Data Files and completed files.

- Use the **Data File Supplied** column to make sure you have the files you need before starting the chapter or exercise indicated in the **Chapter** column.

- Use the **Student Creates File** column to determine the filename you use when saving your new file for the exercise.

- The **Used in** column tells you where a file is used in a chapter.

Use these special instructions for Dreamweaver.

- As you build each website, the exercises in this book will guide you to copy the Data Files you need from the appropriate Data Files folder to the folder where you are storing the website. Your Data Files should always remain intact because you are copying (and not moving) them to the website.

- Some of the files listed in the **Data File Supplied** column are ones that you created or used in a previous chapter, and that are already part of the website you are working on. For instance, if the file tripsmart/amazon_trip.html is listed in the **Data File Supplied** column, this means that you need to use the amazon_trip.html file in the tripsmart site that you already created.

Files used in this book

Adobe Dreamweaver CS4

Chapter	Data File Supplied	Student Creates File	Used In
1	dw1_1.html about_us.swf accommodations.swf activities.swf cafe.swf index.swf shop.swf spa.swf assets/pool.jpg assets/su_background.jpg assets/su_banner.gif		Lesson 2
	dw1_2.html assets/su_banner.gif	about_us.html activities.html cafe.html cruises.html fishing.html index.html spa.html	Lesson 4
	dw1_3.html dw1_4.html assets/blooms_banner.jpg assets/blooms_logo.jpg	annuals.html classes.html index.html newsletter.html perennials.html plants.html tips.html water_plants.html	Skills Review
	dw1_5.html assets/tripsmart_banner.jpg	amazon.html catalog.html destinations.html kenya.html newsletter.html services.html	Project Builder 1
	dw1_6.html assets/cc_banner.jpg	adults.html catering.html children.html classes.html recipes.html shop.html	Project Builder 2

Adobe Dreamweaver CS4 (continued)

Chapter	Data File Supplied	Student Creates File	Used In
	none		Design Project
	none		Portfolio Project
2	dw2_1.html spa.doc assets/su_banner.gif assets/the_spa.jpg		Lesson 2
	dw2_2.html gardening_tips.doc assets/blooms_banner.jpg assets/garden_tips.jpg		Skills Review
	none		Project Builder 1
	none		Project Builder 2
	none		Design Project
	none		Portfolio Project
3	questions.doc		Lesson 1
		su_styles.css	Lesson 2
	dw3_1.html assets/boardwalk.jpg assets/club_house.jpg assets/pool.jpg assets/sago_palm.jpg assets/sports_club.jpg assets/su_banner.gif		Lesson 4
	assets/stripes_back.gif assets/umbrella_back.gif		Lesson 6
	dw3_2.html assets/blooms_banner.jpg assets/daisies.jpg assets/lantana.jpg assets/petunias.jpg assets/verbena.jpg	blooms_styles.css	Skills Review
	dw3_3.html dw3_4.html assets/tripsmart_banner.jpg assets/lion.jpg assets/zebra_mothers.jpg	tripsmart_styles.css	Project Builder 1

Adobe Dreamweaver CS4 (continued)

Chapter	Data File Supplied	Student Creates File	Used In
	dw3_5.html dw3_6.html assets/cc_banner.jpg assets/cranberry_ice.jpg assets/pot_knives.jpg	cc_styles.css	Project Builder 2
	none		Design Project
	none		Portfolio Project
4	dw4_1.html assets/heron_waiting_small.jpg assets/su_banner.gif assets/two_dolphins_small.jpg		Lesson 1
	assets/about_us_down.gif assets/about_us_up.gif assets/activities_down.gif assets/activities_up.gif assets/cafe_down.gif assets/cafe_up.gif assets/home_down.gif assets/home_up.gif assets/spa_down.gif assets/spa_up.gif		Lesson 3
	dw4_2.html dw4_3.html assets/boats.jpg assets/heron_small.jpg		Lesson 5
	dw4_4.html dw4_5.html dw4_6.html dw4_7.html assets/b_classes_down.jpg assets/b_classes_up.jpg assets/b_home_down.jpg assets/b_home_up.jpg assets/b_newsletter_down.jpg assets/b_newsletter_up.jpg assets/b_plants_down.jpg assets/b_plants_up.jpg		Skills Review

Adobe Dreamweaver CS4 (continued)

Chapter	Data File Supplied	Student Creates File	Used In
	assets/b_tips_down.jpg assets/b_tips_up.jpg assets/blooms_banner.jpg assets/fuchsia.jpg assets/iris.jpg assets/water_hyacinth.jpg		
	dw4_8.html dw4_9.html dw4_10.html assets/giraffe.jpg assets/parrot.jpg assets/sloth.jpg assets/tripsmart_banner.jpg assets/water_lily.jpg		Project Builder 1
	dw4_11.html dw4_12.html dw4_13.html assets/cc_banner.jpg assets/cc_banner_with_text.jpg assets/children_cooking.jpg assets/cookies_oven.jpg assets/dumplings1.jpg assets/dumplings2.jpg assets/dumplings3.jpg assets/fish.jpg		Project Builder 2
	none		Design Project
	none		Portfolio Project

Adobe Dreamweaver CS4 (continued)

Chapter	Data File Supplied	Student Creates File	Used In
5	cafe.doc assets/cafe_logo.gif assets/cafe_photo.jpg		Lesson 2
	assets/cheesecake.jpg		Lesson 6
	gardeners.doc assets/flower_bed.jpg assets/gardening_gloves.gif		Skills Review
	assets/hat.jpg assets/pants.jpg assets/vest.jpg		Project Builder 1
	menu items.doc assets/muffins.jpg		Project Builder 2
	none		Design Project
	none		Portfolio Project
6		The Striped Umbrella.ste	Lesson 5
		blooms & bulbs.ste	Skills Review
		TripSmart.ste	Project Builder 1
		Carolyne's Creations.ste	Project Builder 2
	none		Design Project
	none		Portfolio Project

Adobe Flash CS4

Chapter	Data File Supplied	Student Creates File	Used In
1		workspace.fla	Lesson 1
	fl1_1.fla		Lesson 2
		tween.fla	Lesson 3
		layers.fla	Lesson 4
	*layers.fla		Lesson 5
	fl1_2.fla		Skills Review
		demonstration.fla	Project Builder 1
	fl1_3.fla		Project Builder 2
		dpc1.fla	Design Project
			Portfolio Project
2	fl2_1.fla		Lessons 1-4
	fl2_2.fla		Lesson 5
	fl2_3.fla		Skills Review
		ultimatetours2.fla	Project Builder 1
		thejazzclub2.fla	Project Builder 2
		dpc2.fla	Design Project
		portfolio2.fla	Portfolio Project
3	fl3_1.fla		Lesson 1
	fl3_2.fla		Lessons 2-4
	islandview.jpg sailboat.ai	sailing.fla	Lesson 5
	fl3_3.fla BeachScene.jpg		Skills Review
	**ultimatetours2.fla UTLogo.jpg		Project Builder 1
		isa3.fla	Project Builder 2
		dpc3.fla	Design Project
	**portfolio2.fla		Portfolio Project

*Created in a previous Lesson or Skills Review in current chapter

**Created in a previous chapter

Adobe Flash CS4 (continued)

Chapter	Data File Supplied	Student Creates File	Used In
4	fl4_1.fla fl4_2.fla		Lesson 1
	fl4_3.fla		Lesson 2
	fl4_4.fla		Lesson 3
	fl4_5.fla		
	fl4_6.fla		Lesson 4
	fl4_7.fla fl4_8.fla		
	fl4_9.fla		Lesson 5
	fl4_10.fla		Lesson 6
	fl4_11.fla		Skills Review
	**ultimatetours3.fla ship.gif		Project Builder 1
		jumper4.fla	Project Builder 2
		dpc4.fla	Design Project
	**portfolio3.fla		Portfolio Project

*Created in a previous Lesson or Skills Review in current chapter

**Created in a previous chapter

Adobe Flash CS4 (continued)

Chapter	Data File Supplied	Student Creates File	Used In
5	fl5_1.fla		Lesson 1
	fl5_2.fla		Lesson 2
	carSnd.wav		
	beep.wav		
	fl5_3.fla		Lesson 3
	fireworks.mov		
	fl5_4.fla		Lesson 4
	fl5_5.fla		
	fl5_6.fla		Lesson 5
	fl5_7.fla		Lesson 6
	fl5_8.fla		Skills Review
	fl5_9.fla		
	tour-video.mov		
	fl5_10.fla		Project Builder 1
	fl5_11.fla		Project Builder 2
		dpc5.fla	Design Project
	*portfolio4.fla		Portfolio Project

Chapter	Data File Supplied	Student Creates File	Used in
Chapter 1	PS 1-1.psd PS 1-2.tif		Lessons 2–8
		Review.psd	Skills Review
	PS 1-3.psd		Skills Review
	PS 1-4.psd		Project Builder 2
		Critique-1.psd Critique-2.psd	Design Project
Chapter 2	PS 2-1.psd PS 2-2.psd		Lessons 1–4
	PS 2-3.psd PS 2-4.psd		Skills Review
	PS 2-5.psd PS 2-6.psd		Project Builder 1
	PS 2-7.psd PS 2-8.psd		Project Builder 2
	PS 2-9.psd PS 2-10.psd		Design Project
	PS 2-11.psd		Portfolio Project
Chapter 3	PS 3-1.psd PS 3-2.psd PS 3-3.psd PS 3-4.psd PS 3-5.psd PS 3-6.psd		Lessons 1–4
	PS 3-7.psd PS 3-8.tif PS 3-9.tif PS 3-10.tif		Skills Review
	PS 3-11.psd		Project Builder 1
	PS 3-12.psd		Project Builder 2
		Sample Compositing.psd	Design Project
	PS 3-13.psd		Portfolio Project

Adobe Photoshop CS4 (continued)

Chapter	Data File Supplied	Student Creates File	Used in
Chapter 4	PS 4-1.psd		Lessons 1–4, 6-7
	PS 4-2.psd		Lessons 5–6
	PS 4-3.tif		Lesson 7
	PS 4-4.psd PS 4-5.psd PS 4-6.tif		Skills Review
	PS 4-7.psd		Project Builder 1
	PS 4-8.psd		Project Builder 2
	PS 4-9.psd		Design Project
	PS 4-10.psd		Portfolio Project
Chapter 5	PS 5-1.psd		Lessons 1–7
	PS 5-2.psd		Skills Review
	PS 5-3.psd		Project Builder 1
	PS 5-4.psd		Project Builder 2
	PS 5-5.psd		Design Project
		Community Promotion.psd	Portfolio Project

Integration

Chapter	Data File Supplied	Student Creates File	Used In
1	ic_1.psd ic_1.html ic_2.psd		Lesson 1
	ic_3.psd	AZScenes.fla AZScenes.swf	Lesson 2
	*AZScenes.swf	NorthernAZ.html	Lesson 3
	bread-heading.psd bread-photo.psd	food-home.html bread-An.fla bread-An.swf	Skills Review
	ULTours_home.html ULTours-photo.psd ULTours-heading.psd **ultimatetours5.fla **ultimatetours5.swf	ULTours-PhotoAn.fla ULTours-PhotoAn.swf	Project Builder 1
	crab_logo.psd Striped Umbrella site files	crab_Anim.fla crab_Anim.swf	Project Builder 2
	none	dpcIntegration	Design Project
	portfoliohome.html portfolio-heading.psd portfolio-photo.psd **portfolio5.swf **portfolio5.fla	portfolioCase.psd	Portfolio Project

*Created in a previous Lesson or Skills Review in current chapter

**Created in a previous chapter

Absolute path

A path containing an external link that references a link on a web page outside of the current website, and includes the protocol "http" and the URL, or address, of the web page.

ActionScript

The Flash scripting language used by developers to add interactivity to movies, control objects, exchange data, and create complex animations.

Actions Panel

The Flash panel used when you create and edit actions for an object or frame.

Adobe Bridge

A stand-alone application that serves as the hub for the Adobe Create Suite 4. Can be used for file management tasks such as opening, viewing, sorting, and rating files.

Adobe Community Help

A collection of materials such as tutorials, published articles, or blogs, that is part of the Adobe Help content. Adobe CSS Advisor A part of the Adobe website that offers solutions for resolving issues with your pages.

Adobe Flash

A program that is used to create animations and video content for the web.

Adobe Flash Player

A program that must be installed on a computer to view Flash movies.

Adobe Version Cue

Version Cue is used to track versions of a file and monitor file check-in and check-out, which helps ensure efficient workgroup collaboration when sharing files.

Additive colors

A color system in which, when the values of R, G, and B are 0, the result is black; when the values are all 255, the result is white.

Aligning an image

Positioning an image on a web page in relation to other elements on the page.

Alternate text

Descriptive text that can be set to appear in place of an image while the image is downloading or when users place a mouse pointer over an image.

Altitude

A Bevel and Emboss setting that affects the amount of visible dimension.

Anchor point

Joins path segments to delineate changes in direction.

Angle

In the Layer Style dialog box, the setting that determines where a drop shadow falls relative to the text.

Animation

The perception of motion caused by the rapid display of a series of still images.

Anti-aliasing

Partially fills in pixel edges, resulting in smooth-edge type. This feature lets your type maintain its crisp appearance and is especially useful for large type.

AP div tag

A div tag that is assigned a fixed position on a page (absolute position).

AP element

The resulting container that an AP div tag creates on a page.

AP elements panel

Panel in the CSS panel group that is used to control the visibility, name, and Z-Index stacking order of AP elements on a web page.

Apache web server

A public domain, open source web server that is available using several different operating systems including UNIX and Windows.

Application bar

The toolbar located above the Document window which includes menu names (Windows only), a Workspace switcher, and other application commands.

Arrangement

How objects are positioned relative to one another.

Assets

Files that are not web pages, such as images, audio files, and video clips.

Assets folder
A subfolder in which you store most of the files that are not web pages, such as images, audio files, and video clips.

Assets panel
A panel that contains nine categories of assets, such as images, used in a website. Clicking a category button displays a list of those assets.

Asymmetrical balance
Page in which objects are placed unequally on either side of an imaginary vertical line in the center of the page.

Background color
A color that fills the entire web page, a frame, a table, a cell, or a document. In Photoshop, used to make gradient fills and to fill in areas of an image that have been erased. The default background color is white.

Background image
A graphic file used in place of a background color.

Balance
In screen design, balance refers to the distribution of optical weight in the layout. Optical weight is the ability of an object to attract the viewer's eye, as determined by the object's size, shape, color, and so on.

Banners
Graphics that generally appear across the top of the screen that can incorporate a company's logo, contact information, and navigation bars.

Base color
The original color of an image.

Base layer
The bottom layer in a clipping group, which serves as the group's mask.

Baseline
An invisible line on which type rests.

Baseline shift
The distance type appears from its original position.

Behavior
A preset piece of JavaScript code that can be attached to page objects. A behavior tells the page object to respond in a specific way when an event occurs, such as when the mouse pointer is positioned over the object.

Bitmap
A geometric arrangement of different color dots on a rectangular grid.

Bitmap mode
Uses black or white color values to represent image pixels; a good choice for images with subtle color gradations, such as photographs or painted images.

Bitmap type
Type that may develop jagged edges when enlarged.

Blend color
The color applied to the base color when a blending mode is applied to a layer.

Blending mode
Affects the layer's underlying pixels or base color. Used to darken or lighten colors, depending on the colors in use.

BMP
Bitmapped file. A file format used for images that is based on pixels.

Body
The part of a web page that is seen when the page is viewed in a browser window.

Border
An outline that surrounds a cell, a table, or a frame.

Bread crumbs trail
A list of links that provides a path from the initial page opened in a website to the page being viewed.

Brightness
The measurement of relative lightness or darkness of a color (measured as a percentage from 0% [black] to 100% [white]).

Broken links
Links that cannot find the intended destination file for the link.

Browser
Software used to display web pages, such as Microsoft Internet Explorer, Mozilla Firefox, or Safari.

Bullet
A small dot or similar icon preceding unordered list items.

Bulleted list
An unordered list that uses bullets.

Button Symbols
Objects in Flash that appear on the Stage and that are used to provide interactivity, such as jumping to another frame on the Timeline.

Cascading Style Sheet
A file used to assign sets of common formatting characteristics to page elements such as text, objects, and tables.

Cell padding
The distance between the cell content and the cell walls in a table.

Cell spacing
The distance between cells in a table.

Cell walls
The edges surrounding a cell in a table.

Cells
Small boxes within a table that are used to hold text or graphics. Cells are arranged horizontally in rows and vertically in columns.

Character panel
Helps you control type properties. The Toggle the Character and Paragraph panel button is located on the options bar when you select a Type tool.

Child page
A page at a lower level in a web hierarchy that links to a parent page.

Class type
See Custom style.

Clipboard
Temporary storage area, provided by your operating system, for cut and copied data.

Cloaked file
File that is marked to be excluded from certain processes, such as being transferred to the remote site.

Code and Design Views
A web page view that is a combination of Code View and Design View.

Code Inspector
A window that works just like Code view, except that it is a floating window.

Code View
A web page view that shows a full screen with the HTML code for the page. Use this view to read or directly edit the code.

Coding toolbar
A toolbar that contains buttons that are used when working directly in the code.

Color Picker
A feature that lets you choose a color from a color spectrum.

Color Range command
Used to select a particular color contained in an existing image.

Color separation
Result of converting an RGB image into a CMYK image; the commercial printing process of separating colors for use with different inks.

Columns
Table cells arranged vertically.

Comments
Helpful text describing portions of the HTML code, such as a JavaScript function, that are inserted in the code and are not visible in the browser window.

Compositing
Combining images from sources such as other Photoshop images, royalty-free images, pictures taken from digital cameras, and scanned artwork.

Compound type
A type of CSS rule that is used to format a selection.

Contents
The Adobe Help feature that lists topics by category.

Controller
A toolbar that contains the playback controls for a movie.

Coordinate
In Flash, the position on the Stage of a pixel as measured across (X coordinate) and down (Y coordinate) the Stage.

Copyright
A legal protection for the particular and tangible expression of an idea.

Crisp
Anti-aliasing setting that gives type more definition and makes it appear sharper.

Crop
To exclude part of an image. Cropping hides areas of an image without losing resolution quality.

CSS page layout
A method of positioning objects on web pages through the use of containers formatted with CSS styles.

CSS page layout block
A section of a web page defined and formatted using a Cascading Style Sheet.

Custom button
In a form, a button that triggers action that you specifiy on the page.

Custom style
A style that can contain a combination of formatting attributes that can be applied to a block of text or other page elements. Custom style names begin with a period (.). Also known as a class style.

Debug
To find and correct coding errors.

Declaration
The property and value of a style in a Cascading Style Sheet.

Default base font
Size 3 (Dreamweaver). The default font that is applied to any text without an assigned size that is entered on a web page.

Default font color
The color the browser uses to display text, links, and visited links if no other color is assigned.

Default link color
The color the browser uses to display links if no other color is assigned. The default link color is blue.

Defining a Website
Specifying the site's local root folder location to help Dreamweaver keep track of the links among web pages and supporting files.

Definition lists
Lists made up of terms with indented descriptions or definitions.

Delimited files
Database or spreadsheet files that have been saved as text files with delimiters.

Delimiter
A comma, tab, colon, semicolon, or similar character that separates tabular data.

Dependent file
File that another file needs to be complete, such as an image or navigation bar element.

Derivative work
An adaptation of another work, such as a movie version of a book.

Description
A short summary of website content that resides in the Head section.

Deselect
A command that removes the marquee from an area, so it is no longer selected.

Design notes
Separate files in a website that contain additional information about a file.

Design View
The view that shows a full-screen layout and is primarily used when designing and creating a web page.

Diagonal symmetry
A design principle in which page elements are balanced along the invisible diagonal line of the page.

Digital image
A picture in electronic form. It may be referred to as a file, document, picture, or image.

Distance
Determines how far a shadow falls from the text. This setting is used by the Drop Shadow and Bevel and Emboss styles.

Distort filters
Create three-dimensional or other reshaping effects. Some of the types of distortions you can produce include Glass, Pinch, Ripple, Shear, Spherize, Twirl, Wave, and ZigZag.

Div tag
An HTML tag that is used to format and position web page elements.

Dock
A collection of palettes, panels, or buttons surrounded by a dark gray bar. The arrows in the dock are used to maximize and minmize the palettes or panels.

Document toolbar
A toolbar that contains buttons for changing the current web page view, previewing and debugging web pages, and managing files.

Document-relative path
A path referenced in relation to the web page that is currently displayed.

Document window
The large white area in the Dreamweaver workspace where you create and edit web pages.

Documents
Flash, Photoshop, Fireworks, and Dreamweaver files.

Domain name
An IP address expressed in letters instead of numbers, usually reflecting the name of the business represented by the website.

Down Image state
The state of a page element when the element has been clicked with the mouse pointer.

Download time
The time it takes to transfer a file to another computer.

Drop Shadow
A style that adds what looks like a colored layer of identical text behind the selected type. The default shadow color is black.

Drop Zone
A blue outline area that indicates where a palette or panel can be moved.

DSL
Digital Subscriber Line. A type of high-speed Internet connection.

Dual Screen layout
A layout that utilizes two monitors while working in Dreamweaver.

Element
A graphic link that is part of a navigation bar and can have one of four possible appearances.

Embedded CSS style sheet
Styles that are part of an HTML page rather than comprising a separate file.

Embedded video
A video file that has been imported into a Flash document and becomes part of the SWF file.

Enable Cache
A setting to direct the computer system to use space on the hard drive as temporary memory, or cache, while you are working in Dreamweaver.

Expanded Tables Mode
A Dreamweaver mode that displays tables with temporary cell padding and spacing to make it easier to see the table cells.

Export data
To save data that was created in Dreamweaver in a special file format so that you can bring it into another software program.

External CSS style sheet
Collection of rules stored in a separate file that control the formatting of content on a web page. External CSS style sheets have a .css file extension.

External links
Links that connect to web pages in other websites or to an e-mail address.

Extract feature
Used to isolate a foreground object from its background.

Fair use
A concept that allows users to copy all or part of a copyrighted work in support of their First Amendment rights.

Fastening point
An anchor within the marquee. When the marquee pointer reaches the initial fastening point, a small circle appears on the pointer, indicating that you have reached the starting point.

Favorites
Assets that are used repeatedly in a website and are included in their own category in the assets panel.

Feather
A method used to control the softness of a selection's edges by blurring the area between the selection and the surrounding pixels.

Files panel
A window similar to Windows Explorer (Windows) or Finder (Macintosh), where Dreamweaver stores and manages files and folders. The Files panel contains a list of all the folders and files in a website.

Fill
A solid color, a pattern, or a gradient applied to an object.

Filters
Used to alter the look of an image and give it a special, customized appearance by applying special effects, such as distortions, changes in lighting, and blurring.

Flash button objects
Flash graphic and text objects that you can insert onto a web page without having the Flash program installed.

Flash Player
A program that allows Flash movies (.swf and .exe formats) to be viewed on a computer. This a free program from Adobe.

Flash text
A vector-based graphic that contains text.

Flattening
Merges all visible layers into one layer, named the Background layer, and deletes all hidden layers, greatly reducing file size.

Floating workspace
A feature of Adobe products that allows each document and panel to appear in its own window.

Focus group
A marketing tool where a group of people are asked for feedback about a product.

Font
Characters with a similar appearance.

Font combination
A set of three fonts that specifies which fonts a browser should use to display the text on a web page.

Font family
Represents a complete set of characters, letters, and symbols for a particular typeface. Font families are generally divided into three categories: serif, sans serif, and symbol.

Foreground color
Used to paint, fill, and stroke selections. The default foreground color is black.

Frame animation
An animation created by specifying the object that is to appear in each frame of a sequence of frames (also called a frame-by-frame animation).

Frame-by-frame animation
Animation that creates a new image for each frame (also called Frame animation).

Frame label
A text name for a keyframe that can be referenced within ActionScript code.

Frames
Individual cells that make up the Timeline in Flash.

Frameset
Multiple web pages displayed together using more than one frame or window.

FTP
File Transfer Protocol. The process of uploading and downloading files to and from a remote site.

Fuzziness
Similar to tolerance, in that the lower the value, the closer the color pixels must be to be selected.

Gamut
The range of displayed colors in a color model.

GIF file
Graphics Interchange Format file. A GIF is a type of file format used for images placed on web pages that can support both transparency and animation.

Gloss Contour
A Bevel and Emboss setting that determines the pattern with which light is reflected.

Gradient
Two or more colors that blend into each other in a fixed design.

Gradient fill
A type of fill in which colors appear to blend into one another. A gradient's appearance is determined by its beginning and ending points. Photoshop contains five gradient fill styles.

Gradient presets
Predesigned gradient fills that are displayed in the Gradient picker.

Graphic
Picture or design element that adds visual interest to a page.

Graphic symbols
Objects in Flash, such as drawings, that are converted to symbols and stored in the Library panel. A graphic symbol is the original object. Instances (copies) of a symbol can be made by dragging the symbol from the Library to the Stage.

Grayscale image
Can contain up to 256 shades of gray. Pixels can have brightness values from 0 (black) to white (255).

Grayscale mode
Uses up to 256 shades of gray, assigning a brightness value from 0 (black) to 255 (white) to each pixel.

Grids
Horizontal and vertical lines that fill the page and are used to place page elements

Group
A command that manipulates multiple objects as a single selection.

Guide layers
Layers used to align objects on the Stage in a Flash document.

Guides
Horizontal and vertical lines that you create to help you align objects. Guides appear as light blue lines.

Handles
Small boxes that appear along the perimeter of a selected object and are used to change the size of an image.

Head content
The part of a web page that is not viewed in the browser window. It includes meta tags, which are HTML codes that include information about the page, such as keywords and descriptions.

Headings
Six different styles that can be applied to text: Heading 1 (the largest size) through Heading 6 (the smallest size).

Hexadecimal RGB value
A value that represents the amount of red, green, and blue in a color and is based on the Base 16 number system.

Highlight Mode
A Bevel and Emboss setting that determines how pigments are combined.

History panel
Contains a record of each action performed during an editing session. Up to 1000 levels of Undo are available through the History panel (20 levels by default).

Home page
Usually, the first web page that appears when users visit a website.

Horizontal and vertical space
Blank space above, below, and on the sides of an image that separates the image from the text or other elements on the page.

Horizontal symmetry
A design principle in which page elements are balanced side-to-side across the page.

Hotspot
An area that you define in your document to which you can assign a URL (web address) or other type of interactivity. A clickable area on a graphic that, when clicked, links to a different location on the page or to another web page.

HTML
Hypertext Markup Language. A language web developers use to create web pages.

Hue
The color reflected from/transmitted through an object and expressed as a degree (between 0° and 360°). Each hue is identified by a color name (such as red or green).

Hyperlinks
Graphic or text elements on a web page that users click to display another location on the page, another web page on the same website, or a web page on a different website. Hyperlinks are also known as links.

Id type
A type of CSS rule that is used to redefine an HTML tag.

Image-editing program
Used to manipulate graphic images that can be reproduced by professional printers using full-color processes.

Image map
A graphic that has one or more hotspots defined on it that, when clicked, serve as a link that will take the viewer to another location.

Import data
To bring data created in one software program into another application.

Insert panel
Categories of buttons for creating and inserting objects displayed as a drop-down menu.

Instances
Editable copies of symbols after you drag them from the Library panel to the canvas or Stage (in Flash).

Intellectual property
An image or idea that is owned and retained by legal control.

Interactivity
Allows visitors to your website to interact with and affect content by moving or clicking the mouse.

Internal links
Links to web pages within the same website.

Inverse Kinematics
A process using a bone structure that allows objects to be animated in natural ways, such as a character running, jumping or kicking.

IP address
An assigned series of numbers, separated by periods, that designates an address on the Internet.

ISP
Internet Service Provider. A service to which you subscribe to be able to connect to the Internet with your computer.

JavaScript
A web-scripting code that interacts with HTML code to create dynamic content, such as rollovers or interactive forms.

JPEG file
Joint Photographic Experts Group file. A JPEG is a type of file format used for images that appear on web pages. Many photographs are saved with the JPEG file format.

Kerning
Controlling the amount of space between two characters.

Keyframe
A frame that signifies a change in the Time-line of a Flash movie, such as an object being animated.

Keywords
Words that relate to the content of the website and reside in the Head section.

LAN
A local area network.

Landscape orientation
An image with the long edge of the paper at the top and bottom.

Layer
A section within an image on which objects can be stored. The advantage: Individual effects can be isolated and manipulated without affecting the rest of the image. The disadvantage: Layers can increase the size of your file.

Layer comp
A variation on the arrangement and visibility of existing layers within an image; an organizational tool.

Layer group
An organizing tool you use to group layers on the Layers palette.

Layer (Photoshop)
An element that functions like a folder divided into sections that contain objects. A document can be made up of many layers.

Layer style
An effect that can be applied to a type or image layer.

Layer thumbnail
Contains a miniature picture of the layer's content, and appears to the left of the layer name on the Layers panel.

Layers (Flash)
Rows on the Timeline that are used to organize objects and that allow the stacking of objects on the Stage.

Layers panel
Displays all the layers within an active image. You can use the Layers panel to create, delete, merge, copy, or reposition layers.

Leading
An adjustment to the amount of vertical space between lines of text.

Library
A panel containing graphic symbols, button symbols, and animation symbols. You can use multiple Libraries in a document and share Libraries between documents.

Licensing agreement
The permission given by a copyright holder that conveys the right to use the copyright holder's work.

Link
See hyperlink.

Local site
The location of your local root folder where your website files are stored while being developed.

Local root folder
A folder on your hard drive, Flash drive, or floppy disk that holds all the files and folders for the wesbsite.

Logo
A distinctive image used to identify a company, project, or organization. You can create a logo by combining symbols, shapes, colors, and text.

Looping
The number of times an animation repeats.

Luminosity
The remaining light and dark values that result when a color image is converted to grayscale.

Mailto: link
An e-mail address that is formatted as a link that opens the default mail program with a blank, addressed message.

Main Timeline
The primary Timeline for a Flash movie. The main Timeline is displayed when you start a new Flash document.

Marquee
A series of dotted lines indicating a selected area that can be edited or dragged into another image.

Mask
A feature that lets you protect or modify a particular area; created using a marquee.

Mask layer
A layer in a Flash document that is used to cover the objects on another layer(s) and, at the same time, create a window through which you can view various objects on the other layer.

Matte
A colorful box placed behind an object that makes the object stand out.

Menu bar
A bar across the top of the program window that is located under the program title bar and lists the names of the menus that contain commands.

Merge cells
To combine multiple cells in a table into one cell.

Merge Drawing Model
A drawing mode that causes overlapping drawings (objects) to merge, so that a change in the top object, such as moving it, may affect the object beneath it.

Meta data
Information about a file, such as keywords, descriptions, and copyright information.

Meta tags
HTML codes that include information about the page such as keywords and descriptions. Meta tags reside in the head section.

Mode
Represents the amount of color data that can be stored in a given file format, and determines the color model used to display and print an image.

Model
Determines how pigments combine to produce resulting colors; determined by the color mode.

Mono.type spacing
Spacing in which each character occupies the same amount of space.

Morphing
The animation process of changing one object into another, sometimes unrelated, object.

Motion guide layer
A path used to specify how an animated object moves around the Flash Stage.

Motion Tween Presets
Pre-built animations, such as a bouncing effect, that can be applied to objects in Flash.

Motion tweening
The process used in Flash to automatically fill in the frames between keyframes in an animation that changes the properties of an object such as the position, size, or color. Motion tweening works on groups and symbols.

Movement
In screen design, movement refers to the way the viewer's eye moves through the objects on the screen.

Movie clip symbol
An animation stored as a single, reusable symbol in the Library panel in Flash. It has its own Timeline, independent of the main Timeline.

Named anchor
A specific location on a web page that is used to link to that portion of the web page.

Navigation bar
A set of text or graphic links that viewers can use to navigate between pages of a website.

Navigation structure
The way viewers navigate from page to page in a website.

Nested table
A table within a table.

Non-breaking space
A space that is left on the page by a browser.

Non-Websafe colors
Colors that might not be displayed uniformly across computer platforms.

None
Anti-aliasing setting that applies no anti-aliasing, resulting in jagged edges.

Numbered lists
Lists of items that are presented in a specific order and are preceded by numbers or letters in sequence. Also called ordered lists.

Object Drawing Model
A drawing mode that allows you to overlap objects which are then kept separate, so that changes in one object do not affect another object. You must break apart these objects before you can select their stroke and fills.

Objects
The individual elements in a document, such as text or images. In Flash, objects are placed on the Stage and can be edited or manipulated.

Onion skinning
A setting that allows you to view one or more frames before and after in the current frame.

Opacity
Determines the percentage of transparency. Whereas a layer with 100% opacity will obstruct objects in the layers beneath it, a layer with 1% opacity will appear nearly transparent.

Optical center
The point around which objects on the page are balanced; occurs approximately 3/8ths from the top of the page

Ordered lists
Lists of items that must be placed in a specific order and are preceded by numbers or letters.

Orientation
Direction an image appears on the page: portrait or landscape.

Orphaned files
Files that are not linked to any pages in the website.

Outline type
Type that is mathematically defined and can be scaled to any size without its edges losing their smooth appearance.

Over Image state
The state of a page element when the mouse pointer is over the element.

Over While Down Image state
The state of a page element when the mouse pointer is clicked and held over the element.

Panel groups
Groups of panels such as Design, Code, Application, and Files that are displayed through the Window menu. Sets of related panels are grouped together. Also known as Tab groups.

Panels (Dreamweaver)
Individual windows in Dreamweaver that display information on a particular topic, such as Answers or History.

Panels (Flash)
Components in Flash used to view, organize, and modify objects and features in a movie.

Panels (Photoshop)
Floating windows that can be moved and are used to modify objects. Panels contain named tabs, which can be separated and moved to another group. Each panel contains a menu that can be viewed by clicking the list arrow in its upper-right corner.

Parent page
A page at a higher level in a web hierarchy that links to other pages on a lower level called child pages.

Pasteboard
The gray area surrounding the Flash Stage where objects can be placed and manipulated. Neither the pasteboard, nor objects placed on

it appear in the movie unless the objects move onto the Stage during the playing of the movie.

Path (file location)
The location of an open file in relation to any folders in the website.

Path (vector object)
An open or closed line consisting of a series of anchor points.

Persistence of vision
The phenomenon of the eye capturing and holding an image for one-tenth of a second before processing another image.

PICS
Platform for Internet Content Selection. This is a rating system for web pages.

Pixels
Small squares of color used to display a digital image on a rectangular grid, such as a computer screen. Each dot in a bitmapped image that representsa color or shade.

Playhead
An indicator specifying which frame is playing in the Timeline of a Flash movie.

Plug-in
A module that adds features or enhancements to an application.

PNG file
Portable Network Graphics file. A PNG is a file format used for images placed on web pages that is capable of showing millions of colors but is small in file size. The native file format in Fireworks.

Point of contact
A place on a web page that provides viewers a means of contacting a company representative.

Points
Unit of measurement for font sizes. Traditionally, 1 inch is equivalent to 72.27 points. The default Photoshop type size is 12 points.

Portrait orientation
An image with the short edge of the paper at the top and bottom.

PostScript
A programming language created by Adobe that optimizes printed text and graphics.

PPI
Pixels per inch.

Preferences
Used to control the environment using your specifications.

Projector
In Flash, a standalone executable movie, such as a Windows .exe file.

Properties panel (also called Property Inspector)
In Flash, the panel that displays the properties of the selected object, such as size and color) on the Stage or the selected frame. The Properties panel can be used to edit selected properties.

Property inspector
A panel where properties and options specific to a selected tool or command appear. In Dreamweaver, a panel that displays the properties of the selected web page object. In Flash, the Property inspector displays the properties of the selected object on the Stage or the selected frame. You can change an object's properties using the text boxes, drop-down menus, and buttons on the Property inspector. The contents of the Property inspector vary according to the object currently selected.

Proportional spacing
The text spacing in which each character takes up a different amount of space, based on its width.

Public domain
Work that is no longer protected by copyright. Anyone can use it for any purpose.

Publish
The process used to generate the files neces-sary for delivering Flash movies on the web.

Publish a Website
To make a website available for viewing on the Internet or on an intranet.

QuickTime
A file format used for movies and anima-tions that requires a QuickTime Player.

Radial symFmetry
A design principle in which page elements are balanced from the center of the page outward, like the petals of a flower.

Rasterize
Converts a type layer to an image layer.

Reference panel
A panel used to find answers to coding questions, covering topics such as HTML, JavaScript, and Accessibility.

Refresh Local File List Automatically option
A setting that directs Dreamweaver to automatically reflect changes made in your file listings.

Registration point
The point on an object that is used to posi-tion the object on the Stage in a Flash movie.

Regular expressions
Combinations of characters, such as a phrase that begins or ends with a particular word or tag.

Related files
Files that are linked to a document and are necessary for the document to display and function correctly.

Related Files toolbar
A toolbar located below an open document's filename tab that displays the names of any related files.

Relative path
A path used with an internal link to reference a web page or graphic file within the website. In Flash, a path for an external

link or to an object that is based on the location of the movie file.

Relief
The height of ridges within an object.

Remote server
A web server that hosts websites and is not directly connected to the computer housing the local site.

Remote site
A website that has been published to a remote server.

Rendering intent
The way in which a color-management system handles color conversion from one color space to another.

Resolution
The number of pixels per inch in an image. Also refers to an image's clarity and fineness of detail.

Resulting color
The outcome of the blend color applied to the base color.

Rich media content
Attractive and engaging images, interactive elements, video, or animations.

Rollover
An effect that changes the appearance of an object when the mouse rolls over it.

Root folder (local root folder)
A folder used to store all folders and files for a website.

Root-relative path
A path referenced from a website's root folder.

Rows
Table cells arranged horizontally.

Rule of Thirds
The rule of thirds is a design principle that entails dividing a page into nine squares and then placing the page elements of most interest on the intersections of the grid lines.

Rulers
On screen markers that help you precisely measure and position an object. Rulers can be displayed using the View menu.

Rules
Sets of formatting attributes in a Cascading Style Sheet.

Sampling
A method of changing foreground and background colors by copying existing colors from an image.

Sans serif fonts
Fonts that do not have tails or strokes at the end of characters; commonly used in headlines and on web pages.

Saturation
The strength or purity of the color, representing the amount of gray in proportion to hue (measured as a percentage from 0% [gray], to 100% [fully saturated]). Also known as *chroma*.

Scale
The size relationship of objects to one another.

Scene
A Timeline designated for a specific part of a Flash movie. Scenes are a way to organize long movies by dividing the movie into sections.

Screen reader
A device used by the visually impaired to convert written text on a computer monitor to spoken words.

Script Assist
A feature found in the Actions panel which can be used to generate ActionScript without having to write programming code.

Seamless image
A tiled image that is blurred at the edges so that it appears to be all one image.

Search
The Adobe Help feature that allows you to enter a keyword to begin a search for a topic.

Selection
An area in an image that is surrounded by a selection marquee.

Selector
The name or the tag to which style declarations have been assigned.

Serif fonts
Ornate fonts that have a tail, or stroke, at the end of some characters. These tails make it easier for the eye to recognize

words; therefore, serif fonts are generally used in text passages.

Shading
Bevel and Emboss setting that determines lighting effects.

Shadow Mode
Bevel and Emboss setting that determines how pigments are combined.

Shape hints
Indicators used to control the shape of an object as it changes appearance during an animation.

Shape tweening
The process of animating an object so that its shape changes. Shape tweening requires editable graphics.

Sharp
Anti-aliasing setting that displays type with the best possible resolution.

Sharpen More filter
Increases the contrast of adjacent pixels and can focus blurry images.

Show Code and Design views
A combination of Code view and Design view. The best view for correcting errors.

Site map
A graphical representation of how web pages relate to each other within a website.

Size
Determines the clarity of a drop shadow.

Slices
A web element that divides an image into different sections, which allows you to apply rollover behaviors, animation, and URLs to those areas.

Slider
The small icon on the left side of the History panel that you can drag to undo or redo an action.

Smooth
Anti-aliasing setting that gives type more rounded edges.

Soft return
A shortcut key combination that forces text to a new line without creating a new paragraph by creating a <BR> tag.

Source
The image containing the color that will be matched.

Splash screen
A window that displays information about the software you are using.

Split cells
To divide cells into multiple cells.

Spread
Determines the width of drop shadow text.

Spring-loaded keyboard shortcuts
Shortcut keyboard combinations that temporarily change the active tool.

Stage
That area of the Flash workspace that contains the objects that are part of the movie and that will be seen by the viewers.

Standard Mode
A Dreamweaver mode that is used when you insert a table using the Insert Table icon or command.

Standard toolbar
A toolbar that contains icons for some frequently used commands that are also available on the File and Edit menus.

State
Represents the button's appearance based on a mouse action. These include: Up, Over, Down, and Over While Down.

Status bar
The area located at the bottom of the program window (Win) or the image window (Mac) that displays information such as the file size of the active window and a description of the active tool. In Dreamweaver, bar that appears at the bottom of the Dreamweaver document window. The left end of the status bar displays the tag selector, which shows the HTML tags being used at the insertion point location. The right end displays the window size and estimated download time for the page displayed.

Step
Each task performed in the History panel.

Storyboard
A small sketch that represents each page in a website or screen in an application. Like a flowchart, a storyboard shows the relationship of each page or screen to the other pages in the site or screens.

Stroking the edges
The process of making a selection or layer stand out by formatting it with a border.

Strong
Anti-aliasing setting that makes type appear heavier, much like the bold attribute.

Structure
A Bevel and Emboss setting that determines the size and physical properties of the object.

Style Rendering toolbar
A toolbar that allows you to render a web page as different media types (e.g., handheld).

Subtractive colors
A color system in which the full combination of cyan, magenta, and yellow absorb all color and produce black.

Swatches panel
Contains available colors that can be selected for use as a foreground or background color. You can also add your own colors to the Swatches panel.

Symbol
A graphic, animation, or button that represents an object, text, or combination group.

Symbol fonts
Used to display unique characters (such as $, ÷, or ™).

Symmetrical balance
Page in which objects are placed equally on either side of an imaginary vertical line in the center of the page.

T

Tab groups
Sets of related panels that are grouped together. Also known as panel groups.

Table header
Text placed at the top or sides of a table on a web page that is read by screen readers.

Tables
Grids of rows and columns that can be used either to hold tabular data on a web page or as a basic design tool for page layout.

Tabular data
Data arranged in columns and rows and separated by a delimiter.

Tag Selector
A location on the status bar that displays HTML tags for the various page elements, including tables and cells.

Tag type
A type of CSS rule used to redefine an HTML tag.

Target (Dreamweaver)
The location on a web page that the browser displays in full view when an internal link is clicked or the frame that opens when a link is clicked.

Target (Photoshop)
When sampling a color, the image that will receive the matched color.

Templates
Web pages that contain the basic layout for similar pages in the site.

Terms of use
The rules that a copyright owner uses to establish use of his or her work.

Title bar
Displays the program name and filename of the open image. The title bar also contains buttons for minimizing, maximizing, and closing the image.

Tiled image
A small graphic that repeats across and down a web page, appearing as individual squares or rectangles.

Timeline
The component of Flash used to organize and control the movie's contents over time, by specifying when each object appears on the Stage.

Timeline Effect
Pre-built animation effects (such as rotating, fading, and wiping) that can be applied to objects using a dialog box.

Tone
The brightness and contrast within an image.

Tools panel
A panel in Flash, Dreamweaver, and Photoshop separated into categories containing tools and their options.

Tracing image
An image that is placed in the background of a document as a guide to create page elements on top of it, similar to the way tracing paper is used.

Tracking
The insertion of a uniform amount of space between characters.

Trademark
Protects an image, word, slogan, symbol, or design used to identify goods or services.

Transformation point
The point on an object that is used to orient the object as it is being animated and the point that snaps to a motion guide.

Tweening
The process of adding tweened instances and distributing them to frames so that the movement appears more fluid.

Type
Text, or a layer containing text. Each character is measured in points. In PostScript measurement, 1 inch is equivalent to 72 points. In traditional measurement, 1 inch is equivalent to 72.27 points.

Type spacing
Adjustments you can make to the space between characters and between lines of type.

3 D Effects
A Process in Flash that animates 2 D objects through 3 D space with 3 D Transformation tods

U

Unity
In screen design, intra-screen unity has to do with how the various screen objects relate. Inter-screen unity refers to the design that viewers encounter as they navigate from one screen to another.

Unordered lists
Lists of items that do not need to be placed in a specific order and are usually preceded by bullets.

Unvisited links
Links that have not been clicked by the viewer.

Up Image state
The state of a page element when the mouse pointer is not on the element.

Upload
The process of transferring files from a local drive to a web server.

URL
Uniform Resource Locator. An address that determines a route on the Internet or to a web page.

Vector graphics
Mathematically calculated objects composed of anchor points and straight or curved line segments.

Version Cue
See Adobe Version Cue.

View
A particular way of displaying page content. Dreamweaver has three views: Design view, Code view, and Show Code and Design views.

Vignette
A feature in which the border of a picture or portrait fades into the surrounding color at its edges.

Vignette effect
A feature that uses feathering to fade a marquee shape.

Visited links
Links that have been previously clicked, or visited. The default color for visited links is purple.

Web browser
A program, such as Microsoft Internet Explorer or Mozilla Firefox, that lets you display HTML-developed web pages.

Web design program
A program for creating interactive web pages containing text, images, hyperlinks, animation, sound, and video.

Web server
A computer dedicated to hosting websites that is connected to the Internet and configured with software to handle requests from browsers.

Website
Related web pages stored on a server that users can download using a web browser.

Web-safe colors
Colors that display consistently in all browsers and on Macintosh, Windows, and Unix platforms.

White space
An area on a web page that is not filled with text or graphics.

Workspace
The entire window, from the Application bar at the top of the window, to the status bar at the bottom border of the program window. The area in the Dreamweaver program window where you work with documents, movies, tools, and panels.

Workspace switcher (Dreamweaver)
A drop-down menu located in the top right corner on the Application bar that allows you to change the workspace layout.

Workspace switcher (Photoshop)
Button on the Application bar that lets you switch between defined workspaces.

WYSIWYG
An acronym for What You See Is What You Get, meaning that your web page should look the same in the browser as it does in the web editor.

XHTML
eXtensible HyperText Markup Language. The most current standard for developing web pages.

XML
A language used to create the structure of blocks of information, similar to HTML.

XSL
Similar to CSS; the XSL stylesheet information formats containers created with XML.

XSLT
Extensible Stylesheet Language Transformations.

Special Characters, + (plus sign),
PHOTOSHOP 1–28

A

absolute paths, DREAMWEAVER 4–4, 4–5
absolute positioning. *See* AP *entries*
access, remote sites, setting up,
DREAMWEAVER 6–17—6–18
accessibility, DREAMWEAVER 2–5,
FLASH 1–41
alternate text, DREAMWEAVER 3–33
color guidelines, DREAMWEAVER 3–39
tables, DREAMWEAVER 5–19
Accessibility category, Preferences dialog
box, DREAMWEAVER 3–33
accessibility standards, validating,
DREAMWEAVER 6–9
actions, FLASH 3–22—3–29
ActionScript. *See* ActionScript
assigning to drop-down buttons on
animated navigation bars, FLASH
5–19, 5–22
attaching to video control buttons,
FLASH 5–16
frames, FLASH 3–24
gotoframe, assigning to buttons,
FLASH 3–28
play, assigning to buttons, FLASH 3–27
rollover, animated navigation bars,
FLASH 5–19, 5–23
second, assigning to buttons, FLASH
3–29
stop, assigning to frames, FLASH 3–26
Actions panel, FLASH 3–25
Toolbox pane, FLASH 3–26
ActionScript, FLASH 3–22—3–25
Actions panel, FLASH 3–25
AS2 and AS3, FLASH 3–22—3–25
frame labels, FLASH 3–25
active layers
background color, PHOTOSHOP 5–6
inserting layers beneath, PHOTOSHOP
2–10
Add filter icon, FLASH 1–27
additions to selections, PHOTOSHOP 3–13
additive colors, PHOTOSHOP 4–5, 4–6
adjustment layers, PHOTOSHOP 2–4
Adobe Community Help, DREAMWEAVER 1–17
Adobe Flash Encoder, FLASH 5–13

Adobe programs. *See* Dreamweaver *entries;*
Flash *entries;* Photoshop *entries*
Bridge. *See* Bridge
Adobe website, PHOTOSHOP 1–38
Align menu, DREAMWEAVER 3–23
aligning images, DREAMWEAVER 3–23, 3–26
table cells, DREAMWEAVER 5–29, 5–31
aligning text objects, FLASH 2–32
alternate text, DREAMWEAVER 3–29
accessibility, DREAMWEAVER 3–33
editing, DREAMWEAVER 3–32
missing, checking for, DREAMWEAVER
6–9
Altitude setting, Bevel and Emboss style,
PHOTOSHOP 5–21
anchor(s), named, internal links to.
See internal links to named anchors
anchor points, FLASH 2–4
angle, drop shadows, PHOTOSHOP
5–13, 5–14
Angle setting, Bevel and Emboss style,
PHOTOSHOP 5–21
animated navigation bars, FLASH 5–2,
5–18—5–25
assigning actions to drop-down buttons,
FLASH 5–19, 5–22
creating drop-down menus, FLASH
5–18—5–19
frame labels, FLASH 5–19, 5–23
invisible buttons, FLASH 5–19, 5–24—5–25
mask layers, FLASH 5–18—5–19, 5–21
positioning drop-down buttons, FLASH
5–18, 5–20
rollover actions, FLASH 5–19, 5–23
animating text, FLASH 4–42—4–49
adding actions to buttons, FLASH 4–49
copying and pasting frames, FLASH 4–44
fading in text, FLASH 4–47
making text blocks into buttons,
FLASH 4–48
resizing text, FLASH 4–47
rotating text, FLASH 4–46
selecting frames, FLASH 4–44
animations, FLASH 4–1—4–52
creating, FLASH 1–19—1–20
creating using drawing tools, FLASH 1–22
frame rate, FLASH 4–2
frame-by-frame (frame). *See* frame-by-
frame animations

IK objects, FLASH 5–27, 5–30. *See also*
Inverse Kinematics (IK)
motion tweening. *See* motion tweening
movie clips, FLASH 4–40—4–41
object appearance, FLASH 1–21
operation, FLASH 4–2
Photoshop-created text, 1–17
shape tween. *See* shape tween animations
text. *See* animating text
tweened. *See* classic tween animations;
motion tween animations
anti-aliasing, PHOTOSHOP 5–16—5–19
applying, PHOTOSHOP 5–18
methods for using, PHOTOSHOP 5–18
undoing, PHOTOSHOP 5–19
when to apply, PHOTOSHOP 5–16
AP div tags, DREAMWEAVER 5–4
AP elements, DREAMWEAVER 5–4
Apache web server, DREAMWEAVER 6–16
Application bar, DREAMWEAVER 1–4,
PHOTOSHOP 1–16
opening files, PHOTOSHOP 1–11
approach, planning applications or website,
FLASH 1–41
arrangement
elements, PHOTOSHOP 1–21
image composition, PHOTOSHOP 1–19
arranging panels, FLASH 1–6—1–7
assets, DREAMWEAVER 1–20, 1–26
managing using Version Cue,
DREAMWEAVER 6–11
removing from websites,
DREAMWEAVER 3–35
assets folder, saving image files in,
DREAMWEAVER 1–31, 2–14
Assets panel, DREAMWEAVER 3–22—3–23
displaying web-safe colors,
DREAMWEAVER 6–7
Favorites option, DREAMWEAVER 3–25
resizing, DREAMWEAVER 3–23
Site option, DREAMWEAVER 3–25
viewing email links, DREAMWEAVER 2–23
viewing links, DREAMWEAVER 4–9
website maintenance, DREAMWEAVER 6–4
asymmetrical balance, PHOTOSHOP 1–22
Attach External Style Sheet dialog box,
DREAMWEAVER 3–19
audience, planning applications or websites,
FLASH 1–40

background, moving, FLASH 4–27
background color, DREAMWEAVER 2–5,
  PHOTOSHOP 4–6
  active layer, PHOTOSHOP 5–6
  changing, PHOTOSHOP 4–6,
    PHOTOSHOP 4–8—4–9
  default, setting, PHOTOSHOP 4–7
  setting, DREAMWEAVER 2–9
background images
  inserting, DREAMWEAVER 3–34, 3–35,
    3–36
  removing, DREAMWEAVER 3–37
Background layers, PHOTOSHOP 2–4, 2–5
  converting, PHOTOSHOP 2–6
  converting image layers to, PHOTOSHOP
    2–6, 2–7
balance, screen design, FLASH 1–42
balancing
  colors, PHOTOSHOP 4–27, 4–31
  objects, PHOTOSHOP 1–22
banners, DREAMWEAVER 1–12
base color, PHOTOSHOP 4–27
baseline, PHOTOSHOP 5–9
baseline shift, PHOTOSHOP 5–9, 5–11
BCC (Browser Compatibility Check) feature,
  DREAMWEAVER 5–4, 5–13
behaviors, creating div tags,
  DREAMWEAVER 5–2
Behind mode, PHOTOSHOP 4–28
Bevel and Emboss style, PHOTOSHOP
  5–20—5–23
  adding using Layer menu, PHOTOSHOP
    5–22
  settings, PHOTOSHOP 5–20—5–21,
    5–23
Bezier handles, FLASH 4–6, 4–9
Bind tool, FLASH 2–5
bitmap(s), PHOTOSHOP 4–2
bitmap graphics, FLASH 2–2, 3–30, 3–31
bitmap mode, PHOTOSHOP 4–6
Bitmap type, PHOTOSHOP 5–4
Black & White command, PHOTOSHOP 4–22
blend color, PHOTOSHOP 4–27
blending modes, PHOTOSHOP 2–9, 4–27,
  4–28, 4–30
  components, PHOTOSHOP 4–27
blurring, type, PHOTOSHOP 5–25
blurry images, fixing, PHOTOSHOP 4–26
body of web page, DREAMWEAVER 2–5

bone structure, Inverse Kinematics,
  FLASH 5–26—5–27, 5–29
Bone tool, FLASH 2–5, 5–27
border(s), PHOTOSHOP 4–16—4–17
  images, DREAMWEAVER 3–29,
    PHOTOSHOP 4–16, 3–30
  locking transparent pixels, PHOTOSHOP
    4–16
  tables, DREAMWEAVER 5–18
Border command, PHOTOSHOP 3–12
bread crumbs trail, DREAMWEAVER 4–28
Break Apart command, FLASH 3–5, 3–8
Bridge, 1–2, DREAMWEAVER 3–25—3–26,
  PHOTOSHOP 1–9—1–10, 1–11
  accessing Version Cue, PHOTOSHOP
    1–14
  creating PDFs, PHOTOSHOP 1–36
  inserting files, DREAMWEAVER 3–23
  rate and filter, PHOTOSHOP 1–13
  resetting preferences to factory default,
    PHOTOSHOP 1–10
  uses, PHOTOSHOP 1–10, 1–15
  views, PHOTOSHOP 1–10
  Web Gallery, PHOTOSHOP 1–37
Bridge window, PHOTOSHOP 1–11
brightness, PHOTOSHOP 4–5
  adjusting, PHOTOSHOP 4–29
Brightness/Contrast dialog box,
  PHOTOSHOP 4–29
broken links, DREAMWEAVER 2–18
  checking for, DREAMWEAVER 6–6
browser(s). See web browsers
Browser Compatibility Check (BCC) feature,
  DREAMWEAVER 5–4, 5–13
browsing through files, PHOTOSHOP 1–9
Brush tool, FLASH 2–5, 2–11
bullet(s), DREAMWEAVER 3–4
bulleted lists, DREAMWEAVER 3–4
button(s), FLASH 3–16—3–21
  adding actions, FLASH 4–49
  adding sound, FLASH 5–11
  assigning second event to, FLASH 3–29
  attaching actions to video control
    buttons, FLASH 5–16
  creating, FLASH 3–16, 3–18
  drop-down, animated navigation bars.
    See animated navigation bars
  editing, FLASH 3–17, 3–19
  go to frame action, FLASH 3–28

hit area, FLASH 3–20
Insert panel, DREAMWEAVER 1–4
invisible, animated navigation bars,
  FLASH 5–19, 5–24—5–25
making text blocks into, FLASH 4–48
mouse events responded to, FLASH 3–24
play action, FLASH 3–27
previewing, FLASH 3–17
states, FLASH 3–16
testing, FLASH 3–20—3–21
button symbols, FLASH 3–2

camera(s), PHOTOSHOP 1–39
  file formats, PHOTOSHOP 1–5
  getting photos from, PHOTOSHOP 1–13
Cascading Style Sheets (CSSs),
  DREAMWEAVER 2–5, 2–6, 3–2,
  3–10—3–17. See also CSS entries
  adding rules, DREAMWEAVER
    3–20—3–21
  advantages, DREAMWEAVER 3–11
  attaching style sheets, DREAMWEAVER
    3–21
  Class type, DREAMWEAVER 3–10
  Compound type, DREAMWEAVER 3–10
  creating style sheets, DREAMWEAVER
    3–12
  CSS layout blocks, editing,
    DREAMWEAVER 5–15
  CSS Styles panel, DREAMWEAVER 3–10
  embedded (internal) style sheets,
    DREAMWEAVER 3–18—3–19
  embedded styles. See embedded style(s)
  external style sheets. See external
    style sheets
  HTML tags compared, DREAMWEAVER
    2–11
  ID type, DREAMWEAVER 3–10
  inline styles, DREAMWEAVER 3–10
  internal styles. See embedded style(s)
  Tag type, DREAMWEAVER 3–10
  viewing code with Code Navigator,
    DREAMWEAVER 3–16
case-sensitive links, DREAMWEAVER 4–8
cell(s), tables
  aligning images, DREAMWEAVER 5–29,
    5–31
  cell padding, DREAMWEAVER 5–18, 5–29

cell spacing, DREAMWEAVER 5–18, 5–29
cell walls, DREAMWEAVER 5–18
content. *See* cell content
    formatting, DREAMWEAVER 5–32, 5–33,
        5–36
    inserting images, DREAMWEAVER 5–28,
        5–29, 5–30
    merging, DREAMWEAVER 5–23, 5–27
    splitting, DREAMWEAVER 5–23, 5–26
    width, setting, DREAMWEAVER 5–20
cell content
    formatting, DREAMWEAVER 5–32,
        5–33, 5–35
    modifying, DREAMWEAVER 5–37
cell padding, DREAMWEAVER 5–18, 5–29
cell spacing, DREAMWEAVER 5–18, 5–29
cell walls, DREAMWEAVER 5–18
change rate, shape tween animations,
    FLASH 4–31, 4–34
character animations, Inverse Kinematics.
    See Inverse Kinematics (IK)
Character panel, type properties,
    PHOTOSHOP 5–9
Check In/Check Out feature, enabling,
    DREAMWEAVER 6–23—6–24
Check Spelling dialog box,
    DREAMWEAVER 2–17
checking files in and out, DREAMWEAVER
    6–22—6–25
child pages, DREAMWEAVER 1–20
Circle Hotspot Tool, DREAMWEAVER 4–25
Class type styles, DREAMWEAVER 3–10
classic tween animations, FLASH 4–20—4–23
    keyframes, FLASH 4–20
    motion guides, FLASH 4–20—4–21,
        4–22—4–23
    motion tweens compared, FLASH 4–20
    orienting objects to guides, FLASH 4–23
    registration point, FLASH 4–21
    transformation point, FLASH 4–21
Clean Up Word HTML dialog box,
    DREAMWEAVER 2–15
Clear mode, PHOTOSHOP 4–28
Clipboard, PHOTOSHOP 3–2
cloaked files, DREAMWEAVER 6–2
cloaking files, DREAMWEAVER 6–26—6–29
    selected file types, DREAMWEAVER
        6–27, 6–29
closing files, PHOTOSHOP 1–38, 1–39

CMYK mode, PHOTOSHOP 4–6
code. *See* CSS code; HTML code
Code Inspector, DREAMWEAVER 2–27
    viewing HTML code, DREAMWEAVER
        2–25
Code Navigator
    editing rules, DREAMWEAVER 3–16
    viewing CSS code, DREAMWEAVER
        3–16
Code view, DREAMWEAVER 1–7
Coding toolbar, DREAMWEAVER 1–5
collaboration using ConnectNow,
    PHOTOSHOP 4–21
collapsing, panels, FLASH 1–6, 1–8
color(s), PHOTOSHOP 4–1—4–35
    accessibility guidelines,
        DREAMWEAVER 3–39
    active layer background, PHOTOSHOP
        5–6
    adding to grayscale images, PHOTOSHOP
        4–22—4–25
    adding to layers, PHOTOSHOP 2–17
    additive, PHOTOSHOP 4–5, 4–6
    background. *See* background color
    balancing, PHOTOSHOP 4–27, 4–31
    base, PHOTOSHOP 4–27
    bitmaps, PHOTOSHOP 4–2
    blend, PHOTOSHOP 4–27
    brightness, PHOTOSHOP 4–5
    color models, PHOTOSHOP 4–2,
        4–4—4–5
    color modes, PHOTOSHOP 4–2, 4–6
    converting color images to grayscale,
        PHOTOSHOP 4–22, 4–24
    fills and strokes, FLASH 2–15, 2–17
    foreground, PHOTOSHOP 4–6, 4–7
    gradients. *See* gradient(s)
    hexadecimal values, PHOTOSHOP 4–9
    hue, PHOTOSHOP 4–5
    kuler. *See* kuler
    matching, PHOTOSHOP 4–32—4–33
    non-web-safe, DREAMWEAVER 3–35,
        3–39
    pixels, PHOTOSHOP 4–2
    printing images, PHOTOSHOP 1–33
    psychology of color, PHOTOSHOP 4–4
    removing from websites,
        DREAMWEAVER 3–35
    resulting, PHOTOSHOP 4–27

sampling, PHOTOSHOP 4–32
saturation. *See* saturation
selecting. *See* selecting colors
subtractive, PHOTOSHOP 4–6
type, PHOTOSHOP 5–4, 5–7
verifying that colors are web-safe,
    DREAMWEAVER 6–7
Color Balance dialog box, PHOTOSHOP
    4–27, 4–31
Color Burn mode, PHOTOSHOP 4–28
Color Dodge mode, PHOTOSHOP 4–28
color effects, motion tween animations,
    FLASH 4–12
Color Handling list arrow, Print dialog box,
    PHOTOSHOP 1–33
Color mode, PHOTOSHOP 4–28
color mode(s), PHOTOSHOP 4–2, 4–6
    converting color images to grayscale,
        PHOTOSHOP 4–22, 4–23, 4–24
color models, PHOTOSHOP 4–2,
    4–4—4–5
    gamuts, PHOTOSHOP 4–4, 4–5
Color palette, FLASH 2–15
Color panel, changing background color,
    PHOTOSHOP 4–8
Color Picker, PHOTOSHOP 4–10, 4–12
Color Picker dialog box, type color,
    PHOTOSHOP 5–4
Color Range command, PHOTOSHOP 2–12,
    3–17, 3–18
Color Range dialog box, PHOTOSHOP
    2–14, 3–18
color range selections, PHOTOSHOP
    2–12—2–13, 2–14
color separations, PHOTOSHOP 4–6
Colors section, Tools panel, FLASH 1–6
columns, tables, DREAMWEAVER 5–2
    cells. *See* cell(s); tables
    resizing, DREAMWEAVER 5–24
combining images, PHOTOSHOP 3–2
commands. *See also specific
    command names*
    Control menu, FLASH 1–12—1–13
    options, FLASH 1–15
    selecting, PHOTOSHOP 1–16
    shortcuts, FLASH 1–15
comments, inserting into HTML code,
    DREAMWEAVER 2–28
compositing, PHOTOSHOP 3–2

composition of images, PHOTOSHOP 1–19
Compound type styles, DREAMWEAVER
3–10
ConnectNow, PHOTOSHOP 4–21
content
    cells. *See* cell content
    head. *See* head content
    media, rich, DREAMWEAVER 1–13
    page. *See* page content
    target audience, DREAMWEAVER 2–6
Content panel, Bridge, PHOTOSHOP 1–9
Contract command, PHOTOSHOP 3–12
contrast, PHOTOSHOP 1–36
    adjusting, PHOTOSHOP 4–29
Control menu
    commands, FLASH 1–12—1–13
    opening movies, FLASH 1–15
    playing movies, FLASH 1–15
Controller, FLASH 1–13
    opening movies, FLASH 1–15
    playing movies, FLASH 1–15
Convert to Symbol command, FLASH 3–4
Convert to Symbol dialog box, FLASH 3–4,
    3–5, 3–6
converting layers, PHOTOSHOP 2–6, 2–7
Copy command, FLASH 2–20
copying
    drawn objects, FLASH 2–20, 2–22
    files, PHOTOSHOP 1–10
    frames, frame-by-frame animations,
        FLASH 4–27
    layers, PHOTOSHOP 2–16
    motion paths, FLASH 4–14—4–15
    Photoshop PSD files into Dreamweaver,
        DREAMWEAVER 3–28
copying and pasting
    frames, FLASH 4–44
    navigation bars, DREAMWEAVER 4–17,
        4–22
    Photoshop images to Dreamweaver
        documents, INTEGRATION 1–11
    selections, PHOTOSHOP 3–7
copyright, DREAMWEAVER 6–34—6–37
    fair use, DREAMWEAVER 6–35
    intellectual property, DREAMWEAVER
        6–34
    licensing agreements, DREAMWEAVER
        6–35—6–36
    ownership, DREAMWEAVER 6–35

posting copyright notices,
    DREAMWEAVER 6–36—6–37
proper use of work, DREAMWEAVER
    6–35
Crisp anti-aliasing method, PHOTOSHOP 5–17
cropping images, PHOTOSHOP 2–12
CSS(s). *See* Cascading Style Sheets (CSSs)
CSS Advisor, DREAMWEAVER 5–13
CSS blocks, DREAMWEAVER 2–5
CSS code, DREAMWEAVER 3–11, 5–9
    declaration, DREAMWEAVER 3–11
    selector, DREAMWEAVER 3–11
    viewing with Code Navigator,
        DREAMWEAVER 3–16
CSS containers
    adding images, DREAMWEAVER 5–11
    adding text, DREAMWEAVER 5–10
    page layouts. *See* CSS page layout(s)
CSS page layout(s), DREAMWEAVER
    5–2—5–17
    adding images, DREAMWEAVER 5–11
    adding test, DREAMWEAVER 5–10
    creating pages, DREAMWEAVER
        5–6—5–7
    CSS code, DREAMWEAVER 5–9
    div tag content, DREAMWEAVER 5–8
    div tags, DREAMWEAVER 5–4
    editing CSS layout block properties,
        DREAMWEAVER 5–15—5–16
    editing page properties,
        DREAMWEAVER 5–17
    editing styles in CSS layout blocks,
        DREAMWEAVER 5–15
    formatting content in CSS layout blocks,
        DREAMWEAVER 5–13—5–14
CSS page layout blocks
    tables, DREAMWEAVER 5–2
    viewing, DREAMWEAVER 5–5, 5–14
CSS Property inspector, DREAMWEAVER 3–10
CSS rule(s), DREAMWEAVER 3–10
    adding, DREAMWEAVER 3–20—3–21
    applying, DREAMWEAVER 3–14
    code for, DREAMWEAVER 3–11
    editing, DREAMWEAVER 3–12—3–13,
        3–15, 3–17
CSS Rule definition dialog box,
    DREAMWEAVER 3–10
CSS Styles panel, DREAMWEAVER 3–10,
    3–13, 5–12

customizing
    gradients, PHOTOSHOP 4–19
    keyboard shortcuts, PHOTOSHOP 1–18
    Photoshop window, PHOTOSHOP 1–18
    workspace, PHOTOSHOP 1–23
cutting selections, PHOTOSHOP 3–7

Darken mode, PHOTOSHOP 4–28
data loss, preventing, DREAMWEAVER 2–12
date objects, inserting, DREAMWEAVER 2–29
debugging, DREAMWEAVER 1–7
Deco tool, FLASH 2–5
default document type, creating HTML pages,
    DREAMWEAVER 1–27
default font, DREAMWEAVER 2–5
default images folder, setting,
    DREAMWEAVER 1–29
default link colors, DREAMWEAVER 2–5
defects. *See* imperfections
defining remote sites, DREAMWEAVER
    6–14, 6–15
defining websites, DREAMWEAVER 1–20,
    1–24
definition lists, DREAMWEAVER 3–5
defringing layer contents, PHOTOSHOP
    2–13, 2–15
Delete Item icon, Library panel, FLASH 3–11
deleting. *See also* removing
    Design Notes, DREAMWEAVER 6–12
    files from websites, DREAMWEAVER
        3–38
    layers, FLASH 2–39, PHOTOSHOP
        2–9, 2–11
    rows from tables, DREAMWEAVER 5–22
    from selections, PHOTOSHOP 3–13
    selections, PHOTOSHOP 3–7
    states on History panel, PHOTOSHOP
        1–25, 1–27
    symbols, FLASH 3–14
delimited files, DREAMWEAVER 5–34
delimiters, DREAMWEAVER 5–34
dependent files, DREAMWEAVER 6–15
derivative works, DREAMWEAVER 6–35
description(s), DREAMWEAVER 2–5, 2–8
    entering, DREAMWEAVER 2–7, 2–8
Description dialog box, DREAMWEAVER 2–8
deselecting selections, PHOTOSHOP 3–5,
    3–7, 3–9

design guidelines
 interactive, FLASH 1–43
 screen design, FLASH 1–42—1–43
Design Notes, 1–6, DREAMWEAVER 6–5
 6–10—6–13
 associating with files, DREAMWEAVER
  6–11
 deleting, DREAMWEAVER 6–12
 editing, DREAMWEAVER 6–12—6–13
 enabling, DREAMWEAVER 6–10
Design view, DREAMWEAVER 1–7
device resolution, PHOTOSHOP 1–29
Difference mode, PHOTOSHOP 4–28
digital cameras. *See* camera(s)
digital images, PHOTOSHOP 1–2
disabilities, accessibility. *See* accessibility
display, default, changing, PHOTOSHOP
 1–21
displaying. *See also* viewing
 gridlines, FLASH 2–8
 layers, FLASH 2–35, PHOTOSHOP 1–25,
  1–26, 2–40
 panels, PHOTOSHOP 1–22
 rulers, PHOTOSHOP 2–6
 symbol properties, FLASH 3–14
 toolbars, DREAMWEAVER 1–11
Dissolve mode, PHOTOSHOP 4–28
distance, drop shadows, PHOTOSHOP
 5–13, 5–14
distort filters, PHOTOSHOP 5–24, 5–25
Distort option, Free Transform tool, FLASH 2–21
distributing movies, FLASH 1–36—1–39
 creating projector files, FLASH 1–39
 publishing movies for distribution on
  web, FLASH 1–38
div tags, DREAMWEAVER 5–2, 5–4, 5–31
 content, DREAMWEAVER 5–4
docks, DREAMWEAVER 1–6, PHOTOSHOP 1–18
Document properties dialog box, FLASH 1–17
Document toolbar, DREAMWEAVER 1–4—1–5
Document window, DREAMWEAVER 1–4
document-relative paths, DREAMWEAVER 4–5
domain names, DREAMWEAVER 1–24
Down image stats, DREAMWEAVER 4–16
Down state, FLASH 3–16
download time, viewing, DREAMWEAVER 3–22
downloading
 copyright law, DREAMWEAVER 6–34
 files, DREAMWEAVER 6–15

drawing model modes, FLASH 2–2,
 2–14—2–15, 2–19
drawing objects, FLASH 2–1—2–45
 colors, FLASH 2–15, 2–17
 drawing model modes, FLASH 2–2,
  2–14—2–15, 2–19
 gradients, FLASH 2–15, 2–18
 selecting objects, FLASH 2–14, 2–15,
  2–16—2–17
 tools. *See* drawing tools
drawing tools, FLASH 2–4—2–13
 creating objects, FLASH 1–22
 creating vector graphics, FLASH 2–6
 gridlines, FLASH 2–8
 grouped, FLASH 2–6
 options, FLASH 2–6, 2–11—2–12
 positioning objects on Stage,
  FLASH 2–6—2–7
drawn objects, FLASH 2–20—2–27
 copying, FLASH 2–20, 2–22
 flipping, FLASH 2–21, 2–24
 moving, FLASH 2–20, 2–22
 Primitive Rectangle and Oval tools,
  FLASH 2–26—2–27
 reshaping, FLASH 2–23
 reshaping segments, FLASH 2–21
 resizing, FLASH 2–20, 2–23
 rotating, FLASH 2–21, 2–24
 selecting, FLASH 2–25
 skewing, FLASH 2–21, 2–24
 transforming, FLASH 2–20, 2–23
Dreamweaver, PHOTOSHOP 1–5
 inserting Flash movies. *See* inserting
  Flash movies into Dreamweaver
 inserting Photoshop images into
  documents. *See* inserting Photoshop
  images into Dreamweaver documents
Dreamweaver CS4, PHOTOSHOP 1–5
 overview, DREAMWEAVER 1–2
 starting, DREAMWEAVER 1–8—1–9
Dreamweaver workspace, DREAMWEAVER
 1–4—1–10
 Document window, DREAMWEAVER
  1–4
 hiding and displaying toolbars,
  DREAMWEAVER 1–11
 layout, DREAMWEAVER 1–8, 1–9
 panels, DREAMWEAVER 1–6,
  1–10—1–11

Property inspector, DREAMWEAVER
 1–5—1–6
 toolbars, DREAMWEAVER 1–4—1–5
 views, DREAMWEAVER 1–7, 1–10—1–11
drop shadows, PHOTOSHOP 5–12—5–15
 angle, PHOTOSHOP 5–13, 5–14
 applying, PHOTOSHOP 5–12—5–13,
  5–14
 controlling, PHOTOSHOP 5–13, 5–15
 distance, PHOTOSHOP 5–13, 5–14
 size, PHOTOSHOP 5–13, 5–14
 spread, PHOTOSHOP 5–13, 5–14
drop zones, PHOTOSHOP 1–18
drop-down menus, creating, FLASH
 5–18—5–19
Dual Screen layout, DREAMWEAVER 1–9
duotones, PHOTOSHOP 4–23
duplicating. *See* copying
Dust & Scratches dialog box, PHOTOSHOP
 5–27

ease value
 IK, FLASH 5–32
 motion tween animations, FLASH 4–10
edges, stroking, PHOTOSHOP 4–16, 4–27
Edit Symbols command, FLASH 3–4
editing. *See also* modifying
 alternate text, DREAMWEAVER 3–32
 buttons, FLASH 3–17, 3–19
 CSS layout block properties,
  DREAMWEAVER 5–15—5–16
 Design Notes, DREAMWEAVER
  6–12—6–13
 graphics, FLASH 3–31
 image settings, DREAMWEAVER 3–31
 imported Photoshop images,
  INTEGRATION 1–16—1–17
 instances, FLASH 3–5, 3–7—3–8
 motion paths, FLASH 4–8—4–9
 movie clips, FLASH 4–39
 movies from Dreamweaver, 1–22—1–23
 page properties, DREAMWEAVER 5–17
 Photoshop images, INTEGRATION 1–8,
  1–10
 rasterizing type, PHOTOSHOP 5–24
 rules in CSSs, DREAMWEAVER 3–15, 3–17
 styles in CSS layout blocks,
  DREAMWEAVER 5–15

editors, external, resizing graphics,
DREAMWEAVER 3–28
elements
AP. *See* AP element(s)
media, limiting, DREAMWEAVER 2–2
navigation bars, DREAMWEAVER 4–16,
4–20—4–21
Elliptical Marquee tool, PHOTOSHOP 3–5
Email Link dialog box, DREAMWEAVER
2–22
email links. *See* mailto: links
embedded style(s), DREAMWEAVER 3–10
embedded (internal) style sheets,
DREAMWEAVER 3–18—3–19
embedded video, FLASH 5–12, 5–13
emphasis
contrast to add, PHOTOSHOP 1–36
planning applications or website,
FLASH 1–41
Encoder, FLASH 5–13
enhancing images, DREAMWEAVER
3–28—3–29, 3–30
entering text, DREAMWEAVER 2–10,
FLASH 2–28, 2–12, 2–30
Envelope option, Free Transform tool,
FLASH 2–21
Eraser tool, FLASH 2–5
ethics, PHOTOSHOP 1–22
Exclusion mode, PHOTOSHOP 4–28
exiting Photoshop, PHOTOSHOP 1–38
Expand command, PHOTOSHOP 3–12
Expanded Tables mode, DREAMWEAVER
5–18, 5–19, 5–21
exporting
site definitions, DREAMWEAVER 6–30,
6–31
table data, DREAMWEAVER 5–34
eXtensible HyperText Markup Language
(XHTML), DREAMWEAVER 1–2
Extensible Markup Language (XML),
creating and formatting page content,
DREAMWEAVER 5–6
Extensible Style Language (XSL),
creating and formatting page content,
DREAMWEAVER 5–6
Extensible Stylesheet Language
Transformations (XSLT), creating
and formatting page content,
DREAMWEAVER 5–6

external links, DREAMWEAVER 4–2
creating, DREAMWEAVER 4–4, 4–6—4–7
external style sheets, DREAMWEAVER 3–10,
3–18—3–19
Extract command, PHOTOSHOP 2–12
Eyedropper tool, FLASH 2–5
changing background color,
PHOTOSHOP 4–9

Fade command, PHOTOSHOP 4–27
Fade dialog box, PHOTOSHOP 4–30
fading in text, FLASH 4–47
fair use, DREAMWEAVER 6–35
fastening points, PHOTOSHOP 3–4
favorites, DREAMWEAVER 3–22
Favorites option, Assets panel,
DREAMWEAVER 3–22, 3–25
Favorites panel, Bridge, PHOTOSHOP 1–9
feathering, PHOTOSHOP 3–22
file(s)
associating Design Notes with,
DREAMWEAVER 6–11
browsing through, PHOTOSHOP 1–9
checking in and out, DREAMWEAVER
6–22—6–25
cloaked, DREAMWEAVER 6–2. *See also*
cloaking files
closing, PHOTOSHOP 1–38, 1–39
comparing for differences in content,
DREAMWEAVER 6–17
copying, PHOTOSHOP 1–10
creating from scratch, PHOTOSHOP
1–5
deleting from websites, DREAMWEAVER
3–38
delimited, DREAMWEAVER 5–34
dependent, DREAMWEAVER 6–15
downloading, DREAMWEAVER 6–15
flattening, PHOTOSHOP 1–4,
PHOTOSHOP 2–17, 2–21
inserting using Bridge, DREAMWEAVER
3–23
opening, PHOTOSHOP 1–8, 1–11
orphaned. *See* orphaned files
related, DREAMWEAVER 1–5, 1–14
saving, PHOTOSHOP 1–8, 1–10, 1–12
synchronizing, DREAMWEAVER 6–16,
6–21

transferring to and from remote sites,
DREAMWEAVER 6–15, 6–16, 6–20
uploading to remote sites,
DREAMWEAVER 6–15, 6–20
file formats, PHOTOSHOP 1–5
cameras, PHOTOSHOP 1–5
changing, PHOTOSHOP 1–12
graphics, DREAMWEAVER 3–22
video, importing video, FLASH 5–13
File Info dialog box, PHOTOSHOP 1–9
file management, Files panel, DREAMWEAVER
1–27
File Transfer Protocol (FTP), DREAMWEAVER
1–21, 6–14
setting up web server access to FTP sites,
DREAMWEAVER 6–17
filename(s), HTML pages, DREAMWEAVER
2–14
filename extensions, graphics files,
PHOTOSHOP 1–5
Files panel, DREAMWEAVER 1–2, 1–20
checking files in and out,
DREAMWEAVER 6–25
creating root folder, DREAMWEAVER 1–23
file management, DREAMWEAVER 1–27
selecting drives, DREAMWEAVER 1–22
viewing websites, DREAMWEAVER 1–23
fill(s)
color, FLASH 2–15, 2–17
gradient. *See* gradient(s)
Fill Color tool, FLASH 2–5, 2–6
Filmstrip view, Loupe tool, PHOTOSHOP 1–9
filter(s), PHOTOSHOP 4–26—4–27, 4–30.
See also specific filter names
adding to objects, FLASH 1–27—1–28
fixing blurry scanned images,
PHOTOSHOP 4–26
objects, adding filters, FLASH 1–27—1–28
softening filter effects, PHOTOSHOP 4–27
type. *See* type filters
filter effects, text, FLASH 2–31
Filter panel, Bridge, PHOTOSHOP 1–9
FILTERS area, Properties panel, FLASH 2–31
Find and Replace feature, locating non-web-
safe colors using, DREAMWEAVER 6–7
.fla files, FLASH 1–12, FLASH 1–36
Flash, DREAMWEAVER 1–14
Adobe Flash CS4 Professional features,
FLASH 1–2

importing Photoshop documents into.
    See importing Photoshop documents
    into Flash
inserting movies into Dreamweaver.
    See inserting Flash movies into
    Dreamweaver
Flash CS4 Professional
    features, FLASH 1–2
    workspace. *See* Flash workspace
Flash Player, FLASH 1–14
Flash workspace, FLASH 1–4—1–11
    organizing, FLASH 1–10
    panels, FLASH 1–5—1–6, 1–9—1–10
    Stage, FLASH 1–4—1–5, 1–10—1–11
    Timeline, FLASH 1–5, 1–11
    Tools panel, FLASH 1–6—1–8
flattening files, PHOTOSHOP 1–4, 2–17, 2–21
Flip option, Transform menu, FLASH 2–21
flipping
    drawn objects, FLASH 2–21, 2–24
    selections, PHOTOSHOP 3–20
floating documents, change from tabbed
    documents to, PHOTOSHOP 1–12
flowcharts, FLASH 1–42
FLV files, importing. *See* importing video
focus, maintaining, PHOTOSHOP 4–13
focus groups, DREAMWEAVER 2–7
folder(s)
    adding to websites, DREAMWEAVER
        1–26—1–27, 1–28
    cloaking, DREAMWEAVER 6–26—6–27,
        6–28
    creating in Library panel, FLASH
        3–12—3–13
    local, setting up web server access on
        local or network folders,
        DREAMWEAVER 6–18
    local root, DREAMWEAVER 1–20
    names, DREAMWEAVER 1–20
    network, setting up web server access
        on local or network folders,
        DREAMWEAVER 6–18
    organizing items in Library panel folders,
        FLASH 3–13
    root, DREAMWEAVER 1–20, 1–23
    uncloaking, DREAMWEAVER 6–28
folder hierarchy, DREAMWEAVER 1–20
Folder layers, FLASH 2–34, 2–37
Folders panel, Bridge, PHOTOSHOP 1–9, 1–11

font(s), PHOTOSHOP 5–2
    acquiring, PHOTOSHOP 5–5
    changing, DREAMWEAVER 2–11
    changing sizes, DREAMWEAVER 2–11
    choosing, DREAMWEAVER 3–13
    default, DREAMWEAVER 2–5
    measuring size, PHOTOSHOP 5–5
    sans serif, PHOTOSHOP 5–4, 5–5
    serif, PHOTOSHOP 5–4, 5–5
    symbol, PHOTOSHOP 5–5
    vector, PHOTOSHOP 5–4
font combinations, DREAMWEAVER 2–11
font families, PHOTOSHOP 5–4—5–5
foreground color, PHOTOSHOP 4–6
    default, setting, PHOTOSHOP 4–7
formatting
    cell content, DREAMWEAVER 5–32,
        5–35
    cells, DREAMWEAVER 5–32, 5–33, 5–36
    content in CSS layout blocks,
        DREAMWEAVER 5–13—5–14
    text. *See* formatting text
formatting text, DREAMWEAVER
    2–10—2–11, 2–13
    fonts. *See* font(s)
    HTML tags vs. CSS, DREAMWEAVER
        2–11
    lists. *See* list(s)
    ordered lists, DREAMWEAVER 3–9
    paragraphs, DREAMWEAVER 2–11
    Property inspector, DREAMWEAVER 2–11
    unordered lists, DREAMWEAVER 3–7
frame(s), FLASH 1–5
    actions, FLASH 3–24
    stop action, FLASH 3–26
    Timeline, FLASH 1–30—1–31
frame animations. *See* frame-by-frame
    animations
frame labels, FLASH 3–25
    animated navigation bars, FLASH 5–19,
        5–23
frame rate
    animations, FLASH 4–2
    default, FLASH 4–2
    modifying, FLASH 1–35
frame-by-frame animations, FLASH 4–2,
    4–24—4–29
    copying frames, FLASH 4–27
    in-place, creating, FLASH 4–26

keyframes, FLASH 4–24—4–25
    moving background, FLASH 4–27
    moving objects, FLASH 4–28—4–29
    Onion Skin feature, FLASH 4–2, 4–25
Free Transform tool, FLASH 2–4, 2–5,
    2–20—2–21
FTP (File Transfer Protocol), DREAMWEAVER
    1–21, 6–14
FTP sites, setting up web server access,
    DREAMWEAVER 6–17
Full Screen Mode, PHOTOSHOP 1–20
Full Screen Mode with Application Bar,
    PHOTOSHOP 1–20
functionality, planning applications or
    website, FLASH 1–41—1–42
fuzziness setting, Color Range command,
    PHOTOSHOP 3–17

gamuts, color models, PHOTOSHOP 4–4,
    4–5
Gaussian Blur filter, PHOTOSHOP 5–25
GIF (Graphics Interchange Format), 1–4,
    DREAMWEAVER 3–22, 1–5
Gloss Contour setting, Bevel and Emboss
    style, PHOTOSHOP 5–21
go to frame action, buttons, FLASH 3–28
goals, planning applications or website,
    FLASH 1–40
gradient(s), PHOTOSHOP 2–15, 4–6,
    4–18—4–21
    applying, PHOTOSHOP 4–21, 4–23
    creating, FLASH 2–18
    creating from sample color, PHOTOSHOP
        4–20
    customizing, PHOTOSHOP 4–19
    modifying, FLASH 2–18
    presets, PHOTOSHOP 4–19
    text, FLASH 2–33
Gradient Editor dialog box, PHOTOSHOP
    4–19
Gradient Map dialog box, PHOTOSHOP
    4–23
Gradient picker, PHOTOSHOP 4–18, 4–20
Gradient tool, PHOTOSHOP 4–19
Gradient Transform tool, FLASH 2–4, 2–5
graphic file formats, DREAMWEAVER 3–22
graphic symbols, FLASH 3–2
    creating, FLASH 3–4, 3–5

graphics. *See also* image(s)
  bitmap, FLASH 3–30, 3–31
  definition, DREAMWEAVER 3–27
  editing, FLASH 3–31
  importing. *See* importing graphics
  inserting, DREAMWEAVER 3–23, 3–24
  resizing using external editor,
    DREAMWEAVER 3–28
  types, FLASH 3–30, 3–31
  vector, FLASH 3–30, 3–31
Graphics Interchange Format (GIF),
  INTEGRATION 1–4, DREAMWEAVER
  3–22, 1–5
grayscale images, PHOTOSHOP 4–22
  adding color, PHOTOSHOP 4–22—4–25
  duotones, PHOTOSHOP 4–23
grayscale mode, PHOTOSHOP 4–6
grid(s), positioning page content,
  DREAMWEAVER 5–30
gridlines, showing, FLASH 2–8
grouped tools, FLASH 2–6
Grow command, PHOTOSHOP 3–12
guide(s), PHOTOSHOP 3–6
  positioning page content,
    DREAMWEAVER 5–30
  Smart Guides, PHOTOSHOP 3–8
Guide layers, FLASH 2–34, 2–36
  adding objects, FLASH 2–42
  creating guides, FLASH 2–41

Hand tool, FLASH 2–5, 2–6
handles, PHOTOSHOP 3–17
Hard Light mode, PHOTOSHOP 4–28
head content, DREAMWEAVER 2–4—2–5
  description, DREAMWEAVER 2–5, 2–8
  keywords, DREAMWEAVER 2–4, 2–7
  page titles, DREAMWEAVER 2–4, 2–6
Healing Brush tool, PHOTOSHOP 3–17
  options, PHOTOSHOP 3–21
Help feature, DREAMWEAVER 1–13, FLASH
  1–44, 1–16—1–17, 1–45
Help system, PHOTOSHOP 1–28—1–31
  features, PHOTOSHOP 1–28
  finding information, PHOTOSHOP 1–29,
    1–31
  How-To's, PHOTOSHOP 1–30
  topics, PHOTOSHOP 1–28
hex triplets, DREAMWEAVER 2–9

hexadecimal RGB values, DREAMWEAVER 2–9
hexadecimal values, Info panel,
  PHOTOSHOP 4–9
hiding
  layers, FLASH 2–35, PHOTOSHOP 1–25,
    1–26, 2–40
  panels, PHOTOSHOP 1–22
  rulers, PHOTOSHOP 2–6
  toolbars, DREAMWEAVER 1–11
highlight(s), correcting, PHOTOSHOP 4–29
Highlight Mode Contour setting, Bevel and
  Emboss style, PHOTOSHOP 5–21
History panel, DREAMWEAVER 2–24,
  PHOTOSHOP 1–5, 1–25, 2–25, 2–26
  correcting selection errors,
    PHOTOSHOP 3–5
  deleting states, PHOTOSHOP 1–25, 1–27
  undoing anti-aliasing, PHOTOSHOP 5–19
hit area, buttons, FLASH 3–20
Hit state, FLASH 3–16
home pages, DREAMWEAVER 1–12
  creating, DREAMWEAVER 1–27
horizontal rules, DREAMWEAVER 2–20
horizontal space, images, DREAMWEAVER
  3–29, 3–30
hotspots, DREAMWEAVER 4–24
HSB model, PHOTOSHOP 4–5
HTML (Hypertext Markup Language),
  DREAMWEAVER 1–2
HTML body tags, DREAMWEAVER 3–37
HTML code
  inserting comments, DREAMWEAVER
    2–28
  viewing in Code Inspector,
    DREAMWEAVER 2–25
HTML files, FLASH 1–36
HTML pages, filenames, DREAMWEAVER 2–14
HTML table tags, DREAMWEAVER 5–25
HTML tags, CSSs compared, DREAMWEAVER
  2–11
hue, PHOTOSHOP 4–5
Hue mode, PHOTOSHOP 4–28
Hue/Saturation dialog box, PHOTOSHOP
  4–23, 4–25
hyperlink(s), DREAMWEAVER 1–12. *See also*
  link(s)
Hypertext Markup Language (HTML),
  DREAMWEAVER 1–2. *See also* HTML
  entries

ID type styles, DREAMWEAVER 3–10
IK. *See* Inverse Kinematics (IK)
IK objects, FLASH 5–28. *See also* Inverse
  Kinematics (IK)
image(s), DREAMWEAVER 1–12,
  PHOTOSHOP 1–4, 3–2. *See also* graphics
  adding to CSS containers,
    DREAMWEAVER 5–11
  aligning in table cells, DREAMWEAVER
    5–29, 5–31
  background. *See* background images
  borders, DREAMWEAVER 3–29, 3–30
  composition, PHOTOSHOP 1–19
  contiguous, selecting, PHOTOSHOP 1–9
  creating navigation bars using,
    DREAMWEAVER 4–16, 4–17,
    4–18—4–19
  definition, DREAMWEAVER 3–27
  digital, PHOTOSHOP 1–2
  editing settings, DREAMWEAVER 3–31
  enhancing, DREAMWEAVER 3–28—3–29,
    3–30
  horizontal space, DREAMWEAVER 3–29,
    3–30
  inserting in table cells, DREAMWEAVER
    5–28, 5–29, 5–30
  managing, DREAMWEAVER 3–34—3–35,
    DREAMWEAVER 3–38
  orientation, PHOTOSHOP 1–32
  pixels, PHOTOSHOP 1–4
  printing. *See* printing images
  resizing, PHOTOSHOP 1–23
  resolution, PHOTOSHOP 1–29
  sources, PHOTOSHOP 1–2
  tiled, DREAMWEAVER 3–34
  tracing, DREAMWEAVER 5–5
  vertical space, DREAMWEAVER 3–29, 3–30
image files, saving in assets folder,
  DREAMWEAVER 1–31, 2–14
image layers, PHOTOSHOP 2–4
  converting to Background layers,
    PHOTOSHOP 2–6, 2–7
image maps, DREAMWEAVER 1–12,
  4–24—4–27
  creating, DREAMWEAVER 4–24—4–27
  hotspots, DREAMWEAVER 4–24
Image Preview dialog box, 1–4—1–5,
  DREAMWEAVER 3–31
Image Size dialog box, PHOTOSHOP 1–23

image-editing programs, PHOTOSHOP 1–4
imperfections
　　correcting, PHOTOSHOP 3–17, 3–21
　　removing, PHOTOSHOP 3–22
Import dialog box, INTEGRATION
　　1–12—1–13, 1–15
Import Site dialog box, DREAMWEAVER 6–32
Import Video Wizard, FLASH 5–13, 5–14—5–15
importing
　　graphics. See importing graphics
　　Microsoft Office documents,
　　　　DREAMWEAVER 2–15
　　Photoshop documents into Flash. See
　　　　importing Photoshop documents into
　　　　Flash
　　site definitions, DREAMWEAVER 6–30,
　　　　6–32—6–33
　　sound files, file formats, FLASH 5–9
　　table data, DREAMWEAVER 5–34
　　text, DREAMWEAVER 2–15
　　video. See importing video
importing graphics, FLASH 3–30—3–33
　　graphic types, FLASH 3–30, 3–31
importing Photoshop documents into Flash,
　　INTEGRATION 1–12—1–17
　　creating animations using Photoshop-
　　　　created text, INTEGRATION 1–17
　　editing imported images, INTEGRATION
　　　　1–16—1–17
importing video
　　converting file formats, FLASH 5–13
　　embedded video, FLASH 5–12, 5–13
　　Import Video Wizard, FLASH 5–13,
　　　　5–14—5–15
　　progressive downloading, FLASH 5–12
　　streaming video, FLASH 5–12
Info panel, hexadecimal values, PHOTOSHOP
　　4–9
information overload, overcoming,
　　PHOTOSHOP 1–16
Ink Bottle tool, FLASH 2–5
inline styles, DREAMWEAVER 3–10
Insert Navigation Bar dialog box,
　　DREAMWEAVER 4–18—4–19, 4–21
Insert panel, DREAMWEAVER 1–4
inserting Flash movies into Dreamweaver,
　　INTEGRATION 1–18—1–23
　　changing settings from Dreamweaver,
　　　　INTEGRATION 1–21

editing movies from Dreamweaver,
　　INTEGRATION 1–22—1–23
　　playing movies from Dreamweaver,
　　　　INTEGRATION 1–21
　　Properties panel, INTEGRATION
　　　　1–18—1–19
inserting Photoshop images into
　　Dreamweaver documents, 1–4—1–11
　　copying and pasting Photoshop images,
　　　　INTEGRATION 1–4, 1–11
　　Design Notes, INTEGRATION 1–6
　　designating primary external image
　　　　editor, INTEGRATION 1–7
　　editing Photoshop documents,
　　　　INTEGRATION 1–8, 1–10
　　setting up folder structure,
　　　　INTEGRATION 1–6
instances, FLASH 3–2, 3–4—3–5
　　breaking link between symbol and,
　　　　FLASH 3–5, 3–8
　　creating, FLASH 3–5, 3–7
　　editing, FLASH 3–5, 3–7—3–8
integrating Adobe CS4 Web Premium,
　　INTEGRATION 1–1—1–25. See also
　　importing Photoshop documents into Flash;
　　inserting Flash movies into Dreamweaver;
　　inserting Photoshop images into
　　Dreamweaver documents
intellectual property, DREAMWEAVER 6–34,
　　PHOTOSHOP 1–22. See also copyright
interactive design guidelines, FLASH 1–43
internal links, DREAMWEAVER 4–2
　　creating, DREAMWEAVER 4–5, 4–8
　　named anchors. See internal links to
　　　　named anchors
internal links to named anchors,
　　DREAMWEAVER 4–10—4–15
　　creating, DREAMWEAVER 4–11,
　　　　4–14—4–15
　　inserting named anchors, DREAMWEAVER
　　　　4–10, 4–11, 4–12—4–13
internal styles. See embedded style(s)
Internet Service Providers (ISPs),
　　DREAMWEAVER 1–21
inter-screen unity, FLASH 1–43
intra-screen unity, FLASH 1–43
Inverse Kinematics (IK), FLASH 5–2, 5–26—5–33
　　animating IK objects, FLASH 5–27, 5–30
　　bone structure, FLASH 5–26—5–27, 5–29

　　creating movie clips with IK objects,
　　　　FLASH 5–28, 5–31
　　ease value, FLASH 5–32
　　pose layers, FLASH 5–27
　　runtime feature, FLASH 5–28, 5–33
invisible buttons, animated navigation bars,
　　FLASH 5–19, 5–24—5–25
IP addresses, DREAMWEAVER 1–24
ISPs (Internet Service Providers),
　　DREAMWEAVER 1–21
Item Preview window, Library panel, FLASH 3–11

JavaScript (JScript), DREAMWEAVER 2–25
JPEG (Joint Photographic Experts Group) file
　　format, INTEGRATION 1–4, 1–5,
　　DREAMWEAVER 3–22
JScript. See JavaScript (JScript)

kerning, PHOTOSHOP 5–8, 5–10
keyboard shortcuts, DREAMWEAVER 2–10
　　customized, PHOTOSHOP 1–18
　　hidden, finding, PHOTOSHOP 1–31
　　learning shortcut keys, PHOTOSHOP
　　　　1–19
　　navigating Layers panel, PHOTOSHOP 2–9
　　spring-loaded, PHOTOSHOP 1–18
keyframes
　　classic tween animations, FLASH 4–20
　　frame-by-frame animations, FLASH
　　　　4–24—4–25
　　motion tween animations, FLASH 4–6
keywords, DREAMWEAVER 2–4, 2–7
　　entering, DREAMWEAVER 2–7
Keywords dialog box, DREAMWEAVER 2–7
Keywords panel, Bridge, PHOTOSHOP 1–9
kuler
　　coordinating colors, PHOTOSHOP 4–10
　　downloading theme, PHOTOSHOP 4–11
　　from Photoshop, PHOTOSHOP 4–15
　　from web browser, PHOTOSHOP 4–14
Kuler panel, PHOTOSHOP 4–25

Lab model, PHOTOSHOP 4–4, 4–5
landscape orientation, PHOTOSHOP 1–32
Lasso tool, FLASH 2–4, PHOTOSHOP 3–5, 2–5
　　selecting objects, FLASH 2–14

layer(s), FLASH 1–5, PHOTOSHOP 1–24,
PHOTOSHOP 2–1—2–24, 2–34—2–43
active. *See* active layers
adding images from another image,
PHOTOSHOP 2–14
adding text on top of an object, FLASH
2–43
adding to images, PHOTOSHOP
2–8—2–9, 2–10, 2–11
adding to Timeline, FLASH 1–33
adjustment. *See* adjustment layers
color, PHOTOSHOP 2–17
converting, PHOTOSHOP 2–6, 2–7
creating, FLASH 2–38
creating images with multiple layers,
1–14
defringing layer contents, PHOTOSHOP
2–13, 2–15
deleting, FLASH 2–39, PHOTOSHOP 2–9,
2–11
displaying, FLASH 2–35, PHOTOSHOP
1–25, 1–26, 2–40
distributing text to, FLASH 2–37
duplicating, PHOTOSHOP 2–16
Folder, FLASH 2–37
Guide. *See* Guide layers
hiding, FLASH 2–35, PHOTOSHOP 1–25,
1–26, 2–40
hiding panels, PHOTOSHOP 1–25,
1–26
importance, PHOTOSHOP 2–2
locking, FLASH 2–35, 2–40
merging, PHOTOSHOP 2–8
modifying images, PHOTOSHOP 2–2
moving on Layers panel, PHOTOSHOP
1–27
moving to layer groups, PHOTOSHOP
2–19
naming, FLASH 2–35, PHOTOSHOP 2–9,
PHOTOSHOP 2–20, 2–39
number, PHOTOSHOP 2–2
opacity, PHOTOSHOP 2–2, PHOTOSHOP
2–20
organizing, PHOTOSHOP 2–5
rasterized, PHOTOSHOP 2–8
renaming, PHOTOSHOP 2–20
reordering, FLASH 2–38
selections, PHOTOSHOP 2–2
specifying type, FLASH 2–35

styles. *See* drop shadows; layer style(s)
Timeline, FLASH 1–30, 1–31, 1–34
type (text). *See* type layers
types, FLASH 2–34, PHOTOSHOP
2–4—2–5
using imagery from one layer as fill
pattern for another image's type layer,
PHOTOSHOP 5–20
layer comps, PHOTOSHOP 2–18, 2–20
Layer Comps panel, PHOTOSHOP 2–20
layer groups, PHOTOSHOP 2–16—2–17,
2–19
creating, PHOTOSHOP 2–19
organizing layers into, PHOTOSHOP
2–16—2–17, 2–19
Layer menu
adding Bevel and Emboss style,
PHOTOSHOP 5–22
adding layers, PHOTOSHOP 2–10
New command, PHOTOSHOP 2–9
Layer Properties dialog box, FLASH 2–35
layer style(s), PHOTOSHOP 5–5—5–6.
See also drop shadows
applying, PHOTOSHOP 5–5—5–6
Layer Style dialog box, PHOTOSHOP 5–15,
5–22
layer thumbnails, PHOTOSHOP 2–4, 2–5
Layers panel, PHOTOSHOP 1–25, 2–4, 2–5
adding layers, PHOTOSHOP 2–11
displaying layers, PHOTOSHOP 1–25,
1–26
moving layers, PHOTOSHOP 1–27
navigating, PHOTOSHOP 2–9
layout(s)
Dual Screen layout, DREAMWEAVER 1–9
smart design principles, DREAMWEAVER
2–32
web pages, DREAMWEAVER 2–2
workspace, DREAMWEAVER 1–8, 1–9
leading, PHOTOSHOP 5–9
Library panel, FLASH 3–10—3–15
creating folders, FLASH 3–12—3–13
elements, FLASH 3–10—3–11
grouping and ungrouping, FLASH
1–7—1–8, 1–10
multiple, FLASH 3–15
organizing items in folders, FLASH 3–13
symbols, FLASH 3–4, 3–5, 3–6, 3–14
licenses, obtaining, DREAMWEAVER 6–36

licensing agreements, DREAMWEAVER
6–35—6–36
Lighten mode, PHOTOSHOP 4–28
Line tool, FLASH 2–5, 2–9
link(s), DREAMWEAVER 2–18—2–23,
4–1—4–34
broken. *See* broken links
case-sensitive, DREAMWEAVER 4–8
email. *See* mailto: links
external. *See* external links
internal. *See* internal links; internal links
to named anchors
mailto:. *See* mailto: links
navigation bars, DREAMWEAVER 2–19,
2–20
unvisited, DREAMWEAVER 2–5
viewing in Assets panel, DREAMWEAVER
4–9
visited, DREAMWEAVER 2–5
to web pages, DREAMWEAVER 2–21
websites. *See* website links
Link Checker panel, DREAMWEAVER 6–4
link colors, default, DREAMWEAVER 2–5
linking, Microsoft Office documents,
DREAMWEAVER 2–15
list(s), DREAMWEAVER 3–2
bulleted, DREAMWEAVER 3–4
definition, DREAMWEAVER 3–5
numbered, DREAMWEAVER 3–4—3–5
ordered, DREAMWEAVER 3–4—3–5,
3–8—3–9
unordered, DREAMWEAVER 3–4,
3–6—3–7
list box, Library panel, FLASH 3–10
List Properties dialog box, DREAMWEAVER
3–7
loading selections, PHOTOSHOP 3–9
local folders, setting up web server access on
local or network folders, DREAMWEAVER
6–18
local root folder, DREAMWEAVER 1–20
local sites, DREAMWEAVER 1–25
location, selecting, DREAMWEAVER 1–22
locking
layers, FLASH 2–35, 2–40
transparent pixels, PHOTOSHOP 4–16,
4–17
logos, PHOTOSHOP 1–4
Loop Playback command, FLASH 1–13

Loupe tool, PHOTOSHOP 1–9
luminosity, PHOTOSHOP 4–22
Luminosity mode, PHOTOSHOP 4–28

Macintosh platform, PHOTOSHOP 1–2
   adding folders to websites,
      DREAMWEAVER 1–28
   adding pages to websites,
      DREAMWEAVER 1–33
   opening files, PHOTOSHOP 1–8
   right-clicking, PHOTOSHOP 2–11
   starting Dreamweaver, DREAMWEAVER
      1–9
   starting Photoshop, PHOTOSHOP 1–7
Magic Wand tool
   options, PHOTOSHOP 3–17
   selecting by color, PHOTOSHOP 3–16,
      3–19
   settings, PHOTOSHOP 3–19
Magnetic Lasso tool, PHOTOSHOP 3–5,
   3–10, 3–11
mailto: links, DREAMWEAVER 2–18,
   2–22—2–23
   viewing in Assets panel, DREAMWEAVER
      2–23
markup, validating, DREAMWEAVER 6–5
marquee(s), PHOTOSHOP 2–12, 2–14, 3–2,
   3–12—3–15
   changing size, PHOTOSHOP 3–12, 3–13,
      3–14
   modifying, PHOTOSHOP 3–12, 3–13
   moving, PHOTOSHOP 3–13, 3–14
mask(s), PHOTOSHOP 3–22
mask effects, FLASH 5–2, 5–4—5–7
   mask layers, FLASH 5–4—5–6
   masked layers, FLASH 5–4, 5–5, 5–7
mask layers, FLASH 2–34, 5–4—5–6
   animated navigation bars, FLASH
      5–18—5–19, 5–21
   creating, FLASH 5–6
masked layers, FLASH 2–34, 5–4, 5–5
   creating, FLASH 5–7
Match Color dialog box, PHOTOSHOP 4–33
matching colors, PHOTOSHOP
   4–32—4–33
matte, PHOTOSHOP 1–36
Maximized Screen Mode, PHOTOSHOP 1–20
measurement units, PHOTOSHOP 2–6

media elements, limiting, DREAMWEAVER
   2–2
menus. See also specific menu names
   drop-down, creating, FLASH 5–18—5–19
   selecting commands, PHOTOSHOP 1–16
Merge Drawing Model mode, FLASH 2–2,
   2–14
merging
   cells, DREAMWEAVER 5–23, 5–27
   layers, PHOTOSHOP 2–8
meta tags, DREAMWEAVER 2–4
metadata, DREAMWEAVER 6–11
Metadata panel, Bridge, PHOTOSHOP 1–9
Microsoft Office, importing and linking
   documents, DREAMWEAVER 2–15
mobile devices, testing web pages,
   DREAMWEAVER 2–31
Modify Navigation Bar dialog box,
   DREAMWEAVER 4–17
modifying. See also editing
   navigation bars, DREAMWEAVER 4–17,
      4–22—4–23
   web pages, DREAMWEAVER 1–21
   websites, DREAMWEAVER 2–32
monitors
   Dual Screen layout, DREAMWEAVER 1–9
   resolution, PHOTOSHOP 1–29
monotype spacing, PHOTOSHOP 5–8
morphing, shape tween animations, FLASH
   4–30—4–31, 4–33
motion guide(s), FLASH 4–20—4–21,
   4–22—4–23
   orienting objects to, FLASH 4–23
Motion Guide layers, FLASH 2–34
motion paths, FLASH 1–20—1–21,
   4–5—4–6, 4–8—4–9
   copying, FLASH 4–14—4–15
   editing, FLASH 4–8—4–9
   orienting objects to, FLASH 4–13
   reshaping, FLASH 1–21, 1–24—1–25
motion presets, adding, FLASH 1–28—1–29
Motion Presets panel, FLASH 1–21, 1–28
motion tween animations, FLASH 4–2,
   4–4—4–19
   classic tween animations compared,
      FLASH 4–20
   color effects, FLASH 4–12
   creating, FLASH 1–23—1–24, 4–7
   ease value, FLASH 4–10

motion path. See motion paths
   multiple, FLASH 4–18—4–19
   orienting objects to paths, FLASH 4–13
   preset, FLASH 1–28—1–29, 1–21
   property keyframes, FLASH 4–6
   removing, FLASH 4–17
   resizing and reshaping objects,
      FLASH 4–11
   rotating objects, FLASH 4–16
   3D effects, FLASH 5–35
   tween spans, FLASH 4–5
motion tweening, FLASH 1–20—1–21, 4–4
mouse, right-clicking, PHOTOSHOP 2–11
mouse events, button actions responding to,
   FLASH 3–24
Move tool
   changing selections into, PHOTOSHOP
      3–6
   positioning selections, PHOTOSHOP 3–8
moveable guides, PHOTOSHOP 2–5
movement
   moving backgrounds, FLASH 4–27
   screen design, FLASH 1–43
movie(s)
   adding sound, FLASH 5–8—5–9, 5–10
   changing document properties,
      FLASH 1–17
   creating, FLASH 1–18—1–19
   distributing. See distributing movies
   inserting into Dreamweaver. See inserting
      Flash movies into Dreamweaver
   opening, FLASH 1–12, 1–15
   playing, FLASH 1–15
   previewing, FLASH 1–12
   publishing, FLASH 1–36, 1–38
   saving, FLASH 1–14
   testing, FLASH 1–13, 1–16
movie clip(s), FLASH 4–36—4–41
   animating, FLASH 4–40—4–41
   breaking apart graphic symbols,
      FLASH 4–38
   creating, FLASH 4–39
   creating with IK objects, FLASH 5–28,
      5–31
   editing, FLASH 4–39
   IK, FLASH 5–31
   movie clip symbols, FLASH 4–36—4–37
   separating parts of object from graphic,
      FLASH 4–38

INDEX

movie clip symbols, FLASH 3–2, 4–36—4–37
movies
    changing settings from Dreamweaver,
        1–21
    editing from Dreamweaver, 1–22—1–23
    playing from Dreamweaver, 1–21
moving. *See also* positioning
    drawn objects, FLASH 2–20, 2–22
    layers on Layers panel, PHOTOSHOP
        1–27
    layers to layer groups, PHOTOSHOP 2–19
    marquees, PHOTOSHOP 3–13, 3–14
    objects, frame-by-frame animations,
        FLASH 4–28—4–29
    selections, PHOTOSHOP 2–13, 2–15,
        3–6, 3–7, 3–8, 3–11
    Stage, FLASH 1–6, 1–8
moving background, frame-by-frame
    animations, FLASH 4–27
multiple filters, PHOTOSHOP 5–26
multiple images, contiguous, selecting,
    PHOTOSHOP 1–9
multiple Library panels, FLASH 3–15
multiple motion tween animations,
    FLASH 4–18—4–19
Multiply mode, PHOTOSHOP 4–28

name(s), folders, DREAMWEAVER 1–20
Name text box, Library panel, FLASH 3–11
named anchor(s), internal links to. *See*
    internal links to named anchors
Named Anchor dialog box, DREAMWEAVER
    4–12
naming. *See also* renaming
    layers, FLASH 2–35, PHOTOSHOP 2–9,
        2–20, 2–39
navigating Layers panel, PHOTOSHOP 2–9
navigation bars, DREAMWEAVER 1–12,
    2–19, 2–20, 4–16—4–23
    adding elements, DREAMWEAVER
        4–20—4–21
    animated. *See* animated navigation bars
    copying and pasting, DREAMWEAVER
        4–17, 4–22
    creating using images, DREAMWEAVER
        4–16, 4–17, 4–18—4–19
    elements, DREAMWEAVER 4–16,
        4–20—4–21

    modifying, DREAMWEAVER 4–17,
        4–22—4–23
navigation structure, DREAMWEAVER 1–13
    creating, DREAMWEAVER 1–26
    design issues, DREAMWEAVER 4–28
    intuitive, DREAMWEAVER 2–2
Navigator panel, PHOTOSHOP 1–34
Neon Glow filter, PHOTOSHOP 5–27
nested tables, DREAMWEAVER 5–18, 5–23
network folders, setting up web server
    access on local or network folders,
    DREAMWEAVER 6–18
New command Layer menu, PHOTOSHOP 2–9
New CSS Rule dialog box, DREAMWEAVER
    3–12
New dialog box, PHOTOSHOP 1–5
New Document dialog box, DREAMWEAVER
    5–5
New Folder icon, Library panel, FLASH 3–11
New Layer Comp dialog box, PHOTOSHOP
    2–18, 2–20
New Layer dialog box, PHOTOSHOP 2–10
New Symbol command, FLASH 3–4
New Symbol icon, Library panel, FLASH 3–11
New Window command, PHOTOSHOP 1–33
None anti-aliasing method, PHOTOSHOP 5–17
non-web-safe colors, DREAMWEAVER 3–35,
    3–39
    locating using Find and Replace,
        DREAMWEAVER 6–7
Normal layers, FLASH 2–34
numbered lists, DREAMWEAVER 3–4—3–5

object(s)
    adding effects, FLASH 1–21
    adding text on top of, FLASH 2–43
    adding to Guide layers, FLASH 2–42
    drawn. *See* drawn objects
    moving, frame-by-frame animations,
        FLASH 4–28—4–29
    positioning on Stage, FLASH 2–6—2–7
    resizing, FLASH 1–26—1–27
    transparency, FLASH 1–25—1–26
Object Drawing Model, FLASH 2–2
Object Drawing Model mode, FLASH
    2–14—2–15, 2–19
Onion Skin feature, frame-by-frame
    animations, FLASH 4–2, 4–25

opacity
    adjusting, PHOTOSHOP 4–30
    layers, PHOTOSHOP 2–2, 2–20
    PNG files, DREAMWEAVER 3–22
Open As command, PHOTOSHOP 1–8
Open As Smart Object command,
    PHOTOSHOP 1–8
Open dialog box, PHOTOSHOP 1–11
opening
    files, PHOTOSHOP 1–8, 1–11
    movies, FLASH 1–12, 1–15
optical center, PHOTOSHOP 1–22
options, Flash drawing tools, FLASH 2–5,
    2–6, 2–11—2–12
options bar, Photoshop window,
    PHOTOSHOP 1–17
Options menu, Library panel, FLASH 3–10,
    3–11
Options section, Tools panel, FLASH 1–6
ordered lists
    creating, DREAMWEAVER 3–4—3–5,
        3–8
    formatting, DREAMWEAVER 3–9
orientation, images, PHOTOSHOP 1–32
orienting
    objects to guides in classic tween
        animations, FLASH 4–23
    objects to paths in motion tween
        animations, FLASH 4–13
orphaned files, DREAMWEAVER 4–28
    checking for, DREAMWEAVER 6–6
Outline type, PHOTOSHOP 5–4
Output panel, Bridge, PHOTOSHOP 1–10
Oval tool, FLASH 2–5, 2–9
Over image state, DREAMWEAVER
    4–16
Over state, FLASH 3–16
Over while down image state,
    DREAMWEAVER 4–16
Overlay mode, PHOTOSHOP 4–28

page content
    collecting, DREAMWEAVER 1–20—1–21
    editing in CSS layout blocks,
        DREAMWEAVER 5–12—5–17
    positioning, DREAMWEAVER 5–30
    XML and XSL to create and format,
        DREAMWEAVER 5–6

page layout, DREAMWEAVER 2–2
 checking, DREAMWEAVER 5–37
 table and cell width settings for,
  DREAMWEAVER 5–20
 tracing images, DREAMWEAVER 5–5
Page Properties dialog box,
 DREAMWEAVER 2–9
Page Setup dialog box, modifying print
 settings, PHOTOSHOP 1–35
page titles, DREAMWEAVER 1–32, 2–4, 2–6
Paint Bucket tool, FLASH 2–5
palette(s). See panel(s); specific panel names
panel(s), DREAMWEAVER 1–6, FLASH
 1–5—1–6, 1–9—1–10, 1–10—1–11. See
 also specific panel names
 arranging, FLASH 1–6—1–7
 changing, DREAMWEAVER 1–10—1–11
 collapsing, FLASH 1–6, 1–8
 hiding, PHOTOSHOP 1–22
 Photoshop window, PHOTOSHOP
  1–17—1–18
 showing, PHOTOSHOP 1–22
panel groups, DREAMWEAVER 1–6
paragraphs, FLASH 2–29
 formatting, DREAMWEAVER 2–11
parent page, DREAMWEAVER 1–20
Paste command, FLASH 2–20
Pasteboard, FLASH 1–5
pasting. See copying and pasting
paths
 absolute, DREAMWEAVER 4–4, 4–5
 document-relative, DREAMWEAVER
  4–5
 relative, DREAMWEAVER 4–5
 root-relative, DREAMWEAVER 4–5
 type on, PHOTOSHOP 5–28—5–29
PDF(s), creating with Bridge, PHOTOSHOP
 1–36
PDF Presentations, creating, PHOTOSHOP
 1–10
Pen tool, FLASH 2–4—2–5, 2–10
Pencil tool, FLASH 2–10
permissions process, DREAMWEAVER 6–36
photo(s), getting from camera, PHOTOSHOP
 1–13
Photoshop
 choosing versions, PHOTOSHOP 1–33
 exiting, PHOTOSHOP 1–38
 features, PHOTOSHOP 1–4—1–5

importing documents into Flash. See
 importing Photoshop documents into
 Flash
inserting images into Dreamweaver
 documents. See inserting Photoshop
 images into Dreamweaver documents
integrating with Dreamweaver,
 DREAMWEAVER 3–31
 starting, PHOTOSHOP 1–5, 1–6—1–7
Photoshop PSD files, copying into
 Dreamweaver, DREAMWEAVER 3–28
Photoshop window, PHOTOSHOP
 1–16—1–23
 customizing, PHOTOSHOP 1–18
 options bar, PHOTOSHOP 1–17
 panels, PHOTOSHOP 1–17—1–18
 rulers, PHOTOSHOP 1–18
 shortcut keys, PHOTOSHOP 1–18
 status bar, PHOTOSHOP 1–18
 Tools panel, PHOTOSHOP 1–17—1–18
 workspace, PHOTOSHOP 1–16—1–17
Photoshop workspace
 customizing, PHOTOSHOP 1–23
 Photoshop, PHOTOSHOP 1–16—1–17
 Version Cue, PHOTOSHOP 1–14
PICS (Platform for Internet Content Selection)
 ratings, DREAMWEAVER 2–4
pixels, FLASH 2–2, PHOTOSHOP 1–4, 4–2
 transparent, locking, PHOTOSHOP 4–16,
  4–17
Place command, PHOTOSHOP 2–14
planning, FLASH 1–40—1–45
 steps, FLASH 1–40—1–42
 websites. See planning websites
planning websites, DREAMWEAVER
 1–18—1–19
 basic structure, DREAMWEAVER
  1–19—1–20
 checklist, DREAMWEAVER 1–19
platform(s), PHOTOSHOP 1–2. See also
 Macintosh platform; Windows platform
Platform for Internet Content Selection (PICS)
 ratings, DREAMWEAVER 2–4
play action, buttons, FLASH 3–27
Play command, FLASH 1–12
playback system, planning applications or
 website, FLASH 1–41
playhead, FLASH 1–31
playing movies, FLASH 1–15

plus sign (+), Help topics, PHOTOSHOP 1–28
PNG (Portable Network Graphics) file format,
 1–4, DREAMWEAVER 3–22, 1–5
point(s), PHOTOSHOP 5–5
point of contact, DREAMWEAVER 2–18
Point to File icon, DREAMWEAVER 4–11
Polygon Hotspot Tool, DREAMWEAVER 4–25
Polygonal Lasso tool, PHOTOSHOP 3–5
PolyStar tool, FLASH 2–5
Portable Network Graphics (PNG) file format,
 1–4, DREAMWEAVER 3–22, 1–5
portrait orientation, PHOTOSHOP 1–32
pose layers, FLASH 5–27
positioning. See also moving
 drop-down buttons on animated
  navigation bars, FLASH 5–20
 objects on Stage, FLASH 2–6—2–7
 page content, DREAMWEAVER 5–30
posting copyright notices, DREAMWEAVER
 6–36—6–37
PostScript, PHOTOSHOP 5–5
preferences, PHOTOSHOP 1–8
 setting, PHOTOSHOP 1–24
Preferences dialog box, PHOTOSHOP 1–8,
 1–24
 Accessibility category, DREAMWEAVER
  3–33
preventing data loss, DREAMWEAVER 2–12
Preview panel, Bridge, PHOTOSHOP 1–9
previewing
 buttons, FLASH 3–17
 movies, FLASH 1–12
Primitive Oval tool, FLASH 2–5, 2–27
 drawn objects, FLASH 2–26—2–27
Primitive Rectangle tool, FLASH 2–5,
 2–26—2–27
 drawn objects, FLASH 2–26—2–27
Print dialog box, color handling,
 PHOTOSHOP 1–33
printing images, PHOTOSHOP 1–32—1–33
 color handling, PHOTOSHOP 1–33
 contrast, PHOTOSHOP 1–36
 modifying print settings, PHOTOSHOP
  1–35
 orientation, PHOTOSHOP 1–32
 PDFs, PHOTOSHOP 1–36
 Proof Setup, PHOTOSHOP 1–35
progressive downloading, FLASH 5–12
project management, FLASH 1–43

projector files, creating, FLASH 1–39
Proof Setups, PHOTOSHOP 1–35
properties
   CSS layout blocks, editing,
      DREAMWEAVER 5–15—5–16
   tables, setting, DREAMWEAVER 5–21
   text, setting, DREAMWEAVER 2–16
   web pages, DREAMWEAVER 2–5
   web pages, editing, DREAMWEAVER
      5–17
Properties icon, Library panel,
   FLASH 3–11
Properties panel, FLASH 1–6, 1–25
   FILTERS area, FLASH 2–31
   inserting movies into Dreamweaver,
      INTEGRATION 1–18—1–19
   options for shape tween animations,
      FLASH 4–31
   sound effect properties, FLASH 5–9
Property inspector, DREAMWEAVER
   1–5—1–6
   alternate text setting, DREAMWEAVER
      3–32
   formatting cells, DREAMWEAVER 5–32,
      5–33
   formatting text, DREAMWEAVER 2–11
property keyframes, motion tween
   animations, FLASH 4–6
proportional spacing, PHOTOSHOP 5–8
PSD files, copying into Dreamweaver,
   INTEGRATION 1–4, DREAMWEAVER 3–28
psychology of color, PHOTOSHOP 4–4
public domain, DREAMWEAVER 6–35
publishing movies, FLASH 1–36, 1–38
publishing websites, DREAMWEAVER 1–21,
   1–25, 6–14—6–21
   comparing files for differences in content,
      DREAMWEAVER 6–17
   preparation, DREAMWEAVER 6–2
   remote site. See remote sites
   setting up web server access on local or
      network folders, DREAMWEAVER
      6–18
   site usability testing, DREAMWEAVER
      6–19
   synchronizing files, DREAMWEAVER
      6–16, 6–21
purpose, planning applications or websites,
   FLASH 1–40

Quick Selection tool, PHOTOSHOP 3–13,
   3–15

rasterized layers, PHOTOSHOP 2–8
rasterizing type layers, PHOTOSHOP 5–24,
   5–26
rate of change, shape tween animations,
   FLASH 4–31, 4–34
RDS (Remote Development Services),
   DREAMWEAVER 6–16
Rectangle Hotspot Tool, DREAMWEAVER
   4–24—4–25
Rectangle tool, FLASH 2–5, 2–9
Rectangular Marquee tool, PHOTOSHOP 3–5,
   3–7
red eye, removing, PHOTOSHOP 3–20
Reference panel, DREAMWEAVER 2–25, 2–28
registration point, classic tween animations,
   FLASH 4–21
regular expressions, DREAMWEAVER 6–7
related files, DREAMWEAVER 1–5, 1–14
Related Files toolbar, DREAMWEAVER 1–5
relative paths, DREAMWEAVER 4–5
relief, type, PHOTOSHOP 5–25
Remote Development Services (RDS),
   DREAMWEAVER 6–16
remote servers, DREAMWEAVER 1–25
remote sites, DREAMWEAVER 1–25. See also
   web servers
   defining, DREAMWEAVER 6–14, 6–15
   setting up access, DREAMWEAVER
      6–17—6–18
   transferring files to and from,
      DREAMWEAVER 6–15, 6–16, 6–20
   uploading files, DREAMWEAVER 6–15,
      6–20
   viewing, DREAMWEAVER 6–14—6–15,
      6–19
removing. See also deleting
   assets from websites, DREAMWEAVER
      3–35
   background images, DREAMWEAVER 3–37
   colors from websites, DREAMWEAVER
      3–35
   imperfections, PHOTOSHOP 3–22
   motion tween animations, FLASH 4–17
   red eye, PHOTOSHOP 3–20

renaming
   layers, PHOTOSHOP 2–20
   symbols, FLASH 3–14
rendering intents, PHOTOSHOP 4–7
reordering layers, FLASH 2–38
Reports dialog box, DREAMWEAVER 6–4,
   6–5, 6–8, 6–9
reselecting selections, PHOTOSHOP 3–5
reshaping
   drawn objects, FLASH 2–23
   objects in motion tween animations,
      FLASH 4–11
   segments, drawn objects, FLASH 2–21
   text, FLASH 2–33
resizing
   animating text, FLASH 4–47
   Assets panel, DREAMWEAVER 3–23
   drawn objects, FLASH 2–20, 2–23
   graphics using external editor,
      DREAMWEAVER 3–28
   images, PHOTOSHOP 1–23
   layer thumbnails, PHOTOSHOP 2–4
   marquees, PHOTOSHOP 3–12, 3–13,
      3–14
   objects, FLASH 1–26—1–27
   objects in motion tween animations,
      FLASH 4–11
   Stage, FLASH 1–6, 1–8
   table elements, DREAMWEAVER
      5–22—5–25
   text, FLASH 4–47
   text blocks, FLASH 2–30
   Timeline, FLASH 1–11
resolution
   devices, PHOTOSHOP 1–29
   images, PHOTOSHOP 1–29
   monitors, PHOTOSHOP 1–29
resulting color, PHOTOSHOP 4–27
Rewind command, FLASH 1–13
RGB mode, PHOTOSHOP 4–5—4–6
rich media content, DREAMWEAVER 1–13,
   FLASH 1–41
right-clicking, PHOTOSHOP 2–11
rollover(s), DREAMWEAVER 2–25
rollover actions, animated navigation bars,
   FLASH 5–19, 5–23
root folder, DREAMWEAVER 1–20
   creating, DREAMWEAVER 1–23
root-relative paths, DREAMWEAVER 4–5

Rotate and Skew option, Free Transform tool, FLASH 2–21, 2–24
rotating
  drawn objects, FLASH 2–21, 2–24
  objects in motion tween animations, FLASH 4–16
  text, FLASH 4–46
rows, tables
  adding, DREAMWEAVER 5–22
  CSS tables, DREAMWEAVER 5–2
  deleting, DREAMWEAVER 5–22
  resizing, DREAMWEAVER 5–25
rulers
  coordinates, PHOTOSHOP 4–8
  displaying, PHOTOSHOP 2–6
  hiding, PHOTOSHOP 2–6
  Photoshop window, PHOTOSHOP 1–18
  positioning page content, DREAMWEAVER 5–30
rules (lines), horizontal, DREAMWEAVER 2–20
runtime feature, IK, FLASH 5–28, 5–33

sample pages, Dreamweaver, DREAMWEAVER 5–8
sampling, PHOTOSHOP 4–6
  colors, PHOTOSHOP 4–32
sans serif fonts, PHOTOSHOP 5–4, 5–5
saturation, PHOTOSHOP 4–5
Saturation mode, PHOTOSHOP 4–28
Save As command, PHOTOSHOP 1–12
  changing file formats, PHOTOSHOP 1–12
  Save command vs., PHOTOSHOP 1–10
Save As dialog box, PHOTOSHOP 2–21
Save command, Save As command vs., PHOTOSHOP 1–10
Save Selection dialog box, PHOTOSHOP 3–9
Save Workspace dialog box, PHOTOSHOP 1–23
saving
  changes, DREAMWEAVER 2–12
  files, PHOTOSHOP 1–8, PHOTOSHOP 1–10, 1–12
  image files in assets folder, DREAMWEAVER 1–31, 2–14
  movies, FLASH 1–14
  selections, PHOTOSHOP 3–9

scale, PHOTOSHOP 1–19
Scale option, Free Transform tool, FLASH 2–20, 2–23
scanned images, blurry, fixing, PHOTOSHOP 4–26
scanners, PHOTOSHOP 1–39
scenes, FLASH 1–31
screen design guidelines, FLASH 1–42—1–43
Screen mode, PHOTOSHOP 4–28
screen readers, DREAMWEAVER 3–29
screen sizes, testing web pages, DREAMWEAVER 2–31
Search feature, Help system, PHOTOSHOP 1–31
Secure FTP (SFTP), DREAMWEAVER 6–14
Select File dialog box, DREAMWEAVER 2–21
Select text color dialog box, PHOTOSHOP 5–9, 5–11
selecting
  colors. *See* selecting colors
  frames, animating text, FLASH 4–44
  location, DREAMWEAVER 1–22
  menu commands, PHOTOSHOP 1–16
  multiple contiguous images, PHOTOSHOP 1–9
  objects. *See* selecting objects
  parts of graphic symbols, FLASH 4–38
  tools, PHOTOSHOP 1–19, 1–20
  window size, DREAMWEAVER 2–33
selecting colors
  Color Picker, PHOTOSHOP 4–10, 4–12
  Swatches panel, PHOTOSHOP 4–11, 4–12
selecting objects, FLASH 2–14, 2–15
  drawn objects, FLASH 2–25
  Lasso tool, FLASH 2–14
  Selection tool, FLASH 2–14, 2–15, 2–16—2–17
selection(s), PHOTOSHOP 2–12, 2–13, 3–1—3–25
  adding to, PHOTOSHOP 3–13
  changing into Move tool, PHOTOSHOP 3–6
  color range, PHOTOSHOP 2–12—2–13, 2–14
  copying, PHOTOSHOP 3–7
  correcting selection errors, PHOTOSHOP 3–5
  creating, PHOTOSHOP 3–10, 3–11

  cutting, PHOTOSHOP 3–7
  deleting, PHOTOSHOP 3–7
  deselecting, PHOTOSHOP 3–5, 3–7, 3–9
  developing skill for making, PHOTOSHOP 3–10
  drawing, PHOTOSHOP 3–4, 3–5
  fastening points, PHOTOSHOP 3–4
  flipping, PHOTOSHOP 3–20
  layers, PHOTOSHOP 2–2
  loading, PHOTOSHOP 3–9
  making, PHOTOSHOP 2–13, 2–14
  marquees. *See* marquee(s)
  matching colors using, PHOTOSHOP 4–32
  moving, PHOTOSHOP 2–13, 2–15, 3–6, 3–7, 3–8, 3–11
  moving to existing image, PHOTOSHOP 3–11
  pasting, PHOTOSHOP 3–7
  positioning selections, PHOTOSHOP 3–8
  Rectangular Marquee tool, PHOTOSHOP 3–7
  reselecting, PHOTOSHOP 3–5
  saving, PHOTOSHOP 3–9
  selecting by color, PHOTOSHOP 3–16, 3–17, 3–18
  selecting by shape, PHOTOSHOP 3–4—3–11
  selection tools, PHOTOSHOP 3–2
  Smart Guides, PHOTOSHOP 3–8
  subtracting from, PHOTOSHOP 3–13
  transforming, PHOTOSHOP 3–17
  vignette effects, PHOTOSHOP 3–22—3–23
Selection tool, FLASH 2–4, 2–5, 2–14, 2–15, 2–16—2–17, 2–21, 2–25
selection tools, PHOTOSHOP 2–12, 2–13, 3–2, 3–5
  choosing, PHOTOSHOP 3–16
serif fonts, PHOTOSHOP 5–4, 5–5
SFTP (Secure FTP), DREAMWEAVER 6–14
Shading setting, Bevel and Emboss style, PHOTOSHOP 5–20
shadow(s). *See also* drop shadows
  correcting, PHOTOSHOP 4–29
Shadow Mode Contour setting, Bevel and Emboss style, PHOTOSHOP 5–21
Shadows/Highlights dialog box, PHOTOSHOP 4–29

shape(s), selecting by, PHOTOSHOP 3–4, 3–11
shape hints, shape tween animations, FLASH 4–31, 4–35
shape tween animations, FLASH 4–30—4–35
  creating, FLASH 4–32
  morphing effects, FLASH 4–30—4–31, 4–33
  Properties panel options, FLASH 4–31
  rate of change, FLASH 4–31, 4–34
  shape hints, FLASH 4–31, 4–35
shape tweening, FLASH 4–30
Sharp anti-aliasing method, PHOTOSHOP 5–17
Sharpen More filter, PHOTOSHOP 4–27
sharpness, PHOTOSHOP 1–19
shortcut(s), FLASH 1–15
shortcut keys
  Photoshop window, PHOTOSHOP 1–18
  tool(s), PHOTOSHOP 1–18
Show Code and Design views, DREAMWEAVER 1–7
simplicity, DREAMWEAVER 2–2
Single Column Marquee tool, PHOTOSHOP 3–5
Single Row Marquee tool, PHOTOSHOP 3–5
site definition(s), DREAMWEAVER 6–30—6–33
  exporting, DREAMWEAVER 6–30, 6–31
  importing, DREAMWEAVER 6–30, 6–32—6–33
Site Definition dialog box, DREAMWEAVER 6–14, 6–15
Site option, Assets panel, DREAMWEAVER 3–25
site reports, DREAMWEAVER 6–4—6–5
Site Reports panel, DREAMWEAVER 6–8, 6–9
site usability testing, DREAMWEAVER 6–19
size. See also resizing
  drop shadows, PHOTOSHOP 5–13, 5–14
  fonts, PHOTOSHOP 5–5
skewing
  drawn objects, FLASH 2–21, 2–24
  text, FLASH 2–32
sliders, History panel, DREAMWEAVER 2–24
Smart Guides, PHOTOSHOP 3–8
Smart Objects, INTEGRATION 1–5
Smooth anti-aliasing method, PHOTOSHOP 5–17

Smooth command, PHOTOSHOP 3–12
Soft Light mode, PHOTOSHOP 4–28
sound, FLASH 5–2, 5–8—5–11
  adding to buttons, FLASH 5–11
  adding to movies, FLASH 5–8—5–9, 5–10
  synchronizing to video clips, FLASH 5–17
sound file formats, importing into Flash, FLASH 5–9
source, PHOTOSHOP 4–32
spacing, type, PHOTOSHOP 5–8—5–9, 5–10
special effects, FLASH 5–1—5–40. See also animated navigation bars; importing video; Inverse Kinematics (IK); mask effects; sound; 3D Effects; video filters. See filter(s); type filters
specifications, planning applications or website, FLASH 1–41
spell checking, DREAMWEAVER 2–17
spelling errors, correcting, PHOTOSHOP 5–10
splash screens, PHOTOSHOP 1–5
Split Code view, DREAMWEAVER 1–7
splitting cells, DREAMWEAVER 5–23, 5–26
Spot Healing Brush tool, PHOTOSHOP 3–22
Spray Brush tool, FLASH 2–5
  using with symbol, FLASH 2–12—2–13
spread, drop shadows, PHOTOSHOP 5–13, 5–14
spring-loaded keyboard shortcuts, PHOTOSHOP 1–18
Stage, FLASH 1–4—1–5, 1–10—1–11
  increasing size, FLASH 1–6, 1–8
  positioning objects on, FLASH 2–6—2–7
  repositioning, FLASH 1–6, 1–8
  X and Y coordinates, FLASH 2–22
Standard Guide layers, FLASH 2–34
Standard mode, tables, DREAMWEAVER 5–18
Standard toolbar, DREAMWEAVER 1–4
starting
  Dreamweaver, DREAMWEAVER 1–8—1–9
  Photoshop, PHOTOSHOP 1–5, 1–6—1–7
states, navigation bar elements, DREAMWEAVER 4–16
status bar, DREAMWEAVER 1–5
  Photoshop window, PHOTOSHOP 1–18
Step Backward command, undoing anti-aliasing, PHOTOSHOP 5–19
Step Backward One Frame command, FLASH 1–13

Step Forward One Frame command, FLASH 1–13
steps, History pane(s), DREAMWEAVER 2–24
stop action, frames, FLASH 3–26
storyboards, DREAMWEAVER 1–19—1–20, FLASH 1–42
  planning applications or website, FLASH 1–41
streaming video, FLASH 5–12
stroke(s), color, FLASH 2–15, 2–17
Stroke Color tool, FLASH 2–5, 2–6
Stroke dialog box, PHOTOSHOP 4–17
stroking edges, PHOTOSHOP 4–16, 4–17
Strong anti-aliasing method, PHOTOSHOP 5–17
Structure setting, Bevel and Emboss style, PHOTOSHOP 5–20, 5–21
style(s), CSS. See Cascading Style Sheets (CSSs)
Style Rendering toolbar, DREAMWEAVER 1–4—1–5, 3–15
styles, layers. See drop shadows; layer style(s)
Subselection tool, FLASH 2–4, 2–5, 2–21, 2–25
subtractive colors, PHOTOSHOP 4–6
Swatches panel
  adding colors, PHOTOSHOP 4–13
  changing type color, PHOTOSHOP 5–7
  selecting colors, PHOTOSHOP 4–11, 4–12
.swf files, FLASH 1–12, FLASH 1–36. See also movie(s)
  progressive downloading, FLASH 5–12
Switch Design View to Live View button, DREAMWEAVER 1–10
symbol(s), FLASH 3–2, 3–4—3–9
  button. See button(s)
  categories, FLASH 3–2
  creating, FLASH 3–4, 3–5, 3–6
  deleting, FLASH 3–14
  displaying properties, FLASH 3–14
  instances. See instances
  renaming, FLASH 3–14
symbol fonts, PHOTOSHOP 5–5
symmetrical balance, PHOTOSHOP 1–22
synchronizing files, DREAMWEAVER 6–16, 6–21
synchronizing sound to video clips, FLASH 5–17

tabbed documents, change to floating documents, PHOTOSHOP 1–12
table(s), DREAMWEAVER 5–18—5–37
    accessibility preference settings, DREAMWEAVER 5–19
    borders, DREAMWEAVER 5–18
    cells. *See* cell *entries*
    creating, DREAMWEAVER 5–18, 5–19, 5–20—5–21
    CSS layout blocks, DREAMWEAVER 5–2
    Expanded Tables mode, DREAMWEAVER 5–18, 5–19, 5–21
    exporting data, DREAMWEAVER 5–34
    importing data, DREAMWEAVER 5–34
    inserting text, DREAMWEAVER 5–32, 5–34
    modes, DREAMWEAVER 5–18
    nested, DREAMWEAVER 5–18, DREAMWEAVER 5–23
    properties, setting, DREAMWEAVER 5–21
    resizing elements, DREAMWEAVER 5–22—5–25
    rows. *See* rows, tables
Table dialog box, DREAMWEAVER 5–20
table height, resetting, DREAMWEAVER 5–24
table width
    page layout, DREAMWEAVER 5–20
    resetting, DREAMWEAVER 5–24
tag selector, DREAMWEAVER 1–5—1–6
Tag type styles, DREAMWEAVER 3–10
target(s), PHOTOSHOP 4–32
    internal links to named anchors, DREAMWEAVER 4–10
target audience
    content, DREAMWEAVER 2–6
    planning applications or websites, FLASH 1–40
template(s), DREAMWEAVER 2–6
terms of use, DREAMWEAVER 6–35—6–36
testing
    buttons, FLASH 3–20—3–21
    movies, FLASH 1–13, 1–16
    web pages, DREAMWEAVER 1–21, 2–30—2–31, 2–33, 6–5
text, DREAMWEAVER 1–12, FLASH 2–28—2–33. *See also* type
    adding on top of an object, FLASH 2–43
    adding to CSS containers, DREAMWEAVER 5–10

aligning text objects, FLASH 2–32
alternate. *See* alternate text
animating. *See* animating text
    changing attributes, FLASH 2–28, 2–29, 2–30
    changing text blocks, FLASH 2–28
    CSSs, DREAMWEAVER 3–2
    distributing to layers, FLASH 2–37
    entering, DREAMWEAVER 2–10, FLASH 2–28, 2–12, 2–30
    fading in, FLASH 4–47
    filter effects, FLASH 2–31
    formatting. *See* formatting text
    gradients, FLASH 2–33
    importing, DREAMWEAVER 2–15
    inserting in tables, DREAMWEAVER 5–32, 5–34
    paragraphs, FLASH 2–29
    reshaping, FLASH 2–33
    setting properties, DREAMWEAVER 2–16
    skewing, FLASH 2–32
    spell checking, DREAMWEAVER 2–17
    transforming, FLASH 2–29
text blocks
    changing, FLASH 2–28, 2–29, 2–30
    making into buttons, FLASH 4–48
    resizing, FLASH 2–30
Text tool, FLASH 2–5, 2–29, 2–30
texture(s), type, PHOTOSHOP 5–25
Texture filter, PHOTOSHOP 5–25
themes
    consistent, DREAMWEAVER 2–2
    kuler, PHOTOSHOP 4–11
3D effects, FLASH 5–2, 5–34—5–37
    creating, FLASH 5–36—5–37
    motion tweens, FLASH 5–35
    3D tools, FLASH 5–34—5–35
3D Rotation tool, FLASH 2–4, 2–5, 5–34, 5–35, 5–37
3D Translation tool, FLASH 2–4, 2–5, 5–34, 5–36—5–37
thumbnails, viewing, PHOTOSHOP 1–10
tiled images, DREAMWEAVER 3–34
Timeline, FLASH 1–5, 1–11, 1–30—1–35
    elements, FLASH 1–31
    frame labels, FLASH 3–25
    frames, FLASH 1–30—31
    layers, FLASH 1–30, 1–31, 1–33, 1–34

    Layers area, FLASH 2–35, 2–39
    movie clips, FLASH 4–36
    overview, FLASH 1–30, 1–31
    playhead, FLASH 1–31
    resizing, FLASH 1–11
    viewing features, FLASH 1–34
title tab, Library panel, FLASH 3–10
Toggle Sorting Order icon, Library panel, FLASH 3–11
tone, PHOTOSHOP 1–19
    planning applications or website, FLASH 1–41
tool(s), DREAMWEAVER 1–2, PHOTOSHOP 1–17. *See also specific tool names*
    selecting, PHOTOSHOP 1–19, 1–20
    shortcut keys, PHOTOSHOP 1–18
Tool Preset picker
    adding tools, PHOTOSHOP 1–21
    modifying tool presets, PHOTOSHOP 1–21
    selecting tools, PHOTOSHOP 1–20
toolbars. *See also specific toolbar names*
    displaying, DREAMWEAVER 1–11
    hiding, DREAMWEAVER 1–11
Tools panel, FLASH 1–6—1–8, 2–8
    Colors area, FLASH 2–15
    Photoshop window, PHOTOSHOP 1–17—1–18
    views, PHOTOSHOP 1–17
Tools section, Tools panel, FLASH 1–6
tracing images, DREAMWEAVER 5–5
tracking, PHOTOSHOP 5–8—5–9
trademarks, DREAMWEAVER 6–34
transferring files
    Dreamweaver connection options, DREAMWEAVER 6–16
    to and from remote sites, DREAMWEAVER 6–15, 6–16, 6–20
transformation point, classic tween animations, FLASH 4–21
transforming
    drawn objects, FLASH 2–20, 2–23
    text, FLASH 2–29
transparency, objects, FLASH 1–25—1–26
transparent pixels, locking, PHOTOSHOP 4–16, 4–17
treatment, planning applications or website, FLASH 1–41
tween spans, FLASH 1–20, FLASH 4–5

INDEX

tweened animations. See classic tween
   animations; motion tween animations;
   shape tween animations
Twirl dialog box, PHOTOSHOP 5–24, 5–25
type, PHOTOSHOP 1–5, 5–1—5–31. See also
   text
   anti-aliasing, PHOTOSHOP 5–16—5–19
   baseline shift, PHOTOSHOP 5–9, 5–11
   Bevel and Emboss style, PHOTOSHOP
      5–20—5–23
   color, PHOTOSHOP 5–4, PHOTOSHOP 5–7
   creating, PHOTOSHOP 5–6
   filling with imagery, PHOTOSHOP 5–20
   font. See font(s)
   layers. See type layers
   modifying, PHOTOSHOP 5–6
   on path, PHOTOSHOP 5–28—5–29
   purpose, PHOTOSHOP 5–2
   spacing. See type spacing
   types, PHOTOSHOP 5–4
   uses, PHOTOSHOP 5–2
type filters, PHOTOSHOP 5–24—5–27
   blurring imagery, PHOTOSHOP 5–25
   creating special effects, PHOTOSHOP
      5–24, 5–25
   distort, PHOTOSHOP 5–24, 5–25
   modifying settings, PHOTOSHOP 5–27
   multiple, PHOTOSHOP 5–26
   rasterizing type layers, PHOTOSHOP
      5–24, 5–26
   relief, PHOTOSHOP 5–25
   textures, PHOTOSHOP 5–25
type layers, PHOTOSHOP 2–4
   rasterizing, PHOTOSHOP 5–24, 5–26
   using imagery from one layer as fill
      pattern for another image's type layer,
      PHOTOSHOP 5–20
type spacing, PHOTOSHOP 5–8—5–9, 5–10
   kerning, PHOTOSHOP 5–8, 5–10
   leading, PHOTOSHOP 5–9
   monotype, PHOTOSHOP 5–8
   proportional, PHOTOSHOP 5–8
   tracking, PHOTOSHOP 5–8—5–9
type warping, PHOTOSHOP 5–22

uncloaking folders, DREAMWEAVER 6–28
"under construction" pages, DREAMWEAVER
   2–30

Undo command, undoing anti-aliasing,
   PHOTOSHOP 5–19
undoing anti-aliasing, PHOTOSHOP 5–19
unfinished pages, DREAMWEAVER 2–30
units of measurement, PHOTOSHOP 2–6
unity, screen design, FLASH 1–43
Universal Resource Locators. See URLs
   (Universal Resource Locators)
unordered lists
   creating, DREAMWEAVER 3–4, 3–6
   formatting, DREAMWEAVER 3–7
Unsharp Mask filter, PHOTOSHOP 4–26
untitled documents, checking for,
   DREAMWEAVER 6–8
Untitled-1 file, PHOTOSHOP 1–16
unvisited links, DREAMWEAVER 2–5
Up state, FLASH 3–16
Update dialog box, PHOTOSHOP 1–38
updating, web pages, website links,
   DREAMWEAVER 4–30—4–31
uploading files
   excluding selected files, DREAMWEAVER
      6–26—6–29
   to remote sites, DREAMWEAVER 6–15,
      6–20
URLs (Universal Resource Locators),
   DREAMWEAVER 4–4
   typing, DREAMWEAVER 4–6
usability testing, websites, DREAMWEAVER
   6–19
user interface, FLASH 1–42

validating
   accessibility standards, DREAMWEAVER
      6–9
   markup, DREAMWEAVER 6–5
Validation panel, DREAMWEAVER 6–5
vector fonts, PHOTOSHOP 5–4
vector graphics, FLASH 2–2, 3–30, 3–31
   creating, FLASH 2–6
Verdana typeface, PHOTOSHOP 5–4
version(s), Photoshop, PHOTOSHOP 1–33
Version Cue, 1–2, PHOTOSHOP 1–14—1–15
   administrative functions, PHOTOSHOP
      1–15
   asset management, DREAMWEAVER
      6–11
   workspaces, PHOTOSHOP 1–14

vertical space, images, DREAMWEAVER 3–29,
   3–30
video, FLASH 5–2, FLASH 5–12—5–17
   attaching actions to video control
      buttons, FLASH 5–16
   embedded, FLASH 5–12, 5–13
   importing. See importing video
   streaming, FLASH 5–12
   synchronizing sound to video clips,
      FLASH 5–17
view(s), DREAMWEAVER 1–7, 1–10—1–11
   Bridge, PHOTOSHOP 1–10
   changing, DREAMWEAVER
      1–10—1–11
   Tools panel, PHOTOSHOP 1–17
viewing. See also displaying
   CSS layout blocks, DREAMWEAVER 5–5,
      5–14
   download time, DREAMWEAVER 3–22
   images in multiple views, PHOTOSHOP
      1–33
   imported sites, DREAMWEAVER 6–33
   links in Assets panel, DREAMWEAVER
      4–9
   remote sites, DREAMWEAVER
      6–14—6–15, 6–19
   thumbnails, PHOTOSHOP 1–10
   Timeline features, FLASH 1–34
Views section, Tools panel, FLASH 1–6
vignette(s), PHOTOSHOP 3–22—3–23
   creating, PHOTOSHOP 3–22, 3–23
vignette effects, PHOTOSHOP 3–22
visited links, DREAMWEAVER 2–5
Visual Aids, DREAMWEAVER 5–37
Visual Safe Source (VSS), DREAMWEAVER
   6–16
VSS (Visual Safe Source), DREAMWEAVER
   6–16

Warp Text feature, PHOTOSHOP
   5–22
web browsers, DREAMWEAVER 1–2
   cross-browser rendering issues,
      DREAMWEAVER 5–13
   kulers, PHOTOSHOP 4–14
   testing web pages, DREAMWEAVER
      2–31, 2–33
Web Gallery, Bridge, PHOTOSHOP 1–37

web pages
	adding to websites, DREAMWEAVER
		1–27
	links to, DREAMWEAVER 2–21
	opening, DREAMWEAVER 1–12, 1–14
	related files, DREAMWEAVER 1–14
	viewing basic elements, DREAMWEAVER
		1–12—1–13, 1–14—1–15
web servers, DREAMWEAVER 1–21, 6–14.
	See also remote sites
	setting up access, DREAMWEAVER 1–25,
		DREAMWEAVER 6–18
WebDav, DREAMWEAVER 6–16
web-safe color palette, DREAMWEAVER 2–4
website(s), DREAMWEAVER 1–2
website links, DREAMWEAVER 4–28—4–31
	managing, DREAMWEAVER 4–28, 4–29
	updating pages, DREAMWEAVER
		4–30—4–31
website maintenance, DREAMWEAVER
	6–4—6–13
	Assets panel, DREAMWEAVER 6–4
	checking for missing alternate text,
		DREAMWEAVER 6–9
	checking for orphaned files,
		DREAMWEAVER 6–6
	checking for untitled documents,
		DREAMWEAVER 6–8
	checking links, DREAMWEAVER 6–4, 6–6

Design Notes, DREAMWEAVER
	6–10—6–13
site reports, DREAMWEAVER 6–4—6–5
testing pages, DREAMWEAVER 6–5
validating accessibility standards,
	DREAMWEAVER 6–9
validating markup, DREAMWEAVER 6–5
verifying that colors are web-safe,
	DREAMWEAVER 6–7
Welcome screen, FLASH 1–9
white space, DREAMWEAVER 2–2,
	PHOTOSHOP 1–26
Wind dialog box, PHOTOSHOP 5–25
window size, selecting, DREAMWEAVER 2–33
Windows platform, PHOTOSHOP 1–2
	adding folders to websites,
		DREAMWEAVER 1–28
	adding pages to websites,
		DREAMWEAVER 1–32
	hardware requirements, PHOTOSHOP 1–6
	importing Microsoft Office documents,
		DREAMWEAVER 2–15
	linking Microsoft Office documents,
		DREAMWEAVER 2–15
	opening files, PHOTOSHOP 1–8
	starting Dreamweaver, DREAMWEAVER
		1–8
	starting Photoshop, PHOTOSHOP 1–6
workflow process, FLASH 1–44

workspace. *See* Dreamweaver workspace;
	Photoshop workspace
Workspace switcher, DREAMWEAVER 1–8
workspace switcher, PHOTOSHOP
	1–16
WYSIWYG environment, DREAMWEAVER
	5–19

X coordinates, Stage, FLASH 2–22
XHTML (eXtensible HyperText Markup
	Language), DREAMWEAVER 1–2
XML (Extensible Markup Language),
	creating and formatting page content,
	DREAMWEAVER 5–6
XSL (Extensible Style Language), creating and
	formatting page content, DREAMWEAVER
	5–6
XSLT (Extensible Stylesheet Language
	Transformations), creating and formatting
	page content, DREAMWEAVER 5–6

Y coordinates, Stage, FLASH 2–22

Zoom tool, FLASH 2–5, 2–6, 2–25,
	PHOTOSHOP 1–32, 1–34

INDEX

Web Collection Premium Art Credits

Chapter	Art credit for opening pages
Dreamweaver	
Chapter 1	© David Newham/Alamy
Chapter 2	© Josephine Marsden/Alamy
Chapter 3	© Radius Images/Alamy
Chapter 4	© Christopher Scott/Alamy
Chapter 5	© Radius Images/Alamy
Chapter 6	© Darryl Leniuk/Lifesize/Getty Images
Flash	
Chapter 1	© Dimitri Vervitsiotis/Digital Vision/Getty Images
Chapter 2	© Veer
Chapter 3	© Barbara Peacock/Photodisc/Getty Images
Chapter 4	© Stuart Westmorland/Digital Vision/Getty Images
Chapter 5	© Nick Norman/National Geographic Image Collection/Getty Images
Photoshop	
Chapter 1	© Philip and Karen Smith/Digital Vision/Getty Images
Chapter 2	© Jeff Rotman/Digital Vision/Getty Images
Chapter 3	© Paul Souders/Photodisc/Getty Images
Chapter 4	© Plush Studios/Digital Vision/Getty Images
Chapter 5	© David Tipling/Digital Vision/Getty Images
Integration	
Chapter 1	© Veer
Data Files/Glossary/Index	© Georgette Douwma/Photodisc/Getty Images